CONTEMPORARY
WORLD HISTORY

SEVENTH EDITION

CONTEMPORARY WORLD HISTORY

William J. Duiker

The Pennsylvania State University

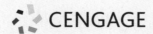
CENGAGE

Australia • Brazil • Canada • Mexico • Singapore • United Kingdom • United States

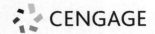

Contemporary World History,
Seventh Edition
William J. Duiker

Senior Product Manager: Joseph D. Potvin

Product Assistant: Haley Gaudreau

Senior Marketing Manager: Valerie A. Hartman

Senior Content Manager: Philip Lanza

IP Analyst: Deanna Ettinger

IP Project Manager: Kellianne Besse

Production Service/Compositor: MPS Limited

Art Director: Sarah Cole

Text & Cover Designer: Sarah Cole

Cover Image: China, Guizhou Province.
Two Miao women in traditional clothes
and headdresses take a selfie.
Westend61/Getty Images.

For product information and technology assistance, contact us at
Cengage Customer & Sales Support, 1-800-354-9706 or
support.cengage.com.

For permission to use material from this text or product,
submit all requests online at
www.cengage.com/permissions.

Library of Congress Control Number: 2019916769

Student Edition:
ISBN: 978-0-357-36486-4

Cengage
200 Pier 4 Boulevard
Boston, MA 02210
USA

Cengage is a leading provider of customized learning solutions with
employees residing in nearly 40 different countries and sales in more
than 125 countries around the world. Find your local representative at
www.cengage.com.

To learn more about Cengage platforms and services, register or
access your online learning solution, or purchase materials for your
course, visit **www.cengage.com**.

Printed in the United States of America
Print Number: 02   Print Year: 2020

ABOUT THE AUTHOR

WILLIAM J. DUIKER is liberal arts professor emeritus of East Asian studies at The Pennsylvania State University. A former U.S. diplomat with service in Taiwan, South Vietnam, and Washington, D.C., he received his doctorate in Far Eastern history from Georgetown University in 1968, where his dissertation dealt with the Chinese educator and reformer Cai Yuanpei. At Penn State, he has written extensively on the history of Vietnam and modern China, including the highly acclaimed *The Communist Road to Power in Vietnam* (revised edition, Westview Press, 1996), which was selected for a Choice Outstanding Academic Book Award in 1982–1983 and 1996–1997. Other published books are *China and Vietnam: The Roots of Conflict* (Berkeley, 1987); *Sacred War: Nationalism and Revolution in a Divided Vietnam* (McGraw-Hill, 1995); and *Ho Chi Minh* (Hyperion, 2000), which was nominated for a Pulitzer Prize in 2001. He is the author, with colleague Jackson Spielvogel, of *World History* (ninth edition, Cengage, 2019). While his research specialization is in the field of nationalism and Asian revolutions, his intellectual interests are considerably more diverse. At Penn State, he served for ten years as Director of International Programs in the College of Liberal Arts, and was awarded a Faculty Scholar Medal for Outstanding Achievement in the spring of 1996. In 2002 the College of Liberal Arts honored him with an Emeritus Distinction Award.

TO JULES F. DIEBENOW (1929–2013),
INVETERATE FELLOW TRAVELER, MENTOR, AND FRIEND.
W.J.D.

BRIEF CONTENTS

DETAILED CONTENTS

HISTORICAL VOICES: DOCUMENTS

MAPS

FEATURES

The twentieth century was an era of paradox. When it began, Western civilization was an emerging powerhouse that bestrode the world like a colossus. Internally, however, the continent of Europe was a patchwork of squabbling states that within a period of less than three decades engaged in two bitter internecine wars that threatened to obliterate two centuries of human progress. As the century came to an end, the Western world had become prosperous and increasingly united, yet there were clear signs that global economic and political hegemony was beginning to shift to the East. In the minds of many observers, the era of Western dominance had come to a close.

In other ways as well, the twentieth century was marked by countervailing trends. While parts of the world experienced rapid industrial growth and increasing economic prosperity, other regions were still mired in abject poverty. The century's final decades were characterized by a growing awareness of not only global interdependence, but also burgeoning ethnic and national consciousness; the period witnessed both the rising power of science and a new era of fervent religiosity and growing doubts about the impact of technology on the human experience.

As the closing chapters of this book indicate, these trends have continued and even intensified in the two decades that have ensued since the advent of the new millennium. The eastward shift of power and influence that had already occurred with the rise of China and Japan has become more pronounced, while the Western democracies have become increasingly mired in economic stagnation, self-doubt, and political disunity. In the meantime, the Technological Revolution, along with the inexorable force of globalization, is exerting an influence on world society similar to that exerted by the Industrial Revolution during the course of the nineteenth century. Although the ultimate effects cannot yet be foreseen, it is increasingly clear that the Enlightenment vision of a world characterized by peace, prosperity, and human freedom can no longer be taken for granted.

Contemporary World History (formerly titled *Twentieth-Century World History*) seeks to chronicle the key events in this revolutionary era while seeking to throw light on some of the underlying issues that have shaped our times. Did the beginning of a new millennium indeed mark the end of the long period of Western dominance? If so, will recent decades of European and American superiority be

followed by a "Pacific century," with economic and political power shifting to the nations of eastern Asia? Will the end of the Cold War eventually lead to a "new world order" marked by global cooperation, or are we now entering an unstable era of ethnic and national conflict? Will the dream of liberal democracy and human freedom give way to a new reality marked by political authoritarianism and social regimentation? Why has a time of unparalleled prosperity and technological advance been accompanied by deep pockets of poverty and widespread doubts about the role of government and the capabilities of human reason? Will the relentless process of globalization lead to a new world civilization or to an era of conflict similar to that brought about by the Industrial Revolution? Although this book does not promise final answers to such questions, it seeks to provide a framework for analysis and a better understanding of some of the salient issues of modern times.

Any author who seeks to encompass in a single volume the history of our turbulent times faces some important choices. First, should the book be arranged in strict chronological order, or should separate chapters focus on individual cultures and societies in order to place greater emphasis on the course of events taking place in different regions of the world? In this book, I have sought to achieve a balance between a global and a regional approach. I accept the commonplace observation that the world we live in is increasingly interdependent in terms of economics as well as culture and communications. Yet the inescapable reality is that this process of globalization is at best a work in progress, as ethnic, religious, and regional differences continue to proliferate and to shape the course of our times. It seems increasingly clear that the oft-predicted transformation of the world into what has been termed a "global village" marked by the inevitable triumph of the democratic capitalist way of life is by no means a preordained vision of the future of the human experience. In fact, influential figures in many countries, from China to Russia and the Middle East, emphatically deny that the forces of globalization will inevitably lead to the worldwide adoption of the Western model and have provided their own formula for the world experience.

There is another reason for avoiding a strictly thematic approach in favor of focusing on the historical experience of different countries and regions as they attempt to navigate the complexities of the contemporary world.

College students today are often not well informed about the distinctive character of civilizations such as China, India, and sub-Saharan Africa. Without sufficient exposure to the historical evolution of such societies, students will assume all too readily that the peoples in these countries have had historical experiences similar to their own and react to various stimuli in a fashion similar to those living in western Europe or the United States. If it is a mistake to ignore the forces that link us together, it is equally erroneous to underestimate the factors that still divide us.

Balancing the global and regional perspectives means that some chapters of this book focus on issues that have a global impact, such as the Industrial Revolution, the era of imperialism, and the two world wars. Others center on individual regions of the world, while singling out contrasts and comparisons that link them to the broader world community. The book is divided into five parts. The first four parts are each followed by a short section labeled "Reflections," which attempts to link events in a broad comparative and global framework. The chapter in the fifth and final part examines some of the common problems of our time—including human inequality, climate change, the population explosion, the impact of technology, and spiritual malaise—and takes a cautious look into the future to explore how such issues might evolve over the course of the twenty-first century.

One issue that has recently attracted widespread discussion and debate among world historians is how to balance the treatment of Western civilization with that given other parts of the world. Until recently, the modern world has usually been viewed by Western historians essentially as the history of Europe and the United States, with other regions treated as mere appendages of the industrial countries. It is certainly true that much of the twentieth century was dominated by events that were initiated in Europe and North America, and in recognition of this fact, the opening chapters in this book focus on the Industrial Revolution and the age of imperialism, both issues directly related to the rise of the West and its impact on the modern world. In recent decades, however, other regions of the world have assumed greater importance, thus restoring a global balance that had existed prior to the scientific and technological revolution that transformed the West in the eighteenth and nineteenth centuries. Later chapters in this book examine this phenomenon in more detail, thus according to regions such as Africa, Asia, and Latin America the importance that they merit today.

In sum, this seventh edition of *Contemporary World History* seeks to present a balanced treatment of the most important political, economic, social, and cultural events of the modern era within an integrated and chronologically ordered synthesis. In my judgment, a strong narrative, linking key issues in a broad interpretive framework, is still the most effective way to present the story of the past to young minds.

Four different feature boxes appear throughout the chapters to supplement the text. **Historical Voices** present documents that illustrate key issues within each chapter. Another feature, **Opposing Viewpoints**, presents a comparison of two or more primary sources to facilitate student analysis of historical documents, including examples such as "Islam in the Modern World: Two Views" (Chapter 5), "Two Visions for India" (Chapter 13), and "Africa: Dark Continent or Radiant Land?" (Chapter 14). **Movies & History** presents a brief analysis of the plot as well as the historical significance, value, and accuracy of eleven films, including such movies as *Lawrence of Arabia* (1962), *Gandhi* (1982), *The Last Emperor* (1987), *The Lives of Others* (2006), and *Persepolis* (2007). New to this edition, **Comparative Illustrations** encourage readers to adopt a comparative approach in their understanding of the human experience. Each of these four different feature presentations includes a Focus Question to help students develop analysis skills in working with documents and images. Extensive maps and illustrations, each positioned at the appropriate place in the chapter, serve to deepen the reader's understanding of the text. "Spot maps" provide details not visible in the larger maps.

The following resources are available to accompany this text.

Instructor's Companion Website   The Instructor's Companion Website, accessed through the Instructor Resource Center (**login.cengage.com**), houses all of the supplemental materials you can use for your course. This includes a Test Bank, Instructor's Manual, and PowerPoint Lecture Presentations.

- Cognero® Test Bank The Test Bank contains multiple-choice, short-answer historical identification, and essay questions for each chapter. Cognero® is a flexible, online system that allows you to author, edit, and manage test bank content for *Contemporary World History*, seventh edition. With Cognero®, you can create multiple test versions instantly and deliver them through your LMS from your classroom or wherever you may be, with no special software installs or downloads required. The following format types are available for download from the Instructor Companion Site: Blackboard, Angel, Moodle, Canvas, and Desire2Learn. You can import these files directly into your LMS to edit, manage questions, and create tests.

- **PowerPoint Lectures** These are ADA-compliant slide decks that collate the key takeaways from the chapter in concise visual formats perfect for in-class presentations or for student review. Each slide deck also includes the chapter's full set of images and maps. New to this edition, the PowerPoints now include six different types of Activity slides to enhance student engagement. The activities include "Think, Pair, Share"; "Quick Check"; "Written Reflection"; "Discussion"; "Diary"; and "Self-Assessment."
- **Instructor's Resource Manual** The Instructor's Resource Manual closely complements the PowerPoint Lecture slides and is focused on supporting instructors who are new to teaching or new to using *Contemporary World History*. It includes instructional objectives, chapter summaries, chapter outlines, brief descriptions of specific chapter features (Historical Voices, Opposing Viewpoints, Movies & History), and notes for using the Activity slides featured in the PowerPoint deck for each chapter.

Cengage.com/student Save your students time and money. Direct them to **cengage.com/student** for a choice in formats and savings and a better chance to succeed in your class. Cengage.com/student, Cengage's online store, is a single destination for more than 10,000 new textbooks, ebooks, study tools, and audio supplements. Students have the freedom to purchase à la carte exactly what they need and when they need it. Students can save up to 70 percent on the ebook electronic version of their textbook.

CENGAGE UNLIMITED We now offer **Cengage Unlimited**, the first-of-its-kind digital subscription designed specifically to lower costs. Students get everything Cengage has to offer—in one place. For $119.99 per term (or $179.99 per year), students have access to:

- Award-winning products proven to boost outcomes and increase engagement

- Over 20,000 digital products, covering 70 disciplines and 675 courses
- A free print rental with any activated digital learning product (like MindTap)
- Dozens of study guides matched to the most common college courses
- Twelve-month free access for up to six ebooks

Currently available in selected markets. For more information, please contact your local Learning Consultant or visit **cengage.com/unlimited**

Doing History: Research and Writing in the Digital Age, 2e (ISBN: 9781133587880) Prepared by Michael J. Galgano, J. Chris Arndt, and Raymond M. Hyser of James Madison University. Whether you're starting down the path as a history major or simply looking for a straightforward, systematic guide to writing a successful paper, this text's "soup to nuts" approach to researching and writing about history addresses every step of the process: locating your sources, gathering information, writing and citing according to various style guides, and avoiding plagiarism.

Reader Program Cengage Learning publishes a number of readers. Some contain exclusively primary sources, others are devoted to essays and secondary sources, and still others provide a combination of primary and secondary sources. All of these readers are designed to guide students through the process of historical inquiry. Visit **cengage.com/history** for a complete list of readers.

Custom Options Nobody knows your students like you, so why not give them a text that tailor-fits their needs? Cengage Learning offers custom solutions for your course—whether it's making a small modification to *Contemporary World History*, 7e, to match your syllabus or combining multiple sources to create something truly unique. Contact your Cengage Learning representative to explore custom solutions for your course.

Acknowledgments

I would like to express my appreciation to the reviewers who have read individual chapters and provided useful suggestions for improvement on this edition, including: Marcus Allen, North Carolina A&T State University; Thomas Apel, Menlo College; Elizabeth Clark, West Texas A&M University; Stephen Gibson, Allegany College of Maryland; Edmund La Clair, Monroe County Community College; Bruce Nye, Front Range Community College; Jeremy Rich, Marywood University; and Laurie Sprankle, The Community College of Allegheny County.

Jackson Spielvogel, coauthor of our textbook *World History*, was kind enough to permit me to use some of his sections in that book for the purposes of writing this one. Several of my other colleagues at Penn State—including E-tu Zen Sun, On-cho Ng, Arthur F. Goldschmidt, and the late Cyril Griffith—have provided me with valuable assistance in understanding parts of the world that are beyond my own area of concentration. Ian Bell, Ruth Petzold, and my daughter Claire L. Duiker have provided useful illustrations. I have also benefited from Nan Johnson's broad understanding of the growth of the women's movement in the United States, and from Jim McMichael for his assistance in understanding the nature of the environmental challenges facing the world today. My Tuesday lunch group, the Knights of the Wobbly Round Table, have provided a useful forum to discuss issues of common concern. To Clark Baxter, whose unfailing good humor, patience, and sage advice so often eased the trauma of textbook publishing, I will always owe my heartfelt thanks. I am also grateful to the history group at Cengage for their assistance in bringing this project to fruition: Joseph Potvin, senior product manager; Philip Lanza, senior content manager; Kate MacLean, learning designer; Haley Gaudreau, product assistant; and Matt Kennedy, Ph.D., subject matter expert. Thanks also to Charu Verma and the team at MPS Limited for production services.

Finally, I am eternally grateful to my wife, Yvonne V. Duiker, Ph.D. Her research and her written contributions on art, architecture, literature, and music have added sparkle to this book. Our many travels together have helped me to understand more fully the wonders and the complexities of the vast world around us. Most important, her presence at my side has added immeasurable sparkle to my life.

William J. Duiker
The Pennsylvania State University

THEMES FOR UNDERSTANDING WORLD HISTORY

As they pursue their craft, historians often organize their material according to themes that enable them to ask and try to answer basic questions about the past. Such is the intention here. This new edition highlights several major themes that I believe are especially important in understanding the course of world history. Thinking about these themes will help students to perceive the similarities and differences among cultures since the beginning of the human experience. You will see these theme labels applied to the various feature boxes appearing throughout the chapters that follow.

Politics & Government

1. *Politics & Government* The study of politics seeks to answer certain basic questions that historians have about the structure of a society: How were people governed? What was the relationship between the ruler and the ruled? What people or groups of people (the political elites) held political power? What actions did people take to guarantee their security or change their form of government?

Art & Ideas

2. *Art & Ideas* We cannot understand a society without looking at its culture, or the common ideas, beliefs, and patterns of behavior that are passed on from one generation to the next. Culture includes both high culture and popular culture. High culture consists of the writings of a society's thinkers and the works of its artists. A society's popular culture encompasses the ideas and experiences of ordinary people. Today, the media have embraced the term *popular culture* to describe the current trends and fashionable styles.

Religion & Philosophy

3. *Religion & Philosophy* Throughout history, people have sought to find a deeper meaning to human life. How have the world's great religions, such as Hinduism, Buddhism, Judaism, Christianity, and Islam, influenced people's lives? How have they spread to create new patterns of culture in other parts of the world?

Family & Society

4. *Family & Society* The most basic social unit in human society has always been the family. From a study of family and social patterns, we learn about the different social classes that make up a society and their relationships with one another. We also learn about the role of gender in individual societies. What different roles did men and women play in their societies? How and why were those roles different?

Science & Technology

5. *Science & Technology* For thousands of years, people around the world have made scientific discoveries and technological innovations that have changed our world. From the creation of stone tools that made farming easier to advanced computers that guide our airplanes, science and technology have altered how humans have related to their world.

Earth & Environment

6. *Earth & Environment* Throughout history, peoples and societies have been affected by the physical world in which they live. Climatic changes alone have been an important factor in human history. Through their economic activities, peoples and societies, in turn, have also made an impact on their world. Human activities have affected the physical environment and even endangered the very existence of entire societies and species.

Interaction & Exchange

7. *Interaction & Exchange* Many world historians believe that the exchange of ideas and innovations is the driving force behind the evolution of human societies. Knowledge of agriculture, writing and printing, metalworking, and navigational techniques, for example, spread gradually from one part of the world to other regions and eventually changed the face of the entire globe. The process of cultural and technological exchange took place in various ways, including trade, conquest, and the migration of peoples.

PART I

NEW WORLD IN THE MAKING

The Crystal Palace in London

Everett Collection

THE RISE OF INDUSTRIAL SOCIETY IN THE WEST

Chapter Outline and Focus Questions

SHEFFIELD SMOKE.
From a Drawing by A. MORROW.

Hulton Archive/Getty Images

IMAGE 1.1 Sheffield became one of England's greatest manufacturing cities during the nineteenth century.

Connections to Today

In your observation, how would you compare the impact of the Industrial Revolution in the European continent with the changes taking place as a result of technological inventions in the world today?

THE TWENTIETH CENTURY was a turbulent era, marked by two violent global conflicts, a bitter ideological struggle between two dominant world powers, explosive developments in the realm of science, and dramatic social change. When the century began, the vast majority of the world's peoples lived on farms, and the horse was still the most common means of transportation. By its end, human beings had trod on the moon and lived in a world increasingly defined by urban sprawl and modern technology.

What had happened to bring about these momentous changes? Although a world as complex as ours cannot be assigned a single cause, a good candidate for consideration is the Industrial Revolution, which began on the British Isles at the end of the eighteenth century and spread steadily throughout the world during the next 200 years. The Industrial Revolution was unquestionably one of the most important factors in laying the foundation of the modern world. It not only transformed the economic means of production and distribution, but also altered the political systems, the social institutions and values, and the intellectual and cultural life of all the societies that it touched. The impact has been both massive and controversial. While proponents have stressed the enormous material and technological benefits that industrialization has brought, critics have pointed out the high costs involved, from growing economic inequality and environmental pollution to the dehumanization of everyday life. Already in the nineteenth century, the German philosopher Karl Marx charged that factory labor had reduced workers to a mere "appendage of the machine," and the English novelist Charles Dickens wrote about an urban environment of factories, smoke, and ashes that seemed an apparition from Dante's Hell.

Today the world is undergoing a vast new social upheaval, spurred on by a revolution in science and technology—most notably in the fields of knowledge and communications. Like its predecessor, the technological revolution has begun to transform the attitudes, the behavioral patterns, and the livelihood of all the world's peoples. Some of the consequences have been beneficial, while others clearly have not. A retrospective look at the dramatic events that took place during the nineteenth century can help us to understand how our own world came into being, as well as to provide us with a glimpse of what the future holds for our species.

1-1 THE INDUSTRIAL REVOLUTION IN GREAT BRITAIN

 Focus Question: What factors appear to explain why Great Britain was the first nation to enter the industrial age?

Why the Industrial Revolution occurred first in Great Britain rather than in another part of the world has been a subject for debate among historians for many decades, and I will briefly address this issue in the Reflection section at the end of Part I of this book. But it is important to note here that a number of distinctive features can help to explain why the transformation from an agricultural to an industrial society began in the British Isles. Certainly,

one key factor was the changing nature of the British political culture. A turbulent period of political strife in the mid-seventeenth century resulted in the weakening of royal authority and the establishment of a constitutional monarchy, in which power was divided equally between the king and parliament. A Declaration of Rights, enacted in 1688, created a new political atmosphere based on the rule of law which shielded individuals and private property from arbitrary seizure and arrest. Under the cover of such protections, an emerging class of landed gentry and merchant capitalists, many of them animated by the Protestant belief that material rewards in this world were a sign of heavenly salvation to come, began to make their contributions to a growing national economy.

A number of other factors contributed to a quickening pace of economic change in late eighteenth-century Britain. First, improvements in agriculture—stimulated by a number of technological innovations—led to a significant increase in food production. British agriculture could now feed more people at lower prices with less labor; even ordinary British families no longer had to use most of their income to buy food, giving them the potential to purchase manufactured goods. At the same time, a rapidly growing population in the second half of the eighteenth century provided a pool of surplus labor for the new factories of the emerging British industrial sector.

Another factor that played a role in promoting the Industrial Revolution in Great Britain was the rapid increase in national wealth. Two centuries of expanding trade with the rest of the world, a product of the settlement and exploitation of the American colonies, as well as growing access to cheap materials from Africa and Asia, had provided Britain with a ready supply of capital for investment in the new industrial machines and the factories that were required to house them (see Chapter 2).[1] Infrastructural changes, such as an effective central bank and well-developed, flexible credit facilities, also contributed. Many early factory owners were merchants and entrepreneurs who had profited from the eighteenth-century cottage industry and now took advantage of new possibilities to expand their horizons.

Not the least of British advantages was the fact that the country was richly supplied with important mineral resources, such as coal and iron ore, soon to be vitally needed in the manufacturing process. Britain was also a small country with ready proximity to the sea, thus making transportation facilities readily accessible. In addition to abundant rivers, from the mid-seventeenth century onward both private and public investment poured into the construction of new roads, bridges, and canals.

A final factor was the appearance during the last decades of the eighteenth century of a number of technological inventions, including the flying shuttle, the spinning jenny, and the power loom, that led to a significant increase in textile production. Cotton had begun to replace wool as the clothing material of choice as awareness of its advantages became public knowledge. But price was an obstacle, because imports of finished goods from India—a major producer of cotton goods for centuries—were expensive. Once mechanized textile factories had begun to appear in Great Britain, the country could provide for its own needs, using cheap cotton fibers imported from South Asia, now increasingly under British domination (see Chapter 2). The cotton textile industry achieved even greater heights of productivity with the invention of the steam engine, which proved invaluable to Britain's Industrial Revolution. The steam engine was a tireless source of power and depended for fuel on a substance—namely, coal—that seemed then to be available in unlimited quantities. The success of the steam engine increased the demand for coal and led to an expansion in coal production. In turn, new processes using coal furthered the development of an iron industry, the production of machinery, and the invention of the railroad. By the first quarter of the nineteenth century, the key elements of a fully industrialized society were in place, and Great Britain—which by 1871 was producing almost one-fifth of all manufactured products in the entire world—was well on its way to earning the popular sobriquet of "the world's workshop."

1-2 THE SPREAD OF THE INDUSTRIAL REVOLUTION

 Focus Question: To what degree did other nations in Europe and North America follow the example of Great Britain in entering the industrial age?

By the turn of the nineteenth century, industrialization had begun to spread to the continent of Europe, where it took a different path than had been followed in Great Britain (see Map 1.1). Unlike the situation in Great Britain, where much of the stimulus for entering the industrial age had been initiated by private entrepreneurs, no independent merchant class existed in Europe, so governments on the European continent were accustomed to playing a major role in economic affairs and continued to do so as the Industrial Revolution got under way, subsidizing inventors, providing incentives to factory owners, and improving the transportation network. By 1850, a network of iron rails (described by the French novelist Émile Zola as a "monstrous great steel skeleton") had spread across much of western and central Europe, while water routes were improved by the deepening and widening of rivers and canals.

Across the Atlantic Ocean, the United States experienced the first stages of its industrial revolution in the first half of the nineteenth century. In 1800, America was still a predominantly agrarian society, as six out of every seven workers were farmers. Sixty years later, only half of all workers were farmers, while the total population had grown from 5 to 30 million people, larger than Great Britain itself.

The initial application of machinery to production was accomplished by borrowing from Great Britain. Soon, however, Americans began to equal or surpass British technical achievements. The Harpers Ferry arsenal, for example, built muskets with interchangeable parts. Because all the individual parts of a musket were identical (for example, all triggers were the same), the final product could be put together quickly and easily; this innovation enabled Americans to avoid the more costly system in which skilled craftsmen fitted together individual parts made separately. The so-called American system reduced costs and revolutionized production by saving labor, an important consideration in a society that had few skilled artisans.

Unlike Britain, the United States was a large country, and the lack of a good system of internal transportation initially seemed to limit American economic development by making the transport of goods prohibitively expensive. This difficulty was gradually remedied, however. Thousands of miles of roads and canals were built linking east and west. The steamboat facilitated transportation on rivers and the Great Lakes and in Atlantic coastal waters. Most important of all in the development of an American transportation system was the railroad. Beginning with 100 miles in 1830, more than 27,000 miles of railroad track were laid in the next thirty years. This transportation revolution turned the United States into a single massive market for the manufactured goods of the northeast, the early center of American industrialization, and by 1860, the United States was well on its way to being an industrial nation.

1-2a The Pace Quickens

During the fifty years before the outbreak of World War I in 1914, the Western world witnessed a dynamic age of material prosperity. Thanks to new industries, new sources of energy, and new technological achievements, a second stage of the Industrial Revolution transformed the human environment and led many people to believe that material progress would improve world conditions and thus bring the problem of world poverty to an end.

The first major change in industrial development after 1870 was the substitution of steel for iron. Steel, an alloy stronger and more malleable than iron, soon became an essential component of the Industrial Revolution

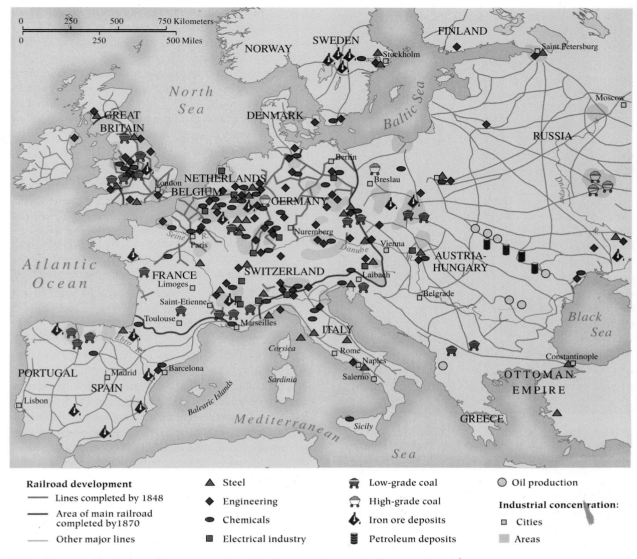

Railroad development
—— Lines completed by 1848
—— Area of main railroad completed by 1870
---- Other major lines

▲ Steel
◆ Engineering
⬭ Chemicals
■ Electrical industry

⛏ Low-grade coal
⛏ High-grade coal
⚒ Iron ore deposits
⬛ Petroleum deposits

◯ Oil production

Industrial concentration:
▫ Cities
▪ Areas

MAP 1.1 The Industrial Regions of Europe at the End of the Nineteenth Century. By the end of the nineteenth century, the Industrial Revolution—in steelmaking, electricity, petroleum, and chemicals—had spurred substantial economic growth and prosperity in western and central Europe; it had also sparked economic and political competition between Great Britain and Germany.

Q *Which parts of Europe became industrialized most quickly in the nineteenth century? Why do you think this was?*

(see Image 1.2). New methods for rolling and shaping steel made it useful in the construction of lighter, smaller, and faster machines and engines, as well as for railways, shipbuilding, and armaments. It also paved the way for the building of the first skyscrapers, a development that would eventually transform the skylines of the cities of the West. In 1860, Great Britain, France, Germany, and Belgium produced 125,000 tons of steel; by 1913, the total was 32 million tons.

The Invention of Electricity Electricity was a major new form of energy that proved to be of great value since it moved relatively effortlessly through space by means of transmitting wires. The first commercially practical generators of electric current were not developed until the 1870s. By 1910, hydroelectric power stations and coal-fired steam-generating plants enabled entire districts to be tied into a single power distribution system that provided a common source of power for homes, shops, and industrial enterprises.

IMAGE 1.2 The Colossus of Paris. When it was completed for the Paris World's Fair in 1889, the Eiffel Tower became, at 1,056 feet, the tallest human-made monument in the world. The colossus, which seemed to be rising from the shadows of the city's feudal past like some new technological giant, symbolized the triumph of the Industrial Revolution and machine-age capitalism, proclaiming the dawn of a new era of endless possibilities and power. Constructed of wrought iron with more than 2.5 million rivet holes, the structure was completed in two years and was paid for entirely by the builder himself, the engineer Gustave Eiffel. From the outset, the monument was wildly popular. Nearly 2 million people lined up at the fair to visit this gravity-defying marvel.

Electricity spawned a whole series of new products. The invention of the incandescent filament lamp opened homes and cities to illumination by electric lights. Although most electricity was initially used for lighting, it was eventually put to use in transportation. By the 1880s, streetcars and subways had appeared in major European cities. Electricity also transformed the factory. Conveyor belts, cranes, machines, and machine tools could all be powered by electricity and located anywhere. Meanwhile, a revolution in communications ensued when Alexander Graham Bell invented the telephone in 1876 and Guglielmo Marconi sent the first radio waves across the Atlantic in 1901.

The Internal Combustion Engine The development of the internal combustion engine had a similar effect. The processing of liquid fuels—petroleum and its distilled derivatives—made possible the widespread use of the internal combustion engine as a source of power in transportation. An oil-fired engine was made in 1897, and by 1902, the Hamburg-Amerika Line had switched from coal to oil on its new ocean liners. By the beginning of the twentieth century, some naval fleets had been converted to oil burners as well.

The internal combustion engine gave rise to the automobile and the airplane. In 1900, world production, initially led by the French, stood at 9,000 cars, but by 1906, Americans had taken the lead. It was an American, Henry Ford, who revolutionized the automotive industry with the mass production of the Model T. By 1916, Ford's factories were producing 735,000 cars a year. In the meantime, air transportation had emerged with the Zeppelin airship in 1900. In 1903, at Kitty Hawk, North Carolina, the Wright brothers made the first flight in a fixed-wing plane powered by a gasoline engine. World War I stimulated the aircraft industry, and in 1919 the first regular passenger air service was established.

Trade and Manufacturing The growth of industrial production depended on the development of markets for the sale of manufactured goods. Competition for foreign markets was keen, and by 1870, European countries were increasingly compelled to focus on promoting domestic demand. Between 1850 and 1900, real wages increased in Britain by two-thirds and in Germany by one-third. A decline in the cost of food combined with lower prices for manufactured goods because of reduced production and transportation costs made it easier for Europeans to buy consumer products. In the cities, new methods for retail distribution—in particular, the department store—were used to expand sales of a whole new range of consumer goods made possible by the development of the steel and electric industries. The desire to own sewing machines, clocks, bicycles, electric lights, and typewriters generated a new consumer ethic that has since become a crucial part of the modern economy.

Meanwhile, increased competition for foreign markets and the growing importance of domestic demand led to a reaction against the free trade that had characterized the European economy between 1820 and 1870. By the 1870s, European governments were returning to the use of protective **tariffs** to guarantee domestic markets for the products of their own industries. At the same time, cartels were being formed to decrease competition internally. In a **cartel**, independent enterprises worked together to control prices and fix production quotas, thereby restraining the kind of competition that led to reduced prices. The Rhenish-Westphalian Coal Syndicate, founded in 1893, controlled 98 percent of Germany's coal production by 1904.

The formation of cartels was paralleled by a move toward larger and more efficient manufacturing plants, especially in the iron and steel, machinery, heavy electric equipment, and chemical industries. The result was a desire to streamline or rationalize production as much as possible. The development of precision tools enabled manufacturers to produce interchangeable parts, which in turn led to the creation of the assembly line for production.

By 1900, much of western and central Europe had entered a new era, characterized by rising industrial production and growing material prosperity. With its capital, industries, and military might, the region dominated the world economy. Eastern and southern Europe, however, was still largely agricultural and relegated by the industrialized countries to providing food and raw materials. The presence of Romanian oil, Greek olive oil, and Serbian pigs and prunes in western Europe served as reminders of an economic division in Europe that continued well into the twentieth century.

1-3 THE EMERGENCE OF A MASS SOCIETY

Focus Question: How did the advent of the Industrial Revolution change the nature of the social class system in Europe?

The new world created by the Industrial Revolution led to the emergence of a **mass society** in western Europe and the United States by the end of the nineteenth century. A mass society meant new forms of expression for the lower classes as they benefited from the extension of voting rights, an improved standard of living, and compulsory elementary education. But there was a price to pay. Urbanization and rapid population growth led to overcrowding in the burgeoning cities and increasing public health problems. Eventually, governments were driven to construct cheap housing for the working classes, thus being forced to step into areas of social engineering that they would never have touched earlier. In the meantime, air and water pollution, a product of the growing use of coal and factory waste, began to rise in industrial areas throughout the continent. In big cities like London and Birmingham, coal particles concentrated in dense fogs often had deadly consequences. For the first time, Europeans began to encounter the environmental costs of the Industrial Revolution. In the meantime, Europeans began for the first time to appreciate the environmental costs of industrialization, as air and water pollution

began to rise in various parts of the continent. In big industrialized cities like London, coal particles concentrated in dense "killer fogs" with deadly human consequences.

1-3a Social Structures

At the top of European society stood a wealthy elite, constituting only 5 percent of the population but controlling between 30 and 40 percent of its wealth. This privileged minority was an amalgamation of the traditional landed aristocracy that had dominated European society for centuries and the emerging upper middle class, sometimes called the bourgeoisie (literally "burghers" or "city people"). Over the course of the nineteenth century, aristocrats coalesced with the most successful industrialists, bankers, and merchants to form a new elite.

Increasingly, aristocrats and the affluent bourgeoisie fused as the latter purchased landed estates to join the aristocrats in the pleasures of country living, while the aristocrats bought lavish town houses for part-time urban life. Common bonds were also created when the sons of wealthy bourgeois families were admitted to the elite schools dominated by the children of the aristocracy. This educated elite assumed leadership roles in the government and the armed forces. Marriage also served to unite the two groups. Daughters of tycoons gained titles, and aristocratic heirs gained new sources of cash. When the American heiress Consuelo Vanderbilt married the duke of Marlborough, the new duchess brought £2 million (approximately $10 million) to her husband.

A New Middle Class Below the upper class was a middle level of the bourgeoisie that included professionals in law, medicine, and the civil service as well as moderately well-to-do industrialists and merchants. The industrial expansion of the nineteenth century also added new vocations to Western society such as business managers, office workers, engineers, architects, accountants, and chemists, who formed professional associations as the symbols of their newfound importance. At the lower end of the middle class were the small shopkeepers, traders, manufacturers, and prosperous peasants. Their chief preoccupation was the provision of goods and services for the classes above them.

The moderately prosperous and successful members of this new mass society shared a certain style of life, one whose values tended to dominate much of nineteenth-century society. They were especially active in preaching their worldview to their children and to the upper and lower classes of their society. This was especially evident in Victorian Britain, often considered a model of middle-class society. It was the European middle classes who accepted and promulgated the importance of progress and science. They believed in hard work, which they viewed as the primary human good, open to everyone and guaranteed to have positive results. They also believed in the good conduct associated with traditional Christian morality.

Such values were often scorned at the time by members of the economic and intellectual elite, and in later years, it became commonplace for observers to mock the Victorian era—the years of the long reign of Queen Victoria (r. 1837–1901) in Great Britain—for its vulgar materialism, cultural philistinism, and conformist values. As the historian Peter Gay has recently shown, however, this harsh portrayal of the "bourgeois" character of the age distorts the reality of an era of complexity and contradiction, with diverse forces interacting to lay the foundations of the modern world.[2]

The Working Class The working classes constituted almost 80 percent of the population of Europe. In rural areas, many of these people were landholding peasants, agricultural laborers, and sharecroppers, especially in eastern Europe. Only about 10 percent of the British population worked in agriculture, however; in Germany, the figure was 25 percent.

There was no homogeneous urban working class. At the top were skilled artisans in such traditional handicraft trades as cabinetmaking, printing, and jewelry making. The Industrial Revolution also brought new entrants into the group of highly skilled workers, including machine-tool specialists, shipbuilders, and metalworkers. Many skilled workers attempted to pattern themselves after the middle class by seeking good housing and educating their children.

Semiskilled laborers, including such people as carpenters, bricklayers, and many factory workers, earned wages that were about two-thirds of those of highly skilled workers (see Historical Voices, "Discipline in the New Factories," p. 9). At the bottom of the hierarchy stood the largest group of workers, the unskilled laborers. They included day laborers, who worked irregularly for very low wages, and large numbers of domestic servants. One of every seven employed persons in Great Britain in 1900 was a domestic servant.

Urban workers did experience a betterment in the material conditions of their lives after 1870. A rise in real wages, accompanied by a decline in many consumer costs, especially in the 1880s and 1890s, made it possible for workers to buy more than just food and housing. Workers' budgets now included money for more clothes and even leisure at the same time that strikes and labor agitation were winning ten-hour days and Saturday afternoons off. The combination of more income and more free time produced whole new patterns of mass leisure.

Among the least attractive aspects of the era, however, was the widespread practice of child labor. Working conditions for underage workers were often abysmal

(see Comparative Illustration, "The Dual Face of the Industrial Revolution," p. 10). According to a report commissioned in 1832 to inquire into the conditions for child factory workers in Great Britain, children as young as six years of age began work before dawn. Those who were drowsy or fell asleep were tapped on the head, doused with cold water, strapped to a chair, or flogged with a stick. Another commission convened in the 1840s described conditions for underage workers in the coal mines as follows: "Chained, belted, harnessed like dogs in a go-cart, black, saturated with wet, and more than half naked—crawling upon their hands and feet, and dragging their heavy loads behind them—they present an appearance indescribably disgusting and unnatural."[3]

1-3b Changing Roles for Women

The position of women during the Industrial Revolution was also changing. During much of the nineteenth century, many women adhered to the ideal of femininity popularized by writers and poets. The British poet Alfred, Lord Tennyson's poem *The Princess* expressed it well:

Man for the field and woman for the hearth:
Man for the sword and for the needle she:
Man with the head and woman with the heart:
Man to command and woman to obey; All else confusion.

The reality was somewhat different. Under the impact of the Industrial Revolution, which created a wide variety of service and white-collar jobs, women began to accept employment as clerks, typists, secretaries, and salesclerks. Compulsory education opened the door to new opportunities in the teaching profession, and the expansion of hospital services enabled more women to find employment as nurses. In some countries in western Europe, women's legal rights increased. Still, most women remained confined to their traditional roles of homemaking and child rearing. The less fortunate were compelled to undertake marginal work as domestic servants or as pieceworkers in sweatshops.

Paradoxically, however, employment in the new textile mills in the United States served as an effective means for young women in New England to escape their homes and establish an independent existence. As one female factory worker expressed it:

Despite the toil we all agree
Out of the mill or in,
Dependent on others we ne'er will be
As long as we're able to spin.[4]

Eventually, however, female textile workers began to organize their efforts to increase wages and improve working conditions, provoking mill owners to move their factories to the southern states, where newly freed slaves provided a rich source of cheap labor.

Discipline in the New Factories

 Which, if any, of the worker regulations described below do you believe would be acceptable to employers and employees in today's labor market? Why?

Family & Society **WORKERS IN THE NEW FACTORIES** of the Industrial Revolution had been accustomed to a lifestyle free of overseers. Unlike the cottage industry, where home-based workers spun thread and wove cloth in their own rhythm and time, the factories demanded a new, rigorous discipline geared to the requirements and operating hours of the machines. This selection is taken from a set of rules for a factory in Berlin in 1844. They were typical of company rules everywhere the factory system had been established.

Factory Rules, Foundry and Engineering Works, Royal Overseas Trading Company

In every large works, and in the coordination of any large number of workmen, good order and harmony must be looked upon as the fundamentals of success, and therefore the following rules shall be strictly observed.

1. The normal working day begins at all seasons at 6 A.M. precisely and ends, after the usual break of half an hour for breakfast, an hour for dinner, and half an hour for tea, at 7 P.M., and it shall be strictly observed. . . .
2. Workers arriving 2 minutes late shall lose half an hour's wages; whoever is more than 2 minutes late may not start work until after the next break, or at least shall lose his wages until then. Any disputes about the correct time shall be settled by the clock mounted above the gatekeeper's lodge. . . .
3. No workman, whether employed by time or piece, may leave before the end of the working day, without having first received permission from the overseer and having given his name to the gatekeeper. Omission of these two actions shall lead to a fine of ten silver groschen payable to the sick fund.
4. Repeated irregular arrival at work shall lead to dismissal. This shall also apply to those who are found idling by an official or overseer, and refused to obey their order to resume work. . . .
6. No worker may leave his place of work otherwise than for reasons connected with his work.
7. All conversation with fellow-workers is prohibited; if any worker requires information about his work, he must turn to the overseer, or to the particular fellow-worker designated for the purpose.
8. Smoking in the workshops or in the yard is prohibited during working hours; anyone caught smoking shall be fined five silver groschen for the sick fund for every such offense. . . .
10. Natural functions must be performed at the appropriate places, and whoever is found soiling walls, fences, squares, etc., and similarly, whoever is found washing his face and hands in the workshop and not in the places assigned for the purpose, shall be fined five silver groschen for the sick fund. . . .
12. It goes without saying that all overseers and officials of the firm shall be obeyed without question, and shall be treated with due deference. Disobedience will be punished by dismissal.
13. Immediate dismissal shall also be the fate of anyone found drunk in any of the workshops. . . .
14. Every workman is obliged to report to his superiors any acts of dishonesty or embezzlement on the part of his fellow workmen. If he omits to do so, and it is shown after subsequent discovery of a misdemeanor that he knew about it at the time, he shall be liable to be taken to court as an accessory after the fact and the wage due to him shall be retained as punishment.

Source: From *Documents of European Economic History* by Sidney Pollard and Colin Holmes (New York: St. Martin's Press, 1968). Copyright © 1968 by S. Pollard and C. Holmes.

Many of the improvements in women's position resulted from the rise of the first feminist movements. **Feminism** in Europe had its origins in the social upheaval of the French Revolution, when some women advocated equality for women based on the doctrine of natural rights. In the 1830s, a number of women in the United States and Europe sought improvements for women by focusing on family and marriage law to strengthen the property rights of wives and enhance their ability to secure a divorce. Later in the century, attention shifted to the issue of equal political rights.

The Dual Face of the Industrial Revolution

Q *How would you compare these contrasting visions of the Industrial Revolution with conditions in the United States today?*

shows prosperous shoppers sampling the wares of a newly erected department store in late-nineteenth century Paris.

Politics & Government

TO MANY CONTEMPORARIES, the Industrial Revolution often appeared to present contrasting visions of the society being produced by its consequences. In Image 1.3a, a woman and a young boy engage in hard labor in a British coal mine. Image 1.3b

IMAGE 1.3a Women and Children in the Mines

Universal History Archive/UniversalImagesGroup/Getty Images

IMAGE 1.3b Shopping at Le Bon Marché

Mary Evans Picture Library/The Image Works

Many feminists believed that the right to vote was the key to all other reforms to improve the position of women.

The struggle to obtain women's suffrage in the United States was spearheaded by the efforts of the social activist Elizabeth Cady Stanton and the Quaker Lucretia Mott, who hosted a meeting on women's rights at Seneca Falls, N.Y. in July 1848. The convention, attended by 300 delegates, drafted a Declaration of Sentiments and passed a number of resolutions calling for the realization of full civil, social, and religious rights for all women in the United States. Although progress was slow, their efforts were finally realized when the 19th amendment to the U.S. Constitution calling for women's right to vote was finally passed in 1920 (see Historical Voices, "A Plea for Women's Rights," p. 11).

The British women's movement was the most vocal and active in Europe, but it was divided over tactics. Moderates believed that women must demonstrate that they would

use political power responsibly if they wanted Parliament to grant them the right to vote. Another group, however, favored a more radical approach. In 1903, Emmeline Pankhurst (1858–1928) and her daughters, Christabel and Sylvia, founded the Women's Social and Political Union, which enrolled mostly middle- and upper-class women. The members of Pankhurst's organization realized the value of the media and used unusual publicity stunts to call attention to their insistence on winning women the right to vote and other demands. They pelted government officials with eggs, chained themselves to lampposts, smashed the windows of department stores on fashionable shopping streets, burned railroad cars, and went on hunger strikes in jail.

Before World War I, demands for women's rights were being heard throughout Europe, although only in Norway, as well as in Australia and New Zealand, did women actually receive the right to vote before 1914. It would take the

A Plea for Women's Rights

 Which of the complaints outlined in the declaration do you feel have not been addressed or corrected today?

Politics & Government IN JULY 1848, a group of over 300 people gathered in the town of Seneca Falls, New York, to demand action on the issue of women's suffrage in the United States. The meeting was organized by the civil rights activist Elizabeth Cady Stanton and her Quaker colleague Lucretia Mott. At the meeting, the delegates drew up a list of demands that were put up for a vote by those in attendance. Some signed the declaration, while others agreed with the document in principle. Still others opposed it in the belief that it might hinder other goals for improving the rights of women in the United States.

The declaration, which was deliberately patterned after the wording of the Declaration of Independence in 1776, aroused considerable controversy at the time, but women's suffrage was finally realized by a constitutional amendment passed by Congress at the end of World War I.

The Declaration of Sentiments

When, in the course of human events, it becomes necessary for one portion of the family of man to assume among the people of the earth a position different from that which they have hitherto occupied, but one to which the laws of nature and of nature's God entitle them, a decent respect to the opinions of mankind requires that they should declare the causes that impel them to such a course...

We hold these truths to be self-evident: that all men and women are created equal; that they are endowed by their Creator with certain inalienable rights; that among these are life, liberty, and the pursuit of happiness... Whenever any form of government becomes destructive of these ends, it is the right of those who suffer from it to refuse allegiance to it, and to insist upon the institution of a new government, laying its foundation on such principles, and organizing its powers in such form, as to them shall seem likely to effect their safety and happiness...

The history of mankind is a history of repeated injuries and usurpations on the part of man toward woman, having in direct object the establishment of an absolute tyranny over her...

He has never permitted her to exercise her inalienable right to the elective franchise. He has compelled her to submit to laws, in the formation of which she had no voice. He has withheld from her rights which are given to the most ignorant and degraded men—both natives and foreigners...

He has taken from her all rights in property, even to the wages she earns.

He has made her, morally, an irresponsible being, as she can commit many crimes with impunity, provided they be done in the presence of her husband. In the covenant of marriage, she is compelled to promise obedience to her husband, he becoming, to all intents and purposes, her master—the law giving him power to deprive her of her liberty, and to administer chastisement.

He has so framed the laws of divorce, as to what shall be the proper causes, and in case of separation, to whom the guardianship of the children shall be given, as to be wholly regardless of the happiness of women—the law, in all cases, going upon a false supposition of the supremacy of man, and giving all power into his hands.

He has monopolized nearly all the profitable employments, and from those she is permitted to follow, she receives but a scanty remuneration. He closes against her all the avenues to wealth and distinction which he considers most honorable to himself. As a teacher of theology, medicine, or law, she is not known.

He has denied her the facilities for obtaining a thorough education, all colleges being closed against her.

He allows her in church, as well as state, but a subordinate position, claiming apostolic authority for her exclusion from the ministry, and, with some exceptions, from any public participation in the affairs of the church.

He has created a false public sentiment by giving to the world a different code of morals for men and women, by which moral delinquencies which exclude women from society, are not tolerated, but deemed of little account in man...

He has endeavored, in every way that he could, to destroy her confidence in her own powers, to lessen her self-respect, and to make her willing to lead a dependent and abject life.

Now, in view of this entire disfranchisement of one-half the people of this country, their social and religious degradation—in view of the unjust laws above mentioned... we insist that [women] have immediate admission to all the rights and privileges which belong to them as citizens of the United States.

Source: Elizabeth Cady Stanton, *A History of Woman Suffrage*, vol. 1 (Rochester, N.Y.: Fowler and Wells, 1889), pp. 70–71.

dramatic upheaval of World War I before male-dominated governments capitulated on this basic issue (see Movies & History, *Suffragette*, below).

1-4 REACTION AND REVOLUTION: THE DECLINE OF THE OLD ORDER

 Focus Questions: What were the major ideas associated with the growth of liberalism and nationalism in nineteenth-century Europe? In the light of the ambiguous character of the term "nationalism," in what conditions should it be applied today?

While the Industrial Revolution shook the economic and social foundations of European society, similar revolutionary developments were reshaping the political map of the European continent. These developments were the product of a variety of factors, including the French Revolution, which broke out in 1789, and the intellectual movement known as the Enlightenment. The French Revolution had severely undermined the traditional concept of hereditary monarchy, as well as the very existence of the traditional system of multinational empires such as Tsarist Russia, the Habsburg monarchy, and the Ottoman Empire, while the Enlightenment gave birth to the idea of the rights of the individual against the power of the state and the church.

With the defeat of French forces under Napoleon Bonaparte at the battle of Waterloo in 1815, the delegates at the Congress of Vienna sought to reinstate the prerevolutionary political system. For years afterward, it appeared that the old order had recovered from the serious threats to its primacy. But by mid-century, traditional Europe was again under attack along a wide front. Arrayed against the conservative forces was a set of new political ideas that began to come into their own in the first half of the nineteenth century and continue to affect the entire world today.

1-4a Liberalism and Nationalism

One of these new political ideas was **liberalism**. Liberalism owed much to the Enlightenment and the American and French Revolutions that erupted at the end of the eighteenth century, all of which proclaimed the autonomy of the individual against the power of the state. Opinions diverged among people classified as liberals—many of them members of the emerging middle class—but all began with a common denominator, a conviction that in both economic and political terms, people should be as free from restraint as possible. Economic liberalism, also known as classical economics, was based on the tenet of *laissez-faire*—the belief that the state should not interfere in the free play of natural economic forces, especially supply and demand. Political liberalism was based on the concept of a constitutional monarchy or constitutional state, with limits on the powers of government and a written charter to protect the basic civil rights of the people. Although they held that people were entitled to equal civil rights, most liberals believed that the right to vote and to hold office should be open only to males who met certain property qualifications.

MOVIES & HISTORY
Suffragette (2015)

Issued in 2015 under director Sarah Gavron, this British film concerns the suffragist movement in Great Britain. The chief actress in the film is the fictitious character Maud Watts (Carey Mulligan), a laundry worker who—as a result of physical abuse at work and in her home—gradually becomes involved in suffragette activities. After hearing a speech by the suffragette leader Emmeline Pankhurst (Meryl Streep) that "deeds, not words" will only give women the right to vote, she and her friends turn to acts of violent destruction. This leads to police violence, imprisonment, and dismissal from her job. After a close colleague is killed while taking part in a public protest, the movement begins to receive more publicity, and the film concludes by noting that women's suffrage began to be achieved in the 1920s.

Focus Features/Courtesy Everett Collection

Do you agree with Maud Watts that if peaceful protest fails to right a social wrong, violent action is justified?

Nationalism was an even more powerful ideology for change in the nineteenth century. The idea arose out of an awareness of being part of a community that had common institutions, traditions, language, and customs. In some cases, that sense of identity was based on shared ethnic or linguistic characteristics. In others, it was the result of a common commitment to a particular religion or culture. Such a community came to be called a "nation," and the primary political loyalty of individuals would be to this "nation" rather than, as was the case in much of Europe at that time, to a dynasty or a city-state or some other political unit. Nationalism did not become a popular force for change until the French Revolution, when the overthrow of the French monarchy under King Louis XV encouraged the popular belief that governments should not be a royal patrimony, but rather should represent the interests of the local population.

Thus, long-divided peoples such as the Germans or the Italians now began to demand national unity in a nation-state with one central government. Subject peoples in Eastern Europe, such as the Poles, the Czechs, and the Hungarians, wanted national self-determination, or the right to establish their own autonomy rather than be subject to a Russian or German minority in a multinational state such as Tsarist Russia or the Habsburg Empire.

1-4b The Revolutions of 1848

At first, the advocates of liberalism and nationalism appeared to march in tandem. When discontent with the Congress of Vienna system began to emerge in the 1830s, the two groups joined forces to topple the conservative government in Paris and install a constitutional monarchy in France. Other uprisings took place in Italy, Poland, and Belgium (although only the latter was successful, leading to a breakaway of the area from the Netherlands). Elsewhere, however, Russian troops successfully crushed a rebellion in Poland, while Austrian forces intervened to uphold reactionary regimes in a number of Italian states.

But the desire for change had not been quenched. In the spring of 1848, a new series of uprisings against established authority broke out in several countries in central and western Europe. The most dramatic was in France, where an uprising centered in Paris overthrew the so-called bourgeois monarchy of King Louis Philippe and briefly brought to power a new republic composed of an alliance of workers, intellectuals, and progressive representatives of the urban middle class.

In Germany, progressive forces began to call for the abolition of the German Confederation (a patchwork of 38 semi-independent kingdoms and principalities that had replaced the archaic Holy Roman Empire after the Congress of Vienna) and the establishment of a new unified state, based on liberal principles, to represent all German-speaking peoples. An assembly of delegates convened in Frankfurt in July to carry through on the demand and draw up a constitution for a future united Germany.

It shortly became clear, however, that optimism about the imminence of a new order in Europe had not been justified. In France, the shaky alliance between workers and the urban bourgeoisie that followed the overthrow of Louis Philippe was ruptured when workers' groups and their representatives in the government began to demand extensive social reforms to provide guaranteed benefits to the poor. Moderates, frightened by rising political tensions in Paris, resisted such demands. Facing the specter of class war, the French nation drew back and welcomed the rise to power of Louis Napoleon, a nephew of Napoleon Bonaparte. Within three years, he declared himself, to general approbation, Emperor Napoleon III. Meanwhile, the demands for reform voiced by the delegates to the Frankfurt Assembly were dismissed by the German rulers, while popular uprisings in several regions of the Italian peninsula failed to unseat autocratic monarchs and overturn the existing political order.

1-4c The Unifications of Italy and Germany

Although the bright hopes of 1848 had seemingly been crushed, the rising force of nationalism was not to be quenched. Nationalist sentiment, at first restricted primarily to the small educated elite, had now begun to spread among the general population as a result of the rise in literacy rates and the increasing availability of books, journals, and newspapers printed in the vernacular languages. Ordinary Europeans, previously unconcerned about political affairs, now became increasingly aware of the nationalist debate and some became actively involved in the political process.

By the 1860s, the growing demand for nationhood finally began to produce results. Italy, long divided into separate kingdoms, was finally united under the kingdom of Piedmont. In Germany, a North German Confederation was formed in 1866 under the leadership of Prussia, its strongest member. Under the urging of Otto von Bismarck (1815–1898), who had been appointed chancellor by King William I (r. 1861–1888), Prussia now sought to bring about the unification of Germany based on a policy of "iron and blood." This more aggressive approach was heralded by many German nationalists who had been stirred up to a fever pitch by the writings of intellectuals such as the philosopher Johann Gottfried Herder, who argued that the German people (the *volk*) had a sacred duty to purify the corrupt old world, as personified by German's perennial rival France. Nationalism had now begun to take on a chauvinistic tinge.

Convinced that the strongest opposition to German hegemony in Europe would come from neighboring France, Bismarck provoked a war with his neighbor in 1870.

After France's crushing defeat, a year later a new German Empire was declared in the Hall of Mirrors at the Palace of Versailles, just outside Paris.

Many German liberals were initially delighted at the unification of their country after centuries of division. But they were soon to discover that the new German Empire would not usher in a new era of peace and freedom. Under Prussian leadership, the new state quickly proclaimed the superiority of authoritarian and militaristic values and abandoned the principles of liberalism and constitutional government. Nationalism had become a two-edged sword, as advocates of a greater Germany began to promote the idea of German expansionism over non-Germanic peoples elsewhere on the continent.

Liberal principles made similarly little headway elsewhere in central and eastern Europe. After the transformation of the Habsburg Empire into the dual monarchy of Austria-Hungary in 1867, the Austrian segment received a constitution that theoretically recognized the equality of the nationalities and established a parliamentary system with the principle of **ministerial responsibility**. But the problem of reconciling the interests of the various nationalities remained a difficult one. The German minority that governed Austria felt increasingly threatened by the Czechs, Poles, and other Slavic groups within the empire, and when representatives of the latter began to agitate for autonomy, the government ignored the parliament and relied increasingly on imperial emergency decrees to govern. On the eve of World War I, the Austro-Hungarian Empire was far from solving its minorities problem (see Map 1.2).

1-4d Roots of Revolution in Russia

To the east, in the vast Russian Empire, neither the Industrial Revolution nor the European Enlightenment had exerted much impact. Always a vast nation situated on the eastern borders of the continent of Europe, at the beginning of the nineteenth century Russia was overwhelmingly rural, agricultural, and autocratic. The Russian tsar was still regarded as a divine-right monarch with unlimited power, although the physical extent of the empire made the claim impracticable. For centuries, Russian farmers had groaned under the yoke of an oppressive system that tied the peasants to poverty conditions and the legal status of serfs under the authority of their manor lord. An enlightened tsar, Alexander II (r. 1855–1881), had sought to alleviate conditions by emancipating the serfs in 1861, but under conditions that left most Russian peasants still poor and with little hope for social or economic betterment. In desperation, the Russian peasants frequently lashed out at their oppressors in sporadic rebellions, but all such uprisings were quelled with brutal efficiency by the tsarist regime.

As we have seen, in western Europe it was the urban bourgeoisie that took the lead in the struggle for change. In preindustrial Russia, the middle class was still small in size and lacking in self-confidence. Some, calling themselves Slavophiles, looked with scorn on their allegedly corrupt counterparts elsewhere in Europe and lauded the purity of traditional Slavic civilization—defined in their eyes by monarchical absolutism and the holy Russian Orthodox Church. Others, however, had traveled to the West and were determined to import Western values and institutions into the Russian environment. At mid-century, a few progressive intellectuals went out to the villages to arouse their rural brethren to the need for change. Known as *narodniks* (from the Russian term *narod*, for "people" or "nation"), they sought to energize the peasantry as a force for the transformation of Russian society. Although many saw the answer to Russian problems in the western European model, others insisted on the uniqueness of the Russian experience and sought to bring about a revitalization of the country on the basis of the communal traditions of the native village.

For the most part, such efforts achieved little. The Russian peasant was resistant to change and suspicious of outsiders. In desperation, some radicals turned to terrorism in the hope that assassinations of public officials would spark tsarist repression, thereby demonstrating the brutality of the system and galvanizing popular anger. Chief among such groups was the Narodnaya Volya ("the People's Will"), a terrorist organization that assassinated Tsar Alexander II in 1881.

The assassination of Alexander II convinced his son and successor, Alexander III (r. 1881–1894), that reform had been a mistake, and he quickly returned to the repressive measures of earlier tsars. When Alexander III died, his son and successor, Nicholas II (r. 1894–1917), began his rule armed with his father's conviction that the absolute power of the tsars should be preserved.

But it was too late, for conditions were changing. Although industrialization came late to Russia, it progressed rapidly after 1890, especially with the assistance of foreign investment. By 1900, Russia had become the fourth-largest producer of steel, behind the United States, Germany, and Great Britain. At the same time, Russia was turning out half of the world's production of oil. Conditions for the working class, however, were abysmal, and opposition to the tsarist regime from workers, peasants, and intellectuals, long frustrated, finally exploded into revolt in 1905. Facing an exhausting war with Japan in Asia (see Chapter 3), Tsar Nicholas reluctantly granted civil liberties and agreed to create a legislative assembly, the Duma, elected directly by a broad franchise. But real constitutional monarchy proved short-lived. By 1907, the

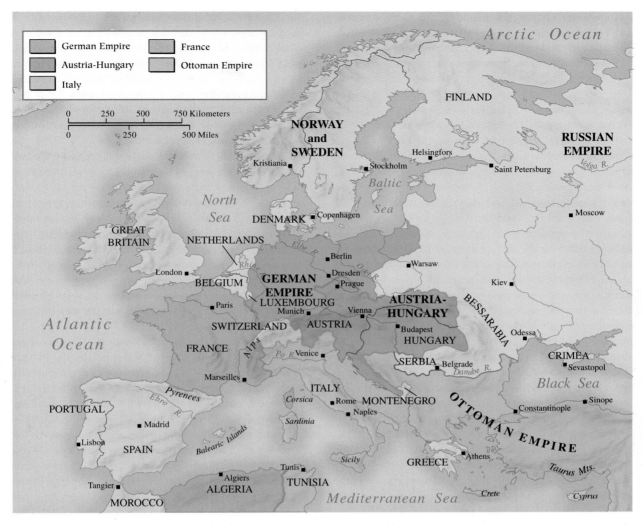

MAP 1.2 **Europe in 1871.** German unification in 1871 upset the balance of power that had prevailed in Europe for more than half a century and eventually led to a restructuring of European alliances. By 1907, Europe was divided into two opposing camps: the Triple Entente of Great Britain, Russia, and France and the Triple Alliance of Germany, Austria-Hungary, and Italy.

 Which of the countries identified on this map could be described as multinational empires?

tsar had curtailed the power of the Duma and fell back on the army and the bureaucracy to rule Russia.

1-4e The Ottoman Empire and Nationalism in the Balkans

Like the Austro-Hungarian Empire, the Ottoman Empire was threatened by the rising nationalist aspirations of its subject peoples. Beginning in the fourteenth century, the Ottoman Turks had expanded from their base in the Anatolian peninsula into the Balkans and southern Russia,

and along the northern coast of Africa. Soon they controlled the entire eastern half of the Mediterranean Sea. But by the nineteenth century, despite state reform programs designed to modernize the empire, increasing social unrest and the intervention of the European powers in Ottoman affairs challenged the legitimacy of the Ottoman state.

Gradually, the emotional appeal of nationhood began to make inroads among the various ethnic and linguistic groups in southeastern Europe. In the course of the nineteenth century, the Balkan provinces of the Ottoman

Empire began to gain their freedom, although the intense rivalry in the region between Austria-Hungary and Russia complicated the process. Greece became an independent kingdom in 1830 after a successful revolt. After Russia's defeat of the Ottoman Empire in 1878, Serbia and Romania were recognized as independent states. Bulgaria achieved autonomous status under Russia's protection, and the Balkan territories of Bosnia and Herzegovina were placed under Austria's. Despite such changes, the force of Balkan nationalism was by no means stilled.

Meanwhile, other parts of the empire began to break away from central control. In Egypt, the ambitious governor Muhammad Ali declared the region's autonomy from Ottoman rule and initiated a series of reforms designed to promote economic growth and government efficiency. During the 1830s, he sought to improve agricultural production and reform the educational system, and he imported machinery and technicians from Europe to carry out the first industrial revolution on African soil. In the end, however, the effort failed, partly because Egypt's manufactures could not compete with those of Europe and also because much of the profit from the export of cash crops went into the hands of conservative landlords.

Measures to promote industrialization elsewhere in the empire had even less success. By mid-century, a small industrial sector, built with equipment imported from Europe, took shape, and a modern system of transport and communications began to make its appearance. By the end of the century, however, the results were meager, and members of the empire's small westernized elite, led by a small group of reformist military officers known as the Young Turks, became increasingly restive (see Chapter 5).

1-5 THE TRIUMPH OF LIBERALISM IN THE WEST

 Focus Questions: What factors do you think are responsible for the triumph of liberal principles in late nineteenth-century western Europe and the United States? Do you think such factors are relevant today?

In western Europe, where democratic principles had already been introduced into the political discussion, and where an affluent urban middle class represented a growing political force, liberal principles experienced a better fate. The British political and economic elites had been frightened by the specter of social revolution that periodically raged on the European continent, and by 1871 the country had a functioning two-party parliamentary system.

The governing Liberal and Conservative parties were both still dominated by a coalition of aristocratic landowners and upper-middle-class business magnates. But both parties also saw the necessity of adopting political reforms to avoid violence and competed in supporting legislation that expanded the right to vote. Reform acts in 1867 and 1884 greatly expanded the number of adult males who could vote, and by the end of World War I, all males over twenty-one and women over thirty had that right.

The political reforms grudgingly enacted in the last half of the nineteenth century led eventually to the growth of **trade unions** and the emergence in 1900 of the Labour Party, which dedicated itself to workers' interests. As a result, the Liberals felt pressure to seek the workers' support by promoting a program of social welfare. The National Insurance Act of 1911 provided benefits for workers in case of sickness or unemployment, to be paid for by compulsory contributions from workers, employers, and the state. Additional legislation provided a small pension for those over seventy and compensation for those injured in accidents at work.

A similar process was under way in France, where the overthrow of Napoleon III's Second Empire in 1870 led to the creation of a republican form of government. France failed, however, to develop a strong parliamentary system on the British two-party model because the existence of a dozen political parties forced the premier to depend on a coalition of parties to stay in power. The Third Republic was notorious for its changes of government. Between 1875 and 1914, there were no fewer than fifty cabinet changes; during the same period, the British had eleven. Nevertheless, the government's political and social reforms gradually won more and more middle-class and peasant support, and by 1914, the Third Republic commanded the loyalty of most French people.

Even in Germany, the situation was changing. Although the levers of power were firmly controlled by a partnership between a conservative landed aristocracy and wealthy industrialists, the country was rapidly becoming urbanized, as the impact of the Industrial Revolution began to seep through the economy. After the formation of the progressive German Social Democratic Party in 1875, several representatives of the working class were elected to the Reichstag, the country's parliament. By the end of the century, a number of reforms had been enacted to benefit the lives of German farmers and workers.

By 1870, Italy had emerged as a geographically united state, but sectional differences (exacerbated by a poverty-stricken south and an industrializing north) weakened any sense of community. Chronic turmoil between labor and industry undermined the social fabric, as did the prevalence of extensive corruption among government officials and the lack of stability created by ever-changing government coalitions. Abroad, Italy's pretensions to great-power status proved equally hollow when it became the first European power to lose a war to an African state, Ethiopia, a humiliation that later led to the costly (but successful) attempt to compensate by conquering Libya in 1911 and 1912.

1-5a The United States and Canada

A similar process took place in the Western hemisphere. Between 1860 and World War I, the United States made the shift from an agrarian to a mighty industrial nation. American heavy industry stood unchallenged in 1900. In that year, the Carnegie Steel Company alone produced more steel than Great Britain's entire steel industry. Industrialization also led to urbanization. While established cities, such as New York, Philadelphia, and Boston, grew even larger, other moderate-size cities, such as Pittsburgh, grew by leaps and bounds because of industrialization and the arrival of millions of immigrants from eastern Europe. Whereas 20 percent of Americans lived in cities in 1860, more than 40 percent did in 1900. One factor underlying the change was a vast increase in agricultural productivity, creating a food surplus that enabled millions of Americans to move from the farm to the factory.

By 1900, the United States had become the world's richest nation and greatest industrial power. Less inclined than their European counterparts to accept government intervention as a means of redressing economic or social ills, Americans experienced both the benefits and the disadvantages of unfettered capitalism. In 1890, the richest 9 percent of Americans owned an incredible 71 percent of all the wealth. Labor unrest over unsafe working conditions, strict work discipline, and periodic cycles of devastating unemployment led workers to organize. By the turn of the twentieth century, one national organization, the American Federation of Labor, emerged as labor's dominant voice. Its lack of real power, however, is reflected in its membership figures: in 1900, it constituted but 8.4 percent of the American industrial labor force. And part of the U.S. labor force remained almost entirely disenfranchised. Although the victory of the North in the Civil War led to the abolition of slavery, political, economic, and social opportunities for the African American population remained limited, and racist attitudes were widespread.

During the so-called Progressive Era after 1900, the reform of many features of American life became a primary issue. At the state level, reforming governors sought to achieve clean government by introducing elements of direct democracy, such as direct primaries for selecting nominees for public office. State governments also enacted economic and social legislation, including laws that governed hours, wages, and working conditions, especially for women and children. The realization that state laws were ineffective in dealing with nationwide problems, however, led to a progressive movement at the national level.

National progressivism was evident in the administrations of Theodore Roosevelt and Woodrow Wilson. Under Roosevelt (1901–1909), the Meat Inspection Act and Pure Food and Drug Act provided for a limited degree of federal regulation of corrupt industrial practices. Wilson (1913–1921) was responsible for the creation of a graduated federal income tax and the Federal Reserve System, which gave the federal government a role in important economic decisions formerly made by bankers. Like many European nations, the United States was moving into policies that extended the functions of the state.

Canada, economically somewhat more homogeneous than its southern neighbor, faced fewer problems in addressing issues related to social and economic equality. The larger issue for Canada was that of national unity. At the beginning of 1870, the Dominion of Canada had only four provinces: Quebec, Ontario, Nova Scotia, and New Brunswick. With the addition of two more provinces in 1871—Manitoba and British Columbia—the Dominion now extended from the Atlantic Ocean to the Pacific. But real unity was difficult to achieve because of the distrust between the English-speaking and the French-speaking peoples of Canada, most of whom lived in the province of Quebec. Fortunately for Canada, Sir Wilfrid Laurier, who became the first French Canadian prime minister in 1896, was able to reconcile Canada's two major groups and resolve the issue of separate schools for French Canadians. Laurier's administration also witnessed increased industrialization and successfully encouraged immigrants from central and eastern Europe to help populate Canada's vast territories.

1-5b Tradition and Change in Latin America

In the three centuries following the arrival of Christopher Columbus in the Western Hemisphere in 1492, South and Central America fell increasingly into the European orbit. Portugal dominated Brazil, and Spain created a vast empire that included most of the remainder of South America as well as Central America. Hence, the entire area is generally described as Latin America. Almost from the beginning, it was a multicultural society composed of European settlers, indigenous American Indians, immigrants from Asia, and black slaves brought from Africa to work on the sugar plantations and in other menial occupations. Intermarriage among the four groups resulted in the creation of a diverse population with a less rigid view of race than was the case in North America. Latin American culture also came to reflect a rich mixture of Iberian, Asian, African, and Native American themes.

The Emergence of Independent States   Until the beginning of the nineteenth century, the various Latin American societies were ruled by colonial officials appointed by monarchical governments in Europe. An additional instrument of control was the Catholic Church, which undertook a major effort to Christianize the indigenous peoples and transform them into docile and loyal subjects of the Portuguese and Spanish Empires. By 1800, however, local elites, mostly descendants of Europeans who had become permanent inhabitants of the Western Hemisphere, became increasingly affected by the spirit of nationalism that had emerged after the Napoleonic era in Europe. During the first quarter of the nineteenth century, under great leaders like Simón Bolívar of Venezuela and José de San Martín of Argentina (see Image 1.4), they launched a series of revolts that led to the eviction of the monarchical regimes and the formation of independent states from Argentina and Chile in the south to Mexico in North America. Brazil received its independence from Portugal in 1825.

Many of the new states were based on the administrative divisions that had been established by the Spanish in the early colonial era. Although all shared the legacy of Iberian culture brought to the Americas by the **conquistadors**, the particular mix of European, African, and indigenous peoples resulted in distinctive characteristics for each country.

One of the goals of the independence movement had been to free the economies of Latin America from European control and to exploit the riches of the continent for local benefit. In fact, however, political independence did not lead to a new era of prosperity for the people of Latin America. Most of the powerful elites in the region earned their wealth from the land and had few incentives to follow the European model of promoting an industrial revolution. As a result, the previous trade pattern persisted, with Latin America exporting raw materials and foodstuffs (wheat and sugar) as well as tobacco and hides in exchange for manufactured goods from Europe and the United States.

Problems of Economic Dependence   With economic growth came a boom in foreign investment. Between 1870 and 1913, British investments—mostly in railroads, mining, and public utilities—grew from £85 million to £757 million, which constituted two-thirds of all foreign investment in Latin America. By the end of the century, however, the U.S. economic presence began to increase dramatically. As Latin Americans struggled to create more

IMAGE 1.4 The Liberators of South America. José de San Martín and Simón Bolívar are hailed as the joint leaders of the South American independence movement. The former focused his campaign on the southern section of the continent, while the Venezuelan Bolívar carried on his activities in the north. This depiction of Bolívar leading impeccably uniformed troops into a campaign is undoubtedly unrealistic.

Q *Given the conditions pertaining at independence, what do you think some of the major challenges to building stable modern societies were for the independence leaders in South America?*

balanced economies after 1900, they concentrated on building a manufacturing base, notably in textiles, food processing, and construction materials.

Nevertheless, the growth of the Latin American economy came largely from the export of raw materials, and the gradual transformation of the national economies in Latin America simply added to the region's growing dependence on the capitalist nations of the West. Modernization was basically a surface feature of Latin American society; past patterns still largely prevailed. Rural elites dominated their estates and their rural workers. Although slavery was abolished by 1888, former slaves and their descendants were still at the bottom of society. The Native Americans remained poverty-stricken, debt servitude was still a way of life, and the region remained economically dependent on foreigners. Despite its economic growth, Latin America was still sorely underdeveloped.

One potential bright spot for the future economic prosperity of Latin America was the discovery of natural rubber in Brazil. Derived from the sap of a tree native to the Amazon River basin, rubber rapidly achieved popularity throughout the world as products made of it—from erasers, footwear, and raincoats to automobile tires— flooded the markets of Europe and the United States. The boom was short-lived, however. After seeds of the rubber tree were secretly shipped to Great Britain in the 1870s, rubber plantations began to be established by European growers in colonial Southeast Asia, and the Brazilian industry—plagued by poor management practices—quickly declined in the first quarter of the twentieth century (see Chapter 2).

The surface prosperity that resulted from the emergence of an export economy had a number of repercussions. One result was the modernization of the elites, who grew determined to pursue their vision of progress. Large landowners increasingly sought ways to rationalize their production methods to make greater profits. As a result, cattle ranchers in Argentina and coffee barons in Brazil became more aggressive entrepreneurs.

Another result of the new prosperity was the growth of a small but increasingly visible middle class—lawyers, merchants, shopkeepers, businessmen, schoolteachers, professors, bureaucrats, and military officers. Living mainly in the cities, these people sought education and decent incomes and increasingly regarded the United States as the model to emulate, especially in regard to industrialization and education.

As Latin American export economies boomed, the working class expanded, and this in turn led to the growth of labor unions, which often advocated the use of the general strike as an instrument for change. By and large, however, the governing elites succeeded in stifling the political influence of the working class by restricting the right to vote. The need for industrial labor also led Latin American countries to encourage European immigrants. Between 1880 and 1914, 3 million Europeans, primarily Italians and Spaniards, settled in Argentina. More than 100,000 Europeans, mostly Italian, Portuguese, and Spanish, arrived in Brazil each year between 1891 and 1900.

Social and Political Changes As in Europe and the United States, industrialization led to urbanization. Buenos Aires (known as the "Paris of South America" for its European atmosphere) had 750,000 inhabitants by 1900 and 2 million by 1914—one-fourth of Argentina's population. By that time, urban dwellers made up 53 percent of Argentina's population overall. Brazil and Chile also witnessed a dramatic increase in the number of urban dwellers.

Latin America also experienced a political transformation after 1870. Large landowners began to take a more direct interest in national politics, sometimes expressed by a direct involvement in governing. In Argentina and Chile, for example, landholding elites controlled the governments, and although they produced constitutions similar to those of the United States and European countries, they were careful to ensure their power by regulating voting rights.

In some countries, large landowners made use of dictators to maintain their interests. Porfirio Díaz, who ruled Mexico from 1876 to 1911, established a conservative government with the support of the army, foreign capitalists, large landowners, and the Catholic Church, all of whom benefited from their alliance. But there were forces for change in Mexico that sought to precipitate a true social revolution. Díaz was ousted from power in 1911 (see Chapter 2), opening an extended era of revolutionary unrest.

Sometimes political instability led to foreign intervention. In 1898, the United States sent military forces in support of an independence movement in Cuba, bringing an end to 400 years of Spanish rule on the island. U.S. occupation forces then remained for several years, despite growing opposition from the local population. The United States also intervened militarily in Nicaragua, Honduras, and the Dominican Republic to restore law and order and protect U.S. economic interests in the region, sparking cries of "Yankee imperialism."

1-6 THE RISE OF THE SOCIALIST MOVEMENT

Focus Questions: How did Karl Marx predict that the Industrial Revolution would affect and change the nature of European society? Were his predictions correct?

One of the less desirable consequences of the Industrial Revolution was the yawning disparity in the distribution of wealth. While industrialization brought increasing affluence to an emerging middle class, it brought grinding hardship to millions of others in the form of low-paying jobs in mines or factories characterized by long working hours under squalid conditions. The underlying cause was clear: because of the rapid population growth taking place in most industrializing societies in Europe, factory owners remained largely free to hire labor on their own terms, based on market forces.

Beginning in the last decades of the eighteenth century, radical groups, inspired by the egalitarian ideals of the

French Revolution, began to seek the means to rectify the problem. Some found the answer in intellectual schemes that envisaged a classless society based on the elimination of private property. Others prepared for an armed revolt to overthrow the ruling order and create a new society controlled by the working masses. Still others began to form trade unions to fight for improved working conditions and higher wages. Only one group sought to combine all of these factors into a comprehensive program to destroy the governing forces and create a new egalitarian society based on the concept of "scientific socialism." The founder of that movement was Karl Marx, a German intellectual who had abandoned an academic career in philosophy to take up radical political activities in Paris.

1-6a The Rise of Marxism

Marxism made its first appearance in 1847 with the publication of a short treatise, *The Communist Manifesto*, written by Karl Marx (1818–1883) and his close collaborator, Friedrich Engels (1820–1895). In the *Manifesto*, the two authors predicted the outbreak of a massive uprising that would overthrow the existing ruling class and bring to power a new revolutionary regime based on their ideas (see Historical Voices, "The Classless Society," p. 21).

Marx, the son of a Jewish lawyer in the city of Trier in western Germany, was trained in philosophy and became an admirer of the German philosopher Georg W. F. Hegel, who viewed historical change as the result of conflict between contending forces. The clash between such forces would eventually lead to synthesis in a new and higher reality.

Marx appropriated Hegel's ideas and applied them to the economic and social conditions of mid-nineteenth-century Europe, where he envisioned an intense struggle between the owners of the means of production and distribution and the oppressed majority who labored on their behalf. In his view, as he put it in *The Communist Manifesto*, "the history of all hitherto existing society is the history of class struggle."[5] During the feudal era, landless serfs rose up to overthrow their manor lords, giving birth to capitalism. In turn, Marx predicted, the **proletariat** (the urban working class) would eventually revolt against subhuman conditions to bring down the capitalist order and establish a new classless society to be called communism. According to Marx, the achievement of communist societies throughout the world would represent the final stage of history.

When revolutions broke out all over Europe in the eventful year of 1848, Marx and Engels eagerly but mistakenly predicted that the uprisings would spread throughout Europe and lead to the destruction of all national borders and the rise of a new revolutionary regime led by workers, dispossessed bourgeois, and communists. When that

did not occur, Marx belatedly concluded that urban merchants and peasants were too conservative by nature to support the workers and would oppose revolution once their own immediate economic demands were satisfied. As for the workers' movement itself, it was clearly still too weak to seize power and could not expect to achieve its own objectives until the workers had become politically more sophisticated and better organized. In effect, Marx concluded that revolution would not take place in western Europe until capitalism had "ripened," leading to a concentration of capital in the hands of a wealthy minority and an "epidemic of overproduction" because of inadequate purchasing power by the impoverished lower classes. Then a large and increasingly alienated proletariat could drive the capitalists from power and bring about a classless utopia.

For the remainder of his life, Marx acted out the logic of these conclusions. From his base in London, he undertook a massive study of the dynamics of the capitalist system, a project that resulted in the publication of the first volume of his most ambitious work, *Das Kapital* (*Capital*), in 1869. In the meantime, he attempted to prepare for the future revolution by organizing the scattered radical parties throughout Europe into a cohesive revolutionary movement, called the International Workingmen's Association (usually known today as the First International), that would be ready to rouse the workers to action when the opportunity came.

Unity was short-lived. Although all members of the First International shared a common distaste for the capitalist system, some preferred to reform it from within (many of the labor groups from Great Britain), whereas others were convinced that only violent insurrection would suffice to destroy the existing ruling class (Karl Marx and the **anarchists** around Russian revolutionary Mikhail Bakunin). Even the radicals could not agree. Marx believed that revolution could not succeed without a core of committed communists to organize and lead the masses; Bakunin contended that the general insurrection should be a spontaneous uprising from below. In 1871, the First International disintegrated.

1-6b Capitalism in Transition

While Marx was grappling with the problems of preparing for the coming revolution, European society was undergoing significant changes. The advanced capitalist states such as Great Britain, France, and the Low Countries (Belgium, Luxembourg, and the Netherlands) were gradually evolving into mature, politically stable societies in which Marx's dire predictions were not being borne out. His forecast of periodic economic crises was correct enough, but his warnings of concentration of capital and the impoverishment of labor were somewhat wide of the mark,

HISTORICAL VOICES

The Classless Society

 How did Marx and Engels define the proletariat? The bourgeoisie? Why did Marxists come to believe that this distinction was paramount for understanding history? For shaping the future?

Politics & Government IN *THE COMMUNIST MANIFESTO*, Karl Marx and Friedrich Engels predicted the creation of a classless society as the end product of the struggle between the bourgeoisie and the proletariat. In this selection, they discuss the steps by which that classless society would be reached.

Karl Marx and Friedrich Engels, *The Communist Manifesto*

A spectre is haunting Europe—the spectre of Communism. All the powers of old Europe have entered into a holy alliance to exorcise this spectre: Pope and Czar, ... French radicals and German police spies.

Where is the party in opposition that has not been decried as Communistic by its opponents in power? Where the opposition that has not hurled back the branding reproach of Communism? ...

Two things result from this fact:

1) Communism is already acknowledged by all European Powers to be itself a Power.
2) It is high time that Communists should openly, in the face of the whole world, publish their views, their aims, their tendencies, and meet this nursery tale of the spectre of Communism with a manifesto of the party itself.

To this end, Communists of various nationalities have assembled in London, and sketched the following Manifesto.

We have seen . . . that the first step in the revolution by the working class is to raise the proletariat to the position of ruling class. . . . The proletariat will use its political supremacy to wrest, by degrees, all capital from the bourgeoisie, to centralize all instruments of production in the hands of the State, i.e., of the proletariat organized as the ruling class; and to increase the total of productive forces as rapidly as possible.

Of course, in the beginning, this cannot be effected except by means of despotic inroads on the rights of property, and on the conditions of bourgeois production; by means of measures, therefore, which appear economically insufficient and untenable, but which, in the course

of the movement, outstrip themselves, necessitate further inroads upon the old social order, and are unavoidable as a means of entirely revolutionizing the mode of production.

These measures will of course be different in different countries.

Nevertheless, in the most advanced countries, the following will be pretty generally applicable:

1. Abolition of property in land and application of all rents of land to public purposes.
2. A heavy progressive or graduated income tax.
3. Abolition of all right of inheritance. . . .
5. Centralization of credit in the hands of the State, by means of a national bank with State capital and an exclusive monopoly.
6. Centralization of the means of communication and transport in the hands of the State.
7. Extension of factories and instruments of production owned by the State. . . .
8. Equal liability of all to labor. Establishment of industrial armies, especially for agriculture.
9. Combination of agriculture with manufacturing industries; gradual abolition of the distinction between town and country, by a more equable distribution of the population over the country.
10. Free education for all children in public schools. Abolition of children's factory labor in its present form. . . .

When, in the course of development, class distinctions have disappeared, and all production has been concentrated in the whole nation, the public power will lose its political character. Political power, properly so called, is merely the organized power of one class for oppressing another. If the proletariat during its contest with the bourgeoisie is compelled, by the force of circumstances, to organize itself as a class, if, by means of a revolution, it makes itself the ruling class, and, as such, sweeps away by force the old conditions of production, then it will, along with these conditions, have swept away the conditions for the existence of class antagonisms and of classes generally, and will thereby have abolished its own supremacy as a class.

In place of the old bourgeois society, with its classes and class antagonisms, we shall have an association, in which the free development of each is the condition for the free development of all.

Source: From Karl Marx and Friedrich Engels, *The Communist Manifesto*.

as capitalist societies began to eliminate or at least reduce some of the more flagrant inequities apparent in the early stages of capitalist development. These reforms occurred because workers and their representatives had begun to use the democratic political process to their own advantage, organizing labor unions and political parties to improve working conditions and enhance the role of workers in the political system. Some of these political parties were led by Marxists, who were learning that in the absence of a social revolution to bring the masses to power, the capitalist democratic system could be reformed from within to improve the working and living conditions of its constituents. In 1889, after Marx's death, several such parties (often labeled "social democratic" parties) formed the Second International, dominated by reformist elements committed to achieving **socialism** within the bounds of the Western parliamentary system.

Marx had also underestimated the degree to which nationalism would appeal to workers in most European countries. Marx had viewed nation and culture as false idols diverting the interests of the oppressed from their true concern, the struggle against the ruling class. In his view, the proletariat would throw off its chains and unite in the sacred cause of "internationalist" world revolution. In reality, workers joined peasants and urban merchants in defending the cause of the nation against its foreign enemies. A generation later, French workers would die in the trenches defending France from workers across the German border.

A historian of the late nineteenth century might have been forgiven for predicting that Marxism, as a revolutionary ideology, was dead. To the east, however, in the vast plains and steppes of central Russia, it was about to be reborn (see Chapter 4).

1-7 TOWARD THE MODERN CONSCIOUSNESS: INTELLECTUAL AND CULTURAL DEVELOPMENTS

 Focus Question: What intellectual and cultural developments opened the way to a modern consciousness in Europe, and how did this consciousness differ from earlier worldviews?

The physical changes that were taking place in societies exposed to the Industrial Revolution were accompanied by an equally significant transformation in the arena of culture. Before 1914, most Westerners continued to believe in the values and ideals that had been generated by the impact of the Scientific Revolution and the Enlightenment. The ability of rational human beings to improve themselves and achieve a better society seemed to be well demonstrated by a rising standard of living, urban improvements, and mass education. Between 1870 and 1914, however, a dramatic transformation in the realm of ideas and culture began to challenge many of these assumptions. A new view of the physical universe, alternative views of human nature, and radically innovative forms of literary and artistic expression shattered old beliefs and opened the way to a more complex view of the human condition. Although the real impact of many of these ideas was not felt until after World War I, they served to provoke a sense of confusion and anxiety before 1914 that would become even more pronounced after the war.

1-7a Developments in the Sciences: The Emergence of a New Physics

A prime example of this development took place in the realm of physics. Throughout much of the nineteenth century, Westerners adhered to the mechanical conception of the universe postulated by the classical physics of Isaac Newton (1642–1727). In this perspective, the universe was a giant machine in which time, space, and matter were objective realities that existed independently of the parties observing them. Matter was thought to be composed of indivisible, solid material bodies called atoms.

But these views began to be questioned at the end of the nineteenth century. Some scientists had discovered that certain elements such as radium and polonium spontaneously gave off rays or radiation that apparently came from within the atom itself. Atoms were therefore not hard material bodies but small worlds containing such subatomic particles as electrons and protons that behaved in a seemingly random and inexplicable fashion. Inquiry into the disintegrative process within atoms became a central theme of the new physics.

Building on this work, in 1900, a Berlin physicist, Max Planck (1858–1947), rejected the belief that a heated body radiates energy in a steady stream but maintained instead that it did so discontinuously, in irregular packets of energy that he called "quanta." The quantum theory raised fundamental questions about the subatomic realm of the atom. By 1900, the old view of atoms as the basic building blocks of the material world was being seriously questioned, and Newtonian physics was in trouble.

Albert Einstein (1879–1955), a German-born patent officer working in Switzerland, pushed these new theories of thermodynamics into new terrain. In 1905, Einstein published a paper setting forth his theory of relativity. According to relativity theory, space and time are not absolute but relative to the observer, and both are interwoven into what Einstein called a four-dimensional space–time continuum. Neither space nor time has an existence independent of human experience. Moreover, matter and energy reflect the relativity of time and space. Einstein concluded that matter was nothing but another form of energy. His epochal formula $E = mc^2$—each particle of matter is equivalent to its mass times the square of the velocity of light—was the key theory explaining the vast energies contained within the atom. It led to the atomic age.

1-7b Charles Darwin and the Theory of Evolution

Equally dramatic changes took place in the biological sciences, where the British scientist Charles Darwin (1809–1882) stunned the world in 1859 with the publication of his book *The Origin of Species*. Drawing from evidence obtained during a scientific expedition to the Galapagos Islands, Darwin concluded that plants and animals were not the finished product of divine creation but evolved over time from earlier and simpler forms of life through a process of **natural selection**. In the universal struggle for existence, only the fittest species survived. Later, Darwin provoked even more controversy by applying his theory of **organic evolution** to human beings. Speculating that modern humans had evolved over millions of years from primates and were thus not the unique creation of God but "a co-descendant with other mammals of a common progenitor," Darwin's theory represented a direct affront to the biblical interpretation of the creation of man as described in the book of Genesis (see Historical Voices, "The Theory of Evolution," p. 24). Critics mocked his ideas as demeaning to human dignity and made scathing references to his own forebears.

But Darwin was not alone in questioning the veracity of the Biblical message relating to the origins of the human species. Prodded by the tendency of the age to question old truths, some began to question the historicity of the life of Jesus, while the German philosopher Friedrich Nietzsche pronounced that "God is dead" and mocked traditional Christian morality as "the best known device for leading mankind by the nose." Paradoxically, the mid-nineteenth century also witnessed a rise in religiosity, especially in the United States and Great Britain, where millions of Christians abandoned established churches to seek refuge in evangelical faiths.

1-7c Sigmund Freud and the Emergence of Psychoanalysis

Although poets and mystics had revealed a world of unconscious and irrational behavior, many scientifically oriented intellectuals under the impact of Enlightenment thought continued to believe that human beings responded to conscious motives in a rational fashion. But at the end of the nineteenth century, the Viennese doctor Sigmund Freud (1856–1939) put forth a series of theories that undermined optimism about the rational nature of the human mind. Freud's thought, like the new physics, added to the uncertainties of the age. His major ideas were published in 1900 in *The Interpretation of Dreams*, which laid the basic foundation for what came to be known as psychoanalysis.

According to Freud, human behavior is strongly determined by the unconscious—former experiences and inner drives of which people are largely oblivious. To explore the contents of the unconscious, Freud relied not only on hypnosis but also on dreams, which were dressed in an elaborate code that needed to be deciphered if the contents were to be properly understood.

Why do some experiences whose influence persists in controlling an individual's life remain unconscious? According to Freud, repression is a process by which unsettling experiences are blotted from conscious awareness but still continue to influence behavior because they have become part of the unconscious. To explain how repression works, Freud elaborated an intricate theory of the inner life of human beings.

Although Freud's theory has had numerous critics, his insistence that a human being's inner life is a battleground of contending forces undermined the prevailing belief in the power of reason and opened a new era of psychoanalysis, in which a psychotherapist assists a patient in probing deep into memory to retrace the chain of repression back to its childhood origins and bring about a resolution of the inner psychic conflict. Belief in the primacy of rational thought over the emotions would never be the same.

1-7d Literature and the Arts: The Culture of Modernity

The revolutions in physics and psychology were paralleled by similar changes in literature and the arts. Throughout much of the late nineteenth century, literature was dominated by Naturalism. Naturalists accepted the material world as real and believed that literature should be realistic. By addressing social problems, writers could contribute to an objective understanding of the world.

The novels of the French writer Émile Zola (1840–1902) provide a good example of Naturalism. Against a backdrop of the urban slums and coalfields of northern France, Zola showed how alcoholism and challenging environments affected people's lives. The materialistic science of his age had an important influence on Zola. He had read Darwin's *Origin of Species* and had been impressed by its emphasis on the struggle for survival and the importance of environment and heredity.

By the beginning of the twentieth century, however, the belief that the task of literature was to represent

The Theory of Evolution

Q *What evidence does Darwin cite to defend his theory of evolution? What is the essence of the theory?*

Science & Technology

DARWIN PUBLISHED HIS THEORY of organic evolution in 1859, followed twelve years later by *The Descent of Man*, in which he argued that human beings, like other animals, evolved from lower forms of life. The theory provoked a firestorm of criticism, especially from the clergy. One critic described Darwin's theory as a "brutal philosophy— to wit, there is no God, and the ape is our Adam."

Charles Darwin, *The Descent of Man*

The main conclusion here arrived at, and now held by many naturalists, who are well competent to form a sound judgment, is that man is descended from some less highly organized form. The grounds upon which this conclusion rests will never be shaken, for the close similarity between man and the lower animals in embryonic development, as well as in innumerable points of structure and constitution, both of high and of the most trifling importance—the rudiments which he retains, and the abnormal reversions to which he is occasionally liable—are facts which cannot be disputed. They have long been known, but until recently they told us nothing with respect to the origin of man. Now when viewed by the light of our knowledge of the whole organic world, their meaning is unmistakable. The great principle of evolution stands up clear and firm, when these groups of facts are considered in connection with others, such as the mutual affinities of the members of the same group,

their geographical distribution in past and present times, and their geological succession. It is incredible that all these facts should speak falsely. He who is not content to look, like a savage, at the phenomena of nature as disconnected, cannot any longer believe that man is the work of a separate act of creation.

He will be forced to admit that the close resemblance of the embryo of man to that, for instance, of a dog—the construction of his skull, limbs and whole frame on the same plan with that of other mammals, independently of the uses to which the parts may be put—the occasional reappearance of various structures, for instance of several muscles, which man does not normally possess . . .—and a crowd of analogous facts—all point in the plainest manner to the conclusion that man is the co-descendant with other mammals of a common progenitor. . . .

Man may be excused for feeling some pride at having risen, though not through his own exertions, to the very summit of the organic scale; and the fact of his having thus risen, instead of having been aboriginally placed there, may give him hope for a still higher destiny in the distant future. But we are not here concerned with hopes or fears, only with the truth as far as our reason permits us to discover it; and I have given the evidence to the best of my ability. We must, however, acknowledge, as it seems to me, that man with all his noble qualities, with sympathy which feels for the most debased, with benevolence which extends not only to other men but to the humblest living creature, with his god-like intellect which has penetrated into the movements and constitution of the solar system— with all these exalted power—Man still bears in his bodily frame the indelible stamp of his lowly origin.

Source: From Charles Darwin, *The Descent of Man* (New York: Appleton, 1876), pp. 606–607, 619.

"reality" had lost much of its meaning. By that time, the new psychology and the new physics had made it evident that many people were not sure what constituted reality anyway. The same was true in the realm of art, where in the late nineteenth century, painters were beginning to respond to ongoing investigations into the nature of optics and human perception by experimenting with radical new techniques to represent the multiplicity of reality. The changes that such cultural innovators produced have since been called **Modernism**.

The first to embark on the challenge were the Impressionists. Originating in France in the 1870s, they rejected indoor painting and preferred to go out to the countryside to paint nature directly. As Camille Pissarro (1830–1903), one of the movement's founders, expressed it: "Don't proceed according to rules and principles, but paint what you observe and feel. Paint generously and unhesitatingly, for it is best not to lose the first impression." The most influential of the Impressionists was Claude Monet (1840–1926), who painted several series of canvases on the same object—such as haystacks, Rouen Cathedral, and water lilies in the garden of his house on the Seine River—in the hope of breaking down the essential lines, planes, colors, and shadows of what the eye observed. His paintings that deal with the interplay of light and reflection on a water surface are considered to be among the wonders of modern painting.

The growth of photography gave artists another reason to reject visual realism. Invented in the 1830s, photography became popular and widespread after George Eastman created the first Kodak camera for the mass market in 1888. What was the point of an artist's doing what the camera did better? Unlike the camera, which could only mirror reality, artists could *create* reality. As in literature, so also in modern art, individual consciousness became the source of meaning. Between the beginning of the new century and the outbreak of World War I in 1914, this search for individual expression produced several new schools of

painting that would have a significant impact on the world of art for decades to come.

In Expressionism, the artist employed an exaggerated use of colors and distorted shapes to achieve emotional expression. Painters such as the Dutchman Vincent van Gogh (1853–1890) and the Norwegian Edvard Munch (1863–1944) were interested not in capturing the optical play of light on a landscape but in projecting their inner selves onto the hostile universe around them. Who cannot be affected by the intensity of van Gogh's dazzling sunflowers or by the ominous swirling stars above a church steeple in his *Starry Night* (1890)?

Another important artist obsessed with finding a new way to portray reality was the French painter Paul Cézanne (1839–1906). Scorning the photographic duplication of a landscape, he sought to isolate the pulsating structure beneath the surface (see Image 1.5). During the last years of his life, he produced several paintings of Mont

IMAGE 1.5 Paul Cézanne, *Bathing Women*. Paul Cézanne (1839–1906) was one of the outstanding figures in modern art, propelling it to seek new ways of expressing reality. Abandoning the one-point perspective of Renaissance painting, he tried to extract the internal dimension underlying the panorama of his canvases. In *Bathing Women*, he is not interested in re-creating the surface details of individual women, but rather the inner pulse of energy emanating from a group of women in harmony with their surroundings. The blue of the lake and the sky is reflected on their skin as they relax, chat, and embrace one another in the midst of a natural scene.

Sainte-Victoire, a mountain located near Aix-en-Provence in the south of France. Although each canvas differed in perspective, composition, and color, they all reflect the same technique of reducing the landscape to virtual geometric slabs of color to represent the interconnection of trees, earth, tiled roofs, mountain, and sky.

Following Cézanne was the Spaniard Pablo Picasso (1881–1973), one of the giants of twentieth-century painting. Settling in Paris in 1904, he and the French artist Georges Braque (1882–1963) collaborated in founding Cubism, the first truly radical approach in representing visual reality. To the Cubist, any perception of an object was a composite of simultaneous and different perspectives.

Modernism in the arts also revolutionized architecture and architectural practices. A new principle known as functionalism motivated this revolution by maintaining that buildings, like the products of machines, should be "functional" or useful, fulfilling the purpose for which they were constructed. Art and engineering were to be unified, and all unnecessary ornamentation was to be stripped away.

The United States took the lead in this effort. Unprecedented urban growth and the absence of restrictive architectural traditions allowed for new building methods, especially in the relatively new city of Chicago. The Chicago school of the 1890s, led by Louis H. Sullivan (1856–1924), used reinforced concrete, steel frames, electric elevators, and sheet glass to build skyscrapers virtually free of external ornamentation. One of Sullivan's most successful pupils was Frank Lloyd Wright (1867–1959), who became known for innovative designs in domestic architecture. Wright's private houses, built chiefly for wealthy patrons, featured geometric structures with long lines, overhanging roofs, and severe planes of brick and stone. The interiors were open spaces and included cathedral ceilings and built-in furniture and lighting features. Wright pioneered the modern American house.

At the beginning of the twentieth century, developments in music paralleled those in painting. Expressionism in music was a Russian creation, the product of composer Igor Stravinsky (1882–1971) and the Ballet Russe, the dance company of Sergei Diaghilev (1872–1929). Together they revolutionized the world of music with Stravinsky's ballet *The Rite of Spring*. When it was performed in Paris in 1913, the savage and primitive sounds and beats of the music and dance caused a near riot among an audience outraged at its audacity.

By the end of the nineteenth century, then, traditional forms of literary, artistic, and musical expression were in a state of rapid retreat. Freed from conventional tastes and responding to the intellectual and social revolution that was getting under way throughout the Western world, painters, writers, composers, and architects launched a variety of radical new ideas that would revolutionize Western culture in coming decades.

MAKING CONNECTIONS

During the course of the nineteenth century, Western society underwent a number of dramatic changes. Countries that were predominantly agricultural in 1750 had by 1900 been transformed into essentially industrial and urban societies. The amount of material goods available to consumers had increased manyfold, and machines were rapidly replacing labor-intensive methods of production and distribution. The social changes were equally striking. Human beings were becoming more mobile and enjoyed more creature comforts than at any time since the Roman Empire. A mass society, based on the principles of universal education, limited government, and an expanding franchise, was in the process of creation.

The Industrial Revolution had thus vastly expanded the horizons and the potential of the human race. It had also broken down many walls of aristocratic privilege and opened the door to a new era based on merit. Yet for some the costs had been high. The distribution of wealth was as unequal as ever, and working and living conditions for millions of Europeans had deteriorated. The psychological impact of such rapid changes had also produced feelings of anger, frustration, and alienation on the part of many who lived through them. Uprooted from their ancestral homes, with the old certainties of religion and science now increasingly under challenge, many faced the future with doubt or foreboding.

Meanwhile, along the borders of Europe—in Russia, in the Balkans, and in the vast Ottoman Empire—the Industrial Revolution had not yet made an impact or was just getting under way. For the most part, traditional values and institutions continued to rule without challenge. Still, the winds of change were beginning to blow from the west, and old autocracies began to find themselves under increasing pressure from ethnic minorities and other discontented subjects even though they continued to resist pressure for reform. As the world prepared to enter a new century, the stage was set for dramatic change.

REFLECTION QUESTIONS

Q What were the major similarities and differences between the first and second stages of the Industrial Revolution?

Q In what ways was the development of industrialization related to the rise of nationalism in nineteenth-century Europe?

Q What were the chief ideas associated with liberalism and nationalism, and how were these ideas put into practice in Europe, Latin America, and Asia in the first half of the nineteenth century?

Q To what extent were the major goals of establishing liberal practices and achieving the growth of political democracy realized in Great Britain, France, Germany, Austria-Hungary, and Russia between 1871 and 1914?

CHAPTER TIMELINE

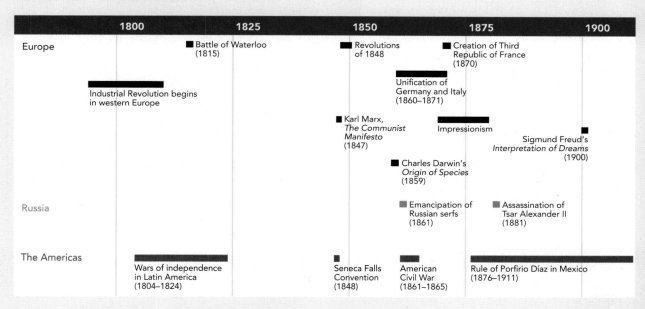

	1800	1825	1850	1875	1900
Europe		Battle of Waterloo (1815)	Revolutions of 1848	Creation of Third Republic of France (1870)	
	Industrial Revolution begins in western Europe		Unification of Germany and Italy (1860–1871)		
			Karl Marx, *The Communist Manifesto* (1847)	Impressionism	Sigmund Freud's *Interpretation of Dreams* (1900)
			Charles Darwin's *Origin of Species* (1859)		
Russia			Emancipation of Russian serfs (1861)	Assassination of Tsar Alexander II (1881)	
The Americas		Wars of independence in Latin America (1804–1824)	Seneca Falls Convention (1848) / American Civil War (1861–1865)	Rule of Porfirio Díaz in Mexico (1876–1911)	

CHAPTER NOTES

1. See Kenneth Pomeranz, *The Great Divergence: China, Europe, and the Making of the Modern World Economy* (Princeton, 2000).
2. See Peter Gay, *Pleasure Wars: The Bourgeois Experience: Victoria to Freud* (New York, 1998).
3. Quoted in Barbara Freese, *Coal: A Human History* (New York, 2003), p. 78.
4. From Stephen Yafa, *Cotton: The Biography of a Revolutionary Fiber* (New York, 2005), p. 94, citing William Moran, *The Belles of New England* (New York, 2002), p. 23.
5. Karl Marx and Friedrich Engels, *The Communist Manifesto* (Middlesex, England, 1985), p. 79.

CHAPTER 2

THE HIGH TIDE OF IMPERIALISM: AFRICA AND ASIA IN AN ERA OF WESTERN DOMINANCE

Chapter Outline and Focus Questions

2-1 The Spread of Colonial Rule

Q What were the causes of the new imperialism of the nineteenth century, and how did new imperialism differ from European expansion in earlier periods of history?

2-2 The Colonial System

Q Do you believe that apologists for Western imperialism in the nineteenth century were justified in claiming that control over non-Western peoples would ultimately be in the latter's best interest?

2-3 India Under the British Raj

Q What were some of the major consequences of British rule in India, and how did they affect the Indian people?

2-4 The Colonial Takeover of Southeast Asia

Q Which Western countries were most active in seeking colonial possessions in Southeast Asia, and what were their motives in doing so?

2-5 Empire Building in Africa

Q What factors were behind the "scramble for Africa," and what impact did it have on the continent?

2-6 Patterns of Resistance to Colonial Conquest

Q How did the indigenous response to the imperialist attacks in Africa and Asia differ from place to place, and how do you account for such differences?

IMAGE 2.1 Revere the conquering heroes: British rule in Africa

Time Life Pictures/The LIFE Picture Collection/Getty Images

Connections to Today

Imperialist nations in the nineteenth century were provoked into expanding their influence into other parts of the world because of their need to obtain access to vital raw materials as well as markets for the manufactured goods produced in their factories at home. Do you think they were justified in doing so, and is that a fair argument for countries to become involved beyond their own borders today?

THERE IS A STATUE OF CECIL RHODES on the campus of Oriel College at Oxford University. Rhodes, an industrial and diamond magnate who became prime minister of the Cape Colony in the 1890s, was one of the most prominent proponents of British imperialist expansion at the end of the nineteenth century.

Eventually, he used some of his wealth to endow the famous Rhodes Scholarships, which provide financial support for deserving students from all over the world to attend Oxford University.

In the fall of 2015, a group of students at Oxford organized protests demanding that Rhodes's statue be removed on the grounds that he was responsible for the enslavement of millions of Africans. To them, he embodied the worst aspects of European colonial rule over the non-Western world. Although similar protests at the University of Cape Town in South Africa had been successful, the student demands at Oxford were denied, as opponents argued that, whatever his faults, Rhodes had been an important historical figure and a major benefactor for the cause of education.

The protest movements at Oxford and Cape Town brought into sharp relief the complex debate over the motives and consequences of a century of Western imperialism. For Rhodes and like-minded contemporaries, European colonial rule had been a necessary step in the arduous task of bringing modern civilization to backward peoples around the world. To critics, in the words of one of the recent protesters, Rhodes was responsible for "stealing land, massacring tens of thousands of black Africans, imposing a regime of unspeakable labor exploitation in the diamond mines and devising pro-apartheid policies."[1]

Rhodes was no apologetic imperialist. When drawing up his last will and testament, he instructed two of his closest friends to use his vast inheritance to bring about the extension of British rule throughout the world, as well as the recovery of the United States as an integral part of the British Empire. A fervent supporter of the imperial vision, Rhodes actively promoted the extension of British rule until his untimely death in 1902.

2-1 THE SPREAD OF COLONIAL RULE

 Focus Question: What were the causes of the new imperialism of the nineteenth century, and how did new imperialism differ from European expansion in earlier periods of history?

Preposterous as Cecil Rhodes's ideas seem to us today, they serve as a graphic reminder of the hubris that characterized the worldview of Rhodes and many of his European contemporaries during the Age of Imperialism, as well as the complex union of moral concern and vaulting ambition that motivated their actions on the world stage. During the nineteenth and early-twentieth centuries, Western colonialism spread throughout much of the non-Western world. Spurred by the demands of the Industrial Revolution, a few powerful states—notably Great Britain, France, Germany, Russia, and the United States—competed avariciously for consumer markets and raw materials for their expanding economies. By the end of the nineteenth century, virtually all of the traditional societies in Asia and Africa were under direct or indirect colonial rule.

2-1a The Myth of European Superiority

To many Western observers at the time, the apparent ease of the European conquest provided a clear affirmation of the innate superiority of Western civilization to its counterparts elsewhere in the world. Influenced by the popular theory of **social Darwinism**, which applied Charles Darwin's theory of natural selection to the evolution of human societies (see Chapter 1 and "2-2a The Philosophy of Colonialism," p. 31), historians in Europe and the United States began to view world history as essentially the story of the inexorable rise of the West, from the glories of ancient Greece to the emergence of modern Europe after the Enlightenment and the Industrial Revolution, to a position of global dominance. The extension of Western influence to Africa and Asia, a process that had gotten underway with the exploratory voyages of European navigators into the Indian Ocean in the early-sixteenth century, was thus viewed as a reflection of Western cultural superiority and represented a necessary step in bringing civilization to the peoples beyond the borders of Europe.

The truth, however, was quite different, for Western global hegemony was a relatively recent phenomenon. Prior to the age of Christopher Columbus at the end of the fifteenth century, Europe was only an isolated appendage of a much larger world system of states stretching across the Eurasian landmass from the Atlantic Ocean to the Pacific. The center of gravity in this trade network was not in Europe or even in the Mediterranean Sea but much farther to the east, in the Persian Gulf and in Central Asia. The most sophisticated and technologically advanced region in the world was not Europe but China, whose proud history could be traced back several thousand years to the rise of the first Chinese state in the Yellow River valley.

As for the transcontinental trade network that linked Europe with the nations of the Middle East, South Asia, and the Pacific basin, maritime commerce throughout the region had not been created by Portuguese and Spanish navigators in the early-sixteenth century but had been gradually developed by local traders from East Africa, Asia, and the Middle East centuries previously. In the meantime, the Mongols had opened up land trade routes from the shores of the Pacific to the bounds of central Europe after their conquest of much of the Eurasian supercontinent in the thirteenth and fourteenth centuries. For centuries, caravan routes and sea lanes stretched across Eurasia and the Indian Ocean between China, Africa, and Europe, carrying not only commercial goods but also ideas and inventions such as the compass, paper, Arabic numerals, and gunpowder. Inventions such as these, many of them originating in China or India, would later play a major role in the emergence of Europe as a major player on the world's stage. Only in the sixteenth century, with the onset of the Age of Exploration, did Europe become important in the process. For the next three centuries, the ships of several European nations crossed the seas in quest of the spices, silks, precious metals, and porcelains of the Orient.

For the first time since the decline of the Roman Empire, beginning in the sixteenth century, Europe became a major player in the global trade network. In a few cases, Europeans—aided by technological advances in shipbuilding and weaponry—engaged in military conquest as a means of seeking their objective. For the most part, however, European nations were satisfied to trade with their Asian and African counterparts from coastal enclaves that they had established along the trade routes that threaded across the seas from the ports along the Atlantic and the Mediterranean Sea to their far-off destinations. In 1800, only the Philippine Islands and parts of the Indian subcontinent and the Indonesian archipelago were under full European control.

2-1b The Advent of Western Imperialism

In the nineteenth century, a new phase of Western expansion into Asia and Africa began. Whereas European aims in the East before 1800 could be summed up in the Portuguese explorer Vasco da Gama's famous phrase "Christians and spices," in the early-nineteenth century, a new relationship took shape: European nations began to view Asian and African societies as a source of industrial raw materials and a market for Western manufactured goods. No longer were Western gold and silver exchanged for cloves, pepper, tea, silk, and porcelain. Now the prodigious output of European factories was sent to Africa and Asia in return for oil, tin, rubber, and the other resources needed to fuel the Western industrial machine.

The Impact of the Industrial Revolution The reason for this change, of course, was the Industrial Revolution. Now industrializing countries in the West needed vital raw materials that were not available at home, as well as a reliable market for the goods produced in their factories. The latter factor became increasingly crucial as capitalist societies began to discover that their home markets could not always absorb domestic output. When consumer demand lagged, economic depression threatened.

As Western economic expansion into Asia and Africa gathered strength during the last quarter of the nineteenth century, it became fashionable to call the process **imperialism**. Although the term *imperialism* has many meanings and can trace its linguistic heritage back to the glories of ancient Rome, when it referred to a multinational state ruled by an emperor who represented one dominant ethnic or religious group, in this instance it referred to the efforts of capitalist states in the West to seize markets, cheap raw materials, and lucrative areas for capital investment beyond traditional Western countries. In this interpretation, the primary motives behind the Western expansion were economic. The best-known promoter of this view was the British political economist John A. Hobson, who in 1902 published a major analysis, *Imperialism: A Study*. In this influential book, Hobson maintained that modern imperialism was a direct consequence of the modern industrial economy. In his view, the industrialized states of the West often produced more goods than could be absorbed by the domestic market and thus had to export their manufactures to make a profit.

The issue was not simply an economic one, however, since economic concerns were inevitably tinged with political ones and with questions of national grandeur and moral purpose as well. In nineteenth-century Europe, economic wealth, national status, and political power went hand in hand with the possession of a colonial empire, at least in the minds of observers at the time. To global strategists of the day, colonies brought tangible benefits in the world of power politics as well as economic profits, and many nations became involved in the pursuit of colonies as much to gain advantage over their rivals as to acquire territory for its own sake.

The relationship between colonialism and national survival was expressed directly in a speech by the French politician Jules Ferry in 1885. A policy of "containment or abstinence," he warned, would set France on "the broad road to decadence" and initiate its decline into a "third- or fourth-rate power." British imperialists agreed. To Cecil Rhodes, the extraction of material wealth from the colonies was only a secondary matter. "My ruling purpose," he remarked, "is the extension of the British Empire."[2] That British Empire, on which (as the saying went) "the sun never set," was the envy of its rivals and was viewed as the primary source of British global dominance during the latter half of the nineteenth century.

Tactics of Conquest With the change in European motives for colonization came a corresponding shift in tactics. Earlier, when their economic interests were more limited, European states had generally been satisfied to deal with existing independent states rather than attempt to establish direct control over vast territories. There had been exceptions where state power at the local level was on the point of collapse (as in India), where European economic interests were especially intense (as in Latin America and the East Indies), or where there was no centralized authority (as in North America and the Philippines). But for the most part, the Western presence in Asia and Africa had been limited to controlling the regional trade network and establishing a few footholds where the foreigners could carry on trade and missionary activity.

After 1800, the demands of industrialization in Europe created a new set of dynamics. Maintaining access to industrial raw materials, such as oil and rubber, and setting up reliable markets for European manufactured products required more extensive control over colonial territories. As competition for colonies increased, the colonial powers sought to solidify their hold over their territories to protect them from attack by their rivals. During the last two decades of the nineteenth century, the quest for colonies became a scramble as all the major European states, now joined by the United States and Japan, engaged in a global land grab. In many cases, economic interests were secondary to security concerns or national prestige. In Africa, for example, the British engaged in a struggle with their rivals to protect their interests in the Suez Canal and the Red Sea. In Southeast Asia, the United States seized the Philippines from Spain at least partly to keep them out of the hands of the Japanese, and the French took over Indochina for fear that it would otherwise be occupied by Germany, Japan, or the United States.

By 1900, virtually all the societies of Africa and Asia were either under full colonial rule or, as in the case of China and the Ottoman Empire, on the point of virtual collapse. Only a handful of states, such as Japan in East Asia, Thailand in Southeast Asia, Afghanistan and Iran in the Middle East, and mountainous Ethiopia in East Africa, managed to escape internal disintegration or political subjection to colonial rule. As the twentieth century began, European hegemony over the ancient civilizations of Asia and Africa seemed complete.

2-2 THE COLONIAL SYSTEM

 Focus Question: Do you believe that apologists for Western imperialism in the nineteenth century were justified in claiming that control over non-Western peoples would ultimately be in the latter's best interest?

Once they had control of most of the world, the colonial powers set out to achieve their primary objective—to exploit the natural resources of the subject areas and to open up markets for manufactured goods and capital investment from the mother country. In some cases, that goal could be realized in cooperation with local political elites, whose loyalty could be earned (or purchased) by economic rewards or by confirming them in their positions of authority and status in a new colonial setting. Sometimes, however, this policy of **indirect rule** was not feasible because local leaders refused to cooperate with their colonial masters or even actively resisted the foreign conquest. In such cases, the local elites were removed from power and replaced with a new set of officials recruited from the mother country.

The distinction between **direct rule** and indirect rule was not always clearly drawn, and many colonial powers vacillated between the two approaches, sometimes in the same colonial territory. The decision often had fateful consequences for the peoples involved. Where colonial powers encountered resistance and were forced to overthrow local political elites, they often adopted policies designed to eradicate the source of resistance and destroy the traditional culture. Such policies often had corrosive effects on the indigenous societies and provoked resentment that not only marked the colonial relationship but even affected relations after the restoration of national independence (see Part V).

The situation in Latin America, which was also affected in various ways by Western imperial expansion in the nineteenth century, was a special case. There the Western powers sought to protect their economic interests and preserve access to crucial raw materials and markets by propping up pseudo-independent regimes. The United States, in particular, sent troops to protect its interests in Central America and the Caribbean on several occasions.

2-2a The Philosophy of Colonialism

To justify their conquests, the colonial powers appealed, in part, to the time-honored maxim of "might makes right." Western powers viewed industrial resources as vital to national survival and security and felt that no moral justification was needed for any action to protect access to them. By the end of the nineteenth century, that attitude received pseudoscientific validity from the concept of social Darwinism, which maintained that only societies that moved aggressively to adapt to changing circumstances would survive and prosper in a world governed by the Darwinist law of "survival of the fittest."

The White Man's Burden Some people, however, were uncomfortable with such a brutal view of the law of nature and sought a moral justification that appeared to benefit the victim. Here again, social Darwinism pointed the way: since human societies, like living organisms, must adapt to survive, the advanced nations of the West were obliged to assist the backward peoples of Asia and Africa so that they, too, could adjust to the challenges of the modern world. Few expressed this view as graphically as the English poet Rudyard Kipling, who called on the Anglo-Saxon peoples (in particular, the United States) to take up the "white man's burden" in Asia (see Opposing Viewpoints, "White Man's Burden, Black Man's Sorrow," p. 33).

Buttressed by such comforting theories, humane souls in Western countries could ignore the brutal aspects of the colonial process and persuade themselves that in the long run, the results would be beneficial to both sides. Some saw the issue primarily in religious terms. During the nineteenth century, Christian missionaries by the thousands went to Asia and Africa to bring the gospel to the "heathen masses." To others, the objective was the more secular one of bringing the benefits of Western democracy and capitalism to the tradition-ridden societies of the Orient. Either way, sensitive Western minds could console themselves with the belief that their governments were bringing civilization to the primitive peoples of the world. If commercial profit and national prestige happened to be by-products of that effort, so much the better. Few were as effective at making the case as the silver-tongued French colonial official Albert Sarraut. Conceding that colonialism was originally an "act of force" taken for material profit, he declared that the end result would be a "better life on this planet" for conqueror and conquered alike.

But what about the possibility that historically and culturally, the societies of Asia and Africa were fundamentally different from those of the West and could not, or would not, be persuaded to transform themselves along Western lines? After all, even Kipling had remarked that "East is East and West is West, and never the twain shall meet." Was the human condition universal, in which case the Asian and African peoples could be transformed, in the quaint American phrase for the subject Filipinos, into "little brown Americans"? Or were human beings so shaped by their history and geographic environment that their civilizations would inevitably remain distinctive from those of the West? If so, a policy of cultural transformation could not be expected to succeed.

Assimilation and Association In fact, colonial theory never decided this issue one way or the other. The French, who were most inclined to philosophize about the problem, adopted the terms **assimilation** (which implied an effort to transform colonial societies in the Western image) and **association** (collaborating with local elites while leaving local traditions alone) to describe the two

alternatives and then proceeded to vacillate between them. French policy in Indochina, for example, began as one of association but switched to assimilation under pressure from liberal elements who felt that colonial powers owed a debt to their subject peoples. But assimilation aroused resentment among the local population, many of whom opposed the destruction of their culture and traditions.

Most colonial powers were not as inclined to debate the theory of colonialism as the French were. The United States, in formulating a colonial policy for the Philippines, adopted a strategy of assimilation in theory but was not quick to put it into practice. The British refused to entertain the possibility of assimilation and generally treated their subject peoples as culturally and racially distinct (as Queen Victoria declared in 1858, her government disclaimed "the right and desire to impose Our conditions on Our subjects").

2-3 INDIA UNDER THE BRITISH RAJ

 Focus Question: What were some of the major consequences of British rule in India, and how did they affect the Indian people?

The first of the major Asian civilizations to fall victim to European predatory activities was India. An organized society (commonly known today as the Harappan civilization) had emerged in the Indus River valley in the fourth and third millennia B.C.E. After the influx of Aryan peoples across the mountains of what is present-day Afghanistan into the Indian subcontinent around 1500 B.C.E., a new civilization based on sedentary agriculture and a regional trade network gradually emerged, with its central focus in the Ganges River basin in north central India. A religious faith brought to the subcontinent by the Aryan people, known today as **Hinduism**, evolved into the dominant religion of the Indian people.

Beginning in the eleventh century, much of northern India fell under the rule of Turkic-speaking people who penetrated into the subcontinent from the northwest and introduced the Islamic religion and civilization. Indian society, however, was not entirely receptive to the new faith. Where **Islam** was fiercely monotheistic, the Indian cosmos was peopled with a multiplicity of deities, each representing different aspects of an all-knowing world spirit known as Brahma. While Islam was egalitarian, and at least technically viewed women as the equal of men in the eyes of God, Indian society since early times had been divided into several classes (known as *varna*, or "color"), each historically identified with a particular economic or

White Man's Burden, Black Man's Sorrow

 According to Kipling, why should Western nations take up the "white man's burden"? What was the "black man's burden," in the eyes of Edmund Morel?

Interaction & Exchange **ONE OF THE JUSTIFICATIONS FOR MODERN IMPERIALISM** was the notion that the supposedly "more advanced" white peoples had the moral responsibility to raise presumably ignorant indigenous peoples to a higher level of civilization. Few captured this notion better than the British poet Rudyard Kipling (1865–1936) in his famous poem *The White Man's Burden*. His appeal, directed to the United States, became one of the most famous sets of verses in the English-speaking world.

That sense of moral responsibility, however, was often misplaced or, even worse, laced with hypocrisy. All too often, the consequences of imperial rule were detrimental to those living under colonial authority. Few observers described the destructive effects of Western imperialism on the African people as well as British journalist Edmund Morel. His book *The Black Man's Burden*, as well as a number of articles written during the first decade of the twentieth century, pointed out some of the more horrific aspects of colonialism in the Belgian Congo. Morel's reports on the brutal treatment of Congolese workers involved in gathering rubber, ivory, and palm oil for export helped to spur the formation of an investigative commission, whose report in 1904 ultimately led to reforms.

Rudyard Kipling, *The White Man's Burden*

Take up the White Man's burden—
Send forth the best ye breed—
Go bind your sons to exile
To serve your captives' need;
To wait in heavy harness,
On fluttered folk and wild—
Your new-caught sullen peoples,
Half-devil and half-child.

Take up the White Man's burden—
In patience to abide,
To veil the threat of terror
And check the show of pride;

By open speech and simple,
An hundred times made plain
To seek another's profit,
And work another's gain.

Take up the White Man's burden—
The savage wars of peace—
Fill full the mouth of Famine
And bid the sickness cease;
And when your goal is nearest
The end for others sought,
Watch Sloth and heathen Folly
Bring all your hopes to nought.

Edmund Morel, *The Black Man's Burden*

It is [the Africans] who carry the "Black man's burden." They have not withered away before the white man's occupation. Indeed . . . Africa has ultimately absorbed within itself every Caucasian and, for that matter, every Semitic invader, too. In hewing out for himself a fixed abode in Africa, the white man has massacred the African in heaps. The African has survived, and it is well for the white settlers that he has. . . .

What the partial occupation of his soil by the white man has failed to do; what the mapping out of European political "spheres of influence" has failed to do; what the Maxim and the rifle, the slave gang, labour in the bowels of the earth and the lash, have failed to do; what imported measles, smallpox and syphilis have failed to do; whatever the overseas slave trade failed to do; the power of modern capitalistic exploitation, assisted by modern engines of destruction, may yet succeed in accomplishing.

For from the evils of the latter, scientifically applied and enforced, there is no escape for the African. Its destructive effects are not spasmodic; they are permanent. In its permanence resides its fatal consequences. It kills not the body merely, but the soul. It breaks the spirit. It attacks the African at every turn, from every point of vantage. It wrecks his polity, uproots him from the land, invades his family life, destroys his natural pursuits and occupations, claims his whole time, enslaves him in his own home.

Sources: Rudyard Kipling, *The White Man's Burden*. From Rudyard Kipling, "The White Man's Burden," *McClure's Magazine* 12 (Feb. 1899). Edmund Morel, *The Black Man's Burden*. From Edmund Morel, *The Black Man's Burden* (New York: Metro Books, 1972).

social function—priests, warriors, merchants, and farmers. Indian women of all classes were viewed legally and socially as occupying a clearly inferior position. Although Indian class distinctions had blurred over time, the system also possessed a religious component that determined not only one's status in society but also one's hope for heavenly salvation. At the bottom of the social and religious scale were the "untouchables," individuals who were assigned to carry out the myriad "unclean" tasks in Indian society.

The Indian people did not belong to one of the classes as individuals, but as part of a larger kinship group, a system of extended families known in English as **castes**. Each caste was identified with a particular *varna*, creating a highly stratified society in which social movement along the scale was extremely unusual; individuals thus lived their entire lives within the boundaries of caste distinctions.

At the end of the fifteenth century, a powerful new force penetrated the Indian subcontinent from the mountains to the north. The Mughals, as they were known, were a Turkic-speaking people whose founding ruler Babur (1483–1530) traced his ancestral heritage back to the great Mongol chieftain Genghis Khan. Although foreigners and Muslims like many of their immediate predecessors, the Mughals nevertheless brought India to a level of political power and cultural achievement that inspired admiration and envy throughout the entire region.

The Mughal Empire reached the peak of its greatness under the famed Emperor Akbar (r. 1556–1605), arguably the greatest monarch in Indian history. Eventually, however, the dynasty began to weaken as Hindu forces in southern India sought to challenge the authority of the Mughal court in Delhi. This process of fragmentation was probably hastened by the growing presence of European traders, who had begun to establish enclaves along the fringes of the subcontinent. By the end of the eighteenth century, the British and the French had begun to seize control of the regional trade routes and to meddle in the internal politics of the subcontinent. Soon nothing remained of the empire but a shell. Into the vacuum left by its final decay stepped the British, who used a combination of firepower and guile to consolidate their power over the subcontinent. Some territories were taken over directly by the East India Company, a privately organized British trading organization which at that time was given authority to administer Asian territories under British occupation, while others were ruled indirectly through their local **maharajas** (see Map 2.1). British rule extended northward as far as present-day Afghanistan, where British fears of Russian expansionism led to a lengthy imperialist rivalry that was popularly labeled "the Great Game."

2-3a The Nature of British Rule

British rule in India brought stability to a region that had recently been wracked by civil strife, as the British adopted reforms that led to a relatively honest and efficient government that in some respects operated to the benefit of the average Indian. For example, heightened attention was given to education. Through the efforts of the British administrator and historian Thomas Babington Macaulay, a new school system was established to train the children of Indian elites, and the British civil service examination was introduced to create a dedicated and honest bureaucracy to help govern the vast country.

British rule also brought an end to some of the more inhumane aspects of Indian tradition. The practice of *sati* (the forced or voluntary cremation of a widow on her husband's funeral pyre) was outlawed, and widows were legally permitted to remarry. Other signs of traditional female inferiority, such as child marriage and women's social and legal dependence on their fathers and husbands, were left essentially untouched. Some Indian husbands of the Hindu faith also kept their wives secluded from public view, according the Muslim practice of **purdah**.

The British also attempted to put an end to the brigandage (known as *thuggee*, which gave rise to the English word *thug*) that had plagued travelers in India throughout much of its history. Railroads, the telegraph, and the postal service were introduced to India shortly after they appeared in Great Britain, all of which would eventually serve to promote the gradual emergence of a modern manufacturing and commercial economy in the country. A new penal code based on the British model was adopted, and health and sanitation conditions were improved.

Agricultural Reforms   In many ways, however, the Indian people paid dearly for the peace and stability brought by the British raj (from the Indian *raja*, or prince). Perhaps the most flagrant cost was economic. In rural areas, the British adopted the *zamindar* system, according to which local landlords were authorized to collect taxes from peasants and turn the taxes over to the government. The British mistakenly anticipated that by continuing the system, they would not only facilitate the collection of agricultural taxes but also create a landed gentry that could, as in Britain itself, become the conservative foundation of an imperial ruling class. But many of the local gentry took advantage of their authority to increase taxes and force the less fortunate peasants to become tenants or lose their land entirely. When rural unrest threatened, the government passed legislation protecting farmers against eviction and unreasonable rent increases, but this measure had little effect outside the southern provinces, where it was originally enacted.

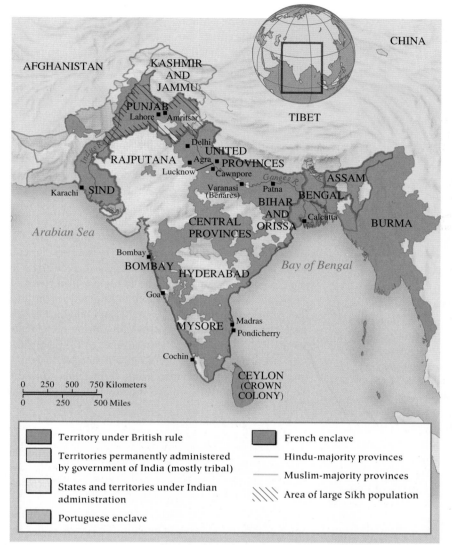

although foreign trade thrived, as Indian goods, notably high-quality cotton textiles, tropical food products, spices, and precious stones, were exported in return for gold and silver. Under the British, limited forms of industrialization took place, notably in the manufacturing of textiles and rope. The first textile mill opened in 1856; seventy years later, there were eighty mills in the city of Bombay (now Mumbai) alone. Nevertheless, the lack of local capital and the advantages given to British imports prevented the emergence of other vital new commercial and manufacturing operations, and the introduction of cheap British textiles put thousands of Bengali women out of work and severely damaged the village textile industry.

A Civilizing Mission? Foreign rule also had an effect on the psyche of the Indian people. Although many British colonial officials sincerely tried to improve the lot of the people under their charge, the government made few efforts to introduce democratic institutions and values to the Indian people. Moreover, British arrogance and contempt for local traditions cut deeply into the pride of many Indians, especially those of high caste who were accustomed to a position of superior status in India (see Movies & History, *A Passage to India*, p. 36). The British raj would pay dearly for its dismissal of Indian customs, when Indian troops serving under British command

MAP 2.1 India Under British Rule, 1805–1931. This map shows the different forms of rule that the British applied in India under their control. The Sikhs, located primarily in the Punjab, were adherents of a religion that began in the sixteenth century as an attempt to reconcile the Hindu and Muslim traditions and ultimately developed into an alternative to both.

Q *Where were the major cities of the subcontinent located, and under whose rule did they fall?*

One particular period of extreme drought in the 1870s, which was probably caused by regional El Nino conditions, resulted in the death of over a million Indians, and was locally blamed on the British authorities for their inaction in the face of the crisis (see Chapter 13 and "16-6 One World, One Environment," p. 417).

Manufacturing British colonialism was also remiss in bringing modern science and technology to India. Industrial development was still in its infancy during the Mughal era,

suddenly revolted against their masters and threatened the very foundations of British rule in India (see "2-6 Patterns of Resistance to Colonial Conquest," p. 47).

By the end of the nineteenth century, some educated Indians became increasingly disillusioned with the failure of the British to live up to their "civilizing mission" and began to clamor for a greater role in the governance of their country. In 1885, a new organization designed to represent the interests of the indigenous population—the Indian National Congress—was born (see Section 5-1c , p. 108).

In 1984, the celebrated director David Lean turned E.M. Forster's famous novel *A Passage to India* (1924) into a feature film. Like the novel, the film traces the adventures of Adela Quested (Judy Davis), a young British woman who visits colonial India during the 1920s. During a visit to local caves, she abruptly accuses an Indian doctor who had accompanied her to the site of rape, although in fact it appears unlikely in the film that the encounter ever took place. At a court trial, however, Adela suddenly recants, and the accused, Doctor Aziz (Victor Bannerjee), is acquitted. Ostracized by the local foreign community, she decides to return to England, while Aziz writes to thank her for marshalling the courage to change her story to affirm his innocence. The film brilliantly portrays the mysterious circumstances surrounding the alleged event, while shedding a harsh light on the racist attitudes prevalent within the British community regarding the surrounding Indian population.

 In this context, why would an accusation of rape become an even more sensitive issue in terms of its effect on Anglo-Indian relations?

2-4 THE COLONIAL TAKEOVER OF SOUTHEAST ASIA

 Focus Question: Which Western countries were most active in seeking colonial possessions in Southeast Asia, and what were their motives in doing so?

Southeast Asia had been one of the first destinations for European fleets en route to the East. Lured by the riches of the Spice Islands (located at the eastern end of the present-day Republic of Indonesia), adventurers from Spain and Portugal sailed to the area in the early-sixteenth century in the hope of seizing control of the spice trade from Arab and Indian merchants. A century later, the lure of profits

had attracted the attention of English and Dutch competitors. By mid-century, the spice trade was fast becoming a monopoly of Dutch mariners, whose sturdy ships and ample supply of capital gave them a significant advantage over their rivals.

Well before the arrival of the first Europeans, however, Southeast Asia had been an active participant in the global trade network, purchasing textiles from India and luxury goods from China in return for spices, precious metals, and various tropical woods and herbs. Although no single empire had ever controlled all of Southeast Asia, several powerful states had emerged in the region since the early centuries of the first millennium C.E. Some, like Sailendra and Srivijaya in the Indonesian archipelago, were primarily trading states. Others, like Vietnam, Angkor, and the Burmese empire of Pagan, were predominantly agricultural, although they too sought actively to participate in the commerce passing through the region. As a result of such trade contacts, most of the emerging states in the area had patterned their political systems and religious beliefs after those practiced on the Indian subcontinent. Only Vietnam, located along the eastern coast of the peninsula, was strongly influenced by China. Eventually, Islam—promoted by Muslim merchants from India and the Middle East—began to make inroads into the southern part of the region.

Fleets from a number of European states had begun patrolling the shipping lanes in the region since the sixteenth century, although in 1800, only two societies in Southeast Asia were under effective colonial rule: the Spanish Philippines and parts of the Indonesian archipelago. The latter would eventually be consolidated into the Dutch East Indies. The British had been driven out of the Spice Islands trade by the Dutch in the seventeenth century and possessed only a small enclave on the southern coast of the island of Sumatra and some territory on the Malay peninsula. The French had actively engaged in trade with states on the Asian mainland, but their activity in the area was eventually reduced to a small missionary effort run by the Society for Foreign Missions. The only legacy of Portuguese expansion in the region was the possession of half of the small island of Timor. The remainder of the region continued to be governed by indigenous rulers.

2-4a The Imposition of Colonial Rule

During the second half of the nineteenth century, however, European interest in Southeast Asia grew rapidly, and by 1900, virtually the entire area was under colonial rule (see Map 2.2). The process began after the Napoleonic wars, when the British, by agreement with the Dutch, abandoned their claims to territorial possessions in the East Indies in return for a free hand in the Malay peninsula.

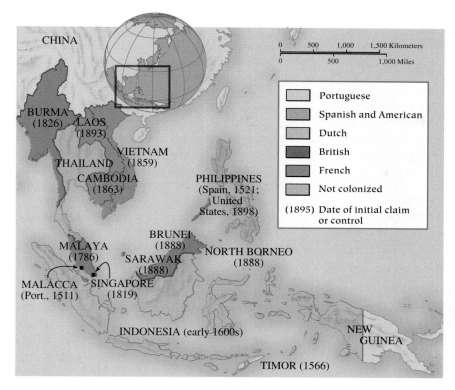

MAP 2.2 **Colonial Southeast Asia.** European colonial rule spread into Southeast Asia between the sixteenth century and the end of the nineteenth.

 What was the strategic significance of Malacca?

In 1819, the colonial administrator Stamford Raffles founded a new British colony on a small island at the tip of the peninsula. Called Singapore ("City of the Lion"), it had previously been used by Malay pirates as a base for raiding ships passing through the Strait of Malacca. When the invention of steam power enabled merchant ships to save time and distance by passing through the strait rather than sailing with the westerlies across the southern Indian Ocean, Singapore became a major stopping point for traffic to and from China and other commercial centers in the region. A few decades later, the British took over the kingdom of Burma and placed it under the colonial administration in India.

The British advance into Burma was watched nervously in Paris, where French geopoliticians were increasingly concerned that their traditional rival might obtain a monopoly on trade with south China. The French maintained a clandestine missionary organization in Vietnam despite harsh persecution by the local authorities, and now began to pressure Vietnamese authorities to allow them commercial access to the country. After many rebuffs, in the late 1850s the French forced the latter to cede territories in the southern part of the country. A generation later,

French rule was extended over the remainder of Vietnam. By the end of the century, French seizure of neighboring Cambodia and Laos had led to the creation of the French-ruled Indochinese Union.

With the French conquest of Indochina, Thailand—then known as Siam—was the only remaining independent state on the Southeast Asian mainland. During the last quarter of the century, British and French rivalry threatened to place the Thai, too, under colonial rule. But under the astute leadership of two remarkable rulers, King Mongkut (later familiar to millions of moviegoers in the West as the monarch in the 1956 film *The King and I*) and his son King Chulalongkorn, the Thai sought to introduce Western learning and maintain relations with the major European powers without undermining internal stability or inviting an imperialist attack. In this case, accommodation proved more effective than violent resistance. In 1896, the British and the French agreed to preserve Thailand as an independent buffer zone between their colonial possessions in Southeast Asia.

The final piece of the colonial edifice in Southeast Asia was put in place in 1898, when U.S. naval forces under Commodore George Dewey defeated the Spanish fleet in Manila Bay on the island of Luzon in the Spanish Philippines. Since gaining independence in the late-eighteenth century, the United States had always considered itself to be an anticolonialist nation, but by the end of the nineteenth century, many Americans believed that the United States was ready to expand abroad. The Pacific islands were the scene of great-power competition and witnessed the entry of the United States on the imperialist stage. Eastern Samoa became the first important American colony; the Hawaiian Islands were the next to fall. Soon after an American naval station had been established at Pearl Harbor in 1887, American settlers gained control of the sugar industry on the islands. When the local Hawaiians tried to reassert their authority, the U.S. Marines were brought in to "protect" American lives. Hawaii was annexed by the United States in 1898 during the era of American nationalistic fervor generated by the

Spanish-American War, which broke out after an explosion damaged a U.S. battleship anchored at Havana on the Spanish-held island of Cuba.

The defeat of Spain in the war of 1898 encouraged the Americans to extend their empire by acquiring Puerto Rico, Guam, and the Philippine Islands. Although President William McKinley justified the seizure of the Philippines on moral grounds, the real reason was to prevent them from falling into the hands of the Japanese. In fact, the Americans (like the Spanish before them) found the islands a convenient jumping-off point for the China trade (see Chapter 3). Although guerrilla forces led by Emilio Aguinaldo fought bitterly against U.S. troops to maintain independence, the resistance collapsed in 1901. President McKinley had his stepping-stone to the rich markets of China.

2-4b Colonial Regimes in Southeast Asia

In Southeast Asia, economic profit was the immediate and primary aim of the colonial enterprise. For that purpose, colonial powers tried wherever possible to work with local elites to facilitate the exploitation of natural resources such as rubber, tin, and oil (see Image 2.2). Indirect rule reduced the cost of training European administrators and had a less corrosive impact on the local culture.

Colonial Administration In the Dutch East Indies, for example, officials of the Dutch East India Company (VOC, from the initials of its Dutch name) entrusted local administration to the indigenous landed aristocracy, known as the *priyayi*. The *priyayi* maintained law and order and collected taxes in return for a payment from the VOC. The British followed a similar practice in Malaya. While establishing direct rule over areas of crucial importance, such as the commercial centers of Singapore and Malacca and the island of Penang, the British signed agreements with local Muslim rulers to maintain princely power in the interior of the peninsula.

In some instances, however, local resistance to the colonial conquest made such a policy impossible. In Burma, faced with staunch opposition from traditionalist forces, the British abolished the monarchy and administered the country directly through their colonial government in India. In Indochina, the French used both direct and indirect means. They imposed direct rule on the southern provinces in the Mekong delta, which had been ceded to France as a colony in 1860. The northern parts of the country, seized in the 1880s, were governed as a protectorate, with the emperor retaining titular authority from his palace in Hué. The French adopted a similar policy in Cambodia and Laos, where local rulers were left in charge with French

IMAGE 2.2 The Production of Rubber. Natural rubber was one of the most important cash crops in the European colonies in Asia. Rubber trees, native to the Amazon River basin in Brazil, were eventually transplanted to Southeast Asia, where they became a major source of profit. Workers on the plantations received few benefits, however. Once the sap of the tree, called latex, was extracted (left photo), it was hardened and pressed into sheets (right photo) and then sent to Europe for refining.

Cultural Influences, East and West

> **Q** *Compare and contrast the artistic styles of these two paintings. What message do they send to the viewer?*

Interaction & Exchange

WHEN EUROPEANS MOVED INTO ASIA in the nineteenth century, some Asians began to imitate European customs for prestige or social advancement. Seen in Image 2.3a, for example, is a young Vietnamese during the 1920s dressed in Western sports clothes, learning to play tennis. Sometimes, however, the cultural influence went the other way. In Image 2.3b, an English nabob, as European residents in India were often called, apes the manner of an Indian aristocrat, complete with harem and hookah, the Indian water pipe. The paintings on the wall, however, are in the European style.

Symbols of the progress of civilization: a tennis player and an athlete, c.1920 (colour litho)/ Vietnamese School (20th century)/INDIVISION CHARMET/Ecole Francaise d'Extreme Orient, Paris, France/Bridgeman Images

IMAGE 2.3a

British Library, London/Werner Forman/Art Resource, NY

IMAGE 2.3b

advisers to counsel them. Even the Dutch were eventually forced into a more direct approach. When the development of plantation agriculture and the extraction of oil in Sumatra made effective exploitation of local resources more complicated, they dispensed with indirect rule and tightened their administrative control over the archipelago. Whatever method was used, colonial regimes in Southeast Asia, as elsewhere, were slow to create democratic institutions. The first legislative councils and assemblies were composed almost exclusively of European residents in the colonies, while the first representatives from the indigenous population were wealthy and thus conservative in their political views (see Comparative Illustration, "Cultural Influences, East and West," above). When Southeast Asians began to complain, colonial officials gradually and reluctantly began to broaden the franchise, but even such liberal thinkers as Albert Sarraut advised patience in awaiting the full benefits of colonial policy. "I will treat you like my younger brothers," he promised, "but do not forget that I am the older brother. I will slowly give you the dignity of humanity."[3]

Economic Development Colonial powers were equally reluctant to shoulder the "white man's burden" in the area of economic development. As we have seen, their primary goals were to secure a source of cheap raw materials and to maintain markets for manufactured goods. So colonial policy concentrated on the export of raw materials—teakwood from Burma; rubber and tin from Malaya; spices, tea, coffee, and palm oil from the East Indies; and sugar and copra from the Philippines.

In some Southeast Asian colonial societies, a measure of industrial development did take place to meet the needs of the European population and local elites. Major manufacturing cities, including Rangoon in lower Burma, Batavia (now renamed Jakarta) on the island of Java, and Saigon in French Indochina, grew rapidly. Although the local middle class benefited in various ways from the Western presence, most industrial and commercial establishments were owned and managed by Europeans or, in some cases, by Indian or Chinese merchants who had long been active in the area. In Saigon, for example, even the manufacture of *nuoc mam*, the traditional Vietnamese fish sauce, was under Chinese ownership. Most urban residents were coolies (laborers, literally "hard labor" in Chinese), factory workers, or rickshaw drivers or eked out a living in family shops as they had during the traditional era.

Rural Policies   Despite the growth of an urban economy, the vast majority of people in Southeast Asia continued to farm the land. Many continued to live by subsistence agriculture, but the colonial policy of emphasizing cash crops for export led to the creation of a form of plantation agriculture in which peasants were recruited to work as wage laborers on rubber and tea plantations owned by Europeans. To maintain a competitive edge, the plantation owners kept the wages of their workers at the poverty level. Many plantation workers were "shanghaied" (the English term originated from the practice of recruiting laborers, often from the docks and streets of Shanghai, by the use of force, alcohol, drugs, or other unscrupulous means) to work on plantations, where conditions were often so inhumane that thousands died. High taxes, enacted by colonial governments to pay for administrative costs or improvements in the local infrastructure, were a heavy burden for poor peasants.

The situation was made even more difficult by the steady growth of the population. Peasants in Asia had always had large families on the assumption that a high proportion of their children would die in infancy. But improved sanitation and medical treatment resulted in lower rates of infant mortality and a staggering increase in population. The population of the island of Java, for example, increased from about a million in the precolonial era to about 40 million at the end of the nineteenth century. Under these conditions, the rural areas could no longer support the growing populations, and many young people fled to the cities to seek jobs in factories or shops. The migratory pattern gave rise to squatter settlements in the suburbs of the major cities.

Imperialism in the Balance   As in India, colonial rule did bring some benefits to Southeast Asia. It led to the beginnings of a modern economic infrastructure, and the development of an export market helped create an entrepreneurial class in rural areas. On the outer islands of the Dutch East Indies (such as Borneo and Sumatra), for example, small growers of rubber, palm oil, coffee, tea, and spices began to share in the profits of the colonial enterprise.

A balanced assessment of the colonial legacy in Southeast Asia must take into account that the early stages of industrialization are difficult in any society. Even in western Europe, industrialization led to the creation of an impoverished and powerless proletariat, urban slums, and displaced peasants driven from the land. In much of Europe, however, the bulk of the population eventually enjoyed better material conditions as the profits from manufacturing and plantation agriculture were reinvested in the national economy and gave rise to increased consumer demand. In contrast, in Southeast Asia, most of the profits were repatriated to the colonial mother country, while displaced peasants fleeing to cities such as Rangoon, Batavia, and Saigon found little opportunity for employment. Many were left with seasonal jobs, with one foot on the farm and one in the factory. The old world was being destroyed, and the new had yet to be born.

2-5 EMPIRE BUILDING IN AFRICA

 Focus Question: What factors were behind the "scramble for Africa," and what impact did it have on the continent?

The last of the equatorial regions of the world to be placed under European colonial rule was the continent of Africa. European navigators had first established contacts with Africans south of the Sahara during the late-fifteenth century, when Portuguese fleets sailed down the Atlantic coast on their way to the Indian Ocean. During the next three centuries, Europeans established port facilities along the coasts of East and West Africa to service their voyages into the Indian Ocean and to engage in limited commercial relations with African societies. Although European exploration of the area was originally motivated by the search for gold, eventually the trade in slaves took precedence, and over the next three centuries several million unfortunate Africans were loaded onto slave ships destined to serve as laborers on the sugar and cotton plantations of the Americas. For a variety of reasons, however, Europeans made little effort to penetrate the vast continent and were generally content to deal with African intermediaries along the coast to maintain their trading relationship. The Western psyche developed a deeply ingrained image of "darkest Africa"—a continent without a history, its people living out their days bereft of cultural contact with the outside world.

2-5a Africa Before Imperialism

There was a glimmer of truth in the Western image of sub-Saharan Africa as a region outside the mainstream of civilization on the Eurasian landmass. Although the continent was the original seedbed of humankind and the site of much of its early evolutionary experience, the desiccation of the Sahara during the fourth and third millennia B.C.E. had erected a major obstacle to communications between the peoples south of the desert and societies elsewhere in the world. The barrier was never total, however. From ancient times, caravans crossed the Sahara from the Niger River basin to the shores of the Mediterranean carrying gold and tropical products in exchange for salt, textile goods, and other manufactured articles from the north. By the seventh century C.E., several prosperous trading societies, whose renown extended to medieval Europe and the Middle East, had begun to arise in the savanna belt (a region of grasslands on the southern edge of the desert) of West Africa.

One crucial consequence of this new trade network was the introduction of Islam to the peoples of the region (see Map 2.3). Arab armies sweeping westward along the coast of the Mediterranean Sea had already brought the message of the Prophet Muhammad as far as Morocco and the Iberian peninsula. Soon, Islamic religion and culture began to cross the Sahara in the baggage of Muslim merchants. Along with the Qur'an, Islam's holy book, the new faith introduced its African converts to a new code of law and ethics—the *Shari'a*—and to the Prophet's uncompromising message of the equality of all in the eyes of God. The city of Timbuktu, on the banks of the Niger River, soon became a major center of Islamic scholarship and schools providing education in the Arabic language.

In the eastern half of the continent, the Sahara posed no obstacle to communication beyond the seas. The long eastern coast had played a role in the trade network of the Indian Ocean since the time of the pharaohs along the Nile. Ships from India, the Persian Gulf, and as far away as China made regular visits to the East African ports of Kilwa, Malindi, and Sofala, bringing textiles, metal goods, and luxury

articles in return for gold, ivory, and various tropical products from Africa. With the settlement of Arab traders along the eastern coast, the entire region developed a new synthetic culture, known as **Swahili**, that combined elements of Arabic and indigenous cultures. Although the Portuguese briefly seized or destroyed most of the existing trading ports along the eastern coast, by the eighteenth century they had been driven out, and local authority was restored.

In the vast interior of the continent, from the Congo River basin southward to the Cape of Good Hope, contacts with the outside world were rare, and the majority of the population lived in autonomous villages organized by clans or a local chieftain; they supported themselves by farming, pastoral pursuits, or hunting and gathering. In a few cases, some of these individual communities had begun to consolidate into small states, which took part in a growing interregional trade network based on the exchange of metal goods and foodstuffs.

2-5b The Growing European Presence in West Africa

By the beginning of the nineteenth century, the horrific slave trade was in decline. One reason was the growing sense of outrage in Europe over the purchase, sale, and exploitation of human beings. Traffic in slaves by Dutch merchants effectively came to an end in 1795 and by Danes in 1803. The slave trade was declared illegal in Great Britain in 1807 and in the United States in 1808. The British began to apply pressure on other nations to follow suit, and most did so after the end of the Napoleonic wars in 1815, leaving only Portugal and Spain as practitioners of the trade south of the equator. Meanwhile, the demand for slaves began to decline in the Western Hemisphere, although an illegal trade in slaves across the Atlantic persisted for some time (see Historical Voices, "Tragedy at Caffard Cove," p. 42). By the 1880s, slavery had been abolished in all major countries of the world.

The decline of the slave trade in the Atlantic during the nineteenth century, however, did not lead to an overall reduction in the European presence in West Africa. On the contrary, European interest in what was sometimes called "legitimate trade" in natural resources increased. Exports of peanuts, timber, hides, and palm oil increased substantially during the first decades of the century, and imports of textile goods and other manufactured products also rose.

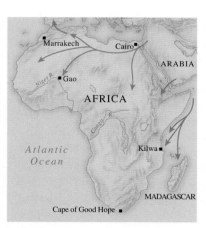

MAP 2.3 The Spread of Islam in Africa

Tragedy at Caffard Cove

 How were the surviving victims of the shipwreck at Caffard Cove dealt with by the government authorities in Martinique? Under what provisions of the law was the decision reached?

Interaction & Exchange **THE SLAVE TRADE WAS DECLARED ILLEGAL** in France in 1818, but the clandestine shipment of Africans to the Americas continued for many years afterward. At the same time, slavery was widely tolerated in the French colonies, especially in the Caribbean, where sugar plantations on the islands of Guadeloupe and Martinique depended on cheap labor for their profits. It was not until 1849 that slavery was abolished throughout the French Empire.

Among the tragic events that characterized the shipment of slaves to the Americas (often called the "Middle Passage"), few are as poignant as the incident described in the passage below, which took place in 1830 on the island of Martinique. The text, which includes passages from the original official report of the incident, is taken from a memorial erected at the site many years later. Laurent Valère, a local sculptor, erected fifteen statues to commemorate the victims. The name of the ship and the name and nationality of the ship's captain, as well as the ultimate fate of the surviving victims, remain a mystery to this day.

The Caffard Memorial

Around noon on the 8th of April 1830, a sailing ship [was observed] carrying out odd maneuvers off the coast of [the town of] Diamant [on the southern coast of Martinique]; at about five P.M. [the vessel] cast anchor off the dangerous coast of nearby Caffard Cove. François Dizac, a resident of the neighborhood and manager of the Plage du Diamant, a plantation owned by the Count de Latournelle, realized that the ship's situation was perilous, but a heavy swell prevented him from launching a boat to warn the captain that the vessel was in imminent danger of running aground. He therefore sent signals that the captain either could not, or chose not, to acknowledge.

At 11 P.M. that evening, anguished cries and cracking sounds suddenly began to shatter the silence of the night. Dizac and a party of slaves from the nearby plantation rushed promptly to the scene, only to encounter a horrifying sight: the ship had been dashed on the rocks and its passengers thrown into the fury of the raging seas.

The rescuers on shore then observed a large number of panic-stricken males clinging desperately to the ship's foremast, which suddenly broke in two, tossing them into the foam or onto the rocks. Broken masts lying on the rocks, fragments of torn sails floating alongside ropes caught in the reef where the ship itself lay on the rocks all provided visual evidence of the frightful incident that had just occurred.

Forty-six bodies, four of whom were white males, were lying amidst the rocks. . . . "I ordered the bodies of the black victims to be buried at a short distance from the shore, then directed that those of the white males be carried to the cemetery of Diamant parish, where they received a Christian burial. I was then taken to the cabin of a certain Borromé, a free man of color, where those black castaways who had been rescued from the shipwreck had been given temporary shelter. Among the victims, six were found to be in such poor condition that they could not be taken to the Latournelle plantation. The other 80 survivors were handed over to the naval authorities at Fort Royal. In all, 86 African captives, of whom 60 were women or girls, were rescued out of a ship's "cargo" estimated at nearly 300 persons.

"I ordered the interrogation of the surviving black castaways by interpreters, and it became clear from their testimony that the ship had been at sea for four months, and that most of the white sailors on board had died during the crossing [of the Atlantic], and that an additional 70 blacks had died from illness and had been thrown overboard during the voyage. Another 260 individuals remained on the ship when it was sunk off the coast of Diamant. . . . Only a few males had thus survived, since all of them were shackled together in the ship's hold with irons on their feet at the time of the wreck."

At that point, a legal issue was raised: what should be done with the surviving castaways who, although they could not be classified as slaves under existing law (since they were victims of illegal trade), yet could not be considered in this colony as men and therefore couldn't be freed. In May 1830, the Privy Council of Martinique ordered that the captured Negroes were to be shipped to Cayenne [the capital of French Guiana] in order to avoid having in the [French] West Indies a special class of people who could not be classified either as slaves or as free individuals. . . .

Thus, in July 1830, a second deportation followed the first, adding to the ordeal of the [African] slaves who had survived the shipwreck at Caffard Cove.

Source: Association de Sauvegarde du Patrimoine du Diamant. Text by Merlande, MOANDA SATURNIN, historian. Translation from the original French by the author.

Stimulated by growing commercial interests in the area, European governments began to push for a more permanent presence along the coast. During the early-nineteenth century, the British established settlements along the Gold Coast (present-day Ghana) and in Sierra Leone, where they attempted to set up agricultural plantations for freed slaves who had returned from the Western Hemisphere or had been liberated by British ships while en route to the Americas. A similar haven for ex-slaves was developed with the assistance of the United States in Liberia. The French occupied the area around the Senegal River near Cape Verde, where they attempted to develop peanut plantations.

The growing European presence in West Africa led to tensions with local governments in the area. British efforts to increase trade with the state of Ashanti, in the area of the present-day state of Ghana, led to conflict in the 1820s, but did not halt their efforts. Most African states, especially those with a fairly high degree of political integration, were able to maintain their independence from this creeping European encroachment, called "**informal empire**" by some historians, but eventually, in 1874, the British stepped in and annexed the Ashanti kingdom as Britain's first African colony of the Gold Coast. At about the same time, the British extended an informal protectorate over warring tribal groups in the Niger delta.

2-5c Imperialist Shadow over the Nile

A similar process was under way in the Nile valley. Ever since the voyages of the Portuguese explorers at the close of the fifteenth century, European trade with the East had been carried on almost exclusively by the route around the Cape of Good Hope at the southern tip of Africa. But from the outset, there was interest in shortening the route by digging a canal east of Cairo, where only a low, swampy isthmus separated the Mediterranean from the Red Sea. The Ottoman Turks, who controlled the area, had considered constructing a canal in the sixteenth century, but nothing was accomplished until 1854, when the French entrepreneur Ferdinand de Lesseps signed a contract to begin construction of the canal, which was completed in 1869 (see Map 2.4). The project brought little immediate benefit to Egypt, however, which was attempting to adopt reforms on the European model under the vigorous rule of the Ottoman official Muhammad Ali. The costs of construction imposed a major debt on the

Egyptian government and forced a growing level of dependence on foreign financial support. When an army revolt against the increasing foreign influence broke out in 1881, the British stepped in to protect their investment (they had bought Egypt's canal company shares in 1875) and set up an informal protectorate that would last until World War I.

Rising discontent in the Sudan added to Egypt's internal problems. In 1881, the Muslim cleric Muhammad Ahmad, known as the Mahdi (in Arabic, the "rightly guided one"), led a religious revolt that brought much of the upper Nile under his control. The famous British general Charles Gordon led a military force to Khartoum to restore Egyptian authority, but his besieged army was captured in 1885 by the Mahdi's troops, thirty-six hours before a British rescue mission reached Khartoum. Gordon himself died in the battle.

The weakening of Turkish rule in the Nile valley had a parallel farther along the Mediterranean coast to the west, where autonomous regions had begun to emerge under local viceroys in Tripoli, Tunis, and Algiers. In 1830, the French, on the pretext of reducing the threat of piracy to European shipping in the Mediterranean, seized the area surrounding Algiers and annexed it to the kingdom of France. By the mid-1850s, more than 150,000 Europeans had settled in the fertile region adjacent to the coast, though Berber resistance continued in the desert to the south. In 1881, the French imposed a protectorate on neighboring Tunisia. Only Tripoli and Cyrenaica (Ottoman provinces that make up modern-day Libya) remained under Turkish rule until the Italians took them in 1911–1912.

2-5d The Scramble for Africa

At the beginning of the 1880s, most of Africa was still independent. European rule was limited to the fringes of the continent, and a few areas, such as Egypt, lower Nigeria, Senegal, and Mozambique, were under various forms of loose protectorate. But the trends were ominous, as the pace of European penetration was accelerating and the constraints that had limited European rapaciousness were fast disappearing.

The scramble began in the mid-1880s, when several European states engaged in what today would be called a feeding frenzy. All sought to seize a piece of African territory before the carcass had been picked clean. By 1900, virtually the entire continent had been placed under one form or another of European rule (see Map 2.5).

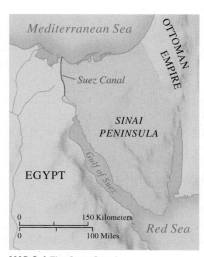

MAP 2.4 The Suez Canal

Mediterranean Sea

OTTOMAN EMPIRE

Suez Canal

SINAI PENINSULA

Gulf of Suez

EGYPT

Red Sea

0   150 Kilometers

0   100 Miles

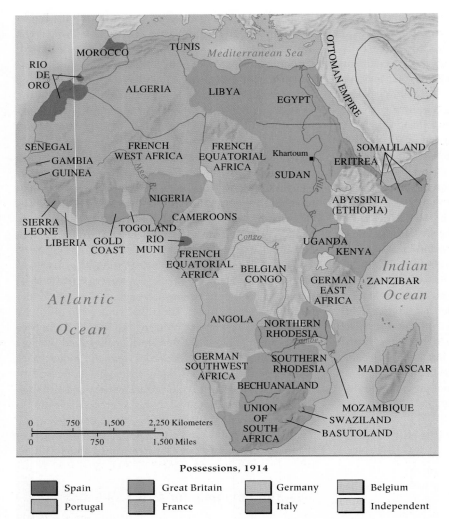

Possessions, 1914

■ Spain	■ Great Britain	■ Germany	■ Belgium
■ Portugal	■ France	■ Italy	□ Independent

MAP 2.5 Africa in 1914. By the beginning of 1900, virtually all of Africa was under some form of European rule. The territorial divisions established by colonial powers on the continent of Africa on the eve of World War I are shown here.

Q *Which European countries possessed the most colonies in Africa? Why did Ethiopia remain independent?*

The Motives What had happened to spark the sudden imperialist hysteria that brought an end to African independence? Economic interests in the narrow sense were not at stake as they had been in South and Southeast Asia: the level of trade between Europe and Africa was simply not sufficient to justify the risks and the expense of conquest. Clearly, one factor was the growing rivalry among the imperialist powers. European leaders might be provoked into an imperialist takeover not by economic considerations but by the fear that another state might do so, leaving them at a disadvantage.

Another consideration might be called the "missionary factor," as European religious interests lobbied with their governments for a colonial takeover to facilitate their efforts to convert the African population to Christianity. In fact, considerable moral complacency was inherent in the process. The concept of the "white man's burden" persuaded many that it was in the interests of the African people to be introduced more rapidly to the benefits of Western civilization. Even the highly respected Scottish missionary David Livingstone had become convinced that missionary work and economic development had to go hand in hand, pleading to his fellow Europeans to introduce the "three Cs" (Christianity, commerce, and civilization) to the continent. How much easier such a task would be if African peoples were under benevolent European rule! There were more prosaic reasons as well. Advances in Western technology and European superiority in firearms made it easier than ever for a small European force to defeat superior numbers. Furthermore, life expectancy for Europeans living in Africa had improved. With the discovery that quinine (extracted from the bark of the cinchona tree) could provide partial immunity from the ravages of malaria, the mortality rate for Europeans living in Africa dropped dramatically in the 1840s. By the end of the century, European residents in tropical Africa faced

The British had consolidated their authority over the Nile valley and seized additional territories in East Africa. The French retaliated by advancing eastward from Senegal into the central Sahara, where they eventually came eyeball to eyeball with the British in the Nile valley. They also occupied the island of Madagascar and other coastal territories in West and Central Africa. In between, the Germans claimed the hinterland opposite Zanzibar, as well as coastal strips in West and Southwest Africa north of the Cape, and King Leopold II of Belgium claimed the Congo.

only slightly higher risks of death by disease than individuals living in Europe.

Under these circumstances, King Leopold of Belgium used missionary activities as an excuse to claim vast territories in the Congo River basin—Belgium, he said, as "a small country, with a small people," needed a colony to enhance its image.[4] The royal land grab set off a desperate race among European nations to stake claims throughout sub-Saharan Africa. Leopold ended up with the territories south of the Congo River, while France occupied areas to the north. Rapacious European adventurers established plantations in the new Belgian Congo to grow rubber, palm oil, and other valuable export products.

The Berlin Conference As rivalry among the competing powers heated up, a conference was convened at Berlin in 1884 to avert war and reduce tensions among European nations competing for the spoils of Africa. It proved reasonably successful at achieving the first objective but less so at the second. During the next few years, African territories were annexed without provoking a major confrontation between Western powers, but in the late 1890s, Britain and France reached the brink of conflict at Fashoda, a small town on the Nile River in the Sudan. The French had been advancing eastward across the Sahara with the transparent objective of controlling the regions around the upper Nile. In 1898, British and Egyptian troops seized the Sudan and then marched southward to head off the French. After a tense face-off between units of the two European countries at Fashoda, the French government backed down, and British authority over the area was secured. Except for Djibouti, a tiny portion of the Somali coast, the French were restricted to equatorial Africa.

2-5e Bantus, Boers, and British in South Africa

Nowhere in Africa did the European presence grow more rapidly than in the south. During the eighteenth century, Dutch settlers from the Cape Colony began to migrate eastward into territory inhabited by local Khoisan- and Bantu-speaking peoples, the latter of whom had recently entered the area from the north. Internecine warfare among the Bantus had largely depopulated the region, facilitating occupation of the land by the Boers, the Afrikaans-speaking farmers descended from the

original Dutch settlers in the seventeenth century. But in the early-nineteenth century, a Bantu people called the Zulus, under the talented ruler Shaka, counterattacked, setting off a series of wars between the Europeans and the Zulus. Eventually, Shaka was overthrown, and the Boers continued their advance northeastward during the so-called Great Trek of the mid-1830s (see Map 2.6). By 1865, the total European population of the area had risen to nearly 200,000 people.

The Boers' eastward migration was provoked in part by the British seizure of the Cape from the Dutch during the Napoleonic wars. The British government was generally more sympathetic to the rights of the local African population than were the Afrikaners, many of whom saw white superiority as ordained by God and fled from British rule to control their own destiny. Eventually, the Boers formed their own independent republics, the Orange Free State and the South African Republic (usually known as Transvaal).

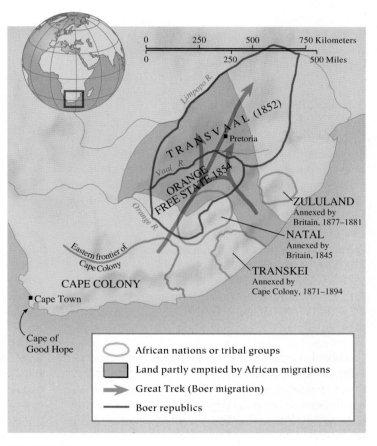

MAP 2.6 The Struggle for Southern Africa. Shown here is the expansion of European settlers from the Cape Colony into adjacent areas of southern Africa in the nineteenth century. The arrows indicate the routes taken by the Afrikaans-speaking Boers.

 Who were the Boers, and why did they migrate eastward?

Much of the African population in these areas was confined to reserves. In the meantime, British troops began to move into areas nearer the coast, sometimes encountering fierce resistance from Zulu warriors.

The Boer War   The discovery of gold and diamonds in the Transvaal complicated the situation. Clashes between the Afrikaner population and foreign (mainly British) miners and developers led to an attempt by Cecil Rhodes, prime minister of the Cape Colony and a prominent entrepreneur in the area, to subvert the Transvaal and bring it under British rule. In 1899, the so-called Boer War broke out between Britain and the Transvaal, which was backed by the Orange Free State. Guerrilla resistance by the Boers was fierce, but the vastly superior forces of the British were able to prevail by 1902. To compensate the defeated Afrikaner population for the loss of independence, the British government agreed that only whites would vote in the now essentially self-governing colony. The Boers were placated, but the brutalities committed during the war (the British introduced an institution later to be known as the concentration camp) created bitterness on both sides that continued to fester for decades.

2-5f Colonialism in Africa

In general, Western economic interests were more limited in Africa than elsewhere. As a result, most colonial governments settled down to govern their new territories with the least effort and expense possible. In many cases, they pursued a form of indirect rule reminiscent of the British approach to the princely states in the Indian peninsula.

British Rule in Nigeria   Nigeria offers a typical example of British-style indirect rule. British officials operated at the central level, but local authority was assigned to Nigerian chiefs, with British district officers serving as intermediaries with the central administration. The local authorities were expected to maintain law and order and to collect taxes from the indigenous population. A dual legal system was instituted that applied African laws to Africans and European laws to foreigners.

One advantage of such an administrative system was that it did not severely disrupt local customs and institutions. At the same time, it was misleading because all major decisions were made by the British administrators while the African authorities served primarily as the means of enforcing the decisions. Moreover, indirect rule served to perpetuate the autocratic system that often existed prior to colonial takeover since there was a natural tendency to view the local aristocracy as the African equivalent of the traditional British ruling class. Such a policy provided few opportunities for ambitious and talented young Africans from outside the traditional elite and thus sowed the seeds for class tensions after the restoration of independence in the twentieth century.

The British in East Africa   The situation was somewhat different in Kenya, which had a relatively large European population attracted by the temperate climate in the central highlands. The local government had encouraged Europeans to migrate to the area as a means of promoting economic development and encouraging financial self-sufficiency. To attract them, fertile farmlands in the central highlands were reserved for European settlement while, as in South Africa, specified reserve lands were set aside for Africans. The presence of a privileged European minority had an impact on Kenya's political development. The European settlers actively sought self-government and dominion status similar to that granted to such former British possessions as Canada and Australia. The British government, however, was not willing to run the risk of provoking racial tensions with the African majority and agreed only to establish separate government organs for the European and African populations.

South Africa   The situation in South Africa, of course, was unique, not only because of the high percentage of European settlers but also because of the division between English-speaking and Afrikaner elements within the European population. In 1910, the British agreed to the creation of the independent Union of South Africa, which combined the old Cape Colony and Natal with the two Boer republics. The new union adopted a representative government, but only for the European population. The African reserves of Basutoland (now Lesotho), Bechuanaland (now Botswana), and Swaziland were subordinated directly to the crown. The union was now free to manage its own domestic affairs and possessed considerable autonomy in foreign relations. Remaining areas south of the Zambezi River, eventually divided into the territories of Northern and Southern Rhodesia, were also placed under British rule. British immigration into Southern Rhodesia was extensive, and in 1922, after a popular referendum, it became a crown colony.

Direct Rule   Most other European nations governed their African possessions through a form of direct rule. The prototype was the French system, which reflected the centralized administrative system introduced in France by Napoleon. As in the British colonies, at the top of the pyramid was a French official, usually known as a governor-general, who was appointed from Paris and governed with the aid of a bureaucracy in the capital city. At the provincial level, French commissioners were assigned to deal with local administrators, but the latter were required to be conversant in French and could be transferred to a new position to meet the needs of the central government.

After World War I, European colonial policy in Africa entered a new and more formal phase, sometimes labeled "high colonialism." Colonial governments paid more attention to improving social services, including education, medicine, sanitation, and communications. More Africans were now serving in colonial administrations, though relatively few were in positions of responsibility. On the other hand, race consciousness probably increased during this period. Segregated clubs, schools, and churches were established as more European officials brought their wives with them and began to raise families in the colonies.

More directly affected by the colonial presence than the small African elite were ordinary Africans, who were subjected to countless indignities reminiscent of Western practices in Asia. While the institution of slavery was discouraged in much of the continent, African workers were routinely exposed to unbelievably harsh conditions as they were put to use as manual laborers to promote the cause of imperialism.

The most flagrant example was in the Belgian Congo. Conditions on the plantations there were so abysmal that an international outcry eventually led to the formation of a commission under British consul Roger Casement to investigate. The commission's report, issued in 1904, helped to bring about reforms (see Opposing Viewpoints, "White Man's Burden, Black Man's Sorrow," p. 33).

Women in Colonial Africa Colonial rule had a mixed impact on the rights and status of women in Africa. Sexual relationships changed profoundly during the colonial era, sometimes in ways that could justly be described as beneficial. Colonial governments attempted to put an end to such traditional practices as forced marriage, bodily mutilation such as clitoridectomy, and **polygyny**. Missionaries introduced women to Western education and encouraged them to organize to defend their interests.

But the colonial system had some unfavorable consequences as well. African women had traditionally benefited from the prestige of **matrilineal** systems and were empowered by their traditional role as the primary agricultural producers in their community. Under colonialism, European settlers not only took the best land for themselves but also, in introducing new agricultural techniques, tended to deal exclusively with males, encouraging the latter to develop lucrative cash crops, while women were restricted to traditional farming methods. Whereas African

men applied chemical fertilizer to the fields, women continued to use manure. While men began to use bicycles, and eventually trucks, to transport goods, women still carried their goods on their heads, a practice that continues today. In British colonies, Victorian attitudes of female subordination led to restrictions on women's freedom, and positions in government that they had formerly held were now closed to them.

2-6 PATTERNS OF RESISTANCE TO COLONIAL CONQUEST

 Focus Question: How did the indigenous response to the imperialist attacks in Africa and Asia differ from place to place, and how do you account for such differences?

Local resistance to the establishment of colonial rule in Asia and Africa took various forms. For the most part, it was led by the existing ruling elites, although in some instances traditionalist forces continued their opposition even after resistance by the indigenous rulers had ceased. In India, for example, many local leaders fought against the expansion of British rule even after the virtual collapse of the Mughal Dynasty. Some, like the local leader Haider Ali, used guerrilla tactics with considerable success. Similarly, after the decrepit monarch in Vietnam had been defeated by a French attack on the capital of Hanoi in 1884, civilian and military officials set up an independent organization called Can Vuong (literally, "save the king") and continued their own resistance campaign without imperial sanction (see Opposing Viewpoints, "To Resist or Not to Resist," p. 48).

Sometimes opposition to Western penetration took the form of peasant revolts. In traditional Asian societies, peasant discontent over high taxes, official corruption, rising debt, and famine had often led to rural uprisings. Such conditions frequently existed under colonialism, since rural conditions often deteriorated as population density increased and peasants were driven off the land to make way for plantation agriculture. Angry peasants then vented their frustration at the foreign invaders.

2-6a Opposition to Colonial Rule in Africa

Because of the continent's sheer size and its ethnic, religious, and linguistic diversity, resistance to the European invaders in Africa was often sporadic and uncoordinated, but fierce nonetheless. The uprising led by the Mahdi in the Sudan was only the most dramatic example. In South Africa, the Zulus engaged in a bitter war of resistance to

To Resist or Not to Resist

 Explain briefly the reasons advanced by each writer to justify his actions. Which argument do you think would have earned more support from contemporaries? Why?

Interaction & Exchange **HOW TO RESPOND TO COLONIAL RULE** could be an excruciating problem for political elites in many Asian countries because resistance often seemed futile while often adding to the suffering of the indigenous population. Hoang Cao Khai and Phan Dinh Phung were members of the Confucian scholar-gentry from the same village in Vietnam. Yet they reacted in dramatically different ways to the French conquest of their country. Their exchange of letters, reproduced here, illustrates the dilemmas they faced.

Hoang Cao Khai's Letter to Phan Dinh Phung

Soon, it will be seventeen years since we ventured upon different paths of life. How sweet was our friendship when we both lived in our village. . . . At the time when the capital was lost and after the royal carriage had departed, you courageously answered the appeals of the King by raising the banner of righteousness. It was certainly the only thing to do in those circumstances. No one will question that.

But now the situation has changed and even those without intelligence or education have concluded that nothing remains to be saved. How is it that you, a man of vast understanding, do not realize this?. . . You are determined to do whatever you deem righteous. . . . But though you have no thoughts for your own person or for your own fate, you should at least attend to the sufferings of the population of a whole region. . . .

Until now your actions have undoubtedly accorded with your loyalty. May I ask however what sin our people have committed to deserve so much hardship? I would understand your resistance, did you involve but your family for the benefit of a large number. As of now, hundreds of families are subject to grief; how do you have the heart to fight on? I venture to predict that, should you pursue your struggle, not only will the population of our village

be destroyed but our entire country will be transformed into a sea of blood and a mountain of bones. It is my hope that men of your superior morality and honesty will pause a while to appraise the situation.

Reply of Phan Dinh Phung to Hoang Cao Khai

In your letter, you revealed to me the causes of calamities and of happiness. You showed me clearly where advantages and disadvantages lie. All of which sufficed to indicate that your anxious concern was not only for my own security but also for the peace and order of our entire region. I understood plainly your sincere arguments.

I have concluded that if our country has survived these past thousand years when its territory was not large, its army not strong, its wealth not great, it was because the relationships between king and subjects, fathers and children, have always been regulated by the five moral obligations. In the past, the Han, the Sung, the Yuan, the Ming time and again dreamt of annexing our country and of dividing it up into prefectures and districts within the Chinese administrative system. But never were they able to realize their dream. Ah! if even China, which shares a common border with our territory, and is a thousand times more powerful than Vietnam, could not rely upon her strength to swallow us, it was surely because the destiny of our country had been willed by Heaven itself.

The French, separated from our country until the present day by I do not know how many thousand miles, have crossed the oceans to come to our country. Wherever they came, they acted like a storm, so much so that the Emperor had to flee. The whole country was cast into disorder. Our rivers and our mountains have been annexed by them at a stroke and turned into a foreign territory.

How can the French not be aware of all the suffering that the rural population has had to endure? Under these circumstances, is it surprising that families should be disrupted and the people scattered?

My friend, if you are troubled about our people, then I advise you to place yourself in my position and to think about the circumstances in which I live. You will understand naturally and see clearly that I do not need to add anything else.

Source: From Truong Buu Lam, *Patterns of Vietnamese Response to Foreign Intervention*, Monograph Series No. 11. Southeast Asian Studies, Yale University, 1967. Dist. By Celler Bookshop, Detroit, MI.

Boer colonists arriving from the Cape Colony. Later they fought with equal determination against the British occupation of their territory and were not finally subdued until the end of the century. In West Africa, the Ashanti ruling class led a bitter struggle against the British with broad-based popular support.

Resistance to the colonial onslaught, therefore, was fairly widespread. The lack of modern weapons, however, was decisive, and African forces eventually suffered defeat after defeat throughout the continent. The first effective modern weapon in the hands of the Europeans was the Gatling gun, a repeating rifle first put in use in the 1860s. But the most fearsome was the Maxim gun, the first recoil-operated machine gun, which had been invented by the American Hiram Stevens in 1883. In the hands of colonial troops it enabled the Europeans to defeat adversaries many times their own size (in the widely quoted words of the British poet Hilaire Belloc: "Whatever happens, we have got The Maxim gun, and they have not.").

The one notable exception was in Ethiopia, where, at the Battle of Adowa in 1896, the modern army of Emperor Menelik III was able to fend off an Italian invasion force with firearms purchased from several European countries, and thus preserve the country's national independence well into the next century (see Image 2.4).

2-6b The Sepoy Uprising

Perhaps the most famous revolt against European authority in the mid-nineteenth century was that of the **sepoys** in India. The sepoys were Indian troops hired by the East India Company to protect British interests in the subcontinent. Unrest within Indian units of the colonial army had been common since early in the century, when it had been sparked by economic issues, religious sensitivities, or nascent anticolonial sentiment. In 1857, new tensions erupted when the British adopted the new Enfield rifle for use by sepoy infantrymen. The rifle was a muzzle-loader that used paper cartridges covered with animal fat and lard; because the cartridge had to be bitten off, it broke strictures against high-class Hindus' eating animal products and Muslim prohibitions against eating pork. Protests among sepoy units in northern India were initially ignored by British authorities and soon turned into a full-scale mutiny, supported by uprisings in various parts of the country. Although the movement lacked clear goals and was eventually suppressed, the revolt frightened the British and led to several reforms, as well as a decision to give precedence for military service to ethnic groups more likely to be loyal to the British, such as the Sikhs of Punjab and the Gurkhas, a mountain people from Nepal. The British also decided to suppress

IMAGE 2.4 The Battle of Adowa. During the 1890s, ambitious Italian leaders—their country only recent reunited—sought to follow the example of their European counterparts by creating their own colony in East Africa. After forcing the kingdom of Ethiopia to cede territories along the coast, in the winter of 1896 they determined to complete their conquest of the entire country. But on March 1, 1897, Ethiopian forces armed with European firearms inflicted a major defeat on the Italian army near the town of Adowa. In the ensuing Treaty of Addis Ababa, Italy formally recognized Ethiopian independence. The victory inspired African resistance leaders for decades, as well as the anonymous artists of this painting, which shows Ethiopian forces, led by their patron St. George on his white horse, matched against their Italian adversaries.

the final remnants of the hapless Mughal Dynasty, which had supported the mutiny, and turn responsibility for the administration of the subcontinent from the East India Company over to the crown.

2-6c The Path of Collaboration

Not all Asians and Africans reacted to the colonial takeover by choosing the path of violent resistance. Some found elements to admire in Western civilization and compared it favorably with their own traditional practices and institutions. The decision to collaborate with the colonial administration was undoubtedly often motivated by self-interest. In those cases, the collaborators might be treated by their compatriots with scorn or even hostility, especially by those who had chosen the path of resistance. On occasion, the decision was undoubtedly reached only after painful consideration of the alternatives. Whatever the circumstances, it often divided friends and families, as occurred with two onetime childhood friends in Vietnam, when one chose resistance, the other collaboration (see Opposing Viewpoints, "To Resist or Not to Resist," p. 48).

Not all colonial subjects, of course, felt required to choose between resistance and collaboration. Most simply lived out their lives without engaging in the political arena. Even so, in some cases their actions affected their country's future. A prime example was Ram Mohan Roy, a brahmin from Bengal, who founded the Brahmo Samaj (Society of Brahma) in 1828 to help his fellow Hindus defend their faith against verbal attacks from British acquaintances. Roy was by no means a hide-bound traditionalist. He opposed such practices as sati and recognized the benefit of introducing the best aspects of European culture into Indian society, but he felt it was important to encourage his compatriots to defend their traditional values against the onslaught of Western civilization. In so doing, he helped promote the first stirrings of nationalist sentiment in nineteenth-century India.

HISTORIANS DEBATE
2-6d Imperialism: Drawing Up the Balance Sheet

Few periods of history are as controversial among scholars and casual observers alike as the era of imperialism. To defenders of the colonial enterprise like the poet Rudyard Kipling, imperialism was the "white man's burden," a disagreeable but necessary phase in the evolution of human society, lifting up the toiling races from tradition to modernity and bringing an end to poverty, famine, and disease. Although its immediate consequences were sometimes unfortunate, they concede, Western imperialism would prove to be ultimately beneficial to colonial powers and subjects alike because it created the conditions for global economic development and the universal application of democratic institutions.

Critics take exception to such views, portraying imperialism as a tragedy of major proportions. The insatiable drive of the advanced economic powers for access to raw materials and markets created an exploitative environment that transformed the vast majority of colonial peoples into a permanent underclass while restricting the benefits of modern technology to a privileged few. Kipling's "white man's burden" was dismissed as a hypocritical gesture to hoodwink the naive and salve the guilty feelings of those who recognized imperialism for what it was – a savage act of rape. They dismiss the Western civilizing mission itself as a fig leaf to cover naked greed and reject the notion that imperialism played a salutary role in hastening the adjustment of traditional societies to the demands of industrial civilization. Rather, it locked them into what many social scientists today describe as a "dependency relationship" with their colonial masters. "Why is Africa (or for that matter Latin America and much of Asia) so poor?" asked one Western critique of imperialism. "The answer is very brief: we have made it poor."[5]

Between these two irreconcilable views, where does the truth lie? It is difficult to provide a simple answer to this question, as the colonial record varied from country to country. In some cases, the colonial experience was probably beneficial in introducing Western technology, values, and democratic institutions into traditional societies with a minimum of social disruption. As its defenders are quick to point out, colonialism often laid the foundation for preindustrial societies to play an active and rewarding role in the global economic marketplace.

Still, the critics have a point. Although colonialism did introduce the peoples of Asia and Africa to new technology and the expanding economic marketplace, it was unnecessarily brutal in its application and all too often failed to realize the exalted claims and objectives of its promoters. Existing social and economic networks—often potentially valuable as a foundation for later development—were ruthlessly swept aside in the interests of providing markets for Western manufactured goods. Potential sources of local industrialization were nipped in the bud to avoid competition for factories in Amsterdam, London, Pittsburgh, or Manchester. Training in Western democratic ideals and practices was ignored out of fear that the recipients might use them as weapons against the ruling authorities.

A fundamental weakness of colonialism, then, was that it was ultimately based on the self-interests of the citizens of the colonial powers. When those interests collided with the needs of the colonial peoples, the former always triumphed. However sincerely the David Livingstones, Albert Sarrauts, and William McKinleys of the world were convinced of the rightness of their civilizing mission, the ultimate result was to deprive the colonial peoples of the right to make their own choices about their destiny. Sophisticated, age-old societies that could have been left to respond to the technological revolution in their own way were thus squeezed dry of precious national resources under the false guise a of a "civilizing mission." As the sociologist Clifford Geertz remarked in his book *Agricultural Involution: The Processes of Economical Change in Indonesia*, the tragedy is not that the colonial peoples suffered throughout the colonial era, but that they suffered for nothing. We shall address this issue again in the Reflections at the end of Part I.

MAKING CONNECTIONS

By the first quarter of the twentieth century, virtually all of Africa and a good part of South and Southeast Asia were under some form of colonial rule. With the advent of the age of imperialism, a global economy was finally established, and the domination of Western civilization over the civilizations of Africa and Asia appeared to be complete.

The imperialist rush for colonies did not take place without opposition. In most areas of the world, local governments and peoples resisted the onslaught, sometimes to the bitter end. But with few exceptions, they were unable to overcome the fearsome new warships and firearms that the Industrial Revolution in Europe had brought into being. Although the material benefits and democratic values of the occupying powers aroused admiration from many observers in much of the colonial world, in the end it was weapons, more than ideas, that ushered in the age of imperialism.

Africa and southern Asia were not the only areas of the world that were buffeted by the winds of Western expansionism in the late nineteenth century. The nations of eastern Asia, and those of Latin America and the Middle East as well, were also affected in significant ways. The consequences of Western political, economic, and military penetration varied substantially from one region to another, however, and therefore require separate treatment. The experience of East Asia will be dealt with in the next chapter. That of Latin America and the Middle East will be discussed in Chapter 24. In these areas, new rivals—notably the United States, Russia, and Japan—entered the scene and played an active role in the process. By the end of the nineteenth century, the rush to secure colonies had circled the world.

REFLECTION QUESTIONS

Q What were the consequences of the new imperialism of the nineteenth century for the colonies of the European powers? How should the motives and stated objectives of the imperialist countries be evaluated?

Q What arguments have been advanced to justify the European takeover of societies in Asia and Africa during the latter part of the nineteenth century? To what degree are such arguments justified?

Q The colonial powers adopted two basic philosophies in seeking to govern their conquered territories in Asia and Africa—assimilation and association. What were the principles behind these philosophies, and how did they work in practice? Which do you believe was more successful?

Q How did the forms of imperialism applied by the advanced industrial powers in the nineteenth century compare with earlier examples of imperial rule as established throughout history? How would you draw up the balance sheet?

CHAPTER TIMELINE

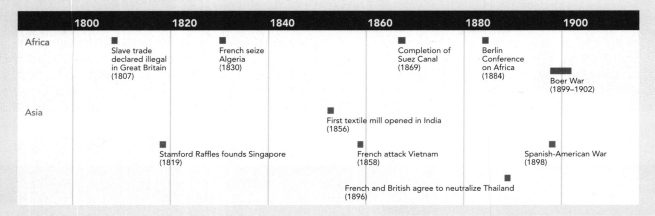

	1800	1820	1840	1860	1880	1900

Africa

Slave trade declared illegal in Great Britain (1807)

French seize Algeria (1830)

Completion of Suez Canal (1869)

Berlin Conference on Africa (1884)

Boer War (1899–1902)

Asia

First textile mill opened in India (1856)

Stamford Raffles founds Singapore (1819)

French attack Vietnam (1858)

Spanish-American War (1898)

French and British agree to neutralize Thailand (1896)

CHAPTER NOTES

1. Quoted in *The New York Times*, January 30, 2016.
2. The quotations are from Henri Brunschwig, *French Colonialism, 1871–1914* (London, 1961), p. 80.
3. Quoted in Louis Roubaud, *Vietnam: La Tragédie Indochinoise* (Paris, 1926), p. 80.
4. Quoted in T. Pakenham, *The Scramble for Africa* (New York, 1991), p. 13.
5. Quoted in Tony Smith, *The Pattern of Imperialism: The United States, Great Britain and the Late-Industrializing World Since 1815* (Cambridge, 1981), p. 81.

SHADOWS OVER THE PACIFIC: EAST ASIA UNDER CHALLENGE

Chapter Outline and Focus Questions

Connections to Today

What lessons can emerging nations today learn from the experiences encountered by China and Japan during the period covered in this chapter?

IMAGE 3.1 The Imperial City in Beijing

IN AUGUST 1793, a British diplomatic mission led by Lord Macartney arrived at the north Chinese port of Dagu and embarked on the road to Beijing. His caravan, which included 600 cases filled with presents for the emperor, bore flags and banners provided by the Chinese that proclaimed in Chinese characters "Ambassador bearing tribute from the country of England." Upon his arrival in the capital, Macartney was admitted into the imperial presence in the Forbidden City but, in spite of the awesome majesty of the surroundings, he refused his hosts' demand that he perform the **kowtow**, a traditional symbol of submission to the emperor. Eventually, the dispute over protocol was resolved with a compromise: Macartney agreed to bend on one knee, a courtesy that he displayed to his own sovereign (see Image 3.1).

To his disappointment, however, the mission was a failure, for Emperor Qianlong rejected the British request for an increase in trade between the two countries, and Macartney left Beijing in October with nothing to show for his efforts. Not until half a century later would the ruling Qing dynasty—at the point

53

of a gun—agree to the British demand for an expansion of commercial ties.

Historians have often viewed the failure of the Macartney mission as a reflection of the disdain of Chinese rulers toward their counterparts in other countries, and their serene confidence in the superiority of Chinese civilization in a world inhabited by barbarians. Indeed it was, for the Emperor dismissed with contempt Macartney's request for regular trade relations. "There is nothing we lack," he noted, adding that "we have never set much store on strange or ingenious objects, nor do we need more of your country's manufactures." As it turned out, however, the Chinese emperor Qianlong's confidence was misplaced, for in the decades immediately following the abortive Macartney mission to Beijing, China faced a growing challenge not only from the escalating power and ambitions of the West but also from its own growing internal weaknesses. Backed by European guns, European merchants and missionaries pressed insistently for the right to carry out their activities in China and the neighboring islands of Japan. Despite their initial reluctance, the Chinese and Japanese governments were eventually forced to open their doors to the foreigners, whose presence and threat to the local way of life escalated rapidly during the final years of the nineteenth century.

3-1 CHINA AT ITS APEX

 Focus Question: Why did the Qing Dynasty decline and ultimately collapse, and what role did the Western powers play in this process?

In 1800, the Qing or Manchu dynasty (1644–1911) appeared to be at the height of its power. The Manchus, a seminomadic people whose original homeland was north of the Great Wall, had invaded North China in the midseventeenth century and conquered the tottering Ming dynasty in 1644. Under the rule of two great emperors, Kangxi (1661–1722) and Qianlong (1736–1795), China had then experienced a long period of peace and prosperity. Its borders were secure, and its culture and intellectual achievements were the envy of the world. Its rulers, hidden behind the walls of the Forbidden City in Beijing, had every reason to describe their patrimony as the Central Kingdom, China's historical name for itself. But a little over a century later, humiliated and harassed by the black ships and big guns of the Western powers, the Qing dynasty, the last in a series that had endured for more than 2000 years, collapsed in the dust (see Map 3.1).

3-1a Changeless China?

Historians once assumed that the primary reason for the rapid decline and fall of the Manchu dynasty was the intense pressure applied to a proud but somewhat complacent traditional society by the modern West. There is indeed some truth in that allegation. On the surface, China had long appeared to be an unchanging society patterned after the Confucian vision of a Golden Age in the remote past. This, in fact, was the image presented by China's rulers, who referred constantly to tradition as a model for imperial institutions and cultural values. That tradition was based firmly on **Confucianism**, a set of ideas that were identified with the ancient philosopher Confucius (551–479 B.C.E.), who emphasized such qualities as obedience, hard work, rule by merit, and the subordination of the individual to the interests of the community. Such principles, which had emerged out of the conditions of a continental society based on agriculture as the primary source of national wealth, had formed the basis for Chinese political and social institutions and values since the rise of the Han dynasty in the late third century B.C.E.

When European ships first appeared off the coast of China in the sixteenth and seventeenth centuries, they brought with them dangerous new ideas and values that were strikingly at variance with those of imperial China. China's rulers soon came to recognize the nature of the threat represented by European Christian missionaries and merchants and attempted to expel the former while restricting the latter to a limited presence in the southern coastal city of Canton. For the next two centuries, China was, at least in intent, an essentially closed society.

It was the hope of influential figures at the imperial court in Beijing that by expelling the barbarians, they could protect Chinese civilization from the virus of foreign ideas. Their effort to freeze time was futile, however, for in reality, Chinese society was already beginning to change under their feet—and changing rather rapidly. Although few observers may have been aware of it at the time, by the beginning of the Manchu era in the seventeenth century, many traditional precepts were becoming increasingly irrelevant in a society that was becoming ever more complex.

Changes in Rural Areas Nowhere was change more evident than in the economic sector. During the early modern period, China was still a predominantly agricultural society, as it had been throughout recorded history. Nearly 85 percent of the people were farmers. In the south, the main crop was rice; in the north, it was wheat or dry crops. But even though China still had few urban centers, the population was beginning to increase rapidly. Thanks to a long era of peace and stability, the introduction of new crops from the Americas, and the cultivation of new, fast-ripening strains

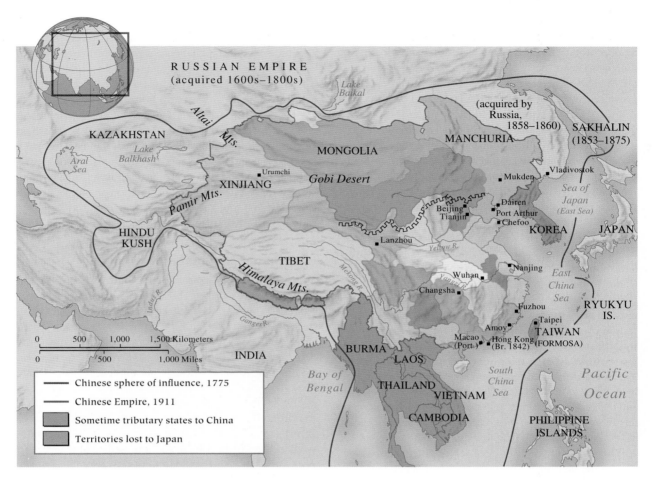

RUSSIAN EMPIRE
(acquired 1600s–1800s)

KAZAKHSTAN

XINJIANG

HINDU
KUSH

MONGOLIA

Gobi Desert

MANCHURIA

(acquired by
Russia,
1858–1860)

SAKHALIN
(1853–1875)

Vladivostok

Mukden

Dairen
Port Arthur
Chefoo

Beijing
Tianjin

Lanzhou

KOREA

JAPAN

Sea of
Japan
(East Sea)

TIBET

Himalaya Mts.

Wuhan

Changsha

Nanjing

Fuzhou

Taipei

Amoy

Macao
(Port.)

Hong Kong
(Br. 1842)

TAIWAN
(FORMOSA)

East
China
Sea

RYUKYU
IS.

INDIA

BURMA

LAOS

THAILAND

CAMBODIA

VIETNAM

South
China
Sea

PHILIPPINE
ISLANDS

Pacific
Ocean

Bay of
Bengal

Chinese sphere of influence, 1775
Chinese Empire, 1911
Sometime tributary states to China
Territories lost to Japan

MAP 3.1 The Qing Empire. Shown here is the Qing Empire at the height of its power in the late-eighteenth century, together with its shrunken boundaries at the moment of its dissolution in 1911.

Q *Where are China's tributary states on the map? How had their status changed by 1911?*

of rice, the Chinese population doubled between the time of the early Qing and the end of the eighteenth century. And it continued to grow during the nineteenth century, reaching the unprecedented level of 400 million by 1900.

Of course, this population increase meant much greater pressure on the land, smaller farms, and an ever-thinner margin of safety in the event of climatic disaster. The imperial court had attempted to deal with the problem by various means—most notably by preventing the concentration of land in the hands of wealthy landowners—but by the end of the eighteenth century, almost all the land that could be irrigated was already under cultivation, and the problems of rural hunger and landlessness became increasingly serious. Not surprisingly, economic hardship quickly translated into rural unrest.

Seeds of Industrialization Another change that took place during the Qing dynasty was the steady growth of

manufacturing and commerce. Trade and manufacturing had existed in China since early times, but they had been limited by a number of factors, including social prejudice, official restrictions, and state monopolies on mining and on the production of such commodities as alcohol and salt. Chinese moral precepts had always viewed trading activities as a somewhat base occupation compared to the sacred responsibilities of feeding the people. Now, taking advantage of the long era of peace and prosperity under the Qing, merchants and manufacturers began to expand their operations beyond their immediate provinces. Trade in silk, metal and wood products, porcelain, cotton goods, and cash crops such as tea and tobacco developed rapidly, and commercial networks began to operate on a regional and sometimes even a national basis.

With the growth of trade came an expansion of commercial contacts and guild organizations nationwide. Merchants began organizing guilds in cities and market towns throughout the country to provide legal protection, an opportunity to do business, and food and lodging for merchants from particular provinces. Foreign trade also expanded, as Chinese merchants, mainly from the coastal provinces of the south, established extensive contacts with countries in Southeast Asia. In many instances, the contacts in Southeast Asia were themselves ethnic Chinese who had settled in the area during earlier centuries.

Some historians have suggested that this rise in industrial and commercial activity would, under other circumstances, have led to an indigenous industrial revolution and the emergence of a capitalist society such as that taking shape in Europe. The significance of these changes should not be exaggerated, however, for there were some key differences between China and western Europe that would have impeded the emergence of industrial capitalism in China. In the first place, although industrial production in China was on the rise, it was still based almost entirely on traditional methods of production. China had no uniform system of weights and measures, and the banking system was still primitive by European standards. The use of paper money, invented centuries earlier, was still relatively limited. There were few paved roads, and the Grand Canal, long the most efficient means of carrying goods between the north and the south, was silting up. As a result, merchants had to rely more and more on the coastal route, where they faced increasing competition from foreign shipping.

There were other, more deep-seated differences as well. The bourgeois class in China was not as independent as its European counterpart. Reflecting an ancient preference for agriculture over manufacturing and trade, the state levied heavy taxes on manufacturing and commerce while seeking to keep agricultural taxes low. Such attitudes were still shared by key groups in the population. Although much money could be made in commerce, most merchants who accumulated wealth used it to buy their way into the ranks of the landed gentry. The most that can really be said, then, is that during the Qing dynasty, China was beginning to undergo major economic and social changes that might have led, even in the absence of external influence, to the eventual emergence of an industrialized society.

3-2 TRADITIONAL CHINA IN TRANSITION

 Focus Question: Why did the Qing Dynasty decline and ultimately collapse, and what role did the Western powers play in this process?

When Western pressure on the Manchu Empire began to increase during the early nineteenth century, it served to exacerbate the existing strains in Chinese society. By 1800, the trade relationship that restricted Western merchants to a small commercial outlet at Canton was no longer acceptable to the British, who were increasingly concerned about the trade imbalance resulting from the growing appetite for Chinese tea in Britain. Their solution was opium. A product more addictive than tea, opium was grown in northeastern India under British East India Company sponsorship and then shipped directly to the Chinese market. Soon demand for the product in South China became insatiable, despite an official prohibition on its use. Bullion now flowed out of the Chinese imperial treasury into the pockets of British merchants and officials.

3-2a Opium and Rebellion

When the Qing attempted to prohibit the opium trade—viewing it as an evil drug that diverted the common people from carrying out their other responsibilities—the British declared war. The Opium War, as it was called, lasted three years (1839–1842) and graphically demonstrated the superiority of British firepower and military tactics (see Image 3.2). After a series of humiliating defeats, China sued for peace and, in the Treaty of Nanjing, agreed to open five coastal ports to British trade, limit tariffs on imported British goods, grant extraterritorial rights to British citizens in China, and pay a substantial indemnity to cover the British costs of the war. Beijing also agreed to cede the small island of Hong Kong (dismissed by a senior British official as a "barren rock") to Great Britain. Nothing was said in the treaty about the opium trade.

Although the Opium War is now considered the beginning of modern Chinese history, it is unlikely that many Chinese at the time would have seen it that way. This was not the first time that a ruling dynasty had been forced to make concessions to foreigners, and the opening of five coastal ports to the British (derisively described by one imperial official as "an insignificant and detestable race")_ hardly constituted a serious threat to the security of the empire. Although a few concerned Chinese argued that the court should learn more about European civilization to find the secret of the British success, others contended that China had nothing to learn from the barbarians, and that borrowing foreign ways would undercut the purity of Confucian civilization.[1]

3-2b The Taiping Rebellion

The Manchus attempted to deal with the problem in the traditional way of playing the foreigners off against each other. Concessions granted to the British were offered to other Western nations, including the United States, and soon thriving foreign concession areas were operating in

IMAGE 3.2 **The Opium War.** Waged between China and Great Britain between 1839 and 1842, the Opium War was China's first major conflict with a European power. Lacking modern military technology, the Chinese suffered a humiliating defeat. In this painting, heavily armed British steamships destroy unwieldy Chinese junks along the Chinese coast. The steamship in the right background is the HMS Nemesis. Built in 1839, it was Britain's first iron-hulled steamship, and its ability to navigate shallow coastal waters inspired Chinese defenders to dub it "the devil ship." China's humiliation at sea was a legacy of its rulers' lack of interest in maritime matters since the middle of the fifteenth century, when Chinese junks were among the most advanced sailing ships in the world.

 Why do you think China was unable to develop military weaponry to fend off the foreign threat?

treaty ports along the southern Chinese coast from Canton in the south to Shanghai, a bustling new port on a tributary of the Yangzi River, in the center.

In the meantime, the Qing court's failure to deal with pressing internal economic problems led to a major peasant revolt that shook the foundations of the empire. On the surface, the so-called Taiping Rebellion owed something to the Western incursion; the leader of the uprising, Hong Xiuquan, was a Christian convert who viewed himself as a younger brother of Jesus Christ and hoped to establish what he referred to as a "Heavenly Kingdom of Supreme Peace" in China. With their ranks swelled by impoverished peasants and other discontented elements throughout the southern provinces, the rebels swept northward, seizing the Yangzi river port of Nanjing in

MAP 3.2 **Area Under Taiping Rebellion Control**

March 1853. The revolt continued for ten more years but gradually lost momentum, and in 1864, the Qing, though weakened, retook Nanjing and destroyed the remnants of the rebel force. The rebellion had cost the lives of millions of Chinese (see Map 3.2).

One reason for the dynasty's failure to deal effectively with internal unrest was its continuing difficulties with the Western imperialists. In 1856, the British and the French, smarting from trade restrictions and limitations on their missionary activities, launched a series of attacks and seized the capital of Beijing in 1860. In the ensuing Treaty of Tianjin, the Qing agreed to humiliating new concessions: legalization of the opium trade, the opening of additional ports to foreign trade, and cession of the peninsula of Kowloon (opposite the island of Hong Kong) to the British.

Practical Learning or Confucian Essence: The Debate over Reform

 Q *Why does journalist Wang Tao believe that the reforms he proposes are necessary? What are Zhang Zhidong's criticisms of such reforms?*

Politics & Government

BY THE LAST QUARTER OF THE NINETEENTH CENTURY, Chinese officials and intellectuals had become increasingly alarmed at the country's inability to counter the steady pressure emanating from the West. Some, like the journalist Wang Tao (1828–1897), asserted that nothing less than a full-scale reform of Chinese society was required, including the adoption of the Western concept of political rights and democratic institutions. Others, like the scholar-official Zhang Zhidong (1837–1909), countered that such values and institutions would not work in China, and that the adoption of Western technology and science would be sufficient to protect the country from collapse. These two excerpts display the depth of disagreement between the two opposing views.

Zhang Zhidong, *Rectification of Political Rights*

The doctrine of people's rights will bring us not a single benefit but a hundred evils. Are we going to establish a parliament? Among the Chinese scholars and people there are still many today who are content to be vulgar and rustic. They are ignorant of the general situation of the world, they do not understand the basic system of the state. They have not the most rudimentary ideas about foreign countries—about the schools, the political systems, military training, and manufacture of armaments. Even supposing the confused and clamorous people are assembled in one house, for every one of them who is clear-sighted, there will be a hundred others whose vision is beclouded; they will converse at random and talks if in a dream—what use will it be?. . . .

Wang Tao, *A General History of France*

Since the National Assembly is established as a public body, not a private one, the people all submit to it. It is like this in all the countries of Europe . . . Under such a [system], those above and those below are at peace with one another and the monarch and his subjects share in the governing. Things can go on for a long time, without getting to the point where people suffer from tyrannical administration and popular support is lost through the avarice and cruelty [of the officials]. For the members of both the upper and the lower assemblies are chosen entirely by the public, and from the time they first put themselves forward [as candidate] they must display fairness and rectitude in order to win. If they should at some point do something that is improper, in flagrant violation of public sentiment and not in accord with popular opinion, the same people who elected them can also remove them. Thus, even if they are inclined to turn a deaf ear to people's criticisms, there are definite bounds to their misconduct. . . .

Sources: From Ssu-yu Teng and John K. Fairbank, *China's Response to the West: A Documentary Survey, 1839–1923* (Cambridge: Harvard University Press, 1954), p. 167. From Paul Cohen, *Between Tradition and Modernity: Wang T'ao and Reform in Late Ch'ing China* (Cambridge: Harvard University Press, 1974, p. 221, citing Fa-kuo chih-lueh (A General History of France, 1890).

3-2c Efforts at Reform

By the late 1870s, the old dynasty was on the verge of collapse. In fending off the Taiping Rebellion, the Manchus had been compelled to rely for support on armed forces under regional command. After quelling the revolt, many of these regional commanders refused to disband their units and, with the support of the local gentry, continued to collect local taxes for their own use. The dreaded pattern of imperial breakdown, so familiar in Chinese history, was beginning to appear once again.

In their weakened state, the Qing rulers finally began to listen to the appeals of reform-minded officials who advocated a new policy called **self-strengthening**, in which Western technology would be adopted while Confucian principles and institutions were maintained intact. This policy, popularly known by its slogan "East for essence, West for practical use," remained the guiding standard for Chinese foreign and domestic policy for nearly a quarter of a century. Some advisers went further and even called for reforms in education and in China's hallowed political institutions (see Opposing Viewpoints, "Practical Learning or Confucian Essence: The Debate over Reform," above).

For the time being, the more cautious arguments won the day. During the last quarter of the century, the Manchus attempted to modernize their military establishment and build up an industrial base without disturbing the essential elements of traditional Chinese civilization. Railroads, weapons arsenals, and shipyards were built, but the value system remained essentially unchanged.

3-2d The Climax of Imperialism in China

In the end, the results spoke for themselves. During the last two decades of the nineteenth century, the European penetration of China, both political and military, intensified. Rapacious imperialists began to bite off territory at the outer edges of the Qing Empire. The Gobi Desert north of the Great Wall, Chinese Central Asia (known in Chinese as Xinjiang), and Tibet, all inhabited by non-Chinese peoples and never fully assimilated into the Chinese Empire, were now gradually removed totally from Beijing's control. In the north and northwest, the main beneficiary was Russia, which took advantage of the dynasty's weakness to force the cession of territories north of the Amur River in Siberia. In Tibet, competition between Russia and Great Britain prevented either power from seizing the territory outright but at the same time enabled Tibetan authorities to revive local autonomy never recognized by the Chinese. On the southern borders of the empire, British and French advances in mainland Southeast Asia removed Burma and Vietnam from their traditional vassal relationship with the Manchu court.

Even more ominous developments were taking place in the Chinese heartland, where European economic penetration led to the creation of so-called **spheres of influence** dominated by diverse foreign powers. Although the imperial court retained theoretical sovereignty throughout the country, in practice its political, economic, and administrative influence beyond the region of the capital was increasingly circumscribed.

The breakup of the Manchu dynasty accelerated during the last five years of the nineteenth century. In 1894, the Qing went to war with Japan over Japanese incursions into the Korean peninsula, which threatened China's long-held suzerainty over the area (see "3-5d Joining the Imperialist Club," p. 70). To the surprise of many observers, the Chinese were roundly defeated, confirming to some critics the devastating failure of the policy of self-strengthening by halfway measures.

More humiliation came in 1897, when Germany, a new entrant in the race for spoils in East Asia, used the pretext of the murder of two German missionaries by Chinese rioters to demand the cession of territories in the Shandong peninsula. The imperial court's approval of this demand set off a scramble for territory by other interested powers. Russia now demanded the Liaodong peninsula with its ice-free harbor at Port Arthur, and Great Britain obtained a 100-year lease on the New Territories, a peninsula on the mainland adjacent to the island of Hong Kong, as well as a coaling station in northern China.

The latest scramble for territory had taken place at a time of internal crisis in China. In the spring of 1898, an outspoken advocate of reform, the progressive Confucian scholar Kang Youwei, won the support of the young emperor Guangxu for a comprehensive reform program (known as the "One Hundred Days") patterned after recent changes initiated in Japan. Without change, Kang argued, China would perish. During the next several weeks, the emperor issued edicts calling for major political, administrative, and educational reforms. Not surprisingly, Kang's ideas for reform were opposed by many conservatives, who saw little advantage to copying the West. Most important, the new program was opposed by the emperor's aunt, the Empress Dowager Cixi, who was the real source of power at court. Cixi had begun her political career as a concubine to an earlier emperor. After his death, she became a dominant force at court and in 1878 placed her infant nephew, the future emperor Guangxu, on the throne. For two decades, she ruled in his name as regent. Cixi interpreted Guangxu's action as a British-supported effort to reduce her influence at court. With the aid of conservatives in the army, she arrested and executed several of the reformers and had the emperor incarcerated in the palace. Kang Youwei managed to flee abroad. With Cixi's palace coup, the so-called One Hundred Days of reform came to an end.

Opening the Door to China During the next two years, foreign pressure on the dynasty intensified (see Map 3.3). With encouragement from the British, who hoped to avert a total collapse of the Manchu Empire, U.S. Secretary of State John Hay presented the other imperialist powers with a proposal to ensure equal economic access to the China market for all nations. Hay also suggested that all powers join together to guarantee the territorial and administrative integrity of the Chinese Empire. When none of the other governments flatly opposed the idea, Hay issued a second note declaring that all major nations with economic interests in China had agreed to an "Open Door" policy in China.

Though probably motivated more by a U.S. desire for open markets than by a benevolent wish to protect China, the **Open Door Notes** did have the practical effect of reducing the imperialist hysteria over access to the China market. That hysteria—the product of decades of mythologizing among Western commercial interests about the "400 million" Chinese customers—had accelerated at the end of the century as fears of China's imminent collapse increased. The "gentlemen's agreement" about the Open Door (it was not a treaty but merely a pious and

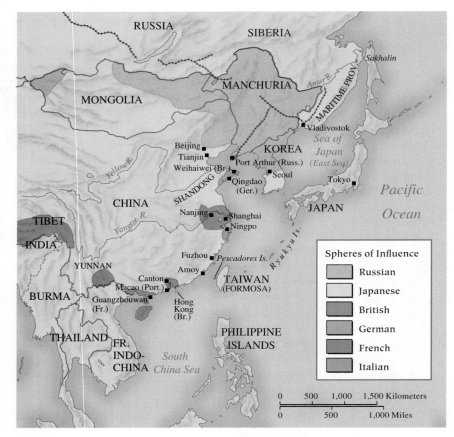

MAP 3.3 Foreign Possessions and Spheres of Influence About 1900. At the end of the nineteenth century, China and its tributary areas were being carved up like a melon by foreign imperialist powers.

Q *Which of the areas marked on the map were removed from Chinese control during the nineteenth century?*

foreign residents and besieged the foreign legation quarter in Beijing until the foreigners were rescued by an international expeditionary force in the late summer of 1900 (see Image 3.3). As punishment, the foreign troops destroyed a number of temples in the capital suburbs, and the Chinese government was compelled to pay a heavy indemnity to the foreign governments involved in suppressing the uprising.

3-2e The Collapse of the Old Order

During the next few years, the old dynasty tried desperately to reform itself. The empress dowager, who had long resisted change, now embraced a number of reforms in education, administration, and the legal system. The venerable **civil service examination** system, a centuries-old merit system for selecting government officials based on knowledge of the Confucian classics, was replaced by a new educational system patterned after the Western model. In 1905, a commission was formed to study constitutional changes, and over the next few years, legislative assemblies were established at the provincial level. Elections for a national assembly were held in 1910.

nonbinding expression of intent) served to diminish fears in Britain, France, Germany, and Russia that other powers would take advantage of China's weakness to dominate the China market.

The Boxer Rebellion   In the long run, then, the Open Door was a positive step that brought a measure of sanity to the imperialist meddling in East Asia. Unfortunately, it came too late to stop the domestic explosion known as the Boxer Rebellion. The Boxers (literally, "righteous and harmonious fists"), so called because of the physical exercises they performed, were members of a secret society operating primarily in rural areas in North China. Provoked by a damaging drought and high levels of unemployment caused in part by foreign economic activity (the introduction of railroads and steamships, for example, undercut the livelihood of boat workers who traditionally carried merchandise on the rivers and canals), the Boxers attacked

Such moves helped shore up the dynasty temporarily, but Qing officials now discovered that the most dangerous period for an authoritarian system is often when it begins to reform itself, because change breeds instability and performance rarely matches rising expectations. Such was the case in China. The emerging new provincial elite, composed of merchants, professionals, and reform-minded gentry, soon became impatient with the slow pace of political change and were disillusioned to find that the new assemblies were intended to be primarily advisory rather than legislative. The government also alienated influential elements by financing railway development projects through lucrative contracts to foreign firms rather than by turning to local investors. The reforms also had little meaning for peasants, artisans, miners, and transportation workers, whose living conditions were

IMAGE 3.3 Justice or mercy? Uncle Sam decides. In the summer of 1900, Chinese rebels known as Boxers besieged Western embassies in the imperial capital of Beijing. Western nations, including the United States, dispatched troops to north China to rescue their compatriots. In this cartoon, which appeared in a contemporary American newsmagazine, China figuratively seeks pardon from a stern Uncle Sam.

Why do you think the United States viewed itself as a mediator in the dispute between China and European imperialist nations?

being eroded by rising taxes and official venality. Rising rural unrest, as yet poorly organized and often centered on secret societies such as the Boxers, was an ominous sign of deep-seated resentment to which the dynasty would not, or could not, respond.

The Rise of Sun Yat-Sen To China's reformist elite, such signs of social unrest were a threat to be avoided; to its tiny revolutionary movement, they were a harbinger of promise. The first physical manifestations of future revolution appeared during the last decade of the nineteenth century with the formation of the Revive China Society by the young radical Sun Yat-sen (1866–1925). Born to a peasant family in a village south of Canton, Sun was educated in Hawaii and returned to China to practice medicine. Soon he turned his full attention to the ills of Chinese society,

leading bands of radicals in small-scale insurrections to attract attention.

At first, Sun's efforts yielded few positive results other than creating a symbol of resistance and the new century's first revolutionary martyrs. But at a convention held in Tokyo in 1905, Sun managed to unite radical groups from across China into the so-called Revolutionary Alliance (Tongmenghui). The new organization's program was based on Sun's **Three People's Principles**: nationalism (meaning primarily the destruction of Manchu rule over China), democracy, and "people's livelihood," which was a program to improve social and economic conditions (see Historical Voices, "Program for a New China," p. 62). Although the new organization was small and relatively inexperienced, it benefited from rising popular discontent with the failure of Manchu reforms to improve conditions in China.

The October Uprising In October 1911, followers of Sun Yat-sen launched an uprising in the industrial center of Wuhan, in central China. With Sun traveling in the United States, the insurrection lacked leadership, but the decrepit government's inability to react quickly encouraged political forces at the provincial level to take measures into their own hands. The dynasty was now in a state of virtual collapse: the dowager empress had died in 1908, one day after her nephew Guangxu; the throne was now occupied by the infant Puyi, the son of Guangxu's younger brother. Sun's party, however, had neither the military strength nor the political support necessary to seize the initiative and was forced to turn to a representative of the old order, General Yuan Shikai (1859–1916). A prominent figure in military circles since the beginning of the century, Yuan had been placed in charge of the imperial forces sent to suppress the rebellion, but now he abandoned the Manchus and acted on his own behalf. In negotiations with representatives of Sun Yat-sen's party (Sun himself had arrived back in China in January 1912), he agreed to serve as president of a new Chinese republic. The old dynasty and the age-old system it had attempted to preserve were no more.

HISTORIANS DEBATE **The 1911 Revolution: Success or Failure?**
Propagandists for Sun Yat-sen's party have often portrayed the events of 1911 as a glorious revolution that brought 2000 years of imperial tradition to an end. But a true revolution does not just destroy an old order; it also brings new political and social forces into power and creates new institutions and values that provide a new framework for a changing society. In this sense, the 1911 revolution did not live up to its name. Sun and his followers were unable to consolidate their gains. The Revolutionary Alliance found the bulk of its support in an emerging urban middle class and set forth a program

Program for a New China

Q *What were Sun Yat-sen's key proposals for the modernization of Chinese society? Why can he be described as a revolutionary rather than a reformer?*

Politics & Government

IN 1905, SUN YAT-SEN united a number of anti-Manchu groups into a single patriotic organization called the Revolutionary Alliance (Tongmenghui). The new organization was eventually renamed the Guomindang, or Nationalist Party. This excerpt is from the organization's manifesto, published in 1905 in Tokyo. Note that Sun believed that the Chinese people were not ready for democracy and required a period of tutelage to prepare them for constitutional political government. This was a formula that would be adopted by many other political leaders in Asia and Africa after World War II.

Sun Yat-sen, Manifesto for the Tongmenghui

By order of the Military Government, . . . the Commander-in-Chief of the Chinese National Army proclaims the purposes and platform of the Military Government to the people of the nation:

Therefore we proclaim to the world in utmost sincerity the outline of the present revolution and the fundamental plan for the future administration of the nation.

1. *Drive out the Tartars:* The Manchus of today were originally the eastern barbarians beyond the Great Wall. They frequently caused border troubles during the Ming dynasty; then when China was in a disturbed state they came inside Shanhaikuan [the eastern terminus of the Great Wall], conquered China, and enslaved our Chinese people. . . . The extreme cruelties and tyrannies of the Manchu government have now reached their limit. With the righteous army poised against them, we will overthrow that government, and restore our sovereign rights.
2. *Restore China:* China is the China of the Chinese. The government of China should be in the hands of

the Chinese. After driving out the Tartars we must restore our national state. . . .
3. *Establish the Republic:* Now our revolution is based on equality, in order to establish a republican government. All our people are equal and all enjoy political rights. . . .
4. *Equalize land ownership:* The good fortune of civilization is to be shared equally by all the people of the nation. We should improve our social and economic organization, and assess the value of all the land in the country. Its present price shall be received by the owner, but all increases in value resulting from reform and social improvements after the revolution shall belong to the state, to be shared by all the people, in order to create a socialist state, where each family within the empire can be well supported, each person satisfied, and no one fail to secure employment. . . .

The above four points will be carried out in three steps in due order. The first period is government by military law. When the righteous army has arisen, various places will join the cause. . . . Evils like the oppression of the government, the greed and graft of officials, . . . the cruelty of tortures and penalties, the tyranny of tax collections, shall all be exterminated together with the Manchu rule. Evils in social customs, such as the keeping of slaves, the cruelty of foot binding, the spread of the poison of opium, should also all be prohibited. . . .

The second period is that of government by a provisional constitution. When military law is lifted in each *hsien* [district], the Military Government shall return the right of self-government to the local people. . . .

The third period will be government under the constitution. Six years after the provisional constitution has been enforced, a constitution shall be made. The military and administrative powers of the Military Government shall be annulled; the people shall elect the president, and elect the members of parliament to organize the parliament.

based generally on Western liberal democratic principles. That class and that program had provided the foundation for the capitalist democratic revolutions in western Europe and North America in the late-eighteenth and nineteenth

centuries, but the bourgeois class in China was too small to form the basis for a new post-Confucian political order. The vast majority of the Chinese people were still illiterate and lived on the land. Sun had hoped to win their support with a land reform program that relied on fiscal incentives to persuade landlords to sell excess lands to their tenants, but the plan was not widely publicized in the countryside, and few peasants had participated in the 1911 revolution. In effect, then, the 1911 uprising was less a revolution than a collapse of the old order. Undermined by imperialism and its own internal weaknesses, the old dynasty had come to an abrupt end before new political and social forces were ready to fill the vacuum.

What China had experienced was part of a historical process that was bringing down traditional empires across the globe, both in regions threatened by Western imperialism and in Europe itself, where tsarist Russia, the Austro-Hungarian Empire, and the Ottoman Empire all came to an end within a few years of the collapse of the Qing (see Chapters 4 and 5). The circumstances of their demise were not all the same, but all four regimes bore responsibility for their common fate because they had failed to meet the challenges posed by the times. All had responded to the forces of economic change and popular participation in the political process with hesitation and reluctance, and their attempts at reform were too little and too late. All paid the supreme price for their folly.

3-3 CHINESE SOCIETY IN TRANSITION

 Focus Question: What political, economic, and social reforms were instituted by the Qing Dynasty during its final decades, and why were they not more successful in reversing the decline of Qing rule?

The growing Western presence in China during the late-nineteenth and early-twentieth centuries had provided the imperial government with an opportunity to take measures to recover from its internal difficulties. The results, however, were meager. Although foreign concession areas in the coastal cities provided a conduit for the importation of Western technology and modern manufacturing methods, the Chinese borrowed less than they might have. Foreign manufacturing enterprises could not legally operate in China until the last decade of the nineteenth century, and their methods had little influence beyond the concession areas. Chinese efforts to imitate Western methods, notably in ship-building and weapons manufacture, were dominated by the government and often suffered from mismanagement.

Equally serious problems persisted in the countryside. The rapid increase in population had led to smaller plots and growing numbers of tenant farmers. Whether per capita consumption of food was on the decline is not clear from the available evidence, but apparently rice as a staple of the diet was increasingly being replaced by less nutritious foods, many of which depleted the soil, already under pressure from the dramatic increase in population. Some farmers benefited from switching to commercial agriculture to supply the markets of the growing coastal cities. The shift entailed a sizable investment, however, and many farmers went so deeply into debt that they eventually lost their land. At the same time, the traditional patron–client relationship was frayed as landlords moved to the cities to take advantage of the glittering urban lifestyle introduced by the West.

3-3a The Impact of Western Imperialism

The advent of the imperialist era in the second half of the nineteenth century thus appeared in a society already facing serious challenges. Whether the Western intrusion was beneficial or harmful is debated to this day. The Western presence undoubtedly accelerated the transformation of the Chinese economy in some ways: the introduction of modern means of production, transport, and communications; the expansion of an export market; and the steady integration of the Chinese market into the nineteenth-century global economy. To many Westerners at the time, it was self-evident that such changes would ultimately benefit the Chinese people. Critics, however, retorted that Western imperialism actually hindered the process of structural change in preindustrial societies like China because the Western powers thwarted the rise of local industrial and commercial sectors in order to maintain colonies and semicolonies as a market for Western manufactured goods and a source of cheap labor and materials. If the West had not intervened, some argued, China would have found its own road to becoming an advanced industrial society.

Whatever the truth of these conjectures, the hesitant efforts of the Qing to cope with these challenges suggest that the most important obstacle to reform was at the top: Qing officials often seemed overwhelmed by the combination of external pressure and internal strife. At a time when other traditional societies, such as Russia, the Ottoman Empire, and Japan, were making attempts to modernize their economies, the Manchu court, along with much of the elite class, still exhibited an alarming degree of complacency at the magnitude of the threat that now faced them.

3-3b Daily Life in Qing China

At the beginning of the nineteenth century, daily life for most Chinese was not substantially different from what it had been in earlier centuries. Most were farmers, living in millions of villages in rice fields and on hillsides throughout the countryside. Their lives were governed by the harvest cycle, village custom, and family ritual. Their roles in society were firmly fixed by the time-honored principles of Confucian social ethics. Male children, at least the more fortunate ones, were educated in the Confucian classics, while females remained in the home or in the fields. All children were expected to obey their parents, and wives to submit to their husbands.

Unlike the situation in many traditional societies, organized religion did not play a major role in the lives of most Chinese. Religious practices were in fact highly eclectic. While some elites followed Confucian tradition in viewing Heaven as more a force of Nature than a personal and transcendent deity, many ordinary Chinese were at least nominally Buddhist—an ethico-religious belief system founded in India during the first millennium B.C.E. and imported into China hundreds of years later.

Buddhist practices were highly personal and focused on individual salvation and betterment, and attendance at religious ceremonies in Buddhist temples normally occurred on an individual basis. Beyond any organized religious system, many Chinese—like their counterparts elsewhere in Asia—believed in a multiplicity of household, community, and Nature deities, some of them loosely subsumed under an ancient belief system known as Daoism (sometimes, Taoism). Significantly, one set of beliefs did not necessarily negate another, and a Chinese could be at once a Confucian, a Buddhist, or a Daoist, depending on the situation.

A visitor to China 100 years later would have seen a very different society, although still recognizably Chinese. Change was most striking in the coastal cities, where the educated and affluent had been visibly affected by the growing Western cultural presence. Confucian social institutions and behavioral norms were declining rapidly in influence, while those of Europe and North America were ascendant. Christianity, introduced by Jesuit priests during the sixteenth century, was growing in popularity, especially among the upwardly mobile. Change was much less noticeable in the countryside, but even there, the customary bonds had been dangerously frayed by the rapidly changing times.

Some of the change can be traced to the educational system. During the nineteenth century, the importance of a Confucian education steadily declined because up to half of the degree holders had purchased their degrees. After 1906, when the government abolished the civil service examinations, a Confucian education ceased to be the key to a successful career, and Western-style education became more desirable. The old dynasty attempted to modernize by establishing an educational system on the Western model with universal education at the elementary level. The plan was too poorly funded to have much effect in the countryside, but it did produce some changes in the large cities, where public schools, missionary schools, and other private institutions educated a new generation of Chinese with little knowledge of or respect for China's venerable history.

3-3c Changing Roles for Women

The status of women was also in transition. During the mid-Qing era, women were still expected to remain in the home. Their status as useless sex objects was painfully symbolized by the practice of foot binding, a custom that had probably originated among court entertainers in the eighth century and later spread to the common people. By the mid-nineteenth century, more than half of all adult women probably had bound feet (see Image 3.4).

Shanghai Barrow Taxi, c.1870s (b/w photo)/Saunders, William (1832–1892)/JOHN HILLELSON COLLECTION/Private Collection/Bridgeman Images

IMAGE 3.4 Women with Bound Feet. To provide the best possible marriage for their daughters, upper-class families began to perform foot binding during the Song dynasty. The two young women shown here are clearly from an upper-class family and are being taken for an outing on a rickshaw. Eventually, the practice of foot binding spread to all social classes in China. Although small feet were supposed to denote a woman of leisure, most Chinese women with bound feet were in the labor force, working mainly in textiles and handicrafts to supplement the family income. During the author's first visit to China during the 1970s, it was not uncommon to see older women with bound feet, even in metropolitan areas.

Q *How would you compare the treatment of women in China with what you have learned about the role of women in other societies at the time?*

During the second half of the nineteenth century, signs of change began to appear. Women began to seek employment in factories—notably in the cotton mills and in the silk industry, established in Shanghai in the 1890s. Some women were active in dissident activities, such as the Taiping Rebellion and the Boxer movement, and a few fought beside men in the 1911 revolution. Qiu Jin, a well-known female revolutionary, wrote a manifesto calling for women's liberation and then organized a revolt against the Manchu government, only to be captured and executed at the age of thirty-two in 1907.

By the end of the century, educational opportunities for women appeared for the first time. Christian missionaries began to open girls' schools, mainly in the foreign concession areas. Although only a relatively small number of women were educated in these schools, they had a significant impact on Chinese society as progressive intellectuals began to argue that ignorant women produced ignorant children. In 1905, the court announced its intention to open public schools for girls, but few such schools ever materialized. The government also began to take steps to discourage the practice of foot binding, initially with only minimal success.

3-4 TRADITIONAL JAPAN AND THE END OF ISOLATION

 Focus Question: How did the Japanese reaction to the Western onslaught differ from that of China, and what were the consequences?

While Chinese rulers were coping with the dual problems of external threat and internal instability, similar developments were taking place in Japan. An agricultural society like its powerful neighbor, Japan had borrowed extensively from Chinese civilization for more than a millennium; its political institutions, religious beliefs, and cultural achievements all bore the clear imprint of the Chinese model. Nevertheless, the Japanese were able to retain not only their political independence but also their cultural uniqueness and had created a distinct civilization.

One reason for the historical differences between China and Japan is that, while China was a large continental country, Japan was a small island nation. Proud of their own considerable cultural achievements and their dominant position throughout the region, the Chinese were traditionally reluctant to dilute the purity of their culture with foreign innovations. Often subject to invasion by nomadic peoples from the north, they viewed culture rather than race as the key factor shaping their sense of identity. By contrast, the island character of Japan undoubtedly had

the effect of strengthening the Japanese sense of ethnic and cultural distinctiveness. Although the Japanese self-image of ethnic homogeneity may not be entirely justified, it enabled them to import ideas from abroad without the risk of destroying the uniqueness of their own culture.

As a result, although the Japanese borrowed liberally from China over the centuries, they turned Chinese ideas and institutions to their own uses. In contrast to China, where a centralized political system was viewed as crucial to protecting the vast country from foreign conquest or internal fractionalization, a decentralized political system reminiscent of the feudal system in medieval Europe held sway in Japan under the hegemony of a powerful military leader, or **shogun**, who ruled with varying degrees of effectiveness in the name of the hereditary emperor. This system lasted until the early-seventeenth century, when a strong shogunate called the Tokugawa rose to power after a protracted civil war. The Tokugawa managed to revitalize the traditional system in a somewhat more centralized form that enabled it to survive for another 250 years.

3-4a A "Closed Country"

One of the many factors contributing to the rise of the Tokugawa was the impending collapse of the old system under the impact of decades of internal civil strife. Another was contact with the West, which had begun with the arrival of Portuguese ships in Japanese harbors in the mid-sixteenth century. After an initial period of hesitation, Japan opened its doors eagerly to European trade and missionary activity, but later Japanese elites became concerned about the corrosive effects of Western religious practices and attempted to evict the foreigners. For the next two centuries, the Tokugawa adopted a policy of "closed country" (to use the contemporary Japanese phrase) to keep out foreign ideas and protect Japanese values and institutions. Only the Dutch—who had little interest in converting their hosts to the Christian faith—were allowed to trade with Japan on a limited basis. Despite such efforts, however, Japanese society was changing from within, and by the early-nineteenth century, it was quite different from what it had been two centuries earlier. Traditional institutions and the aristocratic feudal system were under increasing strain, not only from the emergence of a new merchant class but also from the centralizing tendencies of the powerful shogunate.

Some historians have noted strong parallels between Tokugawa Japan and early modern Europe, which witnessed the emergence of centralized states and a strong merchant class at the same time in history. Certainly, there were signs that the **shogunate system** was becoming less effective. Factionalism and corruption plagued the central bureaucracy. Feudal lords in the countryside (known as **daimyo**, or "great names") reacted to increasing economic pressures by intensifying their exactions from the peasants who farmed their manorial holdings and by engaging in manufacturing and commercial pursuits, such as the sale of textiles, forestry products, and *sake* (Japanese rice wine). As peasants were whipsawed by rising manorial exactions and a series of poor harvests caused by bad weather, rural unrest swept the countryside.

Japan, then, was ripe for change. Some historians maintain that the country was poised to experience an industrial revolution under the stimulus of internal conditions. As in China, the resumption of contacts with the West in the middle of the nineteenth century rendered the question somewhat academic. To the Western powers, the continued isolation of Japanese society was an affront and a challenge. Driven by growing rivalry among themselves and convinced by their own propaganda and the ideology of world capitalism that the expansion of trade on a global basis would benefit all nations, Western nations began to approach Japan in the hope of opening up the country to foreign economic interests.

3-4b The Opening of Japan

The first to succeed was the United States. American ships following the northern route across the Pacific needed a fueling station before completing their long journey to China and other ports in the area. The efforts to pry the Japanese out of their cloistered existence initially failed, but the Americans persisted. In the summer of 1853, an American fleet of four warships under Commodore Matthew C. Perry arrived in Edo Bay (now Tokyo Bay) with a letter from President Millard Fillmore addressed to the shogun (see Image 3.5). A few months later, intimidated

Glasshouse Images/JT Vintage/Alamy stock photo

IMAGE 3.5 Black Ships in Tokyo Bay. The arrival of a U.S. fleet commanded by Commodore Matthew Perry in 1853 caused consternation among many Japanese observers, who were intimidated by the size and ominous presence of the American ships. This nineteenth-century woodblock print shows curious Japanese paddling out to greet the arrivals.

Q *Do you believe that the United States was justified in seeking to pressure Japanese leaders to open the door to foreign commerce?*

officials in the shogunate relented and agreed to the Treaty of Kanagawa, providing for the opening of two ports and the establishment of a U.S. consulate on Japanese soil. In 1858, U.S. Consul Townsend Harris signed a more elaborate commercial treaty calling for the opening of several ports to U.S. trade and residence, an exchange of ministers, and extraterritorial privileges for U.S. residents in Japan. The Japanese soon signed similar treaties with several European nations.

The decision to open relations with the Western barbarians was highly unpopular in some quarters, particularly in regions distant from the shogunate headquarters in Edo. Resistance was especially strong in two key daimyo territories in the south, Satsuma and Choshu, both of which had strong military traditions. In 1863, the "Sat-Cho" alliance forced the hapless shogun to promise to bring relations with the West to an end, but the rebellious groups soon disclosed their own weakness. When Choshu troops fired on Western ships in the Strait of Shimonoseki, the Westerners fired back and destroyed the Choshu fortifications. The incident convinced the rebellious **samurai** ("retainers," the traditional warrior class subordinated to the daimyo lords) of the need to strengthen their own military and intensified their unwillingness to give in to the West. Having strengthened their influence at the imperial court in Kyoto, they demanded the resignation of the shogun and the restoration of the power of the emperor. In January 1868, rebel armies attacked the shogun's palace in Kyoto and proclaimed the restored authority of the emperor. After a few weeks, resistance collapsed, and the venerable shogunate system was brought to an end.

3-5 RICH COUNTRY, STRONG ARMY

 Focus Question: To what degree was the Meiji Restoration a "revolution," and to what extent did it succeed in transforming Japan?

Although the victory of the Sat-Cho faction over the shogunate appeared on the surface to be a triumph of tradition over change, the new leaders soon realized that Japan must modernize to survive and embarked on a policy of comprehensive reform that would lay the foundations of a modern industrial nation within a generation. The symbol of the new era was the young emperor himself, who had taken the reign name Meiji ("enlightened rule") on ascending the throne after the death of his father in 1867. Although the post-Tokugawa period was termed a "restoration," the Meiji ruler was controlled by the new leadership, just as the shogun had controlled his predecessors. In tacit recognition of the real source

of political power, the new capital was located at Edo, which was renamed Tokyo ("Eastern Capital"), and the imperial court was moved to the shogun's palace in the center of the city.

3-5a The Transformation of Japanese Politics

Once in power, the new leaders launched a comprehensive reform of Japanese political, social, economic, and cultural institutions and values. They moved first to abolish the remnants of the old order and strengthen their executive power. To undercut the power of the daimyo, hereditary feudal privileges were abolished in 1871, and the great lords lost title to their lands. As compensation, they were named governors of the territories formerly under their control. The samurai received a lump-sum payment to replace their traditional stipends but were forbidden to wear the sword, the symbol of their hereditary status.

The abolition of the legal underpinnings of the Tokugawa system permitted the Meiji modernizers to embark on the creation of a modern political system based on the Western model. In the Charter Oath of 1868, the new leaders promised to create a new deliberative assembly within the framework of continued imperial rule. Although senior positions in the new government were given to the daimyo, the key posts were dominated by modernizing samurai, known as the **genro**, from the Sat-Cho clique.

During the next two decades, the Meiji government undertook a systematic study of Western political systems. A constitutional commission under Prince Ito Hirobumi traveled to several Western countries, including Great Britain, Germany, Russia, and the United States, to study their political institutions. As the process evolved, a number of factions appeared, each representing different ideas. The most prominent were the Liberals, who favored political reform on the Western liberal democratic model, and the Progressives, who called for a division of power between the legislative and executive branches, with a slight nod to the latter. There was also an imperial party that advocated the retention of supreme authority in the hands of the emperor.

The Meiji Constitution   In the end, the Progressives emerged victorious. The Meiji constitution, adopted in 1890, vested authority in the executive branch, although the imperialist faction was pacified by the statement that the constitution was the gift of the emperor. Members of the cabinet were to be handpicked by the Meiji oligarchs. The upper house of parliament was to be appointed and have equal legislative powers with the lower house, called the Diet, whose members would be elected. The core ideology of the state, called the **kokutai** (national polity), embodied (although in very imprecise form) the concept of the uniqueness of the Japanese system based on the supreme authority of the emperor.

The result was a system that was democratic in form but despotic in practice, modern in external appearance but still recognizably traditional in that power remained in the hands of a ruling oligarchy. The system permitted the traditional ruling class to retain its influence and economic power while acquiescing in the emergence of a new set of institutions and values.

3-5b Meiji Economics

With the end of the daimyo domains, the government needed to establish a new system of land ownership that would transform the mass of the rural population from indentured serfs into citizens. To do so, it enacted a land reform program that redefined the domain lands as the private property of the tillers, while compensating the previous owner with government bonds. One reason for the new policy was that the government needed operating revenues. At the time, public funds came mainly from customs duties, which were limited by agreement with the foreign powers to 5 percent of the value of the product. To remedy the problem, the Meiji leaders added a new agriculture tax, which was set at an annual rate of 3 percent of the estimated value of the land. The new tax proved to be a lucrative and dependable source of income for the government, but it was quite onerous for many farmers, who had previously paid a fixed percentage of their harvest to the landowner. As a result, in bad years, many peasants were unable to pay their taxes and were forced to sell their lands to wealthy neighbors. Eventually, the government reduced the tax to 2.5 percent of the land value. Still, by the end of the century, about 40 percent of all farmers were tenants.

Launching the Industrial Revolution With its budget needs secured, the government turned to the promotion of industry. A small but growing industrial economy had already existed under the Tokugawa. In its early stages, manufacturing in Japan had been the exclusive responsibility of an artisan caste, who often worked for the local daimyo. Eventually, these artisans began to expand their activities, hiring workers and borrowing capital from merchants. By the end of the seventeenth century, manufacturing centers had developed in Japan's growing cities, such as Edo, Kyoto, and Osaka. According to one historian, by 1700, Japan already had four cities with a population over 100,000 and was one of the most urbanized societies in the world.

Japan's industrial sector received a massive stimulus from the **Meiji Restoration**. The government provided financial subsidies to needy industries, imported foreign advisers, improved transport and communications, and established a universal system of education emphasizing applied science. In contrast to China, Japan was able to achieve results with minimum reliance on foreign capital. Although the first railroad—built in 1872—was underwritten by a loan from Great Britain, future projects were all financed locally. Foreign currency holdings came largely from tea and silk, which were exported in significant quantities during the latter half of the nineteenth century.

During the late Meiji era, Japan's industrial sector began to grow. Besides tea and silk, other key industries were weaponry, shipbuilding, and *sake*. From the start, the distinctive feature of the Meiji model was the intimate relationship between government and private business in terms of operations and regulations. Once an individual enterprise or industry was on its feet (or sometimes, when it had ceased to make a profit), it was turned over entirely to private ownership, although the government often continued to play some role even after its direct involvement in management was terminated. Many new entrepreneurs were members of the samurai class, who had lost their livelihood with the destruction of the large daimyo domains and now sought to find their place in the new economy.

Also noteworthy is the effect that the Meiji reforms had on rural areas. As we have seen, the new land tax provided the government with funds to subsidize the industrial sector, but it imposed severe hardship on the rural population, many of whom abandoned their farms and fled to the cities in search of jobs. This influx of people in turn benefited Japanese industry by providing an abundant source of cheap labor. As in early modern Europe, the industrial revolution in Japan was built on the strong backs of the long-suffering peasantry.

3-5c Building a Modern Social Structure

The Meiji Restoration also transformed several other feudal institutions. A key focus of their attention was the army. The Sat-Cho reformers had been struck by the weakness of the Japanese armed forces in clashes with the Western powers and embarked on a major program to create a modern military force that could compete in a social Darwinist world in which only the fittest would survive. The old feudal army based on the traditional warrior class was abolished, and an imperial army based on universal conscription was formed in 1871. The army also played an important role in Japanese society, becoming a means of upward mobility for many rural males.

Education Education also underwent major changes. The Meiji leaders recognized the need for universal education, including instruction in modern technology. After a few years of experimenting, they adopted the American model of a three-tiered system culminating in a series of

The Rules of Good Citizenship in Meiji Japan

 According to the Imperial Rescript, what was the primary purpose of education in Meiji Japan? How did these goals compare with those in China and the West?

Politics & Government **AFTER SEIZING POWER** from the Tokugawa Shogunate in 1868, the new Japanese leaders turned their attention to the creation of a new political system that would bring the country into the modern world. After exploring various systems in use in the West, a constitutional commission decided to adopt the system used in imperial Germany because of its paternalistic character. To promote civic virtue and obedience among the citizenry, the government then drafted an imperial rescript that was to be taught to every schoolchild in the country. The rescript instructed all children to obey their sovereign and place the interests of the community and the state above their own personal desires.

Imperial Rescript on Education, 1890

Know ye, Our subjects:

Our Imperial Ancestors have founded Our Empire on a basis broad and everlasting, and have deeply and firmly implanted virtue; Our subjects ever united in loyalty and filial piety have from generation to generation illustrated the beauty thereof. This is the glory of the fundamental character of Our Empire, and herein also lies the source of Our education. Ye, Our subjects, be filial to your parents, affectionate to your brothers and sisters; as husbands and wives be harmonious, as friends true; bear yourselves in modesty and moderation; extend your benevolence to all; pursue learning and cultivate arts, and thereby develop intellectual faculties and perfect moral powers; furthermore, advance public good and promote common interests; always respect the Constitution and observe the laws; should emergency arise, offer yourselves courageously to the State; and thus guard and maintain the prosperity of Our Imperial state; and thus guard and maintain the prosperity of Our Imperial Throne coeval with heaven and earth. So shall ye not only be Our good and faithful subjects, but render illustrious the best traditions of your forefathers.

The way here set forth is indeed the teaching bequeathed by Our Imperial Ancestors, to be observed alike by Their Descendants and the subjects, infallible for all ages and true in all places. It is Our wish to lay it to heart in all reverence, in common with you, Our subjects, that we may all attain to the same virtue.

Source: Dairoku, Kikuchi. "The Imperial Rescript on Education (1890)." 2–3 in *Japanese Education*. London: John Murray, 1909.

universities and specialized institutes. In the meantime, they sent bright students to study abroad and brought foreign specialists to Japan to teach in the new schools. Much of the content of the new system was inspired by Western models. Yet its ethical foundations, as embodied in the Imperial Rescript on Education promulgated in 1890, had a distinctly Confucian orientation, emphasizing such values as filial piety and loyalty to the emperor (see Historical Voices, "The Rules of Good Citizenship in Meiji Japan," above).

Traditional Values and Women's Rights In traditional Japan, women were constrained by the "**three obediences**" imposed on them: child to father, wife to husband, and widow to son. Husbands could easily obtain a divorce, but wives could not (supposedly, a husband could divorce his spouse if she drank too much tea or talked too much). Marriages were arranged, and the average age of marriage for females was sixteen years. Females did not share inheritance rights with males, and few received any education outside the family.

The Meiji reforms had a significant impact on the role of women in Japanese society. Education was open to them through an educational order in 1872. By the end of the nineteenth century, women were beginning to play a crucial role in their nation's effort to modernize. Urged by their parents to augment the family income as well as by the government to fulfill their patriotic duty, young girls were sent en masse to work in the textile mills. From 1894 to 1912, women made up 60 percent of the Japanese labor force. Thanks to them, by 1914, Japan was the world's leading exporter of silk and dominated cotton manufacturing. If it had not been for the export revenues earned from textile exports, Japan might not have been able to develop its heavy industry and military prowess without an infusion of foreign capital.

Japanese women received few rewards, however, for their contribution to the nation. Traditional values were provided with a firm legal basis in the Constitution of 1890, which restricted the franchise to males, while a civil code adopted in 1898 de-emphasized individual human rights and essentially placed women within the context of their role in the family. In 1900, new regulations prohibited women from joining political organizations or attending public meetings. Beginning in 1905, a group of independent-minded women petitioned the Japanese parliament to rescind this restriction, but it was not repealed until 1922.

3-5d Joining the Imperialist Club

Japan's rapid advance was viewed with proprietary pride and admiration by sympathetic observers around the world. The Japanese, however, did not just imitate the domestic policies of their Western mentors; they also emulated the latter's aggressive approach to foreign affairs. That they adopted this course is perhaps not surprising. In their own minds, the Japanese were particularly vulnerable in the world economic arena. Their territory was small, lacking in resources, and densely populated, and they had no natural outlet for expansion. To observant Japanese, it seemed that the lessons of history were clear. Western nations had amassed wealth and power not only because of their democratic systems and high level of education but also because of their colonies, which provided them with sources of raw materials, cheap labor, and markets for their manufactured products.

Traditionally, Japan had not been an expansionist country. Although some Japanese merchants eagerly participated in the commercial network that stretched southward into the South China Sea, most Japanese had generally been satisfied to remain on their home islands, while the shogunate had even sought to isolate the country from most of its neighbors during the Tokugawa era. Perhaps the most notable exception was a short-lived attempt at the end of the sixteenth century to extend Japanese control over the Korean peninsula.

The Japanese began their program of territorial expansion (see Map 3.4) close to home. In 1874, they claimed compensation from China for fifty-four sailors from the Ryukyu Islands who had been killed by the local population on the island of Taiwan and sent a Japanese fleet to Taiwan to punish the perpetrators. When the Qing dynasty evaded responsibility for the incident while agreeing to pay an indemnity to Japan to cover the cost of the expedition, it weakened its claim to ownership of the island of Taiwan. Japan was then able to claim suzerainty over the Ryukyu Islands, long tributary to the Chinese Empire. Two years later, Japanese naval pressure forced the opening of Korean ports to Japanese commerce.

During the 1880s, as the Meiji leaders began to modernize their military forces along Western lines, Sino-Japanese

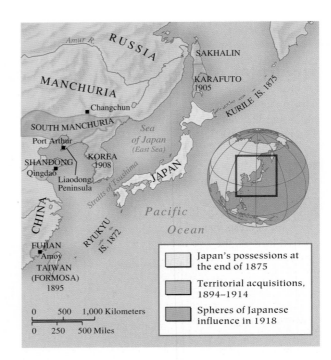

MAP 3.4 Japanese Overseas Expansion During the Meiji Era. Beginning in the late-nineteenth century, Japan ventured beyond its home islands and became an imperialist power. The extent of Japanese colonial expansion through World War I is shown here.

Q *Which parts of the Chinese Empire came under Japanese influence during this period?*

rivalry over Korea intensified. In 1894, China and Japan intervened on opposite sides of an internal rebellion in Korea. When hostilities broke out between the two powers, Japanese ships destroyed the Chinese fleet and seized the Manchurian city of Port Arthur. In the Treaty of Shimonoseki, the Manchus were forced to recognize the independence of Korea, which they had long claimed as a tributary state, and to cede Taiwan and the Liaodong peninsula, with its strategic naval base at Port Arthur, to Japan.

Shortly thereafter, under pressure from the European powers, the Japanese returned the Liaodong peninsula to China, but in the early-twentieth century, they returned to the offensive. Rivalry with Russia over influence in Korea led to increasingly strained relations between the two countries. In 1904, Japan launched a surprise attack on the Russian naval base at Port Arthur, which Russia had taken from China in 1898. Technically, the Japanese armed forces were weaker, but Russia faced difficult logistical problems along its new Trans-Siberian Railway and severe political instability at home (see Chapter 1). In 1905, after Japanese warships sank almost the entire Russian fleet off the coast of Korea, the Russians agreed to a humiliating peace, ceding the strategically located Liaodong peninsula back to Japan, along with southern Sakhalin and the

Kurile Islands. Russia also agreed to abandon its political and economic influence in Korea and southern Manchuria, which now came increasingly under Japanese control. The Japanese victory stunned the world, including the colonial peoples of Southeast Asia, who now began to realize that Europeans were not necessarily invincible.

During the next few years, the Japanese consolidated their position in northeastern Asia, annexing Korea in 1908 as an integral part of Japan. When the Koreans protested the seizure, Japanese reprisals resulted in thousands of deaths. The United States was the first nation to recognize the annexation in return for Tokyo's declaration of respect for U.S. authority in the Philippines, which many American merchant interests viewed as a stepping-stone to the China market. In 1908, the two countries reached an agreement in which the United States recognized Japanese interests in the region in return for Japanese acceptance of the principles of the Open Door. But mutual suspicion between the two countries was growing, sparked in part by U.S. efforts to restrict immigration from all Asian countries. President Theodore Roosevelt, who mediated the Russo-Japanese War, had aroused the anger of many Japanese by turning down a Japanese demand for reparations from Russia. In turn, some Americans began to fear the "yellow peril," manifested by Japanese expansion in East Asia.

3-5e Japanese Culture in Transition

The wave of Western technology and ideas that entered Japan in the second half of the nineteenth century greatly altered the shape of traditional Japanese culture. Literature in particular was affected as European models eclipsed the familiar tales of the Tokugawa era. Dazzled by this "new" literature, Japanese authors began translating and imitating the imported models. Experimenting with Western verse, Japanese poets were at first influenced primarily by the British but eventually adopted such styles as Symbolism, Dadaism, and Surrealism, although some traditional poetry was still composed.

As the Japanese invited technicians, engineers, architects, and artists from Europe and the United States to teach their "modern" skills to a generation of eager students, the Meiji era became a time of massive consumption of Western artistic techniques and styles. Japanese architects and artists created huge buildings of steel and reinforced concrete adorned with Greek columns and cupolas, oil paintings reflecting the European concern with depth perception and shading, and bronze sculptures of secular subjects. European influence even affected the familiar Japanese technique of woodblock printing, as in the print of the Ginza, which uses a traditional technique to depict Tokyo's most modern thoroughfare complete with streetcar and electric lights (see Image 3.6).

Art Resource, NY

IMAGE 3.6 The Ginza in Downtown Tokyo. This 1877 woodblock print shows the Ginza, a major commercial thoroughfare in downtown Tokyo, with modern brick buildings and a horse-drawn streetcar. The centerpiece and focus of public attention is a new electric streetlight. In combining traditional form with modern content, this print symbolizes the unique ability of the Japanese to borrow ideas from abroad while preserving much of the essence of their traditional culture.

Q *Why do you think the Japanese were so quick to imitate Western ways and adopt Western technology?*

Cultural exchange also went the other way as Japanese arts and crafts, porcelains, textiles, fans, folding screens, and woodblock prints became the vogue in Europe and North America. Japanese art influenced Western painters such as Vincent van Gogh, Edgar Degas, and James Whistler, who experimented with flatter compositional perspectives and unusual poses. Japanese gardens, with their exquisite attention to the positioning of rocks and falling water, became especially popular.

After the initial period of mass absorption of Western art, a national reaction occurred at the end of the nineteenth century as many artists returned to pre-Meiji techniques. In 1889, the Tokyo School of Fine Arts (today the Tokyo National University of Fine Arts and Music) was founded to promote traditional Japanese art. Over the next several decades, Japanese art underwent a dynamic resurgence, reflecting the nation's emergence as a prosperous and powerful state. While some artists attempted to synthesize Japanese and foreign techniques, others returned to past artistic traditions for inspiration.

MAKING CONNECTIONS

The Meiji Restoration was one of the great success stories of modern times. Not only did the Meiji leaders put Japan firmly on the path to economic and political development, they also managed to remove the unequal treaty provisions that had been imposed on them at mid-century. Japanese achievements are especially impressive when compared with the difficulties experienced by China, which was not only unable to effect significant changes in its traditional society but had not even reached a consensus on the need for doing so. Japan's achievements more closely resemble those of Europe, but whereas the West needed a century and a half to achieve a significant level of industrial development, the Japanese achieved it in forty years.

The differences between the Japanese and Chinese responses to the West have sparked considerable debate among students of comparative history. Some have argued that Japan's success was partly due to good fortune; lacking abundant natural resources, it was exposed to less pressure from the West than many of its neighbors. Be that as it may, it seems clear that Japanese leaders were much quicker than their Chinese counterparts to recognize the implications of the threat that they faced from the Western onslaught, and quicker to take action to address the challenge. Perhaps, as some historians have suggested, Japan's unique geographic position in Asia was a factor. China, a continental nation with a heterogeneous ethnic composition, was distinguished from its neighbors by its Confucian culture. By contrast, Japan was an island nation, ethnically and linguistically homogeneous, that had never been conquered. Unlike the Chinese, who showed considerable reluctance to abandon key components of their traditional system, the Japanese had little to fear from cultural change in terms of its effect on their national identity. If Confucian culture, with all its accoutrements, was what defined the Chinese gentleman, his Japanese counterpart, in the familiar image, could discard his sword and kimono and don a modern military uniform or a Western business suit and still feel comfortable in both worlds.

Whatever the case, the Meiji Restoration was possible because aristocratic and capitalist elements managed to work together in a common effort to fend off the foreign threat and seek national wealth and power. The nature of the Japanese value system, with its emphasis on practicality and military achievement, may also have contributed. Finally, the Meiji benefited from the fact that the pace of urbanization and commercial and industrial development had already begun to quicken under the Tokugawa. Japan, it has been said, was ripe for change, and nothing could have been more suitable as an antidote for the collapsing old system than the Western emphasis on wealth and power. It was a classic example of challenge and response.

One thing stands out in any analysis of the impact of imperialism in East Asia: almost alone among the societies of Asia and Africa, both China and Japan were able to maintain at least the semblance of national independence during the height of the Western onslaught. For China, once the most advanced country in the world, survival was very much in doubt, as waves of Western political, military, and economic influence lapped at the edges and even the heartland of the Qing Empire. Only Japan responded with vigor and effectiveness, launching a comprehensive reform program that by the end of the century had transformed the island nation into an industrial power in its own right.

What explains the ability of the two major societies in East Asia to avoid total domination by the Western powers? In the case of China, the answer may lie in its sheer size, as well as the fact that rivalry among the covetous industrial nations prevented any single power from placing the almost continental nation within its own orbit. Japan, however, stands out as the one true exception. By its own efforts, it not only fended off the Western challenge, but by the end of the century threatened to become an emerging member of the imperialist club on its own. Whatever the reasons for the difference, as the new century dawned, East Asia was the exception; elsewhere, the industrialized nations' stranglehold on most of the world appeared virtually complete.

REFLECTION QUESTIONS

Q How did China and Japan each respond to Western pressures in the nineteenth century, and what implications did their different responses have for each nation's history?

Q What were some of the key reasons why the Meiji reformers were so successful in launching Japan on the road to industrialization? Which of those reasons also applied to China under the Qing?

Q What impact did colonial rule have on the environment in the European colonies in Asia and Africa during the nineteenth century? Did some of these same factors apply in China and Japan?

Q How did Western values and institutions influence Chinese and Japanese social mores and traditions during the imperialist era?

CHAPTER TIMELINE

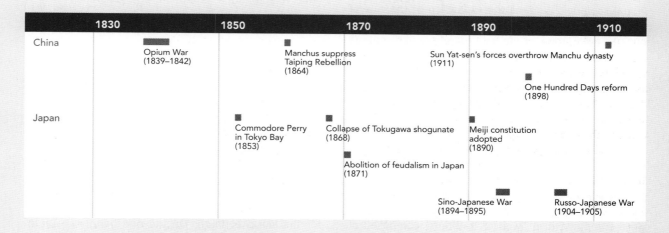

CHAPTER NOTES

1. The quote is from H.F. MacNair, *Modern Chinese History: Selected Readings* (Shanghai: Commercial Press Ltd. 1923), p. 136, and reproduced in F. Schurmann and Orville Schell (eds.), *Imperial Reader: The Decline of the Last Dynasty and the Origins of Modern China* (New York, 1967), pp. 146–147.

PART I
REFLECTIONS

THE NINETEENTH CENTURY witnessed two major developments: the onset of the Industrial Revolution and the ensuing drama of the European domination of the world. The two were clearly related, since the former had created the conditions for the latter. It was, of course, the major industrial powers—Great Britain, France, Germany, and the United States—that took the lead in building the large colonial empires that spanned the globe.

EXPLAINING THE WINNERS AND LOSERS Why some societies were able to master the challenge of industrialization and others were not has been a matter of considerable scholarly debate. Some observers have found the answer in the cultural characteristics of individual societies, such as the expansion of the rule of law in Great Britain, the Protestant work ethic in various parts of Europe, or the tradition of social discipline and class hierarchy in Japan. According to historian David Landes, cultural differences were the key reason why the Industrial Revolution took place first in Europe rather than elsewhere in the world. While admitting that other factors-such as climate and the presence of natural resources-played a role in the process, what was most important, he maintained in his provocative book *The Wealth and Poverty of Nations*, was "work, thrift, honesty, patience, and tenacity," all characteristics that are present to a greater or lesser degree in European civilization. Other societies, he declared, were entangled in a "web of tradition" composed of political authoritarianism, religious prejudice, and a suspicion of material wealth. Thus, they failed to overcome obstacles to rapid economic development. Only Japan, with its own tradition of hard work and self-sacrifice, succeeded in emulating the European experience.[1]

Other observers have taken issue with Landes' cultural thesis and have argued that other considerations played more important roles in determining the winners and losers in the race to achieve economic wealth and power. As we have seen above, historian Kenneth Pomeranz has maintained that the availability of crucial raw materials like coal and water power, along with the capital and experience accumulated during the early stages of European expansion in the early modern era, provided the primary impetus for the Industrial Revolution in Great Britain. The importance of the early modern era was also emphasized by the sociologist Andre Gunder Frank, who argued that the Industrial Revolution was less important as the driving force of the modern age than the age of exploration and expansion—a period marked by Western military conquest and degradation of many non-Western peoples—that preceded it.

It is clear that neither side possesses a monopoly of truth in this debate. Although culture clearly matters, other factors, such as climate and geography—which are certainly crucial in determining a given society's innate capacity to enter the industrial age—are equally if not more important. On the other hand, critics who maintain that imperialism was the main culprit in holding back industrial development in colonial or semicolonial societies in Asia and Africa must take into account the fact that some have succeeded in mounting the ladder of economic success much more successfully than others. What is increasingly evident is that there is no single answer, or solution, to the question.[2]

THE LEGACY OF THE INDUSTRIAL REVOLUTION Whatever the ultimate causes, the advent of the industrial age had a number of lasting consequences for the world at large. On the one hand, the material wealth of those nations that successfully passed through the process increased significantly. In many cases, the creation of advanced industrial societies strengthened democratic institutions and led to a higher standard of living for the majority of the population. The spread of technology and trade outside of Europe created the basis for a new international economic order based on the global exchange of goods.

On the other hand, as we have seen, not all the consequences of the Industrial Revolution were beneficial, even within the industrializing societies themselves. In European society, there were losers as well as winners, and because the print revolution and an increase in literacy rates had made Europeans much more aware of what was taking place around them, public resentment

over the vast disparities in the distribution of wealth was probably much more intense than it had been in earlier centuries. At the same time, the economic and social disruption engendered by the transition from an agricultural to an industrial society led to an increased sense of rootlessness and alienation among much of the population that had not benefitted from the transition.

The Industrial Revolution also created resentment among the nations taking part in the experience. Some countries, notably Great Britain and France, were able to make good use of their advantages to extend their power and influence beyond the borders of Europe. As a result, they were the first and foremost to succeed in the land grab for colonies. Later arrivals, such as Germany, Italy, and Japan, became increasingly resentful at being left out in the search for the spoils of conquest. Inevitably, there would eventually be a reckoning for this disparity in benefits, as we shall see in Part II of this book.

In the meantime, old empires like Imperial Russia, Austria-Hungary, and the Ottoman Turks were not directly exposed to the full impact of the Industrial Revolution during the nineteenth century. Nevertheless, they felt some of its shockwaves, since the dramatic political, economic, and social changes taking place in Western Europe inevitably drew great interest among restive elements far to the east. Some radical groups, like the Narodniks in Russia and the Young Turks in the Ottoman Empire, began to put increasing pressure on their sclerotic monarchies to bring their countries into the modern age. The surge in national consciousness that had originally manifested itself in places like France, Germany, and Italy also began to seep eastward as well, arousing a growing sense of ethnic, linguistic, and cultural awareness among subject peoples like the Poles, the Czechs, and the southern Slavic peoples who had long been voiceless entities living in multiethnic empires. For them, the events taking place in the west were a harbinger of potential future dramatic change.

Looking back from the perspective of our own day, the enduring historical debate over the impact of the Industrial Revolution has taken on an element of particular relevance for our own times. The global economy today is in the throes of another period of what the futurist writer Alvin Toffler once termed a "third wave" of rapid technological change. If the first two great historical transformations he described—the Agricultural and the Industrial Revolutions—each significantly reshaped the political, economic, and social foundations of human society in their own time, the explosion of scientific and technological knowledge that is taking place today has begun to exert an equivalent impact on our own world, revamping the political culture, the economic networks, and the norms and institutions of our contemporary society—and in dramatic and sometimes destructive ways. In a similar manner to the impact of the Industrial Revolution, the current turmoil has been characterized by a substantial degree of what might be called "creative destruction," in which the advent of the New necessarily entails the destruction of much of the Old, thus arousing a considerable sense of unease among many groups in society at large. For those most affected, it is an unsettling experience.[3]

IMPERIALISM: INDUSTRIALIZATION'S "EVIL TWIN"?

What about the impact of the Industrial Revolution beyond the borders of Europe? On balance, did it help or hinder those Asian and African societies who were affected in various ways by the transition to a new industrial era? As we have seen above, the debate over this topic today is as contentious as ever. In recent years it has been a commonplace for many scholars to view the imperialist era through a highly critical lens. It was misguided, they argue, to believe that Western intervention into traditional societies would result in improved conditions and lives; and it was hypocritical to assign benevolent motives to actions that were almost always often patently self-serving.

That viewpoint is not universal, however, as a few recent writers continue to defend the actions taken during the era of imperialism as not only benevolent in their intentions, but salutary in their consequences. In his *Empire: The Rise and Demise of the British World*

Order and the Lessons for Global Power, historian Niall Ferguson argued that while the British performance during the imperial era was by no means flawless, it nonetheless provided subjects of the Empire with many benefits, including the rule of law, free trade, the abolition of slavery, and a long period of global peace. Arguing that the concept of imperialism itself has been unfairly maligned, Ferguson expressed the hope that the United States would take up the mantle left by the British without apology.[4]

It is debatable whether a consensus on this issue will ever be reached, since (as in the case of the Industrial Revolution itself) the consequences of the imperialist era are much too complex to be summed up with facile conclusions. While countries like Japan can be singled out as a success story (keeping in mind that Japan eventually became an imperialist nation in its own right), many others serve as an example of how imperialist intervention probably delayed or distorted their capacity to develop institutions and values appropriate to the modern era. And although colonial rule did ultimately introduce countless traditional societies to the technology, the institutions, and the values that characterize the most advanced nations in the world today, the price was high, as millions of people were uprooted from their traditional environments and exposed to a life marked by poverty and degradation. Although there is not much ground here to reach a scholarly consensus,

it seems that the defenders of imperialism have much to explain.

We shall have cause to return to this topic later in this book, when we evaluate the recent performance of many of those societies once subjugated to imperial rule. For the moment, it is sufficient to note that—two centuries after the opening of the imperialist era—the debate over the wealth and poverty of nations and the means to be used to narrow the differences has continued unresolved into our own day.

Ironically, however, in opening the door for the rest of the world to become more familiar with the momentous events taking place in Europe, the imperialist nations may have sown the seeds of their own ultimate defeat. Colonized peoples eventually learned how to operate within the accepted bounds of European social theories, mobilizing themselves by appeals to new concepts of nationality. Subjugated peoples were thus provided with a weapon that could ultimately be used with great effectiveness against their new masters. In introducing such explosive ideas as liberalism and nationalism—however inadvertently—to their newly conquered subjects, colonial officials soon found themselves riding the tiger of an aroused populace determined to throw them out. And, as the Chinese proverb goes, when you ride a tiger, it's hard to dismount.

NOTES

1. David Landes, *The Wealth and Poverty of Nations: Why Some are So Rich and Some So Poor* (New York: W.W. Norton, 1998.

2. The importance of climate and geography in shaping world history has been emphasized by Jared Diamond in his ground-breaking study *Guns, Germs, and Steel: the Fates of Human Societies* (New York: W.W. Norton, 1997). While I do not necessarily subscribe to all of his conclusions, the author's case for the importance of these two factors is quite persuasive.

3. See Alvin and Heidi Toffler, *Creating a New Civilization: the Politics of the Third Wave* (Atlanta, Ga., 1995). The term "creative destruction" was first applied by the Austrian economist Joseph Schumpeter to describe the operation of the modern capitalist system. I apply it here in a broader socio-historical sense.

4. Niall Ferguson, *Empire: The Rise and Demise of the British World Order and the Lessons for Global Power* (New York: Basic Books, 2003). A similar point of view regarding French imperialism appears in Daniel LeFeuvre, *Pour en Finir avec la Répentance Coloniale* (Paris: Flammerion, 2008). LeFeuvre contends that French colonialism was a child not only of the Industrial Revolution, but of the French Revolution and the Declaration of Rights of Man as well.

PART II

CULTURES IN COLLISION

The Japanese attack on Pearl Harbor, Hawaiian Islands, December 7, 1941

Everett Collection Inc/Alamy Stock Photo

Chapter Outline and Focus Questions

Connections to Today

What lessons do you believe can be learned today about the outbreak of World War I that might enable us to avoid a repeat performance?

IMAGE 4.1 The excitement of war

Mary Evans Picture Library/The Image Works

NEGOTIATIONS AMONG THE GREAT POWERS had been going on for weeks. Anguished messages had been exchanged between Berlin, Vienna, and Saint Petersburg as the crowned heads of three empires—William II of Germany, Francis Joseph of Austria, and Nicholas II of Russia—alternated between threats and appeals as they sought to avoid the outbreak of all-out war in Europe. To many observers at the time, the apparent cause of the sudden international crisis—the assassination of a relatively little-known Austrian official in the town of Sarajevo, in the Balkans—seemed to be almost absurdly insignificant.

The efforts of these world leaders to avoid a direct confrontation, however, were in vain: on August 1, 1914, Germany declared war on Russia. Three days later, France and Great Britain had entered the fray on the side of Russia. Surprisingly, the outbreak of conflict was not generally greeted with high anxiety in the countries involved. Many on both sides even welcomed the prospect of what they expected to be a tidy little war that might be over in a few weeks. For their part, many followers of the philosophy of Karl Marx were convinced that working men and women in Europe would refuse to fight for their capitalist overlords against their counterparts in hostile countries.

A few, however, were more wary. In London, British Foreign Secretary Edward Grey remarked sorrowfully to an acquaintance: "The lamps are going out all over Europe; we shall not see them lit again in our lifetime."[1] As it turned out, his comment was all too prescient. A century of peace and progress was about to come to an end in four years of bloody conflict on the battlefields of Europe. The continent would take more than a generation to recover from the slaughter.

4-1 THE COMING OF WAR

 Focus Question: How did internal Austrian politics influence the outbreak of World War I?

The new century had dawned on a much brighter note. To some contemporaries, the magnificent promise offered by recent scientific advances and the flowering of the Industrial Revolution appeared about to be fulfilled. Few expressed this mood of optimism better than the renowned British historian Arnold Toynbee. In a retrospective look at the opening of a tumultuous century written many years later, Toynbee remarked:

> [We had expected] that life throughout the world would become more rational, more humane, and more democratic and that, slowly, but surely, political democracy would produce greater social justice. We had also expected that the progress of science and technology would make mankind richer, and that this increasing wealth would gradually spread from a minority to a majority. We had expected that all this would happen peacefully. In fact we thought that mankind's course was set for an earthly paradise.[2]

Such bright hopes for the future of humankind were sadly misplaced. In the summer of 1914, simmering rivalries between the major imperialist powers erupted into full-scale war. By the time it ended, Europe had suffered extensive physical destruction and the deaths of millions. Several venerable empires across the continent were in a state of collapse, and the rising power of nationalism appeared unstoppable. Many survivors faced the prospects for the future with a profound sense of pessimism. The Great War, as it came to be called, was an eerie prelude to a tumultuous century marked by widespread violence and dramatic change.

4-1a Rising Tensions in Europe

Between 1871 and 1914, Europeans experienced a long period of peace, as the great powers sought to maintain a fragile balance of power in an effort to avert the reemergence of the destructive forces unleashed during the Napoleonic era. But rivalries among the major world powers continued, and even intensified, leading to a series of crises that might have erupted into a general war. Some of these crises, as we have seen in Chapters 2 and 3, took place outside Europe, as the imperialist nations scuffled for advantage in the race for new colonial territories. But the main focus of European statesmen remained on Europe itself, where the emergence of Germany as the most powerful state on the European continent threatened to upset the fragile balance of power that had been established at the Congress of Vienna in 1815. Fearful of a possible anti-German alliance between France and Russia, German Chancellor Otto von Bismarck signed a defensive treaty with Austria in 1879. Three years later, the alliance was enlarged to include Italy, which was angry with the French over conflicting colonial ambitions in North Africa. The so-called Triple Alliance of 1882 committed the three powers to support the existing political and social order while maintaining a defensive alliance against France.

While Bismarck was chancellor, German policy had been essentially cautious, as he sought to prevent rival powers from conspiring against Berlin. But in 1890 the country's new Emperor William II dismissed the "iron chancellor" from office and embarked on a more aggressive foreign policy dedicated to providing Germany with its rightful "place in the sun." As Bismarck had feared, France and Russia responded by concluding their own military alliance in 1894. By 1907, a loose confederation of Great Britain, France, and Russia—known as the Triple Entente—stood opposed to the Triple Alliance of Germany, Austria-Hungary, and Italy. Europe was divided into two opposing camps that became more and more inflexible and unwilling to compromise. The stage was set for war.

4-1b Crisis in the Balkans, 1908–1913

The dispute that led to world war began in the Balkans, where the decline of Ottoman power had turned the region into a tinderbox of ethnic and religious tensions. In 1908, Austria decided to annex its two protectorates of Bosnia and Herzegovina to prevent them from being seized by neighboring Serbia, a young nation whose leaders had visions of creating a large kingdom that would include most of the southern Slavic-speaking peoples. When Russia backed its protégé Serbia, Germany announced its

MAP 4.1 **Europe in 1914.** By 1914, two alliances dominated Europe: the Triple Entente of Britain, France, and Russia and the Triple Alliance of Germany, Austria-Hungary, and Italy. Russia sought to bolster fellow Slavs in Serbia, whereas Austria-Hungary was intent on increasing its power in the Balkans and thwarting Serbia's ambitions. Thus, the Balkans became the flash point for World War I.

 Which nonaligned nations were positioned between the two alliances?

support of Austria, thus raising the stakes in a potential conflict. The standoff ended when Russia backed down, but tensions within the Balkans had intensified, leading in 1912 and 1913 to a brief and inconclusive struggle for territory among the newly independent states in the region (see Map 4.1). In the meantime, Great Britain and France drew closer to Saint Petersburg.

4-1c **The Outbreak of War**

By now Austrian officials in Vienna had become convinced that Serbia was a mortal threat to their empire and must be crushed. When Archduke Francis Ferdinand (the heir to the Austrian throne) and his wife, Sophia, were assassinated on June 28, 1914, in the Bosnian city of Sarajevo by a member of a Serbian terrorist organization, the Austrian government issued an ultimatum to Serbia, demanding that the latter conduct a full inquiry into the event and root out all signs of anti-Austrian terrorist activity in the country. Serbian leaders, confident of Russian support, rejected Austrian demands as a threat to the country's sovereignty. Austrian leaders—counting on German support and determined not to back down to an insignificant rival—then declared war on Serbia on July 28. Russia, however, was still smarting from its humiliation in the Bosnian crisis of 1908, and thus was determined to support Serbia's cause. On July 28, Tsar Nicholas II ordered a partial mobilization of the Russian army against Austria. But when the Russian general staff informed the tsar that its mobilization plans were based on a war against both Germany and Austria simultaneously, he ordered a full mobilization the next day, even while knowing that the Germans would consider this an act of war against them. As predicted, Berlin responded by demanding that the Russians halt their mobilization within twelve hours. When the Russians ignored the ultimatum, Germany declared war on Russia on August 1. Great Britain and France followed suit in defense of their ally shortly after.

4-2 **THE WORLD AT WAR**

Q **Focus Question:** Why do you think the war did not come to an end within a few weeks, as most observers at the time anticipated?

Before 1914, many political leaders had become convinced that war entailed so many political and economic risks that it was not worth fighting. A highly popular book published in 1910—British economist Norman

Angell's *The Great Illusion*—had argued that the economic costs of a general war would be so high that any rational national leader would seek to avoid provoking one. Many readers were convinced by this reasoning, in the expectation that experienced diplomats could control any situation and prevent the outbreak of war. At the beginning of August 1914, both of these illusions were shattered, but the new illusions that replaced them soon proved to be equally foolish.

4-2a Illusions of Victory, 1914–1915

Europeans went to war in 1914 with remarkable enthusiasm. Government propaganda in every belligerent nation had been successful in stirring up national antagonisms before the war. Now, in August 1914, the urgent pleas of governments for defense against aggressors fell on receptive ears, as most people seemed genuinely convinced that their nation's cause was just. A new set of illusions also fed the general lust for war. In August 1914, almost everyone believed that because of the risk of damage to the regional economy, the war would not last long. People were reminded that most of the major battles in European wars since 1815 had in fact ended in a matter of weeks. Both the soldiers who exuberantly boarded the trains for the war front in August 1914 and the jubilant citizens who bombarded them with flowers as they departed were convinced that that the warriors would be home by Christmas.

German hopes for a quick end to the war rested on a military gamble. The so-called Schlieffen Plan (named after its creator, Alfred von Schlieffen, the German Chief of Staff from 1891 to 1905) had called for the German army to march quickly through the neutral state of Belgium into northern France with a vast encircling movement that would sweep around Paris and surround the bulk of the French army. But the high command had not heeded Schlieffen's advice to place sufficient troops on the western salient near the English Channel to guarantee success, and the German advance was halted only 20 miles from Paris at the First Battle of the Marne (September 6–10), where French troops—many of them rushed to the front in taxis—soon blunted the German offensive.

With Germany's initial thrust blunted, the war quickly turned into a stalemate, as neither the Germans nor the French could dislodge the other from the trenches they had begun to dig for shelter. Two lines of trenches soon extended over 400 miles from the English Channel to the frontiers of Switzerland (see Map 4.2). The Western Front had become bogged down in **trench warfare** that kept both sides immobilized in virtually the same positions for four years.

The War in the East Faced with the intimidating prospect of a two-fronted war, German strategists had counted on achieving a rapid victory on the Western Front before launching their offensive against Russia. But the unexpected success of the French in halting the initial attack changed the equation. At the beginning of the war, the Russian army moved into eastern Germany but was decisively defeated at the Battles of Tannenberg on August 30 and the Masurian Lakes on September 15. The Russians were no longer a threat to German territory. The Austrians, Germany's allies, fared less well initially. After they were defeated by the Russians in Galicia and thrown out of Serbia as well, the Germans came to their aid. A German-Austrian army defeated and routed the poorly equipped Russian army in Galicia and pushed the Russians back 300 miles into their own territory. Russian casualties already stood at 2.5 million killed, captured, or wounded; the Russians had almost been knocked out of the war. Buoyed by their success, the Germans and Austrians, joined by the Bulgarians in September 1915, attacked and eliminated Serbia from the war.

4-2b The Great Slaughter, 1916–1917

By 1916, the early trenches dug in 1914 along the Western front had by now become elaborate systems of defense. Both lines of trenches were protected by barbed-wire entanglements 3 to 5 feet high and 30 yards wide, concrete machine-gun nests, and mortar batteries, supported farther back by heavy artillery. Troops lived in holes in the ground, separated from the enemy by a no-man's land.

The unexpected development of trench warfare baffled military leaders who had been trained to fight wars of movement and maneuver. Military strategists on both sides began to look for technological breakthroughs to end the stalemate. First to do so was Great Britain. Taking advantage of the recent invention of the Caterpillar tractor in the United States, the British introduced tanks (so-called because workers in British factories assembling the new weapon compared them to large water tanks) on the Western Front in 1915. The plan was to combine the tanks with infantry assaults to break through enemy lines and change the balance of forces on the battlefield. Success, however, was elusive. Tank performance was often unreliable, while rapid advances were difficult because of the uneven terrain, pockmarked by trenches and potholes caused by heavy artillery bombardments. Airplanes—just a few years into their development—were utilized primarily for reconnaissance purposes, since their capacity to serve as an offensive weapon was still limited. For the most part, the war in the air was characterized by dogfights between squadrons of fighters on both sides.

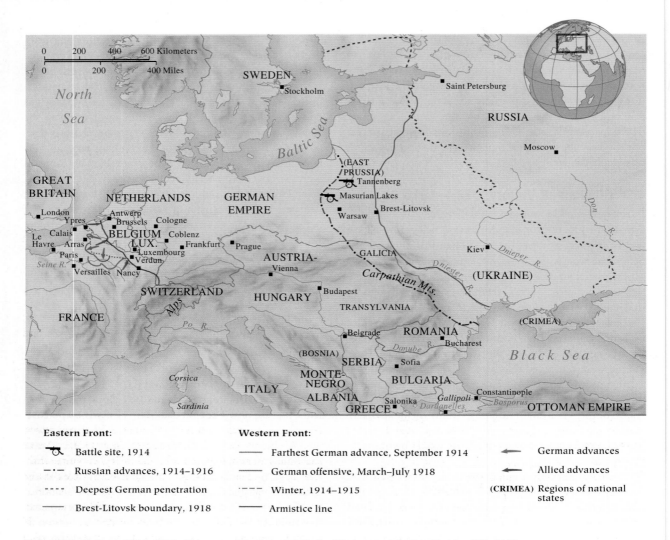

MAP 4.2 World War I, 1914–1918. This map shows how greatly the Western and Eastern Fronts of World War I differed. After initial German gains in the west, the war became bogged down in trench warfare, with little change in the battle lines throughout the war. The Eastern Front was marked by considerable mobility, with battle lines shifting by hundreds of miles.

 How do you explain the difference in the two fronts?

Stymied by limits to their capacity to effectively utilize the latest advances in military technology effectively, military commanders on both sides fell back on continuous attempts to achieve a breakthrough by throwing masses of men against enemy lines that had first been battered by artillery barrages. After "softening up" the enemy in this fashion, a mass of soldiers would climb out of their trenches with fixed bayonets and hope to work their way toward the opposing trenches. The attacks rarely worked, as the machine gun—ever more effective since the invention of the Maxim gun a few years previously—put hordes of men advancing unprotected across open fields at a severe disadvantage. In 1916 and 1917, millions of young men were sacrificed in the search for the elusive breakthrough. In ten months at Verdun in 1916, 700,000 men lost their lives over a few miles of terrain (see Image 4.2).

Warfare in the trenches of the Western Front produced unimaginable horrors. Battlefields were hellish landscapes of barbed wire, shell holes, mud, and injured and dying men. The bright visions of quick victory that had motivated all sides to enlist quickly evaporated (see Opposing Viewpoints, "The Excitement and the Reality of War," p. 84). The introduction of poison gas in 1915 produced new forms of

Hulton Archive/Stringer/Getty Images

IMAGE 4.2 The Horrors of War. The slaughter of millions of men in the trenches of World War I created unimaginable horrors for the participants. For the sake of survival, many soldiers learned to harden themselves against the stench of decomposing bodies and the sight of bodies horribly dismembered by artillery barrages.

Q *Do you think it is understandable that under these conditions, many soldiers on both sides of the conflict would desert their posts or refuse to fight?*

injuries, but the first aerial battles were a rare sideshow and gave no hint of the horrors to come with air warfare in the future.

Soldiers in the trenches also lived with the persistent presence of death. Since combat went on for months, soldiers had to carry on in the midst of countless dead bodies and the remains of men dismembered by artillery barrages. Many soldiers remembered the stench of decomposing bodies and the swarms of rats that grew fat in the trenches. At one point, battlefield conditions became so bad that units of the French army erupted in open mutiny. The high command responded by carrying out widespread executions of suspected ringleaders. Similar events occurred within the armies of the other belligerent countries.

4-2c The Widening of the War

As the war settled into a long, grueling struggle that consumed almost the entire continent, its tentacles began to stretch into other parts of the world as well. Faced with high casualties on the battlefield, the major imperialist

countries began to recruit troops from their colonies to serve on the front lines. Punjabis and Gurkhas from India, Zouaves from North Africa, Cossacks from Central Asia, and infantry units from Australia and New Zealand (tied defensively to Great Britain by their shared membership in the British Commonwealth) fought side by side with their European counterparts. Thousands of others, mainly from Africa and French Indochina, served as laborers on the battlefield or in factories to replace workers who had been drafted into military service. An estimated 80,000 Africans were killed or injured in the war, where they served as front-line troops, workers, or as bearers of provisions at the Front.

The Middle East, in particular, became an important front in the war. German war planners had hoped that the Ottoman Empire, long an influential force in the Middle East, could be persuaded to conduct a holy war that would eliminate British and French influence throughout the region, especially in the Arabian peninsula, where vast oil reserves had recently been discovered. German Emperor William II was personally obsessed with destroying the British Empire, pledging that "if we are to be bled to death, England shall at least lose India."[3]

The Turks, always suspicious of the Russians, eventually agreed to enter the war on the German side, a decision that provoked the British to launch a disastrous attack at Gallipoli, south of Constantinople, in 1915. But Berlin had miscalculated, for the Turks had their own vulnerabilities. In 1917, the dashing but eccentric British adventurer T. E. Lawrence (1888–1935), popularly known as Lawrence of Arabia, incited tribal groups in the Arabian peninsula to revolt against their Ottoman overlords (see Movies & History, *Lawrence of Arabia*, p. 85). Then, in 1918, British forces from Egypt destroyed the rest of the Ottoman Empire in the Middle East. For these campaigns, the British mobilized forces from India, Australia, and New Zealand. The Allies also took advantage of Germany's preoccupations in Europe and lack of naval strength to seize German colonies in Africa. Japan – which had recently signed a defensive treaty with Great Britain – seized a number of German-held islands in the Pacific, and Australia took over German New Guinea (for further discussion of these events, see Chapter 5). Germany's effort to adopt a global strategy to counter British control over the oceans had disastrously failed to achieve its objective.

The Yanks are Coming   Another important factor to the Allied cause was the entry of the United States into the war. At first, the administration of President Woodrow Wilson tried to remain neutral, but that became more difficult as the war dragged on. The naval conflict between Germany and Great Britain was the immediate reason for U.S. concern.

The Excitement and the Reality of War

 According to Stefan Zweig, why did so many Europeans welcome the outbreak of war in 1914? Why had they so badly underestimated the cost?

Politics & Government **THE INCREDIBLE OUTPOURING** of patriotic enthusiasm that greeted the declaration of war at the beginning of August 1914 demonstrated the power that nationalistic feeling had attained at the beginning of the twentieth century. Many Europeans seemed to believe that the war had given them a higher purpose, a renewed dedication to the greatness of their nation. That sense of enthusiasm was captured by the Austrian writer Stefan Zweig in his book *The World of Yesterday*.

The reality of war was entirely different. Soldiers who had left for the front in August 1914 in the belief that they would be home by Christmas found themselves shivering and dying in the vast networks of trenches along the battlefront. Few expressed the horror of trench warfare as well as the German writer Erich Maria Remarque in his famous novel *All Quiet on the Western Front*, first published in a German newspaper in 1928.

Stefan Zweig, *The World of Yesterday*

The next morning I was in Austria. In every station placards had been put up announcing general mobilization. The trains were filled with fresh recruits, banners were flying, music sounded, and in Vienna I found the entire city in a tumult. . . . There were parades in the street, flags, ribbons, and music burst forth everywhere, young recruits were marching triumphantly, their faces lighting up at the cheering. . . .

And to be truthful, I must acknowledge that there was a majestic, rapturous, and even seductive something in this first outbreak of the people from which one could escape only with difficulty. And in spite of all my hatred and aversion for war, I should not like to have missed the memory of those days. As never before, thousands and hundreds of thousands felt what they should have felt in peace time, that they belonged together.

What did the great mass know of war in 1914, after nearly half a century of peace? They did not know war, they had hardly given it a thought. It had become legendary, and distance had made it seem romantic and heroic. They still saw it in the perspective of their school readers and of paintings in museums; brilliant cavalry attacks in glittering uniforms, the fatal shot always straight through the heart, the entire campaign a resounding march of victory—"We'll be home at Christmas," the recruits shouted laughingly to their mothers in August of 1914. . . . A rapid excursion into the romantic, a wild, manly adventure—that is how the war of 1914 was painted in the imagination of the simple man, and the younger people were honestly afraid that they might miss this most wonderful and exciting experience of their lives; that is why they hurried and thronged to the colors, and that is why they shouted and sang in the trains that carried them to the slaughter; wildly and feverishly the red wave of blood coursed through the veins of the entire nation.

Erich Maria Remarque, *All Quiet on the Western Front*

We wake up in the middle of the night. The earth booms. Heavy fire is falling on us. We crouch into corners. . . . Every man is aware of the heavy shells tearing down the parapet, rooting up the embankment and demolishing the upper layers of concrete. . . . Already by morning a few of the recruits are green and vomiting. . . .

No one would believe that in this howling waste there could still be men, but steel helmets now appear on all sides out of the trench, and fifty yards from us a machine-gun is already in position and barking.

The wire-entanglements are torn to pieces. Yet they offer some obstacle. We see the storm-troops coming. . . . We recognize the distorted faces, the smooth helmets: they are French. They have already suffered heavily when they reach the remnants of the barbed wire entanglements.

I see one of them, his face upturned, fall into a wire cradle. His body collapses, his hands remain suspended as though he were praying. Then his body drops clear away and only his hands with the stumps of his arms, shot off, now hang in the wire.

Sources: From *The World of Yesterday* by Stefan Zweig, translated by Helmut Ripperger. Translation copyright 1943 by the Viking Press, Inc. *All Quiet on the Western Front* by Erich Maria Remarque. *Im Westen nichts Neues*, copyright 1928 by Ullstein A. G.; copyright renewed © 1956 by Erich Maria Remarque. *All Quiet on the Western Front*, copyright 1929, 1930 by Little, Brown and Company. Copyright renewed © 1957, 1958 by Erich Maria Remarque. All Rights Reserved.

MOVIES & HISTORY

Lawrence of Arabia (1962)

The conflict in the Middle East produced one of the great romantic heroes of World War I. T. E. Lawrence, a British army officer popularly known as Lawrence of Arabia, organized Arab tribesmen and led them in battle against the Ottoman Turks, who had become allies of the Central Powers (Germany and its allies). Although the military significance of Lawrence's exploits was limited, their long-term implications for the region were enormous. During the peace negotiations that followed the German surrender in November 1918, most Ottoman possessions in the Middle East were replaced by British and French mandates, while the Arabian peninsula embarked on the road to independence under the tribal chieftain Ibn Saud. The political implications of that settlement are still important today.

The movie *Lawrence of Arabia*, directed by the great British filmmaker David Lean, won seven Oscars and made an instant star of actor Peter O'Toole, who played the eccentric Lawrence with mesmerizing perfection. The cinematography and the acting are both superb, and Lean's deft portrayal of the behavior and motives of all participants makes the lengthy film (more than three hours) essential viewing for those interested in comprehending the complex roots of the current situation in the Middle East.

British objectives, as voiced by the British general Viscount Edmund Allenby (played by the veteran actor Jack Hawkins), were unabashedly military in nature—use Arab unrest in the region as a means of taking the Ottomans out of the war. Arab leaders such as Prince

T. E. Lawrence (Peter O'Toole in white) at the head of the Arab tribes.

Faisal—languidly played by the consummate actor Alec Guinness—openly sought their independence from Turkish rule, but initially appeared hopelessly divided. It was Major Lawrence who provided the spark and the determination to knit together a coalition of Arab forces capable of winning crucial victories in the final year of the war. Faisal himself would eventually be chosen by the British to become the king of the artificial state of Iraq.

Lawrence himself remains an enigma—in the movie as in real life. Combining a fervent idealism about the Arab cause with an overweening sense of self-promotion, he played to the end an ambiguous role in the geopolitics of the Middle East. Disenchanted with the postwar peace settlement, he eventually removed himself from the public eye and died in a motorcycle accident in 1935.

Britain took advantage of its superior naval power to impose a naval blockade on Germany. The latter retaliated with a counterblockade enforced by unrestricted submarine warfare. Strong U.S. protests over the German sinking of passenger liners—especially the British ship *Lusitania* on May 7, 1915, when more than 100 Americans lost their lives—forced the German government to suspend unrestricted submarine warfare to avoid further antagonizing the Americans.

In January 1917, however, German naval officers convinced Emperor William II that the renewed use of unrestricted submarine warfare could starve the British into submission within five months. To create a distraction in case the White House should decide to enter the war on the Allied side, German Foreign Minister Alfred von Zimmerman secretly encouraged the Mexican government

to launch a military attack to recover territories lost to the United States in the American Southwest.

The resumption of unrestricted submarine warfare, combined with outrage over the Zimmerman telegram (which had been decoded by the British and provided to U.S. diplomats in London), finally brought the United States into the war on April 6, 1917. Although American troops did not arrive in Europe in large numbers until 1918, the U.S. entry into the war gave the Allies a badly needed psychological boost at a time when their offensive efforts on the Western Front had achieved disappointing results. Then, in November 1917, the Bolshevik Revolution in Russia (see "4-4 Revolution in Russia," p. 90) led to Russia's withdrawal from the war, leaving Germany free to concentrate entirely on the Western Front.

4-2d The Home Front: The Impact of Total War

Because most of the participants had expected the war to be short, they had given little thought to economic problems and long-term wartime needs. Governments had to respond quickly, however, when the war machines failed to achieve their knockout blows and made ever-greater demands for men and matériel. The extension of government power was a logical outgrowth of these needs. Most European countries had already devised some system of mass conscription or military draft. It was now carried to unprecedented heights as countries mobilized tens of millions of young men for that elusive breakthrough to victory.

Throughout Europe, wartime governments also expanded their powers over their economies. Free market capitalistic systems were temporarily shelved as governments experimented with price, wage, and rent controls; the rationing of food supplies and matériel; the regulation of imports and exports; and the nationalization of transportation systems and industries. Compulsory military service was adopted for all eligible males. Some governments even moved toward compulsory employment. In effect, to mobilize the entire resources of the nation for the war effort, European countries had moved toward planned economies directed by government agencies.

Women in World War I   The war also created new roles for women. Because so many men went off to fight at the front, women were called on to take over jobs and responsibilities that had not been available to them before. Overall, the number of women employed in Britain who held new jobs or replaced men rose by 1,345,000. Their occupations included chimney sweeps, truck drivers, farm laborers, and factory workers in heavy industry (see Historical Voices, "Women in the Factories," p. 87). By 1918, some 38 percent of the workers in the Krupp armaments factories in Germany were women.

While male workers expressed concern that the employment of females at lower wages would depress their own wages, women began to demand equal pay legislation. A law passed by the French government in July 1915 established a minimum wage for women home-workers in textiles, an industry that had grown dramatically thanks to the demand for military uniforms. Later in 1917, the government decreed that men and women should receive equal rates for piecework. Despite the noticeable increase in women's wages that resulted from government regulations, women's industrial wages still were not equal to men's wages by the end of the war.

Morale Problems   As the Great War dragged on and both casualties and privations worsened, internal dissatisfaction replaced the patriotic enthusiasm that had marked the early stages of the conflict. By 1916, there were numerous signs that civilian morale was beginning to crack under the pressure of total war. War governments, however, fought back against the growing opposition to the war, as even parliamentary regimes resorted to an expansion of police powers to stifle internal dissent. At the very beginning of the war, the British Parliament passed the Defence of the Realm Act (DORA), which allowed the public authorities to arrest dissenters as traitors. The act was later extended to authorize public officials to censor newspapers by deleting objectionable material and even to suspend newspaper publication. In France, government authorities had initially been lenient about public opposition to the war, but by 1917, they began to fear that open opposition to the war might weaken the French will to fight. When Georges Clemenceau (1841–1929) became premier near the end of 1917, the lenient French policies came to an end, and basic civil liberties were suppressed for the duration of the war. When a former premier publicly advocated a negotiated peace, Clemenceau's government had him sentenced to prison for two years for treason.

4-2e The Last Year of the War

Germany was suffering from morale problems as well, not only on the battlefield but on the home front, where the Allied blockade caused severe privation for civilians and aroused growing discontent over the continuation of the war. The withdrawal of the Russians from the war in March 1918 briefly offered renewed hope for a favorable end to the conflict. Erich von Ludendorff (1865–1937), who guided German military operations, persuaded civilian leaders to make one final gamble—a grand offensive in the west to break the military stalemate. The German attack was launched in March and lasted into July, but an Allied counterattack, supported by the arrival of 140,000 fresh American troops, defeated the Germans at the Second Battle of the Marne on July 18. Ludendorff's gamble had failed. With the arrival of 2 million more American troops on the European continent, Allied forces began to advance steadily toward Germany.

On September 29, 1918, General Ludendorff informed German leaders that the war was lost and recommended that the government sue for peace. When German officials discovered that the Allies were unwilling to negotiate a settlement with the wartime leadership, reforms were instituted to create a liberal government that would be more acceptable to the Allies. But these constitutional reforms came too late for the exhausted and restive German people. On November 3, naval units in Kiel

Women in the Factories

 What did Naomi Loughnan learn about men and lower-class women while working in the munitions factory? What did she learn about herself?

Family & Society **DURING WORLD WAR I,** women were called on to assume new job responsibilities, including factory work. In this selection, Naomi Loughnan, a young, upper-middle-class woman, describes the experiences in a munitions plant that considerably broadened her perspective on life.

Naomi Loughnan, "Munition Work"

We little thought when we first put on our overalls and caps and enlisted in the Munition Army how much more inspiring our life was to be than we had dared to hope. . . . Our long days are filled with interest, and with the zest of doing work for our country in the grand cause of Freedom. As we handle the weapons of war we are learning great lessons of life. In the busy noisy workshops we come face to face with every kind of class, and each one of these classes has something to learn from the others. . . .

Engineering mankind is possessed of the unshakable opinion that no woman can have the mechanical sense. If one of us asks humbly why such and such an alteration is not made to prevent this or that drawback to a machine, she is told, with a superior smile, that a man has worked her machine before her for years, and that therefore if there were any improvement possible it would have been made. As long as we do exactly what we are told and do not attempt to use our brains, we give entire satisfaction, and are treated as nice, good children. Any swerving from the easy path prepared for us by our males arouses the most scathing contempt in their manly bosoms. . . . Women have, however, proved that their entry into the munition world has increased the output. Employers who forget things personal in their patriotic desire for large results are enthusiastic over the success of women in the shops. But their workmen have to be handled with the utmost tenderness and caution lest they should actually imagine it was being suggested that women could do their work equally well, given equal conditions of training—at least where muscle is not the driving force. . . .

The coming of the mixed classes of women into the factory is slowly but surely having an educative effect upon the men. "Language" is almost unconsciously becoming subdued. There are fiery exceptions, who make our hair stand up on end under our close-fitting caps, but a sharp rebuke or a look of horror will often straighten out the most savage. . . . It is grievous to hear the girls also swearing and using disgusting language. Shoulder to shoulder with the children of the slums, the upper classes are having their eyes opened at last to the awful conditions among which their sisters have dwelt. Foul language, immorality and many other evils are but the natural outcome of overcrowding and bitter poverty . . . Sometimes disgust will overcome us, but we are learning with painful clarity that the fault is not theirs whose actions disgust us, but must be placed to the discredit of those other classes who have allowed the continued existence of conditions which generate the things from which we shrink appalled.

Source: From "Munition Work" by Naomi Loughnan in Gilbert Stone, ed., *Women War Workers* (London: George Harrap and Company, 1971), pp. 25, 35, 38.

mutinied, and within days, councils of workers and soldiers were forming throughout northern Germany and taking over civilian and military administrations. Bowing to public pressure, William II abdicated on November 9, and members of the German Socialist Party under Friedrich Ebert (1871–1925) announced the establishment of a republic. Two days later, on November 11, 1918, the new German government agreed to an armistice. The war was over.

The news of the armistice brought tears of joy to the eyes of millions. But the way the conflict had ended—with German armies still fighting on foreign battlefields—was ominous. Rumors soon began to circulate in Germany that its armies had not actually been defeated, but had been "stabbed in the back" by defeatists (many of them Jews or Marxists) who had just established the new republic. The Great War was over, but anger at the result had begun to fester in the minds of millions of Germans.

The final tally of casualties from the war was appalling. Nearly 10 million soldiers were dead, including 5 million on the Allied side and 3.5 million from the Central Powers. Millions more were mutilated from their wounds on the battlefield. Civilian deaths were nearly as high. France, which had borne much of the burden of the war, suffered nearly 2 million deaths, including one out of every four males between eighteen and thirty years of age.

4-3 THE PEACE SETTLEMENT

 Focus Question: What were the primary objectives of U.S. President Woodrow Wilson at the Versailles Peace Conference, and how did they differ from the postwar aims of other Allied nations?

In January 1919, the delegations of twenty-seven victorious Allied nations gathered at the palace of Versailles near Paris to conclude a final settlement of the Great War. Some delegates hoped that this conference would avoid the mistakes made at Vienna in 1815 by aristocrats who rearranged the map of Europe to meet the selfish desires of the great powers. As Harold Nicolson, one of the British delegates, remarked: "We were journeying to Paris not merely to liquidate the war, but to found a New Order in Europe. We were preparing not Peace only, but Eternal Peace. There was about us the halo of some divine mission. . . . For we were bent on doing great, permanent and noble things."[4]

4-3a The Vision of Woodrow Wilson

National expectations, however, made Nicolson's quest for "eternal peace" a difficult one. Over the course of the war, the reasons for fighting had been tacitly transformed from selfish national interests to idealistic principles. No one expressed the latter better than Woodrow Wilson (1856–1924). The American president outlined to the U.S. Congress "Fourteen Points" that he believed justified the enormous military struggle then being waged. Wilson's proposals included "open covenants of peace, openly arrived at" instead of secret diplomacy; the reduction of national armaments to a "point consistent with domestic safety"; and the self-determination of peoples so that "all well-defined national aspirations shall be accorded the utmost satisfaction." Wilson characterized World War I as a people's war waged against "absolutism and militarism," two scourges of liberty that could be eliminated only by creating democratic governments and a "general association of nations" that would guarantee "political independence and territorial integrity to great and small states alike." As the self-proclaimed spokesman for a new world order based on democracy and international cooperation, Wilson

was enthusiastically cheered by many Europeans when he arrived in Europe for the peace conference.

Wilson soon found, however, that his soaring rhetoric did not always match the reality on the ground. In particular, representatives of other states at the conference were guided by considerably more pragmatic motives. The secret treaties and agreements that had been made before and during the war could not be totally ignored, even if they conflicted with Wilson's principle of self-determination. National interests also complicated the deliberations of the conference. In particular, he discovered that two of his key allies were determined to punish their adversaries severely for having provoked the conflict. David Lloyd George (1863–1945), prime minister of Great Britain, had in fact won a decisive electoral victory in December 1918 on a platform of making the Germans pay for this dreadful war.

Georges Clemenceau, the feisty French premier who had led his country to victory, appeared to be even more vindictive. In his view, the French people had borne the brunt of German aggression and deserved security against any possible future attack. To achieve that goal, Clemenceau wanted a demilitarized Germany, vast reparations to pay for the costs of the war, and a separate Rhineland as a buffer state between France and Germany—demands that Wilson viewed as contrary to the principle of national self-determination. The Europeans, he once complained to a colleague, just want to "divide the swag."[5]

Although twenty-seven nations were represented at the Paris Peace Conference, the most important decisions were made by Wilson, Clemenceau, and Lloyd George. Italy was technically considered one of the so-called Big Four powers, but it played a much less important role than the other three countries. Germany was not invited to attend, and Russia could not because it was embroiled in civil war.

Forming the League of Nations   In view of the many conflicting demands at Versailles, it was inevitable that the Big Three would quarrel. Wilson was determined to create a League of Nations to prevent future wars. Clemenceau and Lloyd George were equally determined to punish Germany. In the end, only compromise made it possible to achieve a peace settlement. On January 25, 1919, the conference adopted the principle of the League of Nations (the details of its structure were left for later sessions); Wilson willingly agreed to make compromises on territorial arrangements to guarantee the League's establishment, believing that a functioning League could later rectify bad arrangements. Clemenceau also compromised to obtain some guarantees for French security. He renounced France's desire for a separate Rhineland and instead accepted a defensive alliance with Great Britain and the United States, both of which pledged to help France if it was attacked by Germany.

4-3b The Treaty of Versailles

The final peace settlement at Paris consisted of five separate treaties with the defeated nations—Germany, Austria, Hungary, Bulgaria, and Turkey. The Treaty of Versailles with Germany, signed on June 28, 1919, was by far the most important one. The Germans considered it a harsh peace and were particularly unhappy with Article 231, the so-called **war guilt clause**, which declared Germany (and Austria) responsible for starting the war and ordered Germany to pay **reparations** for all the damage to which the Allied governments and their people had been subjected as a result of the war "imposed upon them by the aggression of Germany and her allies."

The military and territorial provisions of the treaty also rankled the Germans. Germany was required to lower its army to 100,000 men, reduce its navy, and eliminate its air force. German territorial losses included the return of Alsace and Lorraine to France and sections of Prussia to the new Polish state. German territory west and as far as 30 miles east of the Rhine was established as a demilitarized zone and stripped of all armaments or fortifications to serve as a barrier to any future German military moves westward against France. Although outraged by what it considered a "dictated peace," the new German government had no choice but to accept the treaty.

The separate peace treaties made with the other Central Powers extensively redrew the map of eastern Europe (see Map 4.3). Many of these changes merely ratified what the war had already accomplished. Both Germany and Russia lost considerable territory in eastern Europe; the Austro-Hungarian Empire disappeared altogether. New nation-states emerged from the remnants of

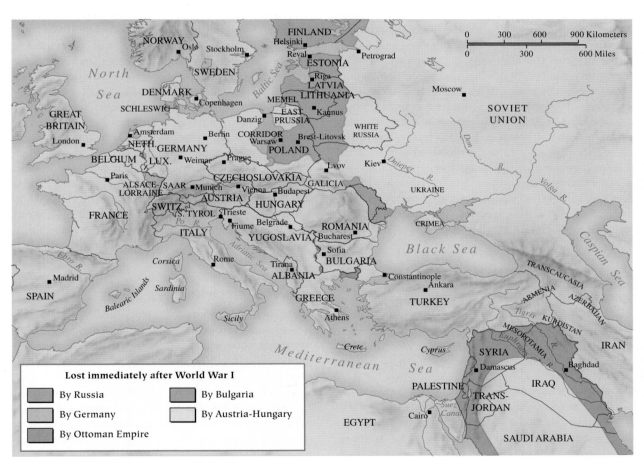

MAP 4.3 Territorial Changes in Europe and the Middle East After World War I. The victorious Allies met in Paris to determine the shape and nature of postwar Europe. At the urging of U.S. President Woodrow Wilson, many nationalist aspirations of former imperial subjects were realized with the creation of several new countries from the prewar territory of Austria-Hungary, Germany, Russia, and the Ottoman Empire.

Q *What new countries emerged in Europe and the Middle East?*

these three empires: Finland, Latvia, Estonia, Lithuania, Poland, Czechoslovakia, Austria, and Hungary. Territorial rearrangements were also made in the Balkans. Romania acquired additional lands from Russia, Hungary, and Bulgaria. Serbia formed the nucleus of a new south Slav state, called Yugoslavia, which combined Serbs, Croats, and Slovenes. The Ottoman Empire was also broken up, remaking the map of the Middle East (see Chapter 5).

Although the Paris Peace Conference was supposedly guided by the principle of self-determination, the mixtures of peoples in eastern Europe made it impossible to draw boundaries along neat ethnic lines. Compromises had to be made, sometimes to satisfy the national interest of the victors. France, for example, had lost Russia as its major ally on Germany's eastern border and wanted to strengthen Poland, Czechoslovakia, Yugoslavia, and Romania as much as possible so that those states could serve as barriers against Germany and Communist Russia. As a result of such compromises, virtually every eastern European state was left with national minorities that could lead to future conflicts: Germans in Poland; Hungarians, Poles, and Germans in Czechoslovakia; and the combination of Serbs, Croats, Slovenes, Macedonians, and Albanians in Yugoslavia all became sources of later conflict. Moreover, the new map of eastern Europe was based on the temporary collapse of power in both Germany and Russia. As neither country accepted the new eastern frontiers, it seemed only a matter of time before both would seek to make changes. In retrospect, the fear expressed by U.S. Secretary of State Robert Lansing that the principle of self-determination aroused hopes that "can never be realized" seems all too justified.

4-4 REVOLUTION IN RUSSIA

 Focus Question: What were the causes of the Russian Revolution of 1917 and why do you believe the Bolsheviks were able to seize and retain power?

One of the more important consequences of the Great War was the impact that it had on Imperial Russia. In the summer of 1914, Tsar Nicholas II had almost appeared to welcome the prospect of a European war. Such a conflict, he hoped, would unite his subjects at a time when his empire was passing through a period of rapid social change and political unrest. The imperial government had survived the popular demonstrations that erupted during the Russo-Japanese War of 1904–1905, although the tsar had been forced to grant a series of reforms in a desperate effort to forestall the collapse of the traditional system (see Chapter 1).

As it turned out, the onset of war served not to revive the Russian monarchy, but rather—as is so often the case with decrepit empires undergoing dramatic change—to undermine its already fragile foundations. World War I halted the trajectory of Russia's economic growth and set the stage for the final collapse of the old order. After stirring victories in the early stages of the war, news from the battlefield turned increasingly grim as poorly armed Russian soldiers were slaughtered by the modern armies of the German emperor. Between 1914 and 1916, 2 million Russian soldiers were killed, and another 4 to 6 million were wounded or captured. The conscription of peasants from the countryside caused food prices to rise and led to periodic bread shortages in the major cities. Workers grew increasingly restive at the wartime schedule of long hours with low pay and joined army deserters in angry marches through the capital of Saint Petersburg (now for patriotic reasons renamed Petrograd).

It was a classic scenario for revolution—discontent in the big cities fueled by mutinous troops streaming home from the battlefield and a rising level of lawlessness in rural areas as angry peasants seized land and burned the manor houses of the wealthy. Even the urban middle class, always a bellwether on the political scene, grew impatient with the economic crisis and the bad news from the front and began to question the competence of the tsar and his advisers. In March 1917 (late February according to the old-style Julian calendar still in use in Russia), government troops fired at demonstrators in the streets of the capital and killed several. An angry mob marched to the Duma (the ineffectual legislative body established after the abortive revolution in 1905), where restive delegates demanded the resignation of the tsar's cabinet.

4-4a The March Uprising

Nicholas II, whose character combined the fatal qualities of stupidity and stubbornness, had never wanted to share the supreme power he had inherited. After a brief period of hesitation, he abdicated, leaving a vacuum that was quickly seized by leading elements in the Duma, who formed a provisional government to steer Russia through the crisis. On the left, reformist and radical political parties—including the Social Revolutionaries (the legal successors of the outlawed terrorist organization **Narodnaya Volya**) and the Russian Social Democratic Labor Party (RSDLP), the only orthodox Marxist party active in Russia—cooperated in creating a shadow government called the Saint Petersburg Soviet. It supported the provisional government in pursuing the war but attempted to compel it to grant economic and social reforms that would benefit the masses.

The March 1917 uprising had brought about the collapse of the monarchy but offered little promise of solving the deeper problems that had led Russia to the brink of civil war. As the crisis continued, radical members of the RSDLP began to hope that a social revolution was at hand.

Marxism had first appeared in Russia in the 1880s. Early Marxists, aware of the primitive conditions in their country, asked Karl Marx himself for advice. The Russian proletariat was oppressed—indeed, brutalized—but small in numbers and unsophisticated. Could agrarian Russia make the transition to socialism without an intervening stage of capitalism? Marx, who always showed more tactical flexibility than the rigid determinism of his system suggested, replied that Russia might be able to avoid the capitalist stage by building on the communal traditions of the Russian village, known as the *mir*.

But as Russian Marxism evolved, its leaders turned more toward Marxist orthodoxy. Founding member George Plekhanov saw signs in the early stages of its industrial revolution that Russia would follow the classic pattern. In 1898, the RSDLP held its first congress.

Lenin and the Bolsheviks During the last decade of the nineteenth century, a new force entered the Russian Marxist movement in the figure of Vladimir Ulyanov, later to be known as Lenin (1870–1924). Initially radicalized by the execution of his older brother for terrorism in 1886, he became a revolutionary and a member of Plekhanov's RSDLP. Like Plekhanov, Lenin believed in the revolution, but he was a man in a hurry. Whereas Plekhanov sought to prepare patiently for revolution by education and mass work, Lenin wanted to build up the party rapidly as a vanguard instrument to galvanize the masses and spur the workers to revolt. In a pamphlet titled *What Is to Be Done?* he proposed the transformation of the RSDLP into a compact and highly disciplined group of professional revolutionaries that would not merely ride the crest of the revolutionary wave but would unleash the storm clouds of revolt.

At the Second National Congress of the RSDLP, held in 1903 in Brussels and London, Lenin's ideas were supported by a majority of the delegates (thus, the term **Bolsheviks**, or "majorityites," for his followers). His victory was short-lived, however, and for the next decade, Lenin was a brooding figure living in exile on the fringe of the Russian revolutionary movement, which was now dominated by the **Mensheviks** ("minorityites"), who opposed Lenin's single-minded pursuit of violent revolution. Scoffing at his more cautious rivals, Lenin declared that revolution was "a tough business" and could not be waged "wearing white gloves and with clean hands."[6]

From his residence in exile in Switzerland, Lenin heard the news of the collapse of the tsarist monarchy and decided to return to Russia. The German government secretly provided him and his followers with a sealed railroad car to travel through Germany, undoubtedly in the hope that his presence would promote instability in Russia. On his arrival in Petrograd in April 1917, Lenin laid out a program for the RSDLP: all power to the **soviets** (locally elected government councils), an end to the war, and the distribution of land to poor peasants. But Lenin's April Theses (see Historical Voices, "All Power to the Soviets," p. 92) were too radical even for his fellow Bolsheviks, who continued to cooperate with the provisional government while attempting to push it to the left. His onetime mentor Plekhanov remarked that Lenin's plans for a general uprising were "delirious."

4-4b The Bolshevik Revolution

During the summer, the crisis worsened, and in July, riots by workers and soldiers in the capital led the provisional government to outlaw the Bolsheviks and call for Lenin's arrest. The "July Days," raising the threat of disorder and class war, aroused the fears of conservatives and split the fragile political consensus within the provisional government. In September, General Lavr Kornilov, commander in chief of Russian imperial forces, launched a coup d'état to seize power from Alexander Kerensky, a lawyer who was now the dominant figure in the provisional government. The revolt was put down with the help of so-called Red Guard units, formed by the Bolsheviks within army regiments in the capital area (these troops would later be regarded as the first units of the Red Army), but Lenin now sensed the weakness of the provisional government and persuaded his colleagues to prepare for revolt. On the night of November 7 (October 25, old style), forces under the command of Lenin's lieutenant, Leon Trotsky (1879–1940), seized key installations in the capital area, while other units loyal to the Bolsheviks, including mutinous sailors from the battleship *Aurora* stationed nearby on the Neva River, stormed the Winter Palace, where supporters of the provisional government were quickly overwhelmed. Alexander Kerensky was forced to flee from Russia in disguise.

The following morning, at a national congress of delegates from soviet organizations throughout the country, the Bolsheviks declared a new socialist order. Moderate elements from the Menshevik faction and the Social Revolutionary Party protested the illegality of the Bolshevik action and left the conference hall in anger. They were derided by Trotsky, who proclaimed that they were relegated "to the dustbin of history."

All Power to the Soviets!

> **Q** *What were the key provisions of Lenin's April Theses? To what degree were they carried out?*

Politics & Government **ON HIS RETURN TO PETROGRAD** in April 1917, the revolutionary Marxist Vladimir Lenin issued a series of proposals designed to overthrow the provisional government and bring his Bolshevik Party to power in Russia. At the time his April Theses were delivered, his ideas appeared to be too radical, even for his closest followers. But the Bolsheviks' simple slogan of "Peace, Land, and Bread" soon began to gain traction on the streets of the capital. By the end of the year, Lenin's compelling vision had been realized, and the world would never be the same again.

Lenin's April Theses, 1917

1. The specific feature of the present situation in Russia is that the country is *passing* from the first stage of the revolution—which, owing to the insufficient class-consciousness and organization of the proletariat, placed power in the hands of the bourgeoisie—to its *second* stage, which must place power in the hands of the proletariat and the poorest sections of the peasants. . . .

   This peculiar situation demands of us an ability to adapt ourselves to the *special* conditions of Party work among unprecedentedly large masses of proletarians who have just awakened to political life. . . .

2. No support for the Provisional Government: the utter falsity of all the promises should be made clear, particularly of those relating to the renunciation of annexations. Exposure in place of the impermissible, illusion-breeding "demand" that *this* government of capitalists should *cease* to be an imperialist government.

The masses must be made to see that the Soviets of Workers' Deputies are the *only possible* form of revolutionary government, and that therefore our task is, as long as *this* government yields to the influence of the bourgeoisie, to present a patient, systematic and persistent explanation of the errors of their tactics, an explanation especially adapted to the practical needs of the masses.

As long as we are in the minority we carry on the work of criticizing and exposing errors and at the same time we preach the necessity of transferring the entire state power to the Soviets of Workers' Deputies, so that the people may overcome their mistakes by experience.

Nationalization of *all* lands in the country, the land to be disposed of by the local Soviets of Agricultural Laborers' and Peasants' Deputies. The organization of separate Soviets of Deputies of Poor Peasants. The setting up of a model farm on each of the large estates (ranging in size from 100 to 300 dessiatines [about 270 to 810 acres], according to local and other conditions, and to the decisions of the local bodies) under the control of the Soviets of Agricultural Laborers' Deputies and for the public account.

Source: V. I. Lenin, *Collected Works*, 4th ed. (Moscow: Progress, 1964), Vol. XXIV, pp. 21–24.

With the Bolshevik Revolution of November 1917, Lenin was now in command (see Image 4.3). His power was tenuous and extended only from the capital to a few of the larger cities, such as Moscow and Kiev, where radicals had waged their own insurrections. There were, in fact, few Bolsheviks in rural areas, where most peasants supported the moderate leftist Social Revolutionaries. On the fringes of the Russian Empire, restive minorities prepared to take advantage of the anarchy to seize their own independence, while supporters of the monarchy began raising armies to destroy the "Red menace" in Petrograd. Lenin was in power, but for how long?

HISTORIANS DEBATE **The Bolshevik Revolution in Retrospect**
The Bolshevik Revolution of 1917 has been the subject of vigorous debate by scholars and students of world affairs. Could it have been avoided if the provisional government had provided more effective leadership, or was it inevitable? Did the November revolution stifle Russia's halting progress toward a Western-style capitalist democracy, or was the Bolshevik victory preordained by the autocratic conditions and lack of democratic traditions in Imperial Russia? Finally, would the Bolsheviks have succeeded in seizing power without Lenin's insistence on carrying it out? Such questions have

IMAGE 4.3 Lenin Addresses a Crowd. Vladimir Lenin was the driving force behind the success of the Bolsheviks in seizing power in Russia and creating the Union of Soviet Socialist Republics. Here Lenin is seen addressing a rally in Moscow in 1917.

Q *Do you find the argument convincing that without the overwhelming strength of Lenin's determination, the Bolshevik Revolution might not have succeeded?*

no simple answers, but some hypotheses are possible. The weakness of the moderate government created by the March revolution was probably predictable, given the political inexperience of the urban middle class, the horrendous conditions in Russia at the time, and the deep divisions within the ruling coalition over issues of peace and war. At the same time, it seems highly unlikely that the Bolsheviks would have possessed the self-confidence to act without the presence of their leader, Vladimir Lenin, who almost single-handedly employed his strength of will to urge his cautious colleagues to make their bid for power. The November revolution in Russia is often cited as a cardinal example of the role that a single individual can sometimes have on the course of history. Without Lenin, it would probably have been left to the army to intervene in an effort to maintain law and order, as would happen, with uncertain consequences, so often elsewhere during the turbulent twentieth century.

In any event, the Bolshevik Revolution was a momentous development for Russia and for the entire world. Not only did it present Western capitalist societies with a

brazen new challenge to their global supremacy, but it also demonstrated that Lenin's concept of revolution, carried through at the will of a determined minority of revolutionary activists "in the interests of the masses," could succeed in a society going through the difficult early stages of the Industrial Revolution. It was a repudiation of orthodox "late Marxism" and a return to Marx's pre-1848 vision of a multiclass revolt leading rapidly from a capitalist to a proletarian takeover (see Chapter 1). It was, in short, a lesson that would not be ignored by radical intellectuals throughout the world, as we shall see in the chapter to follow.

4-4c The Civil War

The Bolshevik seizure of power in Petrograd (soon to be renamed Leningrad after Lenin's death in 1924) was only the first, and not necessarily the most difficult, stage in the Russian Revolution. Although the Bolshevik slogan of "Peace, Land, and Bread" had considerable appeal among workers, petty merchants, and soldiers in the vicinity of the capital and other major cities, the party—only 50,000 strong in November—had little representation in the rural areas, where the majority of the peasants supported the moderate leftist Social Revolutionary Party. On the fringes of the Russian Empire, ethnic minority groups took advantage of the confusion in Petrograd to launch movements to restore their own independence or achieve a position of autonomy within the Russian state. In the meantime, supporters of the deposed Romanov dynasty and other political opponents of the Bolsheviks, known as White Russians, attempted to mobilize support to drive the Bolsheviks out of the capital and reverse the verdict of "Red October." And beyond all that, the war with Germany continued.

Lenin was aware of these problems and hoped that a wave of socialist revolutions in the economically advanced countries of central and western Europe would bring the world war to an end and usher in a new age of peace, socialism, and growing economic prosperity. In the meantime, his first priority was to consolidate the rule of the working class and its party vanguard (now to be renamed the Communist Party) in Russia. The first step was to set up a new order in Petrograd to replace the provisional government that had been created after the March Uprising. For lack of a better alternative, outlying areas were simply informed of the change in government—a "revolution by telegraph," as Leon Trotsky termed it. Then Lenin moved to create new organs of proletarian power, setting up the Council of People's Commissars (the word "commissar," Lenin remarked "smells of revolution") to serve as a provisional government. Lenin was unwilling to share power with moderate leftists who had resisted the Bolshevik coup in November, and he created security forces (popularly called the Cheka, or "extraordinary commission"), which imprisoned and brutally executed opponents of the new regime. In January 1918, the Constituent Assembly, which had been elected on the basis of plans established by the previous government, convened in Petrograd. Composed primarily of delegates from the Social Revolutionary Party and other parties opposed to the Bolsheviks, it showed itself critical of the new regime and was immediately abolished.

Lenin was determined to prevent the Romanov family from becoming a rallying cry for opponents of the new Bolshevik regime. In the spring of 1918, the former tsar and his family were placed under guard in Ekaterinburg, a small mining town in the Ural Mountains. On the night of July 16, the entire family was murdered on Lenin's order. The bodies were dropped into a nearby mine shaft. For decades, rumors persisted that one of Nicholas II's daughters, Anastasia, had survived execution.

In foreign affairs, Lenin's first major decision was to seek peace with Germany in order to permit the new government to focus its efforts on the growing threat posed by White Russian forces within the country. In March 1918, a peace settlement with Germany was reached at Brest-Litovsk, although at enormous cost. Soviet Russia lost nearly one-fourth of the territory and one-third of the population of the prewar Russian Empire. In retrospect, however, Lenin's controversial decision to accept a punitive peace may have been a stroke of genius, for it gained time for the regime to build up its internal strength and defeat its many adversaries still operating in the territories that once composed the empire of the tsars.

Indeed, the odds for a Bolshevik success must have seemed dim in the immediate aftermath of the seizure of power. Lenin himself initially predicted that defeat was likely in the absence of successful revolutionary outbreaks elsewhere in Europe. Support for the Bolsheviks in Russia was limited, and the regime antagonized farmers by the harsh measures it used to obtain provisions for its troops. Although Leon Trotsky showed traces of genius in organizing the Red Army, he was forced to station trusted lieutenants as "political commissars" in army units to guarantee the loyalty of his commanders.

In the end, Lenin's gamble that the Russian people were desperate enough to embrace radical change paid off. The White Russian forces were larger than those of the Red Army, and they were supported by armed contingents sent by Great Britain, France, and the United States to assist in the extinction of the "Red menace." Nevertheless, they were also rent by factionalism and hindered by a tendency to fight "red terror" with "white terror" and to return conquered land to the original landowners, thereby driving many peasants to support the Soviet regime. By 1920, the civil war was over, and Soviet power was secure.

4-5 AN UNCERTAIN PEACE

 Focus Question: Why did the Versailles Peace Conference fail to resolve the problems left over by the war and introduce a new era of democracy and economic progress in Europe?

In the years following the end of World War I, many people hoped that the world was about to enter a new era of international peace, economic growth, and political democracy. In all of these areas, the optimistic hopes of the 1920s failed to be realized.

4-5a The Search for Security

The peace settlement at the end of World War I had tried to fulfill the nineteenth-century dream of nationalism by creating new boundaries and new states out of the now-defunct empires in central and eastern Europe. From the outset, however, the settlement had left many unhappy. Conflicts over disputed border regions between Germany and Poland, Poland and Lithuania, Poland and Czechoslovakia, Austria and Hungary, and Italy and Yugoslavia poisoned mutual relations in eastern Europe for years. Many Germans viewed the peace of Versailles as a dictated peace and vowed to seek its revision.

To its supporters, the League of Nations was the place to resolve such problems. The League, however, proved ineffectual in maintaining the peace. One of the reasons for its weakness was the lack of adequate provisions for enforcement. Because many nations were reluctant to compromise their own national security, the League could use only economic sanctions to halt aggression. The French attempt to strengthen the League's effectiveness as an instrument of collective security by creating a peace-keeping force was rejected by nations that feared giving up any of their sovereignty to a larger international body.

Another reason that the League failed to achieve its promise was that the United States, where many were disillusioned by the disputes at Versailles, failed to join the new organization. The U.S. Senate also rejected President Wilson's proposal for a defensive alliance with Great Britain and France. Two other nations important to the future of the world—Germany and Soviet Russia—were not even members of the League.

France Goes it Alone The weakness of the League of Nations and the failure of both the United States and Great Britain to honor their promise of a defensive military alliance with France led the latter to insist on a strict enforcement of the Treaty of Versailles. This tough policy toward Germany began with the issue of reparations—the payments that the Germans were supposed to make to compensate for the "damage done to the civilian population of the Allied and Associated Powers and to their property," as the treaty asserted. In April 1921, the Allied Reparations Commission settled on a sum of 132 billion marks ($33 billion) for German reparations, payable in annual installments of 2.5 billion (gold) marks. Allied threats to occupy the Ruhr valley, Germany's chief industrial and mining center, induced the new German republic to accept the reparations settlement and to make its first payment in 1921. By the following year, however, facing rising inflation, domestic turmoil, and lack of revenues because of low tax rates, the German government announced that it was unable to pay more. Outraged by what they considered to be Germany's violation of one aspect of the peace settlement, the French government sent troops to occupy the Ruhr valley. If the Germans would not pay reparations, the French would collect reparations in kind by operating and using the Ruhr mines and factories.

French occupation of the Ruhr seriously undermined the fragile German economy. The German government adopted a policy of passive resistance to French occupation that was largely financed by printing more paper money, thus intensifying the inflationary pressures that had already begun at the end of the war. The German mark became worthless (see Image 4.4). Economic disaster fueled political upheavals as communists staged uprisings in October and nationalist elements under the leadership of an as yet little-known army veteran by the name of Adolf Hitler attempted to seize power in Munich in 1923. The following year, a new conference of experts was convened to reassess the reparations problem.

Solving the Reparations Problem

The formation of liberal-socialist governments in both Great Britain and France opened the door to a more conciliatory approach to Germany and the reparations problem. At the same time, a new German government led by Gustav Stresemann (1878–1929) ended the policy of passive resistance and committed Germany to carry out the provisions of the Versailles Treaty while seeking a new settlement of the reparations question.

In August 1924, an international commission produced a new plan for reparations. Named the Dawes Plan after the American banker who chaired the commission, it reduced reparations and stabilized Germany's payments on the basis of its ability to pay. The Dawes Plan also granted an initial $200 million loan for Germany's recovery, which opened the door to heavy American investments in Europe that helped create a new era of European prosperity between 1924 and 1929.

William J. Duiker

IMAGE 4.4 The Cruel Face of Inflation. To pay for reparations, the postwar German government was forced to print paper currency to finance government expenditures. The German mark, once valued at approximately four to the U.S. dollar, rapidly declined in value. By the fall of 1923, German banknotes had become virtually worthless, and sardonic observers remarked that they were only useful as wall paper. Although the inflationary spiral was eventually stemmed, the damage had been done, as millions of Germans became convinced that their hapless government was unable to prevent erstwhile enemies from seeking to cripple their economy. The banknotes shown here, issued—from left to right—in 1908, 1922, and late 1923 graphically illustrate the drastic decline in the value of the German currency.

Q *Why does inflation often pose a severe threat to the well-being of a country?*

The Spirit of Locarno

A new approach to European diplomacy accompanied the new economic stability. A spirit of international cooperation was fostered by the foreign ministers of Germany and France, Gustav Stresemann and Aristide Briand (1862–1932), who concluded the Treaty of Locarno in 1925. This treaty guaranteed Germany's new western borders with France and Belgium. Although Germany's new eastern borders with Poland were conspicuously absent from the agreement, the Locarno pact was viewed by many as the beginning of a new era of European peace. On the day after the pact was concluded, the headline in the *New York Times* read "France and Germany Ban War Forever," and the *London Times* declared "Peace at Last."[7]

Germany's entry into the League of Nations in March 1926 soon reinforced the atmosphere of conciliation engendered at Locarno. Two years later, similar attitudes prevailed in the Kellogg-Briand Pact, drafted by U.S. Secretary of State Frank B. Kellogg and French Foreign Minister Briand. Sixty-three nations signed this accord, in which they pledged "to renounce war as an instrument of national policy." Nothing was said, however, about what would be done if anyone violated the treaty.

The spirit of Locarno was based on little real substance. Germany lacked the military power to alter its western borders even if it wanted to. Pious promises to renounce war without mechanisms to enforce them were virtually worthless. And the issue of disarmament soon proved that paper promises could not bring nations to cut back on their weapons. The League of Nations Covenant had recommended the "reduction of national armaments to the lowest point consistent with national safety." Numerous disarmament conferences, however, failed to achieve anything substantial as states proved unwilling to trust their security to anyone but their own military forces. By the time the World Disarmament Conference finally met in Geneva in 1932, the issue was already dead.

4-5b A Return to Normalcy?

According to Woodrow Wilson, World War I had been fought to make the world "safe for democracy." During the decade that followed the signing of the Treaty of Versailles, there seemed to be some justification for his optimism. Several major European states, as well as a number of the new countries established in eastern Europe, had functioning political democracies. A number of nations, including the United States, broadened the right to vote to include women, and the individual liberties of citizens were strengthened in other ways as well. Even Germany appeared to share in the shift toward political pluralism, as a new republic based in the city of Weimar took steps to establish democratic political institutions under the able leadership of moderate statesmen like Friedrich Ebert (1871–1925) and Gustav Stresemann.

But the "return to normalcy," as Woodrow Wilson's successor, President Warren Harding (1865–1923), called it, was based on fragile economic foundations, as recovery from the four years of bitter conflict was slow and halting. France was only partially successful in reconstructing areas in the northern parts of the country that had been devastated by the Great War. Great Britain went through its own period of painful adjustment. The country had lost many of its markets for industrial products, especially to the United States and Japan. The postwar decline of such staple industries as coal, steel, and textiles led to a rise in unemployment, which reached the 2 million mark by 1922. An economic recovery began in the next few years but proved to be superficial, and unemployment remained at the 10 percent level throughout the decade. Coal miners were especially affected by the decline of the antiquated and inefficient British coal mines, which suffered from a global glut of coal.

In the immediate postwar era, the United States alone continued its gradual emergence as an industrial powerhouse—marked by the rapid development of the motor car industry under the leadership of Henry Ford. An ambitious entrepreneur with innovative ideas, Ford had revolutionized the industry by adopting the continuous assembly line in the factories devoted to the manufacture of his automobiles. With the assembly line operated by a conveyer belt, a new "Model T" car could be assembled in about 90 minutes, as compared with over twelve hours in previous years. By the late 1920s, his River Rouge manufacturing plant was the biggest in the United States and employed more than 100,000 workers, many of whom became prosperous enough to purchase his new automobiles. Some of them were African Americans, who migrated from rural areas in the South to seek employment in the growing factories in the North and the Midwest. With its capacity to produce multiple goods rapidly and at reduced expense, the new factory showed the promise of ending the "boom and bust" cycle of the modern capitalist economy.

There were some social gains as well. A Constitutional amendment to grant women's suffrage, first proposed by the social activist Susan B. Anthony (1820–1906) in 1878, was finally ratified as Congress as the 19th Amendment on August 18, 1920. President Woodrow Wilson, once a skeptic, supported the measure on the grounds that American women, who had actively supported the war effort, should be allowed to vote. Although efforts by activists to introduce other measures to broaden women's rights had mixed results, the more socially permissive culture that thrived in the free-wheeling 1920s helped to liberate American women from the social restrictions that had prevailed in the prewar years. Dress codes were relaxed, and women for the first time began to smoke cigarettes, although at a lesser rate than their male counterparts.

African Americans saw their economic horizons expanded as well, with the opening up of job opportunities in the new factories in the North and the Midwest, although they still faced restrictions on their civil rights, especially in the South, where racial prejudice was still deeply imbedded within the white population. "Whites only" policies were freely proclaimed in hotels, restaurants, and other social establishments. The Ku Klux Klan (KKK), a white supremacist organization that had been established by disgruntled Confederate soldiers shortly after the civil war, continued to operate freely in many southern states, intimidating and frequently terrorizing their black neighbors. Lynchings of African Americans, often accused falsely of crimes, still took place, although perhaps at a lower rate than had been the case during the nineteenth century.

In the meantime, the benefits of U.S. economic expansion in the 1920s were uneven. Rural areas generally did not share in the surface prosperity that had begun to appear in the larger industrialized cities. At the same time, labor organizations fought with only limited success to improve the working conditions and wages of their constituents in the face of legal hurdles and stiff resistance by corporate interests. By the end of the decade, income disparity in the United States was growing, and the initial promise of the "roaring twenties" (as the era had been dubbed by pundits) had begun to fade.

None of the larger Western democracies faced greater challenges than Germany, where the Weimar Republic, burdened by heavy war reparations, had encountered serious economic difficulties from the start. The runaway inflation of 1922 and 1923 mentioned earlier had grave social effects, as widows, orphans, the elderly, army officers, civil servants, and others who lived on fixed incomes all watched their monthly stipends become worthless or their lifetime savings disappear. Ominously, these continuing economic difficulties inexorably pushed the middle class, which still lacked experience in using its political influence to achieve its objectives, toward the young German Communist Party or to rightist parties that were equally hostile to the republic.

4-5c The Great Depression

During the first few years after the end of World War I, there had been some tantalizing signs that Europe was on the path of recovery from the consequences of that devastating conflict. But that illusion was burst in 1929, with the onset of the Great Depression.

Causes Two factors played a major role in the coming of the Great Depression: a downturn in European economies and an international financial crisis created by the collapse of the American stock market in 1929. Already in the mid-1920s, global prices for agricultural goods were beginning to decline rapidly as a result of the overproduction of basic commodities, such as wheat, elsewhere in the world. In 1925, states in central and eastern Europe began to impose tariffs to close their markets to other countries' goods. Meanwhile, an increase in the use of oil and hydroelectricity led to a slump in the coal industry.

Much of the European prosperity in the mid-1920s was built on U.S. bank loans to Germany, but in 1928 and 1929, American investors began to pull money out of Germany to invest in the booming New York stock market. When that market crashed in October 1929, panicky American investors withdrew even more of their funds from Germany and other European markets. The withdrawal of funds seriously weakened the banks of Germany and other central European states. The Credit-Anstalt, Vienna's most prestigious bank, collapsed on May 31, 1931. By that time, trade was slowing down, industrialists were cutting back production, and unemployment was increasing as the ripple effects of international bank failures had a devastating impact on domestic economies.

Repercussions Economic downturns were by no means a new phenomenon in the rise of Western capitalism, but the Great Depression was exceptionally severe and had immediate repercussions. In the United States, great fortunes were lost overnight, and, with consumer demand dropping, industrial production fell dramatically, throwing millions out of work. President Herbert Hoover (1874–1964) responded in the traditional way, signing legislation that imposed high tariffs on imported goods. In Great Britain, when the ruling Labour Party failed to resolve the crisis, it was replaced by a Conservative government which followed the U.S. lead by using the traditional policies of balanced budgets and protective tariffs. France—with a protected market based on small enterprises—was initially less affected by the crisis, but nevertheless began to feel the impact in 1931. For the next several years, six different cabinets were formed as the country faced political chaos.

But the European nation that suffered the most damage from the Depression was probably Germany. Unemployment increased to more than 4 million by the end of 1930. For many Germans, who had already suffered through difficult times in the early 1920s, the democratic experiment represented by the Weimar Republic had appeared to become an outright failure. Some reacted by turning to the ideas of Karl Marx, who had long predicted that capitalism would destroy itself through overproduction. Although communism took on a new popularity, the real beneficiary of the Great Depression in Germany was Adolf Hitler, whose National Socialist German Workers' (Nazi) Party came to power in 1933 (see Chapter 6).

The first reaction of all major Western governments faced with the crisis had been to adopt the traditional policy of tight money, balanced budgets, and a "beggar thy neighbor" policy of high tariffs on foreign goods. But as the Great Depression worsened, the Cambridge University economist John Maynard Keynes (1883–1946) took issue with the traditional view that depressions should be left to work themselves out through the self-regulatory mechanisms of a free economy. Rather, he argued that unemployment stemmed not from overproduction but from a decline in consumer demand, which could most effectively be increased by public works, financed if necessary through **deficit spending** to stimulate production.

IMAGE 4.5 **Brother, Can You Spare a Job?** The Great Depression devastated the world economy and led to a dramatic rise in unemployment throughout the industrialized world. In the United States, manufacturing centers like Chicago, Cleveland, and Detroit were especially hard hit as consumer demand for appliances and automobiles plummeted throughout the decade of the 1930s. In this poignant photograph taken in 1930, an unemployed worker in Detroit pleads for a job at the beginning of the depression. Unfortunately, full recovery would not come until many years later.

Q *What was Roosevelt's strategy to put Americans back to work. Was it successful?*

Such policies, he insisted, could be accomplished only by government intervention in the economy, a measure that most political leaders had long been unwilling to undertake.

Franklin Roosevelt and the New Deal The full force of the Great Depression struck the United States by 1932. In that year, industrial production fell to 50 percent of what it had been in 1929. By 1933, there were 15 million workers unemployed (see Image 4.5). Under these circumstances, Democrat Franklin Delano Roosevelt (1882–1945) was able to win a landslide victory in the presidential election of 1932. A pragmatist who was willing to adopt unorthodox

measures to deal with a crisis situation, FDR (as he was popularly known) rejected a proposal to invoke emergency executive powers to deal with the challenge and pursued a Keynesian policy of active government intervention in the economy that came to be known as the **New Deal**.

Initially, the New Deal attempted to restore prosperity by creating the National Recovery Administration (NRA), which required government, labor, and industrial leaders to work out regulations for each industry. Declared unconstitutional by the Supreme Court in 1935, the NRA was soon superseded by other efforts collectively known as the Second New Deal. Its programs included the Works Progress Administration (WPA), established in 1935, which employed between 2 and 3 million people building bridges, roads, post offices, airports, and other public works. The Roosevelt administration was also responsible for new social legislation that launched the American welfare state. In 1935, the Social Security Act created a system of old-age pensions and unemployment insurance. At the same time, the National Labor Relations Act of 1935 encouraged the rapid growth of labor unions.

The New Deal undoubtedly provided some social reform measures and may even have averted social revolution in the United States by stimulating economic growth through government intervention. But the New Deal did not immediately solve the unemployment problems created by the Great Depression. In May 1937, during what was considered a period of recovery, American unemployment still stood at 7 million; a recession the following year, triggered in part by a decline in public spending, increased that number to 11 million. Discouraged by the slow recovery from the economic downturn, many Americans began to lose confidence in the capitalist system and turned to fascist or communist ideas emanating from Europe. Nativist organizations like the KKK revived in popularity, targeting foreigners, African Americans, Roman Catholics, and Jews as responsible for the ills afflicting American society. Only World War II and the subsequent growth of armaments industries brought American workers back to full employment and eased the crisis.

4-5d Building Socialism in Soviet Russia

In Russia, Bolshevik leaders had their own plans for the future. With their victory over the White Russians in 1920, Lenin and his colleagues could turn for the first time to the challenging task of building the first socialist society in a world dominated by their capitalist enemies. A new Union of Socialist Soviet Republics (U.S.S.R.) was created in 1924 and a constitution was adopted that granted the multiple minority groups that had lived under the old Russian Empire broad legal rights to preserve their own unique cultures. In fact, however, Lenin and his colleagues were determined to remake all Soviet citizens into the vision of the pure "Communist Man," who would live by the slogan, "from each according to his ability, to each according to his need" in helping to build a classless society.

In his writings, Karl Marx had said little about the nature of the final communist utopia or how to get there. He had spoken briefly of a transitional phase, variously known as "raw communism" or "socialism," that would precede the final stage of communism. During this phase, the Communist Party would establish a "dictatorship of the proletariat" to rid society of the capitalist oppressors, set up the institutions of the new order, and indoctrinate the population in the communist ethic. In recognition of the fact that traces of "bourgeois thinking" would remain among the population, profit incentives would be used to encourage productivity (in Marxist terminology, payment would be on the basis of "work" rather than solely on "need"), but major industries would be nationalized and private landholdings eliminated. After seizing power in 1917, however, the Bolsheviks were too preoccupied with survival to give much attention to the future nature of Soviet society. **War communism**—involving the government seizure of major industries, utilities, and sources of raw materials and the requisition of grain from private farmers—was, by Lenin's own admission, just a makeshift policy to permit the regime to mobilize resources for the civil war.

The New Economic Policy   In 1920, it was time to adopt a more coherent approach. The realities were sobering. Lenin's conviction that social revolutions would break out all over Europe at the end of the Great War had proven invalid, as widespread social unrest in many countries gradually gave way to the emergence of stable governments and functioning economies. For the time being, he realized, the new Russia would have to survive on its own.

Soviet Russia, however, was not an advanced capitalist society in the Marxist image, blessed with modern technology and an impoverished but politically aware underclass imbued with the desire to advance to socialism. It was poor and primarily agrarian, and its small but growing industrial sector had been ravaged by years of war. Under the circumstances, Lenin called for caution. He won his party's approval for a moderate program of social and economic development known as the **New Economic Policy**, or NEP. The program was based on a combination of capitalist and socialist techniques designed to increase production through the use of profit incentives while at the same time promoting the concept of socialist ownership and maintaining firm party control over the political system and the overall direction of the economy. The "commanding heights" of the Soviet economy (heavy industry, banking, utilities, and foreign trade) remained in the hands of the state, while private industry and commerce were allowed to operate at the lower levels. The forced requisition of grain, which had caused serious unrest among the peasantry, was replaced by a tax, and land remained firmly in private hands. The theoretical justification for the program was that Soviet Russia now needed to go through its own "capitalist stage" (albeit under the control of the party) before beginning the difficult transition to socialism.

As an economic strategy, the NEP succeeded brilliantly. During the early and mid-1920s, the Soviet economy recovered rapidly from the ravages of war and civil war. A more lax hand over the affairs of state allowed a modest degree of free expression of opinion within the ranks of the party and in Soviet society at large. Under the surface, however, trouble loomed. Lenin had been increasingly disabled by a bullet lodged in his neck from an attempted assassination, and he began to lose his grip over a fractious party. Even before his death in 1924, potential successors had begun to scuffle for precedence in the struggle to assume his position as party leader, the most influential position in the state. The main candidates were Leon Trotsky and a rising young figure from the state of Georgia, Joseph Djugashvili, better known by his revolutionary name, Stalin (1879–1953). Lenin had misgivings about all the candidates hoping to succeed him and suggested that a collective leadership would best represent the interests of the party and the revolution. After his death in 1924, however, factional struggle among the leading figures in the party intensified. Although in some respects it was a pure power struggle, it did have policy ramifications as party factions argued about the NEP and its impact on the future of the Russian Revolution.

At first, the various factions were relatively evenly balanced, but Stalin proved adept at using his position as general secretary of the party to outmaneuver his rivals. By portraying himself as a centrist opposed to the extreme positions of his "leftist" (too radical in pursuit of revolutionary goals) or "rightist" (too prone to adopt moderate positions contrary to Marxist principles) rivals, he gradually concentrated power in his own hands.

In the meantime, the relatively moderate policies of the NEP continued to operate as the party and the state vocally encouraged the Soviet people, in a very un-Marxist manner, to enrich themselves. Capital investment and technological assistance from Western capitalist countries were actively welcomed. Soviet policy-makers were particularly interested in persuading the U.S. carmaker Henry Ford to build an enormous factory in the USSR to produce tractors. With mechanized farm equipment, they concluded, it would be easier to persuade conservative Russian peasants of the benefits of socialism. An observer at the time might reasonably have concluded that the Marxist vision of a world characterized by class struggle had become a dead letter.

Stalin Takes Over Stalin had previously joined with the moderate members of the party to defend the NEP against Trotsky, whose "left opposition" wanted a more rapid advance toward socialism. Trotsky, who had become one of Stalin's chief critics, was expelled from the party in 1927. Then, in 1928, Stalin reversed course: he now claimed that the NEP had achieved its purpose and called for a rapid advance to socialist forms of ownership. Beginning in 1929, a series of new programs changed the face of Soviet society. Private capitalism in manufacturing and trade was virtually abolished, and state control over the economy was extended. The first of a series of five-year plans was launched to promote rapid "socialist industrialization," and in a massive effort to strengthen the state's hold over the agricultural economy, all private farmers were herded onto **collective farms**.

The bitter campaign to collectivize the countryside aroused the antagonism of many peasants and led to a decline in food production, and in some areas to mass starvation. It also further divided the Communist Party and led to a massive purge of party members at all levels who opposed Stalin's effort to achieve rapid economic growth and the socialization of Russian society. A series of brutal purge trials eliminated thousands of "Old Bolsheviks" (people who had joined the party before the 1917 Revolution) and resulted in the conviction and death of many of Stalin's chief rivals. Trotsky, driven into exile, was dispatched by Stalin's assassin in 1940. Of the delegates who attended the National Congress of the CPSU (Communist Party of the Soviet Union) in 1934, fully 70 percent had been executed by the time of the National Congress in 1939. A key component of Stalin's strategy to build socialism was to extract the maximum amount of grain from the Soviet republic of Ukraine. Blessed with a fertile soil that had historically earned it the label of the "bread basket" of Europe, Ukraine (the name can roughly be translated as "frontier") was populated by Slavic peoples who—although related to their Great Russian neighbors—cherished their cultural uniqueness and had often resisted the harsh reality of Russian rule. To win their allegiance, Soviet planners in Moscow initially encouraged them to develop their own cultural traditions under the rule of Moscow, in accordance with Soviet nationality policy.

With the decision to advance rapidly toward socialism in 1928, however, Stalin reversed course and decided to crush all resistance in Ukraine to Soviet rule or state grain requisitions. "Nationalist" elements among the local party leadership, along with "**kulaks**" (prosperous peasants who resisted grain seizures) were arrested and sometimes executed, while forcible grain requisitions led to a vast food shortage and claimed the lives of an estimated four million Ukrainians. Memories of the **Holodomor** (Famine) of 1932–1933 haunted Ukrainians for decades and provoked many of them to welcome the German invasion of the USSR in 1941 (see Chapter 6).

The Legacy of Stalinism By the late 1930s, as the last of the great purge trials came to an end, the Russian Revolution had been in existence for more than two decades. It had achieved some successes. Stalin's policy of forced industrialization had led to rapid growth in the industrial sector, surpassing in many respects what had been achieved in the capitalist years prior to World War I. Between 1918 and 1937, steel production increased from 4 to 18 million tons per year, and hard coal output went from 36 to 128 million tons. New industrial cities sprang up overnight in the Urals and Siberia. The Russian people in general were probably better clothed, better fed, and better educated than they had ever been before. But the cost in human lives had been enormous. Millions had died by bullet or starvation. Thousands, perhaps millions of others, languished in Stalin's concentration camps. The remainder of the population lived in a society now officially described as socialist, under the watchful eye of a man who had risen almost to the rank of a deity, the "great leader" of the Soviet Union, Joseph Stalin. For millions of Soviet citizens, the wartime slogan of "peace, land, and bread" must have seemed a distant memory.

The impact of Stalin on Soviet society in one decade had been enormous. If Lenin had brought the party to power and nursed it through the difficult years of the civil war, it was Stalin, above all, who had mapped out the path to economic modernization and socialist transformation. To many foreign critics of the regime, the Stalinist terror and the autocratic system were an inevitable consequence of the concept of the vanguard party and the centralized state built by Lenin. Others traced Stalinism back to Marx. It was he, after all, who had formulated the idea of the dictatorship of the proletariat, which now provided ideological justification for the Stalinist autocracy. Still others found the ultimate cause in Russian political culture, which, they claimed, had been characterized by autocracy since the emergence of Russian society from Mongol control in the fifteenth century.

Was Stalinism an inevitable outcome of Marxist-Leninist doctrine and practice? Or, as the last Soviet leader Mikhail Gorbachev later claimed (see Chapter 9), were Stalin's crimes "alien to the nature of socialism" and a departure from the course charted by Lenin before his death? Certainly, Lenin had not envisaged a party dominated by a figure who became even larger than the organization itself and who, in the 1930s, almost destroyed the party. On the other hand, recent evidence shows that Lenin was capable of brutally suppressing perceived enemies of the revolution in a way that is reminiscent in manner, if not in scope, of Stalin's actions. In a 1922 letter to a colleague, he declared that after the NEP had served its purpose, "we shall return to the terror, and to economic terror."[8]

It is also true that the state created by Lenin provided the conditions for a single-minded and ruthless leader like Stalin to rise to absolute power. The great danger that neither Marx nor Lenin had foreseen had come to pass: the party itself, the vanguard organization leading the way into the utopian future, had become corrupted. Lenin had sown the seeds; Stalin reaped the harvest.

4-6 THE SEARCH FOR A NEW REALITY IN THE ARTS

 Focus Question: How did the cultural and intellectual trends of the post-World War I era reflect the political and socioeconomic conditions experienced at the time?

The mass destruction brought by World War I precipitated a general disillusionment with Western civilization on the part of artists and writers throughout Europe. Avant-garde art, which had sought to discover alternative techniques to portray reality, now gained broader acceptance as Europeans began to abandon classical traditions in an attempt to come to grips with the anxieties of the new age.

4-6a New Schools of Artistic Expression

A number of the artistic styles that gained popularity during the 1920s originated during the war among alienated intellectuals, who congregated in cafés to decry the insanity of the age and exchange ideas on how to create a new and better world. Among such groups were the **Dadaists**, artists based in neutral Switzerland who sought to destroy the past with a vengeance, proclaiming their right to complete freedom of expression in art.

A flagrant example of Dada's revolutionary approach to art was the decision by French artist Marcel Duchamp (1887–1968) to enter a porcelain urinal in a 1917 art exhibit in New York City. By signing it and giving it a title, Duchamp proclaimed that he had transformed the urinal into a work of art. Duchamp's Ready-Mades (as such art would henceforth be labeled) declared that whatever the

artist proclaimed to be art was art. Duchamp's liberating concept served to open the floodgates of the art world, obliging the entire twentieth century to swim in this free-flowing, exuberant, exploratory, and often frightening torrent.

Probing the Subconscious While Dadaism flourished in Germany during the Weimar era, a school of **Surrealism** was established in Paris to liberate the total human experience from the restraints of the rational world. By using the subconscious—a realm popularized in Freudian psychiatry—Surrealists hoped to resurrect the whole personality and reveal a submerged and illusive reality. Normally unrelated objects and people were juxtaposed in dreamlike and frequently violent paintings that were intended to shock the viewer into approaching reality from a totally fresh perspective. Most famous of the Surrealists was the Spaniard Salvador Dalí (1904–1989), who subverted the sense of reality in his painting by using near-photographic detail in presenting a fantastic and irrational world.

Yet another modernist movement born on the eve of World War I was **Abstract**, or Nonobjective, painting. As one of its founders, Swiss artist Paul Klee (1879–1940), observed, "the more fearful this world becomes, . . . the more art becomes abstract."[9] Two of the movement's principal founders, Wassily Kandinsky (1866–1944) and Piet Mondrian (1872–1944), were followers of Theosophy, a religion that promised the triumph of the spirit in a new millennium. Since they viewed matter as an obstacle to salvation, the art of the new age would totally abandon all reference to the material world. Only abstraction, in the form of colorful forms and geometric shapes floating in space, could express the bliss and spiritual beauty of this terrestrial paradise (see Image 4.6).

A Musical Revolution Musicians joined the search for new revolutionary means of expression. Austrian composer Arnold Schoenberg (1874–1951) rejected the traditional tonal system based on the harmonic triad that had dominated Western music since the Renaissance. To free the Western ear from traditional harmonic progression, Schoenberg substituted a radically new "atonal" system in which each piece established its own individual set of relationships and structure. In 1923, he devised a twelve-tone system in which he placed the twelve pitches of the chromatic scale found on the piano in a set sequence for a musical composition. The ordering of these twelve tones was to be repeated throughout the piece, for all instrumental parts, constituting its melody and harmony. Although such atonal music seems even today incomprehensible to the uninitiated, Schoenberg, perhaps more than any

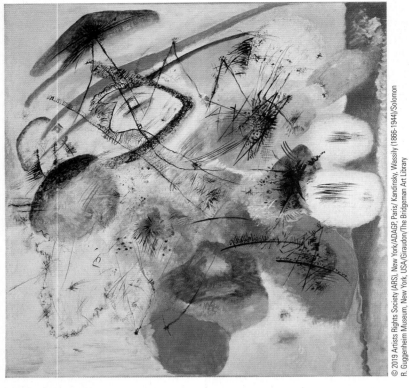

IMAGE 4.6 *Black Lines No. 189,* 1913 (oil on canvas), Wassily Kandinsky. Abstract painting was a renunciation of the material world and a glorification of the spiritual realm. Deeming it no longer necessary to represent objects and people, artists chose to express their emotions solely through color and abstract form. In this painting by Kandinsky, we rejoice in the spring-like swirling splashes of color of the artist's abstract world.

Q *How did abstract art help the viewer to probe the subconscious? Do you think it serves the same purpose today?*

other modern composer, influenced the development of twentieth-century music.

Modernism in Architecture Other fields of artistic creativity, including sculpture, ballet, and architecture, also reflected these new directions. In Germany, a group of imaginative architects called the Bauhaus School created what is widely known as the "international school," which soon became the dominant school of modern architecture. Led by the famous German architect Ludwig Mies van der Rohe (1881–1969), the internationalists promoted a new functional and unadorned style (Mies was widely known for observing that "less is more") characterized by high-rise towers of steel and glass that were reproduced endlessly all around the world during the second half of the century.

For many postwar architects, the past was the enemy of the future. In 1925, the famous French architect Le

Corbusier (1877–1965) advocated razing much of the old city of Paris, to be replaced by modern towers of glass. In his plan, which called for neat apartment complexes separated by immaculate areas of grass, there was no room for people, pets, or nature. Fortunately, the plan was rejected by municipal authorities.

4-6b Culture for the Masses

During the postwar era, writers followed artists and architects in rejecting traditional forms in order to explore the subconscious. In his novel *Ulysses*, published in 1922, Irish author James Joyce (1882–1941) invented the "stream of consciousness" technique to portray the lives of ordinary people through the use of inner monologue. Joyce's technique exerted a powerful influence on literature for the remainder of the century. Meanwhile, some American writers, such as Ernest Hemingway (1899–1961), Theodore Dreiser (1871–1945), and Sinclair Lewis (1885–1951), reflected the rising influence of mass journalism in a new style designed to "tell it like it is." Such writers sought to report the "whole truth" in an effort to attain the authenticity of modern photography.

For much of the Western world, however, the best way to find (or escape) reality was through mass entertainment. The motion picture had been invented at the end of the nineteenth century, but it wasn't until the 1920s that "movies" became solid fixtures in the realm of popular entertainment. The 1930s represented the heyday of the Hollywood studio system in the United States, which in the single year of 1937 turned out nearly 600 feature films. Supplementing the movies were cheap paperbacks and radio, which brought sports, soap operas, and popular music to the mass of the population. The radio was a great social leveler, speaking to all classes with the same voice. Such new technological wonders offered diversion even to the poor while helping to define the twentieth century as the era of the common people. During the 1920s and 1930s, radio and the movies brought new forms of mass culture to millions of people in Europe and North America.

World War I shattered the image of Europe as a modern civilization based on the sturdy pillars of economic prosperity, social harmony, and the rule of law. It also demonstrated that European leaders had overestimated the prevalence of the Enlightenment belief in rational thinking, while ignoring the emotive power of raw nationalism and nativism. Urged on by new propaganda techniques utilized by their own governments, entire populations were manipulated into marching off blindly into a meaningless slaughter.

Who was responsible for the carnage? To the victorious Allied leaders at the time, it was their defeated former adversaries, on whom they imposed harsh terms at the Paris Peace Conference at the end of the war. The losers, on the other hand, were convinced that they had been unfairly punished for simply seeking to occupy their rightful place in the concert of nations. As the Chinese proverb has it, "the winner is king, the loser is rebel."

Eventually, however, many observers began to conclude that the real culprit was the prewar international system itself. The system of nation-states that began to emerge in Europe during the second half of the nineteenth century had led not to cooperation, as many liberals had hoped, but to heightened competition. Persuaded that national survival was based on the twin achievements of industrial prowess and imperialist might, European leaders began to view international politics as a zero-sum game, in which the losers would be consigned to the realm of victims in a social Darwinist universe. Governments that exercised restraint in order to avoid war wound up being publicly criticized for their weakness; those that went to the brink of war to maintain their national interests were often praised for

having preserved national honor. As the British historian John Keegan has noted, for European statesmen in the early twentieth century, "the fear of not meeting a challenge was greater than the fear of war." In any case, by 1914 the major European states had come to believe that their alliances were important for their survival and that their security depended on supporting their allies, even when they took foolish risks.

To make matters worse, the very industrial and technological innovations that had brought the prospect of increased material prosperity for millions had also led to the manufacture of new weapons of mass destruction that would make war a more terrible prospect for those involved, whether military or civilian. If war did come, it would be highly destructive.

The victorious world leaders who gathered at Versailles hoped to forge a peace settlement that would say good-bye to all that. But as it turned out, the turmoil wrought by World War I seemed to open the door to an even greater sense of insecurity. Revolutions in Russia and the Middle East dismembered old empires and created new states that themselves soon gave rise to unexpected problems. Expectations that Europe and the world would return to "normalcy" (i.e., the relatively stable balance of power that had prevailed through much of the nineteenth century) were soon dashed by the failure to achieve a lasting peace, by sudden economic collapse, and by the rise of authoritarian governments that not only restricted individual freedoms but sought even greater control over the lives of their subjects, manipulating and guiding their people to achieve the goals of their totalitarian regimes. In the next chapter, we will examine these events in greater detail.

REFLECTION QUESTIONS

Q What were the underlying causes that led to the outbreak of World War I?

Q What nation, if any, was the most responsible for causing World War I? Why?

Q How did Lenin and the Bolsheviks manage to seize and hold power despite their small numbers?

Q How was World War I the first global war?

CHAPTER TIMELINE

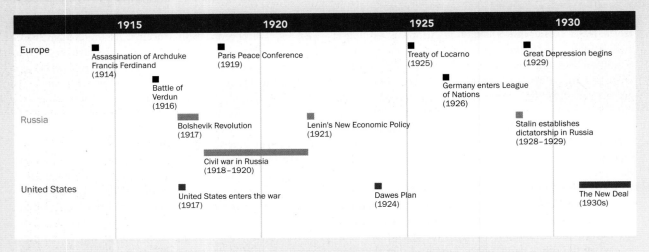

	1915	1920	1925	1930
Europe	Assassination of Archduke Francis Ferdinand (1914)	Paris Peace Conference (1919)	Treaty of Locarno (1925)	Great Depression begins (1929)
	Battle of Verdun (1916)		Germany enters League of Nations (1926)	
Russia	Bolshevik Revolution (1917)	Lenin's New Economic Policy (1921)		Stalin establishes dictatorship in Russia (1928–1929)
	Civil war in Russia (1918–1920)			
United States	United States enters the war (1917)	Dawes Plan (1924)		The New Deal (1930s)

CHAPTER NOTES

1. Cited in Barbara Tuchman, *The Guns of August* (New York, 1962), p. 146.
2. Arnold Toynbee, *Surviving the Future* (New York, 1971), pp. 106–107.
3. Immanuel Geiss, *July 1914: The Outbreak of the First World War: Selected Documents* (Scribner, 1968), No. 135, cited in Niall Ferguson, "The Jihad of 1914" in the *New York Review of Books*, February 13, 2003, p. 21.
4. Harold Nicolson, *Peacemaking, 1919* (Boston and New York, 1933), pp. 31–32.
5. Margaret MacMillan, *Paris 1919: Six Months That Changed the World* (New York, 2001), p. 103.
6. Dmitri Volkogonov, *Lenin: A New Biography* (New York, 1994), p. 22.
7. Quoted in Robert Paxton, *Europe in the Twentieth Century*, 2nd ed. (San Diego, 1985), p. 237.
8. Volkogonov, *Lenin*, p. 3.
9. Quoted in Nikos Stangos, *Concepts of Modern Art: From Fauvism to Postmodernism*, 3rd ed. (London, 1994), p. 44.

NATIONALISM, REVOLUTION, AND DICTATORSHIP: ASIA, THE MIDDLE EAST, AND LATIN AMERICA 1919–1939

Chapter Outline and Focus Questions

5-1 *The Spread of Nationalism in Asia and the Middle East*

Q What were the various stages in the rise of nationalist movements in Asia and the Middle East? How did their experience compare with that of nationalist movements in nineteenth century Europe?

5-2 *Revolution in China*

Q What challenges did China encounter between the two world wars, and what solutions did the Nationalists and the Communists propose to resolve them?

5-3 *Japan Between the Wars*

Q How did Japan address the challenge of nation-building in the first decade of the twentieth century, and why did democratic institutions not take hold more effectively?

5-4 *Nationalism and Dictatorship in Latin America*

Q What problems did the nations of Latin America face in the interwar years? To what degree were they a consequence of foreign influence?

The Tours Congress, Ho Chi Minh (1890–1969) from 'L'Humanite', December 1920 (b/w photo), French Photographer, (20th century)/Bibliotheque Nationale, Paris, France/Archives Charmet/ The Bridgeman Art Library

IMAGE 5.1 Nguyen the Patriot at Tours

ON CHRISTMAS DAY IN 1920, a young Asian man in an ill-fitting rented suit stood up nervously to address the several hundred delegates of the French Socialist Party (FSP) who had gathered in the historic French city of Tours. The speaker introduced himself as Nguyen Ai Quoc, or "Nguyen the Patriot," and he was a Vietnamese subject in the French colony of Indochina.

The delegates had assembled to decide whether the FSP, a political party of Marxist persuasion that had become a member of the Second International (see Chapter 1) would drop its moderate objectives in order to follow the path of violent revolution recommended by the new Bolshevik regime in Soviet Russia. Among those voting in favor of the proposal was Nguyen Ai Quoc, who had decided that only the path of Karl Marx and Lenin could lead to national independence for his compatriots. In future years, operating under the pseudonym of Ho Chi Minh, he would become a founding member of the Vietnamese Communist Party and the public face of a revolutionary movement that would successfully challenge the global power of the United States during the Cold War.

Connections to Today

Do the nations of Asia, the Middle East, and Latin America face today some of the same challenges that affected their counterparts in the first decade of the twentieth century. If so, what are they?

The meeting in Tours was held at a time when resistance to Western imperial rule was on the rise in Asia, and the decision that Nguyen Ai Quoc faced of whether to opt for violent revolution or gradual change was one that would be encountered by colonial peoples throughout the world. As Europeans devastated their own civilization on the battlefields of Europe, the subject peoples in their vast colonial empires were quick to recognize the opportunity to shake free of foreign domination. In those areas, movements for national independence began to take shape. Some were inspired by the nationalist and liberal movements of the West, while others looked to the new Marxist model provided by the victory of the Communists in Soviet Russia, who soon worked to spread their revolutionary vision to African and Asian societies. In the Middle East, World War I ended the rule of the Ottoman Empire and led to the creation of new states, many of which were placed under Western domination.

The nations of Latin America were no longer under direct colonial rule and thus, for the most part, did not face the same degree of challenge as did their counterparts elsewhere. Nevertheless, the economies of many Latin American countries were virtually controlled by foreign interests. A similar situation prevailed in China and Japan, two countries which had managed with some difficulty to retain a degree of political independence despite severe pressure from the West. But the political flux and economic disruption that characterized much of the world during and after World War I had affected Latin America, China, and Japan as well, leading many in these regions to heed the siren call of fascist dictatorship or social revolution. For all the peoples of Asia, the Middle East, and Latin America, the end of the Great War had not created a world safe for democracy, as Woodrow Wilson had hoped, but an age of great peril and uncertainty.

5-1 THE SPREAD OF NATIONALISM IN ASIA AND THE MIDDLE EAST

 Focus Questions: What were the various stages in the rise of nationalist movements in Asia and the Middle East? How did their experience compare with that of nationalist movements in nineteenth century Europe?

Although the West had emerged from World War I relatively intact, its political and social foundations and its self-confidence had been severely undermined by the experience. Within Europe, doubts about the future viability of Western civilization were widespread, especially among the intellectual elite. These doubts were quick to reach the attention of perceptive observers elsewhere and contributed to a rising tide of unrest against Western political domination throughout the colonial and semicolonial world. That unrest took a variety of forms but was most notably displayed in increasing worker activism, rural protest, and, for many, a new awareness of national and ethnic identity.

5-1a Stirrings of Nationhood

Prior to the colonial takeover, most societies outside Europe lacked a clear sense of common purpose or modern nationhood. Many were deeply divided by ethnic, linguistic, and religious differences, while others were united primarily on the basis of religious beliefs, community loyalties, or devotion to hereditary leaders. Although some individuals identified themselves as members of a particular ethnic or linguistic group, many others viewed themselves as subjects of a king, members of a caste, or adherence to a particular village community, tribal affiliation, or lineage group. That lack of sharp focus on their communal identity was obviously a disadvantage as they responded to the challenge from imperialist nations.

The creation of colonies with defined borders and a powerful central government weakened traditional ties and reoriented individuals' sense of political identity. The introduction of Western ideas of citizenship and representative government engendered a new sense of participation in the affairs of government. At the same time, the appearance of a new and foreign elite class based not on hereditary privilege or religious sanction but on alleged racial or cultural superiority aroused a shared sense of resentment among subject peoples, who felt a common commitment to the creation of an independent society. By the first quarter of the twentieth century, political movements dedicated to the overthrow of colonial rule had arisen throughout much of the non-Western world.

The first nationalist movements in Asia and the Middle East, then, were a product of colonialism and, in a sense, a reaction to it. But a sense of being part of a broader community defined by nationality does not emerge full-blown in a society. It begins among a few members of the educated elite (most commonly among articulate professionals such as lawyers, teachers, journalists, and doctors) and spreads gradually to the mass of the population. Only then has a true sense of nationhood been created.

The process of creating modern nations began to take shape at the beginning of the twentieth century and was the product of the convergence of several factors. The most vocal sources of anticolonialist sentiment were found in a new class of westernized intellectuals in the urban centers created by colonial rule. In many cases, this new urban middle class, composed of merchants, petty functionaries, clerks, students, and professionals, had been educated in Western-style schools and spoke European languages. A few had spent time in the West. In any case, they were the first generation of Asians and Africans to possess more than a rudimentary understanding of the institutions and values of the modern West.

The results were paradoxical. On the one hand, this new class admired Western culture and sometimes harbored a deep sense of contempt for traditional ways, many of which had not only failed to fend off the imperial conquest but also appeared to be inadequate to meet the needs of changing times. On the other hand, many strongly resented the gap between ideal and reality, theory and practice, in colonial policy. Although Western political thought exalted democracy, equality, and individual freedom, these values were generally not applied in the colonies, and colonial subjects usually had access to only the most menial positions in the colonial bureaucracy.

Equally important, the economic prosperity of the West was only imperfectly reflected in the colonies. Normally, middle-class colonial subjects did not suffer in the same manner as impoverished peasants or menial workers in coal mines or on sugar or rubber plantations, but they, too, had complaints. They usually qualified only for menial jobs in the government or business. Even when employed, their salaries were normally lower than those of Europeans in similar occupations. The superiority of the Europeans was expressed in a variety of ways, including "whites only" clubs and the use of the familiar form of the language (normally used by adults to children) when addressing members of the local population.

Out of this mixture of hopes and resentments emerged the first stirrings of modern nationalism in Asia and Africa. During the first quarter of the twentieth century, in colonial and semicolonial societies across the entire arc of Asia from the Suez Canal to the shores of the Pacific Ocean, indigenous peoples began to organize political parties and movements seeking reforms or the end of foreign rule and the restoration of independence.

5-1b Modern Nationalism

At first, many of the leaders of these movements did not focus clearly on the idea of nationhood but were motivated primarily to defend the economic interests or religious beliefs of the local population. In Burma, for example, the first expression of modern nationalism came from students at the University of Rangoon, who formed an informal organization to protest against official persecution of the Buddhist religion and British failure to observe local customs in Buddhist temples, such as not removing their footwear.

Calling themselves Thakin (a polite term in the Burmese language meaning "lord" or "master," thereby emphasizing their demand for the right to rule themselves), the students began by protesting against British arrogance and lack of respect for local religious traditions. Eventually, however, they began to focus specifically on the issue of national independence.

A similar movement arose in the Dutch East Indies, where the first quasi-political organization dedicated to the creation of a modern Indonesia, the Sarekat Islam (Islamic Association), began as a self-help society among Muslim merchants to fight against domination of the local economy by Chinese interests. Eventually, activist elements began to realize that the source of the problem was not the Chinese merchants, most of whom were Buddhists, but the colonial presence, and in the 1920s, Sarekat Islam was transformed into a new organization—the Nationalist Party of Indonesia (PNI)—that focused on the issue of national independence. Like the Thakins in Burma, this party would eventually lead the country to independence after World War II.

Independence or Modernization? The Nationalist Quandary

Building a new nation, however, requires more than a shared sense of grievances against the foreign invader. Many other questions need to be answered. By what means was independence to be achieved? Should independence or modernization be the first priority? What kind of political and economic system should be adopted once colonial rule had been overthrown? What national or cultural concept should be adopted as the symbol of the new nation, and which institutions and values should be preserved from the past?

Questions such as these triggered lively and sometimes acrimonious debates among patriotic elements throughout the colonial world. If national independence was the desired end, how could it best be achieved? Could the Westerners be persuaded to leave without resort to violent measures, or would force be required? If the Western presence was potentially beneficial by introducing much-needed reforms in traditional societies, then a gradualist approach made sense. On the other hand, if the colonial regime was an impediment to social and political change, then the first priority, in the minds of many, was to bring it to an end.

Another problem was how to adopt useful Western ideas and institutions while preserving the essential values that defined the indigenous culture. One of the reasons for retaining traditional values was to provide ideological symbols that the common people could understand. If the desired end was national independence, then the new political parties obviously needed to enlist the mass of the population in the common struggle. But how could peasants, plantation workers, fishermen, and shepherds be made to understand complicated and unfamiliar concepts like democracy, industrialization, and nationhood? The problem was often one of communication, for most urban intellectuals had little in common with the teeming population in the countryside. As the Indonesian intellectual Sutan Sjahrir lamented, many westernized intellectuals had more in common with their colonial rulers than with the local population in the rural villages. In a letter to his wife written in 1935, Sjahrir declared that indigenous culture no longer had relevance for those who sought to make their way in the new world:

> Here [in Indonesia] there has been no spiritual or cultural life, and no intellectual progress for centuries. There are the much-praised Eastern art forms but what are these except bare rudiments from a feudal culture that cannot possibly provide a dynamic fulcrum for people of the twentieth century? . . . Our spiritual needs are needs of the twentieth century; our problems and our views are of the twentieth century . . . .[1]

5-1c Gandhi and the Indian National Congress

Nowhere in the colonial world were these issues debated more vigorously than in India (see Map 5.1). Before the Sepoy Uprising, Indian consciousness had focused primarily on the question of religious identity. But in the latter half of the nineteenth century, a stronger sense of national consciousness began to arise, provoked by the conservative policies and racial arrogance of the British colonial authorities.

The first Indians to focus on nationhood were almost invariably upper class and educated. Many of them were from urban areas such as Bombay (now Mumbai), Madras (Chennai), and Calcutta (Kolkata). Some were trained in law and were members of the civil service. At first, many tended to prefer reform to revolution and believed that India needed modernization before it could handle the problems of independence. An exponent of this view was Gopal Gokhale (1866–1915), a moderate nationalist who hoped that he could convince the British to bring about needed reforms in Indian society. Gokhale and other like-minded reformists did have some effect. In the 1880s, the government launched a series of reforms introducing a measure of self-government for the first time. All too often, however, such efforts were sabotaged by local British officials.

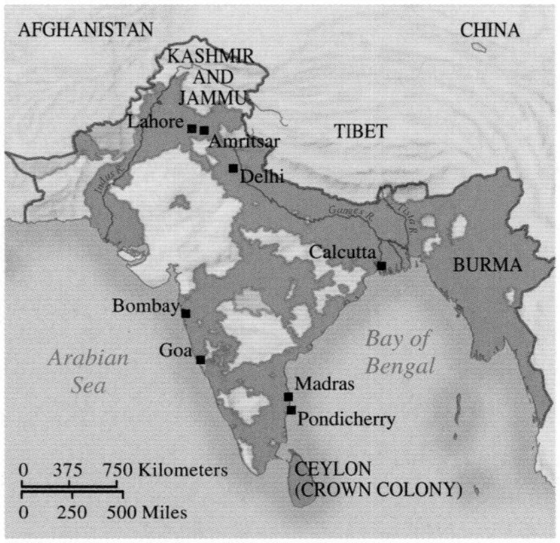

The Indian National Congress The slow pace of reform convinced many Indian nationalists that relying on

British benevolence was futile. In 1885, a small group of Indians met in Bombay to form the Indian National Congress (INC). They hoped to speak for all India, but most were high-caste English-trained Hindus. Like their reformist predecessors, members of the INC did not demand immediate independence and accepted the need for reforms to end traditional abuses like child marriage and *sati* (see Chapter 2). At the same time, they called for an Indian share in the governing process and more spending on economic development and less on military campaigns along the frontier.

The British responded with a few concessions, such as accepting the principle of elective Indian participation on government councils, but in general, change was glacially slow. As impatient members of the INC became disillusioned, radical leaders such as Balwantrao Tilak (1856–1920) openly criticized the British while defending traditional customs like child marriage to solicit support from conservative elements within the local population. Tilak's activities split the INC between moderates and radicals, and he and his followers formed the New Party, which called for the use of terrorism and violence to achieve national independence. Tilak was eventually convicted of sedition.

The INC also had difficulty reconciling religious differences within its ranks. The stated goal of the INC was to seek self-determination for all Indians regardless of class or religious affiliation, but many of its leaders were Hindu and inevitably reflected Hindu concerns. By the first decade of the twentieth century, Muslims began to call for the creation of a separate Muslim League to represent the interests of the millions of Muslims in Indian society.

India's "Great Soul," Mohandas Gandhi In 1915, the return of a young Hindu lawyer from South Africa transformed the movement and galvanized India's struggle for independence and identity. Mohandas Gandhi was born in 1869 in Gujarat, in western India, the son of a government minister. In the late-nineteenth century, he studied in London and became a lawyer. In 1893, he went to South Africa to work in a law firm serving Indian émigrés working as laborers there. He soon became aware of the racial prejudice and exploitation experienced by Indians living in the territory and tried to organize them to protest their living conditions.

MAP 5.1 British India Between the Wars

Nonviolent Resistance On his return to India, Gandhi immediately became active in the independence movement.

MOVIES & HISTORY
Gandhi (1982)

To many of his contemporaries, Mohandas Gandhi—the Mahatma, or "great soul"—was the conscience of India. Son of a senior Indian official from the state of Gujarat, he trained as a lawyer at University College in London. Gandhi first dealt with racial discrimination when he sought to provide legal assistance to Indian laborers living under the apartheid regime in South Africa. On his return to India in 1915, he rapidly emerged as a fierce critic of British colonial rule over his country. His message of *satyagraha*—embodying the idea of a steadfast but nonviolent resistance to the injustice and inhumanity inherent in the colonial enterprise—inspired millions of his compatriots in their long struggle for national independence. It also earned the admiration and praise of sympathetic observers around the world. His death by assassination at the hands of a Hindu fanatic in 1948 shocked the world.

Time, however, has somewhat dimmed his message. Gandhi's vision of a future India was symbolized by the spinning wheel—he rejected the industrial age and material pursuits in favor of the simple pleasures of the traditional Indian village. Since achieving independence, however, India has followed the path of national wealth and power laid out by Gandhi's friend and colleague Jawaharlal Nehru. Gandhi's appeal for religious tolerance and mutual respect at home rapidly gave way to a bloody conflict between Hindus and Muslims that still persists today. On the global stage, his vision of world peace and brotherly love has been similarly ignored, first during the Cold War and more recently by the "clash of civilizations" between Western countries and the forces of militant Islam.

Jawaharlal Nehru (Roshan Seth), Mahatma Gandhi (Ben Kingsley), and Muhammad Ali Jinnah (Alyque Padamsee) confer before the partition of India into Hindu and Muslim states.

It was at least partly in an effort to revive and perpetuate the message of the Mahatma that British filmmaker Richard Attenborough directed the film *Gandhi*. Epic in its length and scope, the film seeks to present a faithful rendition of the life of its subject, from his introduction to apartheid in South Africa at the turn of the century to his tragic death after World War II. Actor Ben Kingsley, son of an Indian father and an English mother, plays the title role with intensity and conviction. The film was widely praised and earned eight Academy Awards, including one for Kingsley as Best Actor.

 Why do you think Gandhi became such a widely admired—if controversial—figure in his lifetime?

Using his experience in South Africa, he set up a movement based on nonviolent resistance (the Indian term was **satyagraha**, "hold fast to the truth") to try to force the British to improve the lot of the poor and grant independence to India. Gandhi was particularly concerned about the plight of the millions of "untouchables" (the lowest social class in traditional India), whom he called **harijans**, or "children of God." When the British attempted to suppress dissent, he called on his followers to refuse to obey British regulations. He began to manufacture his own clothes (dressing in a simple *dhoti* made of coarse homespun cotton) and adopted the spinning wheel as a symbol of Indian resistance to imports of British textiles.

Gandhi, now increasingly known as India's "Great Soul" (*Mahatma*), organized mass protests to achieve his aims, but in 1919, they got out of hand and led to British reprisals. British troops killed hundreds of unarmed protesters in the enclosed square of the city of Amritsar in northwestern India. When the protests began to spread, Gandhi was horrified at the violence and briefly retreated from active politics. Nevertheless, he was arrested for his role in the protests and spent several years in prison.

Gandhi combined his anticolonial activities with an appeal to the spiritual instincts of all Indians (see Movies & History, *Gandhi*, above). Though born and raised a Hindu, he possessed a universalist approach to the idea of God that transcended individual religion, although it was shaped by the historical themes of Hindu religious belief. At a speech given in London in September 1931, he expressed his view of the nature of God as "an indefinable mysterious power that pervades everything . . . , an unseen power which makes itself felt and yet defies all proof."

In 1921, the British passed the Government of India Act to expand the role of Indians in the governing process and transform the heretofore advisory Legislative Council into a bicameral parliament, two-thirds of whose members would be elected. Similar bodies were created at the provincial level. In a stroke, 5 million Indians were enfranchised. But such reforms were no longer enough for many members of the INC, who wanted to follow the new INC leader, Motilal Nehru, in pushing aggressively for full independence. The British exacerbated the situation by increasing the salt tax and prohibiting the Indian people from manufacturing or harvesting their own salt. In 1930, Gandhi, now released from prison, resumed his policy of **civil disobedience** by openly joining several dozen supporters in a 240-mile walk to the sea, where he picked up a lump of salt and urged Indians to ignore the law. Gandhi and many other members of the INC were arrested.

New Leaders for New Challenges   In the 1930s, a new figure entered the movement in the person of Jawaharlal Nehru (1889–1964), son of the INC leader Motilal Nehru. Educated in the law in Great Britain and a *brahmin* (member of the highest social class) by birth, Nehru personified the new Anglo-Indian politician: secular, rational, upper class, and intellectual. In fact, he appeared to be everything that Gandhi was not. With his emergence, the independence movement embarked on dual paths: religious and secular, Indian and Western, traditional and modern (see Comparative Illustration, "Masters and Disciples," p. 111). The dichotomous character of the INC leadership may well have strengthened the movement by bringing together the two primary impulses behind the desire for independence: elite nationalism and the primal force of Indian traditionalism. But it portended trouble for the nation's new leadership in defining India's future path in the contemporary world. In the meantime, Muslim discontent with Hindu dominance over the INC was increasing. In 1940, the Muslim League called for the creation of a separate state based on Islamic principles in the northwest, to be known as Pakistan ("Land of the Pure"). As communal strife between Hindus and Muslims increased, many Indians came to realize with sorrow (and some British colonialists with satisfaction) that British rule was all that stood between peace and civil war.

5-1d Revolt in the Middle East

In the Middle East, as in Europe, World War I hastened the collapse of old empires. The Ottoman Empire, which had dominated the eastern Mediterranean since the seizure of Constantinople in 1453, had been growing steadily weaker since the end of the eighteenth century, troubled by rising governmental corruption, a failure to take advantage of technological advances (such as advanced firearms) introduced from Europe, a decline in the effectiveness of the sultans, and the loss of considerable territory in the Balkans and southwestern Russia. In North Africa, Ottoman authority, tenuous at best, had disintegrated in the nineteenth century, enabling the French to seize Algeria and Tunisia and the British to establish a protectorate over the Nile River valley.

Twilight of the Ottoman Empire   Reformist elements in Istanbul (as Constantinople was officially renamed in 1930), to be sure, had tried to resist the decline. The first efforts had taken place in the eighteenth century, when westernizing forces, concerned at the shrinkage of the empire, had tried to modernize the army. One energetic **sultan**, Selim III (r. 1789–1807), tried to establish a "new order" that would streamline both the civilian and military bureaucracies, but conservative elements in the emperor's private guard, alarmed at the potential loss of their power, revolted and brought the experiment to an end. Further efforts during the first half of the nineteenth century were somewhat more successful and resulted in a series of bureaucratic, military, and educational reforms. New roads were built, the power of local landlords was reduced, and an Imperial Rescript issued in 1856 granted equal rights to all subjects of the empire, whatever their religious preference. In the 1870s, a new generation of reformers seized power in Istanbul and pushed through a constitution aimed at forming a legislative assembly that would represent all the peoples in the state. But the sultan they placed on the throne, Abdulhamid (r. 1876–1909), suspended the new charter and attempted to rule by traditional authoritarian means.

The "Young Turks"   By the end of the nineteenth century, the defunct 1876 constitution had become a symbol of change for reformist elements, now grouped together under the common name **Young Turks**. In 1908, Young Turk elements forced the sultan to restore the constitution, and he was removed from power the following year.

But the Young Turks had appeared at a moment of extreme fragility for the empire. Internal rebellions, combined with Austrian annexations of Ottoman territories

COMPARATIVE ILLUSTRATION

Masters and Disciples

 Q *How do these four leaders compare in terms of their roles in furthering political change in their respective countries?*

Politics & Government **WHEN THE FOUNDERS** of nationalist movements passed leadership over to their successors, the result was often a change in the strategy and tactics of the organizations. In India, when Jawaharlal Nehru (Image 5.2a, on the left) replaced Mahatma Gandhi (wearing a simple Indian dhoti rather than the Western dress favored by his colleagues) as leader of the Indian National Congress, the movement adopted a more secular posture. In China, Chiang Kai-shek (Image 5.2b, standing) took Sun Yat-sen's Nationalist Party in a more conservative direction after Sun's death in 1925.

IMAGE 5.2a Nehru and Gandhi

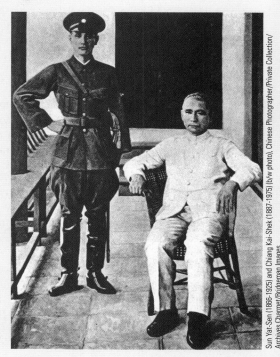

IMAGE 5.2b Sun Yat-Sen and Chiang Kai-Shek

in the Balkans, undermined support for the new government and provoked the army to step in. With most minorities from the old empire now removed from Turkish authority, many ethnic Turks began to embrace a new concept of a Turkish state based on all residents of Turkish nationality.

The final blow to the old empire came during World War I, when the Ottoman government allied with Germany in the hope of driving the British from Egypt and restoring Ottoman rule over the Nile valley. In response, the British declared an official protectorate over Egypt and, aided by the efforts of T. E. Lawrence (Lawrence of Arabia), sought to undermine Ottoman rule in the Arabian peninsula by encouraging Arab nationalists there (see Chapter 4). In 1916, the local governor of Mecca, encouraged by the British, declared Arabia independent from Ottoman rule, while British troops, advancing from Egypt, seized Palestine. In October 1918, having suffered more than 300,000 casualties during the war, the Ottoman Empire negotiated an armistice with the Allied Powers.

During the next two years, Allied diplomats wrestled with how to deal with the remnants of the defeated Ottoman Empire. In 1916, the British and the French had reached a secret agreement to divide up the non-Turkish areas of the empire between themselves. This did not sit well with Woodrow Wilson, who opposed the outright annexation of colonial territories by the victorious Allies. Ultimately, the latter agreed to establish these territories as mandates under the new League of Nations. Mesopotamia and Palestine were assigned to the British, while Syria was given to the

French (see Map 5.2). The Arabian peninsula was dealt with separately, and eventually received its independence as the kingdom of Saudi Arabia in 1932 (see "The Rise of Arab Nationalism," p. 114).

Other aspects of the Treaty of Sèvres, signed in 1920, were even more controversial. Western portions of the Anatolian peninsula were to be occupied by the Greeks in preparation for a future plebiscite to determine the future of the area. Armenia—where the local Christian population had been brutally mistreated by the Turks—was to receive its independence. A proposal for an independent Kurdistan (the Kurds were a non-Arab Muslim people living in mountainous areas throughout the region) was left unresolved.

Mustafa Kemal and the Modernization of Turkey

The impending collapse of the Ottoman Empire energized key elements in Turkey under the leadership of war hero Colonel Mustafa Kemal (1881–1938), who had commanded Turkish forces in their heroic defense of the Dardanelles against a British invasion during World War I. Now he resigned from the army and convoked a national congress that called for the creation of an elected government and the preservation of the remaining territories of the old empire in a new republic of Turkey. Establishing the new capital at Ankara, Kemal's forces drove the Greeks from the Anatolian peninsula and seized Kurdish lands to the east, thus bringing an end to the dream of an independent Kurdistan. The Allies agreed to sign a new Treaty of Lausanne, incorporating these changes. Armenian leaders, still bitter at their mistreatment at the hands of the Turks, decided to join the Soviet Union. In 1923, the last of the Ottoman sultans fled the country, which was now declared a Turkish republic. The Ottoman Empire had finally come to an end.

During the next few years, President Mustafa Kemal (now popularly known as Atatürk, or "Father Turk") attempted to transform Turkey into a modern secular republic. The trappings of a democratic system were put in place, centered on the elected Grand National Assembly, but the president was relatively intolerant of opposition and harshly suppressed critics of his rule. Turkish nationalism was emphasized, and the Turkish language, now written in the Roman alphabet, was shorn of many of its Arabic elements. Popular education was emphasized, old aristocratic titles like *pasha* and *bey* were abolished, and all

MAP 5.2 **The Middle East in 1923**

Turkish citizens were given family names in the European style.

Atatürk also took steps to modernize the economy, overseeing the establishment of a light industrial sector producing textiles, glass, paper, and cement and instituting a five-year plan on the Soviet model to provide for state direction over the economy. Atatürk was no admirer of Soviet communism, however, and the Turkish economy can be better described as a form of state capitalism. He also encouraged the modernization of the agricultural sector through the establishment of training institutions and model farms, but such reforms had relatively little effect on the nation's predominantly conservative rural population.

Perhaps the most significant aspect of Atatürk's reform program was his attempt to limit the power of the Islamic religion and transform Turkey into a secular state. The caliphate (according to which the Ottoman sultan was recognized as the temporal leader of the global Islamic community) was formally abolished in 1924, and the *Shari'a* (Islamic law) was replaced by a revised version of the Swiss law code (see Opposing Viewpoints, "Islam in the Modern World: Two Views," p. 113). The fez (the brimless cap worn by Turkish Muslims) was abolished as a form of headdress, and women were discouraged from wearing the traditional Islamic veil, a practice that symbolized female inferiority with respect to their male counterparts and dated back to the early years of the faith during the life of the Prophet Muhammad. Women received the right to vote in 1934 and were legally guaranteed equal rights with men in all aspects of marriage and inheritance. Education and the professions were now open to both men and women, and some women even began to take part in politics. All citizens were given the right to convert to another religion at will.

The legacy of Mustafa Kemal Atatürk was enormous. Although not all of his reforms were widely accepted in practice, especially by devout Muslims, most of the changes that he introduced were retained after his death in 1938. In virtually every respect, the Turkish republic was the product of his determined efforts to create a modern nation, a Turkish version of the "revolution from above" in Meiji Japan.

Modernization in Iran

In the meantime, a similar process was under way in Persia. Under the Qajar dynasty (1794–1925), the country had not been very successful in resisting Russian advances in the Caucasus or a growing European

Islam in the Modern World: Two Views

 Q *Why did Mustafa Kemal believe that the caliphate no longer met the needs of the Turkish people? Why did Mohammed Iqbal believe that a separate state for Muslims in India would be required? How did he attempt to persuade non-Muslims that this would be to their benefit as well?*

Politics & Government **AS PART OF HIS PLAN** to transform Turkey into a modern society, Mustafa Kemal Atatürk sought to free his country from what he considered to be outdated practices imposed by traditional beliefs. The first selection is from a speech in which he proposed bringing an end to the caliphate, which had been in the hands of Ottoman sultans since the formation of the empire. But not all Muslims wished to move in the direction of a more secular society. Mohammed Iqbal, a well-known Muslim poet in colonial India, was a prominent advocate of the creation of a separate state for Muslims in South Asia. The second selection is from an address he presented to the All-India Muslim League in December 1930, explaining the rationale for his proposal.

Atatürk, Speech to the Assembly (October 1924)

The sovereign entitled Caliph was to maintain justice among the three hundred million Muslims on the terrestrial globe, to safeguard the rights of these peoples, to prevent any event that could encroach upon order and security, and confront every attack which the Muslims would be called upon to encounter from the side of other nations. It was to be part of his attributes to preserve by all means the welfare and spiritual development of Islam. . . .

If the Caliph and Caliphate, as they maintained, were to be invested with a dignity embracing the whole of Islam, ought they not to have realized in all justice that a crushing burden would be imposed on Turkey, on her existence; her entire resources and all her forces would be placed at the disposal of the Caliph? . . .

For centuries our nation was guided under the influence of these erroneous ideas. But what has been the result of it? Everywhere they have lost millions of men. "Do you know," I asked, "how many sons of Anatolia have perished in the scorching deserts of the Yemen? Do you know the losses we have suffered in holding Syria and Egypt and in

maintaining our position in Africa? And do you see what has come out of it? Do you know?"

Those who favor the idea of placing the means at the disposal of the Caliph to brave the whole world and the power to administer the affairs of the whole of Islam must not appeal to the population of Anatolia alone but to the great Muslim agglomerations which are eight or ten times as rich in men.

New Turkey, the people of New Turkey, have no reason to think of anything else but their own existence and their own welfare. She has nothing more to give away to others.

Mohammed Iqbal, Speech to the All-India Muslim League (1930)

It cannot be denied that Islam, regarded as an ethical ideal plus a certain kind of polity . . . has been the chief formative factor in the life history of the Muslims of India. It has furnished those basic emotions and loyalties which gradually unify scattered individuals and groups and finally transform them into a well-defined people. Indeed it is no exaggeration to say that India is perhaps the only country in the world where Islam, as a people-building force, has worked at its best. In India, as elsewhere, the structure of Islam as a society is almost entirely due to the working of Islam as a culture inspired by a specific ethical ideal. . . .

Communalism in its higher aspect, then, is indispensable to the formation of a harmonious whole in a country like India. The units of Indian society are not territorial as in European countries. India is a continent of human groups belonging to different religions. Their behavior is not at all determined by a common race consciousness. Even the Hindus do not form a homogeneous group. The principle of European democracy cannot be applied to India without recognizing the fact of communal groups. The Muslim demand for the creation of a Muslim India within India is, therefore, perfectly justified. . . .

I therefore demand the formation of a consolidated Muslim State in the best interests of India and Islam. For India it means security and peace resulting from an internal balance of power; for Islam an opportunity to rid itself of the stamp that Arabian imperialism was forced to give it, to mobilize its law, its education, its culture, and to bring them into closer contact with its own original spirit and with the spirit of modern times.

Sources: From Atatürk's Speech to the Assembly, pp. 432–433. A speech delivered by Ghazi Mustafa Kemal, President of the Turkish Republic, October 1924; Mohammed Iqbal, Speech to the All-India Muslim League, 1930.

presence farther south. To secure themselves from foreign influence, the Qajars moved the capital from Tabriz to Tehran, in a mountainous area just south of the Caspian Sea. During the mid-nineteenth century, one modernizing shah attempted to introduce political and economic reforms but faced resistance from tribal and religious forces. The majority of Persians were **Shi'ites**, one of the two main branches of Islam (as opposed to **Sunni** Muslims, who predominated in most of the Muslim world). Both Sunnis and Shi'ites adhered to the fundamental principles of Islam, including the "**Five Pillars of Islam**": belief in Allah and Muhammad as his prophet; prayer five times a day and public prayer on Friday at midday to worship Allah; observation of the holy month of Ramadan, including fasting from dawn to sunset; making a pilgrimage, if possible, to Mecca at least once in one's lifetime; and giving alms (zakat) to the poor and unfortunate. The Shi'ites, however, had broken with the mainstream Sunni form of Islam over leadership issues not long after the death of Muhammad and adopted a more strict interpretation of the Muslim faith.

Eventually, the growing foreign presence led to the rise of an indigenous nationalist movement. Its efforts were largely directed against Russian advances in the northwest and growing European influence in the small modern industrial sector, the profits from which left the country or disappeared into the hands of the dynasty's ruling elite. Supported actively by Shi'ite religious leaders, opposition to the regime rose steadily among both peasants and merchants in the cities, and in 1906, popular pressures forced the reigning shah to grant a constitution on the Western model.

As in the Ottoman Empire and Qing China, however, the modernizers had moved before their power base was secure. With the support of the Russians and the British, the shah was able to retain control, and the two foreign powers began to divide the country into separate spheres of influence. One reason for the growing foreign presence in Persia was the discovery of oil reserves in the southern part of the country in 1908. Within a few years, oil exports increased rapidly, with the bulk of the profits going into the pockets of British investors.

In 1921, a Persian army officer by the name of Reza Khan (1878–1944) led a mutiny that seized power in Tehran. The new ruler had originally intended to establish a republic, but resistance from traditional forces impeded his efforts, and in 1925, the new Pahlavi dynasty, with Reza Khan as shah, replaced the now defunct Qajar dynasty. During the next few years, Reza Khan attempted to follow the example of Mustafa Kemal Atatürk in Turkey, introducing a number of reforms to strengthen the central government, modernize the civilian and military bureaucracy, and establish a modern economic infrastructure.

Unlike Atatürk, Reza Khan did not attempt to destroy the power of Islamic beliefs, but he did encourage the establishment of a Western-style educational system and forbade women to wear the veil in public. He granted suffrage to women and encouraged them to get an education. To strengthen the sense of nationalism and reduce the power of Islam, he restored the country's ancient name, Iran, in 1935 and attempted to popularize the symbols and beliefs of pre-Islamic times. Like his Qajar predecessors, however, Reza Khan was hindered by strong foreign influence. When the Soviet Union and Great Britain decided to send troops into the country during World War II, he resigned in protest and died three years later.

Nation Building in Iraq   One consequence of the collapse of the Ottoman Empire was the emergence of a new political entity along the Tigris and Euphrates Rivers, once the heartland of ancient empires. Lacking defensible borders and sharply divided along ethnic and religious lines—a Shi'ite majority in rural areas was balanced by a vocal Sunni minority in the cities and a largely Kurdish population in the northern mountains—the region had been under Ottoman rule since the seventeenth century. With the advent of World War I, the lowland area from Baghdad southward to the Persian Gulf was occupied by British forces, who hoped to protect oil-producing regions in neighboring Iran from a German takeover.

In 1920, the country was placed under British control as the mandate of Iraq under the League of Nations. Civil unrest and growing anti-Western sentiment rapidly dispelled any possible plans for the emergence of an independent government, and in 1921, after the suppression of resistance forces, the British turned titular control of the country to a monarchy under the authority of King Faisal, a resistance leader during World War I and a descendant of the Prophet Muhammad. Faisal relied for support primarily on the politically more sophisticated urban Sunni population, although they represented less than a quarter of the population. The discovery of oil near Kirkuk in 1927 increased the value of the area to the British, who had made the shift from coal to oil for their warships during World War I and now needed a secure access to the rich oil fields of the Middle East. In 1932, the country received its formal independence, although British advisers continued to retain a strong influence over the fragile government.

The Rise of Arab Nationalism   As we have seen, the Arab uprising during World War I helped bring about the demise of the Ottoman Empire. Actually, unrest against Ottoman rule had existed in the Arabian peninsula since the eighteenth century, when the Wahhabi revolt attempted to expel the outside influences and cleanse Islam of corrupt practices that had developed in past centuries. The revolt was eventually suppressed, but the influence of the Wahhabi movement persisted, revitalized in part by resistance to the centralizing and modernizing efforts of reformist elements in the nineteenth century.

World War I offered an opportunity for the Arabs to throw off the shackles of Ottoman rule—but what would replace them? The Arabs were a loose collection of peoples who often did not see eye to eye on what constituted their community. Disagreement over what it means to be an Arab has plagued generations of political leaders who have sought unsuccessfully to knit together the disparate peoples of the region into a single Arab nation.

When the Arab leaders in Mecca declared their independence from Ottoman rule in 1916, they had hoped for British support, but they were sorely disappointed when the British and French assumed control of much of the area as mandates of the League of Nations. To add salt to the wound, the French created a new state of Lebanon along the coastal regions of their mandate of Syria so that the Christian peoples there could be under a Christian administration.

In the early 1920s, a leader of the Wahhabi movement, Ibn Saud (1880–1953), united Arab tribes in the northern part of the Arabian peninsula and drove out the remnants of Ottoman rule. Ibn Saud was a descendant of the family that had led the Wahhabi revolt in the eighteenth century. Devout and gifted, he won broad support among Arab tribal peoples and established the kingdom of Saudi Arabia throughout much of the peninsula in 1932.

At first, his new kingdom, consisting essentially of the vast wastes of central Arabia, was desperately poor. Its financial resources were limited to the income from Muslim pilgrims visiting the holy sites in Mecca and Medina. But during the 1930s, American companies began to explore for oil, and in 1938, Standard Oil made a successful strike at Dahran, on the Persian Gulf. Soon an Arabian-American oil conglomerate, popularly called Aramco, was established, and the isolated kingdom was suddenly inundated by Western oilmen and untold wealth.

The Issue of Palestine   The land of Palestine—once the home of many peoples including the Jews but for centuries thereafter inhabited primarily by Muslim Arabs and a few thousand Christians—became a separate mandate and immediately became a thorny problem for the British. In 1897, the Austrian-born journalist Theodor Herzl (1860–1904) had convened an international conference in Basel, Switzerland, which led to the creation of the World Zionist Organization (WZO). Its aim was to create a homeland for the Jewish people—long dispersed widely throughout Europe, North Africa, and the Middle East—in Palestine, which was then under Ottoman rule.

Over the next decade, Jewish immigration into Palestine increased with WZO support. By the outbreak of World War I, about 85,000 Jews lived in Palestine, representing about 15 percent of the total population. In 1917, responding to appeals from the British chemist Chaim Weizmann, British Foreign Secretary Lord Arthur Balfour issued a declaration saying Palestine was to be a national home for the Jews. The Balfour Declaration, which was later confirmed by the League of Nations, was ambiguous on the legal status of the territory and promised that the decision would not undermine the rights of the non-Jewish peoples currently living in the area. But Arab nationalists were incensed. How could a national home for the Jewish people, a minority, be established in a territory where the majority of the population was Muslim an Arab? (See Opposing Viewpoints, "The Arab and the Jewish Case for Palestine," p. 371.)

After World War I, more Jewish settlers began to arrive in Palestine in response to the promises made in the Balfour Declaration (see Image 5.3). As tensions between the new arrivals and existing Muslim residents began to escalate, the British tried to restrict Jewish immigration into the territory while Palestinian and other Arab voices rejected the concept of a separate state. In a bid to relieve Arab grievances, Great Britain created the separate emirate of Trans-Jordan out of the eastern portion of Palestine. After World War II, it would become the independent kingdom of Jordan. The stage was set for the conflicts that would take place in the region after World War II.

The British in Egypt   Great Britain had maintained a loose protectorate over Egypt since the middle of the nineteenth century, although the area remained nominally under Ottoman rule. London formalized its protectorate in 1914 to protect the Suez Canal and the Nile River valley from possible seizure by the Central Powers. After the war, however, nationalist elements became restive and formed the Wafd Party, a secular organization dedicated to the creation of an independent Egypt based on the principles of representative government. The Wafd received the support of many middle-class Egyptians who, like Kemal Atatürk in Turkey, hoped to meld Islamic practices with the secular tradition of the modern West. Encouraged by the emergence of a more moderate government, Egyptian women began to seek increased freedoms, and a vocal feminist movement was even formed in Cairo in the 1920s. This modernist form of Islam did not have broad appeal outside the cosmopolitan centers, however, and in 1928 the Muslim cleric Hasan al-Bana organized the Muslim Brotherhood, which demanded strict adherence

IMAGE 5.3 European Jewish Refugees. After the 1917 Balfour Declaration promised a Jewish homeland in Palestine, increasing numbers of European Jews emigrated there. Their goal was to build a new life in a Jewish land. Like the refugees aboard this ship, they celebrated as they reached their new homeland. The sign reads, "Keep the gates open, we are not the last"—a reaction to British efforts to slow the pace of Jewish immigration in response to protests by Muslim residents of Palestine.

Q *How did the Balfour Declaration deal with the question of the legal status of the land of Palestine? Has the issue been resolved today?*

to the traditional teachings of the Prophet, as set forth in the Qur'an. The Brotherhood rejected Western ways and sought to create a new Egypt based firmly on the precepts of the *Shari'a*. By the 1930s, the organization had as many as a million members.

5-1e Nationalism and Revolution

Before the Russian Revolution, to most observers in Asia, "westernization" meant the capitalist democratic civilization of western Europe and the United States, not the doctrine of social revolution developed by Karl Marx. Until 1917, Marxism was generally regarded as a utopian idea rather than a concrete system of government. Moreover, Orthodox Marxism appeared to have little relevance to conditions in Asia. Marxist doctrine, after all, declared that a communist society could arise only from the ashes of an advanced capitalism that had already passed through the stage of industrial revolution. From the perspective of Marxist historical analysis, most societies in Asia were still at the feudal stage of development; they lacked the economic conditions and political awareness to achieve a socialist revolution that would bring the working class to power. Finally, the Marxist view of nationalism and religion had little appeal to many patriotic intellectuals in the non-Western world. Marx believed that nationhood and religion were essentially false ideas that diverted the attention

of the oppressed masses from the critical issues of class struggle and, in his phrase, the exploitation of one person by another. Instead, Marx stressed the importance of an "internationalist" outlook based on class consciousness and the eventual creation of a classless society with no artificial divisions based on culture, nation, or religion.

Lenin and the East   The situation began to change after the Russian Revolution in 1917. The rise to power of Lenin's Bolsheviks demonstrated that a revolutionary party espousing Marxist principles could overturn a corrupt, outdated system and launch a new experiment dedicated to ending human inequality and achieving a paradise on earth. In 1920, Lenin proposed a new revolutionary strategy designed to relate Marxist doctrine and practice to non-Western societies. His reasons were not entirely altruistic. Soviet Russia, surrounded by capitalist powers, desperately needed allies in its struggle to survive in a hostile world. To Lenin, the anticolonial movements emerging in North Africa, Asia, and the Middle East after World War I were natural—if temporary—allies of the beleaguered new regime in Moscow. Lenin was convinced that only the ability of the imperialist powers to find markets, raw materials, and sources of capital investment in the non-Western world kept capitalism alive. If the tentacles of capitalist influence in the rest if the world could be severed, imperialism itself would ultimately weaken and collapse.

Establishing such an alliance was not easy, however. Most nationalist leaders in colonial countries belonged to the urban middle class, and many had no interest in promoting the idea of a violent revolution to create a totally egalitarian society. In addition, many still adhered to traditional religious beliefs and were opposed to the atheistic principles of classical Marxism. To provide restive colonized peoples with access to the Bolshevik experiment, Lenin called for the creation of an organization to train agents who would then be dispatched across the world to carry the Marxist message beyond the borders of industrialized Europe. The primary instrument of this effort was the **Communist International**, or **Comintern** for short. Formed in 1919 at Lenin's prodding, the Comintern was a worldwide organization of Communist parties dedicated to the advancement of world revolution. At its headquarters in Moscow, agents from around the world were trained in the precepts of world communism and then sent back to their own countries to form Marxist parties and promote the cause of social revolution. By the end of the 1920s, almost every colonial or semicolonial society in Asia had a party based on Marxist principles. The Soviets had less success in the Middle East, where Marxist ideology appealed mainly to minorities such as Jews and Armenians in the cities, or in sub-Saharan Africa, where Soviet strategists in any case felt that conditions were not sufficiently advanced for the creation of Communist organizations.

Of course, the new doctrine's appeal was not the same in all non-Western societies. In Confucian societies such as China and Vietnam, where traditional belief systems had been badly discredited by their failure to counter the Western challenge, communism had an immediate impact and rapidly became a major factor in the anticolonial movement (see Historical Voices, "The Path of Liberation," p. 118). In Buddhist and Muslim societies, where traditional religion remained strong and actually became a cohesive factor within the resistance movement, communism had less success and was forced to adapt to local conditions to survive. To maximize their appeal and minimize potential conflict with traditional ideas, some Communist parties sought to adjust Marxist doctrine to indigenous values and institutions. In the Middle East, for example, the Ba'ath Party in Syria adopted a hybrid socialism combining Marxism with Arab nationalism. In Africa, radical intellectuals talked vaguely of a uniquely "African road to socialism." In French Indochina, the Vietnamese revolutionary Nguyen Ai Quoc (see the chapter opening vignette, p. 105) sought to clothe the radical objectives of his party behind the screen of a national liberation movement that was allegedly designed to promote Vietnamese independence.

5-2 REVOLUTION IN CHINA

 Focus Question: What challenges did China encounter between the two world wars, and what solutions did the Nationalists and the Communists propose to resolve them?

Overall, revolutionary Marxism had its greatest impact in China, where a group of young radicals, including several faculty and staff members from the prestigious Beijing University, founded the Chinese Communist Party (CCP) in 1921. The rise of the CCP was a consequence of the failed revolution of 1911. When Sun Yat-sen's forces were too weak to consolidate their power, General Yuan Shikai stepped in to fill the vacuum. In China, Sun Yat-sen and his colleagues had accepted Yuan as president of the new Chinese republic in 1911 because they lacked the military force to compete with his control over the army. Moreover, many feared, perhaps rightly, that if the revolt lapsed into chaos, the Western powers would intervene and the last shreds of Chinese sovereignty would be lost. But some had misgivings about Yuan's intentions. As one remarked in a letter to a friend, "We don't know whether he will be a George Washington or a Napoleon."

As it turned out, he was neither. Showing little comprehension of the new ideas sweeping into China from the West, Yuan ruled in a traditional manner, reviving Confucian rituals and institutions and eventually trying to found a new imperial dynasty. Yuan's dictatorial inclinations led to clashes with Sun's party, now renamed the Guomindang, or Nationalist Party. When Yuan dissolved the new parliament, the Nationalists launched a rebellion. When it failed, Sun Yat-sen fled to Japan.

Yuan was strong enough to brush off the challenge from the revolutionary forces but not to turn back the clock of history. He died in 1916 (apparently of natural causes) and was succeeded by one of his military subordinates. For the next several years, China slipped into anarchy as the power of the central government disintegrated and military warlords seized power in the provinces.

5-2a Mr. Science and Mr. Democracy: The New Culture Movement

Although the failure of the 1911 revolution was a clear sign that China was not yet ready for dramatic change, discontent with existing conditions continued to rise in various sectors of Chinese society. The most vocal protests came from radical elements who opposed Yuan Shikai's conservative agenda but were now convinced that political change could not take place until the Chinese people were

The Path of Liberation

> **Q** Why did Ho Chi Minh believe that the Third International was the key to the liberation of the colonial peoples? What were the essential elements of Lenin's strategy for bringing that about?

 Politics & Government

IN 1919, the Vietnamese revolutionary Ho Chi Minh (1890–1969) was living in exile in France, where he first became acquainted with the new revolutionary experiment in Bolshevik Russia. Later he became a leader of the Vietnamese Communist movement. In the following passage, written in 1960, he reminisces about his reasons for becoming a Communist. The Second International mentioned in the text was an organization created in 1889 by moderate socialists who pursued their goal by parliamentary means. Lenin created the Third International, or Comintern, in 1919 to promote violent revolution. Having rallied to Lenin's strategy at the Congress of Tours in 1920, Ho Chi Minh went to Moscow in 1923 to receive training at Comintern headquarters.

Ho Chi Minh, "The Path Which Led Me to Leninism"

After World War I, I made my living in Paris, now as a retoucher at a photographer's, now as a painter of "Chinese antiquities" (made in France!). I would distribute leaflets denouncing the crimes committed by the French colonialists in Vietnam.

At that time, I supported the October Revolution [in Russia] only instinctively, not yet grasping all its historic importance. I loved and admired Lenin because he was a great patriot who liberated his compatriots; until then, I had read none of his books.

The reason for my joining the French Socialist Party was that these "ladies and gentlemen"—as I called my comrades at that moment—had shown their sympathy toward me, toward the struggle of the oppressed peoples. But I understood neither what was a party, a trade union, nor what was Socialism nor Communism.

Heated discussions were then taking place in the branches of the Socialist Party, about the question whether the Socialist Party should remain in the Second International, should a Second-and-a-Half International be founded, or should the Socialist Party join Lenin's Third International? I attended the meetings regularly, twice or three times a week, and attentively listened to the discussion. First, I could not understand thoroughly. Why were the discussions so heated? Either with the Second, Second-and-a-Half, or Third International, the revolution could be waged. What was the use of arguing then? As for the First International, what had become of it?

What I wanted most to know—and this precisely was not debated in the meetings—was: which International sides with the peoples of colonial countries?

I raised this question—the most important in my opinion—in a meeting. Some comrades answered: It is the Third, not the Second International. And a comrade gave me Lenin's "Thesis on the national and colonial questions," published by *l'Humanité*, to read.

There were political terms difficult to understand in this thesis. But by dint of reading it again and again, finally I could grasp the main part of it. What emotion, enthusiasm, clear sightedness, and confidence it instilled in me! I was overjoyed to tears. Though sitting alone in my room, I shouted aloud as if addressing large crowds: "Dear martyrs, compatriots! This is what we need, this is the path to our liberation!"

After that, I had entire confidence in Lenin, in the Third International.

Source: From *Vietnam: History, Documents, and Opinions on a Major World Crisis*, Marvin Gentleman, ed. (New York: Fawcett Publications, 1965), pp. 30–32.

---

more familiar with trends in the outside world. Braving the displeasure of Yuan Shikai and his successors, progressive intellectuals at Beijing University launched the **New Culture Movement**, aimed at abolishing the remnants of the old system and introducing Western values and institutions into China. Using the classrooms of China's most prestigious university as well as the pages of newly established progressive magazines and newspapers, they presented the Chinese people with a heady mix of new ideas, from the philosophy of Friedrich Nietzsche and Bertrand Russell to the educational views of the American John Dewey and the feminist plays of Henrik Ibsen. As such ideas flooded into China, they stirred up a new generation of educated Chinese youth, who chanted "Down with Confucius and sons" and talked of a new era dominated by "Mr. Sai" (Mr. Science) and "Mr. De" (Mr. Democracy).

No one was a greater defender of free thought and speech than the chancellor of Beijing University, Cai Yuanpei:

> So far as theoretical ideas are concerned, I follow the principles of "freedom of thought" and an attitude of broad tolerance in accordance with the practice of universities the world over. . . . Regardless of what school of thought a person may adhere to, so long as that person's ideas are justified and conform to reason and have not been passed by through the process of natural selection, although there may be controversy, such ideas have a right to be presented.[2]

The problem was that appeals for American-style democracy and women's liberation had little relevance to Chinese peasants, most of whom were still illiterate and concerned above all with survival. Consequently, the New Culture Movement did not win widespread support outside the urban areas. It certainly earned the distrust of conservative military officers, one of whom threatened to lob artillery shells into Beijing University to destroy the poisonous new ideas and their advocates.

Discontent among intellectuals, however, was soon joined by the rising chorus of public protest against Japan's efforts to expand its influence on the mainland. During the first decade of the twentieth century, Japan had taken advantage of the Qing's decline to extend its domination over Manchuria and Korea (see Chapter 3). In 1915, the Japanese government insisted that Yuan Shikai accept a series of twenty-one demands that would have given Japan a virtual protectorate over the Chinese government and economy. Yuan was able to fend off the most far-reaching Japanese demands by arousing popular outrage in China, but at the Paris Peace Conference four years later, Japan received Germany's sphere of influence in Shandong Province as a reward for its support of the Allied cause in World War I. On hearing that the Chinese government had accepted the decision, on May 4, 1919, patriotic students, supported by other sectors of the urban population, demonstrated in Beijing and other major cities of the country. Although this "May Fourth Movement," as it came to be called, did not lead to the restoration of Shandong to China, it did alert a substantial part of the politically literate population to the threat to national survival and the incompetence of the warlord government. A sense of Chinese national identity, long suppressed under Manchu rule, was on the rise in the young republic.

By 1920, central authority had almost ceased to exist in China. Two competing political forces now began to emerge from the chaos. One was Sun Yat-sen's Nationalist Party. Driven from the political arena seven years earlier by Yuan Shikai, the party now reestablished itself on the mainland by making an alliance with the warlord ruler of Guangdong Province in South China. From Canton, Sun sought international assistance to carry out his national revolution. The other was the Chinese Communist Party. Following Lenin's strategy, the CCP sought to link up with the more experienced Nationalists. Sun Yat-sen needed the expertise and the diplomatic support that the Soviet Union could provide because his anti-imperialist rhetoric had alienated many Western powers. In 1923, the two parties formed an alliance to oppose the warlords and drive the imperialist powers out of China.

For three years, with the assistance of a Comintern mission in Canton, the two parties submerged their mutual suspicions and mobilized and trained a revolutionary army to march north and seize control of China. The so-called Northern Expedition began in the summer of 1926 (see Map 5.3). By the following spring, revolutionary forces were in control of all Chinese territory south of the Yangtze River, including the major river ports of Wuhan and Shanghai. But tensions between the two parties now surfaced. Sun Yat-sen had died of cancer in 1925 and was succeeded as head of the Nationalist Party by his military subordinate, Chiang Kai-shek (1887–1975) (see Comparative Illustration, "Masters and Disciples," p. 111). Chiang feigned support for the alliance with the Communists but actually planned to destroy them. In April 1927, he struck against the Communists and their supporters in Shanghai, killing thousands. The CCP responded by encouraging revolts in central China and Canton, but the uprisings were defeated and their leaders were killed or forced into hiding.

5-2b The Nanjing Republic

In 1928, Chiang Kai-shek founded a new Republic of China at Nanjing, and over the next three years, he managed to reunify China by a combination of military operations and inducements (referred to his colleagues sardonically as "silver bullets") to various northern warlords to join his movement. One of his key targets was the warlord Zhang Zuolin, who controlled Manchuria under the tutelage of Japan. When Zhang allegedly agreed to throw in his lot with the Nationalists, the Japanese had him assassinated by placing a bomb under his train as he was returning to Manchuria in 1928. The Japanese hoped that Zhang Zuolin's son and successor, Zhang Xueliang, would be more cooperative, but they had miscalculated. Promised a major role in Chiang Kai-shek's government, Zhang Xueliang began instead to integrate Manchuria politically and economically into the Nanjing republic.

Chiang Kai-shek saw the Japanese as a serious threat to Chinese national aspirations but considered them less dangerous than the Communists (he once remarked to

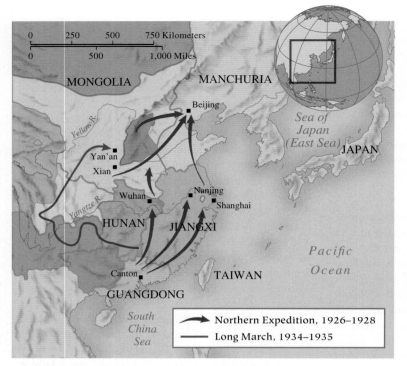

MAP 5.3 The Northern Expedition and the Long March. This map shows the routes taken by the combined Nationalist-Communist forces during the Northern Expedition of 1926–1928. The blue arrow indicates the route taken by Communist units during the Long March led by Mao Zedong.

Q *Where did Mao establish his new headquarters after the Long March? Why?*

an American reporter that "the Japanese are a disease of the skin, but the Communists are a disease of the heart"). After the Shanghai massacre of April 1927, most of the Communist leaders went into hiding in the city, where they attempted to revive the movement in its traditional base among the urban working class. Shanghai was a rich recruiting ground for the party. A city of millionaires, paupers, prostitutes, gamblers, and adventurers, it had led one pious Christian missionary to comment, "If God lets Shanghai endure, He owes an apology to Sodom and Gomorrah."[3] Some party members, however, followed the young Communist organizer Mao Zedong (1893–1976) into a base camp in the hilly areas south of the Yangtze River.

Unlike most other CCP leaders, Mao was convinced that the Chinese revolution must be based on the impoverished peasants in the countryside, not on workers in the big cities. The son of a prosperous farmer, Mao had helped organize a peasant movement in South China during the early 1920s and then served as an agitator in rural villages in his home province of Hunan during the Northern Expedition in the fall of 1926. At that time, he wrote a notorious report to the party leadership suggesting that the CCP support peasant demands for a land revolution. But his superiors refused, fearing that such radical policies would destroy the alliance with the Nationalists (see Historical Voices, "A Call for Revolt," p. 121).

After the spring of 1927, the CCP-Nationalist alliance ceased to exist. Chiang Kai-shek attempted to root the Communists out of their urban base in Shanghai. He succeeded in 1931, when most party leaders, under pressure from Chiang's secret police, were forced to flee Shanghai for Mao's rural redoubt in the rugged hills of Jiangxi Province. Three years later, using their superior military strength, Chiang's troops surrounded the Communist base, inducing Mao's young People's Liberation Army (PLA) to abandon its guerrilla lair and embark on what the Chinese term the Long March, an arduous journey of thousands of miles on foot through mountains, marshes, and deserts to the small provincial town of Yan'an 200 miles north of the modern-day city of Xian in the dusty hills of North China (see Image 5.4). Of the 90,000 who embarked on the journey in October 1934, only 10,000 arrived in Yan'an a year later. Contemporary observers must have thought that the Communist threat to the Nanjing regime had been averted forever.

Meanwhile, Chiang Kai-shek was trying to build a new nation. When the Nanjing republic was established in 1928, Chiang publicly declared his commitment to Sun Yat-sen's Three People's Principles. In a program announced in 1918, Sun had written about the all-important second stage of "political tutelage":

> As a schoolboy must have good teachers and helpful
> friends, so the Chinese people, being for the first
> time under republican rule, must have a farsighted
> revolutionary government for their training. This calls
> for the period of political tutelage, which is a necessary
> transitional stage from monarchy to republicanism.
> Without this, disorder will be unavoidable.[4]

In keeping with Sun's program, Chiang announced a period of political indoctrination to prepare the Chinese people for a final stage of constitutional government. In the meantime, the Nationalists would use their dictatorial power to carry out a land reform program and modernize the urban industrial sector.

A Call for Revolt

Why did Mao Zedong believe that rural peasants could help bring about a social revolution in China? How does his vision compare with the reality of the Bolshevik Revolution in Russia?

Politics & Government

IN THE FALL OF 1926, Nationalist and Communist forces moved north from Canton on their Northern Expedition in an effort to defeat the warlords. The young Communist Mao Zedong accompanied revolutionary troops into his home province of Hunan, where he submitted a report to the CCP Central Committee calling for a massive peasant revolt against the ruling order. The report shows his confidence that peasants could play an active role in the Chinese revolution despite the skepticism of many of his colleagues.

Mao Zedong, "The Peasant Movement in Hunan"

During my recent visit to Hunan I made a firsthand investigation of conditions. . . . In a very short time, . . . several hundred million peasants will rise like a mighty storm, . . . a force so swift and violent that no power, however great, will be able to hold it back. They will smash all the trammels that bind them and rush forward along the road to liberation. They will sweep all the imperialists, warlords, corrupt officials, local tyrants, and evil gentry into their graves. Every revolutionary party and every revolutionary comrade will be put to the test, to be accepted or rejected as they decide. There are three alternatives. To march at their head and lead them? To trail behind them, gesticulating and criticizing? Or to stand in their way and oppose them? Every Chinese is free to choose, but events will force you to make the choice quickly.

The main targets of attack by the peasants are the local tyrants, the evil gentry and the lawless landlords, but in passing they also hit out against patriarchal ideas and institutions, against the corrupt officials in the cities and against bad practices and customs in the rural areas. . . . As a result, the privileges which the feudal landlords enjoyed for thousands of years are being shattered to pieces. . . . With the collapse of the power of the land-lords, the peasant associations have now become the sole organs of authority, and the popular slogan "All power to the peasant associations" has become a reality.

The peasants' revolt disturbed the gentry's sweet dreams. When the news from the countryside reached the cities, it caused immediate uproar among the gentry. . . . From the middle social strata upwards to the Kuomintang [Nationalist] right-wingers, there was not a single person who did not sum up the whole business in the phrase, "It's terrible!" . . . Even quite progressive people said, "Though terrible, it is inevitable in a revolution." In short, nobody could altogether deny the word "terrible." But . . . the fact is that the great peasant masses have risen to fulfill their historic mission. . . . What the peasants are doing is absolutely right; what they are doing is fine! "It's fine!" is the theory of the peasants and of all other revolutionaries. Every revolutionary comrade should know that the national revolution requires a great change in the countryside. The Revolution of 1911 did not bring about this change, hence its failure. This change is now taking place, and it is an important factor for the completion of the revolution. Every revolutionary comrade must support it, or he will be taking the stand of counterrevolution.

Source: From *Selected Works of Mao Tse-Tung* (London: Lawrence and Wishart, Ltd., 1954), vol. 1, pp. 21–23.

But it would take more than paper plans to create a new China. Years of neglect and civil war had severely frayed the political, economic, and social fabric of the nation. There were faint signs of an impending industrial revolution in the major urban centers, but most of the people in the countryside, drained by warlord exactions and civil strife, were still grindingly poor and overwhelmingly illiterate. A westernized middle class had begun to emerge in the cities and formed much of the natural constituency of the Nanjing government. But this new westernized elite, preoccupied with bourgeois values of individual advancement and material accumulation, had few links with the peasants in the countryside or the rickshaw drivers "running in this world of suffering," in the poignant words of a Chinese poet. In an expressive phrase, some critics dismissed Chiang Kai-shek and his chief followers as "banana Chinese"—yellow on the outside, white on the inside.

IMAGE 5.4 Mao Zedong on the Long March. In 1934, the Communist leader Mao Zedong led his bedraggled forces on the famous Long March from southern China to a new location at Yan'an, in the hills just south of the Gobi Desert. The epic journey has ever since been celebrated as a symbol of the willingness of party members to sacrifice for the revolutionary cause. In this photograph, Mao sits astride a white horse as he accompanies his followers on the march. Reportedly, he was the only participant allowed to ride a horse en route to Yan'an.

 How did Mao Zedong's strategy for social revolution in China differ from orthodox Marxist teachings?

The Best of East and West Chiang was aware of the difficulty of introducing exotic foreign ideas into a society still culturally conservative. While building a modern industrial sector and rejecting what he considered the excessive individualism and material greed of Western capitalism, Chiang sought to propagate traditional Confucian values of hard work, obedience, and moral integrity through the officially promoted New Life Movement, sponsored by his Wellesley-educated wife, Mei-ling Soong. In effect, he had revived the old debate over "East for Essence, West for Practical Use" in a new context (see Chapter 3).

Unfortunately for Chiang, the effort to meld Eastern and Western values would be no easy task, because Confucian ideas—at least in their institutional form—had been widely discredited among the Chinese urban elite by the failure of the traditional system to solve the country's festering problems. Moreover, with only a tenuous hold over the provinces, a growing Japanese threat in the north, and a world suffering from the Great Depression, Chiang was facing strong headwinds both inside China and abroad. To make matters worse, he lacked the political acumen and the popular appeal of his mentor, Sun Yat-sen. Fearing Communist influence and distrusting many of his warlord rivals, Chiang repressed all forms of opposition and censored free expression, thereby alienating many intellectuals and political moderates. Because the urban middle class and the landed gentry were his natural political constituency, he shunned programs that would lead to a redistribution of wealth, thus disappointing the vast majority of his constituents, many of whom had felt few benefits from nearly a century of dynastic decline and imperialist interference.

5-2c "Down with Confucius and Sons": Economic, Social, and Cultural Change in Republican China

The transformation of the old order that had begun at the end of the Qing era continued during the early Chinese republic. However, for many of the reasons already mentioned, success was disappointingly slow.

Industrial and Agricultural Development The centerpiece of an advanced economy is a modern manufacturing and commercial sector. Here, the results were disappointing, for the Nanjing government had little success in promoting industrial development, which grew at an average annual rate of only 1 percent or so during the first decade of its existence. Although mechanization had gradually begun to replace manual labor in some traditional industries like textile manufacturing, three-quarters of all industrial goods were still manually produced in the mid-1930s. In addition, traditional Chinese exports, such as silk and tea, were hard-hit by the Great Depression. In the countryside, as well, success was fleeting. A land reform program was enacted in 1930, but it was sabotaged by wealthy landowners—among Chiang's most loyal supporters—and had little impact in reducing rural poverty. Farmers were often victimized by the endemic conflict in the countryside, as well as by high taxes imposed by local warlords. Where similar conditions in Meiji Japan had led to the flight of rural migrants to join the growing labor market in the cities, there was no such option in early Republican China.

Many historians believe that some of the new government's problems can be ascribed to its own missteps. Much of the national wealth was in the hands of senior officials and close subordinates of the ruling elite. High military expenses—a product of Chiang's obsession with eradicating the CCP—consumed half of the budget as a result, few funds were available for social and economic development. Meanwhile, Chiang and his ruling circle appeared oblivious to the need to take decisive steps to alleviate conditions in the countryside. On the other hand, as some observers point out, it is only fair to note that the Nanjing Republic was fated to make its effort to install the foundations of a modern industrial economy in a historically inhospitable climate marked by high global tariffs and vanishing investment funds. Under the best of circumstances, the Nanking government was faced with an enormous challenge in dealing with China's deep-seated economic and social problems. The deadly combination of internal disintegration and foreign pressure now began to coincide with the virtual collapse of the global economic order during the Great Depression and the rise of militant political forces in Tokyo determined to extend Japanese influence and power in an unstable Asia. These forces and the turmoil they unleashed will be examined below.

Social Changes The transformation of the old order that had commenced at the end of the Qing era continued into the period of the early Chinese republic. By 1915, the assault on the old system and values by educated youth was intense. The main focus of the attack was the Confucian concept of the family—in particular, filial piety and the subordination of women. Young people called for the right to choose their own mates and their own careers. Women began to demand rights and opportunities equal to those enjoyed by men.

More broadly, progressives called for an end to the concept of duty to the community and praised the Western individualist ethos. The prime spokesman for such views was the popular writer Lu Xun, whose short stories criticized the Confucian concept of family as a "man-eating" system that degraded humanity. In a famous short story titled "Diary of a Madman," the protagonist remarks:

> I remember when I was four or five years old, sitting in the cool of the hall, my brother told me that if a man's parents were ill, he should cut off a piece of his flesh and

boil it for them if he wanted to be considered a good son. I have only just realized that I have been living all these years in a place where for four thousand years they have been eating human flesh.[5]

Such criticisms did yield some beneficial results. During the early republic, the tyranny of the old family system began to decline, at least in urban areas, under the impact of economic changes and the urgings of the New Culture intellectuals. Women, long consigned to an inferior place in the Confucian world order, began to escape their cloistered existence and seek education and employment alongside their male contemporaries. Free choice in marriage and a more relaxed attitude toward sex became commonplace among affluent families in the cities, where the teenage children of westernized elites adopted the clothing, social habits, and musical tastes of their contemporaries in Europe and the United States (see Historical Voices, "An Arranged Marriage," p. 124).

But as a rule, the new consciousness of individualism and women's rights that marked the early republican era in the major cities did not penetrate to the textile factories, where more than 1 million women worked in conditions resembling slave labor, or to the villages, where traditional attitudes and customs still held sway. Arranged marriages continued to be the rule rather than the exception, and concubinage remained common. According to a survey taken in the 1930s, well over two-thirds of the marriages, even among urban couples, had been arranged by their parents; in one rural area, only three of 170 villagers interviewed had heard of the idea of "modern marriage." Even the tradition of binding the feet of female children continued despite efforts by the Nationalist government to eradicate the practice.

A New Culture Nowhere was the struggle between traditional and modern more visible than in the field of culture. Beginning with the New Culture era during the early years of the first Chinese republic, radical reformists criticized traditional culture as the symbol and instrument of feudal oppression that must be entirely eradicated to create a new China that could stand on its feet with dignity in the modern world.

For many reformers, that new culture must be based on that of the modern West. During the 1920s and 1930s, Western literature and art became popular in China, especially among the urban middle class. Traditional culture continued to prevail among more conservative elements of the population, and some intellectuals argued for the creation of a new art that would synthesize the best of Chinese and foreign culture. But the most creative artists were interested in imitating foreign trends, whereas traditionalists were more concerned with preservation.

HISTORICAL VOICES

An Arranged Marriage

Q Why does Chueh-hsin comply with the wishes of his father in the matter of his marriage? Why were arranged marriages so prevalent in traditional China?

Family & Society

UNDER WESTERN INFLUENCE, Chinese social customs changed dramatically for many urban elites in the interwar years. A vocal women's movement campaigned aggressively for universal suffrage and an end to sexual discrimination. Some progressives called for free choice in marriage and divorce and even for free love. By the 1930s, the government had taken some steps to free women from patriarchal marriage constraints, but life was generally unaffected in the villages, where traditional patterns held sway. This often created severe tensions between older and younger generations, as this passage from a novel by popular twentieth-century writer Ba Jin (BAH JIN) shows.

Ba Jin, *Family*

Brought up with loving care, after studying with a private tutor for a number of years, Chueh-hsin entered middle school. . . . [H]e graduated four years later at the top of his class. He was very interested in physics and chemistry and hoped to study abroad, in Germany. His mind was full of beautiful dreams. At that time he was the envy of his classmates.

In his fourth year at middle school, he lost his mother. His father later married again, this time to a younger woman who had been his mother's cousin. Chueh-hsin was aware of his loss, for he knew full well that nothing could replace the love of a mother. But her death left no irreparable wound in his heart; he was able to console himself with rosy dreams of his future. Moreover, he had someone who understood him and could comfort him—his pretty cousin Mei, "mei" for "plum blossom."

But then, one day his dreams were shattered, cruelly and bitterly shattered. The evening he returned home carrying his diploma, the plaudits of his teachers and friends still ringing in his ears, his father called him into his room and said:

"Now that you've graduated, I want to arrange your marriage. Your grandfather is looking forward to having a great-grandson, and I, too, would like to be able to hold a grandson in my arms. You're old enough to be married; I won't feel easy until I fulfill my obligation to find you a wife. Although I didn't accumulate much money in my years away from home as an official, still I've put by enough for us to get along on. My health isn't what it used to be; I'm thinking of spending my time at home and having you help me run the household affairs. All the more reason you'll be needing a wife. I've already arranged a match with the Li family. The thirteenth of next month is a good day. We'll announce the engagement then. You can be married within the year. . . ."

Chueh-hsin did not utter a word of protest, nor did such a thought ever occur to him. He merely nodded to indicate his compliance with his father's wishes. But after he returned to his own room, and shut the door, he threw himself down on his bed, covered his head with the quilt and wept. He wept for his broken dreams.

He was deeply in love with Mei, but now his father had chosen another, a girl he had never seen, and said that he must marry within the year. . . .

He cried his disappointment and bitterness. But the door was closed and Chueh-hsin's head was beneath the bedding. No one knew. He did not fight back, he never thought of resisting. He only bemoaned his fate. But he accepted it. He complied with his father's will without a trace of resentment. But in his heart he wept for himself, wept for the girl he adored—Mei, his "plum blossom."

Source: Excerpt from "Family" by Ba Jin. Copyright © 1964 Foreign Languages Press, 24 Baiwanzhuang Rd., Beijing 10037, P.R. China.

Literature in particular was influenced by foreign ideas as Western genres like the novel and the short story attracted a growing audience. Although most Chinese novels written after World War I dealt with Chinese subjects, they reflected the Western tendency toward social realism and often dealt with the new westernized middle class (Mao Dun's *Midnight*, for example, described the changing mores of Shanghai's urban elites) or the disintegration of the traditional Confucian family. Most of China's modern authors displayed a clear contempt for the past which, they felt, had been responsible for bringing the country to its current state of decrepitude.

5-3 JAPAN BETWEEN THE WARS

 Focus Question: How did Japan address the challenge of nation-building in the first decade of the twentieth century, and why did democratic institutions not take hold more effectively?

By the beginning of the twentieth century, Japan had made steady progress toward the creation of an advanced society on the Western model. Economic and social reforms launched during the Meiji era led to increasing prosperity and the development of a modern industrial and commercial sector. Although the political system still retained many authoritarian characteristics, optimists had reason to hope that Japan was on the road to becoming a full-fledged democracy.

5-3a Experiment in Democracy

During the first quarter of the twentieth century, the Japanese political system appeared to evolve significantly toward the Western democratic model. Political parties expanded their popular following and became increasingly competitive, while individual pressure groups such as labor unions began to appear in Japanese society, along with an independent press and a bill of rights. The influence of the old ruling oligarchy, the *genro*, had not yet been significantly challenged, however, nor had that of its ideological foundation, which focused on national wealth and power.

The fragile flower of democratic institutions was able to survive throughout the 1920s, often called the era of **Taisho democracy**, from the reign title of the emperor. During that period, the military budget was reduced, and a suffrage bill enacted in 1925 granted the vote to all adult Japanese males. Women remained disenfranchised, but women's associations became increasingly visible during the 1920s, and women were active in the labor movement and in campaigns for various social reforms.

But the era was also marked by growing social turmoil, and two opposing forces within the system were gearing up to challenge the prevailing wisdom. On the left, a Marxist labor movement, which reflected the tensions within the working class and the increasing radicalism among the rural poor, began to take shape in the early 1920s in response to growing economic difficulties. Government suppression of labor disturbances led to further radicalization. On the right, ultranationalist groups called for a rejection of Western models of development and a more militant approach to realizing national objectives. In 1919, radical nationalist Kita Ikki called for a military takeover

and the establishment of a new system bearing a strong resemblance to what would later be called fascism in Europe (see Chapter 6).

This cultural conflict between old and new, indigenous and foreign, was reflected in literature. The restoration of Japanese self-confidence after the victories over China and Russia launched an age of cultural creativity in the early-twentieth century. Fascination with Western literature gave birth to a striking new genre called the "I novel." Defying traditional Japanese reticence, some authors reveled in self-exposure with confessions of their innermost thoughts. Others found release in the "proletarian literature" movement of the early 1920s. Inspired by Soviet literary examples, these authors wanted literature to serve socialist goals and improve the lives of the working class. Finally, some Japanese writers blended Western psychology with Japanese sensibility in exquisite novels reeking of nostalgia for the old Japan. One well-known example is Junichiro Tanizaki's *Some Prefer Nettles* (1929), which delicately juxtaposes the positive aspects of traditional and modern Japan. By the early 1930s, however, military censorship increasingly inhibited literary expression.

5-3b A *Zaibatsu* Economy

Japan also continued to make impressive progress in economic development. Spurred by rising domestic demand as well as a continued high rate of government investment in the economy, the production of raw materials tripled between 1900 and 1930, and industrial production increased more than twelvefold. Much of the increase went into the export market, and Western manufacturers began to complain about the rising competition for markets from the Japanese.

As often happens, rapid industrialization was accompanied by some hardship and rising social tensions. A characteristic of the Meiji model was the concentration of various manufacturing processes within a single enterprise, the **zaibatsu**, or financial clique. Some of these firms were existing merchant companies that had the capital and the foresight to move into new areas of opportunity. Others were formed by enterprising samurai, who used their status and experience in management to good account in a new environment. Whatever their origins, these firms gradually developed, often with official encouragement, into large conglomerates that controlled a major segment of the Japanese industrial sector. According to one source, by 1937 the four largest *zaibatsu* (Mitsui, Mitsubishi, Sumitomo, and Yasuda) controlled 21 percent of the banking industry, 26 percent of mining, 35 percent of shipbuilding, 38 percent of commercial shipping, and more than 60 percent of paper manufacturing and insurance.

This concentration of power and wealth in the hands of a few major industrial combines resulted in the emergence of a form of dual economy: on the one hand, a modern industry characterized by up-to-date methods and massive government subsidies, and on the other, a traditional manufacturing sector characterized by conservative methods and small-scale production techniques.

Concentration of wealth also led to growing economic inequalities. As we have seen, economic growth had been achieved at the expense of the peasants, many of whom fled to the cities to escape rural poverty. That labor surplus benefited the industrial sector, but the urban proletariat was still poorly paid and ill-housed. Rampant inflation in the price of rice led to food riots shortly after World War I. A rapid increase in population (the total population of the Japanese islands increased from an estimated 43 million in 1900 to 73 million in 1940) led to food shortages and the threat of rising unemployment. Intense competition and the global recession in the early 1920s led to a greater concentration of industry and a perceptible rise in urban radicalism. In the meantime, those left on the farm continued to suffer. As late as the beginning of World War II, an estimated half of all Japanese farmers were tenants.

5-3c Shidehara Diplomacy

A final problem for Japanese leaders in the post-Meiji era was the familiar capitalist dilemma of finding sources of raw materials and foreign markets for the nation's manufactured goods. Until World War I, Japan had dealt with the problem by seizing territories such as Taiwan, Korea, and southern Manchuria and transforming them into colonies or protectorates of the growing Japanese empire. That policy had succeeded brilliantly, but it had also begun to arouse the concern and, in some cases, the hostility of the Western nations. China was also becoming apprehensive; as we have seen, Japanese demands for Shandong Province at the Paris Peace Conference in 1919 aroused massive protests in major Chinese cities.

The United States was especially concerned about Japanese aggressiveness. Although the United States had been less active than some European states in pursuing colonies in the Pacific, it had a strong interest in keeping the area open for U.S. commercial activities. Anxiety in Washington about Tokyo's twenty-one demands on China in 1915 led to a new agreement with Japan in 1917, which essentially repeated the compromise provisions of the agreement reached nine years earlier.

In 1922, the United States convened a major conference of nations with interests in the Pacific in Washington, D.C. to discuss problems of regional security. The Washington Conference led to agreements on several issues, but its major accomplishment was the conclusion of a nine-power

treaty recognizing the territorial integrity of China and the Open Door. The other participants induced Japan to accept these provisions by accepting its special position in Manchuria.

During the remainder of the 1920s, Japanese governments attempted to play by the rules laid down at the Washington Conference. Known as Shidehara diplomacy, after the foreign minister (and later prime minister) who attempted to carry it out, this policy sought to use diplomatic and economic means to realize Japanese interests in Asia. But this approach came under severe pressure as Japanese industrialists began to move into new areas of opportunity, such as heavy industry, chemicals, mining, and the manufacturing of appliances and automobiles. Because such industries desperately needed resources not found in abundance locally, the Japanese government came under increasing pressure to find new sources abroad.

The Rise of Militant Nationalism In the early 1930s, with the onset of the Great Depression and growing tensions in the international arena, nationalist forces rose to dominance in the Japanese government. These elements, a mixture of military officers and ultranationalist politicians, were convinced that the diplomacy of the 1920s had failed and advocated a more aggressive approach to protecting national interests in a brutal and competitive world. By the early 1930s, democratic parties and institutions were in full retreat as radical nationalist elements, many of them with connections to the military, sought to take control of the reins of government. We shall discuss the factors involved and the impact of these developments on the international scene in the next chapter.

HISTORIANS
DEBATE ## 5-3d Taisho Democracy: An Aberration?

The dramatic shift in Japanese political culture that occurred in the early 1930s has caused some historians to question the breadth and depth of the trend toward democratic practices in the 1920s. Was Taisho democracy merely a premature attempt at comparative liberalization in a society that was still dominated by the Meiji vision of empire and kokutai? Or was it a natural course of events that was disrupted by the Great Depression, which brought about the rise of militant nationalism and caused the inexorable emergence of democracy in Japan to stall?

Clearly, there is no simple answer to these questions. A process of democratization was taking place in Japan during the first decades of the twentieth century, but without shaking the essential core of the Meiji concept of the state. When the "liberal" approach of the 1920 failed to solve the problems of the day, political forces deeply imbedded in Japanese society expressed growing concerns about the government's current policies in Asia and continued to believe in Japanese uniqueness. With the shallow roots of the democracy movement exposed, the shift toward a more aggressive approach became virtually inevitable.

Still, the course of Japanese history after World War II (see Chapter 9) suggests that the emergence of multiparty democracy in the 1920s was not an aberration, but a natural consequence of evolutionary trends in Japanese society. The seeds of democracy nurtured during the Taisho era were nipped in the bud by the cataclysmic effects of the Great Depression – a tragedy that occurred simultaneously in a number of other countries at the time. In the more conducive climate after World War II, however, a democratic system suitably adjusted to Japanese soil reached full flower.

5-4 NATIONALISM AND DICTATORSHIP IN LATIN AMERICA

 Focus Questions: What problems did the nations of Latin America face in the interwar years? To what degree were they a consequence of foreign influence?

Because most of Latin America had won its independence from European control during the nineteenth century, nationalism and political change took different forms in this area in the years following World War I than they did in Asia and the Middle East. But the region was by no means isolated from the trends occurring throughout the rest of the world. National sentiment in opposition to foreign political and economic influence—and especially U.S. influence—was sometimes intense. And when the Great Depression struck in the late 1920s, the political equation in Latin America was affected in profound ways.

5-4a A Changing Economy

At the beginning of the twentieth century, the economy of Latin America was based largely on the export of foodstuffs and raw materials. Some countries relied on the export earnings of only one or two products. Argentina, for example, depended heavily on the sale of beef and wheat; Chile, on nitrates and copper; Brazil and the Caribbean nations, on sugar; and the Central American states, on bananas. Such exports brought large profits to a few, but for the majority of the population, the returns were meager.

During World War I, exports of some products, such as Chilean nitrates (used to produce explosives), increased dramatically. In general, however, the war led to a decline in European investment in Latin America and a rise in the U.S.

role in the local economies. The United States had already begun to intervene in Latin American politics in the early years of the twentieth century during its construction of the Panama Canal, which dramatically reduced the time and distance needed for ships to pass between the Atlantic and Pacific Oceans.

The Role of the Yankee Dollar By the late 1920s, the United States had replaced Great Britain as the foremost source of foreign investment in Latin America. Unlike the British, however, U.S. investors put their funds directly into production enterprises, causing large segments of the area's export industry to fall into American hands. A number of Central American states, for example, were popularly labeled "banana republics" because of the power and influence of the U.S.-owned United Fruit Company. American firms also dominated the copper mining industry in Chile and Peru and the oil industry in Mexico, Peru, and Bolivia.

Increasing economic power served to reinforce the traditionally high level of U.S. political influence in Latin America, especially in Central America, a region that many Americans considered vital to U.S. national security. American troops occupied parts of both Nicaragua and Honduras to put down unrest or protect U.S. interests there. The growing U.S. presence in the region aroused hostility among Latin Americans, who resented their dependent relationship on the United States, which they viewed as an aggressive imperialist power. Some charged that Washington worked, sometimes through U.S. military intervention, to keep ruthless dictators, such as Juan Vicente Gómez of Venezuela and Fulgencio Batista of Cuba, in power to preserve U.S. economic influence. In a bid to improve relations with Latin American countries, in 1933 President Franklin D. Roosevelt promulgated the **Good Neighbor policy**, which rejected the use of U.S. military force in the region. To underscore his sincerity, Roosevelt ordered the withdrawal of U.S. marines from the island nation of Haiti in 1936. For the first time in thirty years, there were no U.S. occupation troops in Latin America.

Because so many Latin American nations depended for their livelihood on the export of raw materials and food products, the Great Depression of the 1930s was a disaster for the region. In 1930, the value of Latin American exports fell to only half the amount that had been exported in each of the previous five years. Spurred by the decline in foreign revenues, Latin American governments began to encourage the development of new industries to reduce dependence on imports. In some cases—the steel industry in Chile and Brazil, the oil industry in Argentina and Mexico—government investment made up for the absence of local sources of capital.

5-4b The Effects of Dependency

During the late-nineteenth century, most governments in Latin America had been dominated by landed or military elites, who governed by the blatant use of military force. This trend continued during the 1930s as domestic instability caused by the effects of the Great Depression led to the creation of military dictatorships throughout the region, especially in Argentina and Brazil and, to a lesser degree,

in Mexico—three countries that together possessed more than half of the land and wealth of Latin America (see Map 5.4).

Argentina   By no means were all of Latin America's problems the product of foreign influence. Some were self-imposed. In Argentina, autocratic rule by an elite minority had disastrous effects. The government of Argentina, controlled by landowners who had benefited from the export of beef and wheat, was slow to recognize the need to establish a local industrial base. In 1916, Hipólito Irigoyen (1852–1933), head of the Radical Party, was elected president on a program to improve conditions for the middle and lower classes. Little was achieved, however, as the party became increasingly corrupt and identified with the interests of the large landowners. In 1930, the army overthrew Irigoyen's government, but its effort to return to the past and suppress the growing influence of labor unions failed, and in 1946, General Juan Peron—claiming the support of the *descamisados* ("shirtless ones")—seized sole power (see Chapter 8).

Brazil   Brazil followed a similar path. In 1889, the army overthrew the Brazilian monarchy, installed by Portugal decades before, and established a republic. But it was dominated by landed elites, many of whom had grown wealthy through their ownership of coffee plantations. By 1900, three-quarters of the world's coffee was grown in Brazil. As in Argentina, the ruling oligarchy ignored the importance of establishing an urban industrial base. When the Great Depression ravaged profits from coffee exports, a wealthy rancher, Getúlio Vargas (1883–1954), seized power and served as president from 1930 to 1945. At first, Vargas sought to appease the workers by instituting an eight-hour workday and a

MAP 5.4 Latin America in the First Half of the Twentieth Century. Shown here are the boundaries dividing the countries of Latin America after the independence movements of the nineteenth century.

 Which areas remained under European rule?

minimum wage, but influenced by the apparent success of fascist regimes in Europe, he ruled by increasingly autocratic means and relied on a police force that used torture to silence his opponents. His industrial policy was successful, however, and by the end of World War II, Brazil had become Latin America's major industrial power. In 1945, the army, concerned that Vargas was turning increasingly to leftist elements for support, forced him to resign.

Mexico In the early years of the twentieth century, Mexico was in a state of turbulence. Under the rule of the longtime dictator Porfirio Díaz (see Chapter 1), the real wages of the working class had declined. Moreover, 95 percent of the rural population owned no land, and about a thousand families ruled almost all of Mexico. Much of the

Snark/Art Resource, NY

IMAGE 5.5 Emiliano Zapata. Deep-seated poverty in the southern state of Chiapas led one of its own, the young militant Emiliano Zapata, to organize his followers to launch a revolt against wealthy landowners in southern Mexico. After his demands for widespread land reform were rejected, Zapata joined forces with the northern rebel leader Pancho Villa and was killed in a battle with government troops in 1923.

manufacturing sector, and most of the important export industries, was in the hands of foreign owners.

The first rumblings of discontent appeared among members of the intellectual elite, who in the early years of the century began to agitate for political reforms to introduce representative government. They also favored the adoption of measures to improve the lot of the urban and rural poor. In the meantime, violent protests erupted in the countryside. In the poverty-stricken state of Chiapas, the rebel leader Emiliano Zapata (1879–1919) aroused landless peasants, who began seizing the haciendas of wealthy landowners (see Image 5.5). Eventually, Zapata (later made famous to U.S. audiences by the 1952 film *Viva Zapata*, starring Marlon Brando) was able to set up a local revolutionary regime under his own leadership. In the state of Chihuahua, farther to the north, the bandit leader Pancho Villa (1878–1923) terrorized the local power structure and on occasion even crossed the border to launch raids on small towns in the United States.

The growing specter of rural revolt caused great concern among the Mexican power elite, and in 1910 Díaz was forced to resign in favor of the reformist politician Francisco Madero (1873–1913). The latter sought to carry out a program of political reform, but he was unable to keep pace with the rapid change taking place throughout the country. In 1913, Madero was deposed and assassinated by one of Díaz's military subordinates.

For the next several years, Zapata and Pancho Villa continued to be important political forces in Mexico, publicly advocating measures to redress the economic grievances of the poor. But neither had a broad grasp of the challenges facing the country, and power eventually gravitated to a more moderate group of reformists around the Constitutionalist Party. The latter were intent on breaking the power of the great landed families and powerful U.S. corporations, but without engaging in radical land reform or the nationalization of property. After a bloody conflict that cost the lives of thousands, the moderates were able to consolidate power, and in 1917 the party promulgated a new constitution that established a strong presidency, initiated land reform policies, established limits on foreign investment, and set an agenda for social welfare programs. The United States had resisted many of these measures but eventually saw the wisdom of recognizing a government that had successfully avoided the hazards of a vast social revolution, such as had occurred in Russia.

In 1920, the Constitutionalist Party leader Alvaro Obregón assumed the presidency and began to carry out a reform program. But real change did not take place until the presidency of General Lázaro Cárdenas (1895–1970) in 1934. Cárdenas won wide popularity among the peasants by ordering the redistribution of 44 million acres of land controlled by landed elites. He also seized control of the oil industry, which had hitherto been dominated by major U.S. oil companies. Alluding to the Good Neighbor policy, President Roosevelt refused to intervene, and eventually Mexico agreed to compensate the U.S. oil companies for their lost property. It then set up PEMEX, a governmental organization, to run the oil industry. By now, the revolution was democratic in name only, as the ruling political party, known as the Institutional Revolutionary Party (PRI), controlled the levers of power throughout society. Every six years, for more than half a century, PRI presidential candidates automatically succeeded each other in office.

5-4c Latin American Culture

The first half of the twentieth century witnessed a dramatic increase in literary activity in Latin America, a result in part of its ambivalent relationship with Europe and the United States. Many authors, while experimenting with imported modernist styles, felt compelled to proclaim their region's unique identity through the adoption of Latin American themes and social issues. In *The Underdogs* (1915), for example, Mariano Azuela (1873–1952) presented a sympathetic but not uncritical portrait of the Mexican Revolution as his country entered an era of unsettling change.

In their determination to express Latin America's distinctive characteristics, some writers focused on the promise of the region's vast virgin lands and the diversity of its peoples. In *Don Segundo Sombra*, published in 1926, Ricardo Guiraldes (1886–1927) celebrated the life of the ideal *gaucho* (cowboy), defining Argentina's hope and strength through the enlightened management of its fertile earth. Likewise, in *Dona Barbara*, Rómulo Gallegos (1884–1969) wrote in a similar vein about his native Venezuela. Other authors pursued the theme of solitude and detachment, a product of the region's physical separation from the rest of the world.

Latin American artists followed their literary counterparts in joining the Modernist movement in Europe, yet they too were eager to promote the emergence of a new regional and national essence. In Mexico, where the government provided financial support for painting murals on public buildings, the artist Diego Rivera (1886–1957) began to produce a monumental style of mural art that served two purposes: to illustrate the national past by portraying Aztec legends and folk customs and to popularize

IMAGE 5.6 Frida Kahlo: Self-Portrait with Bonito. Frida Kahlo (1907–1954) was one of the most noted Latin American painters of the twentieth century. Born in 1907 of a German father and a Mexican mother, she originally planned on a career in medicine, but turned to art when she married the noted Mexican painter Diego Rivera. By the late 1930s, her distinctive paintings, which combined folk art with elements of Surrealism and radical politics (both she and her husband were members of the Communist Party of Mexico), began to achieve broader popularity. Many of her best-known paintings are self-portraits, and are often used today to explore issues of gender, identity, and postcolonialism.

 Can you think of any other artists whose paintings have taken on strong political connotations?

a political message in favor of realizing the social goals of the Mexican Revolution. His wife, Frida Kahlo (1907–1954), incorporated Surrealist whimsy in her own paintings, many of which were portraits of herself and her family (see Image 5.6).

MAKING CONNECTIONS

The turmoil brought about by World War I not only resulted in the destruction of several of the major Western empires and a redrawing of the map of Europe but also opened the door to political and social upheavals elsewhere in the world. In the Middle East, the decline and fall of the Ottoman Empire led to the creation of the secular republic of Turkey and several other new states carved out of the carcass of the old empire.

Other parts of Asia also witnessed the rise of movements for national independence. In India, Gandhi and his campaign of civil disobedience played a crucial role in his country's bid to be free of British rule. China waged its own dramatic struggle to establish a modern nation as two dynamic political organizations—the Nationalists and the Communists—competed for legitimacy as the rightful heirs of the old order. Japan continued to follow its own path to modernization, which, although successful from an economic point of view, took a menacing turn during the 1930s.

The nations of Latin America faced their own economic problems because of their dependence on exports. Increasing U.S. investments in Latin America contributed to growing hostility against the powerful neighbor to the north. The Great Depression forced the region to begin developing new industries, but it also led to the rise of authoritarian governments, some of them modeled after the fascist regimes of Italy and Germany.

By demolishing the remnants of their old civilization on the battlefields of World War I, Europeans had inadvertently encouraged the subject peoples of their vast colonial empires to begin their own movements for national independence. The process was by no means completed in the two decades following the Treaty of Versailles, but the bonds of imperial rule had been severely strained. Once Europeans began to weaken themselves in the even more destructive conflict of World War II, the hopes of colonial peoples for national independence and freedom could at last be realized. It is to that devastating world conflict that we now turn.

REFLECTION QUESTIONS

Q How did the societies discussed in this chapter deal with the political, economic, and social challenges that they faced after World War I, and how did these challenges differ from one region to another?

Q In what ways did Japan's political system and social structure in the interwar years combine modern and traditional elements? How successful was the attempt to create a modern political system while retaining indigenous traditions of civil obedience and loyalty to the emperor?

Q During the early twentieth century, did conditions for women change for the better or for the worse in the countries discussed in this chapter? Why?

Q Communist parties were established in many Asian societies in the years immediately following the Bolshevik Revolution. How successful were these parties in winning popular support and achieving their goals?

CHAPTER TIMELINE

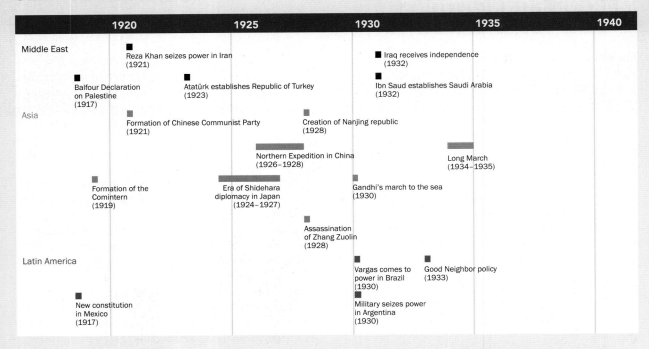

	1920	1925	1930	1935	1940

Middle East

■ Reza Khan seizes power in Iran (1921)

■ Balfour Declaration on Palestine (1917)

■ Atatürk establishes Republic of Turkey (1923)

■ Iraq receives independence (1932)

■ Ibn Saud establishes Saudi Arabia (1932)

Asia

■ Formation of Chinese Communist Party (1921)

■ Creation of Nanjing republic (1928)

▬ Northern Expedition in China (1926–1928)

▬ Long March (1934–1935)

■ Formation of the Comintern (1919)

▬ Era of Shidehara diplomacy in Japan (1924–1927)

■ Gandhi's march to the sea (1930)

■ Assassination of Zhang Zuolin (1928)

Latin America

■ Vargas comes to power in Brazil (1930)

■ Good Neighbor policy (1933)

■ New constitution in Mexico (1917)

■ Military seizes power in Argentina (1930)

CHAPTER NOTES

1. Taken from Sutan Sjahrir and Charles Wolf, Jr., *Out of Exile* (New York: The John Day Company, Inc., 1949), pp. 76–78.

2. Ts'ai Yuan-p'ei, "Ta Lin Ch'in-nan Han," in *Ts'ai Yuan-p'ei Hsiensheng Ch'uan-chi* [Collected Works of Mr. Ts'ai Yuan-p'ei] (Taipei, 1968), pp. 1057–1058.

3. Quoted in Nicholas Rowland Clifford, *Spoilt Children of Empire: Westerners in Shanghai and the Chinese Revolution of the 1920s* (Hanover, N.H., 1991), p. 16.

4. Ibid.

5. Lu Xun, "Diary of a Madman," in *Selected Works of Lu Hsun* (Beijing, 1957), vol. 1, p. 20.

THE CRISIS DEEPENS: THE OUTBREAK OF WORLD WAR II

Chapter Outline and Focus Questions

6-1 *The Rise of Dictatorial Regimes*

Q What are the main characteristics of totalitarian states, and in what key respects do they differ from democratic societies?

6-2 *The Path to War in Europe*

Q Why did other European nations not react more strongly to Germany's aggressive actions during the mid-1930s? Do you think they should have taken further steps to contain the Nazi regime?

6-3 *The Path to War in Asia*

Q What was Japan's justification for its ambitious moves in East Asia during the 1930s? Do you find Tokyo's arguments convincing?

6-4 *The World at War*

Q What were the most important battles fought in the European and Pacific Fronts, and why do you think each was crucial in affecting the course of the war?

6-5 *The Peace Settlement in Europe*

Q How would you compare the peace settlement after World War II with the Treaty of Versailles in 1919? Do you think the settlement signed at Potsdam was better or worse than its predecessor?

Connections to Today

What lessons can be drawn from the rise of dictatorial regimes in Europe during the interwar period, and how can such developments be prevented from arising today?

Doris C. Baker

IMAGE 6.1 Adolf Hitler, founder of the Third Reich

ON JANUARY 30, 1933, President Paul von Hindenburg appointed the rising young politician Adolf Hitler as the new chancellor of Germany. Hitler's rise to power had begun in 1921, when he had founded a new political organization called the National Socialist German Workers' Party—or Nazis, for short—in the southern German city of Munich. The new organization was slow to take root in other parts of the country, but Hitler was an accomplished public speaker, and as Germany entered a state of crisis during the Great Depression, his message of strong leadership, national revival, and territorial expansion soon gained growing popular support. By the early 1930s, the German people had increasingly lost faith in the seemingly inept policies of political leaders in the Weimar republic and began to drift in two opposite directions—toward Hitler's Nazi Party, which promised to cleanse the country of its internal and external enemies, or toward the powerful German Communist Party (GCP), which called for violent revolution to create a socialist state on the pattern of the Bolshevik regime in Russia.

For influential conservative forces in the country, there seemed to be little choice: while nervous about the intentions of the Nazis, they were petrified at the prospect of a communist takeover, so they began to pressure President von Hindenburg to appoint Hitler as the new chancellor of Germany. It was a fateful decision. Within months, Hitler had installed himself as the dictator of a new Third Reich and embarked on a path to rid the country of traitors and make Germany once again the dominant force in Europe. The ensuing conflict not only repeated the horrors of the previous "war to end all wars" but resulted in an even more decisive defeat of German forces on the battlefield. When World War II came to an end in 1945, there could be no further cries of a "stab in the back." Germany, and its capital city of Berlin, lay in ruins.

6-1 THE RISE OF DICTATORIAL REGIMES

 Focus Question: What are the main characteristics of totalitarian states, and in what key respects do they differ from democratic societies?

On February 3, 1933, only four days after he had been appointed chancellor of Germany, Adolf Hitler (1889–1945) met secretly with Germany's leading generals. He revealed to them his desire to remove the "cancer of democracy," create a new authoritarian leadership, and forge a new domestic unity. His foreign policy objectives were equally striking. Since Germany's living space was too small for its people, Hitler said, Germany must rearm and prepare for "the conquest of new living space in the east and its ruthless Germanization."

The rise of Adolf Hitler to supreme power in Germany was not an isolated incident, but part of a pattern that had spread throughout Europe and other parts of the world in the wake of the Great Depression. The apparent triumph of liberal democracy in 1919 had proven to be extremely short-lived. Italy had installed a fascist regime in the 1920s, and the Soviet Union under Joseph Stalin was itself a repressive dictatorial state. A host of other European states, and Latin American countries as well, adopted authoritarian systems, while a militarist regime in Japan moved that country down the path to war. By 1939, only two major states in Europe, France and Great Britain, remained democratic. Even in the United States, the democratic system was under threat, as many Americans began to lose faith in the capitalist system and express an interest in fascism or its reverse image, communism.

Dictatorships, of course, were hardly a new phenomenon as a means of governing human societies, but the type of political system that emerged after World War I did exhibit some ominous new characteristics. The modern **totalitarian state**, whether of the right (as in Germany) or of the left (as in the Soviet Union), transcended the ideal of passive obedience expected in a traditional dictatorship or authoritarian monarchy. It required the active loyalty and commitment of all its citizens to the regime and its goals. Individual freedom was to be subordinated to the collective will of the masses, represented by a single leader and a single party. Modern technology also gave totalitarian states the ability to use unprecedented police powers and communication techniques to impose their wishes on their subjects.

What explains the emergence of this frightening new form of government at a time when the Enlightenment and the Industrial Revolution had offered such bright hopes for the improvement of the human condition? According to the philosopher Hannah Arendt, in her renowned study, *The Origins of Totalitarianism* (1951), the totalitarian state was a direct product of the modern age. At a time when traditional sources of identity, such as religion and the local community, were in decline, alienated intellectuals found fertile ground for their radical ideas among rootless peoples deprived of their communal instincts and their traditional faiths by the corrosive effects of the Industrial Age. The Great Depression, which threw millions into poverty and sowed doubts about the viability of both democratic institutions and the capitalist system, made many observers even more vulnerable to prescriptions calling for a new politics and the remaking of the human condition.

6-1a The Birth of Fascism

In the early 1920s, in the wake of economic turmoil, political disorder, and the general insecurity and fear stemming from World War I, Benito Mussolini (1883–1945) burst upon the Italian scene with the first **fascist** movement in Europe. Mussolini began his political career as a socialist but was expelled from the Socialist Party after supporting Italy's entry into World War I, a position contrary to the socialist principle of ardent neutrality in imperialist wars. In 1919, he established a new political group, the *Fascio di Combattimento*, or League of Combat. It received little attention in the parliamentary elections of 1919, but subsequently when worker strikes and a general climate of class violence broke out, alarmed conservatives turned to the Fascists, who formed armed squads to attack socialist offices and newspapers. On October 29, 1922, after Mussolini and the Fascists threatened to march on Rome if they were not given power, King Victor Emmanuel III (r. 1900–1946) capitulated and made Mussolini prime minister of Italy.

By 1926, Mussolini had established the institutional framework for his Fascist dictatorship. Press laws gave the government the right to suspend any publication that fostered disrespect for the Catholic Church, the monarchy, or the state. The prime minister was made "head of government" with the power to legislate by decree. A police law empowered the police to arrest and confine anybody for both nonpolitical and political crimes without due process of law. In 1926, all anti-Fascist parties were outlawed. By the end of 1926, Mussolini ruled Italy as *Il Duce*, the leader.

Mussolini's regime attempted to mold Italians into a single-minded community by developing Fascist organizations at all levels of society. By 1939, about two-thirds of the population between the ages of eight and eighteen had been enrolled in some kind of Fascist youth group. Activities for these groups included Saturday afternoon marching drills and calisthenics, seaside and mountain summer camps, and youth contests. Beginning in the 1930s, all young men were given some kind of premilitary exercises to develop discipline and provide training for war.

The Fascists also sought to reinforce traditional social attitudes, as is evident in their policies toward women. The Fascists portrayed the family as the pillar of the state and women as the foundation of the family. "Woman into the home" became the Fascist slogan. The role of women was to serve as homemakers and baby producers, "their natural and fundamental mission in life," according to Mussolini, who viewed population growth as an indicator of national strength. The Fascist attitude toward women also reflected a practical consideration: working women would compete with males for jobs in the depression economy of the 1930s. Eliminating women from the market reduced male unemployment.

6-1b Hitler and Nazi Germany

As Mussolini began to lay the foundations of his Fascist state in Italy, a young admirer was harboring similar dreams in Germany. Born on April 20, 1889, Adolf Hitler was the son of an Austrian customs official. He did poorly in secondary school and eventually made his way to Vienna to become an artist, where he gradually developed an avid interest in German nationalism. After World War I, during which he served as a soldier on the Western Front, Hitler moved to the south German state of Bavaria and became actively involved in politics. By then, he had become convinced that the German defeat had been caused by the Jews, for whom he now developed a fervent hatred.

The Roots of Anti-Semitism **Anti-Semitism** was not new to European civilization. Since the Middle Ages, Jews had been portrayed throughout the continent as the murderers of Christ and were often subjected to mob violence and official persecution. Their rights were restricted, and they were physically separated from Christians in separate urban sectors known as ghettos. By the nineteenth century, however, as a result of the ideals of the Enlightenment and the French Revolution, Jews were increasingly granted legal equality in many European countries. Many Jews left the ghettos to which they had been restricted and became assimilated into the surrounding Christian population. Some entered what had previously been the closed world of politics and the professions. Others became successful as bankers, scientists, journalists, and stage performers. Nowhere in Europe did Jews play a more active role in society than in Germany.

Often, however, their achievements provoked envy and distrust. During the last two decades of the nineteenth century, German politicians began to use the criticism of Jews as a means to win the votes of traditional lower-middle-class groups who felt threatened by changing times. Such parties also played on the rising sentiment of racism in German society. Spurred on by the widespread popularity of social Darwinism, some rabid German nationalists promoted the concept of the *Volk* (nation, people, or race) as an underlying idea in German history since the medieval era. Portraying the German people as the successors of the pure "Aryan" race, which they claimed was the true and original creator of Western culture, nationalist groups called for Germany to take the lead in a desperate struggle to save European civilization from the destructive assaults of such allegedly lower races as Jews, blacks, Slavs, and Asians.

Hitler's Rise to Power, 1921–1933 At the end of World War I, Hitler joined the obscure German Workers' Party and transformed it into a new organization called the National Socialist German Workers' Party (NSDAP), or Nazis for short. Hitler worked assiduously to develop the party into a mass political movement with flags, party badges, uniforms, its own newspaper, and its own police force or party militia known as the SA—the *Sturmabteilung*, or Storm Troops. The SA added an element of force and terror to the growing Nazi movement. Hitler's own oratorical skills as well as his populist message were largely responsible for attracting an increasing number of followers.

In November 1923, Hitler staged an armed uprising against the state government in Munich, but the so-called Beer Hall Putsch was quickly crushed, and Hitler was sentenced to prison. During his brief stay in jail, he wrote *Mein Kampf* (*My Struggle*), an autobiographical account of his movement and its underlying ideology. Virulent German nationalism, anti-Semitism, and anticommunism were linked together by a social Darwinian theory of struggle that stressed the right of superior nations to *Lebensraum* ("living space") through expansion and the right of superior individuals to secure authoritarian leadership over the masses.

After Hitler's release from prison, the Nazi Party rapidly expanded to other parts of Germany, increasing from 27,000 members in 1925 to 178,000 by the end of 1929. By 1932, the Nazi Party had 800,000 members and had become the largest party in the Reichstag, the German parliament. No doubt, Germany's economic difficulties were a crucial factor in the Nazis' rise to power. Unemployment had risen dramatically, from 4.35 million in 1931 to 6 million by the winter of 1932. The economic and psychological impact of the Great Depression made extremist parties such as the Nazis and the Communists more attractive. Hitler's appeal to national pride, national honor, and traditional militarism struck chords of emotion in his listeners, and the raw energy projected by his Nazi Party contrasted sharply with the apparent ineptitude emanating from its democratic rivals. As the conservative elites of Germany gradually came to see Hitler as the man who could save Germany from a Communist takeover, President Paul von Hindenburg agreed to allow Hitler to become chancellor on January 30, 1933, and form a new government.

Within two months, Hitler had convinced Hindenburg to issue a decree suspending all basic rights for the full duration of the emergency—declared after a mysterious fire destroyed the Reichstag building in downtown Berlin—thus enabling the Nazis to arrest and imprison anyone without redress. When the Reichstag empowered the government to dispense with constitutional forms for four years while it issued laws that dealt with the country's problems, Hitler became a dictator appointed by the parliamentary body itself. The final step came on August 2, 1934, when Hindenburg died. The office of Reich president was abolished, and Hitler became sole ruler of Germany. Public officials and soldiers were all required to take a personal oath of loyalty to Hitler as the "Führer (leader) of the German Reich and people."

The Nazi State, 1933–1939 Having smashed the Weimar Republic, Hitler now turned to his larger objective, the creation of a totalitarian state that would dominate Europe and possibly the world for generations to come. Mass demonstrations and spectacles were employed to integrate the German nation into a collective fellowship and to mobilize it as an instrument for Hitler's policies (see Movies & History, *Triumph of the Will*). In the economic sphere, the Nazis pursued the use of public works projects and "pump-priming" grants to private construction firms to foster employment and end the depression. But there is little doubt that rearmament contributed far more to solving the unemployment problem. Unemployment, which had stood at 6 million in 1932, dropped to 2.6 million in 1934 and fell below 500,000 in 1937. Although Hitler himself had little interest in either economics or administration, economic factors were operating in his favor, and the German economy began to show

MOVIES & HISTORY
Triumph of the Will (1934)

The documentary entitled *Triumph of the Will* is perhaps the most famous film produced in Germany during the years of the Nazi regime. Directed by the German actress and film maker Leni Riefenstahl, it was produced at the request of Adolf Hitler himself, who hoped that German viewers would be influenced in favor of his new regime, which had taken power a year previously.

The focus in the documentary is on a rally held in 1934 by the Nazi Party in the city of Nuremberg. The event itself was designed to be both a spectacular mass meeting for the participants, and also a powerful propaganda device aimed at conveying to viewers the rising power of National Socialism. The film opens with short introductory titles declaring that the rise to power of Adolf Hitler as the new chancellor marked the rebirth of the German nation. The remainder is devoted to a series of scenes from party rallies, speeches by party leaders, and parades through the city streets with thousands of spectators cheering, and it closes with a speech by the chancellor himself, who appears in almost messianic terms as the savior of the country. To view the film today is to gain some insight into the power of Nazi propaganda in arousing mass support for the regime, and popular adulation for the great leader—Adolf Hitler himself.

 What movies were produced in the United States that might have been effective as propaganda devices in favor of a particular cause?

Universal History Archive/Universal Images Group/Getty Images

steady recovery from its disastrous position during the heart of the Great Depression.

For its enemies, the Nazi totalitarian state had its instruments of terror and repression. Especially important was the SS (*Schutzstaffel*, or "protection echelon"). Originally created as Hitler's personal bodyguard, the SS, under the direction of Heinrich Himmler (1900–1945), came to control all of the regular and secret police forces. Other institutions, including the Catholic and Protestant churches, primary and secondary schools, and universities, were also brought under the control of the state. Criticism from opposition elements in the press was deflected by dismissive comments from regime sources about the "lugenpresse" (the lying press). Nazi professional organizations and leagues were formed for civil servants, teachers, women, farmers, doctors, and lawyers; youth organizations—the *Hitler Jugend* (Hitler Youth) and its female counterpart, the *Bund Deutscher Mädel* (League of German Maidens)—were given special attention.

The Nazi attitude toward women was largely determined by ideological considerations. To the Nazis, men and women were designed by nature to play different roles in society. Men were warriors and political leaders, while women were destined to be wives and mothers. Certain professions, including university teaching, medicine, and law, were considered inappropriate for women. Instead, women were encouraged to pursue professional occupations that had direct practical application, such as social work and nursing (see Image 6.2).

A key goal of the Nazi regime was to resolve "the Jewish question." In September 1935, the Nazis announced new racial laws at the annual party rally in Nuremberg. These laws excluded Jews from German citizenship and forbade marriages and extramarital relations between Jews and German citizens. A more violent phase of anti-Jewish activity was initiated on November 9–10, 1938, the infamous *Kristallnacht*, or night of shattered glass. The assassination of a German diplomat in Paris became the excuse for a Nazi-led destructive rampage against the Jews; synagogues were burned, 7,000 Jewish businesses were destroyed, and at least 100 Jews were killed. Moreover, 20,000 Jewish males were rounded up and sent to concentration camps. Jews were now barred from all public buildings and prohibited from owning, managing, or working in any retail store. Hitler would soon turn to more gruesome measures.

6-1c The Spread of Authoritarianism in Europe

Nowhere had the map of Europe been more drastically altered by World War I than in eastern Europe. The new states of Austria, Poland, Czechoslovakia, and Yugoslavia adopted parliamentary systems, and the preexisting kingdoms of Romania and Bulgaria gained new parliamentary constitutions in 1920. Greece became a republic in 1924. Hungary's government was parliamentary in form but controlled by its landed aristocrats. Thus, at the beginning of the 1920s, the future of political democracy seemed promising. Yet almost everywhere in eastern Europe, parliamentary governments soon gave way to authoritarian regimes.

Several factors helped create this situation. Eastern European states had little tradition of liberalism or parliamentary politics and no substantial middle class to support them. Then, too, these states were predominantly rural and agrarian. Many of the peasants were largely illiterate, and much of the land was still dominated by large landowners who feared the growth of agrarian peasant parties with their schemes for land redistribution. Ethnic conflicts also threatened to tear these countries apart. Fearful of land reform, Communist-led agrarian upheaval, and ethnic conflict, powerful landowners, the churches, and even some members of the small middle class looked to authoritarian governments to maintain the old system. Only Czechoslovakia, with its substantial middle class, liberal tradition, and strong industrial base, maintained its political democracy.

IMAGE 6.2 Women Serving the Nazi Cause. The National Socialist Women's League was the female equivalent of the Nazi Party in Germany. Established in 1931, its responsibilities were to encourage German women to play their assigned roles in Hitler's Germany and—after the outbreak of war in 1939—to provide assistance to the regime on the home front. In public, members were expected to dress in white, and they were encouraged to engage regularly in athletic activities. In 1938, the League had a membership of over 2 million women.

 How would you compare the role of German women in the Third Reich with that of women in the United States during World War II?

In Spain, democracy also failed to survive. Fearful of the rising influence of left-wing elements in the government, in July 1936 Spanish military forces led by General Francisco Franco (1892–1975) launched a brutal and bloody civil war that lasted three years. Foreign intervention complicated the situation. Franco's forces were aided by arms, money, and men from Italy and Germany, while the government was assisted by 40,000 foreign volunteers as well as trucks, planes, tanks, and military advisers from the Soviet Union. After Franco's forces captured Madrid on March 28, 1939, the Spanish Civil War finally came to an end. General Franco soon established a dictatorship that favored large landowners, businessmen, and the Catholic clergy. To concerned observers in Western Europe and the United States, Franco's victory was an ominous sign for the future.

6-1d The Rise of Militarism in Japan

The rise of militant forces in Japan resulted not from a seizure of power by a new political party but from the growing influence of nationalist elements at the top of the political hierarchy. During the 1920s, a multiparty system based on democratic practices appeared to be emerging. Two relatively moderate political parties, the Minseito and the Seiyukai, dominated the Diet and took turns providing executive leadership in the cabinet. Radical elements existed at each end of the political spectrum, but neither militant nationalists nor violent revolutionaries appeared to present a threat to the stability of the system (see Chapter 5).

In fact, the pluralistic political system in Japan was probably weaker than it seemed at the time. Both of the major parties were deeply dependent on campaign contributions from powerful corporations (the *zaibatsu*), and conservative forces connected to the military or the old landed aristocracy were still highly influential behind the scenes. As in the Weimar Republic in Germany during the same period, the actual power base of moderate political forces was weak, and politicians unwittingly undermined the fragility of the system by engaging in bitter attacks on each other.

Political tensions in Japan increased in 1928 when Chiang Kai-shek's forces seized Shanghai and several provinces in central China. In the next few years, Chiang engaged in negotiations with the remaining warlords north of the Yangtze River and made clear his intention to integrate the region, including the three provinces in Manchuria, into the new Nanjing republic. This plan represented a direct threat to military strategists in Japan, who viewed resource-rich Manchuria as the key to their country's expansion onto the Chinese mainland. When Zhang Xueliang, son and successor of the Japanese puppet Zhang Zuolin (see Chapter 5), resisted Japanese threats and decided to integrate Manchuria into the Nanjing republic, the Japanese were shocked. "You forget," Zhang told one Japanese official, "that I am Chinese."[1]

Appeals from Tokyo to Washington for a U.S. effort to restrain Chiang Kai-shek were rebuffed. Militant nationalists in Tokyo, outraged at Japan's loss of influence in Manchuria, began to argue that the Shidehara policy of peaceful cooperation with other nations in maintaining the existing international economic order had been a failure.

The Mukden Incident   In September 1931, acting on the pretext that Chinese troops had attacked a Japanese railway near the northern Chinese city of Mukden, Japanese military units stationed in the area seized control throughout Manchuria. Although Japanese military authorities in Manchuria announced that China had provoked the action, the "Mukden incident," as it was called, had actually been carried out by Japanese saboteurs to create a pretext for intervention. Eventually, worldwide protests against the Japanese action led the League of Nations to send an investigative commission to Manchuria. When the commission issued a report condemning the seizure, Japan angrily withdrew from the League. Over the next several years, the Japanese consolidated their hold on Manchuria, renaming it Manchukuo and placing it under the titular authority of former Chinese emperor and now Japanese puppet, Pu Yi.

Although no one knew it at the time, the Mukden incident would later be singled out by some observers as the opening shot of World War II. The failure of the League of Nations to take decisive action sent a strong signal to Japan and other potentially aggressive states that they might pursue their objectives without the risk of united opposition by the major world powers. Despite its agonizing efforts to build a system of peace and stability that would prevent future wars, the League had failed to resolve the challenges of the postwar era.

Democracy In Crisis   Civilian officials in Tokyo had been horrified by the unilateral actions undertaken by ultranational Japanese military elements in Manchuria, but were cowed into silence. Despite doubts about the wisdom of the Mukden incident, the cabinet was too divided to disavow it, and military officers in Manchuria increasingly acted on their own initiative.

During the early 1930s, civilian cabinets were also struggling to cope with the economic challenges presented by the Great Depression. Already suffering from the decline of its business interests on the mainland, Japan began to feel the impact of the global economic downturn after 1929 when the United States and major European nations raised their tariffs against Japanese imports in a desperate effort to protect local businesses and jobs. The value of Japanese exports dropped by 50 percent from 1929 to 1931, and wages dropped nearly as much. Hardest hit were the farmers as the prices of rice and other staple food crops plummeted. By abandoning the gold standard, Prime Minister Inukai Tsuyoshi was able to lower the price of Japanese goods on the world market, and exports climbed back to earlier levels. But the political parties were no longer able to stem the growing influence of militant nationalist elements.

In May 1932, Inukai Tsuyoshi was assassinated by right-wing extremists. He was succeeded by another moderate, Admiral Saito Makoto, but ultranationalist patriotic societies began to terrorize opponents, assassinating businessmen and public figures identified with the policy of conciliation toward the outside world. Some, like the publicist Kita Ikki, were convinced that the parliamentary system had been corrupted by materialism and Western values and should be replaced by a system that would return to traditional Japanese values and imperial authority. His message "Asia for the Asians" had not won widespread support during the relatively prosperous 1920s but increased in popularity after the Great Depression, which convinced many Japanese that capitalism was unsuitable for Japan.

During the mid-1930s, the influence of the military and extreme nationalists over the government steadily increased. Minorities and left-wing elements were persecuted, and moderates were intimidated into silence. Terrorists put on trial for their part in assassination attempts portrayed themselves as selfless patriots and received light sentences. Japan continued to hold national elections, and moderate candidates continued to receive substantial popular support, but the cabinets were dominated by the military or by civilian advocates of Japanese expansionism. In February 1936, junior officers in the army led a coup in the capital city of Tokyo, briefly occupying the Diet building and other key government installations and assassinating several members of the cabinet. The ringleaders were quickly tried and convicted of treason, but widespread sympathy for the defendants further strengthened the influence of the military in the halls of power.

6-2 THE PATH TO WAR IN EUROPE

 Focus Questions: Why did other European nations not react more strongly to Germany's aggressive actions during the mid-1930s? Do you think they should have taken further steps to contain the Nazi regime?

When Hitler became chancellor on January 30, 1933, Germany's situation in Europe appeared weak. The Versailles Treaty had created a demilitarized zone on Germany's western border that would allow the French to move into the heavily industrialized parts of Germany in the event of war. To Germany's east, smaller states such as Poland and Czechoslovakia had signed defensive treaties with Germany's old rival France. The provisions of the Versailles Treaty, that

limited Germany's army to 100,000 troops with no air force and only a small navy, were still in effect.

Posing as a man of peace in his public speeches, Hitler began to insist that Germany wished only to revise the unfair provisions of Versailles by peaceful means and to take its rightful place among the European states. On March 9, 1935, he announced the creation of a new air force and, one week later, the introduction of a military draft that would expand Germany's army (the *Wehrmacht*) from 100,000 to 550,000 troops. France, Great Britain, and Italy condemned Germany's unilateral repudiation of the Versailles Treaty but failed to take concrete action.

On March 7, 1936, buoyed by his conviction that the Western democracies had no intention of using force to maintain the Treaty of Versailles, Hitler sent German troops into the demilitarized Rhineland. Under the provisions of the treaty, the French had the right to use force against any violation of the demilitarized Rhineland. But Paris would not act without British support, and the British government viewed the occupation of German territory by German troops as a reasonable action by a dissatisfied power. The London *Times*, reflecting the war-weariness that had gripped much of the European public since the end of the Great War, noted that the Germans were only "going into their own back garden."

Meanwhile, Hitler began to reach out for new allies. In October 1935, Mussolini committed Fascist Italy to imperial expansion by invading its old African nemesis Ethiopia. Angered by French and British opposition to the move, Mussolini welcomed Hitler's support and began to draw closer to the German dictator he had once called a buffoon. The joint intervention of Germany and Italy on behalf of General Franco in the Spanish Civil War in 1936 not only drew the two nations closer together, but also created a potential new ally in Madrid. In October 1936, Mussolini and Hitler concluded an agreement that recognized their common political and economic interests. One month later, Germany and Japan concluded the Anti-Comintern Pact and agreed to maintain a common front against communism.

6-2a Stalin Seeks a United Front

From behind the walls of the Kremlin in Moscow, Joseph Stalin undoubtedly observed the effects of the Great Depression with a measure of satisfaction. During the early 1920s, once it became clear that the capitalist states in Europe had managed to survive without socialist revolutions, Stalin decided to improve relations with the outside world as a means of obtaining capital and technological assistance in promoting economic growth in the Soviet Union. But he was undoubtedly aware of his mentor Lenin's prediction that after a brief period of stability in Europe, a new crisis brought on by overproduction and intense competition was likely to occur in the capitalist world. That, Lenin added, would mark the beginning of the next wave of revolution. In the meantime, he declared, "We will give the capitalists the shovels with which to bury themselves."

To Stalin, the onset of the Great Depression was a signal that the next era of turbulence in the capitalist world was at hand, and during the early 1930s, Soviet foreign policy returned to the themes of class struggle and social revolution. When the influence of the Nazi Party reached significant levels in the early 1930s, Stalin viewed it as a pathological form of capitalism and ordered the Communist Party in Germany not to support the fragile Weimar Republic. As for the relatively moderate Socialist Party of Germany, its leaders were derided in Moscow as "red fascists." Hitler would quickly fall, Stalin reasoned, leading to a Communist takeover.

By 1935, however, Stalin had become uneasily aware that Hitler was not only securely in power in Berlin but also represented a potentially serious threat to the Soviet Union. That summer, at a meeting of the Communist International held in Moscow, Soviet officials announced a shift in policy. The Soviet Union would now seek to form united fronts with capitalist democratic nations in Europe against the common danger of Nazism and fascism. Communist parties in capitalist countries and in colonial areas were instructed to cooperate with "peace-loving democratic forces" in forming coalition governments called **Popular Fronts**.

In most capitalist countries, Stalin's move was greeted with suspicion, but in France, a coalition of leftist parties—Communists, Socialists, and Radicals—fearful that rightists intended to seize power, accepted Moscow's offer and formed a Popular Front government in June 1936. The new government succeeded in launching a program for workers, which included the right of collective bargaining, a forty-hour workweek, two-week paid vacations, and minimum wages. But such policies failed to bring an end to the depression, and although it survived until 1938, the Front was for all intents and purposes dead before then, as conservative forces began to organize against the perceived threat of communism in France. Still, France agreed to sign a defensive treaty with Moscow as well as similar agreements with three non-Communist states in eastern Europe (Czechoslovakia, Romania, and Yugoslavia). Soviet negotiations with Great Britain, where influential members of the Conservative Party were wary of entering an embrace with Moscow, achieved little result. The Soviet Union, rebuffed by London and disappointed by Paris, feared that it might be forced to face Hitler alone.

6-2b Decision at Munich

By the end of 1936, the Treaty of Versailles had been virtually scrapped, and Germany had erased much of the stigma of defeat. Hitler, whose foreign policy successes had earned him much internal public acclaim, was convinced that neither the demoralized French nor the British could effectively oppose his plans and decided in 1938 to annex Austria, where pro-German sentiment was strong. By threatening the country with invasion, Hitler coerced the Austrian chancellor into putting Austrian Nazis in charge of the government. The new government promptly invited German troops to enter Austria and assist in maintaining law and order. One day later, on March 13, 1938, Austria formally became a part of Germany.

The annexation of Austria—achieved without severe objections from other European nations—put Germany in position for Hitler's next objective—the destruction of Czechoslovakia. Although the democratic government in Prague was quite prepared to defend itself and was supported by pacts with France and the Soviet Union, Hitler believed that the country's allies would not come to its aid to defend it against a German attack.

His gamble succeeded. On September 15, 1938, Hitler demanded the cession to Germany of the Sudetenland (an area in western Czechoslovakia that was inhabited largely by ethnic Germans) and expressed his willingness to risk "world war" if he was refused. Instead of objecting, the British, French, Germans, and Italians—at a hastily arranged conference held in Munich—reached an agreement that essentially met all of Hitler's demands. German troops were allowed to occupy the Sudetenland as the Czechs, abandoned by their Western allies as well as by the Soviet Union, stood by helplessly (see Map 6.1). The Munich Conference was the high

Annexed Sudetenland, October 1938

Occupied Bohemia and Moravia, March 1939

Poland and Hungary

Annexed Czech territory, 1938 and 1939

MAP 6.1 Central Europe in 1939

The Munich Conference

 What were the opposing views of Churchill and Chamberlain on how to respond to Hitler's demands at Munich? Do these arguments have any wider relevance for other world crises?

Politics & Government | **AT THE MUNICH CONFERENCE**, the leaders of France and Great Britain capitulated to Hitler's demands on Czechoslovakia. When British Prime Minister Neville Chamberlain defended his actions at Munich as necessary for peace, another British statesman, Winston Churchill, characterized the settlement at Munich as "a disaster of the first magnitude." After World War II, political figures in western Europe and the United States would cite the example of appeasement at Munich to encourage vigorous resistance to expansionism by the Soviet Union.

Winston Churchill, Speech to the House of Commons, October 5, 1938

I will begin by saying what everybody would like to ignore or forget but which must nevertheless be stated, namely, that we have sustained a total and unmitigated defeat, and that France has suffered even more than we have. . . . The utmost my right honorable Friend the Prime Minister . . . has been able to gain for Czechoslovakia and in the matters which were in dispute has been that the German dictator, instead of snatching his victuals from the table, has been content to have them served to him course by course. . . . And I will say this, that I believe the Czechs, left to themselves and told they were going to get no help from the Western Powers, would have been able to make better terms than they have got. . . .

We are in the presence of a disaster of the first magnitude which has befallen Great Britain and France. Do not let us blind ourselves to that. . . .

And do not suppose that this is the end. This is only the beginning of the reckoning. This is only the first sip, the first foretaste of a bitter cup which will be proffered to us year by year unless by a supreme recovery of moral health and martial vigor, we arise again and take our stand for freedom as in the olden time.

Neville Chamberlain, Speech to the House of Commons, October 6, 1938

That is my answer to those who say that we should have told Germany weeks ago that, if her army crossed the border of Czechoslovakia, we should be at war with her. We had no treaty obligations and no legal obligations to Czechoslovakia. . . . When we were convinced, as we became convinced, that nothing any longer would keep the Sudetenland within the Czechoslovakian State, we urged the Czech Government as strongly as we could to agree to the cession of territory, and to agree promptly. . . . It was a hard decision for anyone who loved his country to take, but to accuse us of having by that advice betrayed the Czechoslovakian State is simply preposterous. What we did was save her from annihilation and give her a chance of new life as a new State, which involves the loss of territory and fortifications, but may perhaps enable her to enjoy in the future and develop a national existence under a neutrality and security comparable to that which we see in Switzerland today. Therefore, I think the Government deserves the approval of this House for their conduct of affairs in this recent crisis, which has saved Czechoslovakia from destruction and Europe from Armageddon.

Sources: *Parliamentary Debates, House of Commons* (London: His Majesty's Stationery Office, 1938), vol. 339, pp. 361–369; Neville Chamberlain, *In Search of Peace* (New York: Putnam, 1939), pp. 215, 217.

point of Western **appeasement** of Hitler. British Prime Minister Neville Chamberlain returned to England from Munich boasting that the agreement meant "peace in our time." Hitler had promised Chamberlain that he had made his last demand (see Opposing Viewpoints, "The Munich Conference," above).

In fact, Munich confirmed Hitler's perception that the Western democracies were weak and would not fight. He was increasingly convinced of his own infallibility and had

by no means been satisfied at Munich. In March 1939, Hitler suddenly occupied the Czech lands (Bohemia and Moravia), and with his encouragement, the Slovaks, a Slavic people closely related to the Czechs who had always resented the condescending attitude of their neighbors, announced their departure from Czechoslovakia and set up the German puppet state of Slovakia. On the evening of March 15, 1939, Hitler triumphantly declared in Prague that he would be known as the greatest German of them all.

The Western states were now increasingly alarmed by the Nazi threat. Hitler's naked aggression in central Europe had made it clear that his promises were utterly worthless. When he began to demand the return to Germany of Danzig (a primarily German city that had been made a free city by the Treaty of Versailles to serve as a seaport for Poland), Britain recognized the danger and offered to protect Poland in the event of war. Both France and Britain realized that they needed Soviet help to contain Nazi aggression and began political and military negotiations with Stalin. Their distrust of Soviet communism, however, made an alliance unlikely.

Meanwhile, Hitler pressed on in the belief that Britain and France would not go to war over Poland. To preclude an alliance between the western European states and the Soviet Union, which would create the danger of a two-front war, Hitler, ever the opportunist, approached Stalin, who had given up hope of any alliance with Britain and France. The announcement on August 23, 1939, of the Nazi-Soviet Nonaggression Pact shocked the world. The treaty with the Soviet Union gave Hitler the freedom he sought, and on September 1, German forces invaded Poland. A secret protocol divided up the nation of Poland between the two signatories. Two days later, Britain and France declared war on Germany. Europe was again at war.

6-3 THE PATH TO WAR IN ASIA

Focus Questions: What was Japan's justification for its ambitious moves in East Asia during the 1930s? Do you find Tokyo's arguments convincing?

Events in Asia were running parallel to those in Europe. In the years immediately following the Japanese seizure of Manchuria in the fall of 1931, Japanese military forces began to expand gradually into north China (see Map 6.2). Using the tactics of military intimidation and diplomatic bullying rather than all-out attack, Japanese military authorities began to carve out a new "sphere of influence" south of the Great Wall.

Not everyone in Tokyo agreed with this aggressive policy—the young Emperor Hirohito, who had succeeded to the throne in 1926, was initially nervous about possible international repercussions—but right-wing terrorists assassinated some of its key critics and intimidated others into silence.

The United States refused to recognize the Japanese take-over of Manchuria, which Secretary of State Henry L. Stimson declared an act of "international outlawry," but it was unwilling to threaten the use of force. Instead, the Americans sought to avoid confrontation in the hope of encouraging moderate forces in Japanese society. As one senior U.S. diplomat with long experience in Asia warned in a memorandum to the president:

> Utter defeat of Japan would be no blessing to the Far East or to the world. It would merely create a new set of stresses, and substitute for Japan the USSR—as the successor to Imperial Russia—as a contestant (and at least an equally unscrupulous and dangerous one) for the mastery of the East. Nobody except perhaps Russia would gain from our victory in such a war.[2]

For the moment, the prime victim of Japanese aggression was China. At the outset, Chiang Kai-shek attempted to avoid a confrontation with Japan so that he could deal with what he considered the greater threat from the Communists. When clashes between Chinese and Japanese troops broke out on Chinese soil, he sought to appease the Japanese by granting them the authority to administer areas in north China. But, as the Japanese moved steadily southward, popular protests in Chinese cities against Japanese aggression intensified. In December 1936, Chiang was briefly kidnapped by military forces commanded by General Zhang Xueliang, who compelled him to end his military efforts against the Communists in Yan'an and form a new united front against the Japanese. After Chinese and Japanese forces clashed at Marco Polo Bridge, south of Beijing, in July 1937, China refused to apologize, and hostilities spread.

6-3a A Monroe Doctrine for Asia

Japan had not planned to declare war on China, but neither side would compromise, and the 1937 incident eventually turned into a major conflict. The Japanese advanced up the Yangtze valley and seized the Chinese capital of Nanjing, raping and killing thousands of innocent civilians in the process. The full enormity of the horrendous slaughter, which continued for several weeks, only emerged many years after the end of the war. The "Nanjing incident" aroused a deep-seated anger against Japan among the Chinese people that continues to affect relations between the two countries to this day.

MAP 6.2 Japanese Advances into China, 1931–1939

But Chiang Kai-shek refused to capitulate and moved his government upriver to Hankou. When the Japanese seized that city, he retreated further upriver to Chungking, in remote Sichuan Province. Japanese strategists had hoped to force Chiang to join a Japanese-dominated **New Order in East Asia**, comprising Japan, Manchuria, and China. Now they established a puppet regime in Nanjing that would cooperate with Japan in driving Western influence out of East Asia (see Image 6.3). Tokyo hoped eventually to seize resource-rich Soviet Siberia and to create a new **Monroe Doctrine for Asia**, under which Japan would guide its Asian neighbors on the path to development and prosperity. After all, who better to instruct Asian societies on modernization than the one Asian country that had already achieved it? (See Historical Voices, "Japan's Justification for Expansion," p. 144.)

6-3b Tokyo's "Southern Strategy"

During the late 1930s, Japan began to cooperate with Nazi Germany on a plan to launch a joint attack on the Soviet Union and divide up its resources between them.

But when Germany surprised Tokyo by signing the non-aggression pact with the Soviets in August 1939, Japanese strategists—who hadn't been informed of the move in advance—were compelled to reevaluate their long-term objectives. Japan was not strong enough to defeat the Soviet Union alone, as a small but bitter border conflict along the Siberian frontier near Manchukuo had amply demonstrated. So the Japanese began to shift their gaze southward to the vast resources of Southeast Asia—the oil of the Dutch East Indies, the rubber and tin of Malaya, and the rice of Burma and Indochina.

A move southward, of course, would risk war with the European colonial powers and the United States, all of whom had colonial territories in the area. Japan's attack on China in the summer of 1937 had already aroused strong criticism abroad, particularly in Washington, where President Franklin D. Roosevelt threatened in a public speech to "quarantine" the aggressors after Japanese military units bombed a U.S. naval ship operating in China. Fear of involvement in foreign wars was still strong in the United States, however, and a public outcry forced the president to draw back. But when in the summer of 1940

Keystone/Hulton Archive/Getty Images

IMAGE 6.3 A Japanese Victory in China. After consolidating its authority over Manchuria, Japan began to expand into northern China. Direct hostilities between Japanese and Chinese forces began in 1937. This photograph shows victorious Japanese forces in January 1938 riding under the arched Chungshan Gate in Nanjing after they had conquered the Chinese capital city. By 1939, Japan had conquered most of eastern China.

Q *What reasons did the Japanese government give for seeking to control China?*

Japan's Justification for Expansion

 What arguments did Hashimoto Kingoro make in favor of Japanese territorial expansion? What was his reaction to the condemnation of Japan by Western nations?

Politics & Government

ADVOCATES OF JAPANESE EXPANSION justified their proposals by claiming both economic necessity and moral imperatives. Note the familiar combination of motives in this passage written by an extremist military leader in the late 1930s.

Hashimoto Kingoro on the Need for Emigration and Expansion

We have already said that there are only three ways left to Japan to escape from the pressure of surplus population, . . namely emigration, advance into world markets, and expansion of territory. The first door, emigration, has been barred to us by the anti-Japanese immigration policies of other countries. The second door, advance into world markets, is being pushed shut by tariff barriers and the abrogation of commercial treaties. What should Japan do when two of the three doors have been closed against her?

It is quite natural that Japan should rush upon the last remaining door.

It may sound dangerous when we speak of territorial expansion, but the territorial expansion of which we speak does not in any sense of the word involve the occupation of the possessions of other countries, the planting of the Japanese flag thereon, and the declaration of their annexation to Japan. It is just that since the Powers have suppressed the circulation of Japanese materials and merchandise abroad, we are looking for some place overseas where Japanese capital, Japanese skills and Japanese labor can have free play, free from the oppression of the white race.

We would be satisfied with just this much. What moral right do the world powers who have themselves closed to us the two doors of emigration and advance into world markets have to criticize Japan's attempt to rush out of the third and last door?. . .

At the time of the Manchurian incident, the entire world joined in criticism of Japan. They said that Japan was an untrustworthy nation. . . . But the military action taken by Japan was not in the least a selfish one. Moreover, we do not recall ever having taken so much as an inch of territory belonging to another nation. The result of this incident was the establishment of the splendid new nation of Manchuria. The Powers are still discussing whether or not to recognize this new nation, but regardless of whether or not other nations recognize her, the Manchurian Empire has already been established, and now, seven years after its creation, the empire is further consolidating its foundations with the aid of its friend, Japan.

And if it is still protested that our actions in Manchuria were excessively violent, we may wish to ask the white race just which country it was that sent warships and troops to India, South Africa, and Australia and slaughtered innocent natives, bound their hands and feet with iron chains, lashed their backs with iron whips, proclaimed these territories as their own, and still continues to hold them to this very day.

Source: From *Sources of Japanese Tradition* by William Theodore de Bary. Copyright © 1958 by Columbia University Press.

Japan announced its next move—demanding the right to occupy airfields and exploit economic resources in French Indochina—FDR had had enough, and the White House warned the Japanese that it would impose economic sanctions unless Japan withdrew from the area and returned to its borders of 1931 (see Historical Voices, "The Four Freedoms," p. 145).

Not surprisingly, Tokyo viewed the U.S. threat of retaliation as an obstacle to its long-term objectives. Japan badly needed liquid fuel and scrap iron from the United States.

If they were cut off, Japan would have to find them elsewhere. The Japanese were thus caught in a vise. To obtain guaranteed access to the natural resources needed to fuel the Japanese military machine, Japan must risk being cut off from its current source of the raw materials that would be needed in the event of a conflict. After much debate, the Japanese decided to launch a surprise attack on U.S. and European colonies in Southeast Asia in the hope of a quick victory that would cement Japanese dominance in the region.

The Four Freedoms

 To what degree do you feel that President Roosevelt's speech reflects the goals which the United States seeks to project around the world today?

Politics & Government **AS WAR SPREAD IN EUROPE AND ASIA** during the late 1930s, U.S. President Franklin Roosevelt grew increasingly concerned that the United States would inevitably become involved in the conflict. But his efforts to prepare for such an eventuality were thwarted by the reluctance of the American people to enter more "foreign wars." He thus resorted to carefully crafted statements that set forth U.S. concerns over the course of events elsewhere in the world. In a speech to Congress on January 6, 1941, he expressed what he considered to be the core U.S. objectives as the world entered a period of crisis, although he was careful not to commit the country to immediate action. In later years, the address became widely known as the "Four Freedoms" speech.

Franklin D. Roosevelt, Address to Congress, January 6, 1941

In the future days, which we seek to make secure, we look forward to a world founded upon four essential human freedoms.

The first is freedom of speech and expression—everywhere in the world.

The second is freedom of every person to worship God in his own way—everywhere in the world.

The third is freedom from want—which, translated into world terms, means economic understandings which will secure to every nation a healthy peacetime life for its inhabitants—everywhere in the world.

The fourth is freedom from fear—which, translated into world terms, means a world-wide reduction of armaments to such a point and in such a thorough fashion that no nation will be in a position to commit an act of physical aggression against any neighbor—anywhere in the world.

That is no vision of a distant millennium. It is a definite basis for a kind of world attainable in our own time and generation. That kind of world is the very antithesis of the so-called new order of tyranny which the dictators seek to create with the crash of a bomb.

To that new order we oppose the greater conception—the moral order. A good society is able to face schemes of world domination and foreign revolutions alike without fear.

Since the beginning of our American history, we have been engaged in change—in a perpetual peaceful revolution—a revolution which goes on steadily, quietly adjusting itself to changing conditions—without the concentration camp or the quick-lime in the ditch. The world order which we seek is the cooperation of free countries, working together in a friendly, civilized society.

This nation has placed its destiny in the hands and heads and hearts of its millions of free men and women; and its faith in freedom under the guidance of God. Freedom means the supremacy of human rights everywhere. Our support goes to those who struggle to gain those rights or keep them. Our strength is our unity of purpose.

To that high concept there can be no end save victory.

Source: From *Congressional Record*, 1941, Vol. 87, Pt. I. As cited in *World Civilizations*, W.W. Norton Publishing, 1997, All Rights Reserved.

6-4 THE WORLD AT WAR

 Focus Question: What were the most important battles fought in the European and Pacific Fronts, and why do you think each was crucial in affecting the course of the war?

On September 1, 1939, German forces suddenly attacked Poland. Using the tactics of **blitzkrieg**, or "lightning war,"

hundreds of tanks, supported by airplanes, broke quickly through Polish lines and encircled the bewildered Polish troops, whose courageous cavalry units were no match for the mechanized forces of their adversary. Conventional infantry units then moved in to hold the newly conquered territory. Within four weeks, Poland had surrendered. On September 28, 1939, Germany and the Soviet Union officially divided Poland between them. To Hitler's surprise, France and Britain declared war on Germany but took no action during a period of watchful waiting (dubbed the "phony war").

6-4a The War in Europe

Although France had joined with Great Britain in declaring war on Germany after the latter's attack on Poland, the French were ill prepared for the challenge. The political class was badly divided over both domestic and foreign policy (many conservatives, reflecting the slogan "better Hitler than Blum," openly preferred Nazi Germany over the left-leaning Socialists), and the country's military leaders had failed to appreciate the effectiveness of the new mechanized warfare. France therefore took little action when Germany launched a blitzkrieg against Denmark and Norway on April 9, 1940. One month later, however, the Germans went further, attacking the Netherlands, Belgium, and France. German tank divisions broke through the weak French defensive positions in the Ardennes forest and raced across northern France, splitting the Allied armies and trapping French troops and the entire British expeditionary army on the beaches of Dunkirk.

The rapidity of the German advance was stunning, not only to their opponents, but even to the German war planners themselves. In numerical terms, the troops and weapons available to the French and the British significantly outnumbered those of the invaders, but the will to fight, and a grasp of the strategic realities on the battlefield, were all on the side of the Germans. A strong whiff of defeatism could be plainly sensed among the defenders. Only by heroic efforts, and the German military commanders' crucial failure to exploit their advantage, did the British succeed in a gigantic evacuation of 330,000 Allied (mostly British) troops from the European continent. The French capitulated on June 22. German armies occupied about three-fifths of France while the French hero of World War I, Marshal Philippe Petain (1856–1951), established a puppet regime (known as Vichy France) over the remainder. Germany was now in control of western and central Europe (see Map 6.3). Britain had still not been defeated, but it was reeling, and a new wartime cabinet under Prime Minister Winston Churchill debated whether to seek a negotiated peace settlement. Churchill, who doubted that Hitler could be trusted, was opposed.

The Battle of Britain Encouraged by his stunning victories on the European Continent, Hitler turned his attention to the invasion of Great Britain, an operation known as Sealion. An amphibious invasion of Britain could succeed only if Germany gained control of the air. In early August 1940, the *Luftwaffe* (the German air force) launched a major offensive against British air and naval bases, harbors, communication centers, and war industries. The British fought back doggedly, supported by an effective radar system that gave them early warning of German attacks. Nevertheless, the British air force suffered critical losses and was probably only saved by Hitler's sudden change in strategy. In September, in retaliation for a British air attack on Berlin, Hitler ordered a shift from military targets to massive bombing of cities to break British morale. The British rebuilt their air strength quickly and were soon inflicting major losses on *Luftwaffe* bombers. By the end of September, Germany had lost the Battle of Britain, and the invasion of the British Isles had to be abandoned.

The successful outcome of the Battle of Britain provided an enormous boost to British morale in a time of great peril. But behind the scenes, another development was unfolding that would eventually deal a more grievous blow to German prospects for victory. One of the most important weapons in the Allied arsenal was the ability to break the codes produced by the German code machine, known as Enigma. The product of code breakers from several countries, the Ultra project, as it eventually was called, had been initiated a decade earlier but only began to provide consistent access to German plans and actions by the summer of 1940. Eventually, it became an important, if not crucial, factor in several major Allied victories in World War II.

Thwarted in the west by the failure of Operation Sealion, Nazi leaders now pursued a new strategy, which called for Italian troops to capture Egypt and the Suez Canal, thereby closing the Mediterranean to British ships and shutting off Britain's supply of oil. This strategy failed, however, when the British routed the Italian army. Although Hitler responded by sending German troops to the North African theater of war, his primary concern lay elsewhere; he had already reached the decision to fulfill his longtime obsession with the acquisition of territory in the east. In *Mein Kampf*, Hitler had declared that future German expansion must lie in the vast plains of southern Russia.

The Russian Campaign Hitler was now convinced that Britain was remaining in the war only because it anticipated Soviet support. If the Soviet Union were smashed, Britain's last hope would be eliminated. Moreover, the German general staff was convinced that the Soviet Union, whose military leadership had been decimated by Stalin's purge trials, could be defeated quickly and decisively. The invasion of the Soviet Union was scheduled for spring 1941 but was delayed because of problems in the Balkans. Mussolini's disastrous invasion of Greece in October 1940 had exposed Italian forces to attack from British air bases in that country. To secure their Balkan flank, German troops were diverted to the area from the eastern front, where they seized both Yugoslavia and Greece in April 1941. Berlin had already obtained the

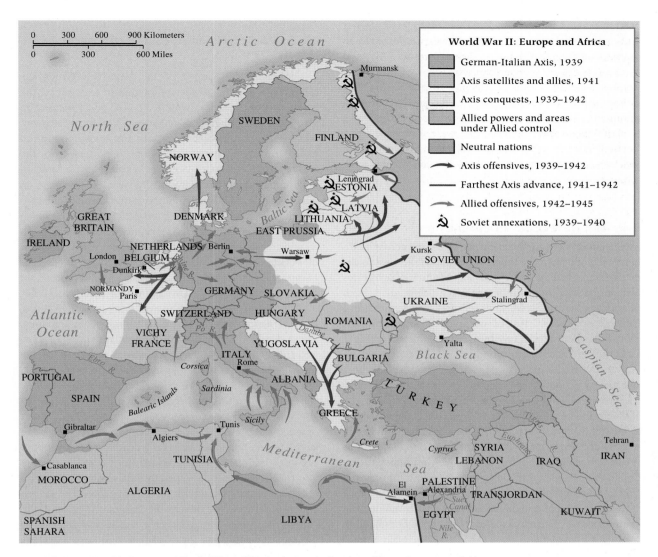

MAP 6.3 World War II in Europe and North Africa. With its fast and effective military, Germany quickly overwhelmed much of western Europe. But Hitler had both overestimated his own country's capabilities and underestimated the determination of his foes. By late 1942, his invasion of the Soviet Union was failing, and the United States had become a major factor in the war. The Allies successfully invaded Italy in 1943 and France in 1944.

 Which countries were neutral, and how did geography help make their neutrality an option?

political cooperation of Hungary, Bulgaria, and Romania. Now reassured that his position in eastern Europe was secure, Hitler ordered an invasion of the Soviet Union on June 22, 1941, in the belief that the Soviets could still be decisively defeated before winter set in. It was a fateful miscalculation.

The massive attack stretched out along an 1,800-mile front. German troops, supported by powerful armored units, advanced rapidly, capturing 2 million Soviet soldiers.

A key reason for their initial success was the surprise factor: Stalin had been alerted by various sources that an attack was imminent, but had dismissed the warnings as British propaganda. By November, one German army group had swept through Ukraine, and a second was besieging Leningrad; a third approached within 25 miles of Moscow, the Russian capital. An early winter and unexpected Soviet resistance, however, brought a halt to the German advance. For the first time in the war, German armies had been stopped. A counterattack in December 1941 by Soviet army units newly supplied with U.S. weapons came as an ominous ending to the year for the Germans. Alarmed by the rapidity of the German advances in Europe, the Roosevelt administration had begun to provide military assistance (known as Lend-Lease) to the Soviet Union via shipments sent around northern Scandinavia to the Soviet port of Murmansk. "We knew we were in trouble," one German war veteran remarked to me many years later, "when we became aware that many Russian soldiers were armed with American rifles."

6-4b The New Order in Europe

By the fall of 1941, the Nazi empire stretched across continental Europe from the English Channel in the west to the outskirts of Moscow in the east. The conquered territories were organized in two different ways. Some areas, such as western Poland, were annexed and transformed into German provinces. Most of occupied Europe, however, was administered indirectly by German officials with the assistance of collaborationist regimes.

Racial considerations played an important role in how conquered peoples were treated. German civil administrations were established in Norway, Denmark, and the Netherlands because the Nazis considered their peoples to be Aryan, or racially akin to the Germans, and hence worthy of more lenient treatment. Latin peoples, such as the occupied French, were given military administrations. But all the occupied territories were exploited for material goods and manpower for Germany's labor needs.

Because the conquered lands in the east contained the living space for German expansion and were populated in Nazi eyes by racially inferior Slavic peoples, Nazi administration there was considerably more ruthless. One million Poles were uprooted and dumped in southern Poland. Hundreds of thousands of ethnic Germans (descendants of peoples who had migrated years earlier from Germany to different parts of southern and eastern Europe) were encouraged to colonize designated areas in Poland. Hitler's grand vision called for a colossal project of social engineering after the war, in which Poles, Ukrainians, and Russians would become slave labor while German peasants settled on the abandoned lands and Germanized them.

Labor shortages in Germany led to the brutal mobilization of foreign labor. After the invasion of the Soviet Union, the 4 million Russian prisoners of war captured by the Germans, along with more than 2 million workers conscripted in France and the Low Countries, became a major source of manpower. By the summer of 1944, 7 million foreign workers had been shipped to Germany, where they constituted 20 percent of Germany's labor force.

Another 7 million were supplying forced labor in their own countries on farms, in industries, and even in military camps.

The Holocaust No aspect of the **Nazi New Order** was more tragic than the deliberate attempt to exterminate the Jewish people of Europe. Until 1939, Nazi policy focused on promoting the "emigration" of German Jews from Germany, while much of the violence against the Jewish population had been privately initiated by Nazis supporters. Once the war began in September 1939, the so-called Jewish problem took on new dimensions. Eventually, Nazi leaders settled on what was called the **Final Solution** to the Jewish problem— the annihilation of the Jewish people. Reinhard Heydrich (1904–1942), head of the SS's Security Service, was given administrative responsibility to carry it out. After the defeat of Poland, Heydrich ordered his special strike forces—the *Einsatzgruppen*—to round up all Polish Jews and concentrate them in ghettos established in a number of Polish cities.

After the invasion of the Soviet Union in June 1941, the *Einsatzgruppen* were transformed into mobile killing units. These death squads followed the regular army's advance into the Soviet Union. Their job was to round up Jews in the villages and execute and bury them in mass graves, often giant pits dug by the victims themselves before they were shot. Even this approach to solving the Jewish problem was soon perceived as inadequate. Instead, the Nazis opted for the systematic annihilation of the European Jewish population in specially built death camps. Jews from occupied countries were rounded up, packed like cattle into freight trains, and shipped to Poland, where six extermination centers were built for this purpose. The largest and most famous was Auschwitz-Birkenau. Zyklon B (the commercial name for hydrogen cyanide) was selected as the most effective gas for quickly killing large numbers of people in gas chambers designed to look like shower rooms to facilitate the cooperation of the victims.

By the spring of 1942, the death camps were in operation. Although initial priority was given to the elimination of the ghettos in Poland, Jews were soon also being shipped from France, Belgium, and the Netherlands and eventually from Greece and Hungary. Despite desperate military needs, the Final Solution had priority in using railroad cars to transport Jews to the death camps.

By the end of the war, the Germans had killed between 5 and 6 million Jews, more than 3 million of them in the death camps (see Image 6.4). Virtually 90 percent of the Jewish populations of Poland, the Baltic countries, and Germany were exterminated. Overall, the **Holocaust** was responsible for the death of nearly two of every three European Jews.

The Nazi terror was not directed solely at the Jews, but was also responsible for the death by shooting, starvation, or overwork of at least another 9 to 10 million people.

IMAGE 6.4 The Holocaust: An Image from Buchenwald. When Allied troops began to occupy Nazi concentration camps in Germany, Austria, and Poland at the end of World War II, they were stunned by the horrific scenes of inhumanity that they observed there: ovens still filled with the charred remains of prisoners, piles of bodies rotting in uncovered graves, and emaciated survivors who greeted the troops with vacant eyes and frequently died within hours or days of their liberation. Some of the most poignant images were deceptively simple, though frightening in their connotations—piles of shoes, eyeglasses, and even children's toys, all left by the victims of the Nazi terror. Shown here are thousands of wedding rings found in a cave near the camp at Buchenwald.

 What were the sources of Nazi hostility to Jewish peoples, and how did they justify their Jewish policy to the German people?

Because the Nazis considered the Gypsies (descendants of migrants who had left southern Asia centuries previously and had never assimilated into the European population), like the Jews, an alien race, they were systematically rounded up for extermination. Civic leaders in many Slavic countries were also arrested and executed. The Nazis also singled out homosexuals for persecution, and thousands lost their lives in concentration camps.

How did the German people react to the gradual transformation of their country from a struggling democracy into a totalitarian state? Studies on the subject undertaken after the end of World War II present mixed explanations. For the majority of Germans who were not directly affected by state-organized repressive policies, the Nazi regime was often viewed, at least initially, quite favorably. As the unemployment rate declined, life in the Third Reich gradually improved for the majority of the population, and many people undoubtedly took pride in their leader's outspoken defense of German culture and the nation's rightful place in the world. At the same time, membership in the Nazi Party or its affiliated organizations provided many benefits, while also representing a safe haven from public criticism and possible arrest. After the outbreak of the war, living conditions began to deteriorate, but by then it was increasingly risky to voice discontent and risk imprisonment, or worse. While many true believers supported the regime to the bitter end, most Germans probably learned to keep their head down and bear privation conditions without complaint.

6-4c War Spreads in Asia

On December 7, 1941, Japanese carrier-based aircraft attacked the U.S. naval base at Pearl Harbor in the Hawaiian Islands. The same day, other units launched assaults on the Philippines and began advancing toward the British colony of Malaya. Shortly thereafter, Japanese forces seized the British island of Singapore, invaded the Dutch East Indies, and occupied a number of islands in the Pacific Ocean. In some cases, as on the Bataan peninsula and the island of Corregidor in the Philippines, resistance was fierce, but by the spring of 1942, almost all of Southeast Asia and much of the western Pacific had fallen into Japanese hands. Placing the entire region under Japanese tutelage, Japan announced its intention to liberate Southeast Asia from Western rule. For the moment, however, Tokyo needed the resources of the region for its war machine and placed its recent conquests on a wartime footing.

Japanese leaders had hoped that their strike at American bases would destroy the U.S. Pacific Fleet and persuade the Roosevelt administration to accept Japanese domination of the Pacific. The American people, in the eyes of Japanese leaders, had been made soft by material indulgence. But the Japanese had miscalculated. Although the administration's failure to anticipate the scope and direction of the Japanese attack aroused legitimate criticism in the United States, the attack on Pearl Harbor galvanized American opinion and won broad support for Roosevelt's war policy. Doubts about the wisdom of engaging in foreign wars quickly evaporated. The United States now joined with European nations and the embattled peoples of Nationalist China in a combined effort to defeat Japan's plan to achieve hegemony in the Pacific.

U.S. Strategy in the Pacific On December 11, 1941, four days after the Japanese attack on Pearl Harbor, Germany committed a major error by declaring war on the United States. Confronted with the reality of a two-front war, President Roosevelt decided that because of the overwhelming superiority of the *Wehrmacht* in Europe, the war effort in that theater should receive priority over the conflict with Japan in the Pacific. Accordingly, U.S. war strategists drafted plans to make maximum use of their new ally in China. An experienced U.S. military commander, Lieutenant General Joseph Stilwell, was appointed as Roosevelt's special adviser to Chiang Kai-shek. His chief assignment was to train Chinese Nationalist forces in preparation for an Allied advance through mainland China toward the Japanese islands. By the fall of 1942, U.S. and British forces were beginning to gather in India for offensive operations into South China through Burma, while U.S. cargo planes continued to fly "over the hump" through the Himalaya Mountains to supply the Chinese government in Chungking with desperately needed war supplies.

In the meantime, the tide of battle began to turn in the Pacific. In the Battle of the Coral Sea in early May 1942, U.S. naval forces stopped the Japanese advance in the Dutch East Indies and temporarily relieved Australia of the threat of invasion. A month later, American carrier planes destroyed all four of the attacking Japanese aircraft carriers near Midway Island and established U.S. naval superiority in the central Pacific, even though almost all of the U.S. planes were shot down in the encounter. The ability of U.S. intelligence operatives to break the Japanese military code by using an offshoot of the Ultra project, code-named "Magic," played a significant role in the victory. Farther to the south, U.S. troops under the command of General Douglas MacArthur launched their own campaign (dubbed "island hopping") by invading the Japanese-held island of New Guinea, at the eastern end of the Dutch East Indies. After a series of bitter engagements in the Solomon Islands from August to November 1942, Japanese fortunes in the area began to fade (see Map 6.4).

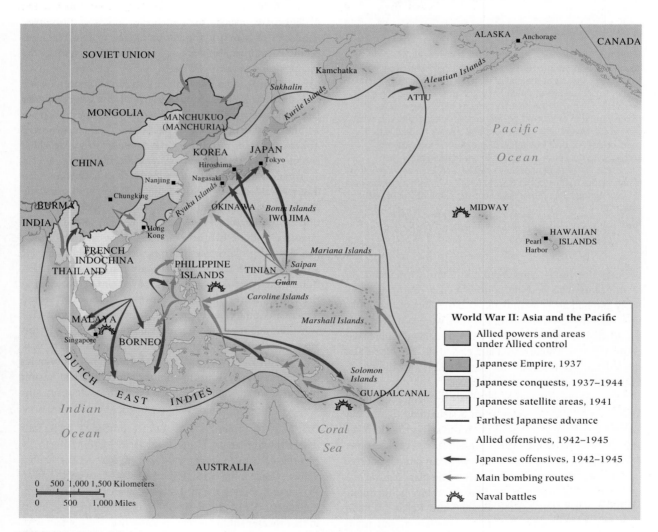

MAP 6.4 World War II in Asia and the Pacific. In 1937, Japan invaded northern China, beginning its effort to create the "Great East Asia Co-Prosperity Sphere." Further expansion led the United States to end iron and oil sales to Japan. Deciding that war with the United States was inevitable, Japan engineered a surprise attack on Pearl Harbor.

Q *Why was control of the islands in the western Pacific of great importance both to the Japanese and to the Allies?*

6-4d The New Order in Asia

Once their military takeover was completed, Japanese policy in the occupied areas of Asia became essentially defensive, as Japan hoped to use its new possessions to meet its burgeoning needs for raw materials, such as tin, oil, and rubber, as well as an outlet for Japanese manufactured goods. To provide an organizational structure for a new Great East Asia Co-Prosperity Sphere, a Ministry for Great East Asia, staffed by civilians, was established in Tokyo in October 1942 to handle relations between Japan and the conquered territories.

Asia for the Asians?   The Japanese conquest of Southeast Asia had been accomplished under the slogan "Asia for the Asians," and many Japanese sincerely believed that their government was liberating the peoples of southern Asia from European colonial rule. Japanese officials in the occupied territories made contact with nationalist elements and promised that independent governments would be established under Japanese tutelage. Such governments were eventually set up in Burma, the Dutch East Indies, Vietnam, the Philippines, and even India.

In fact, however, real power rested with the Japanese military authorities in each territory, and the local Japanese military command was directly subordinated to the Army General Staff in Tokyo. The economic resources of the colonies were exploited for the benefit of the Japanese war machine, while local peoples were recruited to serve in local military units or conscripted to work on public works projects. In some cases, the people living in the occupied areas were subjected to severe hardships. In Indochina, for example, forced requisitions of rice by the local Japanese authorities for shipment abroad created a food shortage that caused the starvation of more than a million Vietnamese in 1944 and 1945.

The Japanese planned to implant a new moral and social order as well as a new political and economic order in the occupied areas. Occupation policy stressed traditional values such as obedience, community spirit, filial piety, and discipline that reflected the prevailing political and cultural bias in Japan, while supposedly Western values such as materialism, liberalism, and individualism were strongly discouraged.

At first, many Asian nationalists took Japanese promises at face value and agreed to cooperate with their new masters. In Burma, an independent government was established in 1943 and subsequently declared war on the Allies. But as the exploitative nature of Japanese occupation policies became increasingly clear, sentiment turned against the new order. Japanese officials sometimes unwittingly provoked resentment by their arrogance and contempt for local customs. In the Dutch East Indies, for example, Indonesians were required to bow in the direction of Tokyo and recognize the divinity of the Japanese emperor, practices that were repugnant to Muslims. In Burma, Buddhist pagodas were sometimes used as military latrines. A generation later, many male Vietnamese still expressed anger at the memory of being severely punished by Japanese officials for urinating in public.

Like German soldiers in occupied Europe, Japanese military forces often had little respect for their subject peoples and viewed the Geneva Convention governing the treatment of prisoners of war as little more than a fabrication of the Western countries to tie the hands of their adversaries. In their conquest of northern and central China, the Japanese freely used poison gas and biological weapons, leading to the deaths of thousands of Chinese citizens. The Japanese occupation of the one-time Chinese capital of Nanjing, described earlier, was especially brutal.

Japanese soldiers were also savage in their treatment of Koreans. Almost 800,000 Koreans were sent overseas, most of them as forced laborers, to Japan. Tens of thousands of Korean women were forced to be "comfort women" (prostitutes) for Japanese troops. The Japanese also made extensive use of both prisoners of war and local peoples on construction projects for their war effort. In building the Burma-Thailand railway in 1943, for example, the Japanese used 61,000 Australian, British, and Dutch prisoners of war and almost 300,000 workers from Burma, Malaya, Thailand, and the Dutch East Indies. An inadequate diet and appalling work conditions in an unhealthy climate led to the deaths of 12,000 Allied prisoners of war and 90,000 local workers by the time the railway was completed. The conditions were later graphically portrayed in the award-winning movie, *The Bridge on the River Kwai*.

Such Japanese behavior created a dilemma for many nationalists in occupied areas, who had no desire to see the return of the colonial powers. Some turned against the Japanese, while others lapsed into inactivity. Some Indonesian patriots tried to have it both ways, feigning support for Japan while attempting to sabotage the Japanese administration. The Communist leader Ho Chi Minh established contacts with U.S. military officials in South China and agreed to provide information on Japanese troop movements in Indochina and to rescue downed American fliers in the area in return for the provision of U.S. training and military equipment for use by his own followers. In Malaya, where Japanese treatment of ethnic Chinese residents was especially harsh, many joined a guerrilla movement against the occupying forces. By the end of the war, little support remained in the region for the erstwhile "liberators."

6-4e The Turning Point of the War, 1942–1943

The entry of the United States into the war created a coalition, called the Grand Alliance, that ultimately defeated the Axis Powers (Germany, Italy, and Japan). Nevertheless, the three major Allies—Britain, the United States, and the Soviet Union—had to overcome mutual distrust before they could operate as an effective alliance. President Roosevelt and Prime Minister Churchill had already agreed on a set of war aims—calling for the self-determination of all peoples—in a meeting held off the coast of Newfoundland in August 1941. But this accord, known as the **Atlantic Charter**, had not been cleared with Moscow. In a bid to allay Stalin's suspicion of U.S. intentions, President Roosevelt declared that the defeat of Germany should be the first priority of the alliance. The United States, through its Lend-Lease program, also sent large amounts of military aid, including $50 billion worth of trucks, planes, and other arms, to the Soviet Union. In 1943, the Allies agreed to fight until the **unconditional surrender** of the Axis Powers. Although some critics feared that the declaration would make the enemy more determined to resist, it also had the effect of making it more difficult for Hitler to divide his foes.

Victory, however, was only in the distant future for the Allied leaders at the beginning of 1942. As Japanese forces advanced into Southeast Asia and the Pacific after crippling the American naval fleet at Pearl Harbor, Axis forces continued the war in Europe against Britain and the Soviet Union. Reinforcements in North Africa enabled the Afrika Korps under General Erwin Rommel to break through the British defenses in Egypt and advance toward Alexandria, a vital seaport in the Nile River delta. In the spring of 1942, a renewed German offensive in the Soviet Union led to the capture of the entire Crimean peninsula, causing Hitler to boast that in two years, German divisions would be on the border of India.

The Battle of Stalingrad   By that fall, however, the war had begun to turn against the Germans. In North Africa, British forces stopped Rommel's troops at El Alamein in the summer of 1942 and then forced them back across the desert. In November, U.S. forces landed in French North Africa and forced the German and Italian troops to surrender in May 1943. Allied war strategists drew up plans for an invasion of Italy, on the "soft underbelly" of Europe. But the true turning point of the war undoubtedly occurred on the Eastern Front, where the German armed forces suffered 80 percent of their casualties during the entire war. After capturing the Crimea, Hitler's generals wanted him to concentrate on the Caucasus and its oil fields, but Hitler

decided that Stalingrad, a major industrial center on the Volga, should be taken as well. Accordingly, German forces advancing in the southern Soviet Union were divided. After three months of bitter fighting, German troops occupied the city of Stalingrad, but Soviet troops in the area, using a strategy of encirclement, now counterattacked. Besieged from all sides, the Germans were forced to surrender on February 2, 1943. The entire German Sixth Army of 300,000 men was lost, with the survivors sent off to prison camps. Soviet casualties were estimated at nearly one million, more than the United States lost in the entire war. By spring, long before Allied troops landed on the European continent, even Hitler knew that the Germans would not defeat the Soviet Union. The *Wehrmacht* was now in full retreat all across the Eastern Front.

Arsenal of Democracy   Although the Battle of Stalingrad was probably the most important single battle in the war, an equally significant development was taking place across the Atlantic, where the growing industrial might of the United States was gradually being transformed from peaceful to wartime uses. By 1943, the United States had become the arsenal of the Allied Powers, producing the military equipment they all needed. At the height of war production in 1943, the nation was constructing six ships a day and $6 billion worth of war-related goods a month. The output of American factories was dispatched not only to the U.S. forces overseas, but to Great Britain, the Soviet Union, and other Allies as well.

Much of the industrial labor was done by American women, who, despite some public opposition, willingly took jobs in factories to replace husbands and brothers who had gone off to war. Long after the return of peace, the face of the fictional "Rosie the Riveter," a poster showing a young woman in overalls flexing her arm muscle at the viewer, was one of the most famous images of the war effort (see Image 6.5). Women also joined the armed forces as WAACs (Women's Army Auxiliary Corps) or served in other civilian occupations once reserved for their fathers and brothers. In addition, more than one million African Americans migrated from the rural South to seek employment in the industrial cities of the North and West. For many Americans, the attack on Pearl Harbor aroused a powerful sense of patriotism that they had never experienced previously in their lifetimes. As the unemployment rate dropped steadily, the U.S. recovery from the Great Depression appeared complete—admittedly at a high cost.

6-4f The Last Years of the War

By the beginning of 1943, the tide of battle had begun to turn against the Axis. On July 10, the Allies crossed the

IMAGE 6.5 Rosie the Riveter. One of the most memorable posters from the wartime era was the graphic art image of "Rosie the Riveter" with the accompanying caption: "We Can Do It!" The poster, which was widely reproduced all over the country at the time, helped to enlist American women to sign up for jobs in factories producing equipment for the war effort. In recent years, a state park honoring the poster has been established in the city of Richmond, California, where thousands of women signed up for jobs in 56 separate industries, including the all-important shipping industry. Such posters were highly effective in encouraging popular support for the war effort in the United States, while the jobs themselves helped to train women to find employment after the war's end.

Mediterranean and carried the war to Italy. After taking Sicily, Allied troops began the invasion of mainland Italy in September. Following the ouster and arrest of Mussolini, a new Italian government offered to surrender to Allied forces. But the Germans, in a daring raid, liberated Mussolini and set him up as the head of a puppet German state in northern Italy while German troops established new defensive lines in the hills south of Rome. Rome finally fell on June 4, 1944. By that time, the Italian war had assumed a secondary role as the Allies opened their long-awaited second front in western Europe. In preparation for a widely anticipated Allied invasion of western Europe, intensive bombing raids levelled German cities, damaging the Nazi industrial capacity and killing thousands of civilians in the process.

Operation Overlord   Since the autumn of 1943, under considerable pressure from Stalin, the Allies had been planning a cross-channel invasion of France (known as Operation Overlord) from Great Britain. Under the direction of U.S. General Dwight D. Eisenhower (1890–1969), five assault divisions landed on the Normandy beaches on June 6, 1944, in history's greatest naval invasion. An initially indecisive German response, due in part to effective Allied disinformation activities, enabled the Allied forces to establish a beachhead, although casualties were heavy. Within three months, they had landed 2 million men and a half-million vehicles that pushed inland and broke through the German defensive lines. Among them were French troops loyal to the French military commander Charles de Gaulle. After the puppet Vichy government was established in the summer of 1940, Colonel de Gaulle had fled the country and founded a Free French movement dedicated to cooperating with the Allies to overturn Nazi domination of the European continent.

After the breakout, Allied troops moved inland, liberating Paris by the end of August. By March 1945, they had crossed the Rhine and advanced into Germany. The Allied advance northward through Belgium encountered greater resistance, as German troops launched a desperate counterattack known as the Battle of the Bulge. The operation introduced a new generation of "King Tiger" tanks more powerful than anything the Allied forces could array against them. The Allies weathered the German attack, however, and in late April, they finally linked up with Soviet units at the Elbe River.

Advance in the East   The Soviets had come a long way since the Battle of Stalingrad in 1943. In the summer of 1943, Hitler had gambled on taking the offensive by making use of the first generation of "King Tiger" tanks. At the Battle of Kursk (July 5–12), the greatest engagement of World War II, involving competing forces numbering more than 3.5 million men, the Soviets soundly defeated the German forces. Soviet forces, now supplied with their own "T-34" heavy tanks, began a relentless advance westward. The Soviets reoccupied Ukraine by the end of 1943; lifted the siege of Leningrad, where more than one million people, the vast majority of them civilians, had died; and moved into the Baltic states by the beginning of 1944. Advancing along a northern front, Soviet troops occupied Warsaw in January 1945 and entered Berlin in April. Meanwhile, Soviet troops along a southern front swept through Hungary, Romania, and Bulgaria.

In January 1945, Hitler moved into a bunker 55 feet under Berlin to direct the final stages of the war. He committed suicide on April 30, two days after Mussolini was shot by partisan Italian forces. On May 7, German commanders surrendered. The war in Europe was over.

6-5 THE PEACE SETTLEMENT IN EUROPE

 Focus Questions: How would you compare the peace settlement after World War II with the Treaty of Versailles in 1919? Do you think the settlement signed at Potsdam was better or worse than its predecessor?

In November 1943, Stalin, Roosevelt, and Churchill, the leaders of the Grand Alliance, met at Tehran (the capital of Iran) to decide the future course of the war. Their major strategic decision involved approval for an American-British invasion of the European continent through France, which Stalin had long demanded; it was scheduled for the spring of 1944. The acceptance of this plan had important consequences. It meant that Soviet and British-American forces would meet in defeated Germany along a north-south dividing line and that eastern Europe would most likely be liberated by Soviet forces. The Allies also agreed to a partition of postwar Germany until denazification could take place. Roosevelt privately assured Stalin that Soviet borders in Europe would be moved westward to compensate for the loss of territories belonging to the old Russian Empire after World War I. Poland would receive lands in eastern Germany to make up for territory lost in the east to the Soviet Union.

6-5a The Yalta Agreement

In February 1945, the three Allied leaders met once again at Yalta, on the Crimean peninsula of the Soviet Union. Since the defeat of Germany was by now a foregone conclusion, much of the attention focused on the war in the Pacific. At Tehran, Roosevelt had sought Soviet military help against Japan, and Stalin had assured him that Soviet forces would be in a position to enter the Pacific war three months after the close of the conflict in Europe. At Yalta, FDR reopened the subject. Development of the atomic bomb was not yet assured, and U.S. military planners feared the possibility of heavy casualties in amphibious assaults on the Japanese home islands. Roosevelt therefore agreed to Stalin's price for military assistance against Japan: possession of Sakhalin and the Kurile Islands, as well as two warm-water ports and railroad rights in Manchuria.

The creation of a new United Nations to replace the now discredited League of Nations was a major U.S. concern at Yalta. Roosevelt hoped to ensure the participation of the Big Three powers in a postwar international organization before difficult issues divided them into hostile camps. After a number of compromises, both Churchill and Stalin accepted Roosevelt's plans for the United Nations organization and set the first meeting for San Francisco in April 1945.

The issues of Germany and eastern Europe were treated less decisively and with considerable acrimony. The Big Three reaffirmed that Germany must surrender unconditionally and created four occupation zones. German reparations were set at $20 billion. A compromise was also worked out in regard to Poland. Stalin agreed to free elections in the future to determine a new government. But the issue of free elections in eastern Europe would ultimately cause a serious rift between the Soviets and the Americans and also become a source of political controversy in the United States. The Allied leaders agreed on an ambiguous statement that interim governments "broadly representative of all democratic elements in the population" would be formed in advance of the scheduling of free elections "responsive to the will of the people."[3] It would soon be clear that Moscow and Washington interpreted the provisions in different ways, a reality that would eventually lead to harsh criticism of Yalta from Roosevelt's opponents in the United States. For his part, FDR was determined to avoid the poisonous feelings left by the Treaty of Versailles after World War I and hoped to win Stalin's confidence as a means of maintaining the Grand Alliance at the close of the war.

6-5b Confrontation at Potsdam

After Yalta, Western relations with the Soviets began to deteriorate rapidly. The Grand Alliance had been one of necessity in which ideological incompatibility had been subordinated to the pragmatic concerns of the war. The Allied Powers' only common aim was the defeat of Nazism. Once this aim had been all but accomplished, the many differences among the Big Three came to the surface.

The Potsdam Conference of July 1945, held in a royal palace just outside Berlin, was the last Allied conference of World War II, and it began under a cloud of mistrust. Roosevelt had died of a cerebral hemorrhage on April 12 and had been succeeded as chief of state by his vice president Harry Truman, while Winston Churchill had been replaced by the new Labour Party prime minister, Clement Attlee. After his arrival at Potsdam, Truman received word that the atomic bomb had been successfully tested. Some historians have argued that this knowledge stiffened Truman's resolve against the Soviets. In any case, there was a new coldness in the relations between the Soviets and the Americans. The Allied leaders disagreed on the status of postwar Germany. Stalin sought absolute security for the USSR, which—in his view—could only be achieved if Germany was sufficiently punished to negate any possibility that it might seek revenge in the future. But Truman, along with many of his advisers, was determined to avoid a punitive peace in the hopes of avoiding a repeat of the bitter experience after World War I.

They also sparred on the future of the newly liberated states of eastern Europe. Truman demanded free elections throughout the region, but Stalin was determined to maintain a string of friendly regimes on its western border and felt that only firm control over the levers of power would guarantee that result. In his view, free elections might result in governments hostile to the Soviet Union. For U.S. officials, the dilemma was clear: as Soviet occupation forces in Eastern Europe had already begun to install pliant regimes in their wake, only an invasion by Western armies could undo developments there, and in the immediate aftermath of the world's most destructive conflict, few people favored such a policy. But the stage was set for a new confrontation, this time between the two major victors of World War II (see Map 6.5).

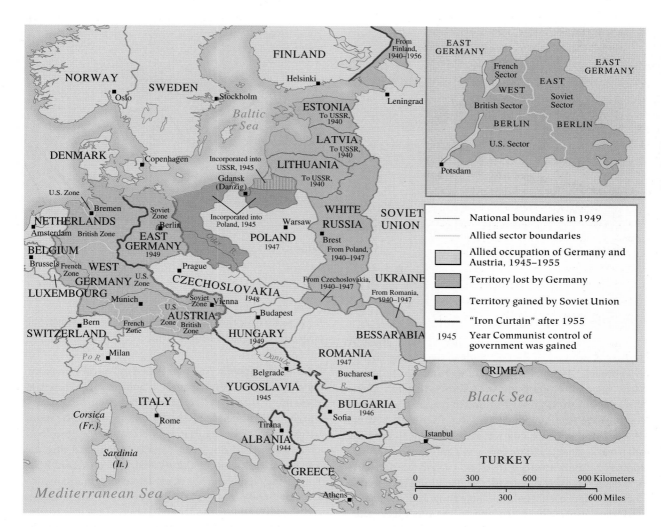

MAP 6.5 Territorial Changes in Europe After World War II. In the last months of World War II, the Red Army occupied much of Eastern Europe. Stalin sought pro-Soviet satellite states in the region as a buffer against future invasions from Western Europe, whereas Britain and the United States wanted democratically elected governments. Soviet military control of the territory settled the question.

Q *Which country gained the greatest territory at the expense of Germany?*

The Bombing of Civilians in World War II

 What was the rationale for bombing civilian populations? Did such bombing achieve its goal?

Family & Society THE MOST DEVASTATING BOMBING of civilians in World War II came near the end of the war when the United States dropped atomic bombs on the Japanese cities of Hiroshima and Nagasaki. Image 6.6a is a panoramic view of Hiroshima that shows the incredible devastation

produced by the atomic bomb. Image 6.6b shows a street in Clydebank, near Glasgow in Scotland, the day after the city was bombed by the Germans in March 1941. Only seven of the city's 12,000 houses were left undamaged; 35,000 of the 47,000 inhabitants became homeless overnight.

IMAGE 6.6a

British Library/HIP/Art Resource, NY

IMAGE 6.6b

Keystone/Hulton Archive/Getty Images

6-5c The War in the Pacific Ends

During the spring and early summer of 1945, the war in Asia continued, although with a significant change in approach. Allied war planners had initially hoped to focus their main effort on an advance through China with the aid of Chinese Nationalist forces trained and equipped by the United States. But Roosevelt became disappointed with Chiang Kai-shek's failure to take the offensive against Japanese forces in China and eventually approved a new strategy to strike toward the Japanese home islands directly across the Pacific. This "island-hopping" approach took an increasing toll on enemy resources, especially at sea and in the air. Meanwhile, new U.S. long-range B-29 bombers unleashed a wave of destruction on all major cities in the Japanese homeland. One massive firebombing raid on Tokyo in March 1945 killed more than 80,000 Japanese and caused such an enormous updraft that a U.S. aviator in one of the last

B-29s to fly over the city was thrown into the air over the target and suffered a broken arm.

Entering the Nuclear Age As Allied forces drew inexorably closer to the main Japanese islands in the summer of 1945, President Harry Truman was faced with an excruciatingly difficult decision. Should he use atomic weapons (at the time, only two bombs were available, and their effectiveness had not been demonstrated) to bring the war to an end without the necessity of an Allied invasion of the Japanese homeland? The deployment of such a weapon could result in thousands of civilian casualties and thereby subject the United States to harsh criticism around the world. On the other hand, invasion of the island of Okinawa in April had resulted in thousands of casualties on both sides, suggesting that an Allied attack on the Japanese home islands could have even bloodier consequences.

After an intense debate within the administration, Truman ultimately approved the use of America's new superweapon. The first bomb was dropped on the city of Hiroshima on August 6. Truman then called on Japan to surrender or expect a "rain of ruin from the air." When the Japanese did not respond, a second bomb was dropped on Nagasaki three days later. The destruction in Hiroshima was incredible. Of 76,000 buildings near the center of the explosion, 70,000 were flattened, and 140,000 of the city's 400,000 inhabitants died by the end of 1945. By the end of 1950, another 50,000 had perished from the effects of radiation (see Comparative Illustration, "The Bombing of Civilians in World War II," p. 156). The dropping of the first atomic bomb introduced the world to the nuclear age.

The nuclear attack on Japan, combined with the news that Soviet forces had launched an attack on Japanese-held areas in Manchuria, did have its intended effect, however. Japan surrendered unconditionally on August 14. World War II was finally over.

HISTORIANS DEBATE **The Debate over the Bomb** In the years following the end of the war, Truman's decision to approve the use of nuclear weapons to compel Japan to surrender aroused considerable controversy. At the time, the decision to drop the bomb was broadly popular in the United States, since it clearly hastened the end of the war and reduced the number of U.S. casualties in the Pacific theater. Although this was the first time that a nuclear weapon had been deployed in a battlefield situation, knowledge of the powerful nature of the new weapon was not widely understood, and most people in the Allied countries probably did not see it as qualitatively much different from many other horrific weapons that had been utilized in the course of the battle. Some of those responsible for developing the weapon, however, were horrified by the civilian casualties in Japan, and feared that it could set a precedent to be followed in future wars.

As time went on, many people began to question Truman's decision to drop the bombs. Critics argued that the decision not only led to thousands of civilian casualties, but also introduced a frightening new weapon that could eventually threaten the survival of the human race. Some suspected that Truman's real purpose in ordering the nuclear strikes was to intimidate the Soviet Union. In Japan, the issue enabled post-war officials to portray their country as a victim, thus relieving them of the responsibility before unleashing the conflict in the first place. Defenders of the decision countered that the human costs of invading the Japanese home islands would have been infinitely higher had the bombs not been dropped and that the Soviet Union would have had ample time to consolidate its control over Manchuria and command a larger role in the postwar occupation of Japan. With the dispute mired in hypothetical outcomes, contrasting statistics, and an unbridgeable gap between morality and realpolitik, there is no apparent solution to the debate, which remains unresolved today.

MAKING CONNECTIONS

World War II was the most devastating total war in human history. Germany, Italy, and Japan had been utterly defeated. Tens of millions of people—soldiers and civilians—had been killed in only six years. Although accurate figures are impossible to come by, Soviet losses alone during the war have been estimated as high as 50 million.[4] In Asia and Europe, countless cities had been reduced to rubble, and millions of people faced starvation as once fertile lands stood neglected or wasted. Untold millions of people had become refugees.

Could the catastrophe of World War II have been avoided? For many years after the end of the conflict, politicians and pundits in the United States frequently evoked the "lessons of Munich" as a guide for U.S. foreign policy during the Cold War. If only the Western democracies had stood up to Hitler's demands at Munich, they argue, the German dictator might have backed down in his demands on Czechoslovakia. The scenario is persuasive, because there is no doubt that the Fuhrer was testing the waters to see how far he could go with his expansionistic strategy. But was it realistic? When facing the prospect of conflict, statesmen and ordinary citizens alike are inevitably conditioned by their own historical experience. And for the generation facing the threat of a new global conflict in 1938, the primary lesson was that provided by the assassination at Sarajevo in 1914—the crucial importance of avoiding a rush to war based on an issue of limited importance, and that might have catastrophic consequences. In 1938, the memory of the Great War was still strong in the minds of many Europeans, and there was little stomach in the popular imagination for a repeat performance. It would take another two years, and the grim prospect of a powerful

Germany on the verge of dominating the entire continent, for reality to set in.

What were the underlying causes of the war? One key factor seems to stand out here: Germany and Japan were two rising capitalist powers who had come late to the scramble for colonies and strongly resented the Versailles Treaty, which had divided the world in a manner favorable to their rivals. Each was determined to overturn the provisions of Versailles at the earliest opportunity. It is probably significant, as well, that both countries cultivated a politics that emphasized imagined and real military traditions. It is no surprise that under the impact of the Great Depression, the effects of which were severe in both countries, fragile democratic institutions were soon overwhelmed by militant forces determined to enhance national wealth and power.

Why then did the Axis Powers lose the war? It is tempting to answer that the Allied countries were victorious because they occupied the moral high ground in the conflict, and that conclusion is certainly not to be dismissed. But other more prosaic factors probably played a more important role in determining the outcome. The ability of Allied intelligence agencies to break the German and Japanese code systems, enabling Allied leaders to anticipate the moves of their adversary on several occasions, was certainly a significant advantage. Equally important, Axis leaders made a number of crucial strategic misjudgments, some of which have been noted in this chapter. Hitler's confidence in his own strategic genius, in particular, led him badly astray on crucial occasions. In the last analysis, however, the tendency of both German and Japanese leaders to underestimate the enormous capacity of the United States and the Soviet Union to harness their industrial and human resources in the war effort was perhaps their greatest mistake. They would pay dearly for their complacency.

REFLECTION QUESTIONS

Q What was the relationship between World War I and World War II, and how did the ways in which the wars were fought differ?

Q How do you account for the early successes of the Germans from 1939 to 1941?

Q How did the Nazis and the Japanese attempt to establish new orders in Europe and Asia after their military victories, and what were the results of their efforts?

Q How did the attempt to arrive at a peace settlement after World War II lead to the beginnings of a new conflict known as the Cold War?

CHAPTER TIMELINE

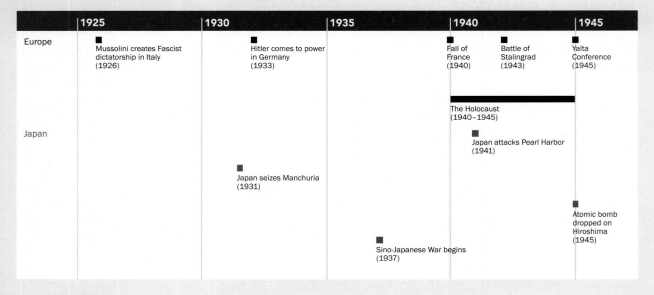

	1925	1930	1935	1940	1945
Europe	Mussolini creates Fascist dictatorship in Italy (1926)	Hitler comes to power in Germany (1933)		Fall of France (1940) Battle of Stalingrad (1943)	Yalta Conference (1945)
				The Holocaust (1940–1945)	
Japan		Japan seizes Manchuria (1931)	Sino-Japanese War begins (1937)	Japan attacks Pearl Harbor (1941)	Atomic bomb dropped on Hiroshima (1945)

CHAPTER NOTES

1. Cited in Jonathon Fenby, *Chiang Kai-shek: China's Generalissimo and the* Nation He Lost (New York, 2003), p. 180.

2. John Van Antwerp MacMurray, quoted in Arthur Waldron, *How the Peace Was Lost: The 1935 Memorandum: "Developments Affecting American Policy in the Far East"* (Stanford, Calif., 1992), p. 5.

3. Cited in Ruhl Bartlett, *The Record of American Diplomacy* (New York, 1952), p. 665.

4. Cited in B. Schwarz, "A Job for Rewrite: Stalin's War," *New York Times,* February 2, 2004.

PART II
REFLECTIONS

IN WORLD WAR II, the European nations for the second time in a generation engaged in a collective orgy of self-flagellation. And, as had occurred on the first occasion, the blood-letting rapidly spread beyond the borders of the European continent to the rest of the world. By 1945, it appeared that the nations at the heart of traditional Western civilization would no longer serve as the main arbiters of world affairs. Instead, two new super-powers from outside the heartland of Europe— the United States and the Soviet Union—took their place. With the decline of the Old World, a new era of global relationships was about to begin.

THE TWO FACES OF NATIONALISM   In the chapters above, we have singled out some of the factors that contributed to the astounding spectacle of self-destruction that engaged the European powers in two bloody interne-cine conflicts within a period of less than a quarter of a century. One key factor was the rise of nationalism. The spirit of nationalism had originally been praised by many Europeans as a positive development in the struggle to create peaceful and unified nation-states throughout the European continent. The concept of the nation-state appeared to represent Enlightenment ideals in

the sense that it would provide peoples everywhere with the opportunity of being governed by those who shared their cultural, linguistic, or ethnic identity.

Yet, as its proponents were soon to discover, nationalism was also potentially divisive in its political ramifications. Most European countries consisted of a patchwork of various ethnic, linguistic, and religious communities, a product of centuries of migrations, wars, and dynastic alliances. Many of these diverse groups lived side by side in the same countries, and even in the same villages, while stubbornly preserving their distinct character. It is hardly surprising, then, that as ethnic, cultural and linguistic awareness increased during the last half of the century, nationalism became a divisive force throughout the European continent, loud and

chauvinist in tone, leading to bitter disputes between and within individual communities and countries. How then could a system of stable nation-states, each based on a single national community, ever emerge from such a bewildering amalgam of cultures and peoples? The peace treaties signed after the Great War replaced one set of territorial boundaries with another, but hardly resolved the underlying problem—the unending competition for resources and living space within the confines of a crowded continent. World War II was the tragic result.

THE TRANSFORMATION OF WARFARE   Another factor that contributed to the violence of the early twentieth century was the Industrial Revolution. The new technology that resulted from the development of advanced industrial economies transformed the nature of war itself. New weapons of mass destruction created the potential for a new kind of warfare that reached beyond the battlefield into the very heartland of the enemy's territory, while the concept of nationalism transformed war from the sport of kings to a matter of national honor and commitment. This trend was amply demonstrated in the two world wars of the twentieth century. Each was a product of antagonisms that had been unleashed by economic competition and growing national consciousness. Each resulted in a level of destruction that severely damaged the material foundations and eroded the popular spirit of the partici-

pants, the victors as well as the vanquished.

In the end, then, industrial prowess and the driving force of nationalism, the very factors that had created the conditions for European global dominance, contained the seeds for its decline. These seeds germinated during the 1930s, when the Great Depression sharpened international competition and mutual antagonisms, and then sprouted in the ensuing conflict, which embraced the entire globe. By the time World War II came to an end, the once-powerful countries of

Europe were exhausted, leaving the door ajar not only for the emergence of the United States and the Soviet Union to global dominance but also for the collapse of the European colonial empires.

CAPITALISM IN TRANSITION A second major event that played a significant role in sharpening the conflicts among the various capitalist societies in Europe was the economic crisis that came to be known as the Great Depression. Sudden economic downturns were by no means a rare occurrence in capitalist societies, but the collapse in the early 1930s was by far the most serious, and its repercussions not only threatened the survival of the capitalist system itself, but also to derail the progress that had been made in building democratic societies throughout the continent of Europe.

Political leaders throughout the Western world adopted different strategies to deal with the situa-

tion. Many relied on a traditional approach, raising tariff barriers and adopting a tight money policy in a bid to put the local economy back on a firm footing. Germany and the Soviet Union turned to command economies, relying on the regimentation of their populations and strict control over the allocation of resources in order to realize goals established by the state.

In the United States, President Roosevelt introduced the New Deal, an ambitious strategy that relied on deficit spending—mainly on social programs—to inject money into the economy and thereby to revive commercial demand.

By the end of the decade, there were signs that a gradual recovery from the Great Depression was underway. By then, however, the damage had been done, as a political crisis brought on by the rise of revanchist regimes like Germany and Japan led to the outbreak of a second global conflict in less than a quarter of a century. World War II—which forced competing nations to engage in a policy of massive borrowing and social regimentation to achieve their objectives—helped to bring a final close to the Great Depression, but at enormous cost. As the war came to a close in 1945, the world faced the future with a high degree of trepidation.

IMPERIALISM AND ITS DISCONTENTS If the dominant motif of the early decades of the twentieth century in Europe had been the intense rivalry among the leading states over primacy in global affairs, the primary challenge in the rest of the world was undoubtedly that of dealing with the ramifications of that struggle. By 1900, a handful of European powers, eventually joined by Japan and the United States, had achieved political mastery over virtually the entire remainder of the world.

It soon became clear to perceptive observers in colonial territories that Western intervention posed an existential threat to the survival of traditional civilizations all over the world. Many realized that the old world was being destroyed, and could not be resurrected. The first generation of nationalist leaders who emerged in the first decades of the twentieth century thus had to accept the inevitability of coming to terms with the new world that had been so forcibly imposed upon them. While vociferously criticizing the exploitative policies practiced by the colonial regimes, they nevertheless began to draw up programs of action that were broadly based on key tenets of modern Western society: the formation of new nations, with defined borders and based on the will of the local population; the creation of modern economies closely linked with the global trade network; the adoption of new social mores that prized individual rights over old social hierarchies; embrace of the new over reverence for the past; and material prosperity over the quest for heavenly salvation. As the old saying has it, they were compelled to accept a new attitude: "if you can't lick 'em, join 'em."

The crisis in European civilization that broke out in the 1930s, however, raised questions about the validity of the Western capitalist model in colonial areas. Some turned to social revolution, with a weather eye out on the progress of the Soviet experiment; others sought ways to synthesize useful elements of traditional civilization with the new Western model. At first, of course, the issue was moot, since the imperialist powers showed no inclination to grant freedom to their subject peoples. But the outbreak of World War II added a new sense of urgency to the situation, since the looming threat to Western colonial empires by the Axis powers raised in the minds of many colonial peoples the enticing prospect of a restoration of independence at the close of the conflict.

LESSONS FROM AN AGE OF CRISIS   Can we draw any lessons from the dramatic events discussed above that might help us to evaluate conditions in the world today? When looking back on the historical era covered in Part II of this book, one salient feature stands out: when making crucial decisions on issues of war and peace, statesmen tended to turn to the recent past for solutions to their dilemmas. Sometimes that decision worked out well, but sometimes it did not. The overconfidence bred of a century of peace, for example, lulled policymakers in 1914 to underestimate the risks of a destructive war. Four years later, the decision to levy a harsh peace on Germany in 1918 created the conditions for a bitter Germany to seek revenge two decades later.

This does not mean that seeking to learn lessons from the past is a fruitless exercise. Postwar leaders in Europe and the United States realized in retrospect that the failure of Western democracies to undertake defensive measures to counter the threat of Nazi Germany had been a drastic mistake, and they applied that lesson, for the most part successfully, during the Cold War. And when the victorious Allies gathered at Potsdam in the summer of 1945, they opted to welcome their former adversaries Germany and Japan back into the family of nations, a decision that turned out reasonably well for all concerned, as we shall see below. There are, then, lessons to be learned from history, but they must be drawn with due respect for changing conditions and cultural differences. As we shall see, for example, the decision by U.S. policymakers to apply the "lessons of Munich" in Southeast Asia during the Cold War had serious limitations (see Chapter 7).

Do the momentous developments that led to the rise of Nazi Germany and other dictatorial regimes in the 1920s and 1930s have relevance today? Although conditions in the contemporary world are quite different from what they were during the Great Depression, there are some similarities that can serve us as warning signs of potential troubles to come. We shall have more to say about this issue in later sections of this book.

PART III

ACROSS THE IDEOLOGICAL DIVIDE

Nixon lectures Soviet Communist Party chief Nikita Khrushchev on the technology of the U.S. kitchen

AP Images

CHAPTER 7

EAST AND WEST IN THE GRIP OF THE COLD WAR

Chapter Outline and Focus Questions

7-1 *The Collapse of the Grand Alliance*

Q Why were the United States and the Soviet Union suspicious of each other after World War II, and what events that took place between 1945 and 1949 heightened the tensions between the two nations?

7-2 *Cold War in Asia*

Q How and why did Mao Zedong and the Communists come to power in China, and what were the Cold War implications of their triumph?

7-3 *From Confrontation to Coexistence*

Q What events led to the era of coexistence in the 1960s, and to what degree did each side contribute to the reduction in international tensions?

7-4 *An Era of Equivalence*

Q Why did the Cold War briefly flare up again in the 1980s, and why did it come to a definitive end at the end of the decade?

The Yalta Conference, February 1945 (photo)/English Photographer, (20th century)/
PETER NEWARK'S PICTURES/Private Collection/Bridgeman Images

IMAGE 7.1 The victorious Allied leaders at Yalta

OUR MEETING HERE IN THE CRIMEA has reaffirmed our common determination to maintain and strengthen in the peace to come that unity of purpose and of action which has made victory possible and certain for the United Nations in this war. We believe that this is a sacred obligation which our Governments owe to our peoples and to all the peoples of the world.[1]

With these ringing words, drafted at the Yalta Conference in February 1945, President Franklin D. Roosevelt, Marshal Joseph Stalin, and Prime Minister Winston Churchill affirmed their common hope that their Grand Alliance, which had brought them victory in World War II, could be sustained in the postwar era. Only through the continuing and growing cooperation and understanding among the three victorious allies, the statement asserted, could a secure and lasting peace be realized that, in the words of the Atlantic Charter, would "afford assurance that all the men in all the lands may live out their lives in freedom from fear and want."

Connections to Today

What relevance does the Cold War have on our world today, and do you feel that a new period of intense ideological competition is likely to occur in our own time?

For himself, Roosevelt hoped that the decisions reached at Yalta would provide the basis for a stable peace in the postwar era and fulfill the promises made in his "Four Freedoms" speech in 1941. Allied occupation forces—American, British, and French in the west and Soviet in the east—were to bring about the end of Axis administration and organize free elections that would lead to democratic governments throughout Europe. To foster an attitude of mutual trust and end the suspicions that had marked relations between the capitalist world and the Soviet Union prior to World War II, Roosevelt tried to reassure Stalin that Moscow's legitimate territorial aspirations and genuine security needs would be adequately met in a durable peace settlement.

It was not to be. Within months after the German surrender, the mutual trust among the victorious allies—if it had ever existed—rapidly disintegrated, and the dream of a stable peace was replaced by the specter of a nuclear holocaust. In time, the long era of intense competition between the United States and the Soviet Union would come to be known as the **Cold War**. As the ideological conflict between Moscow and Washington intensified, the continent of Europe was divided into two armed camps, and the two superpowers, glaring at each other across a deep ideological divide, held the survival of the entire world in their hands.

7-1 THE COLLAPSE OF THE GRAND ALLIANCE

 Focus Question: Why were the United States and the Soviet Union suspicious of each other after World War II, and what events that took place between 1945 and 1949 heightened the tensions between the two nations?

The problems started in Europe. At the end of the war, Soviet military forces occupied all of Eastern Europe and the Balkans (except for Greece, Albania, and Yugoslavia), while U.S. and other Allied forces completed their occupation of the western part of the European continent. Roosevelt had hoped that free elections administered by "democratic and peace-loving forces" would lead to the creation of democratic governments responsive to the aspirations of the local population. But it soon became clear that Moscow and Washington interpreted that phrase in the Yalta agreement differently. When Soviet occupation authorities began forming a new Polish government in Warsaw, Stalin refused to accept the Polish government

in exile—headquartered in London during the war and consisting primarily of representatives of the landed aristocracy who harbored a deep distrust of the Soviets—and instead installed a government composed of Communists who had spent the war in Moscow. Roosevelt complained to Stalin but, preoccupied with other problems, eventually agreed to a compromise whereby two members of the exile government in London were included in the new Communist-dominated regime. A week later, Roosevelt was dead of a cerebral hemorrhage, leaving the challenge to a new U.S. president, Harry Truman (1884–1972), who lacked experience in foreign affairs.

7-1a The Iron Curtain Descends

Similar developments took place elsewhere in Eastern Europe as all of the states occupied by Soviet troops became part of Moscow's sphere of influence. Coalitions of all political parties (except fascist or right-wing parties) were formed to run the government, but within a year or two, the Communist Party in each coalition had assumed the lion's share of power. Key posts in each government, such as Minister of Interior or National Defense, were staffed by Communists. Members of parties who appeared hostile to communist rule were declared "fascist" and placed under arrest.

The next step was the creation of one-party Communist governments. The timetables for these takeovers varied from country to country, but between 1945 and 1947, Communist governments became firmly entrenched in East Germany, Bulgaria, Romania, Poland, and Hungary. In Czechoslovakia, with its strong tradition of democratic institutions, the Communists did not achieve their goals until 1948. In the elections of 1946, the Communist Party became the largest party but was forced to share control of the government with non-Communist rivals. When it appeared that the latter might win new elections early in 1948, the Communists seized control of the government on February 25. All other parties were dissolved, and the Communist leader Klement Gottwald (1896–1953) became the new president of Czechoslovakia.

Yugoslavia was a notable exception to the pattern of growing Soviet dominance in Eastern Europe. The Communist Party there had led the resistance to the Nazis during the war and easily took over power when the war ended. Josip Broz, known as Tito (1892–1980), the leader of the Communist resistance movement, appeared to be a loyal Stalinist. After the war, however, he moved to establish an independent Communist state in Yugoslavia. Stalin had hoped to take control of Yugoslavia, just as he had done in other Eastern European countries. But Tito refused to capitulate to Stalin's demands and gained the support of the people (and some sympathy in the West) by portraying the struggle as one of Yugoslav national freedom. In 1948, Stalin had Yugoslavia formally expelled from the Soviet bloc, and from that point, the country embarked on a neutralist policy in the Cold War (see Map 7.1). In 1958, the Yugoslav party congress asserted that Yugoslav Communists did not see themselves as deviating from communism, only from Stalinism. They considered their more decentralized economic and political system, in which workers could manage themselves and local communes could exercise some political power, closer to the Marxist-Leninist ideal.

To Stalin (who had once boasted, "I will shake my little finger, and there will be no more Tito"), the creation of pliant pro-Soviet regimes throughout Eastern Europe to serve as a buffer zone against the capitalist West may simply have represented his interpretation of the Yalta peace agreement and a reward for sacrifices suffered during the war. In any case, he viewed the idea of "free elections" as a bourgeois affectation and shared Lenin's conviction that power-sharing arrangements between Communist and capitalist parties were a temporary phenomenon that could only lead to full Communist rule. Recent evidence suggests that Stalin did not decide to tighten Communist control over the new Eastern European governments until U.S. actions—notably the promulgation of the Marshall Plan (see "The Marshall Plan," p. 167)—threatened to undermine Soviet authority in the region. If the Soviet leader had any intention of promoting future Communist revolutions in Western Europe—and there is ample indication that he did—such developments would have to await the appearance of a new capitalist crisis a decade or more into the future. As Stalin undoubtedly recalled, Lenin had always maintained that revolutions come in waves, and he was content to wait for the next one to come along.

7-1b The Truman Doctrine and the Beginnings of Containment

In the United States, the Soviet takeover of Eastern Europe represented an ominous development that threatened Roosevelt's vision of a durable peace. Public suspicion of Soviet intentions grew rapidly, especially among the millions of Americans who still had relatives living in Eastern Europe. Winston Churchill was quick to put such fears into words. In a highly publicized speech given to an American audience at Westminster College in Fulton, Missouri, in March 1946, the former British

MAP 7.1 Eastern Europe in 1948

Neutral nations

prime minister declared that an "Iron Curtain" had "descended across the Continent," dividing Germany and Europe itself into two hostile camps. The speech achieved wide publicity in the United States and hardened public opinion against recent Soviet moves around the world. Stalin responded by branding Churchill's speech a "call to war with the Soviet Union." But he need not have worried. Although the changing public attitude among the American people placed increasing pressure on Washington to devise an effective strategy to counter Soviet advances abroad, the American people were in no mood for another war.

The first threat of a U.S.-Soviet confrontation took place in the Middle East. During World War II, British and Soviet troops had been stationed in Iran to prevent Axis occupation of the rich oil fields in that country. Both nations had promised to withdraw their forces after the war, but at the end of 1945, there were ominous signs that Moscow might attempt to use its troops as a bargaining chip to annex Iran's northern territories—known as Azerbaijan—to the Soviet Union. When the government of Iran, with strong U.S. support, threatened to take the issue to the United Nations, the Soviets backed down and removed their forces from that country in the spring of 1946.

A civil war in Greece created another potential arena for confrontation between the superpowers and an opportunity for the Truman administration to take a stand. Communist-led guerrilla forces supported by Tito, who hoped to create a Balkan federation under Yugoslav domination, had taken up arms against the pro-Western government in Athens. Great Britain had initially assumed primary responsibility for promoting postwar reconstruction in the eastern Mediterranean, but in 1947, postwar economic problems caused the British to withdraw from the active role they had been playing in both Greece and Turkey. President Truman, alarmed by British weakness and the possibility of Soviet expansion into the eastern Mediterranean, responded with the **Truman Doctrine**, which said in essence that the United States would provide financial aid to countries that claimed they were threatened by Communist expansion (see Historical Voices, "The Truman Doctrine," p. 167). If the Soviets were not stopped in Greece, Truman declared, then the United States would have to face the spread of communism throughout the free world. As Dean Acheson, the American secretary of state, explained, "Like apples in

HISTORICAL VOICES

The Truman Doctrine

 How did President Truman defend his request for aid to Greece and Turkey? What role did this decision play in intensifying the Cold War?

Politics & Government **BY 1947**, the battle lines in the Cold War had been clearly drawn. This excerpt is taken from a speech by President Harry Truman to the U.S. Congress in which he justified his request for aid to Greece and Turkey. Truman expressed the urgent need to contain the expansion of communism. Compare this statement with that of Soviet leader Leonid Brezhnev presented on p. 230.

Truman's Speech to Congress, March 12, 1947

The peoples of a number of countries of the world have recently had totalitarian regimes forced upon them against their will. The Government of the United States has made frequent protests against coercion and intimidation, in violation of the Yalta agreement, in Poland, Rumania, and Bulgaria. I must also state that in a number of other countries there have been similar developments.

At the present moment in world history nearly every nation must choose between alternative ways of life. The choice is too often not a free one.

One way of life is based upon the will of the majority, and is distinguished by free institutions, representative government, free elections, guarantees of individual liberty, freedom of speech and religion, and freedom from political oppression.

The second way of life is based upon the will of a minority forcibly imposed upon the majority. It relies upon terror and oppression, a controlled press and radio, fixed elections, and the suppression of personal freedoms.

I believe that it must be the policy of the United States to support free peoples who are resisting attempted subjugation by armed minorities or by outside pressures.

I believe that we must assist free peoples to work out their own destinies in their own way.

I believe that our help should be primarily through economic and financial aid which is essential to economic stability and orderly political processes. . . . I therefore ask the Congress for assistance to Greece and Turkey in the amount of $400,000,000.

Source: U.S. Congress, *Congressional Record*, 80th Congress, 1st Session (Washington, D.C.: U.S. Government Printing Office, 1947), Vol. 93, p. 1981.

---

a barrel infected by disease, the corruption of Greece would infect Iran and all the East . . . likewise Africa . . . Italy . . . France. . . . Not since Rome and Carthage has there been such a polarization of power on this earth."[2] It was the first expression of what would later be described as the "domino theory" as a factor in U.S. foreign policy.

The somewhat apocalyptic tone of Acheson's statement was intentional. Not only were the American people in no mood for foreign adventures, but members of the U.S. Congress—in Republican hands for the first time in over a decade—were in an isolationist frame of mind. Only the prospect of a dire threat from abroad, the president's advisers concluded, could persuade the nation to take action. The tactic worked, and Congress voted to provide the aid Truman requested.

As it turned out, however, the U.S. suspicion that Moscow was actively supporting the insurgent movement in Greece was inaccurate. In a private discussion held in 1944, Stalin had conceded to British leader Winston

Churchill that Greece would remain under Western influence after the close of the war, and he was apparently unhappy that Tito was promoting the conflict, not only because he suspected that the latter was attempting to create his own sphere of influence in the Balkans, but also because it risked provoking a direct confrontation between the Soviet Union and the United States in an area that was clearly within the American sphere of influence. "The rebellion in Greece," Stalin declared, "must be crushed."[3]

The Marshall Plan The White House, however, was unaware of Stalin's cautious stance in Moscow, and saw the Soviet dictator's hand behind the unrest in Greece. The proclamation of the Truman Doctrine was soon followed in June 1947 by the European Recovery Program, better known as the **Marshall Plan**. Intended to rebuild prosperity and stability throughout the European continent, this program included $13 billion for the economic recovery of war-torn Europe. Underlying the program was the belief that an economic revival would insulate the peoples of Europe from the appeal of international communism, as well as stimulate economic growth in the United States, which would benefit from European purchases of U.S. goods.

From the Soviet perspective, the Marshall Plan was nothing less than capitalist imperialism, a thinly veiled attempt to buy the support of the smaller European countries, which in return would be expected to submit to economic exploitation by the United States. The White House indicated that the Marshall Plan was open to the Soviet Union and its Eastern European satellite states, but the latter refused to participate. The Soviets, however, were in no position to compete financially with the United States and could do little to counter the Marshall Plan except to tighten their control in Eastern Europe.

7-1c Europe Divided

By 1947, the split in Europe between East and West had become a fact of life. At the end of World War II, the Truman administration had favored a quick end to its commitments in Europe, but fears of Soviet aims caused the United States to play an increasingly important role in European affairs. In an article in *Foreign Affairs* in July 1947, George Kennan, a well-known U.S. diplomat with much knowledge of Soviet affairs, advocated a policy of **containment** against further aggressive Soviet moves. Kennan favored what he termed the "adroit and vigilant application of counter-force at a series of constantly shifting geographical and political points, corresponding to the shifts and maneuvers of Soviet policy." In his view, such a strategy would insulate free nations in other parts of the world from falling into the hands of the Soviet Union without running the risk of a direct conflict with Moscow. After the Soviet blockade of Berlin in 1948 (see below), containment of the Soviet Union became formal U.S. policy.

In the negotiations that took place at the end of the war, the fate of Germany had become a source of heated contention between East and West. Aside from **denazification** and the partitioning of Germany (and Berlin) into four occupied zones, the Allied Powers had agreed on little with regard to the conquered nation. The Soviet Union, hardest hit by the war, took reparations from Germany in the form of booty. By the summer of 1946, nearly six hundred factories in the East German zone had been shipped to the Soviet Union. At the same time, the German Communist Party was reestablished under the control of Walter Ulbricht (1893–1973)

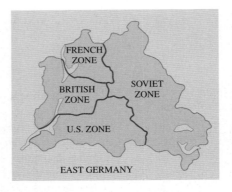

MAP 7.2 Berlin Divided

and was soon in charge of the political reconstruction of the Soviet zone in eastern Germany.

The Berlin Blockade Although the foreign ministers of the four occupying powers (the United States, the Soviet Union, Great Britain, and France) kept meeting in an attempt to arrive at a final peace treaty with Germany, they grew further and further apart. In response, the British, French, and Americans gradually began to merge their zones economically and by February 1948 were making plans for the formation of a national German government. The Soviet Union responded with a blockade of West Berlin that prevented all traffic from entering the city's three western zones through Soviet-controlled territory in East Germany (see Map 7.2). The Soviets hoped to prevent the creation of a separate West German state, which threatened Stalin's plan to create a reunified Germany that could eventually be placed under Soviet control (see Map 7.3).

The Western powers faced a dilemma. Direct military confrontation with Moscow seemed dangerous, and no one wished to risk World War III. Therefore, an attempt to break through the blockade with tanks and trucks was ruled out. The solution was the Berlin Airlift: supplies for the city's inhabitants were brought in by plane. At its peak, the airlift flew 13,000 tons of supplies daily into Berlin. The Soviets, who also wanted to avoid war, did not interfere and finally lifted the blockade in May 1949 (see Image 7.2). But the blockade had severely increased tensions between the United States and the Soviet Union and confirmed the separation of Germany into two states. The Federal Republic of Germany (FRG) was formally created from the three Western zones in September 1949, and a month later, the separate German Democratic Republic (GDR) was established in East Germany. Berlin remained a divided city and the source of much contention between East and West.

Nato and the Warsaw Pact The search for security in the new world of the Cold War also led to the formation of military alliances. The North Atlantic Treaty Organization (**NATO**) was formed in April 1949 when Belgium, Luxembourg, the Netherlands, France, Britain, Italy, Denmark, Norway, Portugal, and Iceland signed a treaty with the United States and Canada (see Map 7.3). All the powers agreed to provide mutual assistance if any one of them was attacked. A few years later, West Germany, Greece, and Turkey joined the alliance. Meanwhile, the U.S. engaged in an arms buildup aimed at preventing the

IMAGE 7.2 **A City Divided.** In 1948, U.S. planes airlifted supplies into Berlin to break the blockade that Soviet troops had imposed to isolate the city. Shown here is a section of the city later to be known as "Checkpoint Charlie" (one of the crossing points between the Western and Soviet zones of Berlin) just as Soviet roadblocks are about to be removed. The banner at the entrance to the Soviet sector reads, ironically, "The sector of freedom greets the fighters for freedom and right of the Western sectors."

 Why did the divided city of Berlin eventually become one of the major flash points of the Cold War?

further expansion of communism anywhere in the world. Truman administration officials were determined to avoid a repeat of the disaster at Munich in 1938.

The Soviet Union and its Eastern European satellites soon followed suit. In 1949, they formed the Council for Mutual Economic Assistance (COMECON) for economic cooperation. Then, in 1955, Albania, Bulgaria, Czechoslovakia, East Germany, Hungary, Poland, Romania, and the Soviet Union organized a formal military alliance, the **Warsaw Pact**. Once again, Europe was tragically divided into hostile alliance systems.

HISTORIANS DEBATE **Who Started the Cold War?** There has been considerable historical debate over who bears responsibility for starting the Cold War. In the 1950s, most scholars in the West assumed that the bulk of the blame must fall on the shoulders of Stalin, whose determination to impose Soviet rule on Eastern Europe snuffed out hopes for freedom and self-determination there and

aroused justifiable fears of Communist expansionist objectives in the West. During the next decade, however, revisionist historians—influenced in part by their opposition to U.S. policies in Southeast Asia—began to argue that the fault lay primarily in Washington, where Truman and his anti-Communist advisers abandoned the precepts of Yalta and sought to encircle the Soviet Union with a tier of pliant U.S. client states. More recently, many historians have adopted a more nuanced view, noting that both the United States and the Soviet Union took some unwise steps that contributed to rising tensions at the end of World War II.

The root of the problem was that both nations were working within a framework conditioned by the past. The rivalry between the two superpowers ultimately stemmed from their different historical perspectives and their irreconcilable political ambitions. As we have seen, intense competition for political and military supremacy had long been a regular feature of Western civilization. The success of the Bolshevik Revolution in 1917 produced an

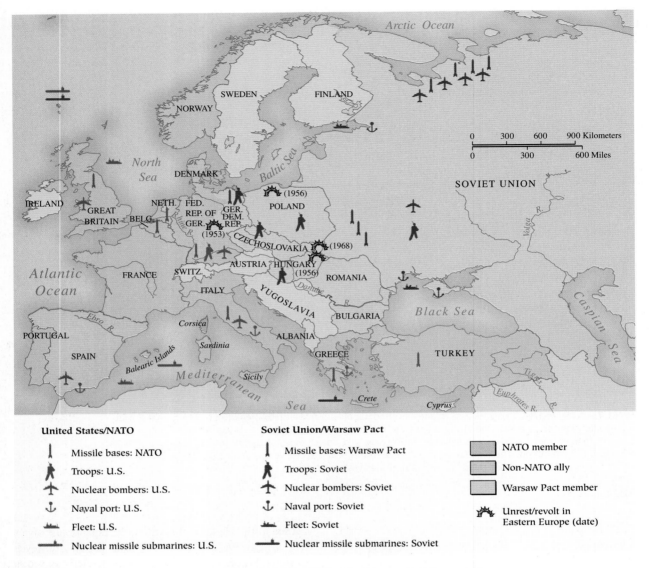

United States/NATO

| Missile bases: NATO |
| Troops: U.S. |
| Nuclear bombers: U.S. |
| Naval port: U.S. |
| Fleet: U.S. |
| Nuclear missile submarines: U.S. |

Soviet Union/Warsaw Pact

| Missile bases: Warsaw Pact |
| Troops: Soviet |
| Nuclear bombers: Soviet |
| Naval port: Soviet |
| Fleet: Soviet |
| Nuclear missile submarines: Soviet |

NATO member

Non-NATO ally

Warsaw Pact member

Unrest/revolt in
Eastern Europe (date)

MAP 7.3 The New European Alliance Systems During the Cold War. This map shows postwar Europe as it was divided during the Cold War into two contending power blocs, the NATO alliance and the Warsaw Pact. Major military and naval bases are indicated by symbols on the map.

 Where on the map was the so-called Iron Curtain?

alternative to the prevailing economic system in Europe, while the Great Depression raised serious questions about the viability of capitalism in satisfying human needs. The United States and the Soviet Union were not only the heirs of that European tradition of power politics; they also represented two contrasting models for the new world that had inevitably emerged after the war. It should come as no surprise, then, that two such competitive systems would not simply struggle to protect their own spheres of influence, but also seek to extend their hegemony and their way of life to the rest of the world. Because of its paramount

need to secure its western border, the Soviet Union was not prepared to give up the advantages it had gained in Eastern Europe from Germany's defeat. But neither were Western leaders prepared to accept without protest the establishment of a system of Soviet satellites that not only threatened the security of Western Europe but also deeply offended Western sensibilities because of its blatant disregard of their concept of human rights, as inherited from the European Enlightenment.

Does this mean that both sides bear equal responsibility for starting the Cold War? A number of revisionist historians have claimed that the U.S. doctrine of containment was an unnecessarily provocative action that aroused Stalin's suspicions and drove him into a position of hostility toward the West. This charge lacks credibility. Although it is understandable that the Soviets were concerned that the United States might use its monopoly of nuclear weapons to attempt to intimidate them (Stalin himself was quoted as saying that the atomic bomb was "a good weapon for threatening people with weak nerves"), information now available from the Soviet archives and other sources makes it increasingly clear, not only that Stalin was determined from the outset to create a system of pliant states along his western border after the war, but also that his suspicions of the West were deeply rooted in his Marxist-Leninist worldview and long predated Washington's enunciation of the doctrine of containment. As his foreign minister, Vyacheslav Molotov, once remarked, Soviet policy was inherently aggressive and would be triggered whenever the opportunity offered. Although Stalin apparently had no master plan to advance Soviet power into Western Europe, he was probably prepared to make every effort to do so once the next revolutionary wave arrived. Under such conditions, it is hardly surprising that Western leaders felt fully justified in reacting to this possibility by strengthening their own lines of defense.

Still, a case can be made that in deciding to respond to the Soviet challenge in a primarily military manner, Western leaders overreacted to the situation and virtually guaranteed that the Cold War would be transformed into an arms race that could conceivably result in a new and uniquely destructive war. George Kennan, the original architect of the doctrine of containment, had initially proposed a primarily political approach and eventually disavowed the means by which the containment strategy was carried out. Other U.S. officials, concerned at the possibility of a Soviet invasion of Western Europe now virtually bereft of U.S. combat troops, believed that a strong military buildup was absolutely necessary.

7-2 COLD WAR IN ASIA

 Focus Question: How and why did Mao Zedong and the Communists come to power in China, and what were the Cold War implications of their triumph?

The Cold War was somewhat slower to make its appearance in Asia. At Yalta, Stalin formally agreed to enter the Pacific war against Japan three months after the close of the conflict with Germany. As a reward for Soviet participation in the struggle against Japan, Roosevelt promised that Moscow would be granted "preeminent interests" in Manchuria (interests reminiscent of those possessed by Imperial Russia prior to its defeat by Japan in 1904–1905) and the establishment of a Soviet naval base at Port Arthur. In return, Stalin promised to sign a treaty of alliance with the Republic of China, thus implicitly committing the Soviet Union not to provide the Chinese Communists with support in a possible future civil war. Although many observers would later question Stalin's sincerity in making such a commitment to the vocally anti-Communist Chiang Kai-shek, in Moscow the decision probably had a logic of its own. Stalin had no particular liking for the independent-minded Mao Zedong (he once derisively labeled the Chinese leader a "radish Communist"—red on the outside and white on the inside—and did not anticipate a Communist victory in the eventuality of a civil war in China. Only an agreement with Chiang Kai-shek—in his mind—could provide the Soviet Union with a strategically vital economic and political presence in North China.

In the course of events, these agreements soon became a dead letter, and the region was sucked into the vortex of the Cold War by the end of the decade. The root of the problem lay not in the agreement at Yalta (as some later charged), but in the underlying weakness of Chiang Kai-shek's regime, a weakness which threatened to create a political vacuum in East Asia that both Moscow and Washington would be tempted to fill.

7-2a The Chinese Civil War

As World War II came to an end in the Pacific, relations between the government of Chiang Kai-shek in China and its powerful U.S. ally had become frayed. Although Roosevelt had hoped that China would be the keystone of his plan for peace and stability in Asia after the war, he eventually became disillusioned with the corruption of Chiang's government and the Chinese leader's unwillingness to risk his forces against the Japanese (Chiang hoped to save them for use against the Communists after the war in the Pacific ended), and China became a backwater as the war came to a close. Nevertheless, U.S. military and economic aid to China had been substantial, and at the war's end, the Truman administration still hoped that it could rely on Chiang to maintain stability and support U.S. postwar goals in the region.

While Chiang Kai-shek wrestled with Japanese aggression and problems of postwar reconstruction, the Communists were building up their liberated base in north China. A wary alliance with Chiang in December 1936 had relieved them from the threat of immediate attack from the south, although Chiang was chronically suspicious of the Communists and stationed troops near Xian to prevent them from infiltrating areas under his control. For their part, Mao hoped to use the volatile conditions in China at the close of the war as a springboard to victory.

Chiang had good reason to fear for the future. During the war, the Communists patiently penetrated Japanese lines and built up their strength in north China. Smaller numbers of Communist units had remained south of the Yangzi River and represented a further irritant. To enlarge their political base, the CCP had carried out what it termed a "mass line" policy designed to win broad popular support by reducing land rents and confiscating the lands of wealthy landlords. Promise the people what they want, Mao reasoned, and they will support you. By the end of World War II, according to Communist estimates 20 to 30 million Chinese were living under their administration, and their People's Liberation Army (PLA) included nearly one million troops.

As the war came to an end, world attention began to focus on the prospects for renewed civil strife in China. Members of a U.S. liaison team stationed in Yan'an during the last months of the war were impressed by the performance of the Communists, and in their reports to Washington some recommended that the United States should support the CCP or at least remain neutral in a possible conflict between Communists and Nationalists for control of China. The Truman administration, though skeptical of Chiang's ability to forge a strong and prosperous country, was increasingly concerned about the spread of communism in Europe and tried to find a peaceful solution through the formation of a coalition government of all parties in China.

The Communist Triumph   The prospects for success were not good. By 1946, full-scale war between the Communists and the Nationalist government, now reinstalled in Nanjing, had resumed. Initially, most of the fighting took place in Manchuria, where newly arrived Communist units began to surround Nationalist forces occupying the major cities. Now Chiang Kai-shek's errors came home to roost. In the countryside, millions of peasants, attracted to the Communists by promises of land and social justice, flocked to serve in the PLA. In the cities, middle-class Chinese, normally hostile to communism, were alienated by Chiang's brutal suppression of all dissent and his government's inability to slow the ruinous rate of inflation or solve the economic problems that it caused. By the end of 1947, almost all of Manchuria was under Communist control.

The Truman administration reacted to the spread of Communist power in China with acute discomfort. Washington had no desire to see a Communist government on the mainland, but it had little confidence in Chiang Kai-shek's ability to realize Roosevelt's dream of a strong, united, and prosperous China. In December 1945,

President Truman sent General George C. Marshall to China in a last-ditch effort to bring about a peaceful settlement. Talks between the protagonists were held, but anti-Communist elements in Nanjing resisted U.S. pressure to join a coalition government with the Chinese Communist Party, while Communist leaders refused Chiang's demand to integrate PLA units into Chiang's army under the latter's leadership. Faced with the failure to forge a peace deal between the contending forces, Marshall left China empty-handed. The United States continued to provide limited military support to Chiang's regime but refused to commit U.S. power to guarantee its survival. The administration's hands-off policy deeply angered many Republican members of Congress, who charged that the White House was "soft on communism" and called for increased military assistance to the Nationalist government.

With morale dropping in Chinese cities, Chiang's troops began to defect to the Communists. Sometimes whole divisions, officers as well as ordinary soldiers, changed sides (one Western observer joked that he knew that Chiang was lost when he observed one of his generals loading his gold and his concubines on an evacuation flight from a Manchurian airport). By 1948, the PLA was advancing south out of Manchuria and had encircled Beijing. Communist troops took the old imperial capital, crossed the Yangzi the following spring, and occupied the commercial hub of Shanghai (see Map 7.4). During the next few months, Chiang's government and 2 million of his followers fled to Taiwan, which the Japanese had returned to Chinese control after World War II. In January 1949, CCP Chairman Mao Zedong announced the establishment of the People's Republic of China (PRC) from the entrance gate to the Imperial City in Beijing.

With the Communist victory in China, Asia became a major theater of the Cold War and an integral element in American politics. In a White Paper (an official government statement) issued by the State Department in the fall of 1949, the Truman administration placed most of the blame for the debacle on Chiang Kai-shek's regime. "The unfortunate but inescapable fact," the authors of the White Paper argued, "is that the ominous result of the civil war in China was beyond the control of the government of the United States." The Communist victory, it added, was "the product of internal Chinese forces, forces which this country tried to influence but could not. A decision was arrived at within China, if only a decision by default."[4]

Republicans in Congress quickly sought to seize political advantage, arguing that Roosevelt had initially betrayed Chiang Kai-shek at Yalta by granting privileges in Manchuria to the Soviet Union. Later, the Truman administration failed to take firm action when Soviet occupation troops in Manchuria had hindered the dispatch of

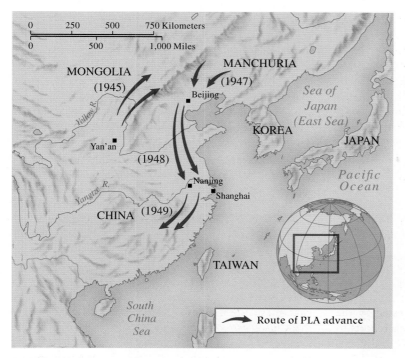

MAP 7.4 **The Chinese Civil War.** After the close of the Pacific war in 1945, the Nationalist government and the Chinese Communists fought a bitter civil war that ended with a Communist victory in 1949. The path of the Communist advance is shown on the map.

 Where did Chiang Kai-shek's government retreat to after its defeat?

Nationalist forces to the area and then provided the PLA with weapons to use against their rivals. Broadening the focus of their criticism, some members of Congress began to charge that a few U.S. diplomats stationed in China were naïve about the threat posed by the CCP, or were even guilty of having sympathy for the Communist cause. A few even questioned the loyalty of General Marshall himself.

Who Lost China? Were such criticisms justified? Was the Truman administration negligent in limiting its assistance to Chiang Kai-shek's government in its moment of extreme peril? One charge, that support from Moscow was a significant factor in the outcome, has been largely discredited in recent years, as sources in Moscow and Beijing have confirmed that in actuality the Soviet Union gave relatively little assistance to the CCP in its postwar struggle against the Nanjing regime. In fact, Stalin—likely concerned at the prospect of a military confrontation with the United States—initially advised Mao against undertaking the effort. Although Communist forces undoubtedly received some assistance from Soviet occupation troops in Manchuria, their victory, as the White Paper contended, ultimately stemmed largely from conditions inside China.

Could the Truman administration have done anything to reverse the result? Although it is always difficult to resolve counterfactual questions, the White House was facing an excruciating dilemma. Although the military forces available to the Nationalist government substantially surpassed those available to the Communists, the government had been seriously weakened by a decade of total war with Japan. For a variety of reasons—some of his own making—Chiang himself had failed to mobilize sufficient popular support for a government which, in the minds of many Chinese, had used the war to enrich itself at the expense of its constituents. Meanwhile, the Communists had taken full advantage of the situation to win the allegiance of millions of Chinese through their own program of land reform and national renewal. In these uncertain conditions, a major commitment of U.S. military support—including the likelihood of American combat troops—would have been a difficult sell to a war-weary populace already nervous about Communist advances in Europe.

Stung by the harsh criticism for its actions, the White House was belatedly forced to respond to its critics. During the spring of 1950, under pressure from Congress and public opinion to define U.S. interests in Asia, the Truman administration adopted a new national security policy that declared that the United States would take whatever steps were necessary to stem the further expansion of communism in the region. Included in its assessment was the need to decide what to do about the island of Taiwan—now occupied by the government-in-exile of Chiang Kai-shek. Containment had come to East Asia.

7-2b Red Star Rising: The New China

In their new capital at Beijing, China's Communist leaders undoubtedly hoped that their accession to power in 1949 would bring about a respite in conflict sufficient to permit their new government to concentrate on domestic goals (see Chapter 12). But their desire for peace was tempered by their determination to erase a century of humiliation at the hands of imperialist powers and to restore the traditional outer frontiers of the Chinese empire. In addition to recovering territories that had previously been

Friends and Enemies

> **Q** *What were Mao Zedong's objectives at the time he exchanged greetings with his two fellow leaders?*

Interaction & Exchange **HANDSHAKES BETWEEN WORLD LEADERS** are not always what they seem. Often, they disguise feelings of deep mutual animosity that have been papered over temporarily in pursuit of short-term goals. In Image 7.3a, Mao Zedong and Chiang Kai-shek exchange a toast during negotiations aimed at finding a solution to the Chinese civil war. In Image 7.3b, Mao shakes hands with Joseph Stalin during the former's visit to Moscow in early 1950. Mao and Stalin, however, did not get along, as Mao reportedly complained to colleagues that obtaining assistance from Stalin was "like taking meat from a tiger's mouth."

IMAGE 7.3a

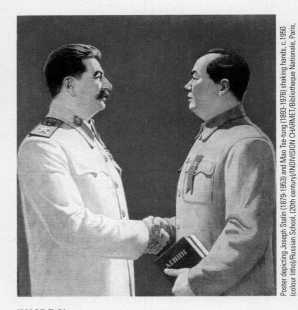

IMAGE 7.3b

Poster depicting Joseph Stalin (1879-1953) and Mao Tse-tung (1893-1976) shaking hands, c.1950 (colour litho)/Russian School, (20th century)/INDIVISION CHARMET/Bibliotheque Nationale, Paris, France/Bridgeman Images

Jack Wilkes/Getty Images

governed by the Manchu dynasty, such as Manchuria, Taiwan, Xinjiang, and Tibet, Chinese leaders also hoped to restore Chinese influence in former tributary areas such as Korea and Vietnam.

It soon became clear that the regime's domestic and foreign policy objectives were not always compatible. Negotiations between Mao Zedong and Stalin held in Moscow in early 1950 were tense (see Comparative Illustration, "Friends and Enemies," above), but led to the signing of a mutual security treaty and Soviet recognition of Chinese sovereignty over Manchuria and Xinjiang (the desolate lands north of Tibet known as Chinese Turkestan because many of the peoples in the area were of Turkish origin), although the Soviets retained a measure of economic influence in both areas. Chinese troops occupied Tibet in 1950 and brought it under Chinese administration for the first time in more than a century. But in Korea and Taiwan, China's efforts to re-create the old imperial buffer zone threatened to provoke new conflicts with foreign powers.

The disagreement over Taiwan was a consequence of the Cold War. As the civil war in China came to an end, the Truman administration appeared determined to avoid entanglement in China's internal affairs and indicated that it would not seek to prevent a Communist takeover of the island, now occupied by Chiang Kai-shek's Republic of China. But as tensions between the United States and the new Chinese government escalated during the winter of 1949–1950, influential figures in the United States began to argue that Taiwan was crucial to U.S. defense strategy in the Pacific. Their efforts were soon to be bolstered by an unexpected event.

7-2c The Korean War

The outbreak of hostilities in Korea also helped bring the Cold War to East Asia. As we saw in Chapter 3, Korea, long a Chinese tributary, became part of the Japanese empire in 1908 and remained so until 1945. Japanese rule had been deeply unpopular in Korea, and its removal from Japanese control had been one of the stated objectives of the Allies in World War II. Accordingly, on the eve of the Japanese surrender in August 1945, the Soviet Union and the United States agreed to divide the country into two separate occupation zones at the 38th parallel (see Map 7.5). They originally planned to hold national elections after the restoration of peace to reunify Korea under an independent government. But as U.S.-Soviet relations deteriorated, two separate governments emerged in Korea, a Communist-led Democratic People's Republic of Korea, or DPRK in the north and the anti-Communist Republic of Korea (ROK) in the south.

Tensions between the two governments ran high along the dividing line, and Kim Il-sung (1912–1994), the Communist leader in the north, asked Moscow to support his plan to use military force to unify the peninsula under his control. Stalin, however, was still unwilling to confront the United States: "If you should get kicked in the teeth," he replied, "I shall not lift a finger. You have to ask Mao for all the help."[5] Mao Zedong, convinced that a new revolutionary wave was on the horizon, gave his blessing to the invasion, despite the misgivings of some of his advisers.

Kim Il-sung, convinced that the United States lacked the stomach for a new war on the Asian mainland, was not deterred by Stalin's refusal of assistance, and on June 25, 1950, North Korean troops took advantage of border skirmishes to launch an invasion of the south. The Truman administration, by now increasingly concerned about Communist intentions in Asia, immediately ordered U.S. naval and air forces to support South Korea, and the United Nations Security Council (with the Soviet delegate absent to protest the failure of the UN to assign China's seat to the new government in Beijing) passed a resolution calling on member nations to jointly resist the invasion in line with the security provisions in the United Nations Charter. By September, UN forces under the command of U.S. General Douglas MacArthur marched northward across the 38th parallel with the aim of unifying Korea under a single non-Communist government.

President Truman worried that by approaching the Chinese border at the Yalu River, the UN troops—the

MAP 7.5 The Korean Peninsula

majority of whom were from the United States—could trigger Chinese intervention, but MacArthur assured him that China would not respond. MacArthur's intelligence sources were mistaken, because in November, Chinese "volunteer" forces intervened on the side of North Korea and drove the UN troops southward in disarray. In a moment of temporary panic, Truman mused in his diary about the necessity of using atomic weapons to avoid a disastrous defeat. Fortunately, a static defense line was eventually established near the original dividing line at the 38th parallel, although the war continued.

To many U.S. officials, the Chinese intervention in Korea—along with the buildup of PLA units on the mainland across from Taiwan—was clear evidence that Beijing intended to promote communism throughout Asia. Immediately after the invasion, President Truman dispatched the U.S. Seventh Fleet to the Taiwan Strait to prevent a possible Chinese invasion of Taiwan. Were White House concerns about China's intentions justified? The available evidence is not conclusive, but in all likelihood China's decision to enter the war was motivated primarily by the fear that hostile U.S. forces might be stationed on the Chinese frontier and perhaps even launch an attack across the border. MacArthur intensified such fears by calling publicly for air attacks (for which he was publicly rebuked, and later dismissed from his position, by President Truman), possibly including nuclear weapons, on Manchurian cities in preparation for an attack on Communist China.

The consequences were particularly costly for China. Not only did the outbreak of war in Korea harden Western attitudes against the new Chinese regime and lead to the country's isolation from contacts with the major capitalist powers. It also strengthened the U.S. commitment to the Nationalist government in Taiwan as the only legal representative of the Chinese people, and led the Truman administration to support its retention of the China seat on the UN Executive Council. As a result, the PRC was cut off from all forms of Western economic and technological assistance and was forced to rely almost entirely on the USSR. For once, Mao Zedong had committed a serious blunder.

7-2d Conflict in Indochina

A cease-fire agreement brought the hostilities in Korea to an end in July 1953, and China quickly signaled its intention to live in peaceful coexistence with other independent countries in the region. But Beijing's gesture of conciliation was undercut by its growing role in a bitter conflict on China's southern flank—in French Indochina. The struggle there had begun shortly after Japan's surrender at the end of World War II, when the Indochinese Communist Party led by Ho Chi Minh (1890–1969)—the new pseudonym of Nguyen Ai Quoc—at the head of a multiparty nationalist alliance called the **Vietminh Front**, seized power in northern and central Vietnam. After abortive negotiations between Ho's government and the French over a proposed "free state" of Vietnam under French tutelage, war broke out in December 1946. French forces occupied the cities and the densely populated lowlands, while the Vietminh took refuge in the mountains. The ICP was renamed the Vietnamese Workers' Party (VWP) to allay suspicions about its ties with Moscow.

For three years, the Vietminh—under firm Communist leadership—waged a "people's war" of national liberation from colonial rule, with their guerrilla forces (no longer supported and supplied by the United States) gradually increasing in size and effectiveness. At the time, however, the conflict in Indochina attracted relatively little attention from world leaders. The Truman administration was uneasy about Ho's long-standing credentials as a Soviet agent, but was equally reluctant to anger anticolonialist elements in the region by intervening on behalf of the French. Moscow had even less interest in the issue. Stalin—still hoping to see the French Communist Party come to power in Paris—ignored Ho's request for recognition of his movement as the legitimate representative of the national interests of the Vietnamese people.

But what had begun as an anticolonial struggle by the Vietminh Front against the French became entangled in the Cold War after the CCP came to power in China. In early 1950, Beijing began to provide military assistance to the Vietminh to burnish its revolutionary credentials and protect its own borders from hostile occupation. The Truman administration, increasingly concerned that a revolutionary "red tide" was sweeping through the region, decided to provide financial and technical assistance to the French, while pressuring them to prepare for an eventual transition to independent non-Communist governments in Vietnam, Laos, and Cambodia. With casualties mounting and the French public tired of fighting the seemingly endless "dirty war" in Indochina, the French agreed to a peace settlement with the Vietminh at the Geneva Conference in 1954. According to the

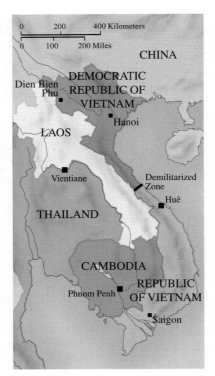

MAP 7.6 Indochina after 1954

treaty, Vietnam was temporarily divided into a northern Communist half (known as the Democratic Republic of Vietnam or DRV) and a non-Communist southern half based in Saigon [eventually to be known as the Republic of Vietnam (or RVN)] (see Map 7.6). Elections throughout the country were to be held in two years to create a unified government. Neighboring Cambodia and Laos were both declared independent under neutral governments. French forces, which had suffered a major defeat at the hands of Vietminh troops at the Battle of Dien Bien Phu in the spring of 1954, were withdrawn from all three countries. As part of the agreement, almost one million refugees, many of them Catholics who feared persecution by the atheist regime about to take power in Hanoi, fled North Vietnam to seek refuge in the South. A smaller number went in the opposite direction to join the fatherly figure known colloquially to his supporters as "Uncle Ho."

China had played an active role in bringing about the agreement and clearly hoped that a settlement would place a friendly government on its southern flank—while also leading to a reduction of tensions in the area. But subsequent efforts to improve relations between China and the United States foundered on the issue of Taiwan. In the fall of 1954, the United States signed a mutual security treaty with the Republic of China guaranteeing U.S. military support in case of an invasion of Taiwan. When Beijing demanded U.S. withdrawal from Taiwan as the price for improved relations, diplomatic talks between the two countries collapsed.

7-3 FROM CONFRONTATION TO COEXISTENCE

 Focus Question: What events led to the era of coexistence in the 1960s, and to what degree did each side contribute to the reduction in international tensions?

The 1950s opened with the world teetering on the edge of a nuclear holocaust. The Soviet Union had detonated its first nuclear device in 1949, and the two blocs—capitalist and socialist—viewed each other across an ideological divide that grew increasingly bitter with each passing year. In the

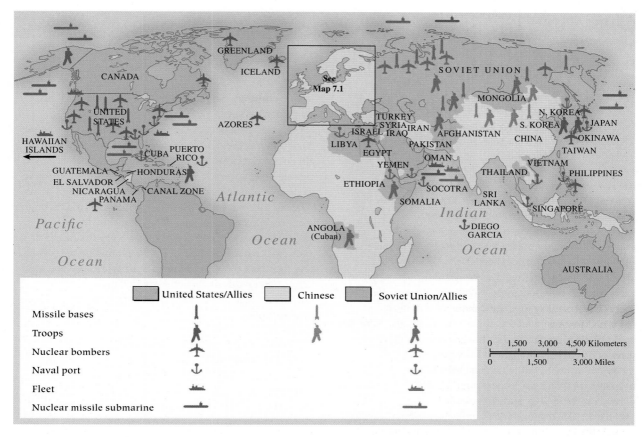

MAP 7.7 The Global Cold War. This map shows the location of the major military bases and missile sites maintained by the contending power blocs at the height of the Cold War.

 Which continents were the most heavily armed, and why?

United States, fear of Communism had reached a fever pitch among the American public, as a "red scare," promoted by Senator Joseph McCarthy, a fiery Republican from the state of Wisconsin, unleashed a frenzied search for Communist sympathizers in all ranks of American society. Dozens of suspected Communists—many of them from Hollywood or in the arts, where left-wing views had been common during the 1930s—were called to testify before the House Un-American Affairs Committee, and a number of witnesses were subsequently dismissed from their jobs. Yet as the decade drew to a close, a measure of sanity had crept into the Cold War, and the leaders of the major world powers began to seek ways to coexist in an increasingly unstable world (see Map 7.7).

7-3a Khrushchev and the Era of Peaceful Coexistence

The first clear sign of an easing of tension occurred after Stalin's death in early 1953. His successor, Georgy

Malenkov (1902–1988), hoped to improve relations with the Western powers so that he could reduce defense expenditures and shift government spending to growing consumer needs. During his campaign to replace Malenkov two years later, Nikita Khrushchev (1894–1971) appealed to powerful pressure groups in the party Politburo (the governing body of the Communist Party of the Soviet Union) by calling for higher defense expenditures, but once in power, he resumed his predecessor's efforts to reduce tensions with the West and improve the living standards of the Soviet people.

In an adroit public relations touch, Khrushchev publicized Moscow's appeal for a new policy of **peaceful coexistence** with the West (see Opposing Viewpoints, "Peaceful Coexistence or People's War?" p. 178). In 1955, he surprisingly agreed to negotiate an end to the postwar occupation of Austria by the victorious Allies and allow the creation of a neutral country with strong cultural and economic ties with the West.

Peaceful Coexistence or People's War?

Q *Why did Nikita Khrushchev feel that the conflict between the socialist and capitalist camps that Lenin had predicted was no longer necessary? How did Lin Biao respond?*

Interaction & Exchange

THE SOVIET LEADER VLADIMIR LENIN had contended that war between the socialist and imperialist camps was inevitable because the imperialists would never give up without a fight. Joseph Stalin agreed, and told colleagues shortly after World War II that a new war would break out in fifteen to twenty years. But Stalin's successor, Nikita Khrushchev, feared that a new world conflict could result in a nuclear holocaust and contended that the two sides must learn to coexist, although peaceful competition would inevitably continue. In this speech given in Beijing in 1959, Khrushchev attempted to persuade the Chinese to accept his views. But Chinese leaders argued that the "imperialist nature" of the United States would never change, and predicted that "people's wars" in the Third World would bring down the structure of imperialism. That argument was presented in a 1966 article by Marshall Lin Biao (LIN BYOW), at that time one of Mao Zedong's (Mao Tse-tung in Wade-Giles transliteration) closest allies.

Nikita Khrushchev, Speech to the Chinese, 1959

Comrades! Socialism brings to the people peace—that greatest blessing. The greater the strength of the camp of socialism grows, the greater will be its possibilities for successfully defending the cause of peace on this earth. The forces of socialism are already so great that real possibilities are being created for excluding war as a means of solving international disputes....

When I spoke with President Eisenhower—and I have just returned from the United States of America—I got the impression that the President of the U.S.A.—and not a few people support him—understands the need to relax international tension....

There is only one way of preserving peace—that is the road of peaceful coexistence of states with different social systems. The question stands thus: either peaceful coexistence or war with its catastrophic consequences. Now, with the present relation of forces between social-ism and capitalism being in favor of socialism, he who

would continue the "cold war" is moving towards his own destruction....

It is not at all because capitalism is still strong that the socialist countries speak out against war, and for peace-ful coexistence. No, we have no need of war at all. If the people do not want it, even such a noble and progressive system as socialism cannot be imposed by force of arms. The socialist countries therefore, while carrying through a consistently peace-loving policy, concentrate their efforts on peaceful construction; they fire the hearts of men by the force of their example in building socialism, and thus lead them to follow in their footsteps. The ques-tion of when this or that country will take the path to socialism is decided by its own people. This, for us, is the holy of holies.

Lin Biao, "Long Live the Victory of People's War"

Many countries and peoples in Asia, Africa, and Latin America are now being subjected to aggression and enslavement on a serious scale by the imperialists headed by the United States and their lackeys.... As in China, the peasant question is extremely important in these regions. The peasants constitute the main force of the national-democratic revolution against the imperialists and their lackeys. In committing aggression against these countries, the imperialists usually begin by seizing the big cities and the main lines of communication. But they are unable to bring the vast countryside completely under their control.... The countryside, and the countryside alone, can provide the revolutionary basis from which the revo-lutionaries can go forward to final victory. Precisely for this reason, Mao Tse-tung's theory of establishing revolu-tionary base areas in the rural districts and encircling the cities from the countryside is attracting more and more attention among the people in these regions.

Taking the entire globe, if North America and Western Europe can be called "the cities of the world," then Asia, Africa, and Latin America constitute "the rural areas of the world." Since World War II, the prole-tarian revolutionary movement has for various reasons been temporarily held back in the North American and West European capitalist countries, while the people's revolutionary movement in Asia, Africa, and Latin America has been growing vigorously. In a sense, the contemporary world revolution also presents a picture of the encirclement of cities by the rural areas. In the final analysis, the whole cause of world revolution hinges on the revolutionary struggles of the Asian, African, and Latin American peoples, who make up the overwhelming majority of the world's population. The socialist countries should regard it as their internationalist duty to support the people's revolutionary struggles in Asia, Africa, and Latin America....

Ours is the epoch in which world capitalism and imperialism are heading for their doom and communism is marching to victory. Comrade Mao Tse-tung's theory of people's war is not only a product of the Chinese revolution, but has also the characteristic of our epoch. The new experience gained in the people's revolutionary struggles in various countries since World War II has provided continuous evidence that Mao Tse-tung's thought is a common asset of the revolutionary people of the whole world.

Sources: From G. F. Hudson et al., eds., *The Sino-Soviet Dispute* (New York: Frederick Praeger, 1961), pp. 61–63, cited in *Peking Review*, No. 40, 1959. From *Nationalism and Communism*, Norman Graebner, ed. Copyright © 1977 by D. C. Heath and Company.

He also called for a reduction in defense expenditures and reduced the size of the Soviet armed forces.

Unrest in Eastern Europe   At first, Khrushchev's overtures were sabotaged by events in Eastern Europe, where popular unrest suddenly erupted in several of Moscow's client states. In 1953, worker strikes broke out in East Germany, and were only quelled by Soviet tanks. In 1956, more broadly based protests erupted over a variety of issues in Poland, forcing the resignation of the then current hard-line Communist leader and his replacement by a more moderate figure. Finally, in October a full-scale popular revolt led to the overthrow of the Stalinist leadership in Hungary. Although reluctant to intervene, Khrushchev ultimately changed his mind and ordered Soviet occupation troops in the country to suppress the uprising (for a more detailed analysis of these events, see Chapter 9). Although the Eisenhower administration reluctantly opted not to intervene, despite the frenzied appeals from protesters, the incident in Hungary fueled Cold War tensions on both sides of the Iron Curtain.

The Berlin Crisis   A new dispute over the divided city of Berlin added to the tension. The Soviets had launched their first intercontinental ballistic missile (ICBM) in August 1957, arousing U.S. fears—fueled by a partisan political debate—of a "missile gap" between the United States and the Soviet Union. Khrushchev attempted to take advantage of the U.S. frenzy over missiles to solve the problem of West Berlin, which had remained an island of prosperity inside the relatively poverty-stricken GDR. Many East Germans sought to escape to West Germany by fleeing through West Berlin—a serious blot on the credibility of the GDR and a potential source of instability in East-West relations. In November 1958, Khrushchev announced that unless the West removed its forces from West Berlin within six months, he would turn over control of the access routes to the East Germans. Unwilling to accept an ultimatum that would have abandoned West Berlin to the Communists, President Eisenhower and the West stood firm, and Khrushchev eventually backed down.

The Spirit of Camp David   Despite such periodic crises in East-West relations, there were tantalizing signs that an era of true peaceful coexistence between the two power blocs could be achieved. As tensions eased in Eastern Europe in the late 1950s, the United States and the Soviet Union initiated a cultural exchange program to enable the peoples of the two blocs to become acquainted with each other's way of life. While Leningrad's Kirov Ballet appeared at theaters in the United States, Benny Goodman's jazz band and Leonard Bernstein's popular film *West Side Story* played in Moscow. During the course of one such exhibit, U.S. Vice President Richard M. Nixon sparred with Khrushchev over the relative merits of capitalist and communist society and culture (see the Part III opening image on p. 163). As a culmination of the current era of good feeling, Nikita Khrushchev visited the United States and had a brief but friendly encounter with President Eisenhower at Camp David, the presidential retreat in northern Maryland. Khrushchev's visit to Hollywood, where he joked with several U.S. movie stars, enabled him to replace the thuggish face of Joe Stalin with a softer image. Predictions of improved future relations led reporters to laud "the spirit of Camp David."

Rivalry in the Third World   Yet Khrushchev could rarely avoid the temptation to gain an advantage over the United States in the competition for influence throughout the world, and this resulted in an unstable relationship that undercut any potential effort to achieve a lasting accommodation between the two superpowers. West Berlin was an area of persistent tension (a boil on the foot of the United States, Khrushchev derisively termed it), and

in January 1961, just as newly elected president John F. Kennedy (1917–1963) took office, Moscow threatened once again to turn over responsibility for the access routes to Berlin from West Germany to the GDR.

Moscow also took every opportunity to promote its interests in the Third World, as the countries of Asia, Africa, and Latin America were then popularly called. Unlike Stalin, Khrushchev viewed the dismantling of colonial regimes in the area as a potential advantage for the Soviet Union and sought especially to exploit anti-American sentiment in Latin America. When neutral-ist leaders like Nehru in India, Tito in Yugoslavia, and Sukarno in Indonesia founded the **Nonaligned Movement** in 1955 as a means of providing an alternative to the two major power blocs, Khrushchev openly sought alliances with strategically important neutralist countries like India, Indonesia, Cuba, and Egypt at a time when Washington's ability to influence events at the United Nations had begun to wane.

In January 1961, just as Kennedy prepared to assume the presidency, relations between Moscow and Washington suddenly took a turn for the worse, when the shooting down of a U.S. reconnaissance plane over Soviet territory provoked a war of words between the two capitals and pro-vided the Soviet leader with a pretense to cancel a planned summit meeting with President Eisenhower (see Movies & History, *Bridge of Spies*, above). Khrushchev then unnerved

the new president at an informal summit meeting, held in Vienna in April, by declaring that Moscow would provide active support to national liberation movements through-out the world. That October, a minor disagreement sud-denly escalated into a brief military standoff—complete with U.S. and Soviet tanks facing each other at oppo-site sides of Checkpoint Charlie—in the heart of Berlin. Increasingly, Washington was also becoming concerned about Soviet meddling in such sensitive trouble spots as Southeast Asia, Central Africa, and the Caribbean.

7-3b The Cuban Missile Crisis and the Move Toward Détente

The Cold War confrontation between the United States and the Soviet Union reached frightening levels during the so-called Cuban Missile Crisis. In 1959, a left-wing revolutionary named Fidel Castro (b. 1926) overthrew the Cuban dictator Fulgencio Batista and established a Soviet-supported totali-tarian regime less than 100 miles off the coast of Florida. As tensions increased between the new government in Havana and the United States, the Eisenhower administration broke relations with Cuba and drafted plans to overthrow Castro, who reacted by drawing closer to Moscow.

Soon after taking office in early 1961, Kennedy approved a plan drafted under his predecessor to support an invasion of Cuba by anti-Castro exiles. But the attempt to land in the Bay of Pigs in southern Cuba was an utter failure. At Castro's request, the Soviet Union then decided to place nuclear missiles in Cuba. But the Kennedy administration was not prepared to allow nuclear weapons within striking distance of the American mainland, although the United States had placed nuclear weapons in Turkey within easy range of the Soviet Union, a fact that Khrushchev was quick to point out. In October 1962, when U.S. intelligence discovered the presence of such missiles, as well as that a Soviet fleet carrying more missiles was heading to Cuba, Kennedy considered several options and ultimately decided to dispatch U.S. warships into the Atlantic to prevent the fleet from reaching its destination.

This approach to the problem was risky but had the benefit of delaying confrontation and giving the two sides time to find a peaceful solution. After a tense standoff during which the two countries came frighteningly close to a direct nuclear confrontation (the Soviet missiles already in Cuba, it turned out, were operational), Khrushchev finally sent a conciliatory letter to Kennedy agreeing to turn back the fleet if Kennedy pledged not to invade Cuba. In a secret concession not revealed until many years later, the president also promised to dismantle U.S. missiles in Turkey. To the world, however (and to an angry Castro), it appeared that Kennedy had bested Khrushchev. "We were eyeball to eyeball," noted U.S. Secretary of State Dean Rusk, "and they blinked."

The outbreak of the Cuban Missile Crisis was a profound shock to millions of Americans. During the late 1950s, fear of Communism had ceased to be a major source of concern among the general populace, partly because of the sudden fall of Senator Joseph McCarthy at Senate hearings, and his death of illness shortly after. Tensions had escalated after the U-2 incident and the disastrous summit meeting in Vienna. Still, many Americans were becoming accustomed to living without the constant fear of war. For those living within the range of the Soviet missiles in Cuba, the dispute was a frightening prospect.

The realization that the world might have been annihilated in a matter of days had a profound effect on both sides. Khrushchev himself was shaken by the willingness of many of his colleagues in the Kremlin to risk total war rather than to cave in to the demands of Moscow's chief class enemy in Washington. A communication hotline between Moscow and Washington was installed in 1963 to expedite rapid communication between the two superpowers in time of crisis. In the same year, the two powers agreed to ban nuclear tests in the atmosphere, a step that served to lessen the tensions between the two nations. Khrushchev, however, paid a heavy price for his decision to resolve the missile crisis, since many of his rivals in the Kremlin began to quietly question his leadership.

In Havana, the spurned Cuban leader Fidel Castro was livid that Moscow had backed down in its confrontation with Washington.

7-3c The Sino-Soviet Dispute

Nikita Khrushchev had launched his slogan of peaceful coexistence as a means of improving relations with the capitalist powers; ironically, one important result of his campaign was to undermine Moscow's ties with its close ally China. During Stalin's lifetime, Beijing had accepted the Soviet Union as the official leader of the socialist camp. After Stalin's death, however, relations began to deteriorate. Part of the reason may have been Mao Zedong's contention that he, as the most experienced Marxist leader in the world, should now be acknowledged as the most authoritative voice within the socialist community. But another determining factor was that just as Soviet policies were moving toward moderation, China's were becoming more radical.

Several other issues were involved, including territorial disputes along the Sino-Soviet border and China's unhappiness with limited Soviet economic assistance. But the key sources of disagreement involved ideology and the Cold War. Chinese leaders were convinced that the successes of the Soviet space program confirmed that the socialists were now technologically superior to the capitalists (the East Wind, trumpeted the Chinese official press, had now triumphed over the West Wind), and they urged Khrushchev to go on the offensive to promote world revolution. More specifically, Beijing wanted Soviet assistance in retaking Taiwan from Chiang Kai-shek. But Khrushchev was trying to improve relations with the West and rejected Chinese demands for support against Taiwan.

By the end of the 1950s, the Soviet Union had begun to remove its advisers from China, and in 1961, the dispute broke into the open. Increasingly isolated, China began to voice its hostility to what Mao described as the "urban industrialized countries" (which included the Soviet Union) and portrayed itself as the leader of the "rural underdeveloped countries" of Asia, Africa, and Latin America in a global struggle against imperialist oppression. In effect, China had applied Mao's famous concept of people's war in an international framework (see Opposing Viewpoints, "Peaceful Coexistence or People's War?" p. 178).

7-3d The Second Indochina War

In the meantime, a new source of Cold War friction was opening up in Southeast Asia with the renewal of conflict in Indochina. The Eisenhower administration had opposed the peace settlement at Geneva in 1954, which divided Vietnam temporarily into two separate regroupment zones, specifically because the provision for future national elections opened up the possibility of placing the entire country under Communist rule. But President Eisenhower had been unwilling to introduce U.S. military forces to continue the conflict without the full support of the British and the French, who preferred to seek a negotiated settlement. In the end, Washington promised not to break the provisions of the agreement but refused to commit itself to the results.

During the next several months, the United States began to provide aid to a new government in South Vietnam. Under the leadership of the anti-Communist politician Ngo Dinh Diem (1901–1963), the Saigon regime began to root out dissidents while refusing to hold the national elections called for by the Geneva Accords. Born in a devoutly Catholic family, Diem hoped to build a solid base of support from his minority co-religionists, whose numbers had been dramatically increased by the thousands of refugees who fled the North at the close of the Franco-Vietminh war. It was widely anticipated, even in Washington, that the Communists would win such elections. In 1959, Ho Chi Minh, despairing of the peaceful unification of the country under Communist rule, reluctantly agreed with headstrong colleagues to resume the strategy of revolutionary war in the south. Late in the following year, a broad political organization that was designed to win the support of a wide spectrum of the population was founded in an isolated part of South Vietnam. Known as the National Liberation Front of South Vietnam, or NLF, it was under the firm leadership of Communist leaders in North Vietnam.

By 1963, South Vietnam was on the verge of collapse. Diem's autocratic methods and his inattention to severe economic inequality had alienated much of the population, and NLF armed forces, popularly known as the **Viet Cong** (Vietnamese Communists), had taken advantage of his missteps to expand their influence throughout rural areas in much of the country. Diem also faced opposition from members of the majority Buddhist community in the South Vietnam, many of whom felt that he favored his fellow-Catholics because they were more solidly supportive of his anti-Communist regime.

By the fall of 1963, opposition to Diem had spilled out into the streets of Saigon, and in early November several dissident South Vietnamese military officers, with the tacit approval of the White House, overthrew Diem's regime, killing him and his brother in the process. But internal factionalism (over the two years following the overthrow of the Diem regime, several coup attempts took place) kept the new military leadership from reinvigorating the struggle against the insurgent forces, and by early 1965, the Viet Cong, their ranks now swelled by

military units infiltrating from North Vietnam, were on the verge of seizing control of the entire country. Fearing that a Communist victory in South Vietnam could lead to the collapse of fragile regimes elsewhere in Southeast Asia—a constant theme in U.S. containment strategy popularly known as the "domino theory"—President Lyndon B. Johnson (1908–1973)—who had occupied the White House on the assassination of John Kennedy in late November 1963—decided to launch bombing raids on the north and dispatch U.S. combat troops to South Vietnam to prevent a total defeat for the anti-Communist government in Saigon (see Opposing Viewpoints, "Confrontation in Southeast Asia," p. 183, and Comparative Illustration, "War in the Rice Paddies," p. 184).

Hanoi responded to the U.S. escalation by infiltrating more of its own regular force troops into the south, and by 1968, the war was a virtual stalemate. Opposition to the war in the United States was growing in intensity, especially among young people, and threatened to unleash an internal revolt within Lyndon Johnson's own Democratic Party. The Communists were not strong enough to overthrow the Saigon regime, whose weakness was shielded by the presence of half a million U.S. troops, but President Johnson was reluctant to engage in all-out war on North Vietnam for fear of provoking a global nuclear conflict. When the Communist-led Tet Offensive (named after the Vietnamese New Year's holiday *Tet*, when the first major attacks took place) shook the fragile stability of the Saigon regime and aroused heightened antiwar protests in the United States, the White House agreed to negotiate, and peace talks began in Paris.

The Conflict in Southeast Asia and The Cold War   Chinese and Soviet leaders had observed the gradual escalation of the conflict in Southeast Asia with mixed feelings. The former were undoubtedly pleased to have a firm Communist ally, one that had in key respects followed the path of Mao Zedong—just beyond their southern frontier. But the Chinese, like their Soviet rivals, were also concerned that bloodshed in South Vietnam might enmesh them in an open confrontation with the United States. In the longer term, Beijing feared that a powerful and ambitious DRV might eventually seek to extend its influence throughout mainland Southeast Asia, an area that China viewed as its own backyard.

Both Moscow and Beijing therefore tiptoed delicately through the minefield of the Indochina conflict. As the war escalated in 1964 and 1965, Soviet leaders assured Washington that they had no interest in seeing the conflict in Indochina escalate into a Great Power confrontation. For its part, Beijing assured Washington privately that China would not directly enter the conflict

Confrontation in Southeast Asia

 How did the NLF justify its claim to represent the legitimate aspirations of the people of South Vietnam? What was President Johnson's counterargument?

Politics & Government | **IN DECEMBER 1960**, the National Liberation Front of South Vietnam (NLF) was born. Composed of political and social leaders opposed to the anti-Communist government, it operated under the direction of the Communist regime in North Vietnam and served as the formal representative of revolutionary forces in the south throughout the remainder of the Vietnam War. When, in the spring of 1965, President Lyndon B. Johnson began to dispatch U.S. combat troops to Vietnam to prevent a Communist victory there, the NLF issued the declaration presented below. The second selection is from a speech that Johnson gave at Johns Hopkins University in April 1965 in response to the NLF.

Statement of the National Liberation Front of South Vietnam (1965)

American imperialist aggression against South Vietnam and interference in its internal affairs have now continued for more than ten years. More American troops and supplies, including missile units, Marines, B-57 strategic bombers, and mercenaries from South Korea, Taiwan, the Philippines, Australia, Malaysia, etc., have been brought to South Vietnam. . . .

The Saigon puppet regime, paid servant of the United States, is guilty of the most heinous crimes. These despicable traitors, these boot-lickers of American imperialism, have brought the enemy into our country. They have brought to South Vietnam armed forces of the United States and its satellites to kill our compatriots, occupy and ravage our sacred soil and enslave our people.

The Vietnamese, the peoples of all Indo-China and Southeast Asia, supporters of peace and justice in every part of the world, have raised their voice in angry protest against this criminal unprovoked aggression of the United States imperialists.

In the present extremely grave situation, the South Vietnam National Liberation Front considers it necessary to proclaim anew its firm and unswerving determination to resist the U.S. imperialists and fight for the salvation of our country. . . . [It] will continue to rely chiefly on its own forces and potentialities, but it is prepared to accept any assistance, moral and material, including arms and other military equipment, from all the socialist countries, from nationalist countries, from international organizations, and from the peace-loving peoples of the world.

Lyndon B. Johnson, "Peace Without Conquest"

The world as it is in Asia is not a serene or peaceful place.

The first reality is that North Viet-Nam has attacked the independent nation of South Viet-Nam. Its object is total conquest.

Of course, some of the people of South Viet-Nam are participating in attack on their own government. But trained men and supplies, orders and arms, flow in a constant stream from north to south.

This support is the heartbeat of the war.

And it is a war of unparalleled brutality. Simple farmers are the targets of assassination and kidnapping. Women and children are strangled in the night because their men are loyal to their government. And helpless villages are ravaged by sneak attacks. Large-scale raids are conducted on towns, and terror strikes in the heart of cities. . . .

Why are these realities our concern? Why are we in South Viet-Nam?

We are there because we have a promise to keep. Since 1954 every American President has offered support to the people of South Viet-Nam. We have helped to build, and we have helped to defend. Thus, over many years, we have made a national pledge to help South Viet-Nam defend its independence.

Our objective is the independence of South Viet-Nam, and its freedom from attack. We want nothing for ourselves—only that the people of South Viet-Nam be allowed to guide their own country in their own way.

We will do everything necessary to reach that objective. And we will do only what is absolutely necessary.

Sources: "Statement of the National Liberation Front of South Vietnam," *New Times* (March 27, 1965), pp. 36–40. Source for Johnson's speech: *Public Papers of the Presidents of the United States: Lyndon B. Johnson, 1965*. Volume I, entry 172, pp. 394–399. Washington D.C.: Government Printing Office, 1966.

War in the Rice Paddies

 How do you think helicopters were used to assist U.S. operations in South Vietnam? Why didn't their use result in a U.S. victory?

Politics & Government

THE FIRST STAGE OF THE VIETNAM WAR consisted primarily of low-level conflicts, as Viet Cong insurgents relied on guerrilla tactics to bring down the U.S.-supported government in Saigon. In 1965, however, President Lyndon Johnson ordered U.S. combat troops into South Vietnam (Image 7.4a) in a desperate bid to prevent a Communist victory in that beleaguered country. The Communist government in North Vietnam responded in kind, sending its own regular forces down the Ho Chi Minh Trail to confront U.S. troops on the battlefield. In Image 7.4b, North Vietnamese troops storm the U.S. Marine base at Khe Sanh (KAY SARN), near the demilitarized zone, in 1968, the most violent year of the war. Although U.S. military commanders believed that helicopters would be a key factor in defeating the insurgent forces in Vietnam, this was one instance when technological superiority did not produce a victory on the battlefield.

IMAGE 7.4a

IMAGE 7.4b

unless U.S. forces threatened its southern border. Beijing also pleased Washington by refusing to cooperate fully with Moscow in shipping Soviet goods to North Vietnam through Chinese territory.

The Road to Peace Richard Nixon (1913–1994) came into the White House in January 1969 on a pledge to bring an honorable end to the Vietnam War. With U.S. public opinion sharply divided on the issue, he began to withdraw U.S. troops while continuing to hold peace talks in Paris. But the centerpiece of his strategy was to improve relations with China and thus undercut Beijing's limited support for the North Vietnamese war effort. During the 1960s, relations between Moscow and Beijing had reached a point of extreme tension, and thousands of troops were stationed on both sides of their long common frontier. To intimidate their Communist rivals, Soviet sources dropped the hint that they might decide to launch a preemptive strike to destroy Chinese nuclear facilities in Xinjiang. Sensing an opportunity to split the onetime allies, Nixon sent his emissary Henry Kissinger on a secret trip to China. Responding to the latter's assurances that the United States was determined to withdraw from Indochina and hoped to improve relations with the mainland regime, Chinese leaders invited President Nixon to visit China in early 1972. Nixon accepted the invitation and the two sides agreed to set aside their differences over Taiwan in order to pursue a better mutual relationship.

Incensed at the apparent betrayal by their close allies, Hanoi continued to adopt an offensive strategy on the battlefield in South Vietnam, although casualties suffered by North Vietnamese troops and their Viet Cong allies continued to escalate. Finally, in January 1973 North Vietnamese leaders decided to accept a temporary settlement of the war.

Later that month a peace treaty was signed in Paris calling for the removal of all U.S. forces from South Vietnam. In return, the Communists agreed to seek a political settlement of their differences with the Saigon regime. But negotiations between North and South over the political settlement soon broke down, and in early 1975, having become convinced that Washington would not intervene, the Communists resumed the offensive. President Gerald Ford, who had risen to the office when Richard Nixon had resigned the presidency the previous summer, provided limited military support to the Saigon regime, but as the end neared, he declared publicly that Vietnam was "a war that was over." At the end of April, under a massive assault by North Vietnamese military forces, the South Vietnamese government surrendered. A year later, the country was unified under Communist rule.

Why had the United States lost the Vietnam War? Debate over U.S. strategy in Vietnam had gone on throughout the war, and continued to break out long after the conflict was over. Many Americans believed that by not taking the war directly to North Vietnam, the White House had forced the U.S. armed forces to fight "with one hand tied behind their backs." But others were convinced that the United States should not have gotten involved in a struggle for national liberation in the first place. Few could be found who defended a policy that had caused heavy casualties, divided America, and achieved no positive result. Many years later, Dean Rusk, secretary of state during both the Kennedy and Johnson administrations, defended U.S. strategy in Vietnam, but admitted that he and his colleagues had probably underestimated the determination of the enemy, while overestimating the patience of the American people. A deeper dive into the evidence suggests a third factor: U.S. policymakers from both parties had consistently overestimated the capacity of their client state in Saigon to defend itself against a highly disciplined adversary. Although countless South Vietnamese citizens fought bravely for years in an effort to prevent a Communist takeover, their leaders in Saigon patently lacked the determination and vision to bring their sacrifices to fruition. In seeking to apply the "lessons of Munich" to a region of the world that few Americans understood or were even aware of, U.S. policymakers were attempting to build a bridge too far. It was a cruel lesson in the dangers of national hubris.

The Communist victory in Vietnam was a severe humiliation for the United States, and it caused untold harm to the social fabric of the country, but in the end its strategic impact was surprisingly limited because of the new relationship with China. Chinese leaders did not seek to take advantage of disarray in U.S. Asian policy, and during the decade after the fall of Saigon, Sino-American relations continued to improve. In 1979, formal diplomatic ties were established between the two countries under an arrangement whereby the United States renounced its mutual security treaty with the Republic of China in return for a pledge from China to seek reunification with Taiwan by peaceful means. By the end of the 1970s, China and the United States had established diplomatic relations, while forging a "strategic relationship" in which each would cooperate with the other against the common threat of Soviet "hegemonism" (China's term for Soviet policy) in Asia.

7-4 AN ERA OF EQUIVALENCE

 Focus Question: Why did the Cold War briefly flare up again in the 1980s, and why did it come to a definitive end at the end of the decade?

When the Johnson administration sent U.S. combat troops to South Vietnam in 1965 in an effort to prevent the expansion of communism in Southeast Asia, Washington's primary concern was with Beijing, not with Moscow. After the Cuban Missile Crisis, the Soviet Union—in the eyes of U.S. officials—had become an essentially conservative power, more concerned with protecting its vast empire than with expanding its borders. In fact, U.S. policymakers periodically sought Soviet assistance in achieving a peaceful settlement of the Vietnam War. As long as Khrushchev was in power, they found a receptive ear in Moscow. Khrushchev did not want to risk a confrontation with the United States in Southeast Asia.

Such was not quite the case with his successor. When Khrushchev was replaced in October 1964 by a new leadership headed by party chief Leonid Brezhnev (1906–1982) and Prime Minister Alexei Kosygin (1904–1980), Soviet attitudes about the Cold War became more ambivalent. On the one hand, the new Soviet leadership had no desire to provoke an open military conflict with the United States. On the other, Moscow was eager to seize advantage of its adversary's discomfort in Southeast Asia and to protect its own interests within the socialist camp. Where possible, it even hoped to expand Soviet influence in the world.

Still, in broad terms Brezhnev and Kosygin generally continued to pursue the Khrushchev line of peaceful coexistence with the West and adopted a cautious posture in foreign affairs. By the early 1970s, a new age in Soviet-American relations had emerged, often referred to as **détente**, a French term meaning a reduction of tensions between the two sides. One symbol of the new relationship was the Anti-Ballistic Missile (ABM) Treaty, often called SALT I (for Strategic Arms Limitation Talks), signed in 1972, in which the two nations agreed to limit their missile systems.

Washington's objective in pursuing the treaty was to make it unlikely that either superpower could win a nuclear exchange by launching a preemptive strike against the other. U.S. officials believed that a policy of "equivalence," in which there was a roughly equal power balance between the two sides, was the best way to avoid a nuclear confrontation. Détente was pursued in other ways as well. When President Nixon took office in 1969, he sought to increase trade and cultural contacts with the Soviet Union. His purpose was to set up a series of "linkages" in U.S.-Soviet relations that would persuade Moscow of the economic and social benefits of maintaining good relations with the West.

The Helsinki Accords of 1975 were a symbol of that new relationship. Signed by the United States, Canada, and all European nations on both sides of the Iron Curtain, these accords recognized all borders in Central and Eastern Europe established since the end of World War II, thereby formally acknowledging for the first time the Soviet sphere of influence. The Helsinki Accords also committed the signatory powers to recognize and protect the human rights of their citizens, a clear effort by the Western states to improve the performance of the Soviet Union and its allies in that area.

7-4a An End to Détente?

Protection of human rights became one of the major foreign policy goals of the next U.S. president, Jimmy Carter (b. 1924). Ironically, just at the point when U.S. involvement in Vietnam came to an end and relations with China began to improve, the mood in U.S.-Soviet relations began to sour.

Renewed Tensions in the Third World There were several reasons. Some Americans had become increasingly concerned about aggressive new tendencies in Soviet foreign policy, notably in Africa, where Soviet influence was on the rise. Moscow sought influence in Somalia, across the Red Sea in South Yemen, and in neighboring Ethiopia, where a Marxist regime took control of the government. Soviet involvement was also on the increase in southern Africa, where an insurgent movement supported by Cuban troops came to power in Angola, once a colony of Portugal.

Then, in 1979, U.S. concerns about Soviet expansionism shifted to the Middle East, where Soviet troops were sent across the border into Afghanistan to protect a newly installed Marxist regime that was facing rising internal resistance from fundamentalist Muslim guerrilla groups. Some U.S. observers suspected that Moscow's motive in deciding to advance into hitherto neutral Afghanistan was to extend Soviet power into the oil fields of the Persian Gulf. To deter such a possibility, the White House promulgated the so-called Carter Doctrine, which declared that the United States would use its military power, if necessary, to safeguard Western access to the oil reserves in the Middle East. As it turned out, U.S. concerns were probably exaggerated, for sources in Moscow later disclosed that the Soviet advance into Afghanistan had little to do with a strategic drive toward the Persian Gulf; rather, it was an effort to increase Soviet influence in a sensitive region increasingly beset with Islamic fervor. Soviet officials feared that the wave of Islamic activism could spread to the Muslim populations in the Soviet republics in central Asia. Now they were emboldened to act, because they were confident that the United States was too distracted by the so-called **Vietnam syndrome** (the public fear of U.S. involvement in another Vietnam-type conflict) to respond.

Other factors also contributed to the growing suspicion of the Soviet Union in the United States. During the era of détente, Washington officials had assumed that Moscow accepted the U.S. doctrine of equivalence—the idea that both sides possessed sufficient strength to destroy the other in the event of a surprise attack. By the end of the 1970s, however, some U.S. defense analysts began to charge that the Soviets were seeking strategic superiority in nuclear weapons and argued for a substantial increase in U.S. defense spending. Such charges, combined with evidence of Soviet efforts in Africa and the Middle East and reports of the persecution of Jews and dissidents in the Soviet Union, helped undermine public support for détente in the United States. These changing attitudes were reflected in the failure of the Carter administration to obtain congressional approval of a new arms limitation agreement (SALT II) signed with the Soviet Union in 1979.

7-4b Countering the Evil Empire

The early years of the administration of President Ronald Reagan (1911–2004) witnessed a return to the harsh rhetoric, if not all of the harsh practices, of the Cold War. President Reagan's anti-Communist credentials were well known. In a speech given shortly after his election in 1980, he referred to the Soviet Union as an "evil empire" and frequently voiced his suspicion of its motives in foreign affairs. Taking issue with the strategy of containment that had guided U.S. foreign policy for three decades, he was determined to apply heavy pressure on Moscow in a bid to force a roll back of its gains around the world. To counter perceived Soviet advantages in strategic weaponry, the White House also began a military buildup that stimulated a renewed arms race. In 1982, the Reagan administration introduced the nuclear-tipped cruise missile, whose ability to fly at low altitudes made it difficult to detect by enemy radar. Reagan also became an ardent exponent of the Strategic Defense Initiative (SDI), nicknamed **Star Wars**. Its purposes were to create a space shield that could destroy incoming missiles, and to force Moscow into an arms race that it could not hope to win. President Reagan's assumptions about Moscow's economic vulnerability were correct: with the price of oil dropping worldwide, Soviet revenues were down sharply, making it not only more difficult for them to pay for food imports, but also to finance their subsidies to failing economies in Eastern Europe. At first, Soviet leaders reacted to the bellicose remarks coming out of Washington by making preparations for war, only to cancel them later in the decade when the White House assured the Kremlin of its peaceful intentions.

The Reagan administration also adopted a more activist stance in the Third World. By providing military support to the devoutly Islamic anti-Soviet insurgents in Afghanistan, the White House helped maintain a Vietnam-like war in Afghanistan that would embed the Soviet Union in its own quagmire. In Central America, where the revolutionary Sandinista regime in Nicaragua was supporting a guerrilla insurgency in nearby El Salvador, the Reagan administration began to provide material aid to the government in El Salvador while simultaneously applying pressure on the Sandinistas by giving support to an anti-Communist guerrilla movement (the **Contras**) in Nicaragua itself. The administration's Central American policy caused considerable controversy in Congress, however, with Democratic critics charging that growing U.S. involvement there could lead to a repeat of the nation's bitter experience in Vietnam.

7-4c Toward a New World Order

In 1985, Mikhail Gorbachev (b. 1931) was elected CPSU general secretary of the Communist Party of the Soviet Union in Moscow. During Brezhnev's last years and the brief tenures of his two successors (see Chapter 9), the Soviet Union had entered an era of serious economic decline, and the dynamic new party chief was well aware that drastic changes would be needed to rekindle the dreams that had inspired the Bolshevik Revolution. During the next few years, he launched a program of restructuring (*perestroika*) to revitalize the Soviet system. As part of that program, he set out to improve relations with the United States and the rest of the capitalist world. When he met with President Reagan in Reykjavik, the capital of Iceland, in 1985, the two leaders agreed to set aside their ideological differences, but Gorbachev was unsuccessful in his effort to persuade Reagan to abandon the Star Wars project (see Image 7.5).

Gorbachev's desperate effort to rescue the Soviet Union from collapse was too little and too late. In 1991, the Soviet Union, so long an apparently permanent fixture on the global scene, suddenly disintegrated. In its place arose several new nations from the ashes of the Soviet Empire. Meanwhile, the string of Soviet satellites in Eastern Europe broke loose from Moscow's grip and declared their independence from Communist rule. The era of the Cold War was over. We shall describe these dramatic events in more detail in Chapter 9.

The end of the Cold War lulled many observers into the seductive vision of a new world order that would be characterized by peaceful cooperation and increasing prosperity. President George H.W. Bush, Reagan's vice

David Hume Kennerly/Getty Images

IMAGE 7.5 Reagan and Gorbachev in Reykjavik. With the election of Mikhail Gorbachev as party general secretary in 1985, Moscow and Washington began to explore the means to reduce tensions between the two great powers. In October of 1986, Gorbachev and U.S. President Ronald Reagan held a summit meeting in Reykjavik, the capital of Iceland, to explore issues of concern to both sides. Although no agreements resulted from the meeting, the atmospherics from the meeting resulted in a new era of good feeling, and soon led to meaningful agreements on arms control and a reduction of tensions in the Cold War.

president and successor in the White House, predicted that a **New World Order**, characterized by peace and prosperity, was in the wings. Sadly, such hopes have not been realized. A bitter civil war in the Balkans in the mid-1990s graphically demonstrated that old fault lines of national and ethnic hostility still divided the post-Cold War world.

Elsewhere, bloody ethnic and religious disputes broke out in Africa and the Middle East. Then, on September 11, 2001, the world entered a dangerous new era when terrorists attacked the nerve centers of U.S. power in New York City and Washington, D.C., inaugurating a new round of tension between the West and the forces of militant Islam.

MAKING CONNECTIONS

At the end of World War II, the two new superpowers, the United States and the Soviet Union, began to compete for global hegemony. Joined by their allies, they faced each other across an ideological divide characterized by high levels of hostility and suspicion. This division began in Europe but soon spread to the rest of the world as nations everywhere were pressured to line up on one side of the ideological ledger, or on the other. For the most part, the competition between the two blocs took place in the political arena, but sometimes—as in Berlin—the risk of a direct confrontation between Moscow and Washington reached crisis proportions. In a few instances as well—notably in Korea and Vietnam—the Cold War became too hot to handle and exploded onto the battlefield. To many contemporary observers, a nuclear confrontation appeared almost inevitable.

As time went on, however, there were tantalizing signs of a thaw in the Cold War. In 1979, China and the United States brought an end to their own mutual animosity and decided to establish mutual diplomatic relations, a consequence of Beijing's decision to focus on domestic reform and stop supporting wars of national liberation. A little over a decade later, the Soviet Union itself collapsed, bringing to a close almost half a century of bitter rivalry between the world's two superpowers. The Cold War had ended without the horrifying vision of a mushroom cloud.

Why had forty years of intense competition between two power blocs ended, not with a bang, but with a whimper in Moscow? Surely, one key factor is the fact that the senior leadership on both sides developed a healthy respect for the enormous destructive power of nuclear weapons and came to realize (sometimes in defiance of their allies or their chief advisers) that the competition should be carried out, as much as possible, in the realm of politics rather than on the battlefield. Another reason is that each side came to envision victory not as a matter of occupying the territory of the enemy, but of transforming its institutions and its value system from within. Both sides accepted the reality of the Iron Curtain and tacitly agreed to avoid

a mutual confrontation to change the balance of forces. Neither side had to win, just not to lose.

How then should we evaluate the effectiveness of U.S. and Soviet foreign policy goals and achievements during the Cold War? The Truman administration latched on to George F. Kennan's doctrine of containment as the most effective means of countering the Soviet threat within months of the end of the resumption of peace. Successive U.S. administrations then continued to follow that strategy for the next thirty years, and it bore fruit when the Soviet regime ultimately collapsed in 1991. Containment did not always succeed as planned, however, notably in Southeast Asia when several presidents miscalculated by seeking to apply the lessons of Munich in South Vietnam. Hardened Cold War warriors might still claim that defeat in Vietnam had at least bought sufficient time for other nations in the region to develop the capacity to stave off the threat of social revolution. Even if that is true, the costs were substantial, not only in lives and resources, but in the lasting damage that it posed to America's global reputation and to its social fabric as well (see Chapter 8).

On the other hand, the balance sheet on Moscow's strategy during the Cold War leaves much to be desired. Lenin's prediction that a social revolution in Europe was inevitable has not yet been validated by the passage of time. More important, perhaps, Moscow's gamble that the Soviet Union could outperform the capitalist democracies in meeting the needs of its citizens proved way off the mark. In the end, it was not military superiority but political, economic, and cultural factors that brought about the triumph of Western civilization over the Marxist vision of a classless utopia.

Then did the United States win the Cold War, as some voices in Washington triumphantly proclaimed when the Soviet Union was collapsing into dust? Perhaps it would be more correct to say that over time the democratic capitalist system as practiced by the United States and many of its allies proved to be more productive, more resilient, and more broadly appealing than did its Marxist rival.

Whatever the case, the world could now shift its focus to other problems of mutual concern. There would now inevitably be a new world order. But what sort of order (or disorder) would it be? These issues will be addressed in the chapters that follow.

REFLECTION QUESTIONS

Q How have historians answered the question of whether the United States or the Soviet Union bears the primary responsibility for the Cold War, and what evidence can be presented on each side of the issue?

Q This chapter has described the outbreak of the Cold War as virtually inevitable given the ambitions of the two superpowers and their ideological differences.

Do you agree? How might the Cold War have been avoided?

Q What disagreements brought about an end to the Sino-Soviet alliance in 1961? Which factors appear to have been most important?

Q How did the wars in Korea and Vietnam relate to the Cold War and affect its course?

CHAPTER TIMELINE

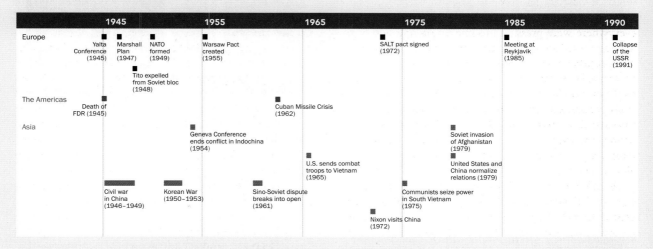

CHAPTER NOTES

1. *Department of State Bulletin*, February 11, 1945, p. 213.
2. Quoted in Joseph M. Jones, *The Fifteen Weeks, February 21–June 5, 1947*, 2nd ed. (New York, 1964), pp. 140–141.
3. Quoted in Misha Glenny, *The Balkans: Nationalism, War, and the Great Powers* (New York, 1999), pp. 543–544.
4. From *United States Relations with China* (Washington, D.C., Department of State, 1949) pp. iii–xvi.
5. Cited in the *New York Review of Books*, June 9, 2011, p. 71.

THE UNITED STATES, CANADA, AND LATIN AMERICA

Chapter Outline and Focus Questions

IMAGE 8.1 President Lyndon Johnson, champion of the Great Society programs, speaking at a ceremony in 1967 commemorating the birth of the 200-millionth U.S. citizen.

Connections to Today

If it is true that the history of American politics tends to shift back and forth on the issue of government intervention into society and the economy, what do you think the trend is today?

ON MAY 22, 1964, President Lyndon B. Johnson gave a policy speech before an audience of students at the University of Michigan in Ann Arbor. He used the occasion to propose a new domestic strategy—to be known as the "Great Society"—to bring about major economic and social reforms in the United States. The aim of these reforms, he said, would be to use the national wealth "to enrich and elevate our national life and to advance the quality of our American civilization."[1]

In his State of the Union address the following January, President Johnson unveiled some of the details of his plan. They included increased funding for education, urban renewal, crime fighting, disease prevention, a new Medicare program, and a war on poverty. Finally, he called for an extension of voting rights to guarantee the franchise to all citizens.

During the next few years, the U.S. Congress enacted many of the programs proposed by the Johnson administration, and the Great Society became a familiar part of the American landscape. A few years, later, however, it came under attack, as a more conservative electorate turned away from expensive welfare programs and endorsed a more modest approach to meeting the social needs of the American people. An era of active government intervention to bring about changes in the fabric of American society had come to an end.

8-1 THE UNITED STATES SINCE 1945

 Focus Question: What are the issues that have most consistently shaped the nature of U.S. politics since the end of World War II?

For a generation after World War II, the legacy of Franklin Roosevelt's New Deal continued to determine the parameters of American domestic politics. The New Deal gave rise to a distinct pattern that signified a basic transformation in American society. This pattern included a dramatic increase in the role and power of the federal government; the rise of organized labor as a significant force in the economy and politics; a commitment to the welfare state, albeit a restricted one (Americans did not have access to universal healthcare as citizens of most other industrialized societies did); a grudging acceptance of the need to resolve problems of minority groups; and a willingness to experiment with deficit spending as a means of stimulating the economy.

8-1a An Era of Prosperity and Social Commitment

One reason for the success of New Deal policies in the postwar era was the general economic recovery that took place in the years following the resumption of peace. A shortage of consumer goods during the war had left Americans with both surplus income and the desire to purchase these goods after the war. Then, too, the growing power of organized labor enabled more and more workers to obtain the wage increases that fueled the growth of the domestic market. Increased government expenditures—based on the theory of English economist John Maynard Keynes that government spending could stimulate a lagging economy to reach higher levels of productivity—along with higher tax rates on the wealthy, also indirectly subsidized the American private enterprise system. Outlays on defense, especially after the Korean War began in 1950, provided money for scientific research in universities and markets for weapons industries. After 1955, tax dollars built a massive system of interstate highways, and tax deductions for mortgages subsidized homeowners. Between 1945 and 1973, real wages grew at an average rate of 3 percent a year, the most prolonged advance in American history.

Also contributing to the economic recovery was the decision by Western leaders to avoid the vicious trade wars that had taken place in the 1930s. The first stage took place in 1947, when twenty-three nations accepted the General Agreement on Tariffs and Trade (GATT); its goal was to lower tariffs and quotas in order to promote free trade on a global basis. To stimulate growth in poorer nations, the International Monetary Fund (IMF) was established to stabilize the global financial system by supervising exchange rates and providing financial and technical assistance to nations encountering economic difficulties. The World Bank was created to provide grants and loans to assist developing countries in building up their infrastructure so that they could compete more effectively in the global marketplace. As the world economy gradually recovered and demand for U.S. manufactures increased (especially in Europe, where the Marshall Plan had stipulated that European aid recipients purchase goods from U.S. manufacturers), the United States assumed the role of workshop of the world, providing jobs for millions of American servicemen returning home from the European and Pacific theaters.

Riding the wave of popular approval for Roosevelt's progressive program, the Democratic Party controlled the White House until 1952, when the Republican candidate and war hero Dwight D. Eisenhower won election to the presidency. Ike, as he was popularly known, was by instinct a fiscal and "small government" conservative, but he tacitly accepted the fundamental premises of the New Deal and even extended them by embarking on the construction of a massive interstate highway system. Although the project was justified on the grounds of national defense, it served as a massive jobs program and stimulated the economy while improving the nation's infrastructure.

The Eisenhower years, however, were clouded by a growing sense of insecurity about the world beyond the borders of the United States (see Chapter 7). The Communist victory in China, the public reaction to which had played an important role in Eisenhower's election to the presidency, aroused fears that Communists had infiltrated the United States. A demagogic senator from Wisconsin, Joseph McCarthy, helped intensify a massive "Red scare" with unsubstantiated allegations that there were hundreds of Communists in high government positions. Congressional hearings on the matter were held by the House Un-American Activities Committee, and dozens of government officials and public figures were accused of radical sympathies or past membership in the Communist Party. A number of film actors and producers were placed on a blacklist that prevented them from finding employment in Hollywood. One U.S. senator even accused General George C. Marshall of treason for his efforts to bring about a truce in the civil war in China.[2]

In the end, McCarthy overplayed his hand when he attacked alleged "Communist conspirators" in the U.S. Army, and he was censured by Congress in 1954. Soon afterward, his anti-Communist crusade came to an end. The pervasive fear of communism and the possibility of a nuclear war, however, remained strong. For those millions of Americans living in major metropolitan areas, the wailing of a siren in the night always conjured up latent fears of a surprise nuclear attack from the Soviet Union. The 1950s were not as tranquil as they have often been portrayed in more recent times.

Toward the Great Society By the late 1950s, economic growth had begun to decline because of the Eisenhower administration's tight money policies, and the Democrats returned to power in 1960 with the election of John F. Kennedy as president. At age forty-three, Kennedy became the youngest elected president in the history of the United States and the first born in the twentieth century. The new administration focused its attention primarily on foreign affairs, but it also adopted policies that inaugurated an extended period of increased economic growth, the result—in part—of lower taxes and a business-friendly atmosphere. But the bright promise of a new era of peace, progress, and prosperity was suddenly shattered on November 22, 1963, when Kennedy was assassinated under mysterious circumstances by Lee Harvey Oswald in Dallas.

Kennedy's successor, Lyndon B. Johnson, who won a new term as president in a landslide in 1964, used his stunning mandate to pursue the growth of the welfare state, first begun in the New Deal. Johnson's Great Society programs included healthcare for the elderly, a "war on poverty" to be fought with food stamps and a "job corps," a new Department of Housing and Urban Development to deal with the problems of the cities, and federal assistance for education.

Focus on Civil Rights The nation had made little progress on improving **civil rights** for African Americans in the years following World War II. The practice of legally segregating blacks from whites (known as Jim Crow laws) was rampant in the South. Blacks in the southern states attended separate schools, ate at separate restaurants, lived in separate communities, and even used separate toilet facilities. That practice, known by the term "separate but equal" had been declared legal by the Supreme Court in a decision reached in 1895.

By the early 1950s, resistance to racial segregation was growing in the African American community, and

in a landmark decision entitled "Brown versus the Board of Education," the Supreme Court in 1954 unanimously struck down the practice of maintaining racially segregated public schools. According to the then recently appointed Chief Justice Earl Warren, "Separate educational facilities are inherently unequal." Support from the U.S. foreign policy establishment was a key factor in promoting the decision, since the treatment of racial minorities was often cited abroad by critics of the United States to point to the falsity of its claim to be a free society in comparison with the Soviet Union.

But it would take more than a single judicial decision to change the hearts and minds of many Americans. White politicians in Southern states refused to eliminate existing segregation laws, basing their defiance on the issue of state's rights. Some African American leaders were also uneasy that the decision could undermine the progress that had been achieved in establishing prestigious black educational institutions across the South. President Eisenhower himself privately expressed his concern that a judicial decision that ran counter to deeply held popular beliefs could result in an uptick in racial violence across the country.

Eisenhower's concerns were soon vindicated. Resistance to integrated schools was fierce in southern states, and on those few occasions when blacks had registered to attend white schools, violence had erupted. The issue came to a head in December 1955, when the black seamstress Rosa Parks refused to give up her seat to a white passenger on a bus in Montgomery, Alabama. When she was evicted from the bus and put in prison, Martin Luther King, Jr. (1929–1968), a young Baptist minister of a local black church, spoke eloquently at the pulpit on behalf of racial equality, while supporting a boycott of segregated buses that lasted over a year. In November 1956, the practice was declared unconstitutional.

By the early 1960s, a number of groups, including King's Southern Christian Leadership Conference (SCLC), were organizing demonstrations and sit-ins across the South to end racial segregation. In August 1963, King led the March on Washington for Jobs and Freedom. This march and King's impassioned plea for racial equality had an electrifying effect on the American people (see Image 8.2). President Kennedy, newly aware of the seriousness of the racial problem in the United States, resolved to act, and the White House initiated legislation to extend civil rights, but the president died before the bill was enacted into law.

On June 21, 1964, three young civil rights workers disappeared while investigating the torching of an African American church in Mississippi. A few weeks later, their bodies were discovered in a partially constructed dam nearby. Although Kennedy's successor Lyndon B. Johnson (LBJ)

IMAGE 8.2 "I Have a Dream." On August 28, 1963 the Reverend Martin Luther King, Jr. spoke before massive crowds in front of the Lincoln Memorial in Washington, D.C. His speech, an appeal to the American people to grant equal rights to their fellow citizens of African heritage, electrified the nation and provided an enormous boost to the cause of racial equality in the United States. It would later be recalled as the "I have a dream" speech.

 Why do you think Martin Luther King selected the Lincoln Memorial as the site of his impassioned address?

had been a senator from the southern state of Texas and had once supported segregation laws, he now recognized the need for action, and decided to take advantage of the uproar caused by the incident to promote the cause of civil rights legislation. In 1964, Congress enacted the Civil Rights Act, which ended segregation and discrimination in the workplace and in all public accommodations. The Voting Rights Act, passed the following year, eliminated racial obstacles to voting in southern states (see Historical Voices, "From Dream to Reality," p. 194).

Outside the South, African Americans had had voting rights for many years, but local patterns of segregation resulted in considerably higher unemployment rates for blacks than for whites, and also left them segregated in huge urban ghettos. Some black leaders, like Malcolm X of the Black Muslims, grew impatient with Martin Luther King's appeals for non-violent protest and began to call for militant action. In the summer of 1965, race riots erupted in the Watts district of Los Angeles and led to thirty-four deaths and the destruction of more than one thousand buildings. After the assassination of Martin Luther King by a white supremacist in 1968, more than 100 cities experienced rioting, including Washington, D.C., the nation's capital. The combination of riots and provocative comments by radical black leaders led to a "white backlash" and a decline in support for civil rights issues among the white population.

A Nation Divided Unfortunately, the passage of legislation designed to bring LBJ's vision of The Great Society to reality coincided with the escalation of the Vietnam War (see Chapter 7). Johnson did not want the war to define his presidency, yet he was determined to avoid a U.S. defeat in Southeast Asia, fearing that it would expose the Democratic Party once again to the charge by Republicans of being "soft on Communism," such as had occurred after the defeat of Republican China over a decade previously. By now, the country was increasingly divided over the war in Vietnam, especially when more and more young Americans—many of them draftees—were being sent into combat (see Image 8.3).

The antiwar protests arose out of a free speech movement that began in 1964 at the University of California at Berkeley as a protest against the impersonality and authoritarianism of the large university. As the Vietnam war progressed and U.S. casualties mounted, protests escalated. Teach-ins, sit-ins, and the occupation of university buildings alternated with more radical demonstrations that increasingly led to violence. Those who supported the protests contended that the antiwar movement helped weaken the willingness of many Americans to continue to support the war. But the combination of antiwar demonstrations and ghetto riots in the cities also provoked many Americans to embrace "law and order," an appeal used effectively by Richard M. Nixon (1913–1994), the Republican presidential candidate,

From Dream to Reality

 Q *What forms of discrimination had been common practice before the passage of The Civil Rights Act of 1964?*

Politics & Government **PURSUANT TO A SPEECH** by President John F. Kennedy in June 1963, the White House had proposed civil rights legislation to guarantee voting rights and protection from discrimination for all Americans, regardless of race, color, sex, or creed. Before Kennedy's assassination in November, the bill had stalled in Congress, but Kennedy's successor, President Lyndon B. Johnson, was able to push the bill through Congress the following year.

The Civil Rights Act of 1964 outlawed many forms of racial discrimination, as can be seen in the document below, but the problem has not yet been resolved, as opponents continue to seek various means to prevent American citizens from exercising their right to vote.

The Civil Rights Act of 1964

Title I – VOTING RIGHTS

(2) No person acting under color of law shall –

    (A) in determining whether any individual is qualified under State law or laws to vote in any Federal election, apply any standard, practice, or procedure different from the standards, practices, or procedures applied under such law or laws to other individuals within the same county, parish, or similar political sub-division who have been found by State officials to be qualified to vote;

    (B) deny the right of any individual to vote in any Federal election because of an error or omission on any record or paper relating to any application, registration, or other act requisite to voting, if such error or omission is not material in determining whether such individual is qualified under State law to vote in such elections; or

    (C) employ any literacy test as a qualification for voting in any Federal election unless (i) such test is administered to each individual and is conducted wholly in writing, and (ii) a certified copy of the test and of the answers given by the individual; is furnished to him within twenty-five days of the submission of his request made within the period of time during which records and papers are required to be retained and preserved pursuant to Title III of the Civil Rights Act of 1960 . . .

DISCRIMINATION BECAUSE OF RACE, COLOR, RELIGION, SEX, OR NATIONAL ORIGIN

SEC 703. (a) It shall be an unlawful employment practice for an employer –

(1) to fail or refuse to hire or to discharge any individual with respect to his compensation, terms, conditions, or privileges of employment, because of such individual's race, color, religion, sex, or national origins; or

(2) to limit, segregate, or classify his employees in any way which would deprive or tend to deprive any individual of employment opportunities or otherwise adversely affect his status as an employee, because of such individual's race, color, religion, sex, or national origin . . . It shall be an unlawful employment practice for a labor organization –

(1) to exclude or to expel from its membership or otherwise to discriminate against, any individual because of his race, color, religion, sex, or national origins;

(2) to limit, segregate or classify its membership, or to clarify or fail or refuse to refer for employment any individual, in any way which would deprive or tend to deprive any individual of employment opportunities, or would limit such employment opportunities or otherwise adversely affect his status as an employee or as an applicant for employment, because of such individual's race, color, religion, sex, or national origin; or

(3) to cause or attempt to cause an employer to discriminate against any individual in violation of this section . . .

Source: *Our Documents: 100 Milestone Documents from the National Archives* (Oxford University Press, 2003), pp. 236–237.

IMAGE 8.3 The Vietnam Veterans Memorial. Often lost in the passions that surrounded the U.S. involvement in the Vietnam War were the countless individual tragedies suffered by loved ones who lost a family member in the conflict. In 1982, construction began on a 300-foot wall on the grounds of the National Mall in Washington, D.C. The wall was designed by the American architect Maya Lin and was dedicated to all the men and women who had fought in the war. The names of more than 58,000 men and women who died in the conflict are inscribed on large slabs of black marble at the site. The reflections of visitors appear on the surface of the wall and represent a means of linking the present and the past together in memory of the experience. An average of three million people visit the site each year.

Coolidge that "the business of government is business." The ideal of equality was fine, but it wasn't the responsibility of the government to enforce it. In fact, growing economic inequality had been grudgingly accepted so long as opportunities for the general public to improve their economic situation were adequate. But when the Great Depression struck with a force that induced despair on millions of Americans, the tide had changed dramatically, and millions of Americans embraced the motives and the policies of the openly interventionist New Deal. By the 1960s, however, most Americans enjoying a new era of unprecedented prosperity, and the pendulum was about to swing once again in the other direction.

Nixon and Watergate Nixon owed his election, at least in part, to the disarray within the Democratic Party over the war in Vietnam, where more than 500,000 U.S. troops were now stationed, and the new president did not seek to reverse the liberal programs—many of them popular with the public—enacted by his predecessors. He even signed the National Environmental Policy Act, which established a national policy for the protection of the environment. Nixon also reduced U.S. involvement in Vietnam by gradually withdrawing American troops and appealing to the "silent majority" of Americans for patience in bringing the conflict to an end. He also broke with his strong anti-Communist past when he visited China in 1972 and opened the door to the eventual diplomatic recognition of that Communist state.

during the election campaign of 1968. By then, the passions of the nation had been consumed by the conflict in Southeast Asia, and in early 1968, Johnson announced that he would not seek re-election. With Nixon's election over the Democratic candidate Hubert Humphrey in 1968, a shift to the right in American politics had begun.

8-1b America Shifts to the Right

There has always been an element of tension between the concepts of liberty and equality in American society, between the desire for individual freedom and the right of every citizen to an equal opportunity to "life, liberty, and the pursuit of happiness" (in the words of the Declaration of Independence). The fact that many early immigrants to the United States had fled their original homes to escape tyrannical governments ensured that their objective on reaching their new home was to secure the freedom to pursue their own destiny. But the concept of equality was somewhat harder to grasp, since for many Americans the essence of Christian teachings was not to question one's station in this life, but to seek salvation in the life to come.

For much of its early history, the American republic had been based on the concept of rugged individualism—epitomized by the famous remark by President Calvin

But on racial issues, Nixon clearly embarked on a new course, dubbed the "southern strategy" by one of his senior advisers. This strategy was dictated in part by the hope for political gain. By signaling to voters in the southern states that the Republican Party was sympathetic to the view that individual states should have the right to decide issues related to civil rights on their own, the White House hoped to pry such voters from their historical alignment with the Democrats that dated back to the Civil War. The Republican strategy also gained some support among Democrats in northern cities, where court-mandated busing to achieve racial integration in schools had produced a white backlash.

But Nixon was paranoid about conspiracies and, despite a landslide victory over the anti-war Democratic candidate George McGovern in the presidential election in 1972, he began to use illegal methods of gaining political intelligence about his political opponents. One of the president's advisers explained that their intention was to "use the available federal machinery to screw our political enemies." Nixon's zeal led to the infamous Watergate scandal—the attempted bugging of Democratic National Headquarters located at the Watergate complex in downtown Washington, D.C. Although Nixon repeatedly lied to the American public about his involvement in the affair, secret tapes of his own conversations in the White House revealed the truth. With a number of Republicans in Congress willing to support the initiation of impeachment proceedings, on August 9, 1974, Nixon resigned from office, an act that saved him from almost certain impeachment and conviction.

The First Oil Crisis   After Watergate and the end of the Vietnam War in 1975, American domestic politics began to focus on economic issues. Gerald R. Ford (1913–2006) became president when Nixon resigned, only to lose in the 1976 election to the Democratic former governor of Georgia, Jimmy Carter, who campaigned as an outsider— and a southerner—against the Washington establishment. Both Ford and Carter faced growing economic problems. The period from 1973 to the mid-1980s was one of economic stagnation, a condition which came to be known as stagflation—a combination of high inflation and high unemployment. In 1984, median family income was 6 percent below that of 1973.

The economic downturn stemmed at least in part from a dramatic rise in oil prices. Oil had been a cheap and abundant source of energy in the 1950s, but by the late 1970s, half of the oil used in the United States came from the Middle East. An oil embargo imposed by the Organization of Petroleum Exporting Countries (OPEC) cartel as a reaction to the Arab-Israeli War in 1973 and OPEC's subsequent raising of prices led to a quadrupling of the cost of oil. By the end of the 1970s, oil prices had increased twentyfold, encouraging inflationary tendencies throughout the entire economy. Although the Carter administration proposed a plan for reducing oil consumption at home while spurring domestic production, neither Congress nor the American people could be persuaded to follow what they regarded as unnecessarily drastic measures.

By 1980, the Carter administration was facing two devastating problems. High inflation and a noticeable decline in average weekly earnings were causing a perceptible drop in American living standards. At the same time, a crisis abroad had erupted when fifty-three Americans were taken hostage by the Iranian government of Ayatollah Khomeini (see Chapter 15). Carter's inability to gain the release of the American hostages led to the perception at home that he was a weak president. His overwhelming loss to Ronald Reagan in the election of 1980 brought forward the chief exponent of conservative Republican policies and a new political order.

Dismantling the Welfare State   The conservative trend accelerated in the 1980s. The election of Ronald Reagan changed the trajectory of American policy on several fronts. Reversing decades of the expanding welfare state, Reagan cut spending on food stamps, school lunch programs, and job programs. At the same time, his administration fostered the largest peacetime military buildup in American history. Total federal spending rose from $631 billion in 1981 to more than $1 trillion by 1986. But instead of raising taxes to pay for the new expenditures, which far outweighed the budget cuts in social areas, Reagan convinced Congress to support supply-side economics. Massive tax cuts were designed to stimulate rapid economic growth and thus produce new revenues in the future.

The American public, weary of high levels of government spending on social issues that never seemed to produce results, found President Reagan's approach appealing and reelected him by overwhelming margins to a second term in 1984. The country experienced an economic upturn that lasted until the end of the decade, but the administration's spending policies also resulted in record government deficits, which loomed as an obstacle to long-term growth. In 1980, the total government debt was around $930 billion; by 1988, the total debt had almost tripled, reaching $2.6 trillion. The inability of George H. W. Bush (b. 1924), Reagan's vice president and successor, to deal with a brief economic downturn contributed to the election of a Democrat, Bill Clinton (b. 1946), in November 1992.

8-1c Seizing the Political Center

The new president was a southerner who claimed to be a "new Democrat"—one who favored fiscal responsibility and a more conservative social agenda—a clear indication that the rightward drift in American politics had not been reversed but only modified by his victory. During his first term in office, Clinton reduced the budget deficit and signed a bill turning many welfare programs back to the states while pushing measures to strengthen education and provide job opportunities for those Americans removed from the welfare rolls. By seizing the center of the American political agenda, Clinton was able to win reelection in 1996, although the Republican Party now held a majority in both houses of Congress.

President Clinton's political fortunes were helped considerably by a lengthy economic revival. Thanks to downsizing and dramatic technological advances, major U.S. corporations began to recover the competitive edge they had lost to Japanese and European firms in previous years.

At the same time, a steady reduction in the annual government budget deficit strengthened public confidence in the performance of the national economy. Although wage increases were modest (partly due to a decline in union membership among American workers), inflation was securely in check, and public confidence in the future was on the rise. Reflecting that confidence in American competitiveness, the administration signed the North American Free Trade Agreement (NAFTA) which reduced mutual tariffs with Canada and Mexico. It also joined the new World Trade Organization (WTO), which replaced GATT.

President Clinton's shift toward the center was motivated in part by confidence that technological developments were about to play a major role in turning the United States into a post-industrial nation. Fears by working-class Americans that jobs in the manufacturing sector would be lost as factory owners fled to lower-salary countries like China and Mexico were dismissed by the White House, which argued that the job losses would be more than compensated for in the new technological economy.

Many of the country's social problems, however, remained unresolved. Although crime rates were down, drug use, smoking, and alcoholism among young people remained high, and the specter of rising medical costs loomed as a generation of baby boomers (so called because they were born during the two decades after World War II when there was a dramatic spike in the number of births) neared retirement age. Americans remained bitterly divided over such issues as abortion and affirmative action programs to rectify past discrimination on the basis of gender, race, or sexual orientation.

President Clinton contributed to the national sense of unease by becoming the focus of a series of alleged financial and sexual scandals that aroused concerns among many Americans that the moral fiber of the country had been severely undermined. Accused of lying under oath in a judicial hearing, he was impeached by the Republican-led majority in Congress. Although the effort to remove Clinton from office failed, his administration was tarnished, and in 2000, Republican candidate George W. Bush (b. 1946), the son of Clinton's predecessor, narrowly defeated Clinton's vice president, Albert Gore, in the race for the presidency. The election was decided at least partly on economic issues. Taking advantage of the failure of the Democrats to address the economic concerns of many working-class Americans, the Republicans wooed them with "values" issues, such as abortion, crime, the role of religion in society, the prevalence of homosexuality, and the right to own a firearm. Still, after entering the White House, President Bush followed his predecessor's playbook and sought to occupy the center of the political spectrum while heeding the concerns of his conservative base.

The Politics of Terrorism On September 11, 2001, Muslim terrorists hijacked four commercial jet planes shortly after they took off from Boston, Newark, and Washington, D.C. Two of the planes were flown directly into the twin towers of the World Trade Center in New York City, causing both buildings to collapse; a third slammed into the Pentagon, near Washington, D.C; and the fourth crashed in a field in central Pennsylvania. About 3000 people were killed, including everyone aboard the four airliners (see Image 16.1 "Terrorist Attack on The World Trade Center in New York City," p. 396). The hijackings were carried out by a terrorist organization known as al-Qaeda, which had been suspected of bombing two U.S. embassies in Africa in 1998 and attacking a U.S. naval ship, the U.S.S. *Cole*, two years later. Its leader, Osama bin Laden (1957–2011), was a native of Saudi Arabia who was allegedly angry at the growing U.S. presence in the Middle East. President Bush vowed to wage an offensive war on terrorism, and in October 2001, with United Nations support, U.S. forces attacked al-Qaeda bases in Afghanistan (see Chapter 15).

The Bush administration had less success in gaining UN approval for an attack on the brutal regime of Saddam Hussein in Iraq, which the White House accused of amassing weapons of mass destruction and providing support to terrorist groups in the region. Nevertheless, in March 2003, U.S. forces invaded Iraq and quickly overthrew the Hussein regime. Initially, the invasion had broad popular support in the United States, but as insurgent activities continued to inflict casualties on U.S. and Allied occupation forces—not to speak of the deaths of thousands of Iraqi civilians—the war became more controversial. The failure to locate the suspected weapons of mass destruction raised questions about the motives behind the administration's decision to invade Iraq. Some Americans called for an immediate pull-out of U.S. troops.

The Bush administration was also dogged by an economic downturn and a number of other domestic problems, including the outsourcing of American jobs to Asian countries (especially to China, which joined the WTO in 2001) and the failure to control illegal immigration from Mexico. But it benefited from the public perception that the Republican Party was more effective at protecting the American people from the threat of terrorism than its Democratic rival. Evangelical Christians—one of the nation's most vocal communities—were also drawn to the Republican Party for its emphasis on traditional moral values and the sanctity of the family and its opposition to abortion. Riding the wave of such concerns, President Bush defeated the Democratic candidate John F. Kerry in the presidential election of 2004.

After the election, the Bush administration sought to rein in the rising cost of domestic spending by presenting new proposals to reform Social Security and the Medicare program. But the public was leery of cuts to popular entitlement programs, and the plans were quickly dropped. In the meantime, the war in Iraq continued to distract the White House from other pressing issues, including a dramatic rise in the price of oil and an exploding national budget deficit. In midterm elections held in the fall of 2006, the Democratic Party seized control of both houses of Congress for the first time in twelve years.

A Historic Milestone   The presidential campaign of 2008 was historic in terms of the major candidates for high office. The nominee of the Democratic Party, Illinois senator Barack Obama (b. 1961), was an African American of mixed parentage. Senator John McCain, the Republican candidate, selected Alaska's female governor Sarah Palin as his running mate. The Republican Party ran strongly on issues of national security, but a sudden financial crisis, brought on by a serious downturn in the housing market and an ensuing credit crunch, put the public focus squarely on the national economy. When the votes were counted, Barack Obama had won a decisive victory over his Republican rival, while Democratic majorities increased in both houses of Congress.

Barack Obama had run on a platform of economic change and social renewal, but his immediate challenge was to reverse the sudden downturn and put the U.S. economy back on a path of steady growth. In the face of Republican opposition, his administration enacted into law a stimulus program to put millions of newly unemployed Americans back to work. But the new president was unwilling to abandon his ambitious social agenda and also pushed through the Patient Protection and Affordable Care Act (ACA)—popularly known as Obamacare—that provided access to inexpensive healthcare to most U.S. citizens. But many Americans were wary of government interference in their lives (one common complaint about the legislation was that is mandated participation even for those who were uninterested in joining), and the ACA failed to achieve broad popular support around the country. Other legislative proposals, including additional stimulus projects and immigration reform, stalled in Congress after Republicans made big gains in the 2010 midterm elections.

The presidential election of 2012 was fought primarily on the state of the nation's economy, which had shown only modest improvement under Obama's stewardship. Mitt Romney, the Republican candidate, ran on a platform of low taxes and a sharp reduction in entitlement spending. But the reelection of President Obama—who called for a balanced approach combining tax increases for wealthy Americans and modest cuts in social spending—suggested that, although many Americans remained distrustful of government, liberal programs like Social Security and Medicare were still widely popular.

During Obama's second term, the national economy continued gradually to improve, although the annual growth rate hovered around only three percent. Social programs provided some protection for the most disadvantaged in American society, but most Americans did not feel much better off than they had been at the start of his first term in office. Meanwhile, rising imports and the outsourcing of factories to countries with low labor costs like China and Mexico led to a steady loss of jobs for many working-class Americans, especially for those in blue collar occupations. Much of the job loss was concentrated in rural areas and in rust-belt cities in the Northeast and the Midwest.

In the meantime, fundamental disagreements between the two major parties over a variety of issues, including the role of government, the social safety net, immigration, abortion, and LGBTQ rights, became increasingly wide. Much of the opposition to President Obama's agenda was led by the so-called **Tea Party**, a loosely organized grassroots movement that became an important force within the opposition Republican Party. Throughout the last years of the Obama presidency, this partisan divide threatened the ability of the political system to deal with the multiple challenges facing the nation.

8-1d Making America Great Again?

As the 2016 presidential election approached, the Democrats nominated Hillary Rodham Clinton, the former first lady who had gone on to represent the state of New York in the U.S. Senate and later served as President Obama's first secretary of state. Clinton was the first woman to serve as the presidential nominee of a major political party in U.S. history. The nomination process to select her Republican challenger was crowded, but the eventual victor was Donald J. Trump, a well-known entrepreneur and TV promoter who based his campaign on a slogan to "Make America Great Again." In the election held in early November, Trump won a surprising victory in the Electoral College, although he had received about three million fewer votes than his Democratic rival.

What were the reasons behind his stunning rise to the presidency? As a candidate, Trump had deliberately run as an outsider to traditional American politics, promising to "drain the swamp" that, in the minds of many of his followers, had long characterized the corrupt and ineffective government in Washington. He had also shrewdly identified a number of key issues that animated the concerns of a wide spectrum of voters, especially in the American heartland: resentment against government interference in the private lives of American citizens; opposition to immigration (especially from across the border with Mexico and from the strife-torn Middle East); and rising public concern at the loss of jobs as countless American factories were relocated overseas. This visceral public anger was focused primarily on a number of key states in the Northeast and the Midwest, states that could become the key to electoral victory or defeat. While the Trump campaign focused on such key battlegrounds, his Democratic opponent appeared to take the support of angry white voters in the Midwest for granted and ran a lackluster campaign that failed to ignite the enthusiasm of voters, many of whom, confident of her inevitable victory, probably stayed at home on election day. The election of Donald J. Trump to the presidency signaled a major change in the direction of American politics. Because this raises so many issues related to the present and future course of our democracy, we shall explore the implications of that change later in this book.

8-2 THE CHANGING FACE OF AMERICAN SOCIETY

 Focus Question: In what major ways has American society evolved over the decades since 1945? Have these changes been for the good or the bad?

Major changes have taken place in American society since the end of World War II. New technologies such as television, jet planes, and the computer have dramatically altered the pace and nature of American life. Increased prosperity has led to the growth of the middle class, the expansion of higher education, and a stunning increase in consumer demand for the products of a mass society. The building of a nationwide system of superhighways, combined with low fuel prices during much of the period, and steady improvements in the quality and operability of automobiles, has produced a highly mobile society in which the average American family moves at least once every five years, sometimes from one end of the continent to the other.

One consequence of this change has been a movement from rural areas and central cities into the suburbs. There has also been an exodus of Americans from the Northeast and Midwest to the "sunbelt" areas of the West and the South, where new industries have resulted in rapid economic growth.

8-2a A Consumer Society, a Permissive Society

These changes in the physical surroundings of the country have been matched by equally important shifts in the social fabric. Boosted by rising incomes, the baby boom generation grew up with higher expectations about their future material prospects than their parents had. The members of this new **consumer society** focused much of their attention on achieving a middle-class lifestyle, complete with a home in the suburbs, two automobiles, and ample time for leisure activities. The growing predilection for buying on the installment plan was an important factor in protecting the national economy from the cycle of "boom and bust" that had characterized the prewar period, but also increased the level of personal debt.

With the introduction of credit cards, the personal debt of the average American skyrocketed, while the savings rate plummeted to its lowest level in decades. By the end of the 1990s, adjustable rate mortgages had become increasingly popular. Inappropriate mortgages were a major factor in the financial crisis that struck the national economy in the fall of 2008, as were risky banking practices. The fact is that millions of Americans, with the encouragement of their political leaders, had become enticed by easy credit terms and were spending beyond their means. When housing prices stopped rising, the number of home foreclosures increased dramatically, triggering a massive financial crisis; the ensuing leap in unemployment led to more foreclosures, and the nation faced its most serious economic recession in decades.

American social mores were also changing. Casual attitudes toward premarital sex (a product in part of the introduction of the birth control pill) and the use of drugs (a practice that increased dramatically during the Vietnam War) marked the emergence of a youth movement in the 1960s that questioned all authority and fostered rebellion against older generations.

In a parallel development, American attitudes toward religion also entered a state of flux. Once a nation marked by a high level of religiosity (many of the early settlers, after all, had fled their original homes in Europe in search of freedom to worship in their own way), after World War II more and more Americans had begun to adopt a more secular life-style; some abandoned formal ties to any established Church. Paradoxically, millions of others—many of them concentrated in rural areas in the Midwest and the South—sought to find greater meaning and purpose in life by seeking a more personal relationship with Christ. To members of the growing Evangelical movement, a more Christian lifestyle was seen as a necessary antidote for avoiding the scourges of crime, drugs, and social alienation increasingly prevalent in American society as a whole.

Despite the growth of religiosity in some sectors of American society, the new social mores were evident in the breakdown of the traditional nuclear family. Divorce rates increased from ten percent in 1960 to over 22 percent twenty years later, so that in the 1980s, one of every two first marriages was likely to end in divorce. Attitudes toward extramarital sex were also changing, and the stigma attached to children born out of wedlock eroded dramatically. At the same time, Americans in general were also becoming more receptive to abortion and LGBTQ rights. In the 2012 elections, several states approved referendums allowing same-sex marriage, and in June 2013, the U.S. Supreme Court struck down restrictive provisions contained in the Defense of Marriage Act, while declaring that the power to define marriage resided in the individual states.

From an economic perspective, one disquieting aspect of this portrait of a changing America is the growing gap that exists between wealthy Americans and everyone else. Beginning with the Reagan administration, which adopted the strategy of supply-side economics in a bid to generate more rapid economic growth, income tax rates on upper-income Americans began falling steadily, while the average American was little better off financially than he was in the early 1960s. According to one statistical measure, since 1980 the annual income of the top 0.01% of the country has gone up an average of over 400 percent, while that of the bottom fifty percent has increased by less than five percent. As a result, the ability of the average American to buy a sufficient amount of consumer goods to keep the factories humming has become increasingly threatened. Like their counterparts in mid-nineteenth century Europe, U.S. corporations have increasingly been driven to seek out foreign markets that can absorb the cornucopia of goods produced in their factories.

The combination of a slowing economy and wage stagnation that has prevailed in recent decades has had a measurable effect on the state of America as a whole. Only the more affluent sectors of society continue to harbor high expectations for their future lifestyle, are able to attend prestigious colleges, and to obtain high-paying jobs after graduation. Most other Americans face narrower horizons. As higher education has become more expensive—a consequence in part of declining government subsidies devoted to public education—fewer young Americans are able to afford the expense of completing a college degree. Lacking the technical skills needed to obtain high-paying jobs in big cities, they are more likely to remain at home—often in small towns and rural areas—and to accept less lucrative forms of employment. Even if they are more religious, they are also more likely to come from broken homes, suffer from serious diseases at a younger age, and to turn to drugs or pain-killers to deal with their afflictions. In 2017, more than 150,000 Americans died from alcohol, drug abuse, or suicide—what are now commonly referred to as deaths of despair. With healthcare costs rising steadily, many Americans cannot afford medical treatment for their physical and emotional needs. Although the Obama administration pushed through an ambitious healthcare plan to help resolve the problem, many people continue to distrust the government to come to their assistance in times of need. As a result, the ladder of upward mobility that once defined American society has been taken away, and many of the poorest Americans are locked in a poverty trap. To some, it seems now that there are now two Americas, with vastly divergent lifestyles and sharply contrasting views on many of the key issues facing the country as a whole.

8-2b The Melting Pot in Action

One of the signature objectives of the Great Society Program was to improve living conditions for African Americans and to hasten their integration into the broader community. Fair housing laws were designed to break up black ghettos and to encourage the emergence of mixed neighborhoods that reflected the broader statistical breakdown of the country as a whole. Affirmative action legislation was passed that required school systems to integrate black students into better-funded white schools, and to require all institutions of higher learning that accepted federal moneys to work toward achieving a better racial balance in their own student populations. But progress on civil rights was not achieved without significant resistance: parents resisted the busing of their students to distant schools in order to achieve racial parity; predominantly white neighborhoods in the inner cities began to suffer from "white flight," as families whose forebears had immigrated from Europe generations before began to abandon their homes to avoid the prospect of living in a racially mixed neighborhood. White students filed lawsuits to complain that their application to attend a university had been rejected to make way for a lesser-qualified African American candidate.

Over the years, some of these concerns have moderated, in great part because the pace of racial integration has slowed down. Truly mixed neighborhoods are still the exception in much of the country, while affirmative action has not fundamentally changed the fact that most students still attend a school composed primarily of children of their own racial identity. The percentage of people of color attending institutions of higher education is still well below that of their white counterparts. Today, much of the attention has shifted to other issues, such as the practice of voter suppression in predominantly black communities, high unemployment levels among young African Americans, police brutality against blacks, and lagging salary levels for blacks in comparison to the remainder of the population. For some of these problems, there appears to be no legislative solution.

One of the primary factors that has helped shape American society in the postwar era has been the increasing pace of new arrivals from abroad. Whereas legal immigration was traditionally based on the percentage of individuals from a particular country already living in the United States, an Immigration Act enacted in 1965 did away with such restrictions, thus bringing about a dramatic increase in immigration levels from non-European countries around the world. Although the majority came from Latin America, substantial numbers arrived from China, Vietnam, and the countries of southern Asia. Whereas about 300,000 immigrants had legally arrived on American shores each year in the 1960s, the annual total increased to over a million forty years later.

Today, illegal immigration—primarily from Mexico but also to a lesser extent from countries in Central America—has become a controversial issue in American politics. Since many undocumented immigrants gravitate to low-paying jobs that are not attractive to most Americans, this influx has usually been tacitly accepted by the public as a necessary evil. In recent years, however, undocumented immigration has increased dramatically, and critics have begun to point to the financial burden that the new arrivals place on the nation's educational and medical systems. Advocates for generous immigrant policies counter that recent arrivals are not a burden, but have become an increasingly indispensable element in the U.S. economy, comprising one-quarter of all farmworkers and 14 percent of all those employed in construction jobs.

Regardless of the outcome of this debate, as more immigrants attain citizenship, they exert a growing influence on U.S. politics. The number of Hispanics living in the United States has increased to 50 million, surpassing African Americans as the largest minority group in the country. More than 16 percent of the total population is Hispanic; of these, almost 30 million are eligible to vote, and their political preferences have proved to be a decisive factor in some recent elections. Moreover, although some recent arrivals gravitate toward areas where there is already a large Hispanic population—such as in counties located along the border with Mexico—their social integration into the broader community is steadily taking place as second- or third-generation Hispanics are increasingly marrying outside their own ethnic group.

Still, immigration is one of the more contentious issues in American politics and, as we have seen above, in 2016 it was highlighted as a key issue by the Republican candidate Donald Trump in his campaign for the presidency. One of his most-discussed campaign promises was to build a concrete wall along the southern border with Mexico to cut back on illegal immigration into the United States. After the election, the issue aroused intense debate in Congress and among the American people, as television news programs provided video reports of refugees from violence-torn countries in Central America streaming northward toward the border to seek entrance into the United States. In one month alone, February 2019, over 70,000 migrants crossed the border to seek asylum into the United States (for a discussion of this issue in a global context, see Chapter 16).

8-2c The Struggle for Sexual Equality

Many of the changes taking place in American life reflect the fact that the role of women has been in a state of transition. Women first began to realize the benefits of the efforts of suffragists like Emily Cady Stanton, Lucretia Watt, and Susan B. Anthony in the years immediately following World War I, when Congress finally enacted the Nineteenth Amendment to the U.S. Constitution. During the 1920s, women's rights activists failed in their effort to achieve a follow-up success with the enactment of an Equal Rights Amendment, but in other ways American women began to experience a new sense of freedom, a reality expressed in the popular image of a young woman on a magazine cover complete with a cigarette in her hand and a dress that ended above her knees. That image of the "liberated woman" survived into the Great Depression, and was eagerly promoted in Hollywood, as the popular films of the 1930s portrayed women as lawyers, aviators, and journalists, all competing on equal terms with their male counterparts.

Following World War II, however, the mood changed, as millions of soldiers returning home from the war sought to resume the jobs that they had abandoned while serving their country abroad. With bitter memories of rampant joblessness during the Great Depression, many women gave up their wartime jobs in offices and factories and returned to their traditional role as homemakers, sparking the "baby boom" of the late 1940s and 1950s. American business interests were only too happy to oblige, taking advantage of the popular new medium of television to promote all the new appliances produced in American factories that the happy housewife required to relieve her of the drudgery that had plagued the lives of their mothers and grandmothers. To underline the point, popular new television series like *I Love Lucy* and *Ozzie and Harriett* portrayed American womanhood happily nestled in the bosom of her family, complete with two (or three) children, a harried husband who was always rushing off to work, and two shiny cars in the family garage.

Unfortunately for the purveyors of that image, many women eventually became restive with their restrictive role as wives and mothers and began to re-enter the workforce at an increasing rate. Unlike the situation before the war, many of the new job-seekers were married. In 1900, for example, married women made up about 15 percent of the

Escaping the Doll's House

 Do you agree that American women had fallen into a "housewife trap" in the years following World War II? Are Betty Friedan's arguments relevant to all American women, or just to women like her?

Family & Society **IN THE FAMOUS PLAY** *A Doll's House* by the Norwegian writer Henrik Ibsen, the fictional housewife Nora Helmer declares her independence from the drudgery of her life as a housewife, leaves her tradition-minded husband, and seeks to take control of her own life. Almost a century later, the author Betty Friedan pled for American women to follow Nora's lead in her 1963 bestseller *The Feminine Mystique*. The author, however, replaces the domineering husband in Ibsen's play with that of a repressive social trope which seeks to bind American womanhood with the shackles of the vision of the happy housewife. Although *The Feminine Mystique* was criticized by some as being irrelevant to the everyday lives of most American working women, it awakened many readers to the reality of their situation and encouraged them to embark on a new path of sexual freedom.

Betty Friedan, *The Feminine Mystique*

"In the fifteen years after World War II, this mystique of feminine fulfillment became the cherished and self-perpetuating core of contemporary American culture. Millions of women lived their lives in the image of those pretty pictures of the American suburban housewife, kissing their husbands goodbye in front of the picture window, depositing their stationwagonsful of children at school, and smiling as they ran the new electric waxer over the spotless kitchen floor. They baked their own bread, sewed their own and their children's clothes, kept their new washing machines and dryers running all day. They changed the sheets on the beds twice a week, instead of once, took the rug-hooking class in adult education, and pitied their poor frustrated mothers, who had dreamed of having a career. Their only dream was to be perfect wives and mothers; their highest ambition to have five children and a beautiful house, their only fight to get and keep their husbands. They had no thought for the unfeminine problems of the world outside the home; they wanted the men to make the major decisions. They gloried in their role as women, and wrote proudly on the census blank: "Occupation: housewife . . ."

The public image, in the magazines and television commercials, is designed to sell washing machines, cake mixes, deodorants, detergents, rejuvenating face creams, hair tints. But the power of that image, on which companies spend millions of dollars for television time and ad space, comes from this: American women no longer know who they are. They are sorely in need of a new image to help them find their identity. As the motivational researchers keep telling the advertisers, American women are so unsure of who they should be that they look to this glossy public image to decide every detail of their lives . . .

The feminine mystique has succeeded in burying millions of American women alive. There is no way for these women to break out of their comfortable concentration camps except by finally putting forth an effort—that human effort which reaches beyond biology, beyond the narrow walls of home, to help shape the future. Only by such a personal commitment to the future can American women break out of the housewife trap and truly find fulfillment as wives and mothers—by fulfilling their own unique possibilities as separate human beings."

Source: Betty Friedan, *The Feminine Mystique* (New York: Dell Publishers, 1963), pp.14, 64–65, and 325.

female labor force. By 1970, their number had increased to 62 percent of working women.

American women were still not receiving equal treatment in the workplace, however, and by the late 1960s, some began to assert their rights and speak as feminists (see Image 8.4). One of the leading advocates of women's rights in the United States was Betty Friedan (1921–2006). A journalist and the mother of three children, Friedan grew increasingly unhappy as she struggled to fulfill the traditional role of housewife and mother. In 1963, she published *The Feminine Mystique*, a book in which she argued that women were systematically being denied equality with men. *The Feminine Mystique* became a bestseller and transformed Friedan into a prominent spokeswoman for women's rights in the United States (see Historical Voices, "Escaping the Doll's House," above).

IMAGE 8.4 The Women's Liberation Movement. In the late 1960s, as women began once again to assert their rights, a revived women's liberation movement emerged. Feminists in the movement maintained that women themselves must alter the conditions of their lives. During this women's liberation rally, some women climbed the statue of Admiral Farragut in Washington, D.C., to exhibit their signs.

Betty Friedan's book hit the newsstands at a highly appropriate time, as many American women had begun to demand greater opportunities to engage in occupations in competition with their male counterparts. The movement quickly became entangled with the youth protest movement against bourgeois culture and the Vietnam War, while provoking strong criticism from advocates of traditional cultural norms throughout the country. The critical response did not halt the momentum unleashed by the feminist movement, however, and women by the millions began to leave their own private doll's house to seek a life beyond the home. In many respects, the decision was based on economic necessity as well as on a choice of life styles, as working families around the country found it increasingly difficult to finance their multiple needs on a single budget.

As women have become more actively involved in the economy, their role in education has increased dramatically as well. Beginning in the 1980s, women's studies programs began to proliferate on college campuses throughout the United States. In recent years, considerably more than half of all students enrolled in institutions of higher learning have been women. The consequences are evident throughout society as a whole, as women are beginning to occupy senior positions in the legal profession, medicine, politics, journalism, and business. According to recent studies, in nearly 20 percent of U.S. households, the wife is the primary breadwinner.

Although women have steadily made gains in terms of achieving true equality in legal rights and economic opportunity in American society, much remains to be done. Efforts during the 1970s to revive the Equal Rights Amendment resulted in passage in both houses of Congress, but the issue has languished in the states. Movements to achieve equal pay for equal work have likewise had only modest success. In recent years, issues of sexism and of sexual assault have received heavy attention in the media. As the result of several cases involving charges against prominent individuals, the **Me Too movement** was formed to bring attention to the problem and bring perpetrators to justice. Passions unleashed by the campaign became embroiled in national politics and contributed to the election of an unprecedented number of women to Congress in 2018.

In recent years, much of the energy in the **women's liberation movement** has focused on maintaining the right to legalized abortion. In 1973, the U.S. Supreme Court's decision in *Roe v. Wade* established the legal right to abortion throughout the United States. That ruling, however, has come under attack from those who believe strongly that abortion is an act of murder against an unborn child, and the issue has remained an important and controversial factor in political campaigns.

The steady progress in the struggle for women's equality has encouraged other groups to seek to imitate that success. LGBTQ rights activists have long faced an uphill battle to achieve equal rights. As public attitudes have gradually evolved on the issue, same-sex marriage has increasingly been accepted in most parts of the country. LGBTQ rights achieved a major success when the Supreme Court ruled in *Obergefell v. Hodges* (2015) that state bans on same-sex marriage were unconstitutional. The struggle to achieve full civil rights for transgender individuals is ongoing.

8-2d The Environment

Historically, the American people have had an ambivalent attitude toward the environment. While paying lip service to the image of "America the Beautiful," in general

Americans have seen nature as an arena open to exploitation for economic purposes. President Theodore Roosevelt was perhaps the first prominent American politician to allude to the importance of conserving wilderness areas from economic exploitation. Known as the "conservation president," Roosevelt doubled the number of sites in the National Park System available for the common enjoyment of the American people. For the remainder of the first half of the twentieth century, however, the nation was preoccupied above all with serious problems at home and abroad and gave little heed to the dangers of environmental damage.

The challenge of preserving the environment first began to engage public opinion in the United States during the 1950s, when rising pollution levels in major cities such as Los Angeles, Chicago, and Pittsburgh, combined with the popularity of Rachel Carson's book *Silent Spring*, aroused concerns over the impact that unfettered industrialization was having on the quality of life and health of the American people. During the next several decades, federal, state, and local governments began to issue regulations directed at reducing smog in urban areas and improving the quality of rivers and streams throughout the country (see Historical Voices, "An Early Warning," p. 205).

In general, most Americans reacted favorably to such regulations, but by the 1980s, the environmental movement had engendered a backlash as some people complained that excessively radical measures could threaten the pace of economic growth and cause a loss of jobs. Around the same time, warnings began to appear from environmentalists about the growing dangers of **global warming**, a phenomenon resulting from the increasing levels of greenhouse gases spewing into the atmosphere from automobiles and factory chimneys around the world (see Chapter 16). In 2006, the documentary film *An Inconvenient Truth* appeared in movie theaters across the country. Produced by Albert Gore, Clinton's vice president and an unsuccessful candidate for the presidency in 2000, it sought to arouse public awareness of the severity of the current climate crisis.

In the presidential elections held two years later, Barack Obama made environmental issues a centerpiece of his campaign, but as the effects of the financial crisis of 2008 rippled through the economy, his administration felt compelled to put economic concerns at the front of the agenda. Some steps to stave off further environmental damage have been taken: government subsidies and tax breaks have assisted start-up companies producing wind and solar energy, and have helped such firms to reduce costs and make their products competitive on the market. A carbon tax to reduce gasoline consumption and punish notorious polluters, however, has been unpopular with the public and has not been promoted on a national basis. In the meantime, new technology has made it possible for energy companies to exploit shale oil deposits found in many parts of the United States. The rapid development of such technology has increased oil stocks in the United States and dramatically reduced the costs of liquid energy. Since liquid energy and coal-fired plants are the chief sources of carbon dioxide pollution in the United States, this has complicated the task of environmentalists to encourage the use of other, less polluting forms of energy.

Climate change, however, does not fluctuate according to the vicissitudes of American politics, and the evidence continues to accumulate that global warming is not simply a theory, as some have maintained, but a looming reality with the capacity to do enormous damage, not only to the United States, but to the entire planet. While the most visible danger appears in a general rise in sea level, which could inundate coastal regions along the eastern and Gulf coasts of the United States, the potential for more frequent and more extreme weather events and the threat of widespread drought conditions would threaten all parts of the country (see Image 8.5).

Although the vast majority of climatologists are in substantial agreement that the statistical rise in global

William J. Duiker

IMAGE 8.5 Rising Seas: An Unavoidable By-product of Global Warming. Coastal flooding will be one of the major consequences of global warming, as melting ice caps and thermal expansion of the world's oceans will cause a significant rise in sea levels in coming years. Human action is often partly responsible for exacerbating the problem, as more and more Americans build vacation homes along the nation's most vulnerable seashores. Shown here, vacation homes built right at the ocean's edge on the Outer Banks of North Carolina weaken vital sand dunes and suffer the consequences during Hurricane Sandy, which swept up the east coast of the United States in 2012.

 What do you think is the best way to prevent massive property damage caused by the frequent hurricanes that strike the coast of the United States?

An Early Warning

 What types of dangerous chemicals do you think are present in the food we eat today? How should the nation seek to shield Americans from such dangers?

Earth & Environment

THE WRITER RACHEL CARSON (1907–1964) was one of America's first environmentalists. At a time when the danger of global warming was not even on the horizon, she sounded an early alarm about the unforeseen environmental consequences of one particular form of human behavior. In her best-selling book entitled *Silent Spring,* published in 1962, she alerted her fellow Americans to the serious environmental and human consequences stemming from the rampant use of chemical pesticides, which were widely used at the time to protect crops from insect damage. Such products, she warned, not only polluted the air, the soil, and the rivers, they also killed off much of the nation's wildlife, including such iconic birds as the American Eagle. Even more dangerous, she wrote, poisons from such products could even be found as carcinogens in food, and thus could be deadly for humans. The most lethal of these chemicals was DDT, a highly effective pesticide which—in large part due to her warnings—was finally banned from use in 1972 by the Environmental Protection Agency (EPA). Tragically, Rachel Carson died of cancer two years later. Fortunately, many of her warnings were heeded, and much of the bird life has returned to our skies. Today, many environmentalists continue to follow her lead as they battle powerful chemical companies over the use of genetically modified organisms (GMOs), widely used in the food industry.

Rachel Carson, *Silent Spring* (1962)

The most alarming of all man's assaults upon the environment is the contamination of air, earth, rivers, and sea with dangerous and even lethal materials. This pollution is for the most part irrecoverable; the chain of evil it initiates not only in the world that must support life but in living tissues is for the most part irreversible. In this now universal contamination of the environment, chemicals are the sinister and little-recognized partners of radiation in changing the very nature of the world—the very nature of its life . . . Chemicals sprayed on croplands or forests or gardens lie long in soil, entering into living organisms, passing from one to another in a chain of poisoning and death. Or they pass mysteriously by underground streams until they emerge and, through the alchemy of air and sunlight, combine into new forms that kill vegetation, sicken cattle, and work unknown harm on those who drink from impure wells.

One of the most sinister features of DDT and related chemicals is the way they are passed on from one organism to another through all the links of the food chain. For example, fields of alfalfa are dusted with DDT; meal is later prepared from the alfalfa and fed to hens; the hens lay eggs which contain DDT. Or the hay, containing residues of 7 to 8 parts per million, may be fed to cows. The DDT will turn up in the milk in the amount of about 3 parts per million, but in butter made from this milk the concentration may run to 65 parts per million. Through such a process of transfer, what started out as a very small amount of DDT may end as a heavy concentration. Farmers nowadays find it difficult to obtain uncontaminated fodder for their milk cows . . .

The poison may also be passed on from mother to offspring. Insecticide residues have been recovered from human milk in samples tested by Food and Drug Administration scientists. This means that the breast-fed human infant is receiving small but regular additions to the load of toxic chemicals building up in his body. It is by no means his first exposure, however: there is good reason to believe this begins while he is still in the womb . . .

It would be unrealistic to suppose that all chemical carcinogens can or will be eliminated from the modern world. But a very large proportion are by no means necessities of life. By their elimination the total load of carcinogens would be enormously lightened, and the threat that one in every four will develop cancer would at least be greatly mitigated. The most determined effort should be made to eliminate those carcinogens that now contaminate our food, our water supplies, and our atmosphere, because these provide the most dangerous type of contact—minute exposures, repeated over and over throughout the years . . .

Source: *Silent Spring* (Boston: Houghton Mifflin, 1962. Fortieth Anniversary Edition), pp. 6, 22–23, 242.

temperatures is at least partly due to human activity, the debate over the issue in the United States has become embroiled in national and local politics, and a minority of Americans remain convinced that the issue is actually a scam promoted by people with ulterior motives. Such skepticism is encouraged by politicians and other individuals and groups who have their own interests at heart. If that continues to be the case, the sense of national urgency that many feel is necessary to cope with the problem will be hard to generate, and nature itself will have to provide the answer.

8-2e Science and Technology

After World War II, the United States emerged as the leading nation in promoting the development of science and technology. Taking advantage of wartime advances in aircraft, weaponry, and electronics, the federal government took the lead in supporting large-scale projects composed of teams of scientists working in ever-larger laboratories, many of them located on university campuses. By 1965 almost 75 percent of all scientific research funds came from the government. Much of this expense was funded by or for the national defense establishment. One of every four scientists and engineers trained in the decades after World War II was engaged in the creation of new weapons systems.

There was no more stunning example of how the new scientific establishment operated than the space race of the 1960s. In 1957, the Soviet Union announced that it had sent the first space satellite, *Sputnik I,* into orbit around the Earth. In response, the United States launched a gigantic project to land a manned spacecraft on the moon within a decade. Massive government funding financed the scientific research and technological advances that attained this goal in 1969.

The postwar alliance of science and technology led to an accelerated rate of technological change that became a fact of life throughout Western society. The emergence of the computer, in particular, has revolutionized American business practices and transformed the way individuals go about their lives and communicate with each other. Although early computers, which required thousands of vacuum tubes to function, were quite large, the development of the transistor and the silicon chip enabled manufacturers to reduce the size of their products dramatically. In 1975, entrepreneur Bill Gates formed Microsoft, promising to put "a computer on every desk." Steve Jobs followed with his competitor Apple a year later.

Bill Gates knew what he was talking about. By the 1990s, the personal computer had become a fixture in businesses, schools, and homes around the country. The Internet— the world's largest computer network—provides millions of people around the world with quick access to immense quantities of information as well as rapid communication and commercial transactions. Major online business corporations like Amazon are revolutionizing the way Americans purchase goods by marketing them on the Internet, rather than through stores and supermarkets. The United States was initially at the forefront of this process, but in recent years, innovation has become a global phenomenon, and U.S. hegemony in the development of computers is being challenged, particularly in Europe and with the rise of its new economic rival China.

Science is also being harnessed to serve other social purposes, including the development of biologically engineered food products, the formulation of new medicines to fight age-old diseases, and the development of alternative fuels to replace oil and the internal combustion engine. Recent interest has focused on the invention of new automobile engines that—like the hybrid models now entering the market—rely on some combination of electrical power and liquid energy. To encourage this process, the Obama administration set higher energy consumption standards for vehicles produced in the United States in future years. The transition from automobiles propelled by internal combustion to vehicles powered entirely by electricity is apparently years away.

The current technological revolution has undoubtedly helped to maintain the healthy growth and functioning of American society, and it has certainly been a key factor in enabling the United States to remain at the forefront among the most advanced nations in the world today. But, as was the case with the Industrial Revolution two centuries ago, success has had mixed blessings. In many sectors of the economy, the new technology is useful precisely because it is cost-effective and replaces human labor. The result can be good for management, since it reduces labor costs and enables them to market their products in an increasingly competitive global marketplace. But it can be bad for the employee who has lost his job or suffered a reduced paycheck, and also for the economy as a whole, since it cuts consumer demand and forces U.S. corporations to look abroad for markets for their goods.

8-3 THE WORLD OF CULTURE

 Focus Question: How have cultural developments reflected the changes taking place in other sectors of U.S. society?

The changing character of American society is vividly reflected in the world of culture, where the postwar era brought forth a new popular culture increasingly oriented toward the interests of young people.

8-3a Art and Architecture

After World War II, the American art world began to experiment with a variety of styles to express reality in new ways. One group of young artists, known as **Abstract Expressionists**, painted large nonrepresentational canvases in an effort to express a spiritual essence beyond the material world. Among the first was Jackson Pollock (1912–1956), who developed the technique of dripping and flinging paint onto a canvas laid on the floor. Pollock's large paintings of swirling colors express the energy of primal forces as well as the vast landscapes of his native Wyoming.

Other artists, concerned that art was being overwhelmed by popular culture, sought to make painting more accessible to the public by portraying aspects of everyday life on canvases. The most famous practitioner of **Pop Art**, as it was called, was Andy Warhol (1930–1987), whose works featured repetitious images of daily items such as soup cans, or even faces of such well-known figures as the *Mona Lisa* and Marilyn Monroe. Another influential figure was Robert Rauschenberg (1925–2008), whose "collages" juxtaposed disparate images and everyday objects—photographs, clothing, letters, even cigarette butts—to reflect the energy and disorder of the world around us.

By the early 1970s, **Postmodernism** became the new vehicle of revolt. Convinced that art should serve society by addressing social inequities relating to race, gender, or sexual orientation, some artists began to experiment with a new technique called **conceptual art**. Using innovative techniques such as photography, video, and even "installations" (machine- or human-made objects, sometimes as large as a room), such artists produced shocking works with the intent of motivating the viewer to political action. A powerful example was the untitled installation by Robert Gober (b. 1954): in its center, a stereotypical statue of the Virgin Mary stands over an open drain while a steel pipe pierces her body. Such a violent violation of the Madonna can be viewed by Christians as depicting the resilience of faith in a world of doubt. For non-Christians, Gober's work represents the indomitable spirit of humanity, which remains intact despite a century of adversity.

In architecture as well, the postwar era has been marked by experimentation and diversity. Tiring of the repetition and impersonality of the international style, innovative American architects have created their own Postmodern skyline, with pyramidal and cupola-topped skyscrapers of blue-green glass and brick, while others have returned to the past by incorporating traditional materials, shapes, and decorative elements into their buildings. Modernist rectangular malls have tacked on Greek columns and entryways shaped like ancient Egyptian pyramids.

8-3b New Concepts in Music

Musical composers also experimented with radically new concepts. One innovator was John Cage (1912–1992), who defined music as the "organization of sound" and included all types of noise in his music. Any unconventional sound was welcomed: electronic buzzers and whines, tape recordings played at altered speeds, or percussion from any household item. His most discussed work, called *4'33"*, was four minutes and thirty-three seconds of silence—the "music" being the sounds the audience heard in the hall during the "performance," such as coughing, the rustling of programs, the hum of air conditioning, and the shuffling of feet.

In the 1960s, **minimalism** took hold in the United States. Largely influenced by Indian music, minimalist composers such as Philip Glass (b. 1937) focus on the subtle nuances in the continuous repetitions of a melodic or rhythmic pattern. Since the 1960s, there has also been much experimental electronic and computer music. Despite the excitement of such musical exploration, however, much of it is considered too cerebral and alien, even by the educated public.

One of the most accomplished and accessible contemporary American composers, John Adams (b. 1947), has labeled much of twentieth-century experimental composition as the "fussy, difficult music of transition." His music blends Modernist elements with classical traditions using much minimalist repetition interspersed with dynamic rhythms. Critics have applauded his operas *Nixon in China* (1987) and *Doctor Atomic* (2005), which dramatizes the anxious countdown to the detonation of the first atomic bomb in New Mexico in 1945.

8-3c New Trends in Literature

Fictional writing in the 1960s reflected growing concerns about the materialism and superficiality of American culture and often took the form of exuberant and comic verbal fantasies. As the pain of the Vietnam War and the ensuing social and political turmoil intensified, authors turned to satire, using black humor and cruelty in the hope of shocking the American public into a recognition of its social ills. Many of these novels—such as Thomas Pynchon's *V.* (1963), Joseph Heller's *Catch-22* (1961), and John Barth's *Sot-Weed Factor* (1960)—were wildly imaginative, highly entertaining, and very different from the writing of the first half of the century, which had detailed the "real" daily lives of small-town or big-city America.

In the 1970s and 1980s, American fiction relinquished the extravagant verbal displays of the 1960s, returning to a more sober exposition of social problems, this time related to race, gender, and sexual orientation. Much of the best fiction explored the moral dimensions of contemporary life from Jewish, African American, feminist, or LGBTQ perspectives. Bernard Malamud (1914–1986), Saul Bellow (1915–2005), and Philip Roth (1933–2018) presented the Jewish American experience, while Ralph Ellison (1914–1994), James Baldwin (1924–1987), and Toni Morrison (1931–2019) dramatized the African American struggle.

Some outstanding women's fiction was written by foreign-born writers from Asia and Latin America, who examined the problems of immigrants, such as cultural identity and assimilation into the American mainstream.

8-3d Popular Culture

Since World War II, the United States has been the most influential force in shaping popular culture in the West and, to a lesser degree, throughout the world. Motion pictures were the primary vehicle for the diffusion of American popular culture in the years immediately following World War II and continued to dominate both European and American markets in the next decades. Although developed in the 1930s, television did not become readily available until the late 1940s. By 1954, there were 32 million sets in the United States as television became the centerpiece of middle-class life. In the 1960s, as television spread around the world, American networks unloaded their products on Europe and developing countries at extraordinarily low prices. Only the establishment of quota systems prevented American television from completely inundating these countries.

The United States has also dominated popular music since the end of World War II. Jazz, blues, rhythm and blues, rock, rap, and hip-hop have been the most popular music forms in the Western world—and much of the non-Western world—during this time. Artists like the late Elvis Presley and Madonna, and all the way up to Beyoncé and Jay Z have become global superstars in the entertainment world. All of these music forms originated in the United States and are rooted in African American musical innovations. These forms later spread to the rest of the world, inspiring local artists, who then transformed the music in their own way.

In the postwar years, sports became a major product of both popular culture and the leisure industry in the United States. The emergence of professional football and basketball leagues, as well as the increasing popularity of their college equivalents, helped to transform sports into something akin to a national obsession. Sports became a cheap form of entertainment for consumers, as fans did not have to leave their homes to enjoy athletic competitions. In fact, some sports organizations initially resisted television, fearing that it would hurt ticket sales. The tremendous revenues possible from television contracts overcame this hesitation, however. As sports television revenue has escalated, many sports have come to receive the bulk of their yearly revenue from broadcasting contracts. Today, sports have become a major force in American society, and individual sports teams—whether amateur or professional—attract the fervent allegiance of millions of devoted supporters.

8-4 CANADA: IN THE SHADOW OF GOLIATH

 Focus Question: To what degree has the recent history of Canada resembled or contrasted with that of its close neighbor the United States?

In many respects, Canada has paralleled the path of the United States in the postwar years. For twenty-five years after World War II, Canada realized extraordinary economic prosperity as it set out on a new path of industrial development. Canada had always had a strong export economy based on its abundant natural resources. Now it also developed electronic, aircraft, nuclear, and chemical engineering industries on a large scale. Some of the Canadian growth, however, was financed by capital from the United States, which resulted in U.S. ownership of many Canadian businesses. While many Canadians welcomed the economic benefits, others feared U.S. economic domination of Canada and its resources.

Canada's close relationship with the United States has been a notable feature of its postwar history. On the other hand, fear of economic domination was joined with worry about playing a subordinate role politically and militarily to its neighboring superpower. Canada agreed to join the North Atlantic Treaty Organization in 1949 and sent military contingents to fight in Korea the following year. But to avoid subordination to the United States or any other great power, Canada has more consistently and actively supported the United Nations and has tended to prefer political to military action as a solution to international problems. Nevertheless, such concerns have not kept Canada from maintaining a special relationship with its southern neighbor. The North American Air Defense Command (NORAD), formed in 1957, was based on close cooperation between the air forces of the two countries for the defense of North America against aerial attack. As another example of their close cooperation, in 1972, Canada and the United States signed the Great Lakes Water Quality Agreement to regulate water quality of the lakes that border both countries.

In general, Canadian politics follows the American pattern, with Liberals and Conservatives alternating periods in office. After 1945, the Liberal Party dominated Canadian politics until 1957, when John Diefenbaker (1895–1979) achieved a Conservative victory. But a major recession returned the Liberals to power, and they created Canada's welfare state by enacting a national social security system (the Canada Pension Plan) and a national health insurance program.

The most prominent Liberal government, however, was that of Pierre Trudeau (1919–2000), who was elected in 1968. Although French Canadian in background, Trudeau was dedicated to Canada's federal union. In 1968, his government passed the Official Languages Act, creating a bilingual federal civil service and encouraging the growth of French culture and language in Canada. In the end, Trudeau's efforts to impose the will of the federal government on the powerful provincial governments alienated voters and led the Liberals to defeat.

For Canada, the vigor of the U.S. economy in the 1980s and 1990s was a mixed blessing, for the American behemoth was all too often inclined to make use of its power to have its way with its neighbors. Economic recession had brought the Conservative Party to power in Canada in 1984, but its decision to privatize many of Canada's state-run corporations and sign a free trade agreement with the United States led to a defeat in national elections in 1993. The Liberals took over with the charge of stimulating the nation's sluggish economy.

The new Liberal government was soon faced with a festering crisis over the French-speaking province of Quebec, where prominent politicians sought to bring about the region's secession from the Canadian confederation (see Map 8.1). In 1976, the Parti Québécois won Quebec's provincial elections and called for a referendum that would enable the provincial government to negotiate Quebec's independence from the rest of Canada. But voters in Quebec rejected the plan in 1995, and debate over Quebec's status continued to divide Canada as the decade came to a close. Provincial elections held in April 2003 delivered a stunning defeat to the Parti Québécois, and the issue declined as a factor in Canadian politics.

In the new century, the game of musical chairs continued. The ruling Liberal Party became plagued by scandals, and in 2006, national elections brought the Conservatives, under new prime minister Stephen Harper (b. 1959), to power in Ottawa. The new

government sought to pursue a policy of limited government and lower tax rates, but such moves resulted in a dramatic increase in the national debt, and in 2015, the Liberals were returned to power under Justin Trudeau (b. 1970), the son of the famous politician Pierre Trudeau. The new prime minister, exhibiting the same form of youthful vigor as his namesake, promised to restore a sense of public morality, to help the poor, and to pursue policies aimed at improving conditions of the indigenous population, many of whom continue to live in impoverished conditions.

8-4a Society and Culture: The Canadian Difference

Canada's many similarities and differences with the United States provide the observer with an instructive means of comparing the distinctive approaches that the two countries have adopted in building modern nations. In both cases, when European migrants first began to arrive in North America, it had already been occupied for millennia by indigenous peoples. Both initially mistreated the native peoples in various ways, exploiting them, sometimes butchering them, or confining them in isolated parts of the country. Eventually, the Canadian government, like the United States, embarked on a program to resettle the indigenous peoples into reserves, and today most of them live in separate Nations, each with its own ethnicity, language, and culture.

As was the case in the United States, the early arrivals from Europe came from a number of separate European countries, but the vast majority of them came from France or the British Isles. Historically, those claiming French extraction tended to settle in the province of Quebec, and have determinedly retained their linguistic and cultural uniqueness by resisting assimilation into the larger English-speaking population. This reality has complicated the challenge for Canada to create a single nation with a unified language and culture, as we have seen above, although in recent years the issue seems to have declined in importance. Meanwhile, English-speaking Canadians living in the western provinces of the country developed their own frontier culture similar in some respects to that in parts of the western United States. Many of them continue to resent Canadian politicians from the more urbanized eastern provinces, who are suspected of seeking to dominate national politics while exploiting the remainder of the country for its natural resources.

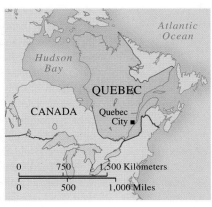

MAP 8.1 Quebec

In general, Canada has exhibited less of the anti-immigrant sentiment that has sometimes prevailed in the United States, a reality that may reflect the fact that Canada has not been exposed to massive immigration—some of it illegal—over its southern border. With its wide-open spaces, the country seems to welcome refugees, although its immigration policy has focused on accepting applicants who possess educational or job skills that are considered important for promoting economic development. The Canadian government is also committed to redistributing sufficient national resources to poorer regions of the country to assist them in providing the necessary services to the local population.

Whatever the reasons, Canada has earned a world-wide reputation for moderation and public concern for the welfare of its citizens that sometimes contrasts with the more laissez-faire policies prevalent in the United States. The Canadian healthcare system is broadly respected for its affordability and its fairness, while social issues like abortion and same-sex marriage have been managed without the acrimony that has often prevailed in the United States. As a result, while Canada is by no means the perfect society, it has earned its reputation as an example of a democracy that works.

MAP 8.2 South America

8-5 DEMOCRACY, DICTATORSHIP, AND DEVELOPMENT IN LATIN AMERICA SINCE 1945

 Focus Question: In what ways have the nations of Latin American sought to rid themselves of the dependency relationship with Europe and the United States which had developed in the late nineteenth century?

The Great Depression of the 1930s caused political instability in many Latin American countries (see Chapter 5), but it also helped transform Latin America from a traditional to a modern economy. Since the nineteenth century, Latin Americans had exported raw materials while buying the manufactured goods of industrialized countries. As a result of the Great Depression, however, export markets virtually vanished, and the revenues available to buy manufactured goods declined. In response, many Latin American countries encouraged the development of new industries to produce goods that were formerly imported. Due to a shortage of capital in the private sector, governments often invested in the new industries, thereby leading, for example, to government-run steel industries in Chile and Brazil and petroleum industries in Argentina and Mexico (see Map 8.2).

8-5a An Era of Dependency

In the 1960s, however, most Latin American countries were still dependent upon the United States, Europe, and Japan for the advanced technology needed for modern industries. To make matters worse, widespread poverty in some countries in Central America and in the Andes limited the size of domestic markets, and many were unable to find markets abroad for their products.

These failures resulted in takeovers by military regimes that sought to curb the demands of the new industrial middle class and the working class that had increased in size and power as a result of industrialization. In the 1960s, repressive military regimes in Chile, Brazil, and Argentina abolished political parties and turned to export-import economies financed by foreigners, while encouraging multinational corporations to invest in local economies. Because these companies were primarily interested in taking advantage of Latin America's raw materials and its abundant supply of cheap labor, their presence often offered little benefit to the local economy and contributed to the region's dependence on the industrially developed nations.

In the 1970s, Latin American regimes grew even more reliant on borrowing from abroad, especially from banks in Europe and the United States. Between 1970 and 1982, debt to foreigners increased from $27 billion to $315.3 billion. By 1982, a number of governments announced that they could no longer pay interest on their debts to foreign banks, and their economies began to crumble. Wages fell, and unemployment skyrocketed. Governments were forced to undertake fundamental reforms to qualify for additional loans, reducing the size of the state sector and improving agricultural production in order to stem the flow of people from the countryside to the cities and strengthen the domestic market for Latin American products. In many cases, these reforms were launched by democratic governments that began to replace the discredited military regimes during the 1980s.

In the 1990s, the opening of markets to free trade and other consequences of the globalization process began to have a growing impact on Latin American economies. As some countries faced the danger of bankruptcy, belt-tightening measures undertaken to reassure foreign investors provoked social protests and threatened to undermine the precarious political stability in the region.

An era of growing political and economic stability that began in the early years of the new century enabled many Latin American states to strengthen democratic institutions and build viable economies. While the tradition that Latin America was the home of the "strong man" was not entirely overcome, a number of countries managed to inaugurate a new era marked by elected governments and non-violent transitions of power. Some South American states—including Argentina, Chile, Brazil, and Paraguay—even elected female presidents. The underlying reasons for this visible strengthening of democratic institutions and practices varied, but strict adherence to term limits, strong watchdog organizations, and an independent judicial system all contributed to the trend.

For the most part, as well, Latin American societies continued to adhere to the tradition of functioning capitalist economies. After the world began to recover from the financial crisis of 2008 (see above), many benefitted from rising global prices for their natural resources or agricultural goods. The emergence of China as an economic powerhouse, in particular, was a significant factor in stimulating economic growth in the region, as its purchases boosted the price of such goods in the global marketplace; Chinese financial investments in local projects like copper mines, fisheries, and port facilities also helped Latin American nations improve their infrastructure base. On the other hand, China's growing involvement in regional trade patterns had a serious downside, since its cheap labor costs undercut efforts by Latin American countries to export their manufactured goods, thus locking them into the disadvantageous position as suppliers of basic commodities to advanced industrial economies elsewhere. As economic growth in China has declined significantly in recent years (see Chapter 10), the effects have been felt in several Latin American countries and placed a strain on their political stability and their capacity to serve the needs of their populations.

Not all political parties in Latin America opted to adopt the capitalist model. In some countries, resentment at economic and social inequities led to the emergence of strong leftist movements or even to social revolution. The most prominent example was Cuba, where in the late 1950s Fidel Castro established a regime based loosely on the Soviet model. Eventually, other revolutionary movements flourished or even came to power in Chile, Uruguay, and parts of Central America as well (see "8-5d The Leftist Variant").

The Role of the Catholic Church The Catholic Church has historically played a significant role in the process of social and political change. A powerful force in Latin America for centuries, the church often applied its prestige on the side of the landed elites, helping them maintain their grip on power. Eventually, however, the church adopted a middle stance in Latin American society, advocating a moderate capitalist system that would respect workers' rights, institute land reform, and provide for the poor. Some Catholics, however, took a more radical path to change by advocating a theology of liberation. Influenced by Marxist ideas, advocates of **liberation theology** believed that Christians must fight to free the oppressed, using violence if necessary. Some Catholic clergy recommended armed rebellions and even teamed up with Marxist guerrillas in rural areas. Other radical priests worked in factories alongside workers or carried on social work among the poor in the slums.

In recent years, the Catholic Church in Latin America has encountered a new challenge in the growth of evangelical Protestant sects. Whereas an estimated 90 percent of the population of the region were traditionally Roman Catholics, today the percentage has declined to under 70 percent. Protestant churches have made significant inroads throughout much of South America and now own the allegiance of almost 20 percent of the population of the continent (see Comparative Illustration, "Shifting Patterns of Religious Belief in Latin America," p. 212). There appear to be several reasons for this shift in allegiance. In some countries like Brazil, one factor advanced for the rising popularity of these sects is the Vatican's stand on issues such as divorce and abortion. In a recent survey, the vast majority of Brazilian Catholics supported the right to abortion in cases of rape or danger to the mother and believed in the use of birth control to limit population growth and achieve smaller families. Many others are concerned over the refusal of the Catholic Church to allow female priests, or to permit male clergy to engage in marriage.

The Behemoth to the North Throughout the postwar era, the United States has cast a large shadow over Latin America. In 1948, the nations of the region formed the Organization of American States (OAS), which was intended to eliminate unilateral action by one state in the internal or external affairs of another state, while encouraging regional cooperation to maintain peace. It did not

Shifting Patterns of Religious Belief in Latin America

Q *How might a spokesperson for the Roman Catholic faith defend the Church against the charge that it does not adequately respond to the needs of its parishioners?*

Religion & Philosophy

IN RECENT YEARS, the historical allegiance of peoples of Latin America to Roman Catholicism has been tested by a variety of factors. Some have left the Church out of disagreement with its teachings; others because they felt it had failed to address adequately some of the social problems that

IMAGE 8.6b

William J. Duiker

IMAGE 8.6a

William J. Duiker

afflict the region. A growing number have joined recently introduced Evangelical faiths because they allegedly offer a greater opportunity for the individual to participate in a truly Christian lifestyle. Many of these new churches are located in small towns, where they compete with the established Catholic Church, such as the one shown in Image 8.6a from a small town in Mexico. But megachurches have also been established in some large cities to address the needs of the faithful, as is the case with the massive church shown in Image 8.6b, recently opened in the city of San Salvador, in Brazil.

end U.S. interference in Latin American affairs, however. The United States returned to a policy of unilateral action when it believed that Soviet agents were attempting to use local Communists or radical reformers to establish governments hostile to U.S. interests. In the 1960s, President Kennedy's Alliance for Progress encouraged social reform and economic development by providing private and public funds to elected governments whose reform programs were acceptable to the United States. But when Marxist-led insurrections began to spread throughout the region, the United States responded by providing massive military aid to anti-Communist regimes to forestall the possibility of a Soviet bastion in the Western Hemisphere.

The foremost example of U.S. interference occurred in Chile, where the Marxist Salvador Allende (1908–1973)

was elected president in 1970. When Allende's government began to nationalize foreign-owned corporations, General Augusto Pinochet (1916–2006), with covert U.S. support, launched a coup d'état, which resulted in the deaths of Allende and thousands of his followers. But Pinochet's flagrant abuse of power led to unrest and eventually, in 1989, to a return of civilian rule.

Since the 1990s, the United States has played an active role in persuading Latin American governments to open their economies to the international marketplace. Though globalization has had some success in promoting prosperity in the region, it has also led to economic dislocation and hardship in some countries, provoking familiar cries of "Yanqui imperialismo" from protest groups and the election in recent years of leftist governments in several countries in the region.

8-5b Nationalism and the Military: The Examples of Argentina and Brazil

The military became the power brokers of twentieth-century Latin America. Especially in the 1960s and 1970s, military leaders portrayed themselves as the guardians of national honor and orderly progress. In the mid-1970s, only Colombia, Mexico, Venezuela, and Costa Rica maintained democratic governments.

A decade later, pluralistic systems had been installed virtually everywhere except in Cuba, Paraguay, and some of the Central American states. The establishment of democratic institutions, however, has not managed to solve all the chronic problems that have plagued the states of Latin America. Official corruption continues in many countries, and the gap between rich and poor is growing, most notably in Brazil and in Venezuela, though leftist regimes in both countries have adopted policies designed to redistribute the wealth.

Argentina Until World War II, a landed oligarchy, composed of wheat and cattle interests and backed by conservative elements in the military, had dominated Argentine politics. But in 1943, some leading military officers grew restive and seized power on their own. When labor unrest broke out, the demagogic army colonel Juan Perón (1895–1974) publicly supported the workers and with their support was elected president in 1946.

Perón pursued a policy of increased industrialization to please his chief supporters—the urban middle class and the *descamisados,* or "shirtless ones," of the working class. At the same time, he sought to free Argentina from foreign investors. The government bought the railways; took over the banking, insurance, shipping, and communications industries; and assumed regulation of imports and exports. But Perón's regime was also authoritarian. His wife, Eva Perón (1919–1952), organized women's groups to support the government while Perón created fascist gangs, modeled after Hitler's Storm Troops, that used violence to intimidate his opponents. But growing corruption in the Perón government and the alienation of more and more people by the regime's excesses encouraged the military to overthrow him in September 1955. Perón went into exile in Spain.

It had been easy for the military to seize power, but they found it harder to rule, especially now that Argentina had a party of *Peronistas* clamoring for the return of the exiled leader. In the 1960s and 1970s, military and civilian governments (the latter closely watched by the military) alternated in power. When both failed to provide economic stability, military leaders decided to allow Juan Perón to return. Reelected president in September 1973, Perón died one year later. In 1976, the military installed a new regime, using the occasion to kill more than 6,000 leftists in what was called the "Dirty War." With economic problems still unsolved, the regime tried to divert popular attention by invading the Falkland Islands in April 1982. Great Britain, which had controlled the islands since the nineteenth century, decisively defeated the Argentine forces. The loss discredited the military and opened the door once again to civilian rule. In 1983, Raúl Alfonsín (1927–2009) was elected president and sought to reestablish democratic processes.

In 1989, however, Alfonsín was defeated in the presidential elections by the Peronist candidate, Carlos Saúl Menem (b. 1930). Initially, the charismatic Menem won broad popularity for his ability to control the army, but when he sought to rein in rampant inflation by curbing government spending, rising unemployment and an economic recession cut into his public acclaim. Plagued with low growth, rising emigration (a growing number of descendants of European settlers were returning to live in Europe), and shrinking markets abroad, the government defaulted on its debt to the International Monetary Fund (IMF) in 2001, initiating an era of political chaos. In May 2003 with the economy in paralysis, Néstor Kirchner (1950–2010) assumed the presidency and sought to revive public confidence. The new president took decisive steps to end the crisis, adopting measures to stimulate economic growth and promote exports. By 2005, the debt to the IMF had been fully paid off. Kirchner also encouraged measures to bring the military officers who had carried out the Dirty War of the 1970s to justice.

Néstor Kirchner's success in stabilizing the Argentine economy, which resulted in a 9 percent increase in the gross domestic product, was undoubtedly a factor in the presidential campaign in 2007, when his wife Cristina Fernández de Kirchner (b. 1953) was elected to succeed him in office. A populist by nature like her husband, the new president aligned herself with other leftist leaders in the region and sought popularity by financing public projects through deficit spending, but growing income inequality, rising inflation—always a threat to prosperity in Argentina—and an energy crisis tarnished the performance of the first female president in the country's history. In 2015, faced with charges of corruption, she was succeeded in office by the mayor of Buenos Aires, Mauricio Macri (b. 1959), who proceeded to govern at the head of a coalition of center-right parties.

Brazil After Getúlio Vargas was forced to resign from the presidency in 1945 (see Chapter 5), a second Brazilian republic came into being. In 1949, Vargas was reelected to the presidency. But he was unable to solve Brazil's economic problems, especially its soaring inflation, and in

1954, after the armed forces called on him to resign, Vargas committed suicide. Subsequent democratically elected presidents had no better success in controlling inflation while trying to push rapid industrialization. In the spring of 1964, the military decided to intervene and took over the government.

The armed forces remained in direct control of the country for twenty years, setting a new economic course by cutting back somewhat on state control of the economy and emphasizing market forces. The new policies seemed to work, and during the late 1960s, Brazil experienced an "economic miracle" as it moved into self-sustaining economic growth, generally the hallmark of a modern economy. Promoters also pointed to the country's success in turning a racially diverse population into a relatively colorblind society.

Rapid economic growth carried with it some potential drawbacks. The economic exploitation of the Amazon River basin opened the region to farming but in the view of some critics threatened the ecological balance not only of Brazil but of the Earth itself. Ordinary Brazilians hardly benefited as the gulf between rich and poor, always wide, grew even wider. At the same time, rapid development led to an annual inflation rate of 100 percent, and an enormous foreign debt added to the problems. Overwhelmed, the generals resigned from power and opened the door for a return to democracy in 1985.

In 1990, national elections brought a new president into office—Fernando Collor de Mello (b. 1949). The new administration promised to reduce inflation with a drastic reform program based on squeezing money out of the economy by stringent controls on wages and prices, drastic reductions in public spending, and cuts in the number of government employees. But Collor de Mello's efforts—reminiscent of Menem's in Argentina—were undermined by reports of official corruption, and he resigned at the end of 1992 after being impeached. In new elections two years later, Fernando Cardoso (b. 1931) was elected president by an overwhelming majority of the popular vote. Cardoso, a member of the Brazilian Social Democratic Party, introduced measures to privatize state-run industries and to reform social security and the pension system. He rode a wave of economic prosperity to reelection in 1998. But economic problems, combined with allegations of official corruption and rising factionalism within the ruling party, undermined his popularity, leading to the victory of the Brazil Workers' Party (BWP) in 2002.

The new president, Luiz Inácio Lula da Silva (b. 1945), a former lathe operator, was enormously popular among the country's working masses and had come to power on a promise to introduce antipoverty programs and reverse his predecessor's policy of privatizing major industries.

On taking office in 2003, however, Lula immediately cautioned his supporters that the party's ambitious plans could not be realized until urgent financial reforms had been enacted. That remark effectively summed up the challenge that the new administration faced: how to satisfy the pent-up demands of its traditional constituency—the millions of Brazilians still living in poverty—while dealing effectively with the realities of exercising power.

During the next few years, the Brazilian economy experienced dramatic growth in several areas: millions of acres of virgin lands were brought under cultivation in the interior, enabling the country to become a major exporter of agricultural products, including wheat, cotton, and soybeans. In late 2007, the government announced the discovery of significant underwater oil reserves off the southeastern coast of the country. Such successes led to growing prosperity for many Brazilian citizens, who took advantage of low interest rates to increase their purchases of automobiles, homes, and consumer goods. Ambitious social programs began to reduce the gap between wealth and poverty—always one of the most visible characteristics of Brazilian society—and it looked as if the country was finally going to overcome the sardonic description frequently applied to it over the years: "Brazil is the country of the future—and always will be." When Lula left office in 2010 after two terms as president, the country was poised to become a hemispheric superpower and had recently announced plans to organize a defensive alliance of Latin American countries similar to NATO.

Lula's protégée and chief of staff, the onetime radical activist Dilma Rousseff (b. 1947), was elected to succeed him as president in 2010 on the promise of building a new "Brazil without Misery." She embraced the antipoverty programs of her predecessor, attempting to clean up the slums—known as *favelas*—that surround every major city, and announced an affirmative action program to increase the percentage of citizens of color in public universities. But the country's recent history of rapid growth was undermined by the global recession, and Rousseff's plans to continue the successes of the Lula years gave way to the reality of a severe recession. In 2016 she was removed from office on the charge of seeking to conceal a budget deficit, and was replaced by an interim president. By then the reputation of the BWP had been tarnished by the rampant corruption and violence that plagued the country (the once-popular Lula was himself imprisoned for money-laundering), and in national elections held in the fall of 2018, victory went to a once-obscure politician named Jair Bolsanaro. The new president disdained the social programs that had been adopted by his predecessors and was openly dismissive of women, the LGBTQ community, and Brazilians of color. Still, Bolsanaro's promise to crack down on widespread crime corruption appealed to a nation weary of leaders who failed to live up to their promises.

8-5c The Mexican Way

During the 1950s and early 1960s, Mexico's ruling party, the Institutional Revolutionary Party (PRI), focused on industrial development. Steady economic growth combined with low inflation and real gains in wages for more and more people made those years appear to be a golden age in Mexico's economic development. But massive student protests in 1968, which turned violent and resulted in hundreds of casualties, were a clear sign of discontent beneath the surface. The protests persuaded PRI leaders to introduce political reforms. The government eased rules for the registration of political parties and allowed greater freedom of debate in the press and universities. But economic problems continued to trouble Mexico.

In the late 1970s, vast new reserves of oil were discovered in Mexico. As sales of oil abroad rose dramatically, the government became increasingly dependent on oil revenues. When world oil prices dropped in the mid-1980s, Mexico was no longer able to make the payments on its foreign debt, which had reached $80 billion in 1982. The government was forced to adopt new economic policies, including the sale of publicly owned companies to private parties.

During the 1990s, Mexican leaders continued the economic liberalization policies of the previous decade, and in 1994 President Carlos Salinas (b. 1948) negotiated the North American Free Trade Agreement (NAFTA) with the United States and Canada. But although NAFTA was highly controversial in the United States because of the fear that U.S. firms would move factories to Mexico, where labor costs are cheaper and environmental standards less stringent, many Mexicans felt that NAFTA was more beneficial to the U.S. economy than to its southern neighbor. An indication of Mexico's continuing economic problems was the rising popular unrest in southern parts of the country. Unhappy farmers, many of them native Amerindians, increasingly protested the endemic poverty and widespread neglect of the needs of the indigenous peoples, who comprise about 10 percent of Mexico's total population of 100 million people.

In 2000, a national election suddenly swept the ruling PRI from power. The new president, Vicente Fox (b. 1942), came to office with high expectations and promised to address the country's many problems, including political corruption, widespread poverty, environmental concerns, and a growing population. But he was hampered both by the PRI, which still controlled many state legislatures and held a plurality in Congress, and by the protest movement in rural areas in the south. Although the movement has since faded, it aroused such a groundswell of support from around the country that Fox found himself under considerable pressure to deal with generations of neglect in solving the problems of Mexico.

The conservative lawyer Felipe Calderón (b. 1962) took over from Fox in December 2006 in a presidential election disputed by his rival, Andrés Manuel López Obrador. With PRI support, Calderón sought to rule from the center, while adopting measures to alleviate poverty and bring about fiscal reform. But his efforts were undermined by the economic slowdown in the United States.

In elections in 2012, the PRI returned to power. The new president, Enrique Peña Nieto (b. 1966), was a charismatic figure who reminded some observers of John F. Kennedy, but he faced enormous challenges. Forty percent of Mexicans lived in poverty, and one in ten earned less than the equivalent of one U.S. dollar a day. At the same time, crime rates were soaring, despite the government's efforts to crack down on the country's powerful drug cartels. Nieto attempted to weaken the drug lords by making use of the Mexican army, but had little success, and his rival Manuel Obrador finally assumed the presidency on a promise to focus on economic development to reduce the problem. Obrador's challenge was heightened by uneasy relations with the United States and the steady flow of refugees from Central American heading toward the border with the United States.

8-5d The Leftist Variant

Most of the countries in Latin America have followed the path laid out by the three examples described above. Military dictatorships have been replaced by elected governments that, at least on paper, follow standard democratic principles. In many cases, though, the influence of traditional ruling elites remains strong, leading to significant levels of popular discontent. In some countries, this has resulted in the emergence of governments dominated by leftist parties influenced by the ideas of Karl Marx. The foremost examples are Cuba and Venezuela.

The Cuban Revolution   An authoritarian regime, headed by Fulgencio Batista (1901–1973) and closely tied economically to U.S. investors, had ruled Cuba since 1934. In the early 1950s, a guerrilla movement—led by Fidel Castro (b. 1926) assisted by Ernesto "Ché" Guevara (1928–1967), an Argentinian who believed that revolutionary upheaval was necessary for change to occur—emerged in the Sierra Maestra. As the rebels gradually gained support, Batista responded with such brutality that he alienated his own supporters. The dictator fled in December 1958, and Castro's revolutionaries seized Havana on January 1, 1959.

As the new regime moved to nationalize key elements of the Cuban economy, relations between Cuba and the United States quickly deteriorated. When the Soviet Union began to provide military and economic aid to Cuba, President Eisenhower directed the Central Intelligence Agency (CIA) to "organize the training of Cuban exiles, mainly in Guatemala, against a possible future day when they might return to their homeland."[3] In October 1960, the United States declared a trade embargo of Cuba, driving Castro closer to the Soviet Union.

On January 3, 1961, the United States broke diplomatic relations with Cuba. The new U.S. president, John F. Kennedy, approved a plan originally drafted by the previous administration to launch an invasion to overthrow Castro's government, but the landing of 1,400 CIA-assisted Cubans in Cuba at the Bay of Pigs on April 17, 1961, turned into a total military disaster. This fiasco encouraged the Soviets to make an even greater commitment to Cuban independence by attempting to place nuclear missiles in the country, an act that led to a showdown with the United States (see Chapter 7).

The missile crisis persuaded Castro that the Soviet Union was unreliable. If revolutionary Cuba was to be secure and no longer encircled by hostile states tied to U.S. interests, it would have to instigate social revolution in the rest of Latin America. He believed that once guerrilla wars were launched, peasants would flock to the movement and overthrow the old regimes. Guevara attempted to launch a guerrilla war in Bolivia but was caught and killed by the Bolivian army in the fall of 1967. The Cuban strategy had failed.

In Cuba, however, Castro's socialist revolution proceeded, with mixed results. The regime provided free medical services for all citizens, and a new law code expanded the rights of women. Illiteracy was wiped out by creating new schools and establishing teacher-training institutes that tripled the number of teachers within ten years. Eschewing the path of rapid industrialization, Castro encouraged agricultural diversification. But the Cuban economy continued to rely on the production and sale of sugar. Economic problems forced the Castro regime to depend on Soviet subsidies and the purchase of Cuban sugar by Soviet bloc countries (see Image 8.7).

The disintegration of the Soviet Union was a major blow to Cuba, as the new government in Moscow no longer had a reason to continue to subsidize the onetime Soviet ally. During the 1990s, Castro began to introduce limited market reforms and to allow the circulation of U.S. dollars. But most Cubans remain locked in poverty, and the system of political repression remained intact. The ageing symbol of the regime, Fidel Castro stayed in power until illness forced him to resign the presidency in 2008. The accession to the presidency of his more pragmatic younger brother, Raúl Castro (b. 1931), opened the door to negotiations with the United States, and in 2014 President Obama announced that the United States would begin normalizing their relationship by lifting the travel ban, opening Cuba to financial investment, and establishing a U.S. embassy in Havana. But with serious ideological differences between the two countries still in place, the relationship remains cool.

Venezuela: The New Cuba? With the discovery of oil in the small town of Cabímas in the early 1920s, Venezuela took its first step toward becoming a major exporter of oil and one of the wealthiest countries in Latin America. At first, profits from "black rain" accrued mainly to the nation's elite families, but in 1976 the oil industry was nationalized, and Venezuela entered an era of national prosperity. But when the price of oil on world markets dropped sharply in the 1980s, the country's economic honeymoon came to an end, and in 1989 President Carlos Andrés Pérez (1922–2010) launched an austerity program that cut deeply into the living standards of much of the population.

After popular demonstrations led to an army crackdown in 1992, restive military forces launched an abortive

IMAGE 8.7 Havana: A Museum for Classic Automobiles. After seizing power in 1959, the regime of Fidel Castro forbade the sale of automobiles in revolutionary Cuba, and even severely restricted imports from Soviet bloc nations. As a result, almost the only vehicles on the streets of Havana were vintage U.S. cars from the 1940s and 1950s, whose owners kept them running with rubber bands and bailing wire. In 2011, the regime suddenly reversed course and authorized the sale and purchase of vehicles. Cuban owners welcomed the decision, which opened up a lucrative market for antique automobiles among buyers in the United States and Europe.

coup to seize power. Five years later, one of the leading members of the plot—a paratroop commander named Hugo Chávez (1954–2013)—was elected president in national elections. Taking advantage of rising oil prices, Chávez launched an ambitious spending program to improve living conditions for the poor. Although such measures earned his regime broad national support, Chávez's efforts to silence critics and strengthen presidential powers—including a program to organize his supporters into "Bolivarian circles" (in honor of the nineteenth-century Venezuelan liberator Simón Bolívar) at the local level—displayed his all-too-evident dictatorial tendencies.

A longtime admirer of Fidel Castro, Chávez strengthened relations with Cuba and encouraged revolutionary movements throughout Latin America. After 2006, he acquired new allies with the election of leftist governments in Bolivia and Ecuador. As an outspoken opponent of "Yanqui imperialismo," he proposed resistance to U.S. proposals for a hemispheric free trade zone, charging that such an organization would operate only for the benefit of the United States. Until his death from cancer in 2013, by using his country's oil wealth as a means of promoting his political objectives, Chávez had replaced Fidel Castro as Washington's most dangerous adversary in Latin America. After Chávez's death, his vice president Nicolás Maduro (b. 1962) was elected president and vowed to continue his predecessor's policies.

But Maduro had the misfortune to inherit leadership in Caracas at a time when global oil prices had begun to drop precipitately. As the country's revenues from oil exports plunged, Maduro refused to cut back on social programs, or on oil subsidies to like-minded countries like Cuba, and the Venezuelan economy suffered the consequences. As internal criticism of the regime escalated, Maduro cracked down on his political opponents, rigged elections, and blamed the United States for the country's difficulties. In early 2019, an opposition leader, the head of the National Assembly Juan Guaidó, claimed to be the only legitimate leader of the country. His claim was supported by the United States and many of Venezuela's neighbors, who were faced with high levels of refugees fleeing across their borders. Russia—always happy to dally with enemies of the United States—has rushed to the support of the beleaguered Maduro, and the situation was at a standoff at the time of this writing.

8-5e Trends in Latin American Culture

Postwar literature in Latin America has been vibrant. Writers such as Jorge Luis Borges (1899–1986), Carlos Fuentes (1928–2012), and Nobel Prize winners Mario Vargas Llosa (b. 1936) and Gabriel García Márquez (1927–2014) are among the most respected literary names of the last half century. These authors often use dazzling language and daring narrative experimentation to make their point. Gabriel García Márquez from Colombia is a master of this style. In *One Hundred Years of Solitude* (1967), he explores the transformation of a small town under the impact of political violence, industrialization, and the arrival of a U.S. banana company. Especially noteworthy is his use of magical realism; the outrageous events that assail the town are related in a matter-of-fact voice, thus transforming the fantastic into the commonplace.

Unlike novelists in the United States and Western Europe, who tend to focus their attention on the interior landscape within the modern personality in an industrial society, fiction writers in Latin America, like their counterparts in Africa and much of Asia, have sought to project an underlying political message. In his epic *The War of the End of the World,* the Peruvian Mario Vargas Llosa condemns the fanaticism and the inhumanity of war. In his novel *The Feast of the Goat* (2001), he expresses his moral outrage at the cruel dictatorship of Fulgencio Trujillo in the Dominican Republic. Others, like Vargas Llosa's countryman, José Maria Arguedas (1911–1969), have championed the cause of the Amerindians and lauded the diversity that marks the ethnic mix throughout the continent. Some have run for high political office as a means of remedying social problems. Some have been women, reflecting the rising demand for sexual equality in a society traditionally marked by male domination. The memorable phrase of the Chilean poet Gabriela Mistral (1889–1957)—"I have chewed stones with woman's gums"—encapsulates the plight of Latin American women.

A powerful example of Postmodern art in Latin America is found in the haunting work of the Colombian sculptor Doris Salcedo (b. 1958). Her art evokes disturbing images of her country's endless civil war and violent drug trade. Salcedo often presents everyday wooden furniture, to which she has applied a thin layer of cement and fragments of personal mementos from the owner's past life: a remnant of lace curtain, a lock of hair, or a handkerchief. Frozen in time, these everyday souvenirs evoke the pain of those who were dragged from their homes in the middle of the night and senselessly murdered. Salcedo's work can be experienced as an impassioned plea to stop the killing of innocent civilians or as the fossilized artifact from some future archaeologist's dig, showing traces of our brief and absurd sojourn on Earth.

MAKING CONNECTIONS

During the second half of the twentieth century, the United States emerged as the preeminent power in the world, dominant in its economic and technological achievements as well as in its military hardware. Although the Soviet Union was a serious competitor in the arms race engendered by the Cold War, its economic achievements paled in comparison with those of the U.S. behemoth.

The engine that drove this juggernaut is a phenomenon that we know as democratic capitalism. And the mechanism that enables the engine of democratic capitalism to function effectively is a symbiotic relationship between the concepts of Liberty and Equality. Too much emphasis on Equality and the freedom to create is stifled, to the detriment of all. But Liberty without restraint allows inequities in the system to proliferate, thus preventing the benefits of the system from permeating all the functioning parts of the mechanism.

The worldwide dominance of the United States was a product of a combination of factors, including the bounty of nature and the good fortune to be protected from disruptive forces by miles and miles of shining sea. Still, the historical capacity of the American system of government to forge an equitable balance between the forces of Liberty and Equality has been one of the nation's foremost keys to success. As we have seen above, that balance is often an uneasy one, as the American political culture has displayed a tendency to swing like a pendulum from one side to the other, while never dwelling for long at either extreme. The sweet spot tends to appear when the pendulum swing is passing through the middle, at a point where Liberty and Equality operate in tandem to the mutual benefit of the population as a whole.

The steady growth of the U.S. economy, while showing periodic signs of slowing in its maturity, has continued well into the new millennium. But recently there have been some warning signs that bear watching: an increasing gap in the distribution of wealth that could ultimately threaten the steady growth in consumer spending; an educational system that all too often fails to produce graduates with either a strong commitment to civic responsibility or the skills needed to master the challenges of a technology-driven economy; and an increasingly dysfunctional political system that increasingly undermines the ability of the government to provide services to a nation of more than 300 million people. By these measurements, the American system of government is in trouble.

Over the course of modern history, the fortunes of Canada and the nations of Latin America have been tied, in many respects, to those of the United States. Still, they have all displayed their own distinctive characteristics. The Canadian political system bears considerable resemblance to that of the United States, including the character of its two major political parties, but the presence of a significant French-speaking minority concentrated in one particular province of the country has complicated efforts to create a nation embodying a single set of cultural symbols. For their part, the countries of Latin America differ substantially from their northern neighbors in terms of both economic performance and political culture—undoubtedly a consequence of their Hispanic heritage. Still, in the last two decades several nations in the region have shown signs of emerging from the shadow of the United States to becoming economic powerhouses in their own right. Foremost among these is Brazil, which—despite its current discontents—continues to show the potential to become the next global economic superpower. At the same time, democratic institutions are steadily taking root throughout the continent. Is Latin America finally reaching a position to take charge of its own destiny?

REFLECTION QUESTIONS

Q Do you agree that the U.S. system of government performs most effectively in bringing benefits to the general population when the balance between the goals of Liberty and Equality are relatively evenly matched? Why or why not?

Q What role has popular culture played in the United States since 1945, and to what extent does it reflect the changes that have taken place in American society?

Q What do you believe are the most important issues that the countries of the Western Hemisphere face today? Are they meeting those challenges effectively, or not?

CHAPTER TIMELINE

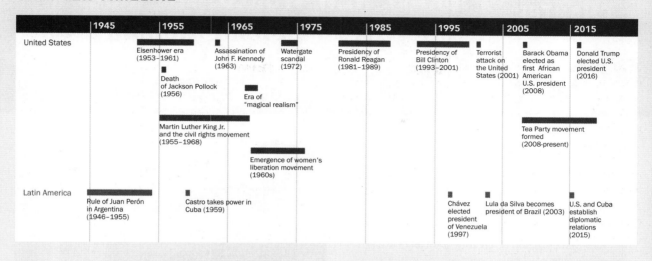

	1945	1955	1965	1975	1985	1995	2005	2015

United States

- Eisenhower era (1953–1961)
- Death of Jackson Pollock (1956)
- Assassination of John F. Kennedy (1963)
- Era of "magical realism"
- Watergate scandal (1972)
- Presidency of Ronald Reagan (1981–1989)
- Presidency of Bill Clinton (1993–2001)
- Terrorist attack on the United States (2001)
- Barack Obama elected as first African American U.S. president (2008)
- Donald Trump elected U.S. president (2016)
- Martin Luther King Jr. and the civil rights movement (1955–1968)
- Emergence of women's liberation movement (1960s)
- Tea Party movement formed (2008–present)

Latin America

- Rule of Juan Perón in Argentina (1946–1955)
- Castro takes power in Cuba (1959)
- Chávez elected president of Venezuela (1997)
- Lula da Silva becomes president of Brazil (2003)
- U.S. and Cuba establish diplomatic relations (2015)

CHAPTER NOTES

1. *Public Papers of the Presidents of the United States: Lyndon B. Johnson,* Bk. 1, 1963–64 (Washington, D.C., 1965), p. 704.
2. To cite a personal example, one of my professors of Political Science was dismissed from his position at my college simply because he had served as a member of a committee that drafted the United Nations Charter.
3. Dwight D. Eisenhower, *The White House Years: Waging Peace, 1956–1961* (Garden City, 1965), p. 533.

BRAVE NEW WORLD: THE RISE AND FALL OF COMMUNISM IN THE SOVIET UNION AND EASTERN EUROPE

Chapter Outline and Focus Questions

9-1 *The Postwar Soviet Union*

Q What, in your view, were the most important reasons why the Soviet Union failed to achieve Karl Marx's dream of creating a society cleansed of the evils of class struggle and the exploitation of man by man?

9-2 *Ferment in Eastern Europe*

Q Why was Soviet strategy to retain its dominance over its client states in Eastern Europe successful for so long?

9-3 *Culture and Society in the Soviet Bloc*

Q How did the culture and society of the states in Eastern Europe differ from those in the Western European countries?

9-4 *The Disintegration of the Soviet Empire*

Q What were the key components of perestroika as espoused by Mikhail Gorbachev during the 1980s? Why did the strategy fail?

9-5 *The New Russia: From Empire to Nation*

Q Why do you think relations between Russia and the United States have deteriorated in the thirty years since the collapse of the Soviet Union? Could the rupture have been avoided?

Connections to Today

Do you share the view that the world is now entering a new phase of the Cold War, with the United States faced off against its traditional rivals, Russia and China?

William J. Duiker

IMAGE 9.1 How to Shop in Moscow

ACCORDING TO KARL MARX, capitalism is a system that involves the exploitation of man by man; under socialism, it is the other way around. That wry joke, an ironic twist on the familiar Marxist saying of the previous century, was typical of popular humor in post–World War II Moscow, where the dreams of a future Communist utopia had faded in the grim reality of life in the Soviet Union.

During the 1950s, the annual rate of economic growth in the Soviet Union exceeded 6 percent, and there were widespread predictions, even in the United States, that the Soviet Union would eventually surpass the United States as the world's preeminent economic power. But Soviet leaders had made a calculated decision to emphasize military spending at the expense of other sectors of the economy, and as growth rates dropped dramatically in the 1980s, the standard of living for Soviet citizens continued to stagnate. Nothing was more symbolic of the difficulties of life in the Soviet Union than the common sight of endless lines of citizens waiting patiently for an opportunity to shop for vital necessities in all Soviet cities (see Image 9.1). For much of the population in the Soviet Union and its Eastern European satellites, the "brave new world" prophesied by Karl Marx remained but a figment of his fertile imagination.

9-1 THE POSTWAR SOVIET UNION

 Focus Question: What, in your view, were the most important reasons why the Soviet Union failed to achieve Karl Marx's dream of creating a society cleansed of the evils of class struggle and the exploitation of man by man?

At the end of World War II, the Soviet Union was one of the world's two superpowers, and its leader, Joseph Stalin, was at the height of his power. As a result of the war, Stalin and his Soviet colleagues were now in control of a vast empire that included Eastern Europe, much of the Balkans, and territory gained from Japan in East Asia (see Map 9.1).

9-1a From Stalin to Khrushchev

World War II had devastated the Soviet Union. Twenty million citizens lost their lives, and cities such as Kiev, Kharkov, and Leningrad suffered enormous physical destruction. As the lands that had been occupied by the German forces were liberated, the Soviet government turned its attention to restoring the nation's economic structures. Nevertheless, in 1945, agricultural production was only 60 percent and steel output only 50 percent of prewar levels. The Soviet people faced incredibly difficult conditions: they worked longer hours than before the war, ate less, and were ill-housed and poorly clothed.

In the immediate postwar years, the Soviet Union removed goods and materials from occupied Germany and extorted valuable raw materials from its satellite states in Eastern Europe. More important, however, to create a new industrial base, Stalin returned to the method he had used in the 1930s—the extraction of development capital from Soviet labor. Working hard for little pay and for precious few consumer goods, Soviet citizens were expected to produce goods for export with little in return for themselves. The incoming capital from abroad could then be used to purchase machinery and Western technology. The loss of millions of men in the war meant that much of this tremendous workload fell upon Soviet women, who performed almost 40 percent of the heavy manual labor.

An Industrial Powerhouse The pace of economic recovery in the postwar Soviet Union was impressive. By 1947, Russian industrial production had attained 1939 levels; three years later, it had surpassed those levels by 40 percent. New power plants, canals, and giant factories were built, and new industrial enterprises and oil fields were established in Siberia and Soviet Central Asia. A new five-year plan, announced in 1946, reached its goals in less than five years. Returning to his prewar forced-draft system, Stalin had created an industrial powerhouse.

Although Stalin's economic recovery policy was successful in promoting growth in heavy industry, primarily for the benefit of the military, consumer goods remained scarce, as long-suffering Soviet citizens were still being asked to sacrifice for a better tomorrow. The development of thermonuclear weapons, MiG fighter jets, and the first space satellite (*Sputnik*) in the 1950s may have elevated the Soviet state's reputation as a world power abroad, but domestically, the Soviet people were shortchanged. Heavy industry grew at a rate three times that of personal consumption. Moreover, the housing shortage was acute, with living conditions especially difficult in the overcrowded cities.

When World War II ended, Stalin had been in power for more than fifteen years. During that time, he had removed all opposition to his rule and emerged as the undisputed master of the Soviet Union. Constantly increasing repression became the hallmark of the regime. In 1946, government decrees subordinated all forms of literary and scientific expression to the political needs of the state. Along with the anti-intellectual campaign came political terror. By the late 1940s, an estimated 9 million people were in Siberian concentration camps.

Increasingly distrustful of competitors, Stalin exercised sole authority and pitted his subordinates against one another. One of these subordinates, Lavrenti Beria, head of the secret police, controlled a force of several hundred thousand agents, leaving Stalin's colleagues completely cowed. As Stalin remarked mockingly on one occasion, "When I die, the imperialists will strangle all of you like a litter of kittens."[1]

Stalin's morbid suspicions even extended to some of his closest colleagues. In 1948, Andrei Zhdanov, his presumed successor and head of the Leningrad party organization, died under mysterious circumstances. The doctors who had attended Zhdanov were charged with causing his death (hence, the label "the doctors' plot"), but most historians believe it was done on Stalin's order. Within weeks, the Leningrad party organization was purged of several top leaders, many of whom were charged with traitorous connections with Western intelligence agencies. In succeeding years, Stalin directed his suspicion at other members of the inner circle, including Foreign Minister Vyacheslav Molotov.

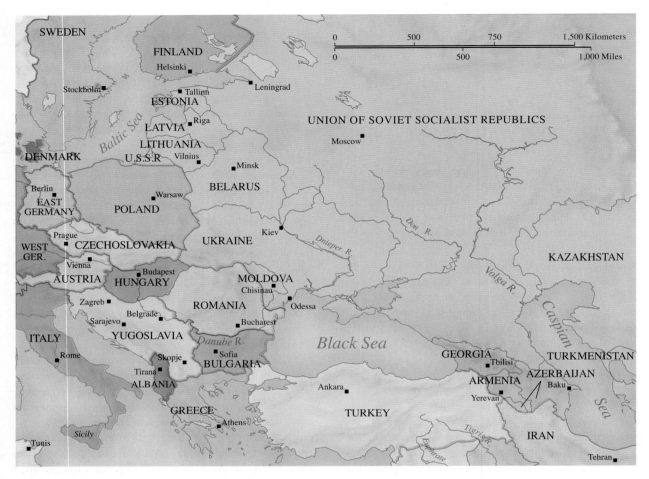

MAP 9.1 The Soviet Union. After World War II, the boundaries of Eastern Europe were redrawn as a result of Allied agreements reached at the Tehran and Yalta Conferences. This map shows the new boundaries that were established throughout the region, placing Soviet power in the center of Europe.

 How had the boundaries changed from the prewar era?

Known as "Old Stone Butt" in the West for his stubborn defense of Soviet security interests, Molotov had been a loyal lieutenant since the early years of Stalin's rise to power. Now Stalin distrusted Molotov and had his Jewish wife sent to a Siberian concentration camp. To colleagues, Stalin privately accused his own foreign minister of being "a hireling of American imperialism."

The Rise and Fall of Nikita Khrushchev Stalin died—presumably of natural causes—in 1953 and, after some bitter infighting within the party leadership (resulting in the arrest and secret execution of the feared Beria) he was succeeded by Georgy Malenkov, a veteran administrator and ambitious member of the Politburo. Malenkov came to power with a clear agenda. In foreign affairs, he hoped to promote an easing of Cold War tensions and improve

relations with the Western powers. For Moscow's Eastern European allies, he advocated a so-called **New Course** in their mutual relations and an end to Stalinist methods of rule. Inside the Soviet Union, he hoped to reduce defense expenditures and assign a higher priority to improving the standard of living. Such goals were laudable and probably had the support of the majority of the Russian people, but they were not necessarily appealing to key pressure groups within the Soviet Union—the army, the Communist Party, the managerial elite, and the security services (now known as the Committee for State Security, or KGB). Malenkov, whose hold on power was always tenuous because of the maneuverings of his rivals in the Kremlin, was soon removed from his position as prime minister, and power shifted to his chief competitor, the new party general secretary, Nikita Khrushchev.

During his struggle for power with Malenkov, Khrushchev had outmaneuvered his rival by calling for heightened defense expenditures and a continuing emphasis on heavy industry. Once in power, however, Khrushchev showed the political dexterity displayed by many an American politician and reversed his priorities. He now resumed his predecessor's efforts to reduce tensions with the West and boost the standard of living of the Russian people. He moved vigorously to improve the performance of the Soviet economy and revitalize Soviet society. By nature, Khrushchev was a man of enormous energy as well as an innovator. In an attempt to loosen the stranglehold of the central bureaucracy over the national economy, he abolished dozens of government ministries and split up the party and government apparatus. Khrushchev also attempted to rejuvenate the stagnant agricultural sector, long the Achilles heel of the Soviet economy. He attempted to spur production by increasing profit incentives and opened "virgin lands" in the Soviet republic of Kazakhstan to bring thousands of acres of new land under cultivation.

Like any innovator, however, Khrushchev had to overcome the inherently conservative instincts of the Soviet bureaucracy, as well as of the mass of the Soviet population. His plan to remove the "dead hand" of the state, however laudable in intent, alienated much of the Soviet official class, and his effort to split the party angered those who saw it as the central force in the Soviet system. Khrushchev's agricultural schemes inspired similar opposition. Although the Kazakhstan wheat lands would eventually demonstrate their importance, progress was slow, and his effort to persuade the Russian people to eat more corn (an idea he had apparently picked up during a visit to the United States) led to the mocking nickname "Cornman." Disappointing agricultural production, combined with high military spending, hurt the Soviet economy. The industrial growth rate, which had soared in the early 1950s, declined dramatically from 13 percent in 1953 to 7.5 percent in 1964.

Khrushchev was probably best known for his policy of **de-Stalinization**. Khrushchev had risen in the party hierarchy as a Stalin protégé, but he had been deeply disturbed by his mentor's excesses and, once in a position of authority, moved to excise the Stalinist legacy from Soviet society. The campaign began at the Twentieth Congress of the Communist Party in February 1956, when Khrushchev gave a long speech criticizing some of Stalin's major shortcomings. The speech apparently had not been intended for public distribution, but it was quickly leaked to the Western press and created a sensation throughout the world (see Historical Voices, "Khrushchev Denounces Stalin," p. 224). During the next few years, Khrushchev encouraged more freedom of expression for writers, artists, and composers, arguing that "readers should be given the chance to make their own judgments" regarding the acceptability of controversial literature and that "police measures shouldn't be used."[2] At Khrushchev's order, thousands of prisoners were released from concentration camps.

Khrushchev's personality, however, did not endear him to higher Soviet officials, who frowned at his tendency to crack jokes and play the clown. Nor were the higher members of the party bureaucracy pleased when Khrushchev tried to curb their privileges. Foreign policy failures further damaged Khrushchev's reputation among his colleagues. Relations with China deteriorated badly under his leadership. His plan to install missiles in Cuba was the final straw (see Chapter 7). While he was away on vacation in 1964, a special meeting of the Soviet Politburo voted him out of office (allegedly because of "deteriorating health") and forced him into retirement. Although a group of leaders succeeded him, real power came into the hands of Leonid Brezhnev (1906–1982), the "trusted" supporter of Khrushchev who had engineered his downfall.

9-1b The Brezhnev Years, 1964–1982

The ouster of Nikita Khrushchev in October 1964 vividly demonstrated the challenges that would be encountered by any Soviet leader sufficiently bold to try to reform the Soviet system. In democratic countries, pressure on the government comes from various sources within society at large—the business community and labor unions, interest groups, and the general public. In the Soviet Union, pressure on government and party leaders originated from sources essentially operating inside the governing system—from the government bureaucracy, the party apparatus (known in Russian as **apparatchiks**), the KGB, and the armed forces.

Leonid Brezhnev, the new party chief, was undoubtedly aware of these realities of Soviet politics, and his long tenure in power was marked, above all, by the desire to avoid changes that might provoke instability, either at home or abroad. Brezhnev was himself a product of the Soviet system. He had entered the ranks of the party leadership under Stalin, and although he was not a particularly avid believer in party ideology—indeed, his years in power gave rise to innumerable stories about his addiction to "bourgeois pleasures," including expensive country houses in the elite Moscow suburb of Zhukovka and fast cars (many of them gifts from foreign leaders)—he was no partisan of reform.

Still, Brezhnev sought stability in the domestic arena. He and his prime minister, Alexei Kosygin (1904–1980), undertook what might be described as a program of "de-Khrushchevization," returning the responsibility for

Khrushchev Denounces Stalin

 What were Stalin's major crimes, according to Khrushchev? To what degree were these problems resolved under later Soviet leaders?

Politics & Government **THREE YEARS AFTER STALIN'S DEATH,** the new Soviet premier, Nikita Khrushchev, addressed the Twentieth Congress of the Communist Party and denounced the former Soviet dictator for his crimes. This denunciation, which caused consternation in Communist parties around the world, was the beginning of a policy of de-Stalinization in the Soviet Union.

Khrushchev Addresses the Twentieth Party Congress, February 1956

Comrades, . . . quite a lot has been said about the cult of the individual and about its harmful consequences. . . . The cult of the person of Stalin . . . became at a certain specific stage the source of a whole series of exceedingly serious and grave perversions of Party principles, of Party democracy, of revolutionary legality.

Stalin absolutely did not tolerate collegiality in leadership and in work and . . . practiced brutal violence, not only toward everything which opposed him, but also toward that which seemed to his capricious and despotic character, contrary to his concepts.

Stalin abandoned the method of ideological struggle for that of administrative violence, mass repressions and terror. . . . Arbitrary behavior by one person encouraged and permitted arbitrariness in others. Mass arrests and deportations of many thousands of people, execution without trial and without normal investigation created conditions of insecurity, fear, and even desperation.

Stalin showed in a whole series of cases his intolerance, his brutality, and his abuse of power. . . . He often chose the path of repression and annihilation, not only against actual enemies, but also against individuals who had not committed any crimes against the Party and the Soviet government. . . .

Many Party, Soviet, and economic activists who were branded in 1937–38 as "enemies" were actually never enemies, spies, wreckers, and so on, but were always honest communists; they were only so stigmatized, and often, no longer able to bear barbaric tortures, they charged themselves (at the order of the investigative judges-falsifiers) with all kinds of grave and unlikely crimes.

This was the result of the abuse of power by Stalin, who began to use mass terror against the Party cadres. . . . Stalin put the Party and the NKVD [the Soviet police agency] up to the use of mass terror when the exploiting classes had been liquidated in our country and when there were no serious reasons for the use of extraordinary mass terror. The terror was directed . . . against the honest workers of the Party and the Soviet state. . . .

Stalin was a very distrustful man, sickly, suspicious. . . . Everywhere and in everything he saw "enemies," "two-facers," and "spies." Possessing unlimited power, he indulged in great willfulness and choked a person morally and physically. A situation was created where one could not express one's own will. When Stalin said that one or another would be arrested, it was necessary to accept on faith that he was an "enemy of the people." What proofs were offered? The confession of the arrested. . . . How is it possible that a person confesses to crimes that he had not committed? Only in one way—because of application of physical methods of pressuring him, tortures, bringing him to a state of unconsciousness, deprivation of his judgment, taking away of his human dignity.

Source: *Congressional Record*, 84th Congress, 2nd session, vol. 102, pt. 7 (June 4, 1956), pp. 9389–9402.

long-term planning to the central ministries and reuniting the Communist Party apparatus. Despite some cautious attempts to stimulate the stagnant farm sector by increasing capital investment in agriculture and raising food prices to increase rural income and provide additional incentives to collective farmers, there was no effort to revise the basic structure of the collective system. In the industrial sector, the regime launched a series of reforms designed to give factory managers (themselves employees of the state) more responsibility for setting prices, wages, and production quotas. These "Kosygin reforms" had little effect, however, because they were stubbornly resisted by the bureaucracy and were eventually adopted by relatively few enterprises within the vast state-owned industrial sector.

A Controlled Society Brezhnev also initiated a significant retreat from Khrushchev's policy of de-Stalinization. Criticism of the "Great Leader" had angered conservatives both within the party hierarchy and among the public at large, many of whom still revered Stalin as a hero of the Soviet system and a defender of the Russian people against Nazi Germany. Many influential figures in the Kremlin feared that de-Stalinization could lead to internal instability and a decline in public trust in the legitimacy of party leadership—the hallowed "dictatorship of the proletariat." Early in Brezhnev's reign, Stalin's reputation began to revive. Although his alleged "shortcomings" were not totally ignored, he was now described in the official press as "an outstanding party leader" who had been primarily responsible for the successes achieved by the Soviet Union.

The regime also adopted a more restrictive policy toward free expression and dissidence in Soviet society. Critics of the Soviet system, such as the physicist Andrei Sakharov, were harassed and arrested or, like the famous writer Alexander Solzhenitsyn—who had written about the horrors of Soviet concentration camps—forced to leave the country (see Historical Voices, "One Day in the Life of Ivan Denisovich," p. 226) . There was also a qualified return to the anti-Semitic policies and attitudes that had marked the Stalin era. Such indications of renewed repression aroused concern in the West and were instrumental in the inclusion of a statement on human rights in the 1975 Helsinki Accords, which guaranteed the sanctity of international frontiers throughout the continent of Europe (see Chapter 7). Performance in the area of human rights continued to be spotty, however, and the repressive character of Soviet society was not significantly altered.

There were, of course, no rival voices to compete with the party and the government in defining national interests. A new state constitution, promulgated in 1977, enshrined the Communist Party as "the leading and guiding force" in the Soviet Union, while Soviet citizens were "obliged to safeguard the interests of the Soviet state, and to enhance its power and prestige."[3] The media were controlled by the state and presented only what the state wanted people to hear. The two major newspapers, *Pravda* ("Truth") and *Izvestiya* ("News"), were the agents of the party and the government, respectively. Cynics joked that there was no news in *Pravda* and no truth in *Izvestiya*. Airplane accidents in the Soviet Union were rarely publicized out of concern that they would raise questions about the quality of the Soviet airline industry. The government made strenuous efforts to prevent the Soviet people from being exposed to harmful foreign ideas, especially modern art, literature, and contemporary Western rock music. When the Summer Olympic Games were held in Moscow

in 1980, Soviet newspapers advised citizens to keep their children indoors to protect them from being polluted with "bourgeois" ideas passed on by foreign visitors. For those Soviet citizens who craved access to the real world behind the shiny platitudes of government propaganda, the only resource was the **samizdat**—unauthorized publications written by dissident elements and passed on illegally from hand to hand behind the backs of the authorities.

For citizens of Western democracies, such a political atmosphere would seem highly oppressive, but for the people in the Soviet republics, an emphasis on law and order was an accepted aspect of everyday life inherited from the tsarist period. Conformism was the rule in virtually every corner of Soviet society, from the educational system (characterized at all levels by rote memorization and political indoctrination) to child rearing (it was forbidden, for example, to be left-handed) and even to yearly vacations (most workers took their vacations at resorts run by their employer, where the daily schedule of activities was highly regimented). Young Americans studying in the Soviet Union reported that friends there were often shocked to hear U.S. citizens criticizing their own president and to learn that they did not routinely carry identity cards.

A Stagnant Economy Soviet leaders also failed to achieve their objective of revitalizing the national economy. Whereas growth rates during the early Khrushchev era had been impressive (prompting Khrushchev during a reception at the Kremlin in 1956 to chortle to an American guest, "We will bury you," referring to the Western countries), under Brezhnev industrial growth declined to an annual rate of less than 4 percent in the early 1970s and less than 3 percent in the period 1975–1980. Successes in the agricultural sector were equally meager. Grain production rose from less than 90 million tons in the early 1950s to nearly 200 million tons in the 1970s but then stagnated at that level (though it should be noted that Soviet statistics were notoriously unreliable).

One of the primary problems with the Soviet economy was the absence of incentives. Salary structures offered little reward for hard labor and extraordinary achievement. Pay differentials operated within a much narrower range than in most Western societies, and there was little danger of being dismissed. According to the Soviet constitution, every Soviet citizen was guaranteed an opportunity to work.

There were, of course, some exceptions to this general rule. Athletic achievement was highly prized, and a gymnast of Olympic stature would receive great rewards in the form of prestige and lifestyle. Senior officials did not receive high salaries but were provided with countless "perquisites," such as access to foreign goods, official

One Day in the Life of Ivan Denisovich

> **Q** What was the author's purpose in writing this literary work? How did it contribute to Khrushchev's destalinization program?

Art & Ideas

ON NOVEMBER 20, 1962, a Soviet magazine published a work by Alexander Solzhenitsyn that unleashed a literary and political furor. The short novel related one day in the life of its chief character, Ivan Denisovich, at a Siberian concentration camp, to which he had been sentenced at the end of World War II for supposedly spying for the Germans while a Soviet soldier. This excerpt narrates the daily journey from the prison camp to a work project through the subzero cold of Siberia. Many Soviets identified with Ivan as a symbol of the suffering they had endured under Stalin.

Alexander Solzhenitsyn, *One Day in the Life of Ivan Denisovich*

There were escort guards all over the place. They flung a semicircle around the column on its way to the power station, their machine guns sticking out and pointing right at your face. And there were guards with gray dogs. One dog bared its fangs as if laughing at the prisoners. The escorts all wore short sheepskins, except for half a dozen whose coats trailed the ground. The long sheepskins were interchangeable: they were worn by anyone whose turn had come to man the watchtowers.

And once again as they brought the squads together the escort recounted the entire power-station column by fives. . . .

Out beyond the camp boundary the intense cold, accompanied by a headwind, stung even Shukhov's face, which was used to every kind of unpleasantness. Realizing that he would have the wind in his face all the way to the power station, he decided to make use of his bit of rag. To meet the contingency of a headwind he, like many other prisoners, had got himself a cloth with a long tape on each end. The prisoners admitted that these helped a bit. Shukhov covered his face up to the eyes, brought the tapes around below his ears, and fastened the ends together at the back of his neck. Then he covered his nape with the flap of his hat and raised his coat collar. The next thing was to pull the front flap of the hat down into his brow. Thus in front only his eyes remained unprotected. He fixed his coat tightly at the waist with the rope. Now everything was in order except for his hands, which were already stiff with cold (his mittens were worthless). He rubbed them, he clapped them together, for he knew that in a moment he'd have to put them behind his back and keep them there for the entire march.

The chief of the escort guard recited the "morning prayer," which every prisoner was heartily sick of:

> "Attention, prisoners. Marching orders must be strictly obeyed. Keep to your ranks. No hurrying, keep a steady pace. No talking. Keep your eyes fixed ahead and your hands behind your backs. A step to right or left is considered an attempt to escape and the escort has orders to shoot without warning. Leading guards, on the double."

The two guards in the lead of the escort must have set out along the road. The column heaved forward, shoulders swaying, and the escorts, some twenty paces to the right and left of the column, each man at a distance of ten paces from the next, machine guns held at the ready, set off too.

Source: Alexander Solzhenitsyn, *One Day in the Life of Ivan Denisovich* (tr. by Ralph Parker), translation copyright 1963 by E.P. Dutton and Victor Gollancz, Ltd. Copyright renewed in 1991 by Penguin USA and Victor Gollancz Ltd.

automobiles with chauffeurs, and entry into prestigious institutions of higher learning for their children. For the elite, it was *blat* (influence) that most often differentiated them from the rest of the population. The average citizen, however, had little material incentive to produce beyond the minimum acceptable level. It is hardly surprising that overall per capita productivity was only about half that realized in most capitalist countries. At the same time, the rudeness of Soviet clerks and waiters toward their customers became legendary.

The problem of incentives existed at the managerial level as well, where the practice of centralized planning discouraged initiative and innovation. Factory managers, for example, were assigned monthly and annual quotas by the **Gosplan** (the "state plan," drawn up by the central planning commission). Because state-owned factories faced little or no competition, factory managers did not care whether their products were competitive in terms of price and quality, as long as the quota was attained. One of the key complaints of Soviet citizens was the low quality of most locally made consumer goods. Knowledgeable consumers quickly discovered that products manufactured at the end of the month were often of lower quality (because factory workers had to rush to meet their quotas at the end of the production cycle) and tried to avoid purchasing them.

Often consumer goods were simply unavailable. Whenever Soviet citizens saw a queue forming in front of a store, they automatically got in line, often without even knowing what the line was for, because they never knew when an item might be available again (see Image 9.1). When they reached the head of the line, most would purchase several of the same item to swap with their friends and neighbors. This "queue psychology," of course, was a time-consuming process and inevitably served to reduce the per capita rate of productivity.

Soviet citizens often tried to overcome the shortcomings of the system by operating "on the left" (the black market). Private economic activities, of course, were illegal in the socialized Soviet system, but many workers took to "moonlighting" to augment their meager salaries. An employee in a state-run appliance store, for example, would promise to repair a customer's television set on his own time in return for a payment "under the table." Otherwise, the repairs might require several weeks. Knowledgeable observers estimated that as much as one-third of the entire Soviet economy operated outside the legal system.

Another major obstacle to economic growth was inadequate technology. Except in the area of national defense, the overall level of Soviet technology was not comparable to that of the West or the advanced industrial societies of East Asia. Part of the problem, of course, stemmed from the issues already described. With no competition, factory managers had little incentive to improve the quality of their products. But another reason was the high priority assigned to defense. The military sector regularly received the most resources from the government and attracted the cream of the country's scientific talent.

There were still other reasons for the gradual slowdown in the Soviet economy. Coal mining was highly inefficient, and only about one-third of the coal extracted actually reached its final destination. Although Soviet oil reserves were estimated to be the largest in the world, for the most part they were located in inaccessible areas of Siberia where extraction facilities and transportation were inadequate. U.S. intelligence reports predicted that a leveling off of oil and gas production could cause severe problems for the future growth of the Soviet economy.

Soviet planners hoped that nuclear energy would eventually take up the slack, but the highly publicized meltdown of a nuclear reactor at Chernobyl in 1986 vividly demonstrated that Soviet technology was encountering difficulties in that area as well. Finally, there were serious underlying structural problems in agriculture. Climatic difficulties (frequent flooding, drought, and a short growing season) and a lack of fertile soil (except in the renowned "black earth" regions of Ukraine) combined with a chronic shortage of mechanized farm equipment and a lack of incentives to prevent the growth of an advanced agricultural economy.

An Aging Leadership   Such problems would be intimidating for any government; they were particularly so for the elderly party leaders surrounding Leonid Brezhnev, many of whom were cautious to a fault. Although some undoubtedly recognized the need for reform and innovation, they were paralyzed by fear of instability and change. The problem worsened during the late 1970s, when Brezhnev's health began to deteriorate.

Brezhnev died in November 1982 and was succeeded by Yuri Andropov (1914–1984), a party veteran and head of the Soviet secret services. During his brief tenure as party chief, Andropov was a vocal advocate of reform, but most of his initiatives were limited to the familiar nostrums of punishment for wrongdoers and moral exhortations to Soviet citizens to work harder. At the same time, material incentives were still officially discouraged and generally ineffective. Andropov had been ailing when he was selected to succeed Brezhnev as party chief, and when he died after only a few months in office, little had been done to change the system. He was succeeded by a mediocre party stalwart, the elderly Konstantin Chernenko (1911–1985). With the Soviet system in crisis, Moscow seemed stuck in a time warp. As one concerned observer told an American journalist, "I had a sense of foreboding, like before a storm. That there was something brewing in people and there would be a time when they would say, 'That's it. We can't go on living like this. We can't. We need to redo everything.'"[4]

9-2 FERMENT IN EASTERN EUROPE

 Focus Question: Why was the Soviet strategy to retain its dominance over its client states in Eastern Europe successful for so long?

The key to security along the Soviet Union's western frontier was the string of satellite states that had been created in Eastern Europe after World War II. Once Communist power had been assured in Warsaw, Prague, Sofia, Budapest, Bucharest, and East Berlin, a series of "little Stalins" put into power by Moscow instituted Soviet-type five-year plans that emphasized heavy industry rather than consumer goods, the collectivization of agriculture, and the nationalization of industry. They also appropriated the political tactics that Stalin had perfected in the Soviet Union, eliminating all non-Communist parties and establishing the standard institutions of repression—the secret police and military forces. Dissidents were tracked down and thrown into prison, while "national Communists" who resisted total subservience to the nation were charged with treason in mass show trials and executed.

Despite such repressive efforts, however, Soviet-style policies aroused growing discontent in several Eastern European societies. Hungary, Poland, and Romania harbored bitter memories of past Russian domination and suspected that Stalin, under the guise of proletarian internationalism, was seeking to revive the empire of the Romanovs. For the vast majority of peoples in Eastern Europe, the imposition of "people's democracies" (a euphemism invented by Moscow to refer to a society in the early stage of socialist transition) resulted in economic hardship and severe threats to the most basic political liberties.

9-2a Unrest in Poland

The first signs of unrest appeared in 1953, when popular riots broke out against Communist rule in East Berlin. The riots eventually subsided, but the virus soon began to spread to neighboring countries. In Poland, public demonstrations against an increase in food prices in 1956 escalated into widespread protests against the regime's economic policies, restrictions on the freedom of Catholics to practice their religion, and the continued presence of Soviet troops (as called for by the Warsaw Pact) on Polish soil. In a desperate effort to defuse the unrest, in October the Polish party leader stepped down and was replaced by Wladyslaw Gomulka (1905–1982), a popular figure who had previously been demoted for his "nationalist" tendencies.

When Gomulka took steps to ease the crisis, the new Soviet party chief, Nikita Khrushchev, flew to Warsaw to warn his Polish colleague against adopting policies that could undermine the "dictatorship of the proletariat" (the Marxist phrase for the political dominance of the party) and even weaken security links with the Soviet Union. After a brief confrontation, during which both sides threatened to use military force to punctuate their demands, Gomulka and Khrushchev reached a compromise according to which Poland would adopt a policy labeled "internal

reform, external loyalty." Poland agreed to remain in the Warsaw Pact and to maintain the sanctity of party rule. In return, Warsaw was authorized to adopt domestic reforms, such as easing restrictions on religious practice and ending the policy of forced collectivization in rural areas.

9-2b The Hungarian Uprising

The developments in Poland sent shock waves throughout the region. In neighboring Czechoslovakia, dissident groups watched the events in Warsaw with fascination but—undoubtedly rendered cautious by the failure of Western countries to come to their aid in previous crises—took no action. The impact was strongest in Hungary, where the methods of the local "little Stalin," Mátyás Rákosi, were so brutal that he had been summoned to Moscow for a lecture and later was forced to resign from office. In late October 1956, student-led popular riots broke out in the capital of Budapest and soon spread to towns and villages throughout the country.

Rakosi's successor, Imre Nagy (1896–1958), was a "national Communist" like Gomulka, and he initially attempted to satisfy popular demands without arousing the anger of Moscow. Unlike his counterpart in Poland, however, Nagy was unable to contain the zeal of leading members of the protest movement, who sought major political reforms and the withdrawal of Hungary from the Warsaw Pact. On November 1, Nagy announced plans for a multi-party government and promised free elections, which, given the mood of the country, would probably have brought an end to Communist rule.

When protesters then raided the headquarters of the Hungarian Communist Party, Khrushchev finally decided that firm action was required (see Image 9.2). Soviet troops, which had just been withdrawn at Nagy's request, returned to Budapest and installed a new government under the more pliant party leader János Kádár (1912–1989). While Kádár rescinded many of Nagy's measures, Nagy sought refuge in the Yugoslav Embassy. A few weeks later, he left the embassy under the promise of safety but was quickly arrested, convicted of treason, and executed. An estimated 200,000 Hungarian citizens crossed the border and sought asylum in neutral Austria.

The dramatic events in Poland and Hungary graphically demonstrated the vulnerability of the Soviet satellite system in Eastern Europe, and many observers throughout the world anticipated an attempt by the United States to intervene on behalf of the freedom fighters in Hungary. After all, the Eisenhower administration had promised that it would "roll back" communism, and radio broadcasts by the U.S.-sponsored Radio Liberty and Radio Free Europe had encouraged the peoples of Eastern Europe to rise up

IMAGE 9.2 **How the Mighty Have Fallen.** In the fall of 1956, Hungarian freedom fighters rose up against Communist domination of their country in the short-lived Hungarian Revolution. Their actions threatened Soviet hegemony in Eastern Europe, however, and in late October, Soviet leader Nikita Khrushchev dispatched troops to quell the uprising. In the meantime, the Hungarian people had demonstrated their discontent by toppling a gigantic statue of Joseph Stalin in the capital of Budapest. Statues of the Soviet dictator had been erected in all the Soviet satellites after World War II. ("W.C." identifies a public toilet in European countries.)

against Soviet domination. In reality, Washington was well aware that U.S. intervention could lead to nuclear war and limited itself to protests against Soviet brutality in crushing the uprising.

The year of discontent was not without its consequences, however. Soviet leaders now recognized that Moscow could maintain control over its satellites in Eastern Europe only by granting them the leeway to adopt domestic policies appropriate to local conditions. Khrushchev had already embarked on this path when, during a visit to Belgrade in 1955, he assured Tito that there were "different roads to socialism." Eastern European Communist leaders now took Khrushchev at his word and adopted reform programs to make socialism more palatable to their subject populations. Even János Kádár, derisively labeled the "butcher of Budapest," managed to preserve many of Imre Nagy's reforms to allow a measure of capitalist incentive and freedom of expression in Hungary.

9-2c The Prague Spring

Czechoslovakia did not share in the thaw of the mid-1950s and remained under the rule of Antonín Novotný (1904–1975), who had been placed in power by Stalin himself. By the late 1960s, however, Novotný's policies had led to widespread popular alienation, and in early 1968, with the support of intellectuals and reformist party members, Alexander Dubček (1921–1992) was elected first secretary of the Communist Party. He immediately attempted to create what was popularly called "socialism with a human face," relaxing restrictions on freedom of speech and the press and the right to travel abroad. Reforms were announced for the economic sector, and party control over all aspects of society was reduced. A period of euphoria erupted that came to be known as the "Prague Spring."

It proved to be short-lived. Encouraged by Dubček's actions, some Czechs called for more far-reaching reforms, including neutrality and withdrawal from the Soviet bloc. To forestall the spread of this "spring fever," the Soviet Red Army, supported by troops from other Warsaw Pact states, invaded Czechoslovakia in August 1968 and crushed the reform movement. Gustáv Husák (1913–1991), a committed Stalinist, replaced Dubček and restored the old order, while Moscow justified its action by issuing what became known as the **Brezhnev Doctrine** (see Historical Voices, "The Brezhnev Doctrine," p. 230).

9-2d The Persistence of Stalinism in East Germany

Elsewhere in Eastern Europe, Stalinist policies continued to hold sway. The ruling Communist government in East Germany, led by Walter Ulbricht (1893–1973), consolidated its position in the early 1950s and became a faithful Soviet satellite. Industry was nationalized and agriculture collectivized. After the 1953 workers' revolt was crushed by Soviet tanks, a steady flight of East Germans to West Germany ensued, primarily through the city of Berlin. According to one estimate, some 3 million people, or almost 20 percent of the total population of the German Democratic Republic, had fled to West Germany by 1961. This exodus of mostly skilled laborers (soon only party chief Ulbricht would be left, remarked one Soviet observer sardonically) created economic problems and in 1961 led the East German government to erect the infamous Berlin Wall separating West from East Berlin, as well as even more fearsome barriers along the entire border with West Germany.

The Brezhnev Doctrine

 How did Leonid Brezhnev justify the Soviet invasion of Czechoslovakia in 1968? Do you find his arguments persuasive?

Politics & Government

IN THE SUMMER OF 1968, when the new Communist Party leaders in Czechoslovakia were seriously considering proposals for reforming the totalitarian system there, the Warsaw Pact nations met under the leadership of Soviet party chief Leonid Brezhnev to assess the threat to the socialist camp. Soon afterward, military forces of several Soviet bloc nations entered Czechoslovakia and imposed a new government subservient to Moscow. The move was justified by the spirit of "proletarian internationalism" and was widely viewed as a warning to China and other socialist states not to stray too far from Marxist-Leninist orthodoxy, as interpreted by the Soviet Union. The principle came to be known as the Brezhnev Doctrine.

A Letter to Czechoslovakia

To the Central Committee of the Communist Party of Czechoslovakia

Warsaw, July 15, 1968

Dear comrades!

On behalf of the Central Committees of the Communist and Workers' Parties of Bulgaria, Hungary, the German Democratic Republic, Poland, and the Soviet Union, we address ourselves to you with this letter, prompted by a feeling of sincere friendship based on the principles of Marxism-Leninism and proletarian internationalism and by the concern of our common affairs for strengthening the positions of socialism and the security of the socialist community of nations.

The development of events in your country evokes in us deep anxiety. It is our firm conviction that the offensive of the reactionary forces, backed by imperialists, against your Party and the foundations of the social system in the Czechoslovak Socialist Republic, threatens to push your country off the road of socialism and that consequently it jeopardizes the interests of the entire socialist system. . . .

We neither had nor have any intention of interfering in such affairs as are strictly the internal business of your Party and your state, nor of violating the principles of respect, independence, and equality in the relations among the Communist Parties and socialist countries. . . .

At the same time we cannot agree to have hostile forces push your country from the road of socialism and create a threat of severing Czechoslovakia from the socialist community. . . . This is the common cause of our countries, which have joined in the Warsaw Treaty to ensure independence, peace, and security in Europe, and to set up an insurmountable barrier against aggression and revenge. . . . We shall never agree to have imperialism, using peaceful or nonpeaceful methods, making a gap from the inside or from the outside in the socialist system, and changing in imperialism's favor the correlation of forces in Europe. . . .

That is why we believe that a decisive rebuff of the anti-Communist forces, and decisive efforts for the preservation of the socialist system in Czechoslovakia are not only your task but ours as well. . . .

We express the conviction that the Communist Party of Czechoslovakia, conscious of its responsibility, will take the necessary steps to block the path of reaction. In this struggle you can count on the solidarity and all-round assistance of the fraternal socialist countries.

Source: *Moscow News,* Supplement to No. 30(917), 1968, pp. 3–6.

After walling off the West, East Germany succeeded in developing the strongest economy among the Soviet Union's Eastern European satellites. In 1971, Walter Ulbricht was succeeded by Erich Honecker (1912–1994), a party hard-liner who was deeply committed to the ideological battle against détente. Propaganda increased, and the use of the Stasi, the secret police, became a hallmark of Honecker's virtual dictatorship. The Stasi had more than 100,000 employees, and its files on suspected subversives reportedly took up 125 miles of shelf space.[5] Aided by this enormous police bureaucracy, Honecker ruled unchallenged for the next eighteen years (see Movies & History, *The Lives of Others,* p. 231).

MOVIES & HISTORY

The Lives of Others (2006)

Directed by Florian Henckel von Donnersmarck, *The Lives of Others* is a German film (*Das Leben der Anderen*) that re-creates the depressing debilitation of East German society under its Communist regime, and especially the Stasi, the secret police. Georg Dreyman (Sebastian Koch) is a successful playwright in the German Democratic Republic (East Germany). Although he is a dedicated socialist who has not offended the authorities, they try to determine whether he is completely loyal by wiretapping his apartment, where he lives with his girlfriend, Christa-Maria Sieland (Martina Gedeck), an actress in some of Dreyman's plays. Captain Gerd Wiesler (Ulrich Mühe) of the Stasi takes charge of the spying operation. The epitome of the perfect functionary, he is a cold, calculating, dedicated professional who is convinced he is building a better society and is only too eager to fight the "enemies of socialism."

Georg Dreyman (Sebastian Koch) examines his Stasi files.

But as he listens to the everyday details of Dreyman's life, Wiesler begins to develop a conscience and becomes sympathetic to the writer. After a close friend of Dreyman's commits suicide, Dreyman turns against the Communist regime and writes an article on the alarming number of suicides in East German society that is published anonymously in *Der Spiegel*, a West German magazine. Lieutenant Colonel Grubitz (Ulrich Tukur), Wiesler's boss, suspects that Dreyman is the author. His girlfriend is brought in for questioning and provides some damning information about Dreyman's involvement. Horrified by what she has done, she commits suicide, but Wiesler, who is now determined to save Dreyman, fudges his reports and protects him from arrest. Grubitz suspects what Wiesler has done and demotes him. The film ends after the fall of the Berlin Wall when the new German government opens the Stasi files. When Dreyman reads his file, he realizes that Wiesler saved his life and writes a book dedicated to him.

The Lives of Others which won an Academy Award for Best Foreign Language Film, brilliantly depicts the stifling atmosphere of East Germany under Communist rule. The Stasi had about 90,000 employees but also recruited a network of hundreds of thousands of informers who submitted secret reports on their friends, family, bosses, and coworkers. Some volunteered the information, but as the film makes clear, others were bribed or blackmailed into collaborating with the authorities. As the movie demonstrates, the Stasi were experts at wiretapping dwellings and compiling detailed written reports about what they heard, including conversations, arguments, jokes, and even sexual activities. Ironically, Ulrich Mühe, who plays Captain Wiesler in the film, was an East German who himself had been spied on by the Stasi.

The film was praised by East Germans for accurately depicting the drab environment of their country and the role of the Stasi in fostering a society riddled by secrecy, fear, and the abuse of power. The dangers of governments that monitor their citizens are apparent and quite relevant in an age of legislation infringing on personal privacy in an attempt to fight terrorism. The police state is revealed for what it is, a soulless and hollow world with no redeeming features or values.

 How does the film capture the drab environment of East Germany? Why do you think East Germans chose to forget the Stasi past?

9-3 CULTURE AND SOCIETY IN THE SOVIET BLOC

Q **Focus Question:** "How did the culture and society of the states in Eastern Europe differ from those in the Western European countries?"

In his occasional musings about the future Communist utopia, Karl Marx had predicted that a classless society would emerge to replace the exploitative and hierarchical systems of feudalism and capitalism. Workers would engage in productive activities and share equally in the fruits of their labor. In their free time, they would produce a new, advanced culture, proletarian in character and egalitarian in content.

9-3a Cultural Expression

The reality in the post-World War II Soviet Union and in Eastern Europe was somewhat different. Beginning in 1946, a series of government decrees made all forms of literary and scientific expression dependent on the state. All Soviet culture was expected to follow the party line. Historians, philosophers, and social scientists all grew accustomed to quoting Marx, Lenin, and, above all, Stalin as their chief authorities. Artworks were required to conform to the communist ideal of "socialist realism," according to which all forms of artistic creativity were expected to reflect the successes of the Soviet system. The public was quick to catch on to the ruse. When architects in Warsaw tried to follow Stalin's aesthetic preferences when they designed a grandiose skyscraper (known officially as the Palace of Culture) that reflected the hubris of the early Soviet period, local residents joked that the best view of the city could be seen from atop the palace, because one could not see the building from there.

Novels and plays, too, were supposed to portray Communist heroes and their efforts to create a better society. No criticism of existing social conditions was permitted. Even distinguished composers such as Dmitri Shostakovich (1906–1975) were compelled to heed Stalin's criticisms, including his view that contemporary Western music was nothing but a "mishmash." Some areas of intellectual activity were virtually abolished; the science of genetics disappeared, and few movies were made during Stalin's final years (see Image 9.3).

Stalin's death brought a modest respite from cultural repression. Writers and artists banned during Stalin's years were again allowed to publish. The writer Ilya Ehrenburg (1891–1967) set the tone with his novel, significantly titled *The Thaw*. Still, Soviet authorities, including Khrushchev, were reluctant to allow cultural freedom to move far beyond official Soviet ideology.

These restrictions, however, did not prevent the emergence of some significant Soviet literature, although authors paid a heavy price if they alienated the Soviet authorities. Boris Pasternak (1890–1960), who began his literary career as a poet, won the Nobel Prize in 1958 for his celebrated novel *Doctor Zhivago*, published in Italy in 1957. But the Soviet government

William J. Duiker

IMAGE 9.3 Stalinist Heroic: An Example of Socialist Realism. Under Stalin and his successors, art was assigned the task of indoctrinating the Soviet population in the public virtues, such as hard work, loyalty to the state, and patriotism. Grandiose statuary erected to commemorate the heroic efforts of the Red Army during World War II appeared in every Soviet city. Here is an example in Minsk, today the capital of Belarus. The flag reads "Forward under the banner of Lenin to the victory of Communism."

condemned Pasternak's anti-Soviet tendencies, banned the novel from the Soviet Union, and would not allow him to accept the prize. The author had alienated the authorities by describing a society scarred by the excesses of Bolshevik revolutionary zeal.

Alexander Solzhenitsyn (1918–2008) caused an even greater furor than Pasternak. Solzhenitsyn had spent eight years in forced-labor camps for criticizing Stalin, and his *One Day in the Life of Ivan Denisovich*, which won him the Nobel Prize in 1970, was an account of life in those camps (see Historical Voices, "One Day in the Life of Ivan Denisovich," p. 226). Later, Solzhenitsyn wrote *The Gulag Archipelago*, a detailed indictment of the whole system of Soviet oppression. Soviet authorities denounced Solzhenitsyn's efforts to inform the world of Soviet crimes against humanity and arrested and expelled him from the Soviet Union after he published *The Gulag Archipelago* abroad in 1973.

Although restrictive policies continued into the late 1980s, some Soviet authors learned how to minimize battles with the censors by writing under the guise of humor or fantasy. Two of the most accomplished and popular Soviet novelists of the period, Yury Trifonov (1925–1981) and Fazil Iskander (1929–2016), focused on the daily struggle of Soviet citizens to live with dignity. Trifonov depicted the everyday life of ordinary Russians with grim realism, while Iskander used humor to poke fun at the incompetence of the Soviet regime.

The situation was similar in the Eastern European satellites, although cultural freedom varied considerably from country to country. In Poland, intellectuals had access to Western publications as well as greater freedom to travel to the West. Hungarian and Yugoslav Communists, too, tolerated a certain level of intellectual activity that was not liked but not prohibited. Elsewhere, intellectuals were forced to conform to the regime's demands.

The socialist camp did participate in modern popular culture. By the early 1970s, there were 28 million television sets in the Soviet Union, although state authorities controlled the content of the programs that the Soviet people watched. Tourism, too, made inroads into the Communist world as state-run industries provided vacation time and governments facilitated the establishment of resorts for workers on the Black Sea and Adriatic coasts.

Spectator sports became a large industry, although they were highly politicized as the result of Cold War divisions. Victory in international athletic events was viewed as proof of the superiority of the socialist system over its capitalist rival. Accordingly, the state provided money for the construction of gymnasiums and training camps and portrayed athletes as superheroes.

9-3b Social Changes in Eastern Europe

The imposition of Marxist systems in Eastern Europe had far-reaching social consequences. Most Eastern European countries made the change from peasant societies to modern industrialized economies. In Bulgaria, for example, 80 percent of the labor force was engaged in agriculture in 1950, but only 20 percent was still working there in 1980. Although the Soviet Union and its Eastern European satellites never achieved the high standards of living of the West, they did experience some improvement. In 1960, the average real income of Polish peasants was four times higher than before World War II. Consumer goods also became more widespread. In East Germany, only 17 percent of families had television sets in 1960, but 75 percent had acquired them by 1972.

True to their creed, Communist leaders in Eastern Europe took steps to divest traditional elites of their economic power base and replaced them with their own supporters. One route to this reversal of roles was through education.

In some countries, the desire to provide equal educational opportunities led to laws that mandated quota systems based on class. In East Germany, for example, 50 percent of the students in secondary schools had to be children of workers and peasants. The sons of manual workers constituted 53 percent of university students in Yugoslavia in 1964 and 40 percent in East Germany, compared to only 15 percent in Italy and 5.3 percent in West Germany. Social mobility also increased. In Poland in 1961, half of the white-collar workers came from blue-collar families. A significant number of judges, professors, and industrial managers stemmed from working-class backgrounds.

Education became crucial in preparing for new jobs in the Communist system and led to higher enrollments in both secondary schools and universities. In Czechoslovakia, for example, the number of students in secondary schools tripled between 1945 and 1970, and the number of university students quadrupled between the 1930s and the 1960s. The type of education that students received also changed. In Hungary before World War II, 40 percent of students studied law, 9 percent engineering and technology, and 5 percent agriculture. In 1970, the figures were 35 percent in engineering and technology, 9 percent in agriculture, and only 4 percent in law.

But as so often happens in programs aimed at creating a new society through social engineering, reality eventually intruded. As the new managers of society, regardless of class background, realized the importance of higher education, they used their power to gain special privileges for their children. By 1971, fully 60 percent of the children of white-collar workers attended a university, and even though blue-collar families constituted 60 percent of the population, only 36 percent of their children attended institutions of higher learning. Even East Germany dropped its requirement that 50 percent of secondary students had to be the offspring of workers and peasants.

This shift in educational preferences demonstrates yet another aspect of the social structure in the Communist world: the emergence of a new privileged class, made up of members of the Communist Party, state officials, high-ranking officers in the military and secret police, and a few special professional groups. The new elite not only possessed political power but also received special privileges, including the right to purchase high-quality goods in special stores, paid vacations at special resorts, access to good housing and superior medical services, and advantages in education and jobs for their children.

9-3c Women in the Soviet Bloc

The system also failed to measure up in its treatment of women. Long after the Bolshevik Revolution had called for true equality of the sexes, men continued to dominate the leadership positions of the Communist parties in the Soviet Union and Eastern Europe. Women did have greater opportunities in the workforce and even in the professions, however. In the Soviet Union, women comprised 51 percent of the labor force in 1980; by the mid-1980s, they constituted 50 percent of the engineers, 80 percent of the doctors, and 75 percent of the teachers and teachers' aides. But many of these were low-paying jobs; most female doctors, for example, worked in primary care and were paid less than skilled machinists. The chief administrators in hospitals and schools were still men.

Moreover, although women were part of the workforce, they were still expected to fulfill their traditional roles in the home. Most women worked what came to be known as the "double shift." After spending eight hours in their jobs, they came home to do the housework and take care of the children. They might spend another two hours a day in long lines at a number of stores waiting to buy food and clothes. Because of the scarcity of housing, they had to use kitchens that were shared by a number of families.

Nearly three-quarters of a century after the Bolshevik Revolution, then, the Marxist dream of an advanced, egalitarian society was as far away as ever. Although in some respects conditions in the socialist camp were an improvement over those before World War II, many problems and inequities were as intransigent as ever.

9-4 THE DISINTEGRATION OF THE SOVIET EMPIRE

 Focus Questions: What were the key components of perestroika as espoused by Mikhail Gorbachev during the 1980s? Why did the strategy fail?

On the death of Konstantin Chernenko in 1985, party leaders selected the talented and vigorously youthful Soviet official Mikhail Gorbachev to succeed him. The new Soviet leader had shown early signs of promise. Born into a peasant family in 1931, Gorbachev combined farmwork with school and received the Order of the Red Banner for his agricultural efforts. This award and his good school record enabled him to study law at the University of Moscow. After receiving his law degree in 1955, he returned to his native southern Russia, where he eventually became first secretary of the Communist Party in the city of Stavropol and then first secretary of the regional party committee. In 1978, Gorbachev was made a member of the party's Central Committee in Moscow. Two years later, he became a full member of the ruling Politburo and secretary of the Central Committee.

During the early 1980s, Gorbachev began to realize the immensity of Soviet problems and the crucial need to transform the system. During a visit to Canada in 1983, he discovered to his astonishment that Canadian farmers worked hard on their own initiative. "We'll never have this for fifty years," he reportedly remarked.[6] On his return to Moscow, he established a series of committees to evaluate the situation and recommend measures to improve the system.

9-4a The Gorbachev Era

With his election as party general secretary in 1985, Gorbachev seemed intent on taking earlier reforms to their logical conclusions. The cornerstone of his reform program was *perestroika*, or "restructuring." At first, it meant only a reordering of economic policy, as Gorbachev called for the beginning of a market economy with limited free enterprise and some private property. For the first time, Soviet farmers were permitted to sell some of their produce on the open market (see Comparative Illustration, "Sideline Industries," p. 235).

COMPARATIVE ILLUSTRATION

Sideline Industries: Creeping Capitalism in a Socialist Paradise

Q *Why did Chinese citizens adopt capitalist reforms in the countryside more enthusiastically than their Soviet counterparts?*

Politics & Government

IN THE LATE 1980s, Communist leaders in both the Soviet Union and China began to encourage their citizens to engage in private commercial activities as a means of reviving moribund economies. In Image 9.4a, a Soviet farmworker displays fruits and vegetables on a street corner in Odessa, a seaport on the Black Sea. In Image 9.4b, a Chinese woman sells her dumplings to passersby in Shandong Province. As her smile suggests, the Chinese took up the challenge of entrepreneurship with much greater success and enthusiasm than their Soviet counterparts did.

IMAGE 9.4a

William J. Duiker

IMAGE 9.4b

William J. Duiker

Initial economic reforms were difficult to implement, however. Radicals criticized Gorbachev for his caution and demanded decisive measures; conservatives feared that rapid changes would be too painful. In his attempt to achieve compromise, Gorbachev often pursued partial liberalization, which satisfied neither faction and also failed to work, producing only more discontent.

Gorbachev soon perceived that in the Soviet system, the economic sphere was intimately tied to the social and political spheres. Any efforts to reform the economy without political or social reform would be doomed to failure. One of the most important instruments of *perestroika* was *glasnost*, or "openness." Soviet citizens and officials were encouraged to openly discuss the strengths and weaknesses of the Soviet Union. This policy could be seen in *Pravda*, the official newspaper of the Communist Party, where disasters such as the nuclear accident at Chernobyl in 1986 and collisions of ships in the Black Sea received increasing coverage, although some Soviet officials continued to deny the reports from Chernobyl as "imperialist propaganda." Soon this type of reporting was extended to include reports of official corruption, sloppy factory work, and protests against government policy. The arts also benefited from the new policy as previously banned works were now allowed to circulate and motion pictures began to depict negative aspects of Soviet life. Music based

9-4 The Disintegration of the Soviet Empire ■ **235**

on Western styles, such as jazz and rock, began to be performed openly. Religious activities, previously banned by Soviet authorities, were once again tolerated.

Political reforms were equally revolutionary. In June 1987, the principle of two-candidate elections was introduced; previously, voters had been presented with only one candidate. Most dissidents, including Andrei Sakharov, who had spent years in internal exile, were released. At the Communist Party conference in 1988, Gorbachev called for the creation of a new Soviet parliament, the Congress of People's Deputies, whose members were to be chosen in competitive elections. It convened in 1989, the first such meeting since 1918. As an elected member of the Congress, Sakharov called for an end to the Communist monopoly of power, and on December 11, 1989, the day he died, he urged the creation of a new, non-Communist party. Early in 1990, Gorbachev legalized the formation of other political parties and struck out Article 6 of the Soviet constitution, which guaranteed the "leading role" of the Communist Party. Hitherto, the position of first secretary of the party was the most important post in the Soviet Union, but as the Communist Party became less closely associated with the state, the powers of this office diminished. Gorbachev attempted to consolidate his power by creating a new state presidency, and in March 1990, he became the Soviet Union's first president. But by now his stature within the country had diminished, and reformist elements who had vociferously welcomed his policies were increasingly skeptical of success. "Russia," one erstwhile optimist lamented to me at the time, "is not ready for democracy."

9-4b Eastern Europe: From Soviet Satellites to Sovereign Nations

The progressive decline of the Soviet Union had a perceptible impact on its neighbors to the west. As before, Poland was at the forefront. For several years, Party leaders had kept food prices as low as possible in order to avoid the outbreak of another round of unrest ("stuff their mouths with sausage," the current Party general secretary had advised). But in the late 1970s, food prices began to rise, sparking popular protests and the emergence of an independent labor union called **Solidarity**. Led by the union leader Lech Wałęsa (b. 1943), Solidarity rode the wave of national spirit heightened by the visit of Polish-born Pope John Paul II in June 1979 and rapidly became an influential force for change. Sensing a threat to its monopoly on power, the regime outlawed the union and declared martial law in 1981, but the movement continued to gain popular support. Gorbachev was worried at the turn of events, but when he made it clear that Moscow would not bail out the regime, Communist leaders in Warsaw then

bowed to the inevitable and permitted free national elections to take place, resulting in the election of Wałęsa as president of Poland in December 1990. Moscow—inspired by Gorbachev's policy of encouraging "new thinking" to improve relations with the Western powers—took no action to reverse the verdict in Warsaw.

In Hungary, as in Poland, the process of transition had begun many years earlier. After crushing the Hungarian revolution of 1956, the Communist government of János Kádár had tried to assuage popular opinion by enacting a series of far-reaching economic reforms (labeled "communism with a capitalist face-lift"), but as the 1980s progressed, the economy sagged, and in 1989, the regime permitted the formation of opposition political parties, leading eventually to the formation of a non-Communist coalition government in elections held in March 1990.

The transition in Czechoslovakia was more abrupt. After Soviet troops crushed the Prague Spring in 1968, hardline Communists under Gustáv Husák followed a policy of massive repression to maintain their power. In 1977, dissident intellectuals, inspired in part by the Helsinki Accords, formed an organization called Charter 77 as a vehicle for protest against violations of human rights. Regardless of the repressive atmosphere, dissident activities continued to grow during the 1980s, and when massive demonstrations broke out in several major cities in 1989, Husák's government, lacking any real popular support, collapsed. At the end of December, in what was termed the "velvet revolution," Husak was replaced by Václav Havel (1936–2011), a dissident playwright who had been a leading figure in Charter 77 (see Historical Voices, "Vaclav Havel: A Call for a New Politics," p. 237).

Similar outbreaks took place in Moscow's southern satellites. In Bulgaria, popular demonstrations led to the removal of the country's long-time Communist Party chief Todor Zhivkov, followed by the installation of a multi-party government. Only in Romania was the transition marked by violence. When protests by the members of the country's ethnic Hungarian minority erupted in mid-December, they were countered with force, but army units mutinied and the unrest quickly spread to the rest of the country. Two weeks later, Romania's long-time dictator Nicolae Ceausescu and his wife were captured and summarily executed.

The Fall of the Berlin Wall But the most dramatic events took place in East Germany, where a persistent economic slump and the ongoing oppressiveness of the regime of Erich Honecker led to a flight of refugees to neighboring countries. The exodus was dubbed by wits as the "Trabi trail," in reference to the ubiquitous if flimsy Trabant automobiles that had been manufactured for years in the GDR.

Vaclav Havel: A Call for a New Politics

 Do you believe that Václav Havel's criticisms of Czech society under Communist rule have relevance to many advanced industrial nations in the world today?

Politics & Government

WITH THE COLLAPSE OF THE COMMUNIST REGIMES in Eastern Europe in the late 1980s, a new generation of leaders began to call for a new political culture to replace the distorted values that had predominated under the "people's democracies." Some pointed to the need for a new perspective, especially a moral one, to face the challenges of a new era. The excerpt below is taken from a speech by Václav Havel, a playwright and a long-time critic of the Communist regime who was elected the new president of Czechoslovakia at the end of 1989.

Address to the People of Czechoslovakia, January 1, 1990

For forty years you heard from my predecessors on this day different variations on the same theme: how our country was flourishing, how many million tons of steel we produced, how happy we all were, how we trusted our government, and what bright perspectives were unfolding in front of us.

I assume you did not propose me for this office so that I, too, would lie to you.

Our country is not flourishing. The enormous creative and spiritual potential of our nations is not being used sensibly. Entire branches of industry are producing goods that are of no interest to anyone, while we are lacking the things we need. A state which calls itself a workers' state humiliates and exploits workers. Our obsolete economy is wasting the little energy we have available. A country that once could be proud of the educational level of its citizens spends so little on education that it ranks today as seventy-second in the world. We have polluted the soil, rivers and forests bequeathed to us by our ancestors, and we have today the most contaminated environment in Europe. . . .

But all this is still not the main problem. The worst thing is that we live in a contaminated moral environment. We fell morally ill because we became used to saying something different from what we thought. We learned not to believe in anything, to ignore one another, to care only about ourselves. Concepts such as love, friendship, compassion, humility or forgiveness lost their depth and dimension, and for many of us they represented only psychological peculiarities, or they resembled gone-astray greetings from ancient times, a little ridiculous in the era of computers and spaceships. Only a few of us were able to cry out loudly that the powers that be should not be all-powerful and that the special farms, which produced ecologically pure and top-quality food just for them, should send their produce to schools, children's homes and hospitals if our agriculture was unable to offer them to all.

The previous regime—armed with its arrogant and intolerant ideology—reduced man to a force of production, and nature to a tool of production. In this it attacked both their very substance and their mutual relationship. It reduced gifted and autonomous people, skillfully working in their own country, to the nuts and bolts of some monstrously huge, noisy and stinking machine, whose real meaning was not clear to anyone. . . .

When I talk about the contaminated moral atmosphere, I am . . . talking about all of us. We had all become used to the totalitarian system and accepted it as an unchangeable fact and thus helped to perpetuate it. In other words, we are all—though naturally to differing extents—responsible for the operation of the totalitarian machinery. None of us is just its victim. We are all also its co-creators. . . .

If we realize this, hope will return to our hearts.

Source: http://old.hrad.cz/president/Havel/speeches/1990/0101_uk.html

Mass demonstrations against the regime took place in the summer and fall of 1989.[7] Although the regime was reluctant to capitulate to popular pressure, one lower-level official appeared confused about how to respond to the crisis, and inadvertently opened the entire border with the West. The Berlin Wall, the most tangible symbol of the Cold War, became the site of a massive celebration, and most of it was dismantled by joyful Germans from both

IMAGE 9.5 The Fall of the Berlin Wall. As communist regimes in Eastern Europe began to crumble during the summer and fall of 1989, popular protests broke out in East Berlin to demand the destruction of the Berlin Wall. In early November, when local communist officials in the eastern zone appeared uncertain over how to deal with the crisis, crowds of Berliners on both sides of the barrier took measures into their own hands. With the fall of the Berlin Wall, one of the most repugnant symbols of the Cold War had been relegated into history.

during the 1930s now burst into flames. As Party officials in Moscow appeared paralyzed by events in Eastern Europe, nationalist movements emerged in all fifteen republics of the Soviet Union. Many of them called for the establishment of sovereign republics and independence from Russian-based rule centered in Moscow. The Soviet army, in disarray since the intervention in Afghanistan, appeared powerless to control the situation.

Gorbachev had made it clear that he supported self-determination, but he was opposed to secession, an act which he believed would be detrimental to the survival of the Soviet Union. Nevertheless, in December 1989, the Communist Party of Lithuania took the first step and declared itself independent of the Communist Party of the Soviet Union.

The final collapse of the Soviet Union was not long in coming. On March 11, 1990, Lithuania announced its independence from Soviet rule. When authorities in Moscow claimed that the declaration was null and void, the Lithuanians ignored the decision.

For the next several months, Gorbachev struggled to cope with the problems unleashed by his reforms, while seeking to appease conservative forces from the army, the Party, and the KGB, who complained about the growing disorder within the country. On August 19, 1991, a group of discontented rightists arrested Gorbachev and attempted to seize the reins of power. Gorbachev's refusal to work with the conspirators, and the resistance of thousands of Russians in Moscow who had grown accustomed to their new liberties, caused the coup to disintegrate. Still, despite renewed pleas from Gorbachev, all fifteen republics soon opted for complete independence (see Map 9.2). Ukraine voted for independence on December 1, 1991. Similar actions got under way in the various Soviet republics in Central Asia, as well as in the Caucasus, where Georgia and Armenia had long chafed under Russian rule. A week later, the leaders of Russia and Belarus announced that the Soviet Union had "ceased to exist" and would be replaced by a "commonwealth of independent states." On Christmas day, Gorbachev resigned and turned over his responsibilities as commander-in-chief to Boris Yeltsin (1931–2007), the

sides of the border (see Image 9.5). In March 1990, free elections led to the formation of a non-Communist government that began to negotiate political and economic reunification with West Germany (for events in Eastern Europe since 1989, see Chapter 10).

9-4c End of Empire

The events in Eastern Europe were being watched closely in Moscow. One of Gorbachev's most serious problems stemmed from the nature of the Soviet Union. The Union of Soviet Socialist Republics was a truly multiethnic country, containing ninety-two nationalities and 112 recognized languages. Previously, the iron hand of the Communist Party, centered in Moscow, had kept a lid on the centuries-old ethnic tensions that had periodically erupted throughout the history of this region. As Gorbachev released this iron grip, tensions resurfaced as ethnic groups took advantage of the new openness to protest what they perceived to be ethnically motivated slights. Long quiescent Muslim peoples in the Soviet republics in Central Asia suddenly became conscious of the social unrest taking place in nearby Afghanistan and throughout the Middle East. In the Baltic republics, memories of the brief era of independence that had been snuffed out by the Nazi-Soviet Pact of 1939 revived. And in Ukraine, simmering anger at Stalin's crackdown

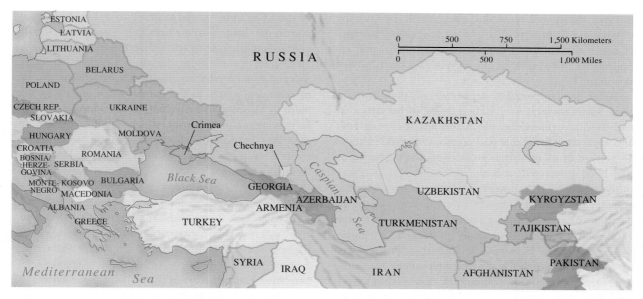

MAP 9.2 Eastern Europe and the Former Soviet Union. After the disintegration of the Soviet Union in 1991, the fifteen constituent Soviet republics declared their independence. This map shows the states that emerged from the former Soviet Union in the 1990s and also from the former Yugoslavia, which disintegrated more slowly in the 1990s and 2000s. The breakaway region of Chechnya is indicated on the map.

 What new nations have appeared in the territory of the old Soviet Union since the end of the Cold War?

president of the new Russian Republic. By the end of 1991, one of the largest empires in world history had come to an end, and fifteen new nations had embarked on an uncertain future.

9-5 THE NEW RUSSIA: FROM EMPIRE TO NATION

 Focus Questions: Why do you think relations between Russia and the United States have deteriorated in the thirty years since the collapse of the Soviet Union? Could the rupture have been avoided?

In Russia, by far the largest of the former Soviet republics, a new power struggle soon ensued. Yeltsin, a one-time engineer who had been dismissed from the Politburo in 1987 for insubordination, was committed to introducing a free market economy as quickly as possible. In December 1991, the Congress of People's Deputies granted him temporary power to rule by decree. But former Communist Party members and their allies in the Congress were opposed to many of Yeltsin's economic reforms and tried to place new limits on his powers.

Yeltsin fought back. After winning a vote of confidence on April 25, 1993, Yeltsin pushed ahead with plans for a new Russian constitution that would abolish the Congress of People's Deputies, create a two-chamber parliament, and establish a strong presidency. A hard-line parliamentary minority resisted and in early October took the offensive, urging supporters to take over government offices and the central television station. Yeltsin responded by ordering military forces to storm the parliament building and arrest hard-line opponents. Yeltsin used his victory to consolidate his power in parliamentary elections held in December.

During the mid-1990s, Yeltsin was able to maintain a precarious grip on power while seeking to implement reforms that would set Russia on a firm course toward a pluralistic political system and a market economy. But the new post-Communist Russia remained as fragile as ever. Burgeoning economic inequality and rampant corruption aroused widespread criticism and shook the confidence of the Russian people in the superiority of the capitalist system over the one that existed under Communist rule. A nagging war in the Caucasus—where the Muslim population of Chechnya sought national independence from Russia—drained the government's budget and exposed the decrepit state of the once vaunted Red Army. In presidential elections held in 1996, Yeltsin was reelected, but the rising popularity of a revived Communist Party and the growing strength of nationalist elements, combined with Yeltsin's precarious health, raised serious questions about the future of the country.

What had happened to derail Yeltsin's plan to transform Soviet society? According to some of his critics, he had tried to achieve too much too fast. Between 1991 and 1995, state firms that had previously provided about 80 percent of all industrial production and employment had been privatized, and the prices of goods (previously subject to government regulation) were allowed to respond to market forces. Only agriculture—where the decision to privatize collective farms had little impact in rural areas—was left substantially untouched. The immediate results were disastrous: industrial output dropped by more than one-third, and unemployment levels and prices rose dramatically. Lacking the strong labor unions and the institutional safeguards that had been installed over a period of decades in modern Western countries, many Russian workers and soldiers were not paid for months on end, and many social services came to an abrupt halt. In rural areas, farmers who in the past had transitioned directly from the communal ownership of the traditional village to the collective farms of the Soviet Union had not been encouraged to develop a culture of entrepreneurship that had sparked the growth of yeoman farmers in most Western countries. At the end of the twentieth century, forty percent of the Russian population was living below the poverty line, as defined by the United Nations.

With the harsh official and ideological constraints of the Soviet system suddenly removed, corruption—labeled by one observer "criminal gang capitalism"—became rampant, and the government often appeared inept in coping with the complexities of a market economy. Few Russians appeared to grasp the realities of modern capitalism and understandably reacted to the inevitable pains that accompanied the transition from the old system by heaping all the blame on the new one. The fact is that Yeltsin had attempted to change the structure of the Soviet system without due regard for the necessity of changing the mentality of the people as well. The result was a high level of disenchantment. A new joke circulated among the Russian people: "We know now that everything they told us about communism was false. And everything they told us about capitalism was true."

9-5a The Putin Era

At the end of 1999, Yeltsin suddenly resigned and was replaced by Vladimir Putin (b. 1952), a former member of the KGB. Putin vowed to bring an end to the rampant corruption and inexperience that permeated Russian political culture and to strengthen the role of the central government in managing the affairs of state. During the succeeding months, the parliament approved his proposal to centralize power in the hands of the federal government in Moscow; in early 2001, he presented a new plan to regulate political parties, which now numbered more than fifty. Parties at both extremes of the political spectrum, from those urging Western-style liberal policies to Gennadi Zyuganov's revived Communist Party, opposed the legislation—without success.

Putin also vowed to bring the breakaway state of Chechnya back under Russian authority and to adopt a more assertive role in international affairs. Growing public anger at Western plans to expand the NATO alliance into Eastern Europe and at the aggressive actions by NATO countries against Serbia in the Balkans (see Chapter 10) gave the new president an opportunity to take measures to restore Russia's position as an influential force in the world. To undercut U.S. dominance on the global scene, Moscow improved relations with neighboring China and simultaneously sought to cooperate with European nations on issues of common concern. To assuage national pride, Putin entered negotiations with such former republics of the old Soviet Union as Belarus and Ukraine to tighten mutual political and economic cooperation.

In addition, Putin steadily pursued measures to strengthen the power of the state over the political system. When critics complained that he was returning to the worst habits of the Soviet era, Putin responded forcefully, noting that while Russia was moving steadily to create conditions for building a democratic society, his government reserved the right to move forward based on its own internal circumstances. "Russia," he said, "can and will independently determine for itself the time frame and the conditions of its movement along that path."[8] Putin's determination to play an active role in that process was clearly demonstrated during the national elections in 2008. Prohibited by the constitution from serving a third term as president, he handpicked a successor—his close ally and United Russia Party member Dmitri Medvedev (b. 1965)—and agreed to serve as prime minister in the new government. Four years later, he was reelected to the presidency amid widespread claims of fraud and voter intimidation. He wasted no time in seeking to strengthen his control over the levers of power by silencing internal critics such as the feminist punk-rock group Pussy Riot. Political rivals have been intimidated, or even assassinated. To those who criticize his tendency to trample on human rights, he is openly contemptuous, declaring that Russia has no intention of following the Western model (see Image 9.6).

IMAGE 9.6 Russia's New Tsar: Vladimir Putin. Vladimir Putin, shown here in 2008 with German Chancellor Angela Merkel, is a one-time KGB agent who was serving in East Berlin at the close of the Cold War. Under his firm rule, Putin has energetically sought to revive the state of Russia to its former prestige under the Romanov Dynasty while rejecting the principles of Western-style liberal democracy as inappropriate for his fellow countrymen.

9-5b Russia Under the New Tsar

Throughout the first decade of the new century, relations between Russia and Western nations steadily deteriorated. Western officials grew increasingly concerned that, under Putin, Russia was reverting to its autocratic past. They were also critical of Moscow's efforts to intimidate the new states along its perimeter, states that had once been under the firm tutelage of the Soviet Union, but which now wished to move out from under Russian domination. For its part, Moscow was irritated at U.S. and European plans to integrate Eastern European countries into the Western alliance. It was especially incensed when the United States and some European governments supported the breakaway region of Kosovo in its bid to achieve independence from Russia's traditional ally Serbia. When dissident elements in Abkhazia and South Ossetia—two restive regions in the newly independent state of Georgia—appealed to Moscow for support against alleged government efforts to engage in ethnic cleansing, Russian military forces entered Georgian territory in support of the rebel forces and extended diplomatic recognition to both regions. Although a cease-fire agreement was eventually reached, the incident strained Moscow's relations with the United States and Western

Europe almost to the breaking point. When the financial crisis struck the global marketplace in the fall of 2008 (see Chapter 8), Moscow reacted with unrestrained pleasure. Flush with foreign currency reserves from its profitable oil exports, Russian officials openly called for the emergence of a new multipolar world no longer dominated by the United States and its European allies. In a bid to fill the vacuum, Moscow sought to use its oil wealth as a political weapon and extended a hand of friendship to a number of Washington's most prominent adversaries, including Iran and Venezuela. Concerned voices in the West expressed alarm at a potential revival of the tensions of the Cold War.

Ukraine: A Nation in Search of Its Identity In February 2014, the relationship between Russia and Western countries finally reached the breaking point, when Russian troops suddenly invaded the Crimea, a peninsula which was by international agreement an integral part of Ukrainian territory, and placed it under Russian rule. The Crimean dispute was rooted in the uneasy historical relationship between the Russian and Ukrainian peoples, and heightened by the fact that the current state of Ukraine is split ethnically and culturally between an eastern half (where the majority of the population is composed of ethnic Russians who feel a strong emotional tie to their mother country) and a western half (consisting primarily of Ukrainians who identify more closely with European culture through their ethnic, cultural, and linguistic ties to the countries of Eastern Europe). Many Ukrainians have historically considered themselves a separate people from Russians, and have been sensitive to patronizing attitudes occasionally expressed by the latter (many of whom have allegedly treated them as country bumpkins lacking in the cultural sophistication of their Russian neighbors).

Under Soviet rule, Crimea was originally governed as a separate territory because of its strategic importance on the Black Sea. The majority of the population were ethnic Russians, mainly because of the presence there of important military facilities. But in 1954 the peninsula was transferred to the Ukrainian Republic (see Map 9.2) for reasons of geographical contiguity. When Ukraine received its independence after the dissolution of the USSR, Crimea was then included within its boundaries.

Many Ukrainians were understandably delighted at the opportunity to seek independence from Russia, and eventually pro-Western leaders in the Ukrainian capital of Kiev sought to undertake steps to join the European Union, and even a closer relationship with NATO (see Chapter 10). Moscow strongly opposed the proposal, however, and its opposition was supported by pro-Russian elements in the eastern Ukraine, who managed to bring about the election of the pro-Moscow politician Viktor Yanukovich to the presidency of the country in 2010. Yanukovich immediately set out to marginalize pro-European politicians and strengthen ties with Moscow, whereupon in February 2014 he was ousted from office after popular protests and forced to seek refuge in Moscow. It was then that Putin and his allies launched the invasion of Crimea and incorporated it back under Russian rule. The UN General Assembly then stepped into the dispute by declaring the unilateral annexation null and void, while Western nations levied stiff trade sanctions on Russia to punish Moscow for its transgression. With the situation currently in a standoff, Ukraine—a nation of over fifty million people occupying the second largest amount of territory on the European continent—still seeks to create its own version of national identity.

Russia Today: Between East and West Today, Putin's Russia is pulling steadily away from the West. In the long debate between Westernizers and traditionalist elements convinced of the uniqueness of Russia over the future direction of the country, the latter are currently winning out. Disillusionment over the country's brief and bitter experience with unbridled capitalism and democracy during the Yeltsin era has tarnished for many the shiny image of Western democracy that briefly prevailed at the end of the Soviet era, and most Russians today appear to prefer a strong government over a weak and divided one. In a recent survey, over fifty percent of respondents expressed a preference for "order" (in Russian, *pryadok*) over a concern for human rights. Almost one-quarter of Russian citizens in the poll would actually approve a return of the Soviet Union.

Vladimir Putin, of course, believes in that assessment. In his mind and that of his supporters, what the Russian people need today is a "national idea," a symbol that will rally public support for the motherland. Putin thinks that he has found the answer in the promotion of nationalism, that brand of patriotism that is built on a combination of pride and resentment: pride in past glories and resentment against the country's many historic foreign enemies. In a cynical ploy that ill befits his own past career as a KGB official, he touts the traditions of the Russian Orthodox Church (ROC)—once ground under heel by Stalin and his apparatchiks in the Soviet secret police—as Russia's answer to the morally corrupt societies in Western Europe and North America. Putin has patronized Church leaders as fellow crusaders seeking to revive pride in the nation's past, while Patriarch Kiril, the current leader of the ROC, has praised Putin as "God's miracle" to the Russian people.

Today, the glories of tsarist Russia, as well as the more recent achievements of the Soviet era, are emphasized in schools, in the official media, in the churches, and in the arts (see Image 9.7). And, as Russia's adversarial relationship with the West intensifies, Putin has gone on the attack, pressuring ex-Soviet republics to refrain from improving relations with the West, using state-controlled Russian cyber experts to interfere in the electoral processes of several Western countries, increasing Russian military capacity, and spreading Moscow's influence abroad by intervening in tense international crises in far-off Latin America and the Middle East.

Like many fellow autocrats past and present, Putin is willing to use history as his handmaiden. Ferocious Russian figures like the sixteenth century tsar Ivan the Terrible—whose name, translated into English, conveys a sense of the brutality of his rule—are softened into strong leaders taking necessary measures to protect Mother Russia from its enemies; meanwhile, more recent events that portray the Soviet Union in a less than favorable light are airbrushed out of existence or ignored: the famine in Ukraine in the 1930s; the Nazi-Soviet Pact of 1939 which teamed-up the USSR with Nazi Germany; and the concentration camps that once held millions of Soviet prisoners.

IMAGE 9.7 **Saint Basil's: Symbol of Imperial Greatness.** Under Soviet rule, religion was severely discouraged, as the Communist regime sought to neutralize potential sources of opposition to its rule. St Basil's Church in Moscow, once a beacon of faith in Holy Russia, was turned into a museum. But the Russian Orthodox faith, long the official religion of Russia under the tsars, has made a comeback in recent years, and St. Basil's is now presented as a symbol of the glories of traditional Russian civilization. President Vladimir Putin has wrapped himself in its mantle by appointing a monk of the church as his spiritual adviser. Located in the heart of Red Square in Moscow, St. Basil's is the most visible symbol of the Orthodox faith in Russia.

incidence of alcoholism, sexual promiscuity, and criminal activities—and it is partly for that reason that many of Putin's compatriots express sympathy with his attempt to restore a sense of pride and discipline in Russian society. He was not alone in his feelings when in the spring of 2005 he expressed the view that the breakup of the Soviet Union was a national tragedy.

Russian Literature Today: A Search for Meaning As is so often the case, the mirror into the heart of a civilization is frequently found in the writings of its serious authors. And in fact, the disarray that has afflicted Russian society since the abrupt collapse of the Soviet Union has been amply reflected in its literary scene. Three of the country's most celebrated writers have presented different perspectives in the Russian people's existential search for meaning.

Svetlana Alexievich (b. 1948) was awarded the Nobel Prize in 2015 for her five-volume set of oral histories portraying the tumultuous lives of respondents from her native Belarus. Early volumes chronicled the laments of Soviet women who anguished over the loss of loved ones in World War II or later in Afghanistan. In succeeding tomes, she interviewed survivors from the nuclear disaster at Chernobyl, many of whom had suffered personally or had lost loved ones in the experience. In the final volume, she recorded the views of older interviewees who, although having suffered through the devastation of World War II and the brutal years under Joseph Stalin, now appear overwhelmed by the societal upheavals that have taken place since the collapse of the Soviet Union. Many of them sought refuge in the past, which to them in retrospect seemed a simpler time, when people weren't consumed by the contemporary rush for creature comforts but stood together to face a common challenge.

For some authors like Vladimir Sorokin (b. 1955), relief from the literary constraints of the Soviet era has led them to revel in hyper-grotesque fiction. Having once faced official criticism for his novels about the limitations of life under Communism, after 1991 he turned the focus of his anger to the excesses of the Putin era. In his novel *The Day of the Oprichnik* (2006), he has used the themes

Dream and Reality Dreams in Moscow of a possible revival of the powerful Soviet empire, however, are probably misplaced. In the first place, Russia—almost totally dependent on petroleum and other natural resources for its wealth—would be among the first to suffer in the event of another serious economic downturn. In the second place, the country is suffering from a multitude of serious structural problems, including widespread corruption, bureaucratic incompetence, a technology gap, and widespread inflation.

Indeed, pride in the recent achievements of the Russian nation is muted these days. Not only have the boundaries of the old Soviet empire shrunk by one-third, but the living standards of the Russian people have declined as well. According to recent statistics, mortality rates have risen by an estimated 40 percent in the last three decades, and the national population is predicted to decline by almost 50 million in the next half-century. Since the early 1980s, marriage rates have fallen by more than 30 percent, and the rate of divorce has increased by a similar measure.

There is a widespread sense of unease in Russia today about the decline of the social order—especially the disintegration of the traditional family and the rising of violence and the grotesque to describe a dysfunctional Russia in the year 2028, when *oprichniks* (the secret police of the sixteenth century tsar Ivan the Terrible) once again control society and practice their murderous ways.

Finally, a popular younger writer, Victor Pelevin (b. 1962), has adopted a satirical style to turn his scorn on the rampant corruption of Russian society today. In *The* *Yellow Arrow* (1993), he portrays the Russian people in a train car full of listless passengers heading heedlessly to an unknown destination. Still programmed in their Soviet-era straightjackets, the characters appear incapable of individual choice or willpower. The novel concludes when Andrei, the protagonist, chooses freedom over passivity and exits the train into an unknown future.

MAKING CONNECTIONS

The Soviet Union had emerged from World War II as one of the world's two superpowers. Its armies had played an instrumental role in the final defeat of the powerful German war machine and had installed pliant Communist regimes throughout Eastern Europe. During the next four decades, the Soviet Union appeared to be secure in its power. Its military and economic performance during the first postwar decade was sufficiently impressive to create an atmosphere of incipient panic in Washington. By the mid-1980s, however, fears that the Soviet Union would surpass the United States as an economic power had long since dissipated, and the Soviet system appeared to be mired in a state of near paralysis. Economic growth had slowed to a snail's pace, corruption had reached epidemic levels, and leadership had passed to a generation of elderly party bureaucrats who appeared incapable of addressing the burgeoning problems that affected Soviet society.

HISTORIANS DEBATE What had happened to tarnish the dream that had inspired Lenin and his fellow Bolsheviks to believe they could create a Marxist paradise? Some historians argue that the ambitious defense policies adopted by the Reagan administration forced Moscow into an arms race it could not afford and thus ultimately led to a collapse of the Soviet economy. Others suggest that Soviet problems were more deeply rooted and would have led to the disintegration of the Soviet Union even without outside stimulation. Both of these explanations have some validity, but the latter contention is surely closer to the mark. For years, if not decades, leaders in the Kremlin had disguised or ignored the massive inefficiencies of the Soviet system. It seems clear in retrospect that the Soviet command economy proved better at managing the early stages of the Industrial Revolution than at moving on to the next stage of an advanced technological society. Lacking incentives, the Soviet people had virtually ceased to work hard, while their leaders in Moscow plowed all of their resources into military hardware. By the 1980s, behind the powerful shield of the Red Army, the system had become an empty shell.

The perceptive Mikhail Gorbachev recognized the crucial importance of instituting radical reforms and hoped that by doing so he could save the socialist system, thus enabling it to compete on more equal terms with the dynamic economies in the West. By then, however, it was too late. Restive minorities that had long resented the suppression of their national or cultural identities under Moscow's heavy hand now saw their opportunity to break away from the Soviet system. Even the Russian people were no longer confident that the bright vision of a Marxist utopia could be transformed into reality.

The dissolution of the Soviet Union and its satellite system in Eastern Europe brought a dramatic end to the Cold War. At the dawn of the 1990s, a generation of global rivalry between two ideological systems had come to a close, and world leaders turned their attention to the construction of what U.S. President George H. W. Bush called the New World Order. In the eyes of many outside observers, the end of the Soviet dream opened the door to a new vision: the entrance of a new Russia and its one-time satellites into the democratic family of nations.

Over the next two decades, Western leaders operated under the assumption that an eastward expansion of the European Union, and even an expanded NATO, was a virtual inevitability. Time, however, has not been favorable to those expectations, and today the world appears to be embarked on a new version of the ideological Cold War that marked the last half of the twentieth century. In retrospect, it was probably unrealistic to expect that in a few short years, Russia could jettison a long tradition of tsarist autocracy and join the Western family of nations based on a set of principles that had taken the latter centuries to achieve. We shall take up these issues in Chapter 10, and in the reflections at the end of Part III.

REFLECTION QUESTIONS

Q How would you evaluate the strategy of containment followed by the United States and its allies during the Cold War. Do you view it as a success, or not?

Q What reasons have been advanced to explain why the Soviet system collapsed in 1991? Which do you think are the most persuasive?

Q Do you believe that the fall of the Soviet Union and its European satellites demonstrates that any form of socialist government is unworkable in the world today? Is capitalism the only effective form of political and economic organization, or are there alternatives?

CHAPTER TIMELINE

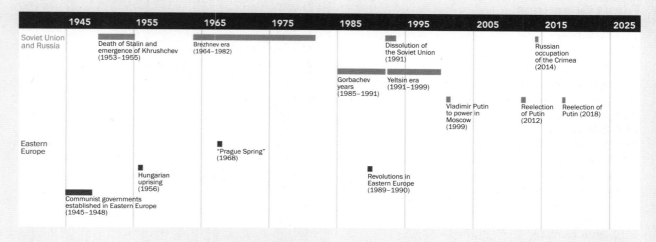

CHAPTER NOTES

1. Vladislav Zubok and Constantine Pleshakov, *Inside the Kremlin's Cold War: From Stalin to Khrushchev* (Cambridge, England, 1996), p. 166.
2. Nikita Khrushchev, *Khrushchev Remembers,* trans. Strobe Talbott (Boston, 1970), p. 77.
3. Excerpts from "The Soviet Constitution of 1977," Novosti Press Agency Publishing House. Moscow 1985.
4. Quoted in Hedrick Smith, *The New Russians* (New York, 1990), p. 30.
5. Cited in Victor Sebestyen, *Revolution 1989: The Fall of the Soviet Empire* (New York, 2009), p. 121.
6. Smith, *The New Russians,* p. 74.
7. Many years later, surviving Trabant automobiles became popular as a collector's item in parts of eastern Germany, perhaps in recollection of a simpler time.
8. C. J. Chivers, "Russia Will Pursue Democracy, but in Its Own Way, Putin Says," *New York Times,* April 26, 2005.

CHAPTER 10

POSTWAR EUROPE: ON THE PATH TO UNITY?

Chapter Outline and Focus Questions

10-1 *Western Europe: Recovery and Renewal*

Q What were the key reasons why European nations were able to recover so quickly from World War II and enter a period of peace and prosperity?

10-2 *The Modern Welfare State: Three European Models*

Q How does the European idea of a welfare state compare with the capitalist system as it is applied in the United States today?

10-3 *Eastern Europe After the Fall of the Iron Curtain*

Q To what degree have Eastern European nations adopted the Western European model since the end of the Cold War? Has their response been successful?

10-4 *Western Europe: The Search for Unity*

Q What are the challenges currently facing the European Union as it attempts to create a strong and united Europe that can play an important role in the world today?

10-5 *Aspects of Society in Postwar Europe*

Q What major social, cultural, and intellectual developments have occurred in Europe since 1945, and how have they changed the character of European society?

10-6 *Aspects of Culture in Postwar Europe*

Q How do recent cultural developments in Europe reflect the broader changes that are taking place in European society?

William Vandivert/Getty Images

IMAGE 10.1 Berlin 1945

Connections to Today

Does a steady level of immigration from foreign countries result in an advantage or a disadvantage for most countries of the world today?

AT THE END OF WORLD WAR II, European civilization was in ruins. Almost 40 million people had been killed in six years. Massive air raids and artillery bombardments had reduced many of the great cities of Europe to rubble. An American general described the German capital of Berlin: "Wherever we looked, we saw desolation. It was like a city of the dead. Suffering and shock were visible in every face. Dead bodies still remained in canals and lakes and were being dug out from under bomb debris." Berlin was not alone in its devastation. Dozens of other cities around Europe had been equally damaged by Allied bombing raids during the war, as air attacks were used for the first time as a deliberate means of intimidating the enemy.

Millions of Europeans now faced starvation as grain harvests were only half of what they had been in 1939. Countless others had been uprooted by the war; now they became "displaced persons," trying to find food and then their way home. The fruits of the Industrial Revolution, when mixed with the heady brew of virulent nationalism and the struggle for empire, were bitter indeed.

In the decades after 1945, Europe not only recovered from the devastating effects of World War II but also experienced an economic resurgence that seemed nothing less than miraculous. At the same time, the historical animosities that had fueled two catastrophic world wars were replaced by a determination to bring about a new united Europe, based on mutual cooperation and equal opportunity for all.

The process is by no means complete, however. As the Cold War came to an end in the early 1990s, ethnic and religious violence broke out in parts of Eastern Europe, undercutting ambitious plans to integrate the nations once isolated behind the Iron Curtain into a broader regional community. In the meantime, Europe's economic problems mounted, as generous welfare programs, combined with slower growth, resulted in growing budget deficits. In 2008, the global financial meltdown rocked the region and pushed several European nations to the edge of national bankruptcy. As a wide-ranging civil crisis in the Middle East led to a flood of migrants seeking entrance into the continent of Europe, popular resistance to the new arrivals led to the emergence of new political parties whose message contains a potential threat to the tradition of democratic pluralism that has flourished in the region for the last several decades. Today, the continent of Europe faces its most serious challenges since the end of World War II.

10-1 WESTERN EUROPE: RECOVERY AND RENEWAL

 Focus Question: What were the key reasons why European nations were able to recover so quickly from World War II and enter a period of peace and prosperity?

In the immediate postwar era, the challenge was clear and intimidating. The peoples of Europe needed to rebuild their national economies and reestablish and strengthen their democratic institutions. They also needed to find the means to cooperate in the face of a potential new threat from the east in the form of the Soviet Union, whose military power had now expanded into the very center of Europe. Above all, they needed to restore their confidence in the continuing vitality and future promise of European civilization—a civilization whose image had been badly tarnished by two bitter internal conflicts in the space of a quarter century.

In confronting the challenge, the Europeans possessed one significant trump card: the support and assistance of the United States. The United States had entered World War II as a major industrial power, but its global influence had been limited by the effects of the Great Depression and a self-imposed policy of isolation that had removed it from active involvement in world affairs. But after the United States helped bring the conflict to a close, the nation bestrode the world like a colossus. Its military power was enormous, its political influence was unparalleled, and its economic potential, fueled by the effort to build a war machine to defeat the Axis Powers, seemed unlimited. When on June 5, 1947, Secretary of State George C. Marshall told the graduating class at Harvard University that the United States was prepared to assist the nations of Europe in the task of recovery from "hunger, poverty, desperation, and chaos," he offered a beacon of hope to a region badly in need of reasons for optimism.

10-1a The Triumph of Democracy in Postwar Europe

With the economic aid of the Marshall Plan, the countries of Western Europe (see Map 10.1) recovered rapidly from the devastation of World War II. Between 1947 and 1950, European countries received $13 billion to be used for new equipment and raw materials. By the late 1970s, industrial production had surpassed all previous records, and Western Europe experienced virtually full employment. Social welfare programs included affordable health care; housing; family allowances to provide a minimum level of material care for children; increases in sickness, accident, unemployment, and old-age benefits; and educational opportunities. Despite economic recessions in the mid-1970s and early 1980s, caused in part by dramatic increases in the price of oil, the economies of Western Europe had never been so prosperous, leading some observers to label the period a "golden age" of political and economic achievement. Western Europeans were full participants in the technological advances of the age and seemed quite capable of standing up to competition from the other global economic powerhouses, Japan and the United States.

In the meantime, confidence in the democratic institutions that had been unable to confront the threat of fascism at the end of the 1930s began to revive. Although local

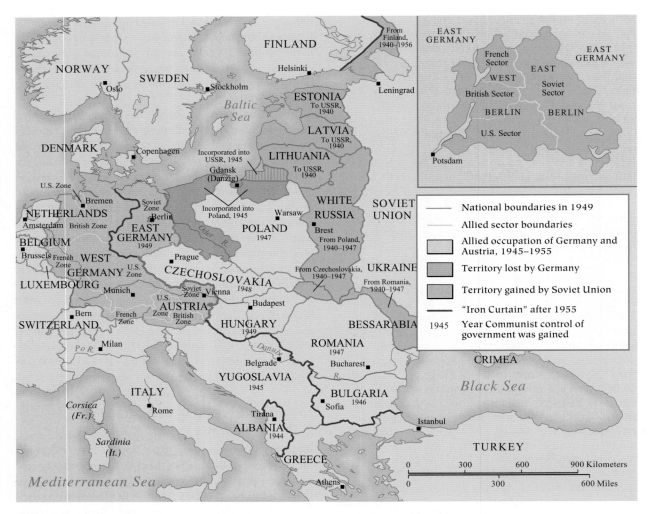

MAP 10.1 Territorial Changes in Europe After World War II. In the last months of World War II, the Red Army occupied much of Eastern Europe. Stalin sought pro-Soviet satellite states in the region as a buffer against future invasions from Western Europe, whereas Britain and the United States wanted democratically elected governments. Soviet military control of the territory settled the question.

 Which country gained the greatest territory at the expense of Germany?

Communist parties received wide support in national elections held in France and Italy immediately after the war, their fortunes waned as economic conditions started to improve. Even Spain and Portugal, which retained their prewar dictatorial regimes well after the end of World War II, established democratic systems in the late 1970s. Moderate political parties, especially the Christian Democrats in Italy and Germany, played a particularly important role in Europe's economic restoration. Overall, the influence of Communist parties declined, although reformist mass parties only slightly left of center, such as the Labour Party in Britain and the Social Democrats in West Germany and France, continued to share power. During the mid-1970s,

a new variety of communism, called Eurocommunism, emerged briefly when Communist parties tried to work within the democratic system as mass movements committed to better government. But by the 1980s, internal political developments in Western Europe and events within the Communist world had combined to undermine the Eurocommunist experiment.

10-1b The Integration of Europe

Since the time of Charlemagne and the formation of the Holy Roman Empire, princes and prelates have dreamed of creating a single European realm united in faith and common purpose against enemies within and without. But the reality of squabbling dynasties, ethnic rivalries, and bitter religious disputes always seemed to get in the way. By the nineteenth century, the rise of nationalism and imperialism threatened the very life of the idea and culminated in the self-destructive wars of the early twentieth century.

It was because of the enormity of the damage inflicted on European society by the two world wars that leading political figures in the post-war era began to draw up plans for a future united Europe. The desire to play a greater role in a world dominated by two superpowers was undoubtedly another factor. In the early 1950s, the first steps were taken with the formation of the Common Market, composed of six nations (France, Germany, Italy, Belgium, the Netherlands, and Luxembourg) within the Western alliance. After further steps toward regional integration, the European Union (EU) was finally created in 1994. The EU did not replace the sovereign powers of its individual members, but it sought to create a common market with no internal borders and freedom of movement from one end of the organization to the other.

From the beginning, however, the inherent tension over jurisdiction between the Union and its component parts has been a nagging problem, and in recent years, has threatened to tear asunder the bonds that unite the nations within the EU, and to disrupt the political consensus within the member nations as well. A more detailed analysis of these issues will appear later in this chapter, and in Chapter 16.

10-2 THE MODERN WELFARE STATE: THREE EUROPEAN MODELS

 Focus Question: How does the European idea of a welfare state compare with the capitalist system as it is applied in the United States today?

The European **welfare state** that began to take shape in the years following World War II represented a distinct effort to combine the social benefits provided by the reformist brand of social democracy (see Chapter 1) with the dynamic qualities of modern capitalism. The results varied from country to country, and not all political parties approved of the social democratic model. Eventually, though, virtually all the nations in Western Europe adopted some elements of the system, which differed sharply from the mostly *laissez-faire* capitalist model practiced in the United States.

10-2a France

The history of France for nearly a quarter century after the war was dominated by one man, Charles de Gaulle (1890–1970), who possessed an unshakable faith in his own historic mission to restore the greatness of the French nation. During the war, de Gaulle, then a colonel in the French army, had assumed leadership of the French government and forces in exile in London, known as the "Free French," as well as the anti-Nazi resistance groups in France itself, and he played an important role in ensuring the establishment of a French provisional government after the war. But immediately following the war, the creation of the Fourth Republic, with a return to a multiparty parliamentary system that de Gaulle considered inefficient, led him to withdraw temporarily from politics. Eventually, he formed the French Popular Movement, a political organization based on conservative principles that blamed the multiparty system for France's chronic political instability and called for a stronger presidency, a goal—and role—that de Gaulle finally achieved in 1958.

Expectations of Grandeur At the time of De Gaulle's election as president, the fragile political stability of the Fourth Republic was shaken by a crisis in Algeria, France's large North African colony. The French army, having suffered a humiliating defeat in Indochina in 1954, was determined to resist demands for independence by Algeria's Muslim majority. Independence was also opposed by the large French community living in Algeria, whose appeals were supported by many senior French military leaders. But a strong antiwar movement among French intellectuals and church leaders led to bitter divisions in France that opened the door to the possibility of civil war. The panic-stricken leaders of the Fourth Republic offered to let de Gaulle take over the government and revise the constitution.

In 1958, de Gaulle drafted a new constitution for the Fifth Republic that greatly enhanced the power of the French president, who now had the right to choose the prime minister, dissolve parliament, and supervise both defense and foreign policy. As the new president, de Gaulle sought to return France to a position of power and influence. Believing that an independent role in the Cold War might enhance France's stature, he pulled France out of the NATO high command. He sought to increase French prestige in the Third World by consenting to Algerian independence despite strenuous opposition from the army and offered French colonies in Africa membership in a new French community of nations under French tutelage. France invested heavily in the nuclear arms race and exploded its first nuclear bomb in 1960.

Although the cost of the nuclear program increased the defense budget, de Gaulle did not neglect the French economy. Economic decision-making was centralized, a reflection of the overall concentration of power undertaken by the Gaullist government. Between 1958 and 1968, the French gross national product (GNP) grew by 5.5 percent annually, faster than the rate of growth in the United States. By the end of the Gaullist era, France was a major industrial producer and exporter, particularly in such areas as automobiles and armaments. Nevertheless, problems remained. The expansion of traditional industries, such as coal and railroads, which had been nationalized, led to large government deficits. The cost of living increased faster than in the rest of Europe.

Shift to the Left Public dissatisfaction with the government's inability to deal with these problems soon led to more violent action. In May 1968, student protests, provoked by France's anachronistic educational system as well as the ongoing war in Vietnam, were followed by a general strike by the labor unions (see "10-5a An Age of Affluence," p. 263). During the spring and summer of 1968, the whiff of tear gas and the sound of police sirens were daily occurrences on the streets of Paris. Although de Gaulle managed to restore order, the events of 1968 seriously undermined popular respect for the aloof and imperious president. Tired and discouraged, de Gaulle resigned from office in April 1969 and died within a year. Yet "le grand Charles," as he was sometimes dubbed derisively by his critics, did make a significant contribution to French governmental institutions by bringing an end to the fractious politics of the prewar era. De Gaulle's successors would enjoy the benefits of a more centralized political system that enabled the chief executive to enact major changes in French society.

During the 1970s, the French economic situation continued to decline, bringing about a political shift to the left. In 1981, the veteran Socialist leader, François Mitterrand (1916–1996), was elected president (see Image 10.2). To resolve France's economic difficulties, he froze prices and wages in the hope of reducing the huge budget deficit and high inflation. Mitterrand also introduced a number of programs to aid workers: an increased minimum wage, expanded social benefits, a mandatory fifth week of paid vacation for salaried workers, a thirty-nine-hour workweek, and higher taxes on the rich. Their success in enacting these measures convinced the Socialists that they could enact more radical reforms. Consequently, the government nationalized the steel industry, major banks, the space and electronics industries, and important insurance firms.

IMAGE 10.2 **François Mitterrand and Margaret Thatcher.** François Mitterrand was the first member of the Socialist Party to serve as President of France after World War II. He was soon forced to move to the center to deal with the problems that he had inherited. Here he is shown with Great Britain's first female prime minister, Margaret Thatcher in a photograph taken in 1986. Thatcher dominated British politics in the 1980s and served in the post longer than any man in modern times.

A Season of Discontent But the Socialist government's efforts to reverse the country's economic decline failed, and when the rate of inflation began to rise, the government froze wages and adopted an austerity program in government spending. By the time he retired in 1995, Mitterrand had become a centrist, in fact if not in name. In 1995 the conservative mayor of Paris, Jacques Chirac (1932–2019), was elected president. By this time, a new element had entered the equation, as public resentment against foreign-born residents had become a growing political reality in France. In 2008 there were nearly 5 million immigrants in the country, nearly 7.5 percent of the total population of 65 million. Many of the recent arrivals were Muslims from North Africa, and thus were identified in the public mind with terrorist actions committed by militant groups based in the Middle East. Spurred by such concerns, many French voters gave their support to Jean-Marie Le Pen's National Front, which openly advocated restrictions on all new immigration and limited the assimilation of immigrants already living in France. In 2002, Le Pen came in second in the race for the French presidency.

In the fall of 2005, youth riots broke out in the crowded suburbs of Paris. Many of the participants were young Muslims protesting their dismal living conditions and the lack of employment opportunities for foreign-born residents in France (see Image 10.5). After the riots subsided, government officials promised to adopt measures to respond to the complaints, but tensions persisted between the growing Muslim community and the remainder of the French population over such issues as the threat of terrorism and the right of female Muslims to wear a head scarf in public schools.

In May 2007, another Conservative, Nicolas Sarkozy (b. 1955), was elected president of France. As minister of the interior under the previous administration, Sarkozy had been critical of the urban protests and promised to crack down on social unrest. Once installed as president, however, he tried to defuse the issue by promising to adopt a Marshall Plan for troubled areas of the country. But the government's options were limited by the realities of an economy struggling with both rising inflation and anemic growth (see "10-5b Rethinking the Welfare State," p. 264). As Europe sought to deal with the effects of the global financial meltdown, in May 2012 Sarkozy was defeated in his bid to win a second term in office, to be replaced by the Socialist François Hollande (b. 1954). The new president took office in a country facing a sluggish economy and an unemployment rate of nearly 20 percent.

As president, Hollande hoped to re-enact elements of his party's socialist program by raising taxes on the wealthy, regulating banks, and bringing an end to the economic crisis caused by the global recession of 2008, which had left European banks exposed to the debts of many of the EU's weaker nations. But when Hollande also tacked to the right by calling for the closure of failing factories and loosening labor regulations to permit corporations to lay off workers, his approval rating dropped dramatically. Hollande's handling of two bloody terrorist attacks in Paris in 2015 temporarily boosted his standing among the public, but he was unable to relieve rising public concern over the nation's steadily declining standard of living, increasing income inequality (one percent of the French population controlled over twenty percent of the national wealth), and a stubbornly high unemployment rate. Widespread anger over the increasing number of immigrants in the country added to his woes. Much of the discontent was centered in what the French call "la France profonde"—loosely translated into English as "the rural heartland of France"—where the job losses, the stagnating incomes, and the hollowing-out of local communities were particularly noticeable.

Overwhelmed by the nation's mounting difficulties and the steady decline in his personal popularity, Hollande decided not to run for reelection in 2017. In the wide-open race to succeed him, it became clear that the traditional alignment of political parties had been shaken by recent events, and two new parties figured prominently in the outcome. The traditional parties—the Conservatives and the Socialists—had been badly discredited for their failure to resolve the nation's discontents, leading to the birth of a new political paradigm.

On the right, Jean-Marie Le Pen's National Front (now renamed the Rassemblement National) had become an increasingly powerful force, with his daughter Marina as its candidate. Meanwhile, a young banker, Emmanuel Macron (b. 1977), formed a new centrist political party known as La Republique en Marche ("the Republic on the Move" in English). The Conservative Party—which had previously accepted the European consensus on economic globalism and neo-liberal social policies—broke with tradition and nominated François Fillon, who based his campaign on a revival of French traditional values, even though he himself had become the subject of a personal scandal. Much of Fillon's support came from Catholics or from individuals who were concerned at the secular character of French society, the decline of the traditional family, and the increasing emphasis on individual rights over that of the community as a whole. Some of his supporters had unsuccessfully attempted to oppose recently adopted legislation proposed by the Socialists that extended legal rights for the LGBTQ community and authorized same-sex marriage.

In the end, Macron's youthful vigor, his public commitment to break the political paralysis in Paris, and his pro-European message appealed to many French voters (as well as to many observers abroad), who elected him as the youngest president in the history of France. Macron entered office with high ambitions to remove many of the various regulations and traditions that, in his view, kept French society in a straight-jacket and undercut its economic competitiveness in the world market. Accordingly, he moved quickly to overhaul the rigid labor code and strengthen the rights of employers to hire and fire workers, while reducing the ability of the nation's powerful labor unions to prevent necessary changes to improve efficiency. Finally, to stimulate lagging investment, he cut state taxes on wealthy citizens.

As he soon discovered, such measures, even though seen as necessary steps to improve the health of the French economy, always take time to reap benefits, while the pain struck the working class immediately, and when the government announced an increase in fuel taxes to cut carbon emissions and thus meet environmental goals required by the EU, discontented workers donned emergency yellow vests (*gilets jaunes*) and took to the streets to protest the increase in fuel prices at the pump. They were soon joined by thousands of other demonstrators bearing similar complaints. Macron reluctantly caved in on the price increase, while promising to adopt measures to improve conditions for the poor. Like so many of his predecessors, Macron had encountered one of the central dilemmas of French politics.

10-2b Germany: Across the Cold War Divide

The unification of the three Western zones into the Federal Republic of Germany (FRG, or West Germany) became a reality in 1949. Konrad Adenauer (1876–1967), the leader of the Christian Democratic Union (CDU), served as chancellor from 1949 to 1963 and became the "founding hero" of the FRG. Adenauer, who had opposed Hitler's regime, sought to revive respect for Germany by cooperating with the United States and the other Western European nations. He was especially desirous of reconciliation with France—Germany's longtime rival. As Cold War tensions increased, concerns about German rearmament subsided, and the FRG became a member of NATO in 1955.

The Economic Miracle Adenauer and his successors did not have the luxury of building upon the rich democratic traditions possessed by many of their counterparts in Western Europe. Germany's only experiment with liberal democracy had been the fragile and much maligned Weimar Republic, which had so easily succumbed to Nazi tyranny in the 1930s. But they were able to reap the benefits of an era of economic expansion and prosperity that Weimar leaders would have envied. In fact, the Adenauer era witnessed a resurrection of the West German economy that was so remarkable it was regarded as an "economic miracle." Although West Germany had only 75 percent of the population and 52 percent of the territory of prewar Germany, by 1955 West Germany's GNP soon exceeded that of prewar Germany. Real wages doubled between 1950 and 1965, even though working hours were cut by 20 percent. Unemployment fell from 8 percent in 1950 to 0.4 percent in 1965. To maintain its economic expansion, West Germany imported hundreds of thousands of "guest" workers, primarily from Italy, Spain, Greece, Turkey, and Yugoslavia.

The Federal Republic had established its capital at Bonn, a sleepy market town on the Rhine River, to erase memories of the Nazi era, when the capital was at Berlin. It also began to make payments to Israel and to Holocaust survivors and their relatives to make some restitution for, in the words of German president Richard von Weizsacker, "the unspeakable sorrow that occurred

in the name of Germany." Unlike their behavior after World War I, most Germans accepted the country's "burden of guilt," and embarked on a quest to replace the prewar German lust for power and *lebensraum* with a dedication to the principles of peace and democracy. A history of Germany that was used frequently as a text for classes at the secondary level presented such ideas ably to a younger generation. It praised the concept of democracy as something that could not function as an ideal, but only if citizens were "thoroughly imbued with democratic attitudes" that are put in practice every day. "We owe it to ourselves," the author declared, "to examine our consciences sincerely and to face the naked truth, instead of minimizing it or glossing over it." That, the author declared, was the way to regain respect in the world.[1]

Willy Brandt and *Ostpolitik* After the Adenauer era ended in the mid-1960s, the Social Democrats became the leading party. By forming a ruling coalition with the small Free Democratic Party, they remained in power until 1982. The first Social Democratic chancellor was Willy Brandt (1913–1992). Brandt was especially successful with his "opening toward the east" (known as *Ostpolitik*), for which he received the Nobel Peace Prize in 1972. On March 19, 1971, Brandt met with Walter Ulbricht, the leader of East Germany, and worked out the details of a treaty that was signed in 1972. This agreement did not establish full diplomatic relations with East Germany but did call for "good neighborly" relations. As a result, it led to greater cultural, personal, and economic contacts between West and East Germany. Despite this success, the discovery of an East German spy among Brandt's advisers caused his resignation in 1974.

His successor, Helmut Schmidt (1918–2015), was more of a technocrat than a reform-minded socialist and concentrated on the economic problems brought about largely by high oil prices between 1973 and 1975. Schmidt was successful in eliminating a deficit of 10 billion marks in three years. In 1982, when the coalition of Schmidt's Social Democrats with the Free Democrats fell apart over the reduction of social welfare expenditures, the Free Democrats joined with the Christian Democratic Union of Helmut Kohl (1930–2017) to form a new government.

Germany United: The Party's Over With the end of the Cold War, West Germany faced a new challenge. Chancellor Helmut Kohl had benefited greatly from an economic boom in the mid-1980s. Gradually, however, discontent with the Christian Democrats increased, and by 1988, their political prospects seemed diminished. But unexpectedly, the 1989 revolution in East Germany led in 1990 to the reunification of the two Germanies (see Chapter 9), making the new Germany, with its 79 million people, the leading power in Europe. Reunification, accomplished during Kohl's administration, brought rich political dividends to the Christian Democrats. In the first all-German federal election, Kohl's Christian Democrats won 44 percent of the vote, and their coalition partners, the Free Democrats, received 11 percent.

But the euphoria over reunification soon dissipated as the realization set in that the revitalization of the old German Democratic Republic (GDR) would take far more money than was originally thought, and Kohl's government was soon forced to face the politically undesirable task of raising taxes substantially. Moreover, the virtual collapse of the economy in eastern Germany led to extremely high levels of unemployment and severe discontent. Even today, unemployment in eastern Germany is double that in the old West Germany, while wages average only about 80 percent of those in the west (see Image 10.3).

Increasing unemployment in turn led to growing resentment against foreigners. For years, foreigners seeking asylum or employment found a haven in Germany because of its extremely liberal immigration laws. In 1992, more than 440,000 immigrants came to Germany seeking asylum, 123,000 of them from former Yugoslavia alone. Attacks against foreigners by right-wing extremists—many of them espousing neo-Nazi beliefs—killed seventeen people in 1992 and became an all too frequent occurrence in German life.

East Germans were also haunted by another memory from their recent past. The opening of the files of the secret police (the Stasi) showed that millions of East Germans had spied on their neighbors and colleagues, and even their spouses and parents, during the Communist era (see Movies & History, *The Lives of Others*, p. 231). A few senior Stasi officials were put on trial for their past actions, but many Germans preferred simply to close the door on an unhappy period in their lives.

As the old century came to a close, Germans struggled to cope with the challenge of building a new, united nation. To reduce the debt incurred because of economic reconstruction in the east, the government threatened to cut back on many of the social benefits Germans had long been accustomed to receiving. This in turn increased resentments that had already appeared between eastern and western Germany. Residents of the old East Germany still often express regrets about reunification, which is commonly referred to there by the more neutral term "Die Wende," meaning the "turn" or "change."[2]

In 1998, voters took out their frustrations at the ballot box. Helmut Kohl's conservative coalition was defeated in national elections, and a new prime minister, Social Democrat Gerhard Schröder (b. 1944), came into office. Schröder had no better luck than his predecessor at reviving the economy, however. In 2003, with nearly 5 million workers unemployed, the government announced plans to scale back welfare benefits that had long been a familiar part of life for the German people. In 2005, national elections brought the Christian Democrats back into power under the leadership of Germany's first woman chancellor, Angela Merkel (b. 1954). Having lived much of her life under communism in East Germany, Merkel supported measures to curb government spending while relying increasingly on the capitalist marketplace. On the other hand, she pursued social

IMAGE 10.3 An Abandoned Factory in East Germany. This abandoned factory on the banks of the Elbe River in eastern Germany stands as a bleak symbol of the economy that the FRG inherited when it embarked on the assimilation of the territories of the old GDR. Much of the industrial sector in East Germany was inefficient and rapidly collapsed once it came into competition with its counterparts in the West. Derelict factories like this one litter the landscape and symbolize the failure of Marxism in Germany.

William J. Duiker

measures like health care reform while seeking to play a leading role in the affairs of the European Union. There, she soon encountered new challenges when Greece and other fellow members of the European Union (see "10-4b The European Union," p. 261) were unable to pay their debts and turned to wealthy nations in northern Europe to stave off the threat of bankruptcy. Many Germans resented having to bail out their neighbors, and Merkel shared that view. Still, she led the EU in efforts to resolve the continuing financial problems faced by Greece and other members from southern Europe like Italy, Spain, and Portugal. Elected as chancellor three times, she became the longest-serving head of state in the EU (see Image 9.6, p. 241).

But when a brutal civil war broke out in Syria in 2015, Merkel risked her popularity by taking the lead in encouraging fellow European countries to accept the thousands of refugees from Syria that were arriving in Europe by land and by sea. As a result, she came under heavy criticism from some fellow Germans for having accepted many of these migrants as part of the European continent's effort to try to ease the humanitarian crisis in the Middle East. Anti-immigration sentiment came primarily, but not exclusively, from Germans living in the former eastern zone, where high levels of unemployment proved stubbornly difficult to eradicate. Part of the reason for the job losses was that the German government had committed itself to relieving the country from its reliance on coal for meeting its electricity requirements. The eastern sections of Germany had traditionally been reliant on the mining of soft coal deposits for their livelihood, while many of the factories that operated under Communist rule had been shuttered because of inefficiency (see Image 10.3).

In Germany, as in neighboring France, the rise of anti-immigration sentiment has led to the realignment of politics and the emergence of a new political party called Alternative for Germany (AfD). This new organization has managed to win popular support away from both Merkel's party and the Social Democrats. At the other end of the political spectrum, many young Germans have become disenchanted with the two major political parties and have gravitated over to the Green Party, a relatively recent political organization founded on environmental issues. Although the country has long been identified with the movement to clean up the environment, it is still highly dependent on coal, and suffers severely from automobile pollution. Some observers compare the emergence of the AfD as a force in German politics with the situation in the 1930s, when anti-foreign sentiment played a significant role in the rise of the Nazi movement, but early signs suggest that the comparison

may be overdrawn (see Historical Voices, "Manifesto for Germany," p. 255).

Today, Angela Merkel—who for long has served as a stabilizing fixture in Europe—has begun to lose support among her constituents, and she has acknowledged such sentiments by announcing that she will not seek re-election as the head of her Christian Democratic Party. As she prepares to leave the stage, the German political scene is showing distinct signs of a break-up of the familiar party designations that have endured since the end of World War II.

10-2c Great Britain

The end of World War II left Britain with massive economic problems. In elections held immediately after the war, the Labour Party overwhelmingly defeated Winston Churchill's Conservative Party. The Labour Party had promised far-reaching reforms, particularly in the area of social welfare—an appealing platform in a country with a tremendous shortage of consumer goods and housing. Clement Atlee (1883–1967), the new prime minister, was a pragmatic reformer rather than the leftist revolutionary that Churchill had warned against during the election campaign. His Labour government proceeded to enact reforms that created a modern welfare state.

The establishment of the British welfare state began with the **nationalization** of the Bank of England, the coal and steel industries, public transportation, and public utilities such as electricity and gas. In the area of social welfare, in 1946 the new government enacted the National Insurance Act and the National Health Service Act. The insurance act established a comprehensive social security program and nationalized medical insurance, thereby enabling the state to subsidize the unemployed, the sick, and the aged. The health act created a system of **socialized medicine** that forced doctors and dentists to work with state hospitals, although private practices could be maintained. This measure was especially costly for the state, but within a few years, 90 percent of the medical profession was participating.

Imperial Sunset The cost of building a welfare state at home forced the British to reduce expenses abroad. This meant dismantling the British Empire and reducing military aid to such countries as Greece and Turkey, a decision that inspired the enunciation of the Truman Doctrine in Washington (see Chapter 7). Economic necessity, and not just pressure from colonial nationalist movements, brought an end to the British Empire.

Continuing economic problems brought the Conservatives back into power from 1951 to 1964. Although they

Manifesto for Germany

 Do the principles established in this manifesto conform in major respects with the liberal consensus established in most Western countries since the end of World War II. If not, how might they differ?

Politics & Government THE MASSIVE INFLUX OF REFUGEES from the Middle East in recent years has tested the capacity of all the countries in Europe to absorb immigrants from foreign lands. Although the majority of the population of the European Continent has been receptive to the new arrivals, the sense of public unease at rising levels of refugees from Muslim countries is palpable, and each incident of Islamic terrorism seems to heighten the sense of concern. Alternative for Germany is only one of several new political parties that have emerged in response to the situation. In the preamble to the manifesto that is presented here, the drafters emphasize their commitment to liberal democratic principles, but also refer to their insistence that their country should remain a "German nation."

Alternative for Germany, Manifesto Preamble

1. **Courage to stand up for Germany.**
2. **We are not subjects but free citizens.**
3. **We are liberals and conservatives.**
4. **We are free citizens of our nation.**
5. **We are staunch supporters of democracy.**

We have come together as citizens with different backgrounds, experience, qualifications and political careers. In spite of our differences, we believe in a common vision, and that the time to stand up and act has arrived. We share a firm conviction that citizens have the right to true political alternatives, not only those presented by the political class.

No longer can we remain idle and observe the breaches of justice and the rule of law, the destruction of the constitutional state, and irresponsible political actions which clash with sound economic principles. Similarly, we are no longer willing to accept the enforcement of the so-called Euro rescue package, which has rekindled long-forgotten prejudices and hostilities between the peoples of Europe. Therefore, we have decided to offer Germany and all its citizens a true political alternative, which covers all aspects of life.

As free citizens we believe in direct democracy, the separation of powers, the rule of law, social market economics, subsidiarity, federalism, family values, and German cultural heritage, as democracy and freedom are vested in our common cultural values and historical tradition. The recollect of the revolutions of 1848 and 1989 drive our civil protest and the determination to complete our national unity in freedom, and create a Europe of sovereign and democratic nation states, united in peace, self-determination and good-neighborliness.

We commit ourselves with all our energy to restoring these principles, and fundamentally reform our country in the spirt of freedom and democracy. We maintain an open mind toward other nations and cultures, but wish to be and remain German at heart. Therefore, we shall continuously strive to uphold human dignity, support families with children, retain our Western Christian culture, and maintain our language and traditions in a peaceful democratic, and sovereign nation state for the German people.

We will have reached our goal when government and all its institutions once again become servants to all citizens in our country, which all members of government swear in the official oath to the constitution:

"I swear that I will dedicate my efforts to the well-being of the German people, promote their welfare, protect them from harm, uphold and defend the German Constitution and the laws of the Federation, perform my duties conscientiously and do justice to all."

Source: "The Political Programme of the Alternative for Germany," p. 6. Approved at the Federal Party Congress held in Stuttgart, Germany, on April 30–May 1, 2016.

---

favored private enterprise, the Conservatives accepted the new system and even extended it, undertaking an ambitious construction program to improve British housing. Although the British economy had recovered from the war, it had done so at a slower rate than other European countries. This slow recovery masked a long-term economic decline caused by a variety of factors, including trade union demands for wages that rose faster than productivity and the unwillingness of factory owners to invest in modern industrial machinery and to adopt new methods. Underlying the immediate problems, however, was a deeper issue. As a result of World War II, Britain had lost much of its prewar revenue from abroad but was left with a burden of debt from its many international commitments.

Between 1964 and 1979, Conservatives and Labour alternated in power. Both parties faced seemingly intractable problems. Although separatist movements in Scotland and Wales were overcome, a dispute between Catholics and Protestants in Northern Ireland was marked by violence as the rebel Irish Republican Army (IRA) staged a series of dramatic terrorist acts in response to the suspension of Northern Ireland's parliament in 1972 and the establishment of direct rule by London. The problem of Northern Ireland remained unresolved. Nor was either party able to deal with Britain's ailing economy. Great Britain's years in the sun, it appeared, were long past.

"Thatcherism": The Conservatives in Ascendance   In 1979, after five years of Labour government and worsening economic problems, the Conservatives returned to power under Margaret Thatcher (1925–2013), the first woman prime minister in British history (see Movies & History, *The Iron Lady*). Thatcher pledged to lower taxes, reduce the government bureaucracy, limit social welfare, restrict union power, and end inflation. The "Iron Lady," as she was called, did break the power of the labor unions. Although she did not eliminate the basic components of the social welfare system, she used austerity measures to control inflation. "Thatcherism," as her economic policy was termed, improved the British economic situation, but at a price. The south of England, for example, prospered, but the old industrial areas of the Midlands and north declined and were beset by high unemployment, poverty, and sporadic violence. Cutbacks in funding for education seriously undermined the quality of British schools, long regarded as among the world's finest.

In foreign policy, Thatcher took a hard-line approach against communism. She oversaw a large military buildup aimed at replacing older technology and reestablishing Britain as a world policeman. In 1982, when Argentina attempted to take control of the Falkland Islands (one of Britain's few remaining colonial outposts, known to Argentines as the Malvinas) 300 miles off its coast, the British successfully rebuffed the Argentines, although at considerable economic cost and the loss of 255 lives. The Falklands War, however, did generate popular support for Thatcher, as many in Britain reveled in memories of the nation's glorious imperial past.

MOVIES & HISTORY
The Iron Lady (2011)

Directed by Phyllida Lloyd, the film *The Iron Lady* is a joint British-French docudrama that was produced in 2011. The character of Margaret Thatcher was played by the renowned American actress Meryl Streep (and, in her youth, by Alexandra Roach).

A controversial figure in British politics, Thatcher was born the daughter of a grocer in the town of Grantham. As a student, she fought against class and gender prejudice to earn a degree at Oxford. After joining the Conservative Party, she won election to Parliament and was eventually named Secretary of Education under Prime Minister Edward Heath. In 1979 she became the first female prime minister of the United Kingdom. Over a twelve-year period, she overcame prejudice from many of her male colleagues to put her indelible stamp on British politics, promoting a tight money policy, reform of the labor unions, and the privatization of state-owned industries. Tough-minded in foreign affairs as in the domestic arena, she opposed European integration and the unification of Germany, and dispatched British military forces to oppose an invasion of the British-held Falkland Islands by Argentina.

It was never easy. Her effort to dismantle the British welfare state resulted in a rise in the unemployment rate and a number of workers' strikes. At the end of her reign as prime minister, she was forced to resign as prime minister by Conservative colleagues and suffered from ill health in her declining years.

As a film, *The Iron Lady* earned mixed reviews from critics, and unfortunately—considering that her historical significance depends almost entirely on her role as a woman in the public arena—spends more time on her marriage to Denis Thatcher (1915–2003) than on her long career in politics, but Meryl Streep deservedly won an Oscar for her stellar performance of this unusual woman.

 What do you think a film about Margaret Thatcher should focus on?

The Era of Tony Blair While Thatcher dominated politics in the 1980s, the Labour Party, beset by divisions between its moderate and radical wings, offered little effective opposition. But in 1990, Labour's fortunes revived when the Conservative government attempted to replace local property taxes with a flat-rate tax payable by every adult to his or her local authority. Although Thatcher contended that this would make local government more responsive to popular needs, many argued that this was nothing more than a poll tax that would enable the rich to pay the same rate as the poor. After anti-tax riots broke out, Thatcher's once legendary popularity plummeted to an all-time low. At the end of November, a revolt within her own party caused Thatcher to resign as prime minister. Her replacement was John Major (b. 1943), whose Conservative Party won a narrow victory in the general elections held in April 1992.

The new prime minister sought to continue his predecessor's policies—privatizing the nation's railroad system in 1994—but his lackluster leadership failed to capture the imagination of many Britons, and in new elections in May 1997, the Labour Party won a landslide victory. The new prime minister, Tony Blair (b. 1953), was a moderate whose youth and energy immediately instilled a new vigor into the political scene. Adopting centrist policies reminiscent of those followed by President Bill Clinton in the United States (Blair entitled his program the "Third Way," a position somewhere between the free market practices in the United States and the paternalistic welfare systems on the European continent), his party dominated the political arena into the new century.

Riding on a wave of economic prosperity, the Labour government passed legislation to introduce a minimum wage and address child poverty. But a continued deterioration of public services—notably in the areas of education, transportation, and health care—steadily eroded Blair's popular appeal. His decision to support the U.S.-led invasion of Iraq in 2003 was also not popular with the British public. The failure of the opposition Conservative Party to field a popular candidate kept him in power for nearly a decade, but in 2007 he stepped down from office and was replaced by his fellow Labour Party leader, Gordon Brown (b. 1951).

A Partnership in Peril In 2010, in the wake of climbing unemployment and a global financial crisis, the Labour Party's thirteen-year rule ended when the Conservative Party candidate David Cameron (b. 1966) became prime minister on the basis of a coalition with the Liberal Democrats. Cameron promised to reduce the government debt by cutting government waste and social services and overhauling the health care system. Cameron's austerity measures, however, exacted a heavy price, as the British economy went into recession.

Still, the Cameron government passed a number of significant legislative measures, reducing social welfare benefits, eliminating the amount of available housing for those on public assistance, and privatizing parts of the country's National Health Service. But Cameron defied Conservative sentiment by passing a Marriage Act in 2013, which authorized marriage by same-sex couples. Riding on his early legislative successes, he earned a second term in 2015, on the promise of calling a popular referendum on the UK's membership in the European Union. Cameron had encountered strong resistance from within his own party regarding the trade and immigration policies enforced by the EU, and he then gambled that a referendum would strengthen his hands in negotiating the terms of Britain's membership in the EU. But on July 23, 2016, British voters surprised everyone by opting to leave the EU in a measure known as the British Referendum Act—but more commonly dubbed Brexit (a combination of the words "Britain" and "Exit").

The votes in favor of or opposed to leaving the EU were not distributed equally across the British Isles. Support for exit was particularly strong in the Midlands, a region in central England that had suffered heavily as British industry declined during the latter half of the twentieth century. In southern England and around the sprawling suburbs of London—where a younger and ethnically diverse population benefitted from the country's membership in the EU—a more cosmopolitan attitude prevailed. Voters in Scotland, where support for a potential separation from the United Kingdom was relatively strong, also tended to view the European Union as a useful balance against an allegedly oppressive government in London.

The uneasiness of the British people with regard to the growing size of the local immigrant population did not originate with the refugee crisis in the Middle East, but dated back to the 1950s, when a gradual influx of refugees took place from Britain's ex-colonies, primarily from South Asia, as those nations became independent after World War II. In recent years, however, the flow increased dramatically as migrants already on the continent of Europe took advantage of Britain's membership in the EU to seek residence there.

The vote in favor of leaving the EU (which passed by a very narrow margin) thus created a significant amount of turmoil in the UK and led to the resignation of its instigator, Prime Minister David Cameron. His replacement, the country's second female prime minister Theresa May (b. 1956), was faced with tough choices, and only a brief period of time to carry it out. The trade relationship with individual members of the EU had to be renegotiated, as well as laws relating to the movement of people into and out of the UK. Her own constituents in the Conservative Party were badly split, not only over whether to leave the European Union, but how to carry it out. Some members of Parliament wanted a "hard Brexit" (by which all ties with the EU would be severed), while others preferred a compromise (a "soft Brexit"), whereby Great Britain would retain some trade ties with the Union. Still others, fearing disaster if the split were carried through, hoped for a second referendum to give the British public another opportunity to reconsider the fate of their nation.

Faced with these stark choices, Prime Minister May attempted to come up with an equitable agreement that would satisfy a majority of the members in Parliament, as well as the British populace itself, on the terms of the separation. But Jeremy Corbyn, the current leader of the Labour Party, was reluctant to take a firm stand on the issue one way or the other, leading some members of his own party, exasperated with his failure to stake out a position, to form their own grouping. As a new Conservative prime minister, the hard-line Brexit-supporter Boris Johnson (b. 1964), took office in the summer of 2019, the ultimate fate of Brexit remained unclear.

10-3 EASTERN EUROPE AFTER THE FALL OF THE IRON CURTAIN

 Focus Question: To what degree have Eastern European nations adopted the Western European model since the end of the Cold War? Has their response been successful?

The collapse of the Communist governments in Eastern Europe during the revolutions of 1989 brought a wave of euphoria to Europe. New governments quickly emerged throughout the region and worked diligently to scrap the remnants of the old system and introduce the democratic procedures and market systems they believed would revitalize their scarred lands (see Chapter 9). But this process proved to be neither simple nor easy.

In the first place, most Eastern European countries had little or no experience with democratic systems. Then, too, ethnic divisions, which had troubled these areas before World War II and had been forcibly submerged under Communist rule, reemerged with a vengeance. Finally, the rapid conversion to market economies also proved painful. The adoption of "shock

therapy" austerity measures produced much suffering. Unemployment, for example, climbed to over 13 percent in Poland in 1992.

Nevertheless, within a few years many of these states had begun to make a successful transition to both free markets and political democracy. In Poland, Aleksander Kwasniewski (b. 1954), although a former Communist, was elected president in November 1995 and pushed Poland toward an increasingly prosperous free market economy. His success brought about his reelection in October 2000. In Czechoslovakia, the shift to non-Communist rule was complicated by old problems, especially ethnic issues. Although Czechs and Slovaks spoke closely related languages, they had different historical experiences, leading to sensitivity on the part of the Slovaks over living in a state dominated by the more sophisticated Czechs. In the end, the two sides accepted a peaceful division of the country. On January 1, 1993, Czechoslovakia split into the Czech Republic and Slovakia (see Map 10.2). Václav Havel was elected the first president of the new Czech Republic.

10-3a Tragedy in the Balkans: The Disintegration of Yugoslavia

But the most difficult transition to the post-Cold War era in Eastern Europe occurred in Yugoslavia. From its beginning in 1919, Yugoslavia had been an artificial creation composed of uneasy neighbors with a long history of mutual animosity. After World War II, the dictatorial Marshal Tito had managed to hold its six republics and two autonomous provinces together. But after his death in 1980, no strong leader emerged, and his responsibilities passed to a collective state presidency dominated by the League of Communists of Yugoslavia. At the end of the 1980s, Yugoslavia was caught up in the reform movements sweeping through Eastern Europe. The League of Communists collapsed, and new parties quickly emerged.

The Yugoslav political scene was complicated by the development of separatist movements. In 1990, the republics of Slovenia, Croatia, Bosnia-Herzegovina, and Macedonia began to lobby for a new federal structure of Yugoslavia that would fulfill their separatist desires. But Slobodan Milošević (1941–2006), Tito's successor who had become the leader of the Serbian Communist Party in 1987 and had managed to stay in power by emphasizing his commitment to Serbian nationalism, asserted that these republics could be independent only if new border arrangements were made to accommodate the Serb minorities in the republics who did not want to live outside the boundaries of Serbia. Serbs constituted

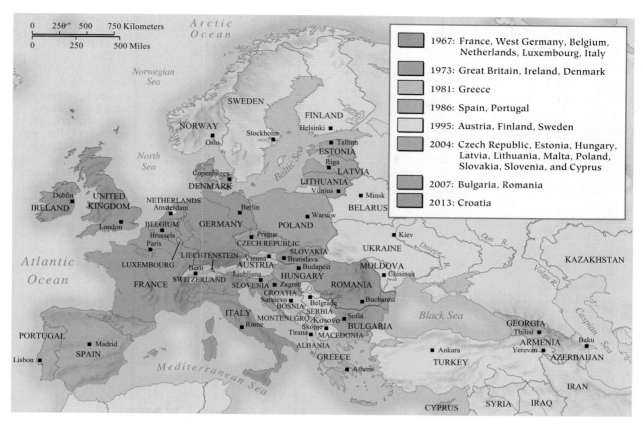

MAP 10.2 **The European Union, 2013.** Beginning in 1957 as the European Economic Community, also known as the Common Market, the union of European states seeking to integrate their economies has gradually grown from six members to twenty-eight in 2013. The European Union has achieved two major goals—the creation of a single internal market and a common currency—although it has been less successful at working toward common political and foreign policy goals.

 What additional nations do you think will eventually join the European Union? Why?

Legend:
- 1967: France, West Germany, Belgium, Netherlands, Luxembourg, Italy
- 1973: Great Britain, Ireland, Denmark
- 1981: Greece
- 1986: Spain, Portugal
- 1995: Austria, Finland, Sweden
- 2004: Czech Republic, Estonia, Hungary, Latvia, Lithuania, Malta, Poland, Slovakia, Slovenia, and Cyprus
- 2007: Bulgaria, Romania
- 2013: Croatia

about 12 percent of Croatia's population and 32 percent of Bosnia's.

After negotiations among the six republics failed, Slovenia and Croatia declared their independence in June 1991. Milošević's government sent the Yugoslavian army, which it controlled, into Slovenia, without much success. In September 1991, it began a full assault against Croatia. Increasingly, the Yugoslavian army was becoming the Serbian army, while Serbian irregular forces played a growing role in military operations. Before a cease-fire was arranged, the Serbian forces had captured one-third of Croatia's territory in brutal and destructive fighting (see Image 10.4).

The recognition of Slovenia, Croatia, and Bosnia-Herzegovina as independent nations by many European states and the United States early in 1992 did not stop the Serbs from turning their guns on Bosnia. By mid-1993,

Serbian forces had acquired 70 percent of Bosnian territory. The Serbian policy of **ethnic cleansing**—killing or forcibly removing Bosnian Muslims from their lands—revived memories of Nazi atrocities in World War II. Nevertheless, despite worldwide outrage, European governments failed to take a decisive and forceful stand against these Serbian activities, and by the spring of 1993, the Muslim population of Bosnia was in desperate straits. As the fighting spread, European nations and the United States began to intervene to stop the bloodshed, and in the fall of 1995, a fragile cease-fire agreement was reached at a conference held in Dayton, Ohio. An international peacekeeping force was stationed in the area to maintain tranquility and monitor the accords.

Peace in Bosnia, however, did not bring peace to Yugoslavia. A new war erupted in 1999 over Kosovo, which had been made an autonomous province within

IMAGE 10.4 Incident at Vukovar. In the fall of 1991, Serbian forces crossed the Danube River and put the Croatian city of Vukovar under siege. After three months of bitter fighting, Serbian troops entered the city and evacuated the Croatian members of the local population to concentration camps. Several thousand residents were killed in the fighting. After the end of the war, the city gradually began to recover, but many parts of the city have not yet been rebuilt, and houses pockmarked with bullet holes are still a common sight in much of the town center. A cemetery containing the graves of war casualties, as shown here, now sits on the outskirts of the town. Vukovar today is one of the more graphic symbols of the horrors of the recent Balkan wars.

Yvonne V. Duiker

Yugoslavia by Tito in 1974. Kosovo's inhabitants were mainly ethnic Albanians. But many Serbs considered it sacred territory because in the fourteenth century Serbian forces had been defeated there by the Ottoman Turks in an epic battle.

In 1989, Yugoslav President Milošević stripped Kosovo of its autonomous status and outlawed any official use of the Albanian language. In 1993, some groups of ethnic Albanians founded the Kosovo Liberation Army (KLA) and began a campaign against Serbian rule in Kosovo. When Serb forces began to massacre ethnic Albanians in an effort to crush the KLA, the United States and its NATO allies sought to arrange a settlement. When Milošević refused to sign the agreement, the United States and its NATO allies began a bombing campaign that forced the Yugoslavian government into compliance. In the elections of 2000, Milošević himself was ousted from power and was later put on trial by an international tribunal for war crimes against humanity for his ethnic cleansing policies. The truncated country of Yugoslavia briefly changed its name to Serbia and Montenegro, but that union came to an end in 2006 as Montenegro and Serbia became independent states. Kosovo received its independence in 2007, against the vigorous opposition of Serbia and its traditional ally Russia. Today the region is slowly returning to peacetime conditions, although historical animosities lie just beneath the surface.

10-4 WESTERN EUROPE: THE SEARCH FOR UNITY

 Focus Question: What are the challenges currently facing the European Union as it attempts to create a strong and united Europe that can play an important role in the world today?

As we have seen, the divisions created by the Cold War led the nations of Western Europe to form the North Atlantic Treaty Organization in 1949. But military cooperation was not the only kind of unity fostered in Europe after 1945. The destructiveness of two world wars caused many thoughtful Europeans to consider the need for additional forms of integration. National feeling was still too powerful, however, for European nations to give up their political sovereignty. Consequently, the quest for unity initially focused primarily on the economic arena rather than the political one.

10-4a The Curtain Rises: The Creation of the Common Market

In 1951, France, West Germany, the Benelux countries (Belgium, the Netherlands, and Luxembourg), and Italy formed the European Coal and Steel Community (ECSC). Its purpose was to create a common market for coal and steel products among the six nations by eliminating tariffs and other trade barriers. The success of the ECSC encouraged its members to proceed further, and in 1957, they created the European Atomic Energy Community (EURATOM) to further European research on the peaceful uses of nuclear energy.

In the same year, the same six nations signed the Rome Treaty, which created the European Economic Community (EEC), also known as the Common Market. The EEC eliminated mutual customs barriers and created a large free-trade area protected from the rest of the world by a common external tariff. By promoting free trade, the EEC also encouraged cooperation and standardization in many aspects of the six nations' economies. All the member nations benefited economically.

Europeans moved toward further integration of their economies after 1970. The European Economic Community expanded in 1973 when Great Britain, Ireland, and Denmark gained membership in what its members now began to call the European Community (EC). By 1986, three more members—Spain, Portugal, and Greece—had been added. The economic integration of the members of the EC led to cooperative efforts in international and political affairs as well. The foreign ministers of the twelve members consulted frequently and provided a common front in negotiations on important issues.

10-4b The European Union

By 1992, the EC included nearly 350 million people and constituted the world's largest single trading bloc, transacting almost one-quarter of the world's commerce. In the early 1990s, EC members drafted the Treaty on European Union (known as the Maastricht Treaty, after the city in the Netherlands where the agreement was reached), seeking to create a true economic and monetary union of all members of the organization (see Historical Voices, "Toward a United Europe," p. 262). The treaty would not take effect, however, until all members agreed. On January 1, 1994, the European Community became the European Union (EU).

One of its first goals was to introduce a common currency, called the euro. But problems soon arose. Voters in many countries opposed the austerity measures that their governments would be compelled to take to reduce growing budget deficits. Germans in particular feared that replacing the rock-solid mark with a common European currency could lead to economic disaster. Yet the logic of the new union appeared inescapable if European nations were to improve their capacity to compete with the United States and the powerful industrializing nations of the Pacific Rim. On January 1, 2002, twelve members of the European Union (including all of the major European states except Great Britain) abandoned their national currencies in favor of the euro. The move hastened the transition of the EU into a single economic entity capable of competing in world markets with the United States and major Asian nations.

10-4c Plans for Expansion: A Bridge Too Far?

In the meantime, plans got under way to extend the EU into Eastern Europe, where several nations were just emerging from decades of domination by the Soviet Union. In the lingering euphoria over the collapse of the Cold War divide, in December 2002, the EU voted to add ten new members—Cyprus, the Czech Republic, Estonia, Hungary, Latvia, Lithuania, Malta, Poland, Slovakia, and Slovenia. They joined the organization in 2004. Bulgaria and Romania joined in 2007, and the addition of Croatia in 2013 increased the size of the EU to twenty-eight members (see Map 10.2).

Now, however, the momentum has begun to shift as the consequences of EU expansion and membership have become clear to all sides. In recent years the EU has created a looser grouping called an "Eastern Partnership" with six potential members—Georgia, Ukraine, Armenia, Azerbaijan, Moldova, and Belarus. With political conditions in the area currently unstable as a result of Russia's opposition to the plan, there is no current intention to risk a direct confrontation with Moscow on the issue. For political leaders in Eastern European countries, the countervailing pressures from East and West make important decisions difficult to achieve. For example, Aleksander Vukic, the current president of Serbia, hopes to join the European Union to reap the economic benefits it will provide, but is reluctant to anger Russia. For his part, Putin has cited the deep historical friendship that has long characterized the relationship between the two countries, and has dangled an offer to provide cheap natural gas as a lure to persuade the Serbs to reject membership in the EU.

The fact is, not all observers are convinced that European integration is a good thing. Some Eastern Europeans have begun to fear that their countries will be dominated by capital investment from their prosperous neighbors, while many Western Europeans have expressed concerns at the influx of low-wage workers from newer members. The recent refugee crisis in the Middle East has caused great consternation in several Eastern European countries, where concern over protecting their ethnic and national identity is always at the forefront. The decision by Great Britain to resign from the EU has undoubtedly caught the attention of several countries on the European continent, although the fallout in the UK from the referendum itself may cause Eastern European leaders to have second thoughts about going through the same process themselves. All in all, a

HISTORICAL VOICES

Toward a United Europe

 What are the key provisions of the Treaty of Maastricht? How do they appear to infringe on traditional standards of national sovereignty?

Politics & Government IN DECEMBER 1991, the nations of Europe took a significant step on the road to unity when they drafted the Treaty of Maastricht, which created the structure for a new European Union. The new organization, which represented a significant step beyond the forms of economic cooperation that had previously existed, envisaged integration in the fields of foreign and security policies and cooperation in the areas of justice and domestic affairs. In the years since the treaty was established, the European Union has successfully created a common currency—the euro—but resolving many of the other obstacles to unity has proved to be a severe challenge. Some of the key provisions of the treaty are presented here.

The Treaty of Maastricht

Article A

By this Treaty, the High Contracting Parties establish among themselves a European Union, hereinafter called "the Union."

This Treaty marks a new stage in the process of creating an ever closer union among the peoples of Europe, in which decisions are taken as closely as possible to the citizen.

The Union shall be founded on the European Communities, supplemented by the policies and forms of cooperation established by this Treaty. Its task shall be to organize, in a manner demonstrating consistency and solidarity, relations between the Member States and between their peoples.

Source: http://europa.eu.int/en/record/mt/titlel.html.

Article B

The Union shall set itself the following objectives:

- to promote economic and social progress which is balanced and sustainable, in particular through the creation of an area without internal frontiers, through the strengthening of economic and social cohesion and through the establishment of economic and monetary union, ultimately including a single currency in accordance with the provisions of this Treaty;
- to assert its identity on the international scene, in particular through the implementation of a common foreign and security policy including the eventual framing of a common defence policy, which might in time lead to a common defence;
- to strengthen the protection of the rights and interests of the nationals of its Member States through the introduction of a citizenship of the Union;
- to develop close cooperation on justice and home affairs. . . .

Article F

1. The Union shall respect the national identities of its Member States, whose systems of government are founded on the principles of democracy.
2. The Union shall respect fundamental rights, as guaranteed by the European Convention for the Protection of Human Rights and Fundamental Freedoms signed in Rome on 4 November 1950 and as they result from the constitutional traditions common to the Member States, as general principles of Community law.
3. The Union shall provide itself with the means necessary to attain its objectives and carry through its policies.

true sense of a unified Europe is still lacking among the population throughout the region, and the rising anti-foreign sentiment across the continent and anger at government belt-tightening are warning signs that advocates of further integration will ignore at their peril.

The application of Turkey to join the EU, which has been pending for many years, has only added to these concerns. Although the Turkish government has sought to assuage European criticisms of its record in the area of human rights (notably in the treatment of its Kurdish minority), many Europeans remain uneasy about the prospect of admitting an Islamic nation of more than 70 million people into an organization of predominantly Christian nations already facing serious concerns over their growing Muslim minorities. With Turkish politics becoming more authoritarian under President Recep Erdogan, Turkey's admission is no longer under serious consideration within the EU. In turn, many Turks now scorn the proposal to join a weakened Europe and seek to redirect their efforts to serving as a bridge to the Middle East (see Chapter 15).

Plans for a transition to a more unified structure for Europe have also encountered resistance. In 2005, voters in several EU countries rejected the draft of a new constitution that would have strengthened the political and economic integration of the nations within the EU. Shaken by popular resistance to their proposals to strengthen the central apparatus of the EU, European leaders lowered their expectations. A new treaty, signed by all members in Lisbon in December 2007 and ratified by all members three years later, provided the organization with a permanent president who will serve for a thirty-month term and have the primary duty of representing the EU abroad. How effective the new executive will be remains to be seen, as resistance to the organization's determination to enforce common requirements relating to economic and immigration issues is growing among many member states.

What Role for NATO?   Meanwhile, the NATO alliance continues to serve as a powerful force for European unity. Yet it too faces new challenges as Moscow's former satellites in Eastern Europe have clamored for membership in the hope that it would spur economic growth and reduce the threat from a revival of Russian expansionism. In 1999, the Czech Republic, Hungary, and Poland joined the alliance, and the Baltic states—once part of the Soviet Union—followed suit several years later. Some observers have expressed concern, however, that an expanded NATO will not only reduce the cohesiveness of the organization but also provoke Russia into a new posture of hostility to the outside world. Western plans to construct U.S. missile defense sites in several Eastern European countries have encountered violent hostility in Moscow, while the Russian invasion of Georgia in 2008 inspired alarm in many Eastern European capitals over its implications for Russian expansionism in the future.

Russia's dispute with Ukraine and its subsequent invasion of Crimea have similarly forced NATO countries to rethink possible plans to expand membership deep into regions that Moscow views as its own backyard. Few Western observers believe that a direct confrontation with Russia over Ukraine is in anyone's best interest. And although some Eastern European nations—notably Poland and the small Baltic states—are eager to place their country's defenses under the umbrella of NATO, Western governments approach the issue today with a high degree of caution.

10-5 ASPECTS OF SOCIETY IN POSTWAR EUROPE

 Focus Question: What major social, cultural, and intellectual developments have occurred in Europe since 1945, and how have they changed the character of European society?

Socially, intellectually, and culturally, Western Europe changed significantly during the second half of the twentieth century. Although many trends represented a continuation of prewar developments, in other cases the changes were quite dramatic, leading some observers in the 1980s to begin speaking of the gradual emergence of a postmodern age. Recent developments, however, have led some observers to fear that the postwar vision of a united, peaceful, and prosperous Europe may be fading.

10-5a An Age of Affluence

Nothing changed in the postwar years as much as the material lives of Europe's inhabitants. In the decades after World War II, products such as automobiles, computers, televisions, jet planes, contraceptive devices, and advanced surgical techniques all dramatically and quickly altered the pace and nature of human life. Called variously a technocratic society, an affluent society, or the consumer society, postwar Europe was characterized by changing social values and new attitudes toward the meaning of the human experience.

The structure of European society was also altered in major respects after 1945. Especially noticeable were changes in the composition of the middle class. Traditional occupations such as merchants and the professions (law, medicine, and the universities) were greatly augmented by a new group of managers and technicians, as large companies and government agencies employed increasing numbers of white-collar supervisory and administrative personnel. In most cases, success depended on specialized knowledge acquired from some form of higher education. Since their jobs usually depended on their skills, these individuals took steps to ensure that their children would be similarly educated.

Changes occurred in other areas as well. Especially noticeable was the dramatic shift from the countryside to the cities. The number of people in agriculture declined by 50 percent. Yet the industrial working class did not expand. In West Germany, industrial workers made up 48 percent of the labor force throughout the 1950s and 1960s. Thereafter, the number of industrial workers began to dwindle as the number of white-collar service employees increased. At the same time, a substantial increase in their real wages enabled the working classes to aspire to the consumption patterns of the middle class. Buying on the installment plan, introduced in the 1930s, became widespread in the 1950s and gave workers a chance to imitate the middle class by buying such products as televisions, washing machines, refrigerators, vacuum cleaners, and stereos. But the most visible symbol of mass consumerism was the automobile. Before World War II, cars were reserved mostly for the upper classes. In 1948, there were 5 million cars in all of Europe, but by 1957, the number had tripled. By the mid-1960s, there were almost 45 million.

Rising incomes, combined with shorter working hours, created an even greater market for **mass leisure** activities. Between 1900 and 1980, the workweek was reduced from sixty hours to about forty hours (or even less in some countries), and the number of paid holidays increased. All aspects of popular culture—music, sports, media—became commercialized and offered opportunities for leisure activities, including concerts, sporting events, and television viewing.

Another very visible symbol of mass leisure was the growth of tourism. Before World War II, most people who traveled for pleasure were from the upper and middle classes. After the war, the combination of more vacation time, increased prosperity, and the flexibility provided by package tours with their lower rates and low-budget rooms enabled millions to expand their travel possibilities. By the mid-1960s, some 100 million tourists were crossing European borders each year. In recent years, the number has increased dramatically.

What had brought about the dramatic change that had taken place in Western Europe during a period once described by the French demographer Jean Fourastié as the "thirty glorious years" following the end of World War II? Several factors were at work: a long era of peace under the protection of the U.S. military umbrella; the emergence of stable governments dedicated to moderate economic policies and a peaceful transition of power; a steady increase in economic growth resulting initially from investment funds provided by the Marshall Plan; lower tariffs engineered and enforced by international agreement; and a system of social benefits supported by all major political parties that provided consumer confidence and a market for goods produced in factories throughout the region. While there were pockets of poverty and periodic outbreaks of social discontent—notably during the era of youth rebellion in the late 1960s—they could easily be described as growth pains rather than endemic weaknesses in the system.

10-5b Rethinking the Welfare State

Beginning in the early years of the new century, however, the promise created by the "thirty glorious years" began to look more like a mirage. What had happened to derail Europe's steady progress toward a peaceful and prosperous future? One factor was certainly the increased competition coming from inexpensive consumer goods imported from developing countries seeking to find their own road to the good life. Another warning sign was the gradual appearance of a demographic crunch. By the end of the twentieth century, birth rates had fallen well below replacement levels in several nations of the EU. While there were undoubtedly several reasons for this uncomfortable development, a couple of reasons stand out. As European women began to enter the workforce, they were forced to delay or forego the experience of raising children. At the same time, families increasingly relied on two wage earners in order to support a middle-class lifestyle. As time went on, the number of active workers available to support each retiree thus began steadily to decline. Today people of working age in Europe outnumber retired persons by only three to one; by mid-century, the ratio is predicted to decline to about two to one (by comparison, the current ratio in the United States is about five to one). In some cases, as in Italy, the total population is actually declining. To counter such worrying trends, several European governments reluctantly began to raise the retirement age or to reduce the size of pensions for retirees. Buffeted by these changes, the middle class is shrinking throughout Europe as the wages have stagnated and social benefits have shrunk. In the meantime, by comparison the wealthy have prospered, although to a lesser degree than has occurred in the United States. The survival of the European welfare state rests in the balance.

One byproduct of this statistical trend was an increase in the inflow of immigrant labor from Eastern Europe and North Africa. Most of the new arrivals entered employment in menial jobs that were by then scorned by many Western Europeans. Linguistic and cultural differences were also barriers preventing the assimilation of these new residents into the broader society. Today, with the creation of "open frontiers" under the Treaty of Maastricht, the flow of immigrants into the European Union has increased dramatically, thus arousing the concerns of many European citizens that the cultural character of their individual nations is at risk.

One measure that some European governments have adopted to counter the trend toward lower birth rates has been to provide financial incentives to encourage families to have more children. Some European politicians see other benefits in such a policy: in Hungary, for example, the current government has introduced such incentives in the hope of strengthening the local culture by reducing the need for immigrants from the Middle East. So far, however, that technique has had limited effect, since with average incomes declining in most countries on the continent, many women need to work to help augment the family income. Europe is in a demographic trap, and there is no easy way out.

10-5c Beware of Greeks Seeking Gifts

As if the challenges discussed above were not sufficient, the EU was sideswiped by a new crisis in the fall of 2008, as the shockwaves of the global financial meltdown began to ripple through the continent. Most affected was Greece, where the beleaguered government in Athens announced that it could no longer pay its bills.

The fragility of the Greek government's finances stemmed from a number of deep-seated factors: high government expenditures (an unusually high percentage of the population was on the government payroll, many in sinecure positions); low revenues (resulting partly from chronic tax evasion); and, finally, a weak export market (due in part to the fact that the national currency was unrealistically based on the stronger euro). Under heavy pressure from the leaders of other EU countries (notably Germany) to adopt stringent austerity measures in order to qualify for bank loans, the Greek government sought to comply, but its efforts led to popular unrest and an economic free fall.

The EU's difficulties in dealing with financial problems in Greece were compounded by the fact that a number of other European countries—most notably those in the southern tier of the continent like Italy, Spain, Portugal, and Cyprus—were facing serious economic problems of their own. In fact, many EU member countries had ignored the provisions of the Treaty of Maastricht requiring them to limit their national debt, and now faced the possibility of a financial meltdown that, in size and scope, could transcend that just experienced by the government of Greece. In the past, the easiest solution to resolve such a crisis was to devalue the local currency, thus increasing exports while making imports more expensive. With most EU nations now using the euro, that option was removed. The spreading crisis was a vivid reminder to European leaders of the dangers inherent in trying to apply a one-size-fits-all system to nations with highly divergent cultures and economic profiles. As the region scrambled to defuse the spreading financial epidemic, the end result cannot yet be foreseen.

At the root of the current economic malaise is an incontrovertible fact: under current conditions, Europe—even more than the United States—is on a path toward bankruptcy. The slowdown in the European economy in the past two decades, combined with the changing social fabric, has already begun to erode the region's long-standing commitment to the concept of the welfare state. Growth rates in coming years are almost uniformly projected to drop. But as European governments have been compelled to consider reducing some of the vaunted social benefits that their citizens now view as a birthright, such measures have run into strong popular resistance, and have led, in many cases, to a change in governments.

The situation is equally perilous in Eastern Europe, where nations with fragile democracies and weak economies are faced with problems of slow growth, low productivity, and high unemployment. Nations like Bulgaria, Hungary, and Romania have lost the limited economic security provided by their past membership in the Soviet bloc and must fend for themselves in a global market dominated by economic powerhouses like China, India, and Brazil. To remain competitive in global trade, several have chosen to reject the euro and thus maintain their own national currencies. Still, prospects for matching the economic prosperity of their western neighbors are relatively bleak.

10-5d Democracy Under Stress

An important consequence of the declining economic prospects for the countries composing the European Union is the potential effect that the trend can have on the stability of the political culture. As we have seen, the popular consensus supporting moderate parties on the Right and on the Left—Conservatives and Democratic Socialists—has dramatically eroded in recent years, as new movements have emerged with platforms based on opposition to immigration, dislike of the unifying requirements of the European Union, and a corresponding focus on the importance of national identity. Many of these parties are populist in tone and practice—that is, they emphasize what they term "the will of the people" (i.e., their own followers) in contrast to the allegedly faceless bureaucrats at EU headquarters in Brussels. In Western European countries like France, Germany, and Great Britain, such forces have already become influential on the political scene, but their proponents do not yet occupy positions of power. In other countries like Italy and Greece, where the number of immigrants arriving has reached unmanageable proportions, they have formed governments and are actively seeking to carry through on their promises. Curiously, openly leftist parties with a commitment to carry out social revolution have not yet won popular favor, but the ingredients for such a development are already present.

Not surprisingly, the shift away from a commitment to pluralist democracy is even more starkly evident in Eastern Europe, where democratic traditions are not deeply rooted, allowing populist governments to attack their critics in the press, limit academic freedoms, and pack the judicial system with like-minded judges. In Hungary, the Fidesz party led by the current president Viktor Orban has openly declared its opposition to immigration and has based its popularity on a naked appeal to Hungarian nationalism. In Poland, the Law and Justice Party seeks to limit cultural pluralism while protecting the country's predominantly Catholic heritage. Curiously, Poland would seem to be protected from such trends, since it has one of the more dynamic economies in Eastern Europe and has benefitted financially from its membership in the EU. Real wages have also risen substantially, although the benefits have been felt primarily by the middle class in the large cities. In Poland, as in other parts of the world today, cultural issues sometimes trump economic ones.

Playing the Terrorism Card   One of the obvious reasons for the high level of public resistance to immigration from the Middle East and North Africa is the threat and frequency of terrorist acts committed by Muslim extremists on the European continent. Many Europeans—as elsewhere—tend to equate Islam with terrorism and instinctively fear the Muslims that they observe in cities and towns around the continent. The terrorists themselves are aware of this instinctive reaction and deliberately take advantage of it in order to incite hostile feelings

between the two groups. A key challenge in easing such fears is the reality that many Muslim residents in Europe are compelled by economic necessity to live in Muslim-majority ghettos in the suburbs of major cities like Berlin, Paris, and London. Sometimes popular anger can erupt into violence for seemingly minor reasons and thus inflame feelings on both sides (see Image 10.5). European governments have periodically sought to find solutions to the problem, but cultural and religious suspicions inherently run deep on both sides, and every act of terrorism makes a solution more difficult to find.

Fortunately, not all the trends in Europe today are on the negative side of the ledger. The flood of immigrants from the Middle East and North Africa has dropped dramatically since 2015, when over one million asylum seekers crossed the frontier into European territory. Agreements worked out with Turkey and Libya to cut the flow are a prime reason for the decline in arrivals. And, despite the visible evidence that resistance to EU policies is high in some areas, public opinion surveys suggest that the majority of Europeans still believe that membership in the organization is beneficial to their country, and to themselves. As Great Britain lurches uncontrollably toward some form of Brexit, the prospects of a future outside the community of Europe no longer looks so enticing to observers elsewhere.

10-5e Social Changes: A Transvaluation of Values?

At the end of World War II, Europe in many respects was still a very traditional society. Most people still lived out their existence within a short distance from their childhood homes. Family was still a key feature in their social lives, and the church was a major factor in determining their religious beliefs. Physically, as well, most Europeans still lived the manner their parents had, and their grandparents before them. Higher education was still largely the preserve of the wealthier classes—in 1950, only 3 or 4 percent of young people were enrolled in a university. Few Europeans had cars or television sets, their indoor heating facilities were meager, and their toilet facilities were still out of doors. In rural areas, they often relieved themselves in the family stable.

Within a generation, daily life in Western Europe had changed dramatically. By the late 1950s and the 1960s, automobiles—often the smaller and cheaper varieties like the Volkswagen Beetle, the Morris Minor, and the Fiat—became a familiar sight on increasingly crowded streets and highways. Television sets, telephones, indoor plumbing, and central heating became more commonplace in

IMAGE 10.5 Days of Anger. In the late fall of 2005, violent youth riots suddenly erupted in the primarily Muslim suburbs of more than 300 cities and towns across France, leaving a trail of shattered shop windows and burned automobiles in their wake. While not all the protesters were Muslims—some were students unhappy at crowded schools and limited employment opportunities—the outbreak served to highlight the growing difficulties of assimilating the country's five million Muslims—many of whom are faced with limited employment opportunities and institutionalized racism—into French society.

middle-class homes. Church attendance began to decline, and more Europeans began to leave the small towns to settle in the big cities.

To cope with economic challenges, European governments also began to foster greater equality of opportunity in higher education by eliminating fees, and universities experienced an influx of students from the middle and lower classes. Enrollments grew dramatically. In France, 4.5 percent of young people went to a university in 1950; by 1965, the figure had increased to 14.5 percent. Overall, enrollments in European universities more than tripled between 1940 and 1960.

With growth, however, came problems. Overcrowded classrooms, unapproachable professors, and authoritarian administrators aroused student resentment. Education was often limited to the Liberal Arts or the professions, and did not prepare many students adequately for their future employment in the economic world. This discontent led to an outburst of student revolts in the late 1960s. In the spring of 1968, student unrest erupted in Paris, where rampaging youths burned automobiles in the streets, occupied buildings, and demanded structural changes, not only in education but in other allegedly outdated social institutions as well. When urban workers, angry at their stagnating salaries, joined the protests, the government instituted a hefty wage hike. When the workers grudgingly returned to their jobs, the government sent the gendarmes into the streets to suppress the remaining student protesters. Eventually, they too resentfully returned to their classes, leaving the streets littered with burned-out autos.

In part, the student protests were an extension of the disruptions in American universities in the mid-1960s, which were often sparked by student opposition to the Vietnam War. In a broader sense, however, young protesters also criticized other aspects of Western society, such as its relentless focus on material possessions, and many expressed concern about becoming cogs in the large and impersonal bureaucratic jungles of the modern world. But other factors were important as well. One source of resentment was the lingering influence of traditional social values in European society, where a rigid code of manners and morals dating from the previous century still reigned supreme. A graffito that I observed sprayed on the wall of a building in Paris in the summer of 1968 put it well: "Culture is the inversion of life." Throughout Western Europe, young people began to flout the social codes of the past, engaging publicly in casual sex and experimenting with hallucinatory drugs. Although such behavior was more prevalent in the large cities than in rural areas, the new permissiveness seeped into the culture at large. Divorce rates increased dramatically, while premarital and extramarital sexual experiences also rose substantially. Although the student revolutionaries had lost the battle in the streets of Paris, their ideas had begun to prevail in the wider world of European society.

Although some remnants of the anti-bourgeois culture of the 1960s still exist today, they are no longer representative of the social attitudes of most Europeans. As economic growth slowed, job opportunities declined, and the fear of being too bourgeois began to be replaced by fear of not making it into the ranks of the bourgeoisie. In areas outside the major cities, there is today a palpable unease at what has been lost with the steady decline of the traditional way of life. As the focus on the individual has replaced the traditional focus on the family and the community, a sense of social and moral emptiness prevails, along with distrust of external forces exemplified by the so-called "faceless bureaucrats" who now make all the important decisions from their offices in Brussels.

For Europeans living in small towns and villages, there is often a visual component to this emotional sense of loss of an imagined way of life—the shuttering of the local bakery and butcher shop, as local residents now do their shopping in the large "centres commerciales" on the outskirts of town. To many older residents, the town square is no longer a comfortable haven for discussing daily topics with neighbors, but seems to be filled with foreign women dressed in **hijabs** (a traditional form of female dress among Muslims). Political parties running on a platform of returning to the presumed "good life," as harbored in memories of the past, have undoubtedly benefitted from this sense of melancholy nostalgia as the world changes rapidly around them. The more the current technological revolution guarantees that the idealized past can never be reconstituted, the more appealing it looks in retrospect, and many politicians are more than willing to play on such emotions.

10-5f Expanding Roles for Women

The changing role of women in European society has obviously been a major contributing factor in this process. Although some women pursued professional careers and other respected vocations in the 1920s and 1930s, the place for most women was still in the home. Half a century later, there were almost as many women as men in the European workplace, many of them employed in professions hitherto reserved for men.

But the increased number of women in the workforce has not changed some old patterns. Working-class women in particular still earn salaries lower than those paid to men for equal work. Women still tend to enter traditionally female jobs. Many European women also still face the double burden of earning income on the one hand and raising a family and maintaining the household on the other.

The participation of women in World Wars I and II helped them to achieve one of the major aims of the nineteenth-century feminist movement—the right to vote. After World War I, governments in many countries—Sweden, Great Britain, Germany, Poland, Hungary, Austria, and Czechoslovakia—acknowledged the contributions of women to the war effort by granting them suffrage. Women in France and Italy finally gained the right to vote in 1945.

After World War II, however, European women tended to fall back into the traditional roles expected of them, and little was heard of feminist concerns. But with the student upheavals of the late 1960s came a renewed interest in feminism, or the women's liberation movement, as it was now called. Inspired by the writings of the French author Simone de Beauvoir (1908–1986), whose feminist tract entitled *The Second Sex*, pointed out that women were second-class citizens living in a male-dominated world, women in Europe began to demand true equality with men (see Historical Voices, "The Voice of the Women's Liberation Movement," p. 269). Realizing that women must take responsibility for transforming the fundamental conditions of their lives, feminists formed "consciousness-raising" groups to further awareness of women's issues and to campaign for the legalization of both contraception and abortion. A French law passed in 1968 legalized the sale of contraceptive devices. In 1979, abortion became legal in France. Even in countries where the Catholic Church remained strongly opposed to contraception and legalized abortion, legislation allowing them passed in the 1970s and 1980s.

As a result of such efforts, the presence of women in the workforce in Europe has been steadily on the rise. Women have also entered new employment areas. Greater access to universities and professional schools has enabled women to take jobs in law, medicine, government, business, and education. Still, economic inequality often prevails; women are paid lower wages than men for comparable work and receive fewer promotions to positions in management. The most visible sign of women's progress was the election in 1995 of Angela Merkel to the position of chancellor of Germany. She has remained in that position for more than two decades.

10-5g The Environment

By the 1970s, serious ecological problems had become all too apparent in the crowded countries of Western Europe. Air pollution, produced by nitrogen oxide and sulfur dioxide emissions from road vehicles, power plants, and industrial factories, was causing respiratory illnesses and having corrosive effects on buildings and historical monuments such as the Louvre in Paris and the Parthenon in Athens. Many rivers, lakes, and seas had become so polluted that they posed serious health risks. Dying forests (such as the famous Black Forest in southern Germany) and disappearing wildlife alarmed more and more people.

Although the environmental movement first began to gain broad public attention in the United States, the problem was more serious in Europe, with its higher population density and high levels of industrial production in such countries as Great Britain and West Germany. The problem was compounded by the lack of antipollution controls in the industrial sectors of the Soviet satellite states to the east. Air pollution from factories in nearby Czechoslovakia, for example, often made the air in the Austrian capital of Vienna dangerous to breathe.

Growing ecological awareness gave rise to Green movements and Green parties throughout Europe in the 1970s. Most started at the local level and then gradually extended their activities to the national level, where they became formally organized as political parties. As in the United States, however, the movement has been hindered by concerns that strict environmental regulations could sap economic growth and exacerbate unemployment. National rivalries and disagreements over how to deal with rising levels of pollution along international waterways such as the Rhine River have also impeded cooperation. Nevertheless, public alarm over the potential effects of global warming has focused attention on the global character of environmental issues, and since the 1980s, the members of the EU have been among the foremost supporters of efforts to establish tougher standards to control environmental pollution on a worldwide basis. Today wind farms are a familiar sight on the horizons of Europe, as the region seeks to wean itself from reliance on coal resources to fuel its electricity grids. Europeans have also taken the lead in promoting public transportation as a means of reducing automobile congestion in major cities. One of the most visible examples was the decision by the municipal government in Paris to establish a public bicycle program for use by residents and visitors to reduce carbon dioxide emissions in the city (see Comparative Illustration, "Cleaning up the Environment," p. 270).

The Voice of the Women's Liberation Movement

> *What did Simone de Beauvoir mean by the "second sex"? By "the Other"? What is the difference between being a "thing" and having an "authentic existence"? According to de Beauvoir, how do women fall prey to the former?*

Art & Ideas

SIMONE DE BEAUVOIR was an important figure in the emergence of the postwar women's liberation movement in Europe. Like Betty Friedan, her counterpart in the United States, she played a key role in arousing the determination of women to demand an equal place with men in the home and the workplace. But where Friedan had painted American women as slaves to their homes and their possessions, Simone de Beauvoir lamented their dependence on men, and on the male tendency to view women as "the Other."

Simone de Beauvoir, *The Second Sex*

Now, woman has always been man's dependent, if not his slave; the two sexes have never shared the world in equality. And even today woman is heavily handicapped, though her situation is beginning to change. Almost nowhere is her legal status the same as man's, and frequently it is much to her disadvantage. Even when her rights are legally recognized in the abstract, long-standing custom prevents their full expression in the mores. In the economic sphere men and women can almost be said to make up two castes; other things being equal, the former hold the better jobs, get higher wages, and have more opportunity for success than their new competitors. In industry and politics men have a great many more positions and they monopolize the most important posts. In addition to all this, they enjoy a traditional prestige that the education of children tends in every way to support, for the present enshrines the past—and in the past all history has been made by men. At the present time, when women are beginning to take part in the affairs of the world, it is still a world that belongs to men—they have no doubt of it at all and women have scarcely any. To decline to be the *Other*, to refuse to be a party to a deal—this would be for women to renounce all the advantages conferred upon them by their alliance with the superior caste. Man-the-sovereign will provide woman-the-liege with material protection and will undertake the moral justification of her existence; thus, she can evade at once both economic risk and the metaphysical risk of a liberty in which ends and aims must be contrived without assistance. Indeed, along with the ethical urge of each individual to affirm his subjective existence, there is also the temptation to forgo liberty and become a thing. This is an inauspicious road, for he who takes it—passive, lost, ruined—becomes henceforth the creature of another's will, frustrated in his transcendence and deprived of every value. But it is an easy road; on it one avoids the strain involved in undertaking an authentic existence. When man makes of woman the *Other*, he may, then, expect her to manifest deep-seated tendencies toward complicity. Thus, woman may fail to lay claim to the status of subject because she lacks definite resources, because she feels the necessary bond that ties her to man regardless of reciprocity, and because she is often very well pleased with her role as the *Other*.

Now, what peculiarly signalizes the situation of woman is that she—a free and autonomous *being* like all human creatures—nevertheless finds herself living in a world where men compel her to assume the status of the *Other*.

Source: From *The Second Sex* by Simone de Beauvoir, trans. H. M. Parshley. Copyright 1952 and renewed 1980 by Alfred A. Knopf, Inc.

10-6 ASPECTS OF CULTURE IN POSTWAR EUROPE

> **Focus Question:** How do recent cultural developments in Europe reflect the broader changes that are taking place in European society?

Since the end of World War II, Europe has tended to follow the pattern of the United States in that a once dominant "elite" culture has gradually given way to a more popular culture directed toward the mass of the population. Nevertheless, even though most Europeans, like Americans, prefer popular literature, rock music, and the movies, what is sometimes called **high culture** (such as serious fiction and nonfiction, art, and classical music) continues to be produced and to exert significant influence on the broader society.

10-6a Postwar Literature

The most influential literary fashion in the immediate postwar period was **Existentialism**. The French intellectual

Cleaning Up the Environment

 Q *Do you support programs such as the ones described here to cut down on carbon dioxide levels in the environment in the United States?*

Earth & Environment

LACKING THE AMPLE RESERVES of liquid energy possessed by other industrial powerhouses like Russia and the United States, the nations of the European Union have attempted to reduce their dependence on foreign sources of oil and natural gas by developing alternative energy supplies. Image 10.6a shows an Austrian wind farm located on the flat plains extending eastward to the Hungarian border. A brisk wind, known to locals as the *fohn*, sweeps down from the Alps and heads toward the flatlands of Eastern Europe. European cities are also combating carbon dioxide emissions by encouraging the use of bicycles. In Paris, a public bicycle program called the *Velib*, short for "free bike," was inaugurated in 2007 with 10,000 bikes and 700 rental stations. Today the program has increased to over 17,000 bikes and approximately 1,200 rental stations, as seen in Image 10.6b, where visitors and citizens can rent a bicycle by the hour.

William J. Duiker

IMAGE 10.6a

William J. Duiker

IMAGE 10.6b

Jean-Paul Sartre (1905–1980) was perhaps most closely identified with the Existential movement, whose fundamental premise was the absence of a god in the universe, thereby denying that humans had any preordained destiny. Humans were thus deprived of any absolute purpose or meaning, set adrift in an absurd world. Often reduced to despair and depression, the protagonists of Sartre's literary works were left with only one reason for hope—themselves and their ability to voluntarily reach out and become involved in their community. In the early 1950s, Sartre became a devout Marxist, hitching his philosophy of freedom to one of political engagement in the Communist ideal.

Sartre's contemporary, Albert Camus (1913–1960), reached similar conclusions on the meaning of life. In his seminal novel, *The Stranger* (1942), the protagonist, having stumbled through a lethargic existence, realizes just before dying that regardless of the absurdity of life, humans still have the opportunity to embrace the joyful dimensions of experience—in his case, the warmth and splendor of the Algerian skies. Neither a political activist nor an ideologue, Camus broke with Sartre and other French leftists after the disclosure of the Stalinist atrocities in the Soviet gulags.

The existentialist world view found expression in the Paris of the 1950s in the "theater of the absurd." One of its foremost proponents was the Irish dramatist Samuel Beckett (1906–1990), who lived in France. In his trail blazing play *Waiting for Godot* (1952), two nondescript men eagerly await the appearance of someone who never arrives. While they wait, they pass the time exchanging hopes and fears, with humor, courage, and touching friendship. This waiting represents the existential meaning of life, which is found in the daily activities and fellowship of the here and now, despite the absence of any absolute salvation for the human condition.

Postmodernism   Beginning in the 1960s, many Europeans became disenchanted with political systems of any kind and began to question the validity of reason, history, progress, and universal truths. The negation of prewar ideologies, now applied to all branches of learning, fused into a new doctrine of skepticism called **deconstruction**, which described a world in which human beings have lost their status as free agents dealing with universal verities and are reduced to empty vessels programmed by language and culture.

The philosophical skepticism reflected in this new approach quickly manifested itself in European literature as authors grappled with new ways to present reality in an uncertain and nonsensical world. Whereas the Modernists at the beginning of the twentieth century had celebrated the power of art to benefit humankind, placing their faith in the written word, much of the new "Postmodern" literature reflected the lack of belief in anything, especially the written word.

Following in the footsteps of the Modernists, French authors in the 1960s experimented so radically with literary forms and language that they pushed fiction well beyond its traditional limits of rational understanding. In the "new novel," for example, authors like Alain Robbe-Grillet (1922–2008) and Nathalie Sarraute (1900–1999) delved deeply into stream-of-consciousness writing, literally abandoning the reader in the disorienting obsessions of the protagonist's unconscious mind.

Some authors, however, preferred to retrieve literary forms and values that Modernists had rejected, choosing to tell a "good" chronological story that entertained as well as delivered a moral message. Graham Greene (1904–1991) was one of Britain's more prolific, popular, and critically acclaimed authors of the century. He succeeded in combining psychological and moral depth with enthralling stories, often dealing with political conflicts set in exotic locales. A longtime critic of the United States, Greene forecast the American defeat in Vietnam in his 1955 novel *The Quiet American.*

Several other European authors also combined a gripping tale and a fresh exciting narrative with seriousness of intent. In 1959, *The Tin Drum* by Günter Grass (1927–2015) blasted German consciousness out of the complacency that had been induced by the country's postwar economic miracle. The novel reexamined Germany's infatuation with Hitler and warned German readers of the ever-present danger of repeating the evils of the past.

In recent years, some European authors have abandoned the preoccupation with the elusiveness of knowledge and meaning and have sought to re-engage with the real world and its problems. In *The Cave* (2001), the Portuguese novelist José Saramago (1922–2010) focused on global issues, such as the erosion of individual cultures stemming from the tyranny of globalization, which, in his view, had not only led to the exploitation of poor countries but had also robbed the world's cultures of their uniqueness. Like Grass, Saramago believed strongly in the Western humanist tradition and viewed authors as society's moral guardians and political mobilizers.

As always, France has produced a number of interesting writers. Jean-Marie Le Clézio (b. 1940), born in France but having resided abroad for much of his life, has made good use of his cosmopolitan experience in his novels by addressing ecological concerns and the effects of globalization on traditional culture. The Romanian-born German writer Herta Muller (b. 1953) won the Nobel Prize in 2009 for her novels depicting the hardships and injustice of life under a totalitarian regime.

10-6b Music and the Arts

Since the end of World War II, serious music has witnessed a wide diversity of experimental movements, each searching for new tonal and rhythmic structures. Striving to go beyond Arnold Schoenberg's atonality, European composers like the French Pierre Boulez (1925–2016) and the German Karlheinz Stockhausen (1928–2007) set out to free their music from the traditional constraints of meter, form, and dynamics. They devised a new procedure called serialism, which is a mathematical ordering of musical components that, once set in motion, essentially writes itself automatically. More recently, the young British composer Thomas Adès (b. 1971) has earned critical acclaim for his musical compositions, which display radiant harmonies and pulsating energy.

In the visual arts, experimentalism, such as the recently popular installation art, is also widely practiced in Europe today, but some painters continue to use the traditional canvas to explore political and social issues relevant to their times. Some, like the Anglo-Irish painter Francis Bacon (1909–1992), sought to portray the horrors of World War II. In a 1946 canvas entitled *Painting*, Bacon portrayed the silent scream of a trapped man crouching beneath Neville Chamberlain's famous umbrella, symbol of the appeasement of Adolf Hitler. In the background, a bloody carcass on a crucifix vividly represents the butchery of war. Also of note is the German Anselm Kiefer (b. 1945), whose large canvases contrast Germany's past accomplishments with the calamity of the Holocaust (see Image 10.7). In *The Book*, he offers a desolate postapocalyptic landscape dominated by a large book made of lead. The book represents regeneration, as humankind's intellectual achievements and indomitable spirit triumph over the ravages of the twentieth century.

IMAGE 10.7 The Holocaust Memorial in Berlin. The "Memorial to the Murdered Jews of Europe" was built in the years 2003 and 2004 in the heart of the Nazi capital of Berlin, only a few blocks from the Brandenburg Gate. The memorial, designed by architect Peter Eisenman and engineer Burro Happold, consists of a series of over 2,700 concrete slabs arranged in a grid pattern and measuring up to 4.7 meters in height. Although many have speculated about the underlying symbolism of the design, the builders insist that it has no special significance. Still, visitors offer a variety of interpretations, with many remarking that the experience produces a sense of uneasiness, uncertainty, or entrapment, sentiments that certainly can conjure up recollections of the Holocaust itself. A "Place of Information" located under the memorial contains the names of over 3 million Jews who died at the hands of the Hitler regime before and during World War II.

Q *What kind of memorial do you think would be most appropriate to foster a better understanding of a tragedy such as the Holocaust?*

MAKING CONNECTIONS

During the immediate postwar era, Western Europe emerged from the ashes of World War II and achieved a level of political stability and economic prosperity unprecedented in its long history. By the 1970s, European leaders were beginning to turn their attention to bringing about further political and economic unity among the nations in the region. With the signing of the Maastricht Treaty in 1994, a schedule had been established to put the dream into effect, and many advocates of European unity were optimistic that the long era of division and mutual animosity could be put to an end.

But with the new century, the pains of transition have become more apparent, as it has become clear that long-standing structural and cultural differences stand in the way of regional unification. The structural problem is related to the question of how to maintain a high level of prosperity and productivity in a time of rapid technological change, social dislocation, and heightened levels of competition from abroad. The cultural challenge is probably even more difficult, since it requires a greater degree

of recognition on the part of EU officials and the general population alike that the inherent capacity to build stable and resilient democratic capitalist societies differs significantly from one country to another, based on their own historical experience.

The decision to expand the European Union into Eastern Europe has opened up new issues to confront, as many of the one-time Soviet satellites do not share the economic prosperity or the democratic traditions of their neighbors to the west. The EU has sought to establish rigid regulations that apply uniformly throughout the continent, but it is probably unrealistic to expect eastern nations to live up to the lofty expectations of more advanced industrial societies who entered their own scientific, intellectual, and industrial revolutions several hundred years ago. In the meantime, the continent is undergoing an economic crisis, as growing budget deficits bring into question the defining feature of the EU—the concept of the welfare state. A truly united Europe still remains a long way off.

REFLECTION QUESTIONS

Q What were the major successes and failures of the Western European democracies between 1945 and 2016?

Q What directions did Eastern European nations take after they became free from Soviet control? Why did they react as they did?

Q What are the major challenges facing the nations of Europe today? Why?

CHAPTER TIMELINE

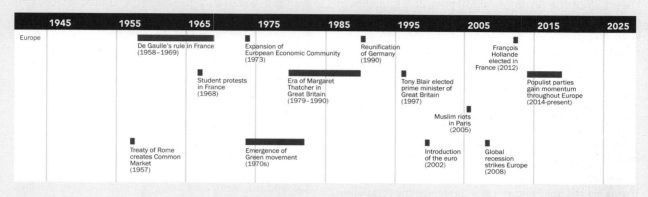

	1945	1955	1965	1975	1985	1995	2005	2015	2025

Europe

De Gaulle's rule in France (1958–1969)

Expansion of European Economic Community (1973)

Reunification of Germany (1990)

François Hollande elected in France (2012)

Student protests in France (1968)

Era of Margaret Thatcher in Great Britain (1979–1990)

Tony Blair elected prime minister of Great Britain (1997)

Populist parties gain momentum throughout Europe (2014-present)

Muslim riots in Paris (2005)

Treaty of Rome creates Common Market (1957)

Emergence of Green movement (1970s)

Introduction of the euro (2002)

Global recession strikes Europe (2008)

CHAPTER NOTES

1. Hannah Vogt, *The Burden of Guilt* tr. Herbert Strauss, (Oxford, 1964) pp. 283–286.

2. Cited in Michael Slackman, "For Some Germans, Unity Is Still Work in Progress," *New York Times*, October 1, 2010.

PART III
REFLECTIONS

AS WORLD WAR II CAME TO AN END, most survivors of that bloody struggle felt that they could afford to face the future with at least a measure of cautious optimism. With the death of Adolf Hitler in his bunker in Berlin, there were reasons to hope that the bitter rivalry that had marked relations among the Western powers would finally be put to an end and that the wartime alliance of the United States, Great Britain, and the Soviet Union could be maintained into the postwar era. In the meantime, the peoples of Asia and Africa could envision the possibility that the colonial system would soon come to an end, ushering in a new era of political stability and economic development on a global scale.

Three quarters of a century later, it is clear that these hopes have been only partly realized. In the decades following the war, the capitalist nations in the West managed to recover from the extended economic depression that had contributed to the start of World War II and advanced to a level of economic prosperity never before seen in world history. The bloody conflicts that had erupted among European nations during the first half of the twentieth century came to an end, and Germany and Japan—the primary instigators of World War II— developed pluralist systems of government and were

fully integrated into the world community. At the same time, the era of imperialism gradually came to a close, enabling newly independent nations in Africa and Asia to seek to regain control over their own destinies.

THE IRON CURTAIN DESCENDS The postwar prospects for a stable, peaceful world and an end to balance-of-power politics, however, were soon dashed by the emergence of the grueling and sometimes tense ideological struggle between the socialist and capitalist blocs, a competition headed by the only remaining great powers, the Soviet Union and the United States. Although the two superpowers were able to avoid a nuclear confrontation, the postwar world was divided into two heavily armed camps in a balance of terror that on at least one occasion—the Cuban Missile Crisis—brought the world briefly to the brink of nuclear holocaust.

Europe again became divided into hostile camps as the Cold War rivalry between the United States and the Soviet Union forced the European nations to ally with one or the other of the superpowers. The creation of two mutually antagonistic military alliances—NATO in 1949 and the Warsaw Pact in 1955—confirmed the new division of Europe, while a divided Germany, and within it a divided Berlin, remained the Cold War's most visible symbols. Repeated crises over the status of Berlin only intensified the fears on both sides of the ideological divide.

On the eastern side of the Iron Curtain, there were few reasons for optimism. Soviet domination, both political and economic, had snuffed out the first stirrings of democracy in that region and seemed so complete that many doubted it could ever be undone. Although popular uprisings in Poland and Hungary in 1956 and in Czechoslovakia in 1968 were vivid reminders that Marx's vision of a utopian society remained only a dream, communism appeared, at least for the time being, too powerful to be dislodged. The Helsinki

Accords, signed in 1975, was a tacit admission by the West that the Iron Curtain had apparently taken on a near-permanent status.

The confrontation between Washington and Moscow soon had repercussions throughout the world, for although the Cold War had begun in Europe, it soon spread to Asia as the Communist Party rose to power in China. By the mid-1950s, the bitter ideological rivalry between the two camps had taken on such a global character that events in such disparate areas as Southeast Asia, Central America, and the Middle East could send shock waves through world capitals everywhere. To most knowledgeable observers, the Cold War between the socialist and the capitalist blocs had become a permanent condition that was likely to affect the destiny of the human experiment for decades, if not generations, to come.

AND THE WALL CAME TUMBLING DOWN

Nevertheless, to the world's astonishment, the Soviet Union and its system of satellites abruptly collapsed in the late 1980s, leading to the end of the multinational Soviet Empire and the emergence of a string of truly independent states in Eastern Europe. The Communist Party in China managed to remain in power, but only by abandoning the key tenets of its longtime leader Mao Zedong and adopting major components of the capitalist system (see Chapter 12).

The sudden end of the Cold War spurred hopes for the emergence of a new era marked by rising global prosperity and peaceful cooperation among nations. But it soon became clear that such optimistic expectations were unjustified. The end of the tense ideological struggle did not lead to a new era of peace, but instead unleashed long-dormant ethnic and religious forces in various parts of the world, producing a new round of civil conflicts and a rising level of terrorist activity reminiscent of the latter part of the nineteenth century. Clearly, the Cold War had not irrevocably changed the trajectory of modern history.

At the same time, the expectation that Russia, which had for so long viewed its western neighbors with an uneasy mixture of envy, suspicion, and fear, would finally be ushered into the family of prosperous and democratic nations was also dashed, as the fragile sprouts of democracy in Moscow were ripped out by an ambitious and devious new tsar in the Kremlin. Russia once again turned its back on the West and turned its attention to the task of rebuilding its old empire.

Is the current tension between Russia and the Western nations an indication that a new ideological Cold War is in the offing? Strictly speaking, it seems an unlikely prospect, since the current regime in Moscow does not appear to be turning its lonely eyes to either Vladimir Lenin or Karl Marx. Nevertheless, Vladimir Putin and his acolytes are eagerly promoting their own model to other countries undergoing the difficult transition to technologically advanced industrialized societies. Based on the twin pillars of political autocracy and a naked appeal to national pride, the current system in place in Russia today serves as a seductive lure to political forces everywhere that seek to pursue their own version of wealth and power. At a time when people in many Western countries are currently questioning the effectiveness of their own democratic institutions, the autocratic model offered by Putin and his cohorts is not to be easily dismissed.

AFFLUENCE AND ITS DISCONTENTS

In the advanced Western nations, the combination of domestic tranquility and rapid economic growth brought an unprecedented level of prosperity to millions of people who were now able to enjoy the "good life" that had once been restricted to a small minority of the population. In the United States, the ability to "buy on the installment plan" or use a credit card made it possible for average Americans, for the first time, to spend well beyond their means. Soon other countries began to follow the American example, thereby laying the groundwork for a global network of material consumption.

Meanwhile, steady improvements in the realm of civil rights and gender equality accompanied the advancements in economic welfare. In most Western countries, legislation protecting the legal rights of ethnic minorities was enacted into law, while women began to enjoy new opportunities in employment and social equality. Still, there was much left to be done, because by no means did all peoples in the advanced countries in the capitalist world share in the affluence of the last half of the twentieth century. Many lacked access to the cornucopia of goods produced by the capitalist machine. This was especially the case for members of minority groups and people who made a living by manual labor. Although political leaders sometimes tried to extend the benefits of prosperity to their disadvantaged constituents, they had only limited success, and virtually all the advanced capitalist nations still had areas of poverty as the twentieth century came to an end.

The global financial crisis that began in the fall of 2008, and the slow recovery that followed it, has only widened the gap between rich and poor. Wages for middle-income and poorer workers have stagnated over the past few years, and unemployment has sometimes reached dangerous proportions. Even those currently living on a comfortable income worry that their prospects for retirement security may be threatened by the growing deficits run up in many of the countries throughout the Western world.

In the past, periods of economic prosperity in advanced capitalist countries have often been followed by difficult times, and the ebb and flow of politics in such societies has often reflected the tendency to undertake periodic corrections to maintain a balance between liberty and equality. Laissez-faire policies in good times are followed by an era of government intervention to encourage the market to correct serious inequities. While such a system is not perfect, it does serve over the long run to maintain a rough balance in the economy and in society as a whole. Today, however, some of the drags on broad-based prosperity and economic growth (such as labor-saving technology, a demographic crunch, and the perils of a free trade system) have made it more difficult for political leaders to maintain a balance. Without such a correction, the welfare state, many observers fear, may soon by a thing of the past.

Economic inequities are not the only challenge facing Western capitalist nations today. Equally important, economic affluence has given rise to its own set of problems. The single-minded focus on the accumulation of material possessions, an intrinsic characteristic of the capitalist ethos, has helped to promote high levels of productivity in offices and factories, but at the same time it has produced a spiritual malaise among individual members of society, who increasingly ask whether life has any meaning and purpose beyond the sheer accumulation of things. While the spread of scientific knowledge has eroded religious belief in some sectors of society, it has caused others to question the value of science and to retreat into the certainties of faith.

At the same time, increasing social mobility has undermined the traditional basic structural units of human society—the family and the community. The individual feels increasingly cast off into the sea of life with no moorings.  Modernity, as postwar society in the advanced countries is now commonly described, appears to offer no answer to the search for meaning in life beyond an unconfirmed and complacent belief in the Enlightenment doctrine of progress. Many turn to religion to fill the gap.

Looming over the current scene is a relative new challenge—the specter of dramatic climate change. Although the problem has not caught public attention until recent years, there is a growing awareness that environmental degradation and global warming present a serious threat to peoples and societies around the world, and many governments are beginning to seek remedies to address the situation. Recognition, however, is by no means universal, nor is everyone agreed on the urgency of the issue. We shall examine these issues, and how they will affect the peoples of the world in the new millennium, in Part V of this book.

PART IV

THIRD WORLD RISING

Beijing, China skyline

Vittoriano Rastelli/Getty Images

TOWARD THE PACIFIC CENTURY? JAPAN AND THE LITTLE TIGERS

Chapter Outline and Focus Questions

Connections to Today

Do you believe that nations in other parts of the world can imitate the progress made by Japan and the Little Tigers in future years, or were they uniquely qualified by culture or circumstance to surmount their challenges?

Keystone/Getty Images

IMAGE 11.1 General Douglas MacArthur and Emperor Hirohito, September 1945

THEY WERE AN UNLIKELY PAIR. The tall, lean American Douglas MacArthur looked every bit the famous warrior-general that he was as he towered over the diminutive and seemingly self-effacing Emperor Hirohito standing by his side. But the meeting between the U.S. general and the emperor of Japan on September 27, 1945, memorialized in the photograph, was a significant event in the history of post-World War II Asia. The discussions between MacArthur, recently appointed proconsul of the U.S. occupation regime in Japan, and Emperor Hirohito, the divine ruler of imperial Japan, signaled to the world that the United States' policy toward its defeated adversary would be relatively benign, rather than punitive as the Allied demand for the "unconditional surrender" of Japan had suggested. The new relationship between conqueror and conquered, which would soon blossom into a full-fledged alliance, opened the door to a series of dramatic changes in postwar East Asia.

Four decades later, Japan had emerged as the second greatest industrial power in the world, democratic in form and content and a source of stability throughout the region. Praise of the so-called Japanese miracle became a growth industry in academic circles in the United States, and Japan's achievement spawned a number of Asian imitators. Known as the "Little Tigers," the four industrializing societies of Taiwan, Hong Kong, Singapore, and South Korea achieved considerable success by following the path originally charted by Japan. Along with Japan, they became economic powerhouses and ranked among the world's top seventeen trading nations. Other nations in Asia and elsewhere took note and began to adopt the Japanese formula. For the first time, nations outside the ranks of the Western democracies had carried through their own economic miracle. It is no wonder that the rapid rise of Japan into the ranks of the world's most advanced and prosperous democracies caught the attention of observers, who relentlessly heralded the coming of the "Pacific Century."

11-1 JAPAN: ASIAN GIANT

 Focus Question: How did the Allied occupation after World War II change Japan's political, economic, and cultural institutions, and what remained unchanged?

For five years after the war in the Pacific, Japan was governed by an Allied administration under the command of U.S. General Douglas MacArthur (1880–1964). The occupation regime, which consisted of the Far Eastern Commission in Washington, D.C., and the four-power Allied Council in Tokyo, was dominated by the United States, although the country was technically administered by a new Japanese government. As commander of the occupation administration, MacArthur was responsible for demilitarizing Japanese society, destroying the Japanese war machine, trying Japanese civilian and military officials charged with war crimes, and laying the foundations of postwar Japanese society.

During the war, senior U.S. officials had discussed whether to insist on the abdication of Emperor Hirohito (r. 1926–1989) as the symbol of Japanese imperial expansion. During the summer of 1945, the United States rejected a Japanese request to guarantee that the position of the emperor would be retained in any future peace settlement and reiterated its demand for unconditional surrender. After the war, however, the United States agreed to the retention of the emperor after he agreed publicly to renounce his divinity. Although many historians have suggested that Hirohito opposed the war policy of his senior

advisers, some recent studies have contended that he supported it, although perhaps with misgivings.

11-1a The Occupation Era

Under MacArthur's firm tutelage, Japanese society was remodeled along Western lines. The centerpiece of occupation policy was the promulgation of a new constitution to replace the Meiji Constitution of 1889. The new charter, which was drafted by U.S. planners and imposed on the Japanese despite their objections to some of its provisions, was designed to transform Japan into a peaceful and pluralistic society that would no longer be capable of waging offensive war. The constitution specifically renounced war as a national policy, and Japan unilaterally agreed to maintain armed forces only sufficient for self-defense. Perhaps most important, the constitution established a parliamentary form of government based on a bicameral legislature, an independent judiciary, and a universal franchise; it also reduced the power of the emperor and guaranteed human rights.

But more than a written constitution was needed to demilitarize Japan and set it on a new course. Like the Meiji leaders in the late nineteenth century, occupation administrators wished to transform Japanese social institutions and hoped that their policies would be accepted by the Japanese people as readily as those of the Meiji period had been. The Meiji reforms, however, had been crafted to reflect Japanese traditions and had set Japan on a path quite different from that of the modern West. Some Japanese observers believed that a fundamental reversal of trends begun with the Meiji Restoration would be needed before Japan would be ready to adopt the Western capitalist, democratic model.

To undercut the mystique of the state represented by the Meiji concept of kokutai (which had embodied the idea of the uniqueness of Japan and the supreme authority of the emperor), Allied officials also sought to remodel the educational system along American lines so that it would turn out independent individuals rather than automatons subject to manipulation by the central government. Wartime textbooks were cleansed of their propagandistic content or completely scrapped, and the 1890 imperial rescript on education emphasizing the concept of loyalty to the state was repealed. Cultural items as familiar to Americans as Coca Cola, chewing gum, and baseball were strongly encouraged.

One of the sturdy pillars of Japanese militarism had been the giant business cartels, known as *zaibatsu*. Allied policy was designed to break up the *zaibatsu* into smaller units in the belief that corporate concentration, in Japan as in the United States, not only hindered competition but was inherently undemocratic and conducive to political authoritarianism. Occupation planners also intended to promote the formation of independent labor unions, lessen the power of the state over the economy, and provide a mouthpiece for downtrodden Japanese workers. Economic inequality in rural areas was to be reduced by a comprehensive land reform program that would turn the land over to the people who farmed it.

Dream and Reality   The Allied program was an ambitious and even audacious plan to remake Japanese society and has been justly praised for its clear-sighted vision and altruistic motives. Parts of the program, such as the constitution, the land reform program, and the educational system, succeeded brilliantly. But as other concerns began to intervene, changes and compromises were made that have become more controversial. In particular, with the rise of Cold War sentiment in the United States in the late 1940s, the goal of decentralizing the Japanese economy gave way to the desire to make Japan a key partner in the effort to defend East Asia against international communism. Convinced of the need to promote economic recovery in Japan, U.S. policymakers began to show more tolerance for the *zaibatsu*. Concerned at growing radicalism within the new labor movement, where left-wing elements were gaining strength, U.S. occupation authorities placed less emphasis on the independence of the labor unions.

Cold War concerns also affected U.S. foreign relations with Japan. On September 8, 1951, the United States and other former belligerent nations signed a peace treaty restoring Japanese independence. In turn, Japan renounced any claim to such former colonies or territories as Taiwan (which had been returned to the Republic of China), Korea (which, after a period of joint Soviet and U.S. occupation, had become two independent states), and southern Sakhalin and the Kurile Islands (which had been ceded to the Soviet Union). The Soviet Union refused to sign the treaty on the grounds that it had not been permitted to play an active role in the occupation. On the same day, the Japanese and Americans signed a defensive alliance and agreed that the United States could maintain military bases on the Japanese islands. Japan was now formally independent, but in a new dependency relationship with the United States. A provision in the new constitution renounced war as an instrument of national policy and prohibited the raising of an army (see Historical Voices, "Japan Renounces War," p. 281).

11-1b The Transformation of Modern Japan: Politics and Government

Thus, by the early 1950s, Japan had regained at least partial control over its own destiny (see Map 11.1).

Although it was linked closely to the United States through the new security treaty and the new U.S.-drafted constitution, Japan was now essentially free to move out on its own. As the world would soon discover, the Japanese adapted quickly to the new conditions. From a semifeudal society with autocratic leanings, Japan rapidly progressed into one of the most stable and advanced democracies in the world.

The Allied occupation administrators started with the conviction that Japanese expansionism was directly linked to the institutional and ideological foundations of the Meiji Constitution. Accordingly, they set out to change Japanese politics into something closer to the pluralistic approach used in most Western nations. The concepts of universal suffrage, governmental accountability, and a balance of power among the executive, legislative, and judicial branches that were embodied in the constitution of 1947 have held firm, and Japan today is a stable and mature democratic society with a literate and politically active electorate and a government that usually seeks to meet the needs of its citizens.

Yet a number of characteristics of the current Japanese political system reflect the tenacity of the

MAP 11.1 Modern Japan. Shown here are the four main islands that comprise the contemporary state of Japan.

 Why do you think most of the largest cities in Japan are located along the western coast of the country?

Japan Renounces War

 Q *What is the current status of Article 9 of the Japanese Constitution? Why are some observers demanding that this provision be changed?*

Politics & Government **ON MAY 3, 1947,** a new Japanese constitution went into effect to replace the Meiji Constitution of 1890. The process of drafting the document had taken place under the watchful guidance of General Douglas MacArthur, the supreme commander of the Allied Powers, who was determined to guarantee that the militaristic tendencies of the prewar Japanese government would not be resurrected in the postwar era. This point of view was explicitly included in the new constitution. According to Article 9 of the new charter, Japan renounced war as an instrument of national policy and eventually decided to maintain only a limited number of so-called self-defense forces to protect itself against external attack. From that time on, Japan relied on the United States for its protection and security.

Excerpts from the Japanese Constitution of 1947

We, the Japanese people, acting through our duly elected representatives in the National Diet, determined that we shall secure for ourselves and our posterity the fruits of peaceful cooperation with all nations and the blessings of liberty throughout this land, and resolved that never again shall we be visited with the horrors of war through the action of government, do proclaim that sovereign power resides with the people and do firmly establish this Constitution. Government is a sacred trust of the people, the authority for which is derived from the people, the powers of which are exercised by the representatives of the people, and the benefits of which are enjoyed by the people. This is a universal principle of mankind upon which this Constitution is founded. We reject and revoke all constitutions, laws, ordinances, and rescripts in conflict herewith.

We, the Japanese people, desire peace for all time and are deeply conscious of the high ideals controlling human relationship, and we have determined to preserve our security and existence, trusting in the justice and faith of the peace-loving peoples of the world. We desire to occupy an honored place in an international society striving for the preservation of peace, and the banishment of tyranny and slavery, oppression and intolerance for all time from the earth. We recognize that all peoples of the world have the right to live in peace, free from fear and want.

We believe that no nation is responsible to itself alone, but that laws of political morality are universal; and that obedience to such laws is incumbent upon all nations who would sustain their own sovereignty and justify their sovereign relationship with other nations.

We, the Japanese people, pledge our national honor to accomplish these high ideals and purposes with all our resources.

Chapter I. The Emperor

Article 1. The Emperor shall be the symbol of the State and of the unity of the people, deriving his position from the will of the people with whom resides sovereign power. . . .

Chapter II. Renunciation of War

Article 9. (1) Aspiring sincerely to an international peace based on justice and order, the Japanese people forever renounce war as a sovereign right of the nation and the threat or use of force as a mean of settling international disputes.

(2) In order to accomplish the aim of the preceding paragraph, land, sea, and air forces, as well as other war potential, will never be maintained. The right of belligerency of the state will not be recognized.

Source: From the Japanese Constitution of 1947. Accessed at: http://history.hanover.edu/texts/1947con.html.

traditional political culture. Although postwar Japan has had a multiparty system with two major parties, the Liberal Democrats and the Socialists, in practice there was a "government party" and a permanent opposition—the Liberal Democrats, who had presided over an era of growing material prosperity, were not voted out of office for thirty years. The ruling Liberal Democratic Party included several factions, but disputes usually involved personalities rather than substantive issues. Many of the leading Liberal Democrats controlled factions on a patron-client basis, and decisions on key issues, such as who should assume the prime ministership, were decided by a modern equivalent of the *genro* oligarchs.

That tradition changed suddenly in 1993 when the ruling Liberal Democrats, shaken by persistent reports of corruption and cronyism between politicians and business interests, failed to win a majority of seats in parliamentary elections. Morihiro Hosokawa (b. 1938), the leader of one of several newly created parties in the Japanese political spectrum, was elected prime minister. He promised to launch a number of reforms to clean up the political system. The new coalition government quickly split into feuding factions, however, and in 1995, the Liberal Democratic Party returned to power. Successive prime ministers failed to carry out promised reforms, and in 2001, Junichiro Koizumi (b. 1942), a former minister of health and welfare, was elected prime minister on a promise that he would initiate far-reaching reforms to fix the political system and make it more responsive to the needs of the Japanese people. His charisma raised expectations that he might be able to bring about significant changes, but bureaucratic resistance to reform and chronic factionalism within the Liberal Democratic Party largely thwarted his efforts. In 2009, three years after he left office, the Liberal Democrats were again voted out of power. But the government's response to a massive tsunami that struck the mainland island of Honshu in 2011 highlighted the ineptitude of the ruling Democratic Party (a center-left party that had been formed in 1998), and in 2012 the Liberal Democrats returned to power under Prime Minister Shinzō Abe (b. 1954). The Abe government has tried to revive the lagging Japanese economy by stimulating competition and adopting new fiscal policies, but his foreign policy has aroused unease elsewhere in Asia because of his often-voiced desire to revise the Japanese constitution so that the country can play a more active military role in the region (see "Atoning for the Past," p. 285).

Japan, Incorporated   One of the major characteristics of the Japanese political system has been the centralizing tendencies that it inherited from the Meiji period. The government is organized on a unitary rather than a federal basis; the local administrative units, called prefectures, have few of the powers of states in the United States. Moreover, the central government plays an active and sometimes intrusive role in various aspects of the economy, mediating management–labor disputes, establishing price and wage policies, and subsidizing vital industries and enterprises producing goods for export. This government intervention in the economy has traditionally been widely accepted and is often cited as a key reason for the efficiency of Japanese industry and the emergence of the country as an industrial giant.

11-1c The Economy

Nowhere are the changes in postwar Japan so visible as in the economic sector, where the nation has developed into a major industrial and technological power in the space of a century, surpassing such advanced Western societies as Germany, France, and Great Britain. Here indeed is the Japanese miracle in its most concrete manifestation. Although Japanese success has often been described as a direct product of the policies adopted during the occupation period, the process actually began over a century ago in the single-minded determination of the Meiji modernizers to create a rich country and a strong state. Their initial motive was to ensure Japan's survival against Western imperialism, but this defensive urge evolved into a desire to excel and, during the years before World War II, to dominate. That desire led to the war in the Pacific and, in the eyes of some observers, still contributes to Japan's problems with its trading partners in the world today.

As we have seen, the officials of the Allied occupation identified the Meiji economic system with centralized power and the rise of Japanese militarism. Accordingly, MacArthur's planners set out to break up the *zaibatsu* and decentralize Japanese industry and commerce. But with the rise of Cold War tensions, the policy was scaled back in the late 1940s, and only the nineteen largest conglomerates were affected. In any event, the new antimonopoly law did not hinder the formation of looser ties between Japanese companies, and as a result, a new type of informal relationship, sometimes called the **keiretsu**, or "interlocking arrangement," began to take shape after World War II. Through such arrangements among suppliers, wholesalers, retailers, and financial institutions, the *zaibatsu* system was reconstituted under a new name.

The occupation administration had more success with its program to reform the agricultural system. Half of the population still lived on farms, and half of all farmers were still tenants. Under a stringent land reform program in the late 1940s, all lands owned by absentee landlords and all cultivated landholdings over an established maximum were sold on easy credit terms to the tenants. The maximum size of an individual farm was set at 7.5 acres, while an additional 2.5 acres could be leased to tenants. The reform program created a strong class of yeoman farmers, and tenants declined to about 10 percent of the rural population.

The Japanese Miracle During the next fifty years, Japan re-created the stunning results of the Meiji era. At the end of the Allied occupation in 1950, the Japanese gross domestic product was about one-third that of Great Britain or France. Thirty years later, it was larger than both put together and well over half that of the United States. For years, Japan was the greatest exporting nation in the world, and its per capita income equaled or surpassed that of most advanced Western states. In terms of education, mortality rates, and health care, the quality of life in Japan now matches or is superior to that in the United States or the advanced nations of Western Europe.

By the mid-1980s, the economic challenge presented by Japan had begun to arouse increasing concern in both official and private circles in Europe and the United States. Explanations for the phenomenon tended to fall into two major categories. Some analysts pointed to cultural factors. The Japanese have over time developed a culture of cooperation with one another. Traditionally hardworking and frugal, they are more inclined to save than to consume, a trait that boosts the saving rate and labor productivity.[1] The Japanese are also family oriented and therefore spend less on government entitlement programs for the elderly, who normally live with their children. Like all Confucian societies, the Japanese value education, and consequently, the labor force is highly skilled. Finally, Japan is a homogeneous society in which people share common values and respond in similar ways to the challenges of the modern world.

Others cited more practical reasons for Japanese success. Paradoxically, Japan benefited from the total destruction of its industrial base during World War II because it did not face the problem of antiquated plants that plagued many industries in the United States. Under the terms of its constitution and the security treaty with the United States, Japan spends less than 1 percent of its gross domestic product on national defense, whereas the United States has averaged over 4 percent. But the most important factor, according to many observers, was that the Japanese government actively sought to promote business interests rather than hindering them. Some analysts charged that Japan used unfair trade practices, subsidizing exports through the Ministry of International Trade and Industry (**MITI**), dumping goods at prices below cost to break into a foreign market, maintaining an artificially low standard of living at home to encourage exports, and unduly restricting imports from other countries.

There was some truth on both sides of the argument. Undoubtedly, Japan benefited from its privileged position beneath the U.S. nuclear umbrella as well as from its ability to operate in a free trade environment that provided both export markets and access to Western technology. The Japanese also took a number of practical steps to improve their competitive position in the world and the effectiveness of their economic system at home. On the other hand, many of these steps were possible precisely because of the cultural factors described here. The tradition of loyalty to the firm, for example, derives from the communal tradition in Japanese society. The concept of sacrificing one's personal interests to those of the state, though not necessarily rooted in the traditional period, was certainly fostered by the *genro* oligarchy during the Meiji era.

The Miracle Tarnished By the 1990s, however, the Japanese economy had begun to run into serious difficulties, raising the question of whether the vaunted Japanese model was as appealing as many observers had earlier declared. A rise in the value of the yen hurt exports and burst the bubble of investment by Japanese banks that had taken place under the umbrella of government protection. At the same time, exports—long the driving force behind the emergence of Japan into the world's second largest economy—began to face increasing competition from hungry and aggressive rivals such as South Korea and Taiwan. With a much smaller domestic market than the United States has, the Japanese economy slipped into a long-term recession that has not yet entirely abated.

These economic difficulties have placed heavy pressure on some of the highly praised features of the Japanese economy. The tradition of lifetime employment created a bloated white-collar workforce and has made downsizing difficult. Today, job security is on the decline as increasing numbers of workers are being laid off. Around 16 percent of the population lives in poverty, a figure only slightly lower than the United States. Unfortunately, the burden has fallen disproportionately on women, who lack seniority and continue to suffer from various forms of discrimination in the workplace.

Ironically, some observers ascribe the country's recent economic difficulties to political factors that were once viewed as an advantage. The practice of providing the central government with an influential role in managing the economy has recently come under fire, as Japanese corporations that once sought government protection from imports have now begun to argue that deregulation is needed to enable Japanese firms to innovate in order to keep up with international competition. Such reforms, however, have been resisted by powerful government ministries in Tokyo, which are accustomed to playing an active role in national affairs.

Some point out that as the Japanese economy gradually opens up to the world market, exposure to foreign economic competition may improve the performance of Japanese manufacturers. In recent years, Japanese consumers have become increasingly concerned about the quality of some of their domestic products, causing one cabinet minister to complain about the "sloppiness and complacency" of Japanese firms (even the Japanese automaker Toyota has faced quality problems in its best-selling fleet of motor vehicles). One apparent reason for the quality problems is the cost-cutting measures adopted by Japanese companies to meet the challenges from abroad.

11-1d A Society in Transition

During the occupation, Allied planners set out to change social characteristics that they believed had contributed to Japanese aggressiveness before and during World War II. The new educational system removed all references to filial piety, patriotism, and loyalty to the emperor, and emphasized the individualistic values of Western civilization. The new constitution and a revised civil code attempted to achieve true gender equality by removing the remaining legal restrictions on women's rights to obtain a divorce, hold a job, or change their domicile. Women were guaranteed the right to vote and were encouraged to enter politics.

An Emphasis on Conformity Such efforts to remake Japanese behavior through legislation have had mixed success. Since the end of World War II, Japan has unquestionably become a more individualistic and egalitarian society. Freedom of choice in marriage and occupation is taken for granted, and social mobility, though less extensive than in the United States, has increased considerably. Although the Allied occupation policy established the legal framework for these developments, primary credit must be assigned to the evolution of the Japanese themselves into an urbanized and technologically advanced industrial society.

At the same time, many of the distinctive characteristics of traditional Japanese society have persisted, in somewhat altered form, to the present day. The emphasis on loyalty to the group and community relationships, for example, is reflected in the continued strength of corporate loyalties in contemporary Japan. Even though competition among enterprises in a given industry is often quite vigorous, social cohesiveness among both management and labor personnel is exceptionally strong within each individual corporation, although, as we have seen, that attitude has eroded somewhat in recent years.

One possible product of this attitude may be the relatively egalitarian nature of Japanese society in terms of income. A chief executive officer in Japan receives, on average, about twenty times the salary of the average worker, compared with more than two hundred times in the United States. The disparity between wealth and poverty

is also generally less in Japan than in most European countries and certainly less than in the United States.

Japan's welfare system also differs profoundly from its Western counterparts. Applicants are required to seek assistance first from their own families, and the physically able are ineligible for government aid. As a result, less than 1 percent of the population receives welfare benefits, compared with more than 10 percent who receive some form of assistance in the United States. Outside observers attribute the difference to several factors, including low levels of drug addiction and illegitimacy in Japan, as well as the importance of the work ethic and family responsibility.

Emphasis on the work ethic remains strong. The tradition of hard work is implanted at a young age by the educational system. The Japanese school year runs for 240 days, compared to 180 days in the United States, and work assignments outside class tend to be more extensive (according to one source, a Japanese student averages about five hours of homework per day). Competition for acceptance into universities is intense, and many young Japanese take cram courses to prepare for the "examination hell" that lies ahead. The results are impressive: the literacy rate in Japanese schools is almost 100 percent, and Japanese schoolchildren consistently earn higher scores on achievement tests than children in other advanced countries. At the same time, this devotion to success has often been accompanied by bullying by teachers and what Americans might consider an oppressive sense of conformity (see Historical Voices, "Growing Up in Japan," p. 285).

Some young Japanese find suicide the only escape from the pressures emanating from society, school, and family. Parental pride often becomes a factor, with "education mothers" pressuring their children to work hard and succeed for the honor of the family. Ironically, once a student is accepted into college, the amount of work assigned tends to decrease because graduates of the best universities are virtually guaranteed lucrative employment offers. Nevertheless, the early training instills an attitude of deference to group interests that persists throughout life. Some outside observers, however, believe such attitudes can have a detrimental effect on individual initiative.

By all accounts, independent thinking is on the increase in Japan, and some schools are beginning to emphasize creativity over rote learning. In some cases, it leads to antisocial behavior, such as crime or membership in a teen gang. Usually, it is expressed in more indirect ways, such as the recent fashion among young people of dyeing their hair brown (known in Japanese as "tea hair") (see Comparative Illustration, "From Conformity to Counterculture," p. 286). Because the practice is banned in many schools and generally frowned on by the older generation (one police chief dumped a pitcher of beer on a student with brown hair

HISTORICAL VOICES

Growing Up in Japan

 What is the apparent purpose of these regulations? How do they differ from standards of behavior in schools in the United States?

Family & Society **JAPANESE SCHOOLCHILDREN** are exposed to a much more regimented environment than U.S. children experience. Most Japanese schoolchildren, for example, wear black-and-white uniforms to school. These regulations are examples of rules adopted by middle school systems in various parts of Japan. The Ministry of Education in Tokyo concluded that these regulations were excessive, but they are probably typical.

School Regulations: Japanese Style

1. Boys' hair should not touch the eyebrows, the ears, or the top of the collar.
2. No one should have a permanent wave, or dye his or her hair. Girls should not wear ribbons or accessories in their hair. Hair dryers should not be used.
3. School uniform skirts should be _____ centimeters above the ground, no more and no less (differs by school and region).
4. Keep your uniform clean and pressed at all times. Girls' middy blouses should have two buttons on the back collar. Boys' pant cuffs should be of the prescribed width. No more than 12 eyelets should be on the shoes. The number of buttons on a shirt and tucks in a shirt are also prescribed.
5. Wear your school badge at all times. It should be positioned exactly.
6. Going to school in the morning, wear your book bag strap on the right shoulder; in the afternoon on the way home, wear it on the left shoulder. Your book case thickness, filled and unfilled, is also prescribed.
7. Girls should wear only regulation white underpants of 100% cotton.
8. When you raise your hand to be called on, your arm should extend forward and up at the angle prescribed in your handbook.
9. Your own route to and from school is marked in your student rule handbook; carefully observe which side of each street you are to use on the way to and from school.
10. After school you are to go directly home, unless your parent has written a note permitting you to go to another location. Permission will not be granted by the school unless the other location is a suitable one. You must not go to coffee shops. You must be home by _____ o'clock.
11. It is not permitted to drive or ride a motorcycle, or to have a license to drive one.
12. Before and after school, no matter where you are, you represent our school, so you should behave in ways we can all be proud of.

Source: *The Material Child: Coming of Age in Japan and America* by Merry White.

that he noticed in a bar), many young Japanese dye their hair as a gesture of independence and a means of gaining acceptance among their peers. When seeking employment or getting married, however, they return their hair to its natural color.

Atoning for the Past Lingering social problems also need to be addressed. Minorities such as the *eta* (hereditary outcasts in traditional Japan, now known as the *Burakumin*) and Korean residents in Japan continue to be subjected to legal and social discrimination. For years, official sources were reluctant to divulge that thousands of Korean women were conscripted to serve as "comfort women" (prostitutes) for Japanese soldiers during the war, and many Koreans living in Japan contend that such condescending attitudes toward minorities continue to exist. Representatives of the "comfort women" have demanded both financial compensation and a formal letter of apology from the Japanese government for the treatment they received during the Pacific War. Negotiations over the issue have been under way for several years.

The **Ainu** are another ethnic minority group that has been left behind in the country's headlong rush into modernity. Descendants of the original settlers on the islands, they were eventually overwhelmed by later arrivals from the mainland and now live for the most part in

COMPARATIVE ILLUSTRATION

From Conformity to Counterculture

Q *How would you compare the social requirements and privileges of Japanese children with those of other cultures that we have encountered in this text?*

Family & Society

TRADITIONALLY, SCHOOLCHILDREN IN JAPAN have worn uniforms to promote conformity with the country's communitarian social mores. In Image 11.2a, young students dressed in identical uniforms are on a field trip to Kyoto's Nijo Castle, built in 1603 by the founder of the Tokugawa dynasty. Recently, however, a youth counterculture has emerged in Japan. Image 11.2b shows fashion-conscious teenagers with "tea hair"—heirs of Japan's long era of affluence—revel in their expensive hip-hop outfits, platform shoes, and layered dresses. Such dress habits symbolize the growing revolt against conformity in contemporary Japan.

William J. Duiker

Barry Cronin/Getty Images

IMAGE 11.2a

IMAGE 11.2b

isolated communities on the northern island of Hokkaido. Long ignored by a government that sought to proclaim the ethnic homogeneity of the Japanese people, in 2008 they were finally recognized as a distinct indigenous culture. Whether their new status will enable the Ainu—currently numbering about 24,000 people—to claim compensation for past ill treatment and present neglect is still an open question.

Japan's behavior during World War II has been an especially sensitive issue. During the early 1990s, critics at home and abroad charged that textbooks printed under the guidance of the Ministry of Education did not adequately discuss the atrocities committed by the Japanese government and armed forces during World War II. Other Asian governments were particularly incensed at Tokyo's failure to accept responsibility for such behavior and demanded a formal apology. The government expressed remorse, but only in the context of the aggressive actions of all colonial powers during the imperialist era. In the view of many Japanese, the actions of their government during the Pacific War were a form of self-defense. When new textbooks were published that openly discussed instances of Japanese wartime misconduct, including sex slavery, the use of slave labor, and the Nanjing massacre (see Chapter 6), many Japanese were outraged and initiated a campaign to delete or tone down references to atrocities committed by imperial troops during the Pacific War. At times, members of the government have exacerbated the controversy;

Prime Minister Koizumi did so by attending ceremonies at shrines dedicated to the spirits of Japan's war dead, as did members of Prime Minister Abe's cabinet in 2013.

The issue is not simply an academic one, for fear of a revival of Japanese militarism is still strong in the region, where Japan's relations with other states have recently been strained by disputes with South Korea and China over ownership of small islands in the China Sea. The United States has not shared this concern, however, and applauded Japan's recent decision to enhance the ability of its self-defense forces to deal with potential disturbances within the region. The proper role of the military has provoked vigorous debate in Japan, where some observers have argued that their country should adopt a more assertive stance toward the United States and China and play a larger role in Asian affairs.

Women in Japanese Society   One of the more tenacious legacies of the past in Japanese society is sexual inequality. Although women are now legally protected against discrimination in employment, very few have reached senior levels in business, education, or politics. In the words of one Western scholar, they remain "acutely disadvantaged," though, ironically, in a recent survey of Japanese business executives, a majority declared that women were smarter than men. Women now make up more than 50 percent of the workforce, but most are in retail or service occupations, and on average they are paid only about half as much as men.[2] There is a feminist movement in Japan, but it has none of the vigor and mass support of its counterpart in the United States.

Most women in Japan consider being a homemaker the ideal position. In the home, a Japanese woman has considerable responsibility. She is expected to be a "good wife and wise mother" and has the primary responsibility for managing the family finances and raising the children. Japanese husbands (known derisively in Japan as the "wet leaf tribe") perform little work around the house, spending an average of nine minutes a day on housework, compared to twenty-six minutes for American husbands. At the same time, Japanese divorce rates are well below those of the United States.

The Demographic Crisis   Many of Japan's current dilemmas stem from its growing demographic problems. Today, Japan has the highest proportion of people older than sixty-five of any industrialized country—almost 23 percent of the country's total population. By the year 2024, an estimated one-third of the Japanese population will be over the age of sixty-five, and the median age will be fifty, ten years older than the median in the United States. This demographic profile is due both to declining fertility and a low level of immigration. Immigrants make up only 1 percent of the total population of Japan. Together, the aging population and the absence of immigrants are creating the prospect of a dramatic labor shortage in coming years. Nevertheless, prejudice against foreigners persists in Japan, and the government remains reluctant to ease restrictions against immigrants from other countries in the region.

Japan's aging population has many implications for the future. Traditionally, it was the responsibility of the eldest child in a Japanese family to care for aging parents, but that system is beginning to break down because of limited housing space and the growing tendency of working-age women to seek jobs in the marketplace. The proportion of Japanese older than sixty-five years of age who live with their children has dropped from 80 percent in 1970 to about 50 percent today. At the same time, public and private pension plans are under increasing financial pressure, partly because of the low birthrate and the graying population.

11-1e Religion and Culture

As in the West, increasing urbanization has led to a decline in the practice of organized religion in Japan, although evangelical sects have proliferated in recent years. The largest and best-known sect is Soka Gakkai, a lay Buddhist organization that has attracted millions of followers and formed its own political party, the Komeito. Many Japanese also follow **Shinto**, a traditional faith based on the belief in the existence of spirits in Nature that was once identified with reverence for the emperor and the state.

Western literature, art, and music have also had a major impact on Japanese society. After World War II, many of the writers who had been active before the war resurfaced, but now their writing reflected demoralization. Many were attracted to existentialism, and some turned to hedonism and nihilism. For these disillusioned authors, defeat was compounded by fear of the Americanization of postwar Japan. One of the best examples of this attitude was the novelist Yukio Mishima (1925–1970), who led a crusade to stem the tide of what he described as America's "universal and uniform 'Coca-Colonization'" of the world in general and Japan in particular.[3] Mishima's ritual suicide in 1970 was the subject of widespread speculation and transformed him into a cult figure.

One of Japan's most serious-minded contemporary authors is Kenzaburo Oe (b. 1935). His work, rewarded with a Nobel Prize for Literature in 1994, focuses on Japan's ongoing quest for modern identity and purpose. His characters reflect the spiritual anguish precipitated by the collapse of the imperial Japanese tradition and the subsequent adoption of Western culture—a trend that Oe contends has culminated in unabashed materialism, cultural decline, and a moral void. Yet unlike Mishima, Oe does not wish to restore the imperial traditions of the past but rather seeks to regain spiritual meaning by retrieving the sense of communality and innocence found in rural Japan.

Haruki Murakami (b. 1949), one of Japan's most popular authors today, was one of the first to discard the introspective and somber style of the earlier postwar period. Characters in his novels typically take the form of a detached antihero, reflecting the emptiness of corporate life in contemporary Japan. In *The Wind-Up Bird Chronicle* (1997), Murakami highlights the capacity for irrational violence in Japanese society and the failure of the nation to accept its guilt for the behavior of Japanese troops during World War II.

Since the 1970s, increasing affluence and a high literacy rate have contributed to a massive quantity of publications, ranging from popular potboilers to first-rate fiction. Much of this new literature deals with the common concerns of all affluent industrialized nations, including the effects of urbanization, advanced technology, and mass consumption. A wildly popular genre is the "art-manga," or graphic novel. Some members of the youth counterculture have used manga to rebel against Japan's rigid educational and conformist pressures.

Other aspects of Japanese culture have also been influenced by Western ideas, although without the intense preoccupation with synthesis that is evident in literature. Western music is very popular in Japan, and scores of Japanese classical musicians have succeeded in the West. Even rap music has gained a foothold among Japanese youth, although without the association with sex, drugs, and violence that it has in the United States. Although some of the lyrics betray an attitude of modest revolt against the uptight world of Japanese society, most lack any such connotations.

11-1f The Japanese Difference

Whether the unique character of modern Japan will endure is unclear. Confidence in the Japanese "economic miracle" has been shaken by the long recession, and there are indications of a growing tendency toward hedonism and individualism among Japanese youth. Older Japanese frequently complain that the younger generation lacks their sense of loyalty and willingness to sacrifice. There are also signs that the concept of loyalty to one's employer may be beginning to erode among Japanese youth. Some observers have predicted that with increasing affluence Japan will become more like the industrialized societies in the West. Although Japan is

unlikely to evolve into a photocopy of the United States, the image of millions of dedicated "salarymen" heading off to work with their briefcases and their pinstriped suits may no longer be an accurate portrayal of reality in contemporary Japan.

11-2 TAIWAN: THE OTHER CHINA

Focus Question: Why do you think the Republic of China has fared better on the island of Taiwan than it did when it controlled the mainland?

It did not take long for other countries in East Asia to attempt to imitate the Japanese success. To Japan's south, the Republic of China on the island of Taiwan was one of the first to do so (see Map 11.2).

After retreating to Taiwan following their defeat by the Communists, Chiang Kai-shek and his followers established a new capital at Taipei and set out to build a strong and prosperous nation based on Chinese traditions and the principles of Sun Yat-sen. The government, which continued to refer to itself as the Republic of China (ROC), contended that it remained the legitimate representative of the Chinese people and that it would eventually return in triumph to the mainland.

The Nationalists had much more success on Taiwan than they had achieved on the mainland. In the relatively secure environment provided by a security treaty with the United States, signed in 1954, and the comforting presence of the U.S. Seventh Fleet in the Taiwan Strait, the ROC was able to concentrate on economic growth without worrying about a Communist invasion. The regime possessed a number of other advantages that it had not enjoyed in Nanjing. Fifty years of efficient Japanese rule had left behind a relatively modern economic infrastructure and an educated population, although the island had absorbed considerable damage during World War II and much of its agricultural produce had been exported to Japan at low prices. With only a small population to deal with (about 7 million in 1945), the ROC could make good use of foreign assistance and the efforts of its own energetic people to build a modern industrialized society.

The government moved rapidly to create a solid agricultural base. A land reform program, more effectively designed and implemented than the one introduced

MAP 11.2 Modern Taiwan

in the early 1930s on the mainland, led to the reduction of rents, while landholdings larger than 3 acres were purchased by the government and resold to the tenants at reasonable prices. As in Meiji Japan, the previous owners were compensated by government bonds. The results were gratifying: food production doubled over the next generation and began to make up a substantial proportion of exports.

In the meantime, the government strongly encouraged the development of local manufacturing and commerce. By the 1970s, Taiwan was one of the most dynamic industrial economies in East Asia. The agricultural proportion of the gross domestic product declined from 36 percent in 1952 to only 9 percent thirty years later. At first, the industrial and commercial sector was composed of relatively small firms engaged in exporting textiles and food products, but the 1960s saw a shift to heavy industry, including shipbuilding, steel, petrochemicals, and machinery, and a growing emphasis on exports. The government played a major role in the process, targeting strategic industries for support and investing in infrastructure. At the same time, as in Japan, the government stressed the importance of private enterprise and encouraged foreign investment and a high rate of internal saving. By the mid-1980s, more than three-quarters of the population lived in urban areas.

11-2a From Dictatorship to Democracy

In contrast to the People's Republic of China (PRC) on the mainland, the ROC actively maintained Chinese tradition, promoting respect for Confucius and the ethical principles of the past, such as hard work, frugality, and filial piety (see Image 11.3). Although there was some corruption in both the government and the private sector, income differentials between the wealthy and the poor were generally less than elsewhere in the region, and the overall standard of living increased substantially. Health and sanitation improved, literacy rates were quite high, and an active family planning program reduced the rate of population growth. Nevertheless, the total population on the island increased to about 20 million in the mid-1980s.

In one respect, however, Chiang Kai-shek had not changed: increasing prosperity did not lead to the democratization of the political process. The Nationalists continued to rule by emergency decree and refused to permit the

IMAGE 11.3 What's in a Name? The National Chiang Kai-shek Memorial Hall in Taipei. While the Chinese government on the mainland attempted to destroy all vestiges of traditional culture, the Republic of China on Taiwan has sought to preserve the cultural heritage as a link between past and present. This policy is graphically displayed in the mausoleum for Chiang Kai-shek in downtown Taipei, shown in this photograph. The mausoleum, with its massive entrance gate, not only glorifies the nation's leader, but recalls the grandeur of old China. In 2007, the mausoleum was controversially renamed the National Taiwan Democracy Memorial Hall in a bid by the government to downplay the island's historical ties to the mainland. In response to protests from Beijing, in 2008 the name was changed back to the National Chiang Kai-shek Memorial Hall.

Q *Why do you think Chinese leaders in Beijing complained about the change in title for the mausoleum?*

formation of opposition political parties on the grounds that the danger of invasion from the mainland had not subsided. Propaganda material from the PRC was rigorously prohibited, and dissident activities (promoting either rapprochement with the mainland or the establishment of an independent Republic of Taiwan) were ruthlessly suppressed. Although representatives to the provincial government of the province of Taiwan were chosen in local elections, the central government (technically representing the entire population of China) was dominated by mainlanders who had fled to the island with Chiang in 1949.

Some friction developed between the mainlanders (as the new arrivals were called), who numbered about 2 million, and the indigenous Taiwanese, who, except for a small number of aboriginal peoples in the mountains, were mostly ethnic Chinese whose ancestors had emigrated to the island during the Qing dynasty. While the mainlanders were dominant in government and the professions, the indigenous Taiwanese were prominent in commerce. Mainlanders tended to view the local population with a measure of condescension, and at least in the early years, intermarriage between members of the two groups was rare. Many Taiwanese remembered with anger the events of March 1947, when Nationalist troops had killed hundreds of Taiwanese demonstrators in Taipei. More than one thousand leading members of the local Taiwanese community were arrested or killed in the subsequent repression. By the 1980s, however, these fissures in Taiwanese society had begun to diminish; by that time, an ever-higher proportion of the population had been born on the island and identified themselves as Taiwanese.

11-2b Crafting a Taiwanese Identity

During the 1980s, the ROC slowly began to evolve toward a more representative form of government—a process that was facilitated by the death of Chiang Kai-shek in 1975. Chiang Ching-kuo (1910–1988), his son and successor, was less concerned about the danger from the mainland and more tolerant of free expression. On his death, he was succeeded as president by Lee Teng-hui (b. 1923), a native Taiwanese. By the end of the 1980s, democratization was under way, including elections and the formation of legal opposition parties. The first fully free national elections, held in 1992, resulted in a bare majority for the Nationalists over strong opposition from the Democratic Progressive Party (DPP).

But political liberalization had its dangers; some leading Democratic Progressives began to agitate for an independent Republic of Taiwan, a possibility that aroused concern within the Nationalist government in Taipei and frenzied hostility in the PRC. In the spring of 2000, DPP candidate Chen Shui-bian (b. 1950) was elected to the presidency, ending half a century of Nationalist Party rule on Taiwan. His elevation to the position angered Beijing, which noted that in the past he had called for an independent Taiwanese state. Chen backed away from that position and called for the resumption of talks with the PRC, but Chinese leaders remain suspicious of his intentions and reacted with hostility to U.S. plans to provide advanced military equipment to the island. In the meantime, charges of official corruption and economic problems began to erode support for the DPP on the island. The return to power of the Nationalist Party under Ma Ying-jeou (b. 1950) in 2008 and his reelection as president in 2012 temporarily eased relations with mainland China, but when the DPP returned to office in 2016 under the country's first woman president, Tsai Ing-wen, tensions began to increase once again.

Whether Taiwan will remain an independent state or be united with the mainland cannot be predicted at this time. Although diplomatic ties have been severed (see Chapter 12), the United States continues to provide defensive military assistance to the Taiwanese armed forces and has made it clear that it supports self-determination for the people of Taiwan. It has also declared that it expects the final resolution of the dispute to take place by peaceful means. The outcome thus depends in good measure on developments in the PRC. Economic and cultural contacts between Taiwan and the mainland have been increasing, but the Taiwanese—who have followed recent events in Hong Kong closely (see "11-4 Singapore and Hong Kong: the Littlest Tigers," p. 292)—have shown no inclination to accept Beijing's offer of "one country, two systems," under which Taiwan would accept the PRC as the legitimate government of China in return for autonomous control over the affairs of Taiwan. The unresolved future of the island remains one of the most delicate problems in the region of East Asia.

11-3 KOREA: A PENINSULA DIVIDED

Focus Question: What factors have contributed to the economic success achieved by South Korea in the years following the end of World War II?

While the world was focused on the economic miracle occurring on the Japanese islands, another miracle of sorts was taking place on the Asian mainland. In 1953, the Korean peninsula was exhausted from three years of bitter fraternal war, a conflict that took the lives of an estimated

4 million Koreans on both sides of the 38th parallel and turned as much as one-quarter of the population into refugees. Although a cease-fire was signed at Panmunjom in July 1953, it was a fragile peace that left two heavily armed and mutually hostile countries facing each other suspiciously (see Map 11.3).

North of the truce line was the Democratic People's Republic of Korea (PRK), a police state under the dictatorial rule of Communist leader Kim Il-sung (1912–1994). To the south was the Republic of Korea, under the equally autocratic President Syngman Rhee (1875–1965), a fierce anti-Communist who had led the resistance to the northern invasion and now placed his country under U.S. military protection. But U.S. troops could not protect Rhee from his own people, many of whom resented his reliance on the political power of the wealthy landlord class. After several years of harsh rule, marked by government corruption, fraudulent elections, and police brutality, demonstrations broke out in the capital city of Seoul in the spring of 1960 and forced him into retirement.

MAP 11.3 The Korean Peninsula Since 1953

11-3a The Korean Model

The Rhee era was followed by a brief period of multiparty democratic government, but in 1961, General Park Chung Hee (1917–1979) came to power through a coup d'état. The new regime promulgated a new constitution, and in 1963, Park was elected president of a civilian government. He set out to foster an economic recovery after decades of foreign occupation and civil war. Adopting the nineteenth-century Japanese slogan "Rich Country and Strong State," Park built up a strong military while relying on U.S. and later Japanese assistance to help build a strong manufacturing base in what had been a predominantly agricultural society. Because the private sector had been relatively weak under Japanese rule, the government played an active role in the process by instituting a series of five-year plans that targeted specific industries for development, promoted exports, and funded infrastructure development. Under a land reform program, large landowners were required to sell all their farmland above 7.4 acres to their tenants at low prices.

The program was a solid success. Benefiting from the Confucian principles of thrift, respect for education, and hard work (during the 1960s and 1970s, South Korean workers spent an average of sixty hours a week at their jobs), as well as from Japanese capital and technology, Korea gradually emerged as a major industrial power in East Asia. The economic growth rate rose from less than 5 percent annually in the 1950s to an average of 9 percent under Park. The largest corporations—including Samsung, Daewoo, and Hyundai—were transformed into massive conglomerates called *chaebol*, the Korean equivalent of the *zaibatsu* of prewar Japan. Taking advantage of relatively low wages and a stunningly high rate of saving, Korean businesses began to compete actively with the Japanese for export markets in Asia and throughout the world. Per capita income also increased dramatically, from less than $90 (in U.S. dollars) annually in 1960 to $1,560 (twice that of Communist North Korea) twenty years later.

But like many other countries in the region, South Korea was slow to develop democratic principles. Although his government functioned with the trappings of democracy, Park continued to rule by autocratic means and suppressed all forms of dissidence. In 1979, Park was assassinated. But after a brief interregnum of democratic rule, in 1980 a new military government under General Chun Doo Hwan (b. 1931) seized power. The new regime was as authoritarian as its predecessors, but after student riots in 1987, by the end of the decade opposition to autocratic rule had spread to much of the urban population.

National elections were finally held in 1989, and South Korea reverted to civilian rule. Successive presidents sought to rein in corruption while cracking down on the *chaebols* and initiating contacts with the Communist regime in the PRK on possible steps toward eventual reunification of the peninsula. After the Asian financial crisis in 1997, economic conditions temporarily worsened, but they have since recovered, and the country is increasingly competitive in world markets today. In elections held in 2012, South Korea elected its first woman president—Park Guen-hye (b. 1952), the daughter of Park Chung Hee. Later, however, she was removed from office on the charge of corruption.

In the meantime, relations with North Korea, now on the verge of becoming a nuclear power, remain tense. Multinational efforts to persuade the regime to suspend its nuclear program continue, although North Korea claimed to have successfully conducted a nuclear test in 2009. To add to the uncertainty, the regime faced a succession crisis, when Kim Jong-il (1941–2011), the son and successor of founder Kim Il-sung, died suddenly in 2011 and was replaced by his inexperienced son, Kim Jong-un (b. 1984). In the uncertainty following the emergence of a new leader in North Korea, tensions with the South erupted once again, as the communist leadership in that impoverished country continues to view the outside world with suspicion. A program run by the North Korean regime to develop an intercontinental ballistic missile system with nuclear warheads has led to increased tensions in the region. In a bid to defuse the issue, bilateral meetings between Kim and U.S. president Donald Trump have taken place in Singapore and Vietnam, but so far without positive result.

William J. Duiker

IMAGE 11.4 Mending the Safety Net in South Korea. Until recently, it was common for South Korean parents to live with their eldest son's family in their senior years, a practice that was viewed as a reward for their past sacrifices in raising their children. But with the country now transformed into an industrial and urbanized society, this social contract has eroded. As their children move into the cities, older Koreans are often left to fend for themselves in rural areas. Because the government has not yet established an adequate social security network the elderly are often left in desperate straits. Show here are a group of elderly women visiting a Buddhist shrine in Pusan.

11-3b South Korea: The Little Tiger with Sharp Teeth

South Korea today is one of the most competitive economies in the world. Its manufactures rival in popularity those of other East Asian nations for predominance in global markets. Japanese observers complain about the country's "hungry spirit," which steals jobs from Japanese workers. Some critics inside the country, however, worry that Koreans put too much emphasis on achieving success and that many children spend so much time preparing for college entrance examinations that they are deprived of a normal childhood. The recent effort by Lee Myung-bak (b. 1941), who served as president from 2008 to 2012, to enforce a five-day workweek was motivated, in part, by the same considerations.

Whether the Korean people's drive to get ahead in life is seen as a benefit or a disadvantage, there is no doubt that, like many of its counterparts in East Asia, South Korea is changing rapidly. A predominantly rural nation at the end of World War II, it is now a manufacturing powerhouse. Though it has historically had a homogeneous population, it now hosts a growing foreign population, many of whom are low-wage workers and young women brought in from other parts of Asia to marry Koreans living in rural areas, where the shortage of marriageable Korean women is acute. The traumatic effect of the transformation of South Korea from a rural to an urban society is ably described by author Kyung-Sook Shin (b. 1963) in her recent novel

entitled *Please Look After Mom*. The disappearance of the protagonist's mother in the book represents the loss of the country's traditional values and lifestyles (see Image 11.4).

Whereas some older Koreans undoubtedly feel betrayed by the transition to a more contemporary lifestyle, many of their younger contemporaries decry the continuing pressure to conform to traditional mores. Han Kang (b. 1970) describes the revolt of a young wife's in her *The Vegetarian* (2007), who—by adopting a meat-free diet—provokes a violent outburst of anger from her husband and expulsion from her family.

11-4 SINGAPORE AND HONG KONG: THE LITTLEST TIGERS

 Focus Question: What factors do you think most contributed to the emergence of the tiny state of Singapore as a major factor in Asian affairs?

The smallest but by no means the least successful of the Little Tigers are Singapore and Hong Kong. Both are essentially city-states with large populations densely packed into small territories. Singapore, once a British crown colony and briefly a part of the state of Malaysia, is now an independent nation (see Map 11.4). Hong Kong was a British colony until it was returned to PRC control, but with autonomous status, in 1997. In recent years, both have emerged as industrial powerhouses with standards of living well above the level of their neighbors.

MAP 11.4 The Republic of Singapore

The success of Singapore must be ascribed in good measure to the will and energy of its political leaders. When it became independent in August 1965, Singapore was in a state of transition. Its longtime position as an entrepôt for trade between the Indian Ocean and the South China Sea was declining in importance. With only 618 square miles of territory, much of it marshland and tropical jungle, Singapore had little to offer but the frugality and industriousness of its predominantly overseas Chinese population. But a recent history of political radicalism, fostered by the rise of influential labor unions, had frightened away foreign investors.

Within a decade, Singapore's role and reputation had dramatically changed. Under the leadership of Prime Minister Lee Kuan Yew (1923–2015), once the firebrand leader of the radical People's Action Party, the government encouraged the growth of an attractive business climate while engaging in massive public works projects to feed, house, and educate the nation's 2 million citizens. The major components of success have been shipbuilding, oil refineries, tourism, electronics, and finance—the city-state has become the banking hub of the entire region.

Like the other Little Tigers, Singapore has relied on a combination of government planning, entrepreneurial spirit, export promotion, high productivity, and an exceptionally high rate of saving to achieve industrial growth rates of nearly 10 percent annually during the last quarter of the twentieth century. Unlike some other industrializing countries in the region, it has encouraged multinational corporations to provide much-needed capital and technological input. Population growth has been controlled by a stringent family planning program, and literacy rates are among the highest in Asia.

As in the other Little Tigers, an authoritarian political system has provided a stable environment for economic growth. Until his retirement in 1990, Lee Kuan Yew and his People's Action Party dominated Singaporean

MAP 11.5 Hong Kong

politics, and opposition elements were intimidated into silence or arrested. The prime minister openly declared that the Western model of pluralist democracy was not appropriate for Singapore and lauded the Meiji model of centralized development. Confucian values of thrift, hard work, and obedience to authority have been promoted as the ideology of the state. The government has had a passion for cleanliness and at one time even undertook a campaign to persuade its citizens to flush the public urinals. In 1989, the local *Straits Times*, a government mouthpiece, published a photograph of a man walking sheepishly from a row of urinals. The caption read "Caught without a flush: Mr. Amar Mohamed leaving the Lucky Plaza toilet without flushing the urinal."[4]

Today, Singapore is the most prosperous and well-educated country in Asia, with a highly competitive industrial sector, advanced social services, and a well-educated population. To provide space for a growing population, additional land is being reclaimed from the surrounding South China Sea, and a new botanical garden contains a futuristic group of tall towers that could provide sustenance for local residents in environmentally sound conditions (see Image 11.5).

But economic success is beginning to undermine the authoritarian foundations of the system as a more sophisticated citizenry begins to demand more political freedoms and an end to government paternalism. Lee Kuan Yew's successor, Goh Chok Tong (b. 1941), promised a "kinder, gentler" Singapore, and political restrictions on individual behavior are gradually being relaxed. In the spring of 2000, the government announced the opening of a speaker's corner, where citizens would be permitted to express their views, provided they obtained a permit and did not break the law. While this was a small step, it provided a reason for optimism that a more pluralistic political system will gradually emerge under the current prime minister, Lee Hsien Loong (b. 1952), the son of Lee Kuan Yew. After he assumed office in 2004, the government announced plans to relax restrictions on freedom of speech and assembly in the small island state. Today the people of Singapore enjoy increasing freedoms, although potential opposition elements continue to be rigorously suppressed.

The future of Hong Kong is not so clear-cut (see Map 11.5). As in Singapore, sensible government

IMAGE 11.5 **Singapore: Asia's City of the Future.** Since achieving its independence in 1965, the city-state of Singapore has emerged as one of the most modern and efficiently run cities in Southeast Asia, if not the world. A recent symbol of this achievement is located on recently reclaimed land in the harbor, where eighteen so-called supertrees have been constructed in a public park adjacent to downtown skyscrapers. Built of concrete and steel, with wire rods for branches, these artificial trees rise up as much as 50 meters in height and are festooned with more than 160,000 tropical plants divided among 200 species. Fed by numerous solar panels and rainwater catches, these hanging gardens offer a look at the future as human communities seek to find ever more innovative ways to feed their growing populations.

policies and the hard work of its people have enabled Hong Kong to thrive. At first, the prosperity of the colony depended on a plentiful supply of cheap labor. Inundated with refugees from the mainland during the 1950s and 1960s, the population of Hong Kong burgeoned to more than 6 million. Many of the newcomers were willing to work for starvation wages in sweatshops producing textiles, simple appliances, and toys for the export market. More recently, Hong Kong has benefited from increased tourism, manufacturing, and the growing economic prosperity of neighboring Guangdong Province, the most prosperous region of the PRC. In one respect, Hong Kong has differed from the other societies discussed in this chapter in that it has relied on an unbridled free market system rather than active state intervention in the economy. At the same time, by allocating substantial funds for transportation, sanitation, education, and public housing, the government has created favorable conditions for economic development.

Unlike the other Little Tigers, Hong Kong remained under colonial rule until very recently. British authorities did little to foster democratic institutions or practices, and most residents of the colony cared more about economic survival than political freedoms. In talks between representatives of Great Britain and the PRC, the Chinese leaders made it clear they were determined to have Hong Kong return to mainland authority in 1997, when the British ninety-nine-year lease over the New Territories, the food basket of the colony of Hong Kong, ran out. The British agreed, on condition that satisfactory arrangements could be made for the welfare of the population. The Chinese promised that for fifty years, the people of Hong Kong would live under a capitalist system and be essentially self-governing. Recent statements and actions by Chinese leaders, however, have raised questions about the degree of autonomy Hong Kong will receive under Chinese rule, which began on July 1, 1997 (see Historical Voices, "Return to the Motherland," p. 295). Opposition forces have been periodically harassed, and in 2012 the Hong Kong government, which normally reflects pressures from Beijing, sought to install new educational guidelines similar to those applied in China. Faced with severe public protests, local officials rescinded the order. More recently, a decision by the local government to extradite Hong Kong residents who have been charged with certain types of crimes for trial on the mainland has provoked widespread popular demonstrations against the decision.

HISTORIANS DEBATE 11-4a The East Asian Miracle: Fact or Myth?

What explains the striking ability of Japan and the four Little Tigers to transform themselves into export-oriented societies capable of competing with the advanced nations of Europe and the Western Hemisphere? Some historians point to the traditional character traits of Confucian societies, such as thrift, a work ethic, respect for education, and obedience to authority. In a recent poll of Asian executives, more than 80 percent expressed the belief that Asian values differ from those of the West, and most said that these values have contributed significantly to the region's recent success. Others placed more emphasis on deliberate steps taken by government and economic leaders to meet the political, economic, and social challenges their societies face.

Return to the Motherland

 To what degree are the people of Hong Kong self-governing under these regulations? How do the regulations infringe on the freedom of the population?

Politics & Government

AFTER LENGTHY NEGOTIATIONS, in 1984 China and Great Britain agreed that on July 1, 1997, Hong Kong would return to Chinese sovereignty. Key sections of the agreement are included here. In succeeding years, authorities of the two countries held further negotiations. Some of the discussions raised questions in the minds of residents of Hong Kong as to whether their individual liberties would indeed be respected after the colony's return to China. These concerns have been amply justified in recent years.

The Joint Declaration on Hong Kong

The Hong Kong Special Administrative Region will be directly under the authority of the Central People's Government of the People's Republic of China. The Hong Kong Special Administrative Region will enjoy a high degree of autonomy, except in foreign and defense affairs, which are the responsibility of the Central People's Government.

The Hong Kong Special Administrative Region will be vested with executive, legislative, and independent judicial power, including that of final adjudication. The laws currently in force in Hong Kong will remain basically unchanged.

The Government of the Hong Kong Special Administrative Region will be composed of local inhabitants. The chief executive will be appointed by the Central People's Government on the basis of the results of elections or consultations by the chief executive of the Hong Kong Special Administrative Region for appointment by the Central People's Government. . . .

The current social and economic systems in Hong Kong will remain unchanged, and so will the lifestyle. Rights and freedoms, including those of the person, of speech, of the press, of assembly, of association, of travel, of movement, of correspondence, of strike, of choice of occupation, of academic research, and of religious belief will be ensured by law. . . . Private property, ownership of enterprises, legitimate right of inheritance, and foreign investment will be protected by law.

Source: Kevin Rafferty, *City on the Rocks* (New York: Penguin, 1991).

There seems no reason to doubt that cultural factors connected to East Asian social traditions have contributed to the economic success of these societies. Certainly, habits such as frugality, industriousness, and subordination of individual desires have all played a role in their governments' ability to concentrate on the collective interest. Political elites in these countries have been highly conscious of these factors and willing to use them for national purposes. Prime Minister Lee Kuan Yew of Singapore deliberately fostered the inculcation of such ideals among the citizens of his small nation and often lamented the decline of Confucian values among the young.

As this chapter has shown, however, without active encouragement by political elites, such traditions cannot be effectively harnessed for the good of society as a whole. As we will see in Chapter 12, the creative talents of the Chinese people were not efficiently utilized under Mao Zedong during the frenetic years of the Cultural Revolution. Only when Deng Xiaoping and other pragmatists took charge and began to place a high priority on economic development were the stunning advances of recent decades achieved.

One other factor should be taken into account. Japan and the little Tigers were operating within a regional framework highly conducive to rapid economic development. The Little Tigers received substantial inputs of capital and technology from the advanced nations of the West (Taiwan and South Korea from the United States, Hong Kong and Singapore from Britain). Japan relied to a greater degree on its own efforts, but received a significant advantage by being placed under the U.S. security umbrella and guaranteed access to market and sources of raw materials in a region dominated by U.S. naval power. Without an eager market in Europe and the United States for consumer goods produced in Asian factories, the miracle would certainly not have occurred. In effect, the rapid rise of East Asia in the postwar era was no miracle, but a fortuitous combination of favorable cultural factors and deliberate human action.

11-5 ON THE MARGINS OF ASIA: POSTWAR AUSTRALIA AND NEW ZEALAND

 Focus Question: How has the geographical location of Australia and New Zealand affected their history and culture? Do you think they should be considered a part of the region of Southeast Asia?

Technically, Australia and New Zealand are not part of Asia, and throughout their short history, both countries have identified culturally and politically with the West rather than with their Asian neighbors. Their political institutions and values are derived from Europe, and their economies resemble those of the advanced countries of the world rather than the preindustrial societies of much of Southeast Asia. Legal ties with the United Kingdom have been loosened since the end of World War II, but citizens in both countries recently rejected a proposal to form republics, thus retaining the British monarch as their own titular head of state. Both are currently members of the British Commonwealth and of the U.S.-led ANZUS (Australia, New Zealand, and the United States) alliance.

Yet trends in recent years have been drawing both states, especially Australia, closer to Asia. In the first place, immigration from East and Southeast Asia has increased rapidly. More than one-half of current immigrants to Australia come from East Asia, and about 7 percent of the population of about 18 million people is now of Asian descent. In New Zealand, residents of Asian descent represent only about 3 percent of the population of 3.5 million, but about 12 percent of the population are Māori, Polynesian peoples who settled on the islands about a thousand years ago. Second, trade relations with Asia are increasing rapidly. About 60 percent of Australia's export markets today are in East Asia, and the region is the source of about one-half of its imports. Asian trade with New Zealand is also on the increase.

In recent years, both countries have been relatively receptive to immigration from Asia, although Australia maintained a "White Australia" policy until 1973. One reason—in the case of Australia—is to increase the population density in its vast territories, although resistance to the policy has been more vocal in recent years. The country's treatment of its aboriginal minority has always left much to be desired, and that continues to be the case.

Both countries maintain strong economic ties with China, but Beijing's rising strength in the region is cause for concern, and was undoubtedly a factor in the agreement reached in 2011 to station 2,500 U.S. troops in Australia. Both countries face the geographical challenge of balancing their European traditions with the reality of their location at the edge of the Eurasian supercontinent.

MAKING CONNECTIONS

In the years following the end of World War II, the peoples of the Pacific Rim emerged from a decade of war to face the challenge of building stable and prosperous independent states. Initially, progress was slow, as new political leaders were forced to deal with the legacy of imperialism, economic dislocation, and internal disagreements over their visions for the future. By the end of the century, a small number of nations in East Asia were well on their way to laying the foundations of advanced industrial societies. They were the first states outside Europe and the Western hemisphere to do so.

It took a little longer for Japan and the Little Tigers to develop stable and mature political systems based on democratic principles and the rule of law. Some observers complained that economic growth in the region has sometimes been achieved at the cost of political freedom and individual human rights, and it is true that, until recently, government repression of opposition has been common throughout East Asia except in Japan. In addition, the rights of national minorities and women are often still limited in comparison with the advanced countries of the West. Still, Japan, South Korea, and Taiwan today have functioning democracies with stable political parties that replace each other in power without recourse to violence, and the latter two have elected women to the highest posts in the land. Singapore has not yet followed their example, as senior political leaders argue that a fully democratic political system is not appropriate in the country's present state of development.

In any event, it should be kept in mind that progress in political pluralism and human rights has taken a long time to be realized in Europe and North America and even now frequently fails to match expectations. A rising standard of living, increased social mobility, and a changing regional environment brought about by the end of the Cold War should go far to enhance political freedoms and promote social justice in the countries bordering the western Pacific.

REFLECTION QUESTIONS

Q Why do you think Japan and the Little Tigers have been so successful in their efforts to build advanced industrial societies?

Q How has independence affected the role of women in southern and eastern Asia? How does the position of women in the region compare with that of their counterparts elsewhere?

Q How have the nations in the region dealt with the challenge of integrating their ethnic and religious minorities into their political systems?

CHAPTER TIMELINE

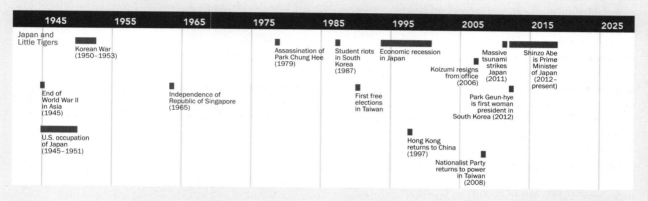

CHAPTER NOTES

1. Younger Japanese save only about 6 percent of their annual income, whereas their parents saved 25 percent. *Far Eastern Economic Review*, April 2005.
2. In 2003, only about 8 percent of managers in Japanese firms were women, compared with 46 percent in the United States. *New York Times*, July 25, 2003.
3. Yukio Mishima and Geoffrey Bownas, eds., *New Writing in Japan* (Harmondsworth, England, 1972), p. 16.
4. Stan Seser, "A Reporter at Large," *New Yorker*, January 13, 1992, p. 44.

Chapter Outline and Focus Questions

12-1 *China Under Mao Zedong*

Q How would you sum up Mao Zedong's political beliefs? Why do you think the Chinese people eventually rejected them?

12-2 *From Mao to Deng*

Q How did China under the leadership of Deng Xiaoping seek to change the policies followed under his predecessor Mao Zedong? How might Deng have justified these changes in terms of Marxist-Leninist ideology?

12-3 *Serve the People: Chinese Society Under Communism*

Q How do the policies adopted by Chinese leaders differ from those adopted by their counterparts in Japan and elsewhere in the Pacific Rim?

12-4 *China's Changing Culture*

Q How would you describe the various ways that Chinese culture has evolved in the years since the end of World War II?

Connections to Today

To what degree do the ideas of Karl Marx and Vladimir Lenin continue to resonate in China today? Does the Communist Party just utilize Marxist ideology as a means of maintaining power, or is its commitment sincere?

Chairman Mao is the Red Sun in our Hearts, August 1969 (colour litho), Chinese School, (20th century)/ Private Collection/© The Chambers Gallery, London/The Bridgeman Art Library

毛主席是我们心中的红太阳

（庆祝建国十七周年）

大型彩色文献纪录片　　　中央新闻纪录电影制片厂　　八一电影制片厂 联合摄制　　中国电影发行放映公司发行

IMAGE 12.1 Art during the Great Proletarian Revolution depicts Mao Zedong as a Chinese demigod

"A REVOLUTION IS NOT A DINNER PARTY, or writing an essay, or painting a picture, or doing embroidery; it cannot be so refined, so leisurely and gentle, so temperate and kind, courteous, restrained, and magnanimous. A revolution is an insurrection, an act of violence by which one class overthrows another."[1] With these words—written in 1926, at a time when the Communists, in cooperation with Chiang Kai-shek's Nationalist Party, were embarked on their Northern Expedition to defeat the warlords and reunify China—the young revolutionary Mao Zedong warned his colleagues that the road to victory in the struggle to build a Communist society would be arduous and would inevitably involve acts of violence against the class enemy.

In the mid-1960s, more than fifteen years after the Communist seizure of power in China, Mao's words continued to resonate, as the country entered a new era of revolutionary violence, known as the Great Proletarian Cultural Revolution. For several years, legions of his supporters, many of them young activists known as Red Guards, scoured Chinese society for traitorous elements who supposedly opposed Mao's teachings by "following the capitalist road." Mao was now worshiped by the Chinese people as a virtual living god, and some of his writings, drawn up into a set of his pithy sayings called the Little Red Book, were viewed as holy writ and were read—even memorized—by millions of his compatriots.

12-1 CHINA UNDER MAO ZEDONG

 Focus Questions: How would you sum up Mao Zedong's political beliefs? Why do you think the Chinese people eventually rejected them?

In the fall of 1949, China was at peace for the first time in twelve years. The newly victorious Chinese Communist Party (CCP), under the leadership of its chairman, Mao Zedong, turned its attention to consolidating its power base and healing the wounds of war. Its long-term goal was to construct a socialist society, but its leaders realized that popular support for the revolution was based on the party's platform of honest government, land reform, social justice, and peace rather than on the utopian goal of a classless society. Accordingly, the new regime initially followed Soviet precedent in adopting a moderate program of political and economic recovery known as New Democracy.

12-1a New Democracy

Under **New Democracy**—patterned roughly after Lenin's New Economic Policy in Soviet Russia in the 1920s (see Chapter 4)—the capitalist system of ownership was retained in the industrial and commercial sectors. A program of land redistribution was adopted, but the collectivization of agriculture was postponed. Only after the CCP had consolidated its rule and brought a degree of prosperity to the national economy would the difficult transformation to a socialist society begin.

In following Soviet precedent, Chinese leaders tacitly recognized that time and extensive indoctrination would be needed to convince the Chinese people of the superiority of socialism. In the meantime, the party would rely on capitalist profit incentives to spur productivity. Manufacturing and commercial firms were permitted to remain in private hands, but they were placed under stringent government regulations and were encouraged to form "joint enterprises" with the government. To win the support of the poorer peasants, who made up

the majority of the population, the land reform program that had long been in operation in "liberated areas" was now expanded throughout the country. This strategy was designed not only to win the gratitude of the rural masses but also to undermine the political and economic influence of counterrevolutionary elements still loyal to Chiang Kai-shek.

In some ways, New Democracy was a success. About two-thirds of the peasant households in the country received property under the land reform program and thus had reason to be grateful to the new regime. Spurred by official tolerance for capitalist activities and the end of the civil war, the national economy began to rebound, although agricultural production still lagged behind both official targets and the growing population, which was increasing at an annual rate of more than 2 percent. But the picture had a number of blemishes. In the course of carrying out land redistribution, thousands, if not millions, of landlords and rich farmers lost their lands, their personal property, their freedom, and sometimes their lives. Many of those who died had been tried and convicted of "crimes against the people" in tribunals set up in towns and villages around the country. As Mao himself later conceded, many were innocent of any crime, but in the eyes of the party, their deaths were necessary to destroy the power of the landed gentry in the countryside. "You can't make an omelet," he remarked laconically, "without breaking eggs."

12-1b The Transition to Socialism

Originally, the CCP's leaders intended to follow the Leninist formula of delaying the building of a fully socialist society until China had a sufficient industrial base to permit the mechanization of agriculture. In 1953, they launched the nation's first five-year plan (patterned after earlier Soviet plans), which called for substantial increases in industrial output. Lenin had believed that the promise of mechanization would give Russian peasants an incentive to join collective farms, which, because of their greater size, could better afford to purchase expensive farm machinery. But the enormous challenge of providing tractors and reapers for millions of rural villages eventually convinced Mao Zedong and some of his colleagues that it would take years, if not decades, for China's infant industrial base to meet the burgeoning needs of a modernizing agricultural sector. He therefore decided to begin collectivization immediately, in the hope that collective farms would increase food production and release land, labor, and capital for the industrial sector.

Accordingly, beginning in 1955, the Chinese government launched a new program to transform the country into a socialist society. Virtually all private farmland was collectivized, although peasant families were allowed to retain small plots for their private use (a Chinese version of the private plots adopted in the Soviet Union). In addition, most industry and commerce were nationalized, as joint enterprises were transformed into fully socialist ones.

On paper, the results were impressive. Collectivization was achieved without arousing the massive peasant unrest that had occurred in the Soviet Union during the 1930s, perhaps because the Chinese government followed a policy of persuasion rather than compulsion (Mao remarked that Stalin had "drained the pond to catch the fish") and because the land reform program had already earned the support of millions of rural Chinese. But the hoped-for production increases did not materialize, and in 1958, at Mao's insistent urging, party leaders approved a more radical program known as the **Great Leap Forward**. Existing rural collectives, normally the size of a traditional village, were combined into vast "people's communes," each containing more than 30,000 people. These communes were to be responsible for all administrative and economic tasks at the local level. The party's official slogan promised "Hard work for a few years, happiness for a thousand."[2]

Mao hoped this program would mobilize the population for a massive effort to accelerate economic growth and ascend to the final stage of communism before the end of the twentieth century. It is better, he said, to "strike while the iron is hot" and advance the revolution without interruption. Some party members were concerned that this ambitious program would threaten the government's rural base of support, but Mao argued that Chinese peasants were naturally revolutionary in spirit:

> [The Chinese rural masses are] first of all, poor, and secondly, blank. That may seem like a bad thing, but it is really a good thing. Poor people want change, want to do things, want revolution. A clean sheet of paper has no blotches, and so the newest and most beautiful words can be written on it, the newest and most beautiful pictures can be painted on it.[3]

Those words, of course, were *socialism* and *communism*.

The Great Leap Forward was a disaster. Administrative bottlenecks, bad weather, and peasant resistance to the new system (which, among other things, attempted to eliminate work incentives and destroy the traditional family as the basic unit of Chinese society) combined to drive food production downward, and over the next few years, as many as 15 million people may have died of starvation. Many peasants were reportedly reduced to eating the bark off trees and in some cases allowing infants to starve. In 1960, the commune experiment was essentially abandoned.

Although the commune structure was retained, ownership and management were returned to the collective level. Mao was severely criticized by some of his more pragmatic colleagues (one remarked bitingly that "one cannot reach Heaven in a single step"), causing him to complain that he had been relegated to the sidelines "like a Buddha on a shelf."

12-1c The Great Proletarian Cultural Revolution

But Mao, still an imposing figure within the CCP, was not yet ready to abandon either his power or his dream of an egalitarian society. In 1966, he returned to the attack, mobilizing discontented youth and disgruntled workers and party members into revolutionary units (soon to be known as Red Guards) who were urged to take to the streets to cleanse Chinese society—from local schools and factories to government ministries in Beijing—of impure elements who in Mao's mind were guilty of "taking the capitalist road." Supported by his wife, Jiang Qing (1914–1991), and other radical party figures, Mao launched China on a new forced march toward communism.

The so-called **Great Proletarian Cultural Revolution** lasted for ten years, from 1966 to 1976. Some Western observers interpreted it as a simple power struggle between Mao and some of his key rivals such as head of state Liu Shaoqi (1898–1969) and Deng Xiaoping (1904–1997), the party's general secretary. Both were removed from their positions, and Liu later died, allegedly of torture, in a Chinese prison. But real policy disagreements were involved. One reason Mao had advocated the Great Leap Forward was to bypass the party and government bureaucracy, which in his view had lost their revolutionary zeal and were primarily concerned with protecting their power. Now he and his supporters feared that capitalist values and the remnants of "feudalist" Confucian ideas and practices would undermine ideological fervor and betray the revolutionary cause. Mao himself was convinced that only an atmosphere of constant revolutionary fervor, or **uninterrupted revolution** as he called it, could enable the Chinese to overcome their past lethargy and achieve the final stage of utopian communism. "I care not," he once wrote, "that the winds blow and the waves beat. It is better than standing idly in a courtyard."

His opponents worried that Mao's "heaven-storming" approach could delay economic growth and antagonize the people. They argued for a more pragmatic strategy that would give priority to nation building over the ultimate Communist goal of spiritual transformation. But with Mao's supporters now in power, the CCP carried out vast economic and educational reforms that virtually

eliminated any remaining profit incentives, established a new school system that emphasized "Mao Zedong thought," and stressed practical education at the elementary level at the expense of specialized training in science and the humanities in the universities. School learning was discouraged as a legacy of capitalism, and Mao's famous *Little Red Book,* composed partly of Maoist aphorisms to encourage good behavior and revolutionary zeal, was hailed as the most important source of knowledge in all areas.

The radicals' efforts to destroy all vestiges of traditional society were reminiscent of the Reign of Terror in revolutionary France, when the Jacobins sought to destroy organized religion and even created a new revolutionary calendar to replace the traditional Christian system. Red Guards rampaged through the country attempting to eradicate the "four olds" (old thought, old culture, old customs, and old habits). They destroyed temples and religious sculptures; they tore down street signs and replaced them with new ones carrying revolutionary names. At one point, the city of Shanghai even ordered that the significance of

colors in stoplights be changed so that red (the revolutionary color) would indicate that traffic could move.

But a mood of revolutionary enthusiasm is difficult to sustain. Key groups, including party bureaucrats, urban professionals, and many military officers, did not share Mao's belief in the benefits of uninterrupted revolution and constant turmoil. Many were alienated by the arbitrary actions of the Red Guards, who indiscriminately accused and brutalized their victims in a society where legal safeguards had almost entirely vanished (see Movies & History, *The Last Emperor*, above). Whether the Cultural Revolution led to declining productivity is a matter of debate. Inevitably, however, the sense of anarchy and uncertainty caused popular support for the movement to erode, and when the end came with Mao's death in 1976, the vast majority of the population may well have welcomed its demise (see Image 12.2).

Personal accounts by young Chinese who took part in the Cultural Revolution show that their initial enthusiasm often turned to disillusionment. In *Son of the Revolution,* Liang Heng tells how at first he helped friends organize

Make Revolution!

 How do the tactics of the Red Guards compare with those employed by the cadres during the land reform program in the early 1950s? To what degree did they succeed in remaking the character of the Chinese people?

Politics & Government IN 1966, MAO ZEDONG unleashed the power of revolution on China. Rebellious youth in the form of Red Guards rampaged through all levels of society, exposing anti-Maoist elements, suspected "capitalist roaders," and those identified with the previous ruling class. In this poignant excerpt, Nien Cheng (nee-uhn CHUHNG), the widow of an official of Chiang Kaishek's regime, describes a visit by Red Guards to her home during the height of the Cultural Revolution.

Nien Cheng, *Life and Death in Shanghai*

Suddenly the doorbell began to ring incessantly. At the same time, there was furious pounding of many fists on my front gate, accompanied by the confused sound of hysterical voices shouting slogans. The cacophony told me that the time of waiting was over and that I must face the threat of the Red Guards and the destruction of my home. . . .

I stood up to put the book on the shelf. A copy of the Constitution of the People's Republic caught my eye. Taking it in my hand and picking up the bunch of keys I had ready on my desk, I went downstairs.

At the same moment, the Red Guards pushed open the front door and entered the house. There were thirty or forty senior high school students, aged between fifteen and twenty, led by two men and one woman much older.

The leading Red Guard, a gangling youth with angry eyes, stepped forward and said to me, "We are the Red Guards. We have come to take revolutionary action against you!"

Though I knew it was futile, I held up the copy of the Constitution and said calmly, "It's against the Constitution of the People's Republic of China to enter a private house without a search warrant."

The young man snatched the document out of my hand and threw it on the floor. With his eyes blazing, he said, "The Constitution is abolished. It was a document written by the Revisionists within the Communist Party. We recognize only the teachings of our Great Leader Chairman Mao." . . .

Another young man used a stick to smash the mirror hanging over the blackwood chest facing the front door.

Mounting the stairs, I was astonished to see several Red Guards taking pieces of my porcelain collection out of their padded boxes. One young man had arranged a set of four Kangxi wine cups in a row on the floor and was stepping on them. I was just in time to hear the crunch of delicate porcelain under the sole of his shoe. The sound pierced my heart. Impulsively I leapt forward and caught his leg just as he raised his foot to crush the next cup. He toppled. We fell in a heap together. . . .

The young man whose revolutionary work of destruction I had interrupted said angrily, "You shut up! These things belong to the old culture. They are the useless toys of the feudal emperors and the modern capitalist class and have no significance to us, the proletarian class. . . . Our Great Leader Chairman Mao taught us, 'If we do not destroy, we cannot establish.' The old culture must be destroyed to make way for the new socialist culture."

Source: From *Life and Death in Shanghai* by Nien Cheng (New York: Penguin, 1986).

Red Guard groups: "I thought it was a great idea. We would be following Chairman Mao just like the grownups, and Father would be proud of me. I suppose I too resented the teachers who had controlled and criticized me for so long, and I looked forward to a little revenge."[4] Later, he had reason to repent. His sister ran off to join the local Red Guard group. Prior to her departure, she denounced her mother and the rest of her family as "rightists" and

enemies of the revolution. The family home was regularly raided by Red Guards, and their father was severely beaten and tortured for having three neckties and "Western shirts." Books, paintings, and writings were piled in the center of the floor and burned before his eyes. On leaving, a few of the Red Guards helped themselves to his monthly salary and his transistor radio (see Historical Voices "Make Revolution!" above).

IMAGE 12.2 Punishing China's Enemies during the Cultural Revolution. During the Great Proletarian Revolution, individuals classified as "class enemies" were often seized and publicly humiliated to set an example for observers. In this photograph from the 1960s, Red Guards parade a victim wearing a dunce cap through the streets of Beijing before instilling further punishment. In many cases, these enemies of the state were subjected to torture and even execution.

 Why do you think the United States and other democratic nations do not punish wrong-doers by inflicting such public humiliation on them?

12-2 FROM MAO TO DENG

Focus Questions: How did China under the leadership of Deng Xiaoping seek to change the policies followed under his predecessor Mao Zedong? How might Deng have justified these changes in terms of Marxist-Leninist ideology?

In September 1976, Mao Zedong died at the age of eighty-three. After a short but bitter succession struggle, the pragmatists led by Deng Xiaoping seized power from the radicals and brought the Cultural Revolution to an end. Mao's widow, Jiang Qing, and three other leading radicals (derisively called the "Gang of Four" by their opponents) were put on trial and sentenced to death or to long terms in prison. The egalitarian policies of the previous decade were reversed, and a new program emphasizing economic modernization was introduced.

12-2a The Four Modernizations

Under the leadership of Deng, who installed his supporters in key positions throughout the party and the government, attention focused on what were called the **Four Modernizations:** industry, agriculture, technology, and national defense. Deng had been a leader of the faction that opposed Mao's program of rapid socialist transformation, and during the Cultural Revolution, he had been forced to perform menial labor to "sincerely correct his errors." But Deng continued to espouse the pragmatic approach and reportedly once remarked, "Black cat, white cat, what does it matter so long as it catches the mice?" Under the program of Four Modernizations, many of the restrictions against private activities and profit incentives were eliminated, and people were encouraged to work hard to benefit themselves and Chinese society. The government popularized the idea that all Chinese would prosper, although not necessarily at the same speed. Familiar slogans such as "Serve the people" and "Uphold the banner of Marxist-Leninist-Maoist thought" were replaced by new ones repugnant to the tenets of Mao Zedong thought: "Create wealth for the people" and "Time is money." The party announced that China was still at the "primary stage of socialism" and might not reach the state of utopian communism for generations.

Crucial to the program's success was the government's ability to attract foreign technology and capital. For more than two decades, China had been isolated from technological advances taking place elsewhere in the world. Although China's leaders understandably prided themselves on their nation's capacity for "self-reliance," their isolationist policy had been exceedingly costly for the national economy. China's post-Mao leaders blamed the country's backwardness on the "ten lost years" of the Cultural Revolution, but the "lost years," at least in technological terms, extended back to 1949 and in some respects even before. Now, to make up for lost time, the government encouraged foreign investment and sent thousands of students and specialists abroad to study capitalist techniques.

By adopting this pragmatic approach in the years after 1976, China made great strides in ending its chronic problems of poverty and underdevelopment. Per capita income roughly doubled during the 1980s; housing, education, and sanitation improved; and both agricultural and industrial output skyrocketed. But critics, both Chinese and foreign, complained that Deng Xiaoping's program had failed to achieve a "fifth modernization": democracy. Official sources denied such charges and spoke proudly of restoring "socialist legality" by doing away with the arbitrary punishments applied during the Cultural Revolution. Deng himself encouraged the Chinese people to speak out against earlier excesses. In the late 1970s, ordinary citizens began to paste posters criticizing the abuses of the past on the so-called Democracy Wall near Tiananmen Square in downtown Beijing.

Yet it soon became clear that the new leaders would not tolerate any direct criticism of the CCP or of Marxist-Leninist ideology. Dissidents were suppressed, and some were sentenced to long prison terms. Among them was the well-known astrophysicist Fang Lizhi, who spoke out publicly against official corruption and the continuing influence of Marxist-Leninist concepts in post-Mao China, telling an audience in Hong Kong that "China will not be able to modernize if it does not break the shackles of Maoist and Stalinist-style socialism." Fang immediately felt the weight of official displeasure. He was refused permission to travel abroad, and articles that he submitted to official periodicals were rejected.

The problem began to intensify in the late 1980s, as more Chinese began to study abroad and more information about Western society reached educated individuals inside the country. Rising expectations aroused by the economic improvements of the early 1980s led to increasing pressure from students and other urban residents for better living conditions, relaxed restrictions on study abroad, and increased freedom to select employment after graduation.

12-2b Incident at Tiananmen Square

As long as economic conditions for the majority of Chinese were improving, other classes did not share the students' discontent, and the government was able to isolate them from other elements in society. But in the late 1980s, an overheated economy led to rising inflation and growing discontent among salaried workers, especially in the cities. At the same time, corruption, nepotism, and favored treatment for senior officials and party members were provoking increasing criticism. In May 1989, student protesters carried placards demanding Science and Democracy (reminiscent of the slogan of the May Fourth Movement, whose seventieth anniversary was celebrated in the spring of 1989), an end to official corruption, and the resignation of China's aging party leadership. These demands received widespread support from the urban population and led to massive protests in Tiananmen Square.

The demonstrations in Beijing and other major cities were greeted with less enthusiasm in rural areas, where economic conditions had been steadily improving during the 1980s and where memories of the disruptive era of the Great Proletarian Cultural Revolution were still strong. In my own travels through central China during the Tiananmen crisis, I encountered much enthusiasm for the protest movement among urban young people, but many older Chinese reacted to the events with unease or

even with disdain. Several remarked to me that the student protests reminded them of the unruly behavior of the Red Guards twenty years previously, and some declared that it was the responsibility of young Chinese to remain in school. The legacy of the Cultural Revolution may be one reason why many Chinese today continue to prize social stability over individual freedom.

The demonstrations divided the Chinese leaders. Reformist elements around party general secretary Zhao Ziyang were sympathetic to the protesters, but veteran leaders such as Deng saw the students' demands for more democracy as a disguised call for an end to the CCP's rule (see Opposing Viewpoints, "Students Appeal for Democracy," p. 305). After some hesitation, the government sent tanks and troops into Tiananmen Square to crush the demonstrators. Dissidents were arrested, and the regime once again began to stress ideological purity and socialist values. Although the crackdown provoked widespread criticism abroad, Chinese leaders insisted that economic reforms could only take place in conditions of party leadership and political stability.

Deng and other aging party leaders turned to the army to protect their base of power and suppress what they described as "counterrevolutionary elements." Deng was undoubtedly counting on the fact that many Chinese, particularly in rural areas, feared a recurrence of the disorder of the Cultural Revolution and craved economic prosperity more than political reform. In the months following the confrontation, the government issued new regulations requiring courses on Marxist-Leninist ideology in the schools, winnowed out dissidents in the intellectual community, and made it clear that while economic reforms would continue, the CCP's monopoly of power would not be allowed to decay. Harsh punishments were imposed on those accused of undermining the Communist system and supporting its enemies abroad.

12-2c Riding the Tiger

After Tiananmen, party leaders began to realize the complexity of maintaining control and stability in a rapidly changing society. "When you ride the tiger," goes an ancient Chinese proverb, "it's hard to dismount." Accordingly, in the 1990s the government sought to nurture urban support by reducing the rate of inflation and guaranteeing the availability of consumer goods in demand among the rising middle class. Under Deng Xiaoping's successor, Jiang Zemin (JAHNG zuh-MIN) (b. 1926), the government promoted rapid economic growth, while cracking down harshly on political dissent. Massive construction projects, including a nationwide rail network, modern airports, and dams to provide hydroelectric power, were initiated throughout the country. As industrial production

Students Appeal for Democracy

 Q *What were the key demands of the protesters in Tiananmen Square? Were they approved by the Chinese government?*

Politics & Government **IN THE SPRING OF 1989,** thousands of students gathered in Tiananmen Square in downtown Beijing to provide moral support to their many compatriots who had gone on a hunger strike in an effort to compel the Chinese government to reduce the level of official corruption and enact democratic reforms, opening the political process to the Chinese people. The first selection is from an editorial published on April 26 by the official newspaper *People's Daily*. Fearing that the student demonstrations would get out of hand, as had happened during the Cultural Revolution, the editorial condemned the protests for being contrary to the Communist Party. On May 17, student leaders distributed flyers explaining the goals of the movement to participants and passersby, including the author of this text. The second selection is from one of these flyers.

IMAGE 12.3 Student protesters gather in Tiananmen Square in May 1989.

People's Daily Editorial, April 26, 1989

This is a well-planned plot . . . to confuse the people and throw the country into turmoil. . . . Its real aim is to reject the Chinese Communist Party and the socialist system at the most fundamental level. . . . This is a most serious political struggle that concerns the whole Party and nation.

"Why Do We Have to Undergo a Hunger Strike?"

By 2:00 P.M. today, the hunger strike carried out by the petition group in Tiananmen Square has been under way for 96 hours. By this morning, more than 600 participants have fainted. When these democracy fighters were lifted into the ambulances, no one who was present was not moved to tears.

Our petition group now undergoing the hunger strike demands that at a minimum the government agree to the following two points:

1. To engage on a sincere and equal basis in a dialogue with the "higher education dialogue group." In addition, to broadcast the actual dialogue in its entirety. We absolutely refuse to agree to a partial broadcast, to empty gestures, or to fabrications that dupe the people.
2. To evaluate in a fair and realistic way the patriotic democratic movement. Discard the label of "trouble-making" and redress the reputation of the patriotic democratic movement.

It is our view that the request for a dialogue between the people's government and the people is not an unreasonable one. Our party always follows the principle of seeking truths from actual facts. It is therefore only natural that the evaluation of this patriotic democratic movement should be done in accordance with the principle of seeking truths from actual facts.

Our classmates who are going through the hunger strike are the good sons and daughters of the people! One by one, they have fallen. In the meantime, our "public servants" are completely unmoved. Please, let us ask where your conscience is.

Sources: "People's Daily" Editorial from *People's Daily* Editorial, April 26, 1989; from a flyer in the archives of William J. Duiker.

continued to rise, living standards, at least in urban areas, soon followed, and outside observers began to predict that China would become one of the economic superpowers of the twenty-first century.

But now a new challenge arose, as lagging farm income, official corruption, and increasing environmental problems began to spark resentment in the countryside. Highly sensitive to the historic record that suggested that peasant revolt was often the harbinger of dynastic collapse, party leaders sought to contain the issue with a combination of the carrot and the stick. The problem was complicated, however, by the fact that with the rise of cell phones and the Internet, the Chinese people were becoming much more aware of events taking place around them. As the public exchange of ideas rapidly increased in the new electronic age, dissidents found a forum to voice their views, while countless ordinary people were newly enabled to exchange information on incidents and issues that official sources wished to suppress. Although the regime scrambled to arrest or intimidate key dissidents and limit public access to events taking place in China and around the world, it was facing an uphill battle.

New leaders installed in 2002 appeared aware of the magnitude of the challenge. Hu Jintao (b. 1943), the new party general secretary and head of state, called for further reforms to open up Chinese society, reduce the level of corruption, and bridge the yawning gap between rich and poor. But the new policies did not entirely fulfill expectations. Although the economy continued to grow rapidly during the first decade of the new millennium, many of the key issues of public concern remained unresolved, and as party elders gathered in the fall of 2012 to select a new slate of leaders for the next decade, it was clear that rapid economic growth, by itself, was not a panacea for China's ills.

In the fall of 2010, Xi Jinping (b. 1953), the son of one of Mao Zedong's closest comrades, was elected president of the People's Republic of China. As a young man, Xi had spent time in the United States and he was generally viewed as a pragmatist, but it soon became clear that he was determined to adopt an ambitious agenda to attack the country's problems and bring to fruition what he described as "the Chinese dream," a slogan that appeared to reflect above all the traditional imperial goal of wealth and power. Although one of his most highly publicized objectives was to target the rampant corruption within the senior ranks of the party, he undercut his message by simultaneously taking steps to strengthen the state-owned enterprises, a sector of the economy which was not only marked by inefficiency but was also the source of much of the wealth in the hands of many leading government and party officials.

Xi was also quick to attack potential adversaries, at home and abroad. Internally, he cracked down on critics who sought—in his words—"to negate the legitimacy of the long-term rule of the CCP." Externally he adopted an aggressive posture against perceived threats to national security from hostile Western forces and ideas. As he began his second term in office, President Xi continued to consolidate his power by persuading colleagues to eliminate the two-term limitation on the presidency, while seeking to "ride the tiger" of China's long-term growth into a major world power.

12-2d Back to Confucius?

Through this period of trial and error, senior leaders have remained steadfast in their belief that the Communist Party must remain the sole political force in charge of carrying out the revolution. Ever fearful of chaos, they are convinced that only a firm hand at the tiller can keep the ship of state from crashing onto the rocks. At the same time, they have tacitly come to recognize that Marxist exhortations are no longer an effective means of enforcing social discipline. Accordingly, they have increasingly turned to the time-honored nostrum of Confucian principles—notably, hard work, obedience to a superior, and sacrifice for the general good—as a tool to influence political and social attitudes. Ceremonies celebrating the birth of Confucius now receive official sanction, and hallowed social virtues such as righteousness, propriety, and filial piety are widely cited as an antidote to the tide of allegedly antisocial behavior.

In a striking departure from the precepts of Marxist internationalism, official sources in Beijing have also turned to Chinese history to defend their assertion that China is unique and will not follow the path of "peaceful evolution" (to use their term) toward a future democratic capitalist society. In words that turn the teachings of Mao Zedong on their head, President Xi has quoted the ideas of some of China's ancient thinkers, while declaring that the party is "the loyal inheritor and promoter of China's traditional culture." The virtues of ancient Chinese society are extolled, while the United States is publicly ridiculed for the allegedly dysfunctional character of its own democratic system of government.

Chasing the Chinese Dream   The regime has also begun to rely on another familiar tactic to retain control— stoking the fires of nationalism. Although Chinese leaders have never been shy in defending what are now labeled their "core interests" within the Pacific Rim, they have tended to adopt cautious policies in practice. Recently, however, China has begun to play an increasingly

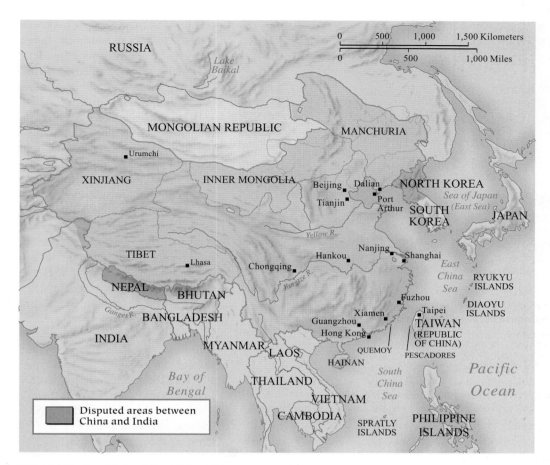

MAP 12.1 **The People's Republic of China.** This map shows China's current boundaries. Major regions are indicated in capital letters.

 In which regions are there movements against Chinese rule?

assertive role in the region. It has not been shy in seeking to counter U.S. influence in East and Southeast Asia, and has aroused concern by claiming sole ownership over the Spratly (sprat-LEE) Islands in the South China Sea and over the Diaoyu (DYOW-you) Islands (also claimed by Japan, which calls them the Senkakus) near Taiwan (see Map 12.1). To strengthen their presence in the area, the PRC has recently built artificial islands not far off the coast of the Philippines and has made no secret of its determination to create a deep-water navy that can compete with potential rivals over influence within the region. In the meantime, relations with the United States over the island of Taiwan, always a matter of considerable sensitivity on both sides, have become increasingly tense.

In 2013, President Xi Jinping announced an ambitious new foreign policy program known originally as the "One Belt, One Road Initiative." Described by Chinese sources as an effort to "enhance regional connectivity and embrace a brighter future," it consists of an offer by China to help finance roads, bridges, and port facilities throughout the Eurasian supercontinent and on to the continent of Africa. Although a number of countries throughout the region have accepted the Chinese offer of providing infrastructure assistance, to many observers, China's new posture raises suspicions that Beijing is once again preparing to flex its muscles as it did periodically in the imperial era. Indeed, there is no doubt that Chinese strategists view the program as providing the country with political influence and access to precious raw materials necessary to achieve President Xi's "Chinese dream." Beijing argues that such actions represent legitimate efforts to resume China's rightful role in the affairs of the region. After a century of humiliation at the hands of the Western powers and

IMAGE 12.4 **The Potala Palace in Tibet.** Tibet was a distant and reluctant appendage of the Chinese empire during the Qing Dynasty. Since the Communist Party's rise to power in 1949, the regime in Beijing has consistently sought to integrate Tibet into the People's Republic of China. Resistance to Chinese rule, however, has been widespread. In recent years, the Dalai Lama, the leading religious figure in Tibetan Buddhism, has attempted without success to persuade Chinese leaders to allow a measure of autonomy for the Tibetan people. In 2008, massive riots by frustrated Tibetans took place in the capital city of Lhasa (LAH-suh) just before the opening of the Olympic Games in Beijing. The Potala Palace, symbol of Tibetan identity, was constructed in the seventeenth century in Lhasa and serves today as the foremost symbol of the national and cultural aspirations of the Tibetan people.

million Muslims in Xinjiang have been sent forcibly to re-education camps to prevent them from listening to the siren call of Islamic fundamentalism.

In the meantime, the regime has been looking with growing uneasiness on the increasing interest in religious faith within the Chinese population. Christian churches that have not agreed to follow rigid state requirements have been closed, and their followers are subjected to official persecution. Chinese leaders are particularly suspicious of evangelical sects like the Falun Gong religious movement, which the regime had attempted to eliminate as a potentially serious threat to its authority. But the rise in church attendance among the population, as well as increasing interest in historically Chinese faiths like Buddhism and Daoism, is an additional indication that with the disintegration of the old Maoist utopia, the Chinese people will need more than a pallid version of Marxism-Leninism or a revived Confucianism to fill the gap.

neighboring Japan, the nation, in Mao's famous words at the Gate of Heavenly Peace in 1949, "has stood up," and no one will be permitted to humiliate it again.

Most Chinese appear to approve of their government's assertive role in world affairs. In recent years, a fervent patriotism seems to be on the rise in China, actively promoted by the party as a means of holding the country together. The decision by the International Olympic Committee to award the 2008 Summer Games to Beijing led to widespread celebration throughout the country. The event symbolized China's emergence as a major national power on the world stage. A large majority also support China's insistence that the island of Taiwan should be returned to the control of the motherland.

Pumping up the spirit of patriotism, however, is not the solution to all problems. Unrest is growing among China's national minorities: in Xinjiang, where restless Muslim peoples are observing with curiosity the emergence of independent Islamic states in Central Asia, and in Tibet, where the official policy of quelling separatist sentiment has led to the violent suppression of Tibetan culture and an influx of thousands of ethnic Chinese immigrants (see Image 12.4). In recent years, up to one

12-3 SERVE THE PEOPLE: CHINESE SOCIETY UNDER COMMUNISM

 Focus Question: How do the social policies adopted by Chinese leaders differ from those adopted by their counterparts in Japan and elsewhere in the Pacific Rim?

Enormous changes took place in Chinese society after the Communist rise to power in 1949. Yet beneath the surface of rapid change were tantalizing hints that much of the old China still endured. The political system was still essentially autocratic, the people were trained to obey their leaders, and the governing class consisted of a small elite trained in a single doctrine. Despite all the efforts of Mao Zedong and his colleagues, the ideas of "Confucius and sons" had still not been irrevocably discarded. China under communism remained a society that was still in many respects enthralled by its past.

12-3a The Politics of the Mass Line

Nowhere was this uneasy balance between the old and the new more clearly demonstrated than in politics and government. In its broad outlines, the new political system followed the Soviet pattern. Yet from the start, CCP leaders made it clear that the Chinese model would differ from the Soviet in important respects. Whereas the Bolsheviks had severely distrusted nonrevolutionary elements in Russia and established a minority government based on the radical left, Mao and his colleagues were more confident that—at least initially—they possessed the basic support of the majority of the Chinese people. Under New Democracy, the party attempted to reach out to all progressive classes in the population to maintain the alliance that had brought it to power in the first place.

The primary link between the regime and the population was the system of "mass organizations," representing peasants, workers, women, religious groups, writers, and artists. The party had established these associations during the 1920s to mobilize support for the revolution. Now they served as a conduit between party and people, enabling the leaders to assess the attitude of the masses while at the same time seeking their support for the party's programs. Behind this facade of representative institutions stood the awesome power of the CCP.

Initially, this "mass line" system worked fairly well. Although opposition to the regime was ruthlessly suppressed and there was no pretense at Western-style democracy, China finally had a government that appeared to be "for the people." Farmland had been distributed on a more equitable basis among the rural population, and exploitative landlords had been punished. Corrupt officials and bureaucratic mismanagement and arrogance had by no means been entirely eliminated, but the new ruling class came preponderantly from the workers and peasants and was more willing than its predecessors to listen to the complaints and aspirations of its constituents.

But the adoption of the Great Leap Forward betrayed a fundamental weakness in the policy of the mass line. While declaring his willingness to listen to the concerns of the population, Mao was also determined to build a utopian society based on Marxist-Leninist principles. Popular acceptance of nationalization and collectivization during the mid-1950s indicates that the Chinese people were not entirely hostile to cooperative ownership, but when those programs were carried to an extreme during the Great Leap Forward, many Chinese, even within the party, resisted and forced the government to abandon the program.

The failure of the Great Leap Forward split the CCP and led to the revolutionary disturbances of the following decade. Some of Mao's associates had opposed his radical approach and now sought to adopt a more cautious road to nation building. To Mao, such views were a betrayal of the party's revolutionary principles. The Cultural Revolution, which he launched in 1966, can be seen above all as his attempt to cleanse the system of its impurities and put Chinese society back on the straight road to egalitarian communism.

In turning his ire on the establishment, Mao found willing ears among the mass of the population, as popular discontent was stirring in many sectors of society. Young people in particular, alienated by the lack of job opportunities and a program that shipped millions of youths to rural areas of the country to work with villagers or carry out massive building projects, flocked to his cause and served with enthusiasm in the Red Guard organizations that became the shock troops of the revolution. Laborers angered by arrogant superiors or harsh working conditions often served as willing allies. But the enthusiasms aroused by the Cultural Revolution did not last, and a period of reaction inevitably set in. In China, revolutionary fervor gave way to a new era in which belief in socialist ideals was replaced by a more practical desire for material benefits.

12-3b Economics in Command

Deng Xiaoping recognized the need to restore a sense of "socialist legality" and credibility to a system that was on the verge of breakdown and hoped that rapid economic growth would satisfy the Chinese people and prevent them from demanding political reforms. Mindful of the disruptive consequences of the period of turmoil just experienced, the post-Mao leaders demonstrated a willingness to emphasize economic performance over ideological purity. To stimulate the stagnant industrial sector, which had been under state control since the end of the era of New Democracy, they reduced bureaucratic controls over state industries and allowed local managers to have more say over prices, salaries, and quality control. Productivity was encouraged by permitting bonuses to be paid for extra effort, a policy that had been discouraged during the Cultural Revolution. State firms were no longer guaranteed access to precious resources and were told to compete with each other for public favor and even to export goods on their own initiative. The regime also tolerated the emergence of a small private sector. Unemployed youth were encouraged to set up restaurants, bicycle or radio repair shops, and handicraft shops on their own initiative. At first, such enterprises were legally limited to seven employees—to prevent exploitation—but eventually the restrictions were relaxed.

Finally, the regime opened up the country to foreign investment and technology. The Maoist policy of self-reliance was abandoned, and China openly sought the advice of foreign experts and the money of foreign capitalists. Special economic zones were established in urban centers near the coast (ironically, many were located in the old nineteenth-century treaty ports), where lucrative concessions were offered to encourage foreign firms to build factories. The tourist industry was encouraged, and students were sent abroad to study.

The new leaders especially stressed educational reform. The system adopted during the Cultural Revolution, emphasizing practical education and ideology at the expense of higher education and modern science, was rapidly abandoned (Mao's *Little Red Book* was even withdrawn from circulation and could no longer be found on bookshelves), and a new system based generally on the Western model was instituted. Admission to higher education was based on success in merit examinations, and courses on science and mathematics received high priority.

Agricultural Reform   No economic reform program could succeed unless it included the countryside. Three decades of socialism had done little to increase food production or to lay the basis for a modern agricultural sector. China, with a population numbering one billion in the mid-1970s, could still barely feed itself. Peasants had little incentive to work and few opportunities to increase production through mechanization, the use of fertilizer, or better irrigation.

Under Deng Xiaoping, agricultural policy made a rapid about-face. Under the new **rural responsibility system**, adopted shortly after Deng had consolidated his authority, collectives leased land on contract to peasant families, who paid a quota as rent to the collective. Anything produced on the land above that payment could be sold on the private market or consumed. To soak up excess labor in the villages, the government encouraged the formation of so-called sideline industries, a modern equivalent of the traditional cottage industries in premodern China. Peasants raised fish or shrimp, made consumer goods, and even assembled living room furniture and appliances to sell to their newly affluent compatriots (see Comparative Illustration, "Sideline Industries," p. 235).

The reform program had a striking effect on rural production. Grain production increased rapidly, and farm income doubled during the 1980s. Yet it also created problems. In the first place, income at the village level became more unequal as some enterprising farmers (known locally as "ten thousand-dollar" households) earned profits several times those realized by their less fortunate or less industrious neighbors. When some farmers discovered they could earn more by growing cash crops or other specialized commodities, they devoted less land to rice and other grain crops, thereby threatening to reduce the supply of China's most crucial staple. Finally, the agricultural policy threatened to undermine the government's population control program, which party leaders viewed as crucial to the success of the Four Modernizations.

The Population Control Program   Since a misguided period in the mid-1950s when Mao had argued that more laborers would result in higher productivity, China had been attempting to limit the growth of its population, which chronically threatened to outstrip the country's food supply. By 1970, the government had launched a stringent family planning program—including education, incentives, and penalties for noncompliance—to persuade the Chinese people to limit themselves to one child per family. The program did have some success, and the rate of population growth was drastically reduced in the early 1980s. The rural responsibility system, however, undermined the program because it encouraged farm families to pay the penalties for having additional children in the belief that their labor would increase the family income and provide the parents with greater security in their old age (one family reportedly named its second child "Dianshi"—or "television set" in English—because, as the father explained, that is what he would have purchased had he not been required to pay the penalty). Eventually, the program was relaxed, and rural families were legally permitted to have a second child if the first child was a girl. Nevertheless, the basic program continued for many years, and in 2008 the regime announced that it would remain in force for at least another decade. By that time, China's population, estimated at about 1.4 billion in 2012, was projected to begin to decline.

China: The New Industrial Powerhouse   Still, the overall effects of the modernization program have been impressive. The standard of living improved for the majority of the population. Where a decade earlier, the average Chinese had struggled to earn enough to buy a bicycle, radio, watch, or washing machine, by the late 1980s, many were able to purchase videocassette recorders, refrigerators, and color television sets. Yet the rapid growth of the economy created its own problems: inflationary pressures, greed, envy, increased corruption, and—most dangerous of all for the regime—rising expectations. Young people in particular resented restrictions on employment (most young people in China were still required to accept the jobs that are offered to them by the government or school officials) and opportunities to study abroad. Disillusionment ran high, especially in the cities, where lavish living by officials and rising prices for goods aroused widespread alienation and cynicism and laid the groundwork for the massive protest demonstrations in 1989.

Since the 1990s, industrial growth rates have continued to be high as Chinese exports have surged and domestic capital has become increasingly available. The government finally recognized the need to close down inefficient state enterprises, and by the end of the decade, the private sector, with official encouragement, accounted for more than 10 percent of the nation's gross domestic product. A stock market opened, and with the country's entrance into the World Trade Organization (WTO) in 2001, China's prowess in the international marketplace improved dramatically.

The dramatic growth of the Chinese economy has continued unabated during the first two decades of the new century, and today China has the second-largest economy in the world and is the largest exporter of goods. Even the global economic crisis that struck the world in the fall of 2008 did not derail the Chinese juggernaut, which quickly recovered from the drop in demand for Chinese goods in countries suffering from the economic downturn. Flushed with cash, the government and the Chinese economic elite have extended their vision abroad, investing in hotels, holiday resorts, port facilities, and infrastructure projects all around the world.

At the same time, China today possesses a large and increasingly affluent middle class and a burgeoning domestic market for consumer goods. The vast majority of urban Chinese now own a color television set, a refrigerator, and a washing machine. Over one-third own their homes, and nearly as many have an air conditioner. For the more affluent, a private automobile is increasingly a possibility, and in 2010, more vehicles were sold in China than in the United States.

Still, as capitalist governments in the West discovered long ago, running an advanced industrial economy can be a tricky proposition, and rapid economic change never comes without cost. To maintain public support, the regime has pumped up the economy to keep growth rates at high levels, and exports have been the key to keeping Chinese factories open and busy. There are warning signs, however, that the global economy is now entering what may be an extended slowdown; as a result, the market for Chinese exports has been dropping, and the country's annual growth rate has declined to an annual rate of only 6 percent. In the meantime, a trade dispute with the United States has prompted the Trump administration to levy tariffs on imports from China, leading some major international corporations to consider moving their manufacturing facilities out of the country. With millions of workers now being laid off, whether the Chinese consumer can pick up the slack has become an open question.

To complicate the equation, demographic conditions are rapidly changing. The reduction in birthrates since the 1980s has begun to create a labor shortage, putting upward pressure on workers' salaries. As a result, China is facing inflation in the marketplace and thus has begun to encounter increased competition from exports produced by factories located in lower-wage countries in South and Southeast Asia. In 2018, the government suddenly discontinued its birth-control program in the hope of avoiding a massive labor shortage in coming years. Even so, China—like Europe—will begin to suffer from a demographic crunch in the near future, with momentous implications for the future.

Discontent has also been on the rise in the countryside, where farmers earn only about half as much as their urban counterparts. Efforts to assuage rural concerns by increasing the official purchase price for grain were discontinued when the subsidy program became too expensive. China's entry into the World Trade Organization was greeted with great optimism but has been of little benefit to farmers facing the challenges of cheap foreign imports. Taxes, environmental problems, and local corruption add to their complaints, and land seizures by the government or by local officials are a major source of anger in rural communities.

In desperation, millions of rural Chinese have left for the big cities, where many of them have been unable to find steady employment and are forced to live in squalid conditions in crowded tenements or in the sprawling suburbs. Millions of others remain on their farms and attempt to augment their income by producing for the market or, in accordance with recent legal changes, by increasing the size of their families. A new land reform law passed in 2008 authorizes farmers to lease or transfer land use rights, although in principle all land in rural areas belongs to the local government.

An Environmental Time Bomb Another factor that has begun to hinder China's rush to economic advancement is the impact of rapid industrialization on the environment. With the rising population, fertile land is in increasingly short supply (China's population has doubled since 1950, but only two-thirds as much irrigable land is available). Soil erosion is a major problem, especially in the north, where over-cultivation of the land is reducing soil fertility, and thousands of acres of irrigable fields are overrun by sands from the Gobi Desert each year (see Image 12.5). Water pollution is also widespread. An ambitious plan to transport water by canals from the Yangzi River to the more arid northern provinces has run into a number of roadblocks. Another massive project to construct dams on the Yangzi River has sparked protests from environmentalists, as well as from local peoples forced to migrate from the area.

Meanwhile, air pollution is ten times the level in the United States, contributing to growing health concerns.

IMAGE 12.5 The Mountain of Singing Sands. This spectacular sand mountain is located on the outskirts of one of the Silk Road's most famous caravan stops—the city of Dunhuang. But while its physical beauty and the tantalizing sounds made by the wind as it passes over the sand make it one of the most popular tourist attractions in China, Mingsha Mountain also symbolizes one of the country's most serious environmental issues. In Dunhuang, as elsewhere, drifting sands from nearby deserts are encroaching on precious farmlands, desperately needed to feed China's growing population. Much of the problem is created by overgrazing of surrounding pasture lands.

Coal is widely used for heating, electricity, and other purposes, although the government has attempted, with limited success, to wean the economy from its reliance from that source. To add to the challenge, more than 700,000 new cars and trucks appear on the country's roads each year. To reduce congestion on roadways, China is constructing an extensive rail network for high-speed bullet trains that will connect all the major regions in the country.

12-3c Chinese Society in Flux

At the root of Marxist-Leninist ideology is the idea of building a new citizen free from the prejudices, ignorance, and superstition of the "feudal" era and the capitalist desire for self-gratification. This new citizen would be characterized not only by a sense of racial and sexual equality but also by a selfless desire to contribute his or her utmost for the good of all. In the words of Mao Zedong's famous work "The Foolish Old Man Who Removed the Mountains," the people should "be resolute, fear no sacrifice, and surmount every difficulty to win victory."[5]

Out with the Old, In with the New! For Mao and his colleagues, the first order of business was to remake Chinese society as a means of creating the new citizen. Like the progressive intellectuals of the New Culture movement a generation previously, the leaders of the new regime believed that old values, old attitudes, and old customs were the foremost obstacle to their ambitious political objectives. At the root of the problem, in their view, was the time-honored Confucian emphasis on the family, headed by the patriarch, as the key component in Chinese society. To the Communists, loyalty to the family, a crucial element in the Confucian social order, undercut loyalty to the state and to the dictatorship of the proletariat. Thus, their long-run objective was to destroy the influence of the traditional family system.

During the early 1950s, they took a number of steps to bring a definitive end to the old system in China. Women were permitted to vote and encouraged to become active in the political process. At the local level, an increasing number of women became active in the CCP and in collective organizations. In 1950, a new marriage law guaranteed women equal rights with men. Most important, perhaps, it permitted women for the first time to initiate divorce proceedings against their husbands. Within a year, nearly one million divorces had been granted.

At first, the government moved carefully on other family issues to avoid alienating its supporters in the countryside. When collective farms were established in the mid-1950s, each member of a collective accumulated "work points" based on the number of hours worked during a specified time period. Payment for work points was made not to the individual but to the family head. The payments, usually in the form of ration coupons, could then be spent at the collective community store. Because the payments went to the head of the family, the traditionally dominant position of the patriarch was maintained. When people's communes were established in the late 1950s, however, payments went to the individual.

Ending the Politics of Dependency During the radical era of the Great Leap Forward, children were encouraged to report to the authorities any comments by their parents that criticized the system. Such practices continued during the Cultural Revolution, when children were expected to report on their parents, students on their teachers, and employees on their superiors. By encouraging the traditionally oppressed elements in society—the young, the female, and the poor—to voice their bitterness, Mao was clearly hoping to break the long Chinese tradition of dependency. In his view, the traditional Confucian **five relationships** (subordination of son to father, wife to husband, younger to older brother, and subject to ruler, and the proper relationship of friend to friend) forced individuals to swallow their anger and frustration ("to eat bitterness" in the Chinese phrase) and accept the hierarchical norms established by Confucian ethics. Such denunciations had been issued against landlords and other "local tyrants" during the era of land reform. During the Cultural Revolution, they were applied to other authority figures in Chinese society.[6]

The Family System Revives The post-Mao era has brought a decisive shift away from revolutionary utopianism and a return to the pragmatic approach to social engineering. For the vast majority of Chinese, this is undoubtedly a welcome development; the era of generational warfare destroyed millions of lives, and few lamented its passing. Under the post-Mao leadership, family relationships once more became a private affair.

As with all social changes, however, the return to a more traditional approach has had a price. Although in the large cities attitudes toward women, marriage, and the family have evolved in line with trends in Western countries, in rural areas the old norms about filial piety and the five relationships sometimes still hold sway. Arranged marriages, nepotism, and the mistreatment of females (for example, under the one-child program, many parents in rural areas reportedly killed female infants in the hope that the next child would be a son) have returned, although such behavior most likely persisted under the cloak of revolutionary purity for a generation. Expensive weddings are now increasingly common, along with the payment of a dowry to the family of the groom. Prostitution and sex crimes against women also appear to be on the rise. To discourage sexual abuse, the government now seeks to provide free legal services for women living in rural areas.

Women in China today do possess some advantages compared to their Western counterparts. Because men outnumber women in Chinese society (among infants, there are 118 males to every 100 females in today's China), women can afford to be more particular in selecting a husband. Young men often complain that without an automobile or an apartment to offer as an incentive, they find it difficult to locate a wife (see Historical Voices, "Love and Marriage in China," p. 314). Indeed, the problem of rootless young males, often with limited employment opportunities, is an issue of increasing concern for China's leaders today. Still,

China today is still essentially a male-dominated society, as is clearly demonstrated in the preponderance of males in leadership positions in the Communist Party and in senior positions elsewhere in society.

Much of the new prosperity is a consequence of the trend toward privatization and a more capitalistic free enterprise system. But there is also a price to pay for this change. Under the Maoist system, the elderly and the sick received retirement benefits and health care from the state or the collective organizations. Today, with the collectives no longer playing such a social role and more workers operating in the private sector, the safety net has been removed. No longer does every Chinese citizen have an "iron rice bowl" (a common phrase denoting guaranteed employment as well as health, education, and retirement benefits). The government has attempted to fill the gap by enacting a social security law, but because of a lack of funds, eligibility has been limited primarily to individuals living in urban areas. Those living in the countryside—who still represent over half of the population—are essentially unprotected, prompting legislation in 2010 to provide modest pensions and medical insurance to the poorest members of society. Yet much more needs to be done, for as the population ages, the lack of an adequate retirement system represents a potential time bomb. It is predicted that the median age of the Chinese population will rise from 33 in 2005 to 45 at mid-century. In the process, the ratio of workers to retirees will drop from 6 to 1 to about 2 to 1. The regime recently attempted to ease the problem, when it promulgated a new law requiring adult children (many of them living in the cities) to provide occasional visits and necessary care to their aging parents in the countryside.

Lifestyle Changes: From Mao to Mod With the end of the Great Proletarian Cultural Revolution, the party leadership turned away from the Maoist-inspired puritanical ethic and embraced the ideal of material consumption. Following the new slogans that urged them to "create wealth for the people" (a new version of the revolutionary slogan "serve the people") and proclaimed "to get rich is glorious," enterprising Chinese began to concentrate on improving their standard of living. For the first time, millions of Chinese saw the prospect of a house or an urban flat with a washing machine, television set, and indoor plumbing. Young people whose parents had given them patriotic names such as Build the Country, Protect Mao Zedong, and Assist Korea began to choose more elegant and cosmopolitan names for their own children. Some names, such as Surplus Grain or Bring a Younger Brother, expressed hope for the future.

The growing emphasis on material accumulation in contemporary Chinese society has predictably led to an

Love and Marriage in China

 Do you think the marriage described here is successful? Why or why not? What do you think this woman feels about her marriage?

Family & Society **"WHAT MEN CAN DO, WOMEN CAN ALSO DO."**
So said Chairman Mao as he "liberated" and masculinized Chinese women to work alongside men. Women's individuality and sexual freedom were sacrificed for the collective good of his new socialist society. Marriage, which had traditionally been arranged by families for financial gain, was now dictated by duty to the state. The Western concept of romantic love did not enter into a Chinese marriage, as this interview of a schoolteacher by the reporter Zhang Xinxin in the mid-1980s illustrates. According to recent surveys, the same is true today.

Zhang Xinxin, *Chinese Lives*

My husband and I never did any courting—honestly! We registered our marriage a week after we'd met. He was just out of the forces and a worker in a building outfit. They'd been given a foreign-aid assignment in Zambia, and he was selected. He wanted to get his private life fixed up before he went, and someone introduced us. Seeing how he looked really honest, I accepted him.

No, you can't say I didn't know anything about him. The person who introduced us told me he was a Party member who'd been an organization commissar. Any comrade who's good enough to be an organization cadre is politically reliable. Nothing special about our standing of living—it's what we've earned. He's still a worker, but we live all right, don't we?

He went off with the army as soon as we'd registered our marriage and been given the wedding certificates. He was away three years. We didn't have the wedding itself before he went because we hadn't got a room yet.

Those three years were a test for us. The main problem was that my family was against it. They thought I was still only a kid and I'd picked the wrong man. What did they have against him? His family was too poor. Of course I won in the end—we'd registered and got our wedding certificates. We were legally married whether we had the family ceremony or not.

We had our wedding after he came back in the winter of 1973. His leaders and mine all came to congratulate us and give us presents. The usual presents those days were busts of Chairman Mao. I was twenty-six and he was twenty-nine. We've never had a row.

I never really wanted to take the college entrance exams. Then in 1978 the school leadership got us all to put our names forward. They said they weren't going to hold us back: the more of us who passed, the better it would be for the school. So I put my name forward, crammed for six weeks, and passed. I already had two kids then. . . .

I reckoned the chance for study was too good to miss. And my husband was looking after the kids all by himself. I usually only came back once a fortnight. So I couldn't let him down.

My instructors urged me to take the exams for graduate school, but I didn't. I was already thirty-four, so what was the point of more study? There was another reason too. I didn't want an even wider gap between us: he hadn't even finished junior middle school when he joined the army.

It's bad if the gap's too wide. For example, there's a definite difference in our tastes in music and art, I have to admit that. But what really matters? Now we've set up this family we have to preserve it. Besides, look at all the sacrifices he had to make to see me through college. Men comrades all like a game of cards and that, but he was stuck with looking after the kids. He still doesn't get any time for himself—it's all work for him.

We've got a duty to each other. Our differences? The less said about them the better. We've always treated each other with the greatest respect.

Of course some people have made suggestions, but my advice to him is to respect himself and respect me. I'm not going to be like those men who ditch their wives when they go up in the world.

I'm the head of our school now. With this change in my status I've got to show even more responsibility for the family. Besides, I know how much he's done to get me where I am today. I've also got some duties in the municipal Women's Federation and Political Consultative Conference. No, I'm not being modest. I haven't done anything worth talking about, only my duty.

We've got to do a lot more educating people. There have been two cases of divorce in our school this year.

Source: From *Chinese Lives: An Oral History of Contemporary China*, by Zhang Xinxin and Sang Ye, copyright © 1987 by W. J. F. Jenner and Delia Davin.

Then and Now: Changing Clothing Styles in China

Q *Does the apparent improvement in living conditions over the past generation suggested by these photographs justify the claim by the Chinese government that centralized leadership by the Communist Party is necessary to improve the lives of its citizens? Why or why not?*

Art & Ideas **FOR THE LONGTIME VISITOR TO CHINA,** the change in clothing styles that has taken place in China since the end of the Cultural Revolution is striking. In Image 12.6a, taken in the 1970s, a group of college students pose for a photograph in front of their classroom at the Beijing Teacher's College. Image 12.6b shows a group of young Chinese on the Bund in Shanghai, complete with their designer handbags and their hand-held electronic devices. The forest of skyscrapers in the Pudong (Poo-DOONG) district looms in the background. As the illustration suggests, the Japanese fashion of "tea hair" (see Chapter 11) has caught on among young people in China as well.

IMAGE 12.6a

IMAGE 12.6b

increased focus on the needs and wants of the individual, as opposed to that of the group. On the positive side, it also tends to produce citizens possessed with greater creativity and independence of spirit. On the other hand (as Mao undoubtedly worried), it can also lead to hedonistic behavior and a reluctance to endure sacrifices in the interests of the larger community. Many older Chinese blame the latter tendency at least partly on the regime's "one-child" policy. With most families limited to a single offspring, many parents overindulged their children, who were sometimes derided by critics as spoiled "little emperors."

The new attitudes have also been reflected in physical appearance. For a generation after the civil war, clothing had been restricted to the traditional baggy "Mao suit" in olive drab or dark blue, but by the 1980s, young people craved such fashionable Western items as designer jeans, trendy sneakers, and sweat suits (see Comparative Illustration, "Then and Now," above). Cosmetic surgery to create a more buxom figure or a more Western facial look became increasingly common among affluent young women in the cities. Many had the epicanthic fold over their eyelids removed or even enlarged their noses—a curious decision in view of the tradition of referring derogatorily to foreigners as "big noses." Prosperity, however, has its own price, as the problem of obesity, especially among younger Chinese, has skyrocketed in recent years. "China's waistlines," goes one recent pun, "are growing faster than the nation's gross domestic product."

The shift from Marxism toward the worship of consumerism is having another predictable effect by giving birth to a growing sense of rootlessness in Chinese society, especially among the young, who did not live through the difficult years prior to the death of Mao Zedong. Incidents of random terrorism, once rare, are on the rise, and many young people are openly materialistic in their attitude and—to the discomfort of party leaders—are correspondingly cynical about politics. For many of them, feverish exhortations from the party leadership to "work hard and sacrifice for the achievement of the Chinese dream" fall on deaf ears.

IMAGE 12.7 The Revival of Buddhism in China. For over half a century, Communist Party leaders attempted to root out all forms of religious faith among their compatriots. Yet today, religious belief is alive and well in China, as various forms of religion are thriving throughout the country, despite efforts by current leaders to contain it. Shown here is a procession of Buddhist monks in a temple in the city of Shanghai.

Q *What are some of the reasons why religious faith is reviving in China today?*

The growing popularity of organized religion in today's China is undoubtedly one consequence. As the government has become somewhat more tolerant of religious belief, some Chinese have returned to the traditional Buddhist faith or to folk religions, and Buddhist and Taoist temples are once again crowded with worshippers (see Image 12.7). Despite official efforts to suppress its more evangelical forms (see "Chasing the Chinese Dream," p. 308), Christianity has become increasingly popular as well; like the "rice Christians" of the past, many now view it as a symbol of success and cosmopolitanism.

12-4 CHINA'S CHANGING CULTURE

Q **Focus Question:** How would you describe the various ways that Chinese culture has evolved in the years since the end of World War II?

During the first half of the twentieth century, Chinese culture was strongly influenced by currents from the West (see Chapter 5). The rise to power of the Communists in 1949 added a new dimension to the debate over the future of culture in China. The new leaders rejected the Western attitude of "art for art's sake" and, like their Soviet counterparts, viewed culture as an important instrument of indoctrination. The standard would no longer be aesthetic

quality or the personal preference of the artist but "art for life's sake," whereby culture would serve the interests of socialism.

12-4a Culture in a Revolutionary Era

At first, the new emphasis on socialist realism did not entirely extinguish the influence of traditional culture. Mao and his colleagues tolerated—and even encouraged—efforts by artists to synthesize traditional ideas with socialist concepts and Western techniques. During the Cultural Revolution, however, all forms of traditional culture came to be viewed as reactionary. Socialist realism became the only acceptable standard in literature, art, and music. All forms of traditional expression were forbidden, and the deification of Mao and his central role in building a Communist paradise became virtually the only acceptable form of artistic expression.

Characteristic of the changing cultural climate in China was the experience of author Ding Ling. Born in 1904 and educated in a school for women set up by leftist intellectuals during the hectic years after the May Fourth Movement, she became involved in party activities in the 1930s. She then settled in Yan'an, where she wrote her most famous novel, *The Sun Shines over the Sangan River* (1948), which described the CCP's land reform program in favorable terms. It was awarded the Stalin Prize three years later.

During the early 1950s, Ding Ling was one of the most prominent literary lights of the new China, but in the more ideological climate at the end of the decade, she was attacked for her individualism and her criticism of the party. Although temporarily rehabilitated, during the Cultural Revolution she was sentenced to hard labor on a commune in the far north and was not released until the late 1970s after the death of Mao. Crippled and in poor health, she died in 1981. Ding Ling's fate mirrored the fate of thousands of progressive Chinese intellectuals who, despite their efforts, were not able to satisfy the constantly changing demands of a repressive regime.

12-4b Art and Architecture

After Mao's death, Chinese culture was finally released from the shackles of socialist realism. In painting, where for a decade the only acceptable standard for excellence was praise for the party and its policies, the new permissiveness led to a revival of interest in both traditional and Western forms. Although some painters continued to blend Eastern and Western styles, others imitated trends from abroad, experimenting with a wide range of previously prohibited art styles, including Cubism and abstract painting.

In the 1980s, some of the more avant-garde examples of contemporary art shocked the Chinese public and provoked the wrath of the party, leading the government to declare that henceforth it would regulate all art exhibits. More recently, some Chinese artists, such as the world-famous Ai Weiwei (b. 1957), have aggressively challenged the government's authority. In response, the government razed Ai's art studio in Shanghai in 2011. Eventually he was taken into police custody on charges related to tax evasion. He was subsequently released, but the government is maintaining a close watch on his activities. Nonetheless, Chinese contemporary art has expanded exponentially, attracting international attention and commanding exorbitant prices on the world market.

In recent years, China has invested heavily in transportation infrastructure and has erected endless blocks of apartment complexes to house the steady stream of migrants into the cities. This has led to an explosive building boom, highlighted by the projects connected with the 2008 Olympic Games in Beijing and spreading outward to China's many megacities. At a dizzying pace, renowned architects, both Chinese and foreign, are executing some of the new century's most original and experimental architectural designs. The gleaming forest of skyscrapers currently rising in Shanghai's Pudong district is the quintessential example (see Image 16.1).

12-4c Literature

The limits on freedom of expression have been most apparent in literature. During the early 1980s, party leaders encouraged Chinese writers to express their views on the mistakes of the past, and a new "literature of the wounded" began to describe the brutal and arbitrary character of the Cultural Revolution. Such efforts quickly drew the ire of the authorities, who continued to insist that only the positive aspects of Chinese society be presented. Still, a few writers brave the displeasure of party leaders by portraying the shortcomings of the current system.

One such writer is Mo Yan (the pen name of Guan Moye) (b. 1955), whose novels *The Garlic Ballads* (1988) and *Life and Death Are Wearing Me Out* (2008) expose the rampant corruption of contemporary Chinese society, the roots of which he attributes to one-party rule. He received the Nobel Prize in Literature in 2012. Like Mo Yan, Yan Lianke (b. 1958) addresses the suffering of

Chinese peasants and what he views as the moral depravity resulting from the country's unbridled embrace of capitalism. But Yan has no nostalgia for the Maoist era. In *Lenin's Kisses* (2004), he is critical of both the Great Leap Forward and the Cultural Revolution. In *The Day the Sun Died* (2015), he portrays the Chinese people as sleep-walkers, so completely programmed by the state that they are incapable of confronting the atrocities that have been committed in the name of the revolution. Not surprisingly, his novels are banned in China, and have been published in Taiwan.

Another author who lays bare the realities of contemporary China is Jiang Rong (the pen name of Lü Jiamin) (b. 1946). In his gripping novel *Wolf Totem* (2007), Jiang describes an example of rural injustice in Inner Mongolia, as Han Chinese migrants are flooding into the area and traditional ecological practices are sacrificed on the altar of rapid economic growth.

Public awareness of the existence of such social ills is accelerated by the pervasiveness of the Internet. A new mass literature, much of it written by and intended for China's new urban youth, explores the aspirations and frustrations of a generation obsessed with material consumption and the right of individual expression. The regime has sought to strike back by sponsoring films and operas—such as a new opera on the Long March—that portray the history of the party in glorious terms, clearly seeking to instill the younger generation with a patriotic fervor matching the decade of the Cultural Revolution.

HISTORIANS DEBATE

12-4d Confucius and Marx: What Explains the Tenacity of Tradition in China?

Why has communism survived in China, albeit in a substantially altered form, when it failed in Eastern Europe and the Soviet Union? This question has aroused the interest of many historians of China. One of the primary factors is probably cultural. Although the doctrine of Marxism-Leninism originated in Europe, many of its main precepts, such as the primacy of the community over the individual and the denial of the concept of private property, run counter to recent trends in Western civilization. This inherent conflict is especially evident in the societies of central Europe, which were influenced to varying degrees by Enlightenment philosophy and the Industrial Revolution and thus resisted the efforts by Stalin and his successors to force-feed them with the communist ideology of Karl Marx. These forces were weaker farther to the east, where submission to authority and reliance on communal property were common features of society, although

Western ideas had begun to penetrate tsarist Russia by the end of the nineteenth century.

In contrast, Marxism-Leninism found a more receptive climate in China and other countries in the region influenced by Confucian tradition. In its political culture, the Communist system exhibits many of the same characteristics as traditional Confucianism—a single truth, an elite governing class, and an emphasis on obedience to the community and its governing representatives. Although a significant and influential minority of the Chinese population—primarily urban and educated—finds the idea of personal freedom against the power of the state appealing, such concepts have little meaning in rural villages, where the interests of the community have always been emphasized over the desires of the individual. It is no accident that Chinese leaders now seek to reintroduce many of the precepts of State Confucianism to bolster a fading belief in the existence of a future Communist paradise.

Party leaders today are banking on the hope that China can be governed as it has always been—by an elite class of highly trained professionals dedicated to pursuing a predefined objective. Their task is complicated, however, by the fact that real changes are taking place in China today. Although the youthful protesters in Tiananmen Square were comparable in some respects to the reformist elements of the early republic—in the sense that their demands were more relevant to the educated minority in the country than to the mass of the population—the China of today is fundamentally different from that of the early twentieth century. Literacy rates and the standard of living are far higher, the pressures of outside powers are less threatening, and China has entered its own industrial and technological revolution. Many Chinese depend more on independent talk radio and the Internet for news and views than on the official media. Whereas Sun Yat-sen, Chiang Kai-shek, and even Mao Zedong broke their lances on the rocks of centuries of tradition, poverty, and widespread resistance to change, the present leaders rule a country much more aware of the world and China's place in it. Although the shift in popular expectations may be gradual, China today is embarked on a journey to a future for which the past no longer provides a roadmap.

MAKING CONNECTIONS

For four decades after the end of World War II, the two major Communist powers appeared to have become permanent features on the international landscape. Suddenly, in the late 1980s, both entered a period of internal crisis that shook the foundations of both countries. Soon thereafter, the Soviet Union collapsed, while Communist rule in China was shaken by the massive protest demonstrations held in Tiananmen Square in Beijing. But, to the surprise of many, the Communist regime in China managed to survive the crisis and today stands at the height of its power.

One reason for the striking success of China's post-Mao leaders is that they accepted the necessity to imitate a number of lessons that they had picked up from the capitalist playbook. With the death of Mao Zedong and the rise to power of the Communist veteran Deng Xiaoping in the late 1970s, the trajectory of the Chinese revolution changed dramatically: from an emphasis on ideology to an emphasis on pragmatism, from a policy of isolation and economic self-sufficiency to a willingness to join the community of nations and participate in the global marketplace. Whereas under Mao Zedong, material acquisition was viewed as evidence of "taking the capitalist road," under Deng and his colleagues, to "get rich" was "glorious."

In their effort to make up for the "ten lost years" of the Great Proletarian Cultural Revolution and transform China from a primarily agricultural society into an advanced industrial economy, leaders in Beijing benefitted from a number of factors, including an ample supply of cheap labor, a relatively well-educated population endowed with a strong work ethic and—not least—from an international community that was prepared to encourage China's entry into the global marketplace. The reason why the Western nations were willing to open the door to China were no mystery. The one-time closed country would now not only open its vast market to foreign consumer goods, by providing the world with a cornucopia of cheap consumer goods, China would help to relieve inflationary pressures around the world, thus providing benefits to its new trading partners as well as enriching itself. In the meantime, Western leaders hoped that increasing prosperity would convince Chinese leaders to become more receptive to the liberal democratic model.

Another key to China's successful transformation lies in its ability to obtain advanced technology from its trading partners abroad. Determined to gain access to the gigantic Chinese market (the resemblance to the rush by nineteenth-century European imperialist nations to sell products to the "400 million Chinese customers" is unavoidable), Western governments and business corporations willingly provided China with access to many of the secrets of their own success. Chinese leaders in Beijing were only too happy to oblige, and some must have recalled the famous statement by Lenin during the 1920s that the capitalists were willing to sell the very shovels with which to bury themselves.

Chinese leaders today would undoubtedly insist on a "second rail" to their strategy of achieving wealth and power in the new millennium. When President Xi Jinping promotes his vision of the "Chinese dream" today, he elaborates on that commitment with a second one: that China will never follow its capitalist rivals in adopting a pluralistic democracy, as anticipated by so many political leaders and pundits in the West (the term used by the Chinese to describe that assumption is "peaceful evolution"). Rather, it will follow a familiar Chinese trajectory by establishing a political system based on the benevolent but dominating role of a ruling party, operating this time not under the guidance of State Confucianism, but of the doctrine of Karl Marx.

But does China today bear any resemblance to the philosophy espoused by that German philosopher who lived in a vastly different world almost two centuries ago? For all intents and purposes, the answer is no. Where Marx declared that national identity and loyalty would eventually give way to the spirit of proletarian internationalism, Xi Jinping and his colleagues blatantly appeal to traditional nationalist symbols to drum up public support for their policies. And where Karl Marx envisioned the emergence of a "Communist Man" who would work not for his own personal benefit but only "according to his need," China today is a highly acquisitive society with more billionaires than any country other than the United States. Many years ago, Deng Xiaoping conceded to his followers that Communism would be a long time coming to China. Under President Xi Jinping, the vision of the Communist Man is on life support.

What is left of the Marxist worldview in China is the Leninist concept of the omnipotent Communist Party, dedicated to maintaining power internally and projecting the might of the state on the international stage. At a time when the appeal of pluralistic democracy has been shaken in many parts of the world, President Xi and his colleagues are undoubtedly gambling that other nations aspiring for their place in the sun may begin to look at the Chinese model, not its Western counterpart.

REFLECTION QUESTIONS

Q Why do you think communism has survived in China, when it failed to survive in the Soviet Union?
Q How have six decades of Communist rule affected the concept of the family in China? How does the current state of the family in China compare with the family in other parts of the world?

Q How has the current generation of leadership in China made use of traditional values to solidify Communist control over the country? To what degree has this approach contradicted the theories of Karl Marx?

CHAPTER TIMELINE

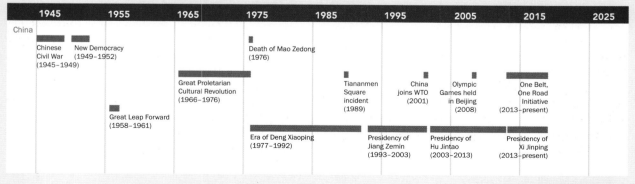

	1945	1955	1965	1975	1985	1995	2005	2015	2025
China									

Chinese Civil War (1945–1949)

New Democracy (1949–1952)

Death of Mao Zedong (1976)

Great Leap Forward (1958–1961)

Great Proletarian Cultural Revolution (1966–1976)

Tiananmen Square incident (1989)

China joins WTO (2001)

Olympic Games held in Beijing (2008)

One Belt, One Road Initiative (2013–present)

Era of Deng Xiaoping (1977–1992)

Presidency of Jiang Zemin (1993–2003)

Presidency of Hu Jintao (2003–2013)

Presidency of Xi Jinping (2013–present)

CHAPTER NOTES

1. "Report on an Investigation of the Peasant Movement in Hunan (March 1927)," *Quotations from Chairman Mao Tse-tung* (Beijing, 1976), p. 12.

2. Quoted in Stanley Karnow, *Mao and China: Inside China's Revolution* (New York, 1972), p. 95.

3. Quoted from an article by Mao Zedong in the journal *Red Flag*, June 1, 1958. See Stuart R. Schram, *The Political Thought of Mao Tse-tung* (New York, 1963), p. 253. The quotation "strike while the iron is hot" is from Karnow, *Mao and China*, p. 93.

4. Liang Heng with Judith Shapiro, *Son of the Revolution* (New York, 1983).

5. "The Foolish Old Man Who Removed the Mountains," *Quotations from Chairman Mao*, p. 182.

6. According to many of Mao Zedong's biographers, as a young man Mao had been severely dominated by his dictatorial father, and perhaps acted out his hatred of parental authority for the remainder of his life.

CHAPTER 13

NATIONALISM TRIUMPHANT: THE EMERGENCE OF INDEPENDENT STATES IN SOUTH AND SOUTHEAST ASIA

Chapter Outline and Focus Questions

13-1 *South Asia*

Q How did Mahatma Gandhi's and Jawaharlal Nehru's goals for India differ, and what role did each leader's views play in shaping modern India?

13-2 *Southeast Asia*

Q What kinds of problems have the nations of Southeast Asia had to face since 1945, and how did they attempt to solve them?

IMAGE 13.1 The Petronas Towers in Kuala Lumpur, Malaysia

William J. Duiker

Connections to Today

How would you compare the policies adopted by the nations discussed in this chapter with those followed by the so-called Little Tigers, as discussed in Chapter 11? Are the countries in South and Southeast Asia following a path toward economic development and political stability today?

AT THE DAWN OF THE NEW MILLENNIUM, first-time visitors to the Malaysian capital of Kuala Lumpur were astonished to observe a pair of twin towers thrusting up above the surrounding buildings into the clouds. The Petronas Towers rise 1,483 feet from ground level; they were the world's tallest buildings at the time of their completion in 1998. (They have since been surpassed by other structures such as Taipei 101, in Taiwan, the Shanghai World Financial Center, and Burj Khalifa, in Dubai.)

Beyond their status as an architectural achievement, the Petronas Towers announced the emergence of Southeast Asia as a major player on the international scene. It is no accident that the foundations were laid on the site of the Selangor Cricket Club, once a symbol of British colonial hegemony in Southeast Asia. "These towers," commented one local official, "will do wonders for Asia's self-esteem and confidence, which I think is very important, and which I think at this moment are at the point of takeoff."[1]

That the nations of the Pacific Rim would become a driving force in global development was all but unimaginable in the decades immediately following the end of World War II, when bitter conflicts in Korea and Vietnam and unstable conditions elsewhere in the region were visible manifestations of a region in turmoil. Yet today, many of the countries in Asia have become models of successful nation building characterized by economic prosperity and political stability. Several cities in the region, including Hong Kong, Singapore, Tokyo, and Shanghai, have become major capitals of finance and monuments of economic prowess, rivaling the traditional centers of New York, London, Berlin, and Paris. They have heralded the opening of what has been called the "Pacific Century."

13-1 SOUTH ASIA

 Focus Question: How did Mahatma Gandhi's and Jawaharlal Nehru's goals for India differ, and what role did each leader's views play in shaping modern India?

In 1947, nearly two centuries of British colonial rule in South Asia came to an end when two new independent nations, India and Pakistan, came into being. Under British authority, the subcontinent had been linked ever more closely to the global capitalist economy. Yet as in other areas of Asia and Africa, the experience brought only limited benefits to the local peoples. Little industrial development took place, and the bulk of the profits went into the pockets of Western entrepreneurs.

For half a century, nationalist forces had been seeking reforms in colonial policy and the eventual overthrow of colonial power. But the peoples of South Asia did not regain their independence until after World War II.

13-1a The End of the British Raj

During the 1930s, the nationalist movement in India was severely shaken by factional disagreements between Hindus and Muslims. The outbreak of World War II subdued these sectarian clashes, but they erupted again after the war ended in 1945. Battles between Hindus and Muslims broke out in several cities, and Muhammad Ali Jinnah (1876–1948), leader of the Muslim League, demanded the creation of a separate state for each group. Meanwhile, the Labour Party, which had long been critical of the British colonial legacy on both moral and economic grounds, had come to power in Britain, and the new prime minister, Clement Attlee, announced that power would be transferred to "responsible Indian hands" by June 1948. But the imminence of independence did not dampen communal strife. As riots escalated, the British reluctantly accepted the inevitability of partition and declared that on August 15, 1947, two independent nations—predominantly Hindu India and Muslim Pakistan—would

be established. Pakistan would be divided between the main area of Muslim habitation in the Indus River valley in the west and a separate territory in eastern Bengal 2,000 miles to the east. Although Mohandas "Mahatma" Gandhi warned that partition would provoke "an orgy of blood,"[2] he was increasingly regarded as a figure of the past, and his views were ignored.

The British instructed the rulers in the princely states to choose which state they would join by August 15, but problems arose in predominantly Hindu Hyderabad, where the nawab (governor) was a Muslim, and mountainous Kashmir, where a Hindu prince ruled over a Muslim population. After independence was declared, millions of Hindus and Muslims fled across the new borders, resulting in violence and the deaths of more than a million people. One of the casualties was Gandhi, who was assassinated on January 30, 1948, as he was going to morning prayer (see Movies & History, *Gandhi*, p. 109). The assassin, a Hindu militant, was apparently motivated by Gandhi's opposition to a Hindu India.

13-1b Independent India

With independence, the Indian National Congress, now commonly known as the Congress Party, moved from opposition to the responsibility of power under Jawaharlal Nehru (1889–1964), the new prime minister. The prospect must have been intimidating. The vast majority of India's 400 million people were poor and illiterate. The new nation encompassed a significant number of ethnic groups and fourteen major languages. Although Congress leaders spoke bravely of building a new nation, Indian society still bore the scars of past wars and divisions.

The government's first problem was to resolve disputes left over from the transition period. The rulers of Hyderabad and Kashmir had both followed their own preferences rather than the wishes of their subject populations. Nehru was determined to include both states within India. In 1948, Indian troops invaded Hyderabad and annexed the area. India also occupied most of Kashmir, but at the cost of creating an intractable problem that has poisoned relations with Pakistan to the present day.

An Experiment in Democratic Socialism Under Nehru's leadership, India adopted a political system on the British model, with a figurehead president and a parliamentary form of government. A number of political parties operated legally, but the Congress Party, with its enormous prestige and charismatic leadership, was dominant at both the central and the local levels. It was ably assisted by the Indian civil service, which had been created during the era of British colonial rule and provided solid expertise in the arcane art of bureaucracy.

Two Visions for India

 What are the key differences between these two views of the future of India? Why do you think Nehru's vision triumphed over that of Mahatma Gandhi?

Politics & Government

ALTHOUGH JAWAHARLAL NEHRU AND MOHANDAS GANDHI agreed on their desire for an independent India, their visions of the future of their homeland were dramatically different. Nehru favored industrialization to build material prosperity, whereas Gandhi praised the virtues of local self-government. The first excerpt is from a speech by Nehru; the second is from an article written by Gandhi and now published in his *Collected Works*.

Nehru's Socialist Creed

I am convinced that the only key to the solution of the world's problems and of India's problems lies in socialism, and when I use this word I do so not in a vague humanitarian way but in the scientific economic sense. . . . I see no way of ending the poverty, the vast unemployment, the degradation and the subjection of the Indian people except through socialism. That involves vast and revolutionary changes in our political and social structure, the ending of vested interests in land and industry, as well as the feudal and autocratic Indian states system. That means the ending of private property, except in a restricted sense, and the replacement of the present profit system by a higher ideal of cooperative service. . . . In short, it means a new civilization, radically different from the present capitalist order. Some glimpse we can have of this new civilization in the territories of the U.S.S.R. Much has happened there which has pained me greatly and with which I disagree, but I look upon that great and fascinating unfolding of a new order and a new civilization as the most promising feature of our dismal age.

Mohandas Gandhi, "Nonviolent Democracy: Control by the People of Themselves and Their Government"

Independence must begin at the bottom. Thus, every village will be a republic or *panchayat* [traditional village council] having full powers. It follows, therefore, that every village has to be self-sustained and capable of managing its affairs even to the extent of defending itself against the whole world. . . . Ultimately, it is the individual who is the unit. . . .

In this structure composed of innumerable villages, there will be ever widening, never ascending circles. Life will not be a pyramid with the apex sustained by the bottom. But it will be an oceanic circle whose centre will be the individual always ready to perish for the village, the latter ready to perish for the circle of villagers, till at last the whole becomes one life composed of individuals, never aggressive in their arrogance but ever humble, sharing the majesty of the oceanic circle of which they are integral units.

Therefore, the outermost circumference [that is, the national government] will not wield power to crush the inner circle but will give strength to all within and derive its own strength from it.

Sources: From *Sources of Indian Tradition*, 2nd ed. Edited by Stephen Hay, vol. II (New York: Columbia University Press, 1988), pp. 256, 317–318.

Nehru had been influenced by British socialism and patterned his economic policy roughly after the program of the British Labour Party. The state took over ownership of the major industries and resources, transportation, and utilities, while private enterprise was permitted at the local and retail levels. Farmland remained in private hands, but rural cooperatives were officially encouraged. The government also sought to avoid excessive dependence on foreign investment and technological assistance. All businesses were required by law to have majority Indian ownership.

In other respects, Nehru was a devotee of Western materialism. He was convinced that to succeed, India must industrialize. In advocating industrialization, Nehru departed sharply from Gandhi, who believed that materialism was morally corrupting and that only simplicity and nonviolence (as represented by the traditional Indian village and the symbolic spinning wheel) could save India, and the world itself, from self-destruction (see Opposing Viewpoints, "Two Visions for India," above). Gandhi, Nehru complained, "just wants to spin and weave."

The primary themes of Nehru's foreign policy were anticolonialism and antiracism. Under his guidance, India took a neutral stance in the Cold War and sought to provide leadership to all newly independent nations in Asia,

Africa, and Latin America. At the Bandung Conference, held in Indonesia in 1955, India promoted the concept of a bloc of "Third World" countries that would provide a balance between the capitalist world and the Communist bloc. It also sought good relations with the new People's Republic of China. India's neutrality put it at odds with the United States, which during the 1950s was trying to mobilize all nations against what it viewed as the menace of international communism.

Relations with Pakistan continued to be troubled. India refused to consider Pakistan's claim to Kashmir, even though the majority of the people there were Muslim. Tension between the two countries persisted, erupting into war in 1965. In 1971, when riots against the Pakistani government broke out in East Pakistan, India intervened on the side of East Pakistan, which declared its independence as the new nation of Bangladesh (see Map 13.1).

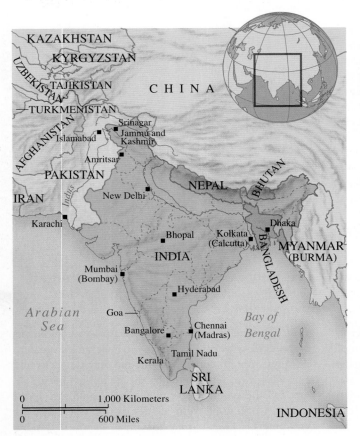

MAP 13.1 Modern South Asia. This map shows the boundaries of all the states in contemporary South Asia. India, the largest in area and population, is highlighted.

Q *Which of the countries on this map have a Muslim majority?*

The Post-Nehru Era Nehru's death in 1964 aroused concern that Indian democracy was dependent on the Nehru mystique. When his successor, a Congress Party veteran, died in 1966, Congress leaders selected Nehru's daughter, Indira Gandhi (no relation to Mahatma Gandhi), as the new prime minister. Gandhi (1917–1984) was inexperienced in politics, but she quickly showed the steely determination of her father.

Like Nehru, Indira Gandhi embraced democratic socialism and a policy of neutrality in foreign affairs, but she was more activist than her father. To combat rural poverty, she nationalized banks, provided loans to peasants on easy terms, built low-cost housing, distributed land to the landless, and introduced electoral reforms to enfranchise the poor.

Gandhi was especially worried by India's growing population and in an effort to curb the growth rate adopted a policy of forced sterilization. This policy proved unpopular, however, and, along with growing official corruption and Gandhi's authoritarian tactics, led to her defeat in the general election of 1975, the first time the Congress Party had failed to win a majority at the national level.

A minority government of procapitalist parties was formed, but within two years, Gandhi was back in power. She now faced a new challenge, however, in the rise of religious strife. The most dangerous situation was in the Punjab, where militant **Sikhs** were demanding autonomy or even independence from India (the Sikh religion was created in the sixteenth century to incorporate elements of both Islam and Hinduism into the new faith). Gandhi did not shrink from a confrontation and ordered an attack on Sikh rebels hiding in their Golden Temple in the city of Amritsar. The incident aroused widespread anger among the Sikh community, and in 1984, Sikh members of Gandhi's personal bodyguard assassinated her.

By now, Congress politicians were convinced that the party could not remain in power without a member of the Nehru family at the helm. Indira Gandhi's son Rajiv (1944–1991), a commercial airline pilot with little interest in politics, was persuaded to replace his mother as prime minister. Rajiv lacked the strong ideological and political convictions of his mother and grandfather and allowed a greater role for private enterprise. But his government was criticized for cronyism, inefficiency, and corruption, as well as insensitivity to the poor.

Rajiv Gandhi also sought to play a role in regional affairs, mediating a dispute between the government in Sri Lanka and Tamil rebels (known as the **Elam Tigers** or Tamil Tigers), who were ethnically related to the majority population in southern India.

Sri Lanka (formerly Ceylon) had been granted independence by the British in 1950 under a government formed by its majority Buddhist population, but two of the island's minority groups—Hindus (most of whom were known as Tamils) and Muslims—were restive under Buddhist rule. The decision to intervene in the bitter civil war cost Gandhi his life: while campaigning for reelection in 1991, he was assassinated by a member of the Elam Tiger organization. India faced the future without a member of the Nehru family as prime minister.

During the early 1990s, Congress remained the leading party, but the powerful hold it had once had on the Indian electorate was gone. New parties, such as the militantly Hindu Bharatiya Janata Party (BJP), actively vied with Congress for control of the central and state governments. Growing political instability at the center was accompanied by rising tensions between Hindus and Muslims, who composed about 15 percent of the total population of the country.

When a coalition government formed under Congress leadership collapsed, the BJP, under Prime Minister A. B. Vajpayee (1924–2018), ascended to power in 1998 and played on Hindu sensibilities to build its political base. The new government based its success on an aggressive program of privatization in the industrial and commercial sectors and made a major effort to promote the nation's small but growing technological base. But BJP leaders had underestimated the discontent of India's less affluent citizens (an estimated 350 million Indians earned less than one U.S. dollar a day), and in the spring of 2004, a stunning defeat in national elections forced the Vajpayee government to resign. The Congress Party returned to power at the head of a coalition government based on a commitment to maintain economic growth while carrying out reforms in rural areas, including public works projects and hot lunch programs for all primary school children.

But sectarian strife between Hindus and Muslims, as well as pervasive official corruption, continued to bedevil the government. In the fall of 2008, a terrorist attack in the city of Mumbai left nearly 200 dead and raised serious questions about the effectiveness of Indian security procedures. Indian officials charged that the inspiration for the attack came from Pakistan. The Congress Party remained in power after national elections held the following year, but in 2014, the BJP stormed back into power under Prime Minister Narendra Modi on a program calling for rapid economic growth, a crackdown on endemic corruption, and a strengthening of the country's role in international affairs. For many Indians, however, the BJP was still most identified by its emphasis on Hinduism as the defining characteristic of the Indian nation (a concept known as **Hindutva**, or "Hinduness").

Militant Hindu groups with tacit approval from BJP officials have provoked clashes with Muslims and with other minority groups such as Dalits (the lowest class in traditional Hindu society, once known as "untouchables") and the country's small Christian community.

In the spring of 2019, nearly one billion Indian citizens were eligible to vote in national elections to determine the future course of the country. The BJP's campaign was based on a promise of rapid economic growth and Hindu revivalism. The Congress Party, now led by the latest member of the Gandhi family, Rajiv's son Rahul (b. 1970), ran on a platform of ethnic diversity and affirmative action for disadvantaged groups. Water shortages and dropping prices for farm products have angered the country's millions of agricultural workers and raised questions about the BJP's ability to deliver on its economic promises, but its defense of Hinduism remains widely popular among the majority of Indian voters, and the party won a stunning victory in the election, thus raising questions about the future direction of the second largest country in the world today.

13-1c The Land of the Pure: Pakistan Since Independence

When Pakistan achieved independence in August 1947, it was, unlike its neighbor India, in all respects a new nation, based on religious conviction rather than historical or ethnic tradition. The unique state united two separate territories 2,000 miles apart. West Pakistan, including the Indus River basin and the West Punjab, was perennially short of water and was populated by dry crop farmers and peoples of the steppe. East Pakistan was made up of the marshy deltas of the Ganges and Brahmaputra Rivers. Densely populated with rice farmers, it was the home of the artistic and intellectual Bengalis.

The peoples of West Pakistan were especially diverse and included, among others, Pashtuns, Baluchis, and Punjabis. The Pashtuns are organized on a tribal basis and have kinship ties with the majority population across the border in neighboring Afghanistan. Many are nomadic and cross the border on a regular basis with their flocks. The Baluchis straddle the border with Iran, while the region of Punjab was divided between Pakistan and India at the moment of independence.

Even though the new state was an essentially Muslim society, its first years were marked by intense internal conflicts over religious, linguistic, and regional issues. Muhammad Ali Jinnah's vision of a democratic state that would assure freedom of religion and equal treatment for all was opposed by those who advocated a state based on Islamic principles, and eventually Islamic law became the basis for the legal and social system.

Ethnic and territorial differences also plagued the new nation. Many residents of East Pakistan felt that the government, based in the west, ignored their needs. In 1952, riots erupted in East Pakistan over the government's decision to adopt Urdu, a language derived from Hindi and used by Muslims in northern India, as the national language of the entire country. Most East Pakistanis spoke Bengali, an unrelated language. Tensions persisted, and in March 1971, East Pakistan declared its independence as the new nation of Bangladesh. Pakistani troops attempted to restore the central government's authority in the capital of Dhaka, but rebel forces supported by India went on the offensive, and the government bowed to the inevitable and recognized independent Bangladesh.

The breakup of the union between East and West Pakistan undermined the fragile authority of the military regime that had ruled Pakistan since 1958 and led to its replacement by a civilian government under Zulfikar Ali Bhutto (1928–1979). But now religious tensions came to the fore, despite a new constitution that made a number of key concessions to conservative Muslims. In 1977, a new military government under General Zia ul Ha'q (1924–1988) came to power with a commitment to make Pakistan a truly Islamic state. Islamic law became the basis for social behavior as well as for the legal system. Laws governing the consumption of alcohol and the role of women were tightened in accordance with strict Muslim beliefs. But after Zia was killed in a plane crash, Pakistanis elected Benazir Bhutto (1953–2007), the daughter of Zulfikar Ali Bhutto and a supporter of secularism who had been educated in the United States. In 1990 she too was removed from power by a military regime, on charges of incompetence and corruption. Reelected in 1993, she attempted to crack down on opposition forces but was removed once again on similar charges. Her successor soon came under fire for the same reason and in 1999 was ousted by a military coup led by General Pervez Musharraf (b. 1943), who promised to restore political stability and honest government.

In September 2001, Pakistan became the focus of international attention when a coalition of forces arrived in neighboring Afghanistan to overthrow the Taliban regime and destroy the al-Qaeda terrorist network. Despite considerable support for the Taliban among his constituents, President Musharraf pledged his help in bringing terrorists to justice. He also promised to return his country to the secular principles espoused by Muhammad Ali Jinnah. But the situation was complicated by renewed tensions over Kashmir, which led to a series of violent clashes between Muslims and Hindus in India. In 2008, Pakistan returned to civilian rule through democratic elections, but the political influence of the military remained paramount. The current president, Imran Khan (b. 1952), an ex-cricket star and a leader of the centrist Justice Movement Party, has pledged to improve economic conditions in the country, while cracking down on powerful militant groups and seeking to cut back on the influence of Islamic radicals in the country's religious schools.

Whoever holds the reins of power in Pakistan faces a number of challenges in coping with the multitude of problems affecting the country today. In a nation where much of the rural population still professes loyalty to traditional tribal leaders, the sense of national identity remains fragile, while military elites who have long played a central role in Pakistani politics continue to press their own agenda. The influence of radical Islam has been growing, and in recent years it has peaked because of the war in Afghanistan and anger over India's suppression of its Muslim minority. Half of the entire population lives in poverty, and illiteracy is widespread. The government is on the verge of bankruptcy because of inadequate tax revenues and declining exports. Massive flooding of the Indus River in 2010 killed nearly 2,000 people and left millions homeless. Plagued by the continuing dispute over Kashmir, relations with India remain fragile, and chronic conflicts among the various ethnic and religious groups undermine the search for stability.

13-1d Poverty and Pluralism in South Asia

The leaders of the new states that emerged in South Asia after World War II faced a number of problems. The peoples of South Asia were still overwhelmingly poor and illiterate, and the sectarian, ethnic, and cultural divisions that had plagued Indian society for centuries had not dissipated.

The Politics of Communalism   Perhaps the most sincere effort to create democratic institutions was in India, where the new constitution called for social justice, liberty, equality of status and opportunity, and fraternity. All citizens were guaranteed protection from discrimination on the grounds of religious belief, race, caste, gender, or place of birth.

In theory, then, India became a full-fledged democracy on the British parliamentary model. In actuality, a number of distinctive characteristics made the system less than fully democratic in the Western sense but may also have enabled it to survive. As we have seen, under Nehru and his immediate successors India became in essence a one-party state. By leading the independence movement, the Congress Party had gained massive public support, which enabled it to retain its preeminent position in Indian politics for three decades. The party also avoided being identified as a party exclusively for the Hindu majority by including prominent non-Hindus among its leaders and favoring measures to protect minority groups such as Sikhs, untouchables, and Muslims from discrimination.

After Nehru's death in 1964, however, problems emerged that had been disguised by his adept maneuvering. One problem was the familiar one of a party too long in power. Party officials became complacent and all too easily fell prey to the temptations of corruption and pork-barrel politics. As a result, the party's aura has faded, and it is viewed today by most Indians as merely one among several competing groups in the political arena.

Another reason for the decline of the Congress Party's political standing was the growing power of **communalism**. Beneath the surface unity of the new republic lay age-old ethnic, linguistic, and religious divisions. From the outset, language was an especially knotty problem. Because of India's vast size and complex history, no national language had ever emerged. Hindi was the most prevalent, but it was the native language of less than one-third of the population. During the colonial period, English had served as the official language of government, and many non-Hindi speakers suggested making it the official language. But English was spoken only by the educated elite, and it represented an affront to national pride. Eventually, India recognized fourteen official tongues.

Bitter feelings that bedeviled relations among the country's various religious communities, originally sparked by the bloody events that took place during the transition to independence, also began to intensify. As we have seen, Gandhi's uncompromising approach to Sikh separatism led to her assassination by her own bodyguards in 1984. Under her son Rajiv, sectarian disputes between India's Hindu majority and the minority Muslim community also began to increase. The issue came to international attention in the 1980s, when Hindu militants demanded the destruction of a mosque that had been built during the Mughal dynasty on a traditional Hindu holy site at Ayodhya, in northern India, where a Hindu temple had previously existed. In 1992, Hindu demonstrators destroyed the mosque and erected a temporary Hindu temple at the site, provoking scattered clashes between Hindus and Muslims throughout the country. In protest, rioters in neighboring Pakistan destroyed a number of Hindu shrines in that country. In 2010, an Indian court ordered that the land that had contained the mosque be divided between the Hindu and Muslim plaintiffs, and the issue died down.

The rise of the BJP as a political force added fuel to the fire, as militant Hindu groups began to demand a state that would cater to the Hindu majority, who now numbered more than 700 million people in the country. The historical achievements of India's Mughal dynasty were downplayed, and some school textbooks were rewritten to reflect a more Hindu-oriented version of history, including the dubious contention that the Indus Valley Civilization, an early polity that arose in the valley of the Indus River about 5,000 years ago, had been founded by Aryan peoples, ancestors of most present-day Hindus. Even the country's small Christian community has been affected. In the eastern state of Orissa, pitched battles have broken out between Hindus and Christians over efforts by the latter to win converts to their faith. At the time, India's Congress Party prime minister Manmohan Singh (b. 1932) lamented what he labeled an assault on India's "composite culture."[3]

The Economy Jawaharlal Nehru's answer to the social and economic inequality that had long afflicted the subcontinent was socialism. He instituted a series of five-year plans, which led to the creation of a relatively large and reasonably efficient industrial sector, centered on steel, vehicles, and textiles. Industrial production almost tripled between 1950 and 1965, and per capita income rose by 50 percent between 1950 and 1980, although it was still less than $300 (U.S. dollars).

By the 1970s, however, industrial growth had slowed. The lack of modern infrastructure was a problem, as was the rising price of oil, most of which had to be imported. The relative weakness of the state-owned sector, which grew at an annual rate of only about 2 percent in the 1950s and 1960s, versus 5 percent for the private sector, also became a serious obstacle.

India's major economic weakness, however, was in agriculture. At independence, mechanization was almost unknown, fertilizer was rarely used, and most farms were small and uneconomical because of the Hindu tradition of dividing the land equally among all male children. As a result, the vast majority of the Indian people lived in conditions of abject poverty. Landless laborers outnumbered landowners by almost two to one. The government attempted to relieve the problem by redistributing land to the poor, limiting the size of landholdings, and encouraging farmers to form voluntary cooperatives. But all three programs ran into widespread opposition and apathy.

Another problem was rapid population growth. Even before independence, the country had had difficulty supporting its people. In the 1950s and 1960s, the population grew by more than 2 percent annually, twice the nineteenth-century rate. Beginning in the 1960s, the Indian government sought to curb population growth. Indira Gandhi instituted a program combining monetary rewards and compulsory sterilization, but popular resistance undermined the program, which was scaled back in the 1970s. One factor in the continued population growth has been a decline in the death rate, especially the rate of infant mortality. Nevertheless, as a result of media popularization

Say No to McDonald's and KFC!

Why does the author of this article oppose the introduction of Western-style fast-food restaurants in India? Do you think her complaints apply in the United States as well?

Interaction & Exchange

ONE OF THE CONSEQUENCES of Rajiv Gandhi's decision to deregulate the Indian economy has been an increase in the presence of foreign corporations, including U.S. fast-food restaurant chains. Their arrival set off a storm of protest in India: from environmentalists concerned that raising grain for chickens is an inefficient use of land, from religious activists angry at the killing of animals for food, and from nationalists anxious to protect the domestic market from foreign competition. The protests went unheeded, however, and fast-food restaurants, many of them under Indian ownership, have become an increasingly visible presence on the urban scene. Most cater to local tastes by avoiding beef products and offering many vegetarian dishes. This piece, which appeared in the *Hindustan Times*, was written by Maneka Gandhi, a daughter-in-law of Indira Gandhi and a onetime minister of the environment who has emerged as a prominent rival of Sonia Gandhi, the widow of Rajiv Gandhi and the Congress Party president.

Why India Doesn't Need Fast Food

India's decision to allow Pepsi Foods Ltd. to open 60 restaurants in India—30 each of Pizza Hut and Kentucky Fried Chicken—marks the first entry of multinational, meat-based junk-food chains into India. If this is allowed to happen, at least a dozen other similar chains will very quickly arrive, including the infamous McDonald's.

The implications of allowing junk-food chains into India are quite stark. As the name denotes, the foods served at Kentucky Fried Chicken (KFC) are chicken-based and fried. This is the worst combination possible for the body and can create a host of health problems, including obesity, high cholesterol, heart ailments, and many kinds of cancer. Pizza Hut products are a combination of white flour, cheese, and meat—again, a combination likely to cause disease. . . .

Then there is the issue of the environmental impact of junk-food chains. Modern meat production involves misuse of crops, water, energy, and grazing areas. In addition, animal agriculture produces surprisingly large amounts of air and water pollution.

KFC and Pizza Hut insist that their chickens be fed corn and soybeans. Consider the diversion of grain for this purpose. As the outlets of KFC and Pizza Hut increase in number, the poultry industry will buy up more and more corn to feed the chickens, which means that the corn will quickly disappear from the villages, and its increased price will place it out of reach for the

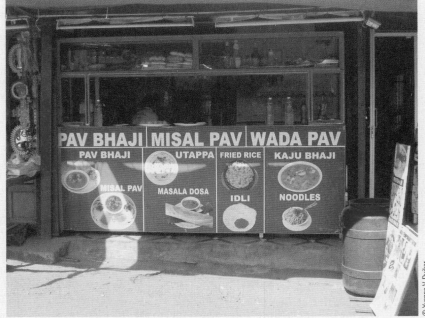

IMAGE 13.2 Fast Food, Indian Style. Some of the popular international fast-food chains like McDonald's and Kentucky Fried Chicken have begun to make their appearance in large Indian cities like Mumbai and New Delhi, despite the criticism by some observers that they would encourage bad health habits and hurt local restaurants. Their familiar logos are rarely seen in smaller towns and in rural areas, however, where many Indians cannot afford their prices or prefer to eat at roadside stalls serving a variety of tasty local dishes, as this small restaurant in the state of Goa attests.

common man. Turning corn into junk chicken is like turning gold into mud. . . .

It is already shameful that, in a country plagued by famine and flood, we divert 37 percent of our arable land to growing animal fodder. Were all of that grain to be consumed directly by humans, it would nourish five times as many people as it does after being converted into meat, milk, and eggs. . . .

Of course, it is not just the KFC and Pizza Hut chains of Pepsi Foods Ltd. that will cause all of this damage. Once we open India up by allowing these chains, dozens more will be eagerly waiting to come in. Each city in America has an average of 5,000 junk-food restaurants. Is that what we want for India?

Source: From *World Press Review* (September 1995), p. 47.

and better government programs, the trend today, even in poor rural villages, is toward smaller families. The average number of children a woman bears has been reduced from six in 1950 to three today. As has occurred elsewhere, the decline in family size began among the educated and is gradually spreading throughout Indian society. Still, the population of India has reached over 1.3 billion people, and the country is on target to surpass China and become the world's most populous nation by the year 2025.

The so-called **green revolution** that began in the 1960s helped reduce the severity of the population problem. The introduction of more productive, disease-resistant strains of rice and wheat doubled grain production between 1960 and 1980. But the green revolution also increased rural inequality. Only the wealthier farmers were able to purchase the necessary fertilizer, while poor peasants were often driven off the land. Millions fled to the cities, where they lived in vast slums, working at menial jobs or even begging for a living.

After the death of Indira Gandhi in 1984, her son Rajiv proved more receptive to foreign investment and a greater role for the private sector in the economy. India began to export more manufactured goods, including computer software. The pace of change has accelerated under Rajiv Gandhi's successors, who have continued to transfer state-run industries to private hands. These policies have stimulated the growth of a prosperous new middle class, now estimated at more than 100 million. Consumerism has soared, and sales of television sets, automobiles, DVD players, and cellphones have increased dramatically. Equally important, Western imports are being replaced by new products manufactured in India with Indian brand names.

One consequence of India's entrance into the industrial age is the emergence of a small but vibrant technological sector that provides many important services to the world's advanced nations. The city of Bangalore in southern India has become an important technological center, benefiting from low wages and the presence of skilled labor with proficiency in the English language. It has also become a symbol of the "outsourcing" of jobs from the United States and Europe that has led to an increase in middle-class unemployment throughout the Western world.

Nevertheless, Nehru's dream of a socialist society remains strong. State-owned enterprises still produce about half of all domestic goods, and high tariffs continue to stifle imports. Nationalist parties have played on the widespread fear of foreign economic influence to make it difficult for large multinational corporations, such as the retail giant Walmart, to break into the Indian market. A few years ago, a combination of religious and environmental groups attempted unsuccessfully to prevent Kentucky Fried Chicken from establishing outlets in major Indian cities (see Historical Voices, "Say No to McDonald's and KFC!" p. 328).

As in the industrialized countries of the West, economic growth in India has been accompanied by serious damage to the environment. Water and air pollution have led to illness and death for many Indians, and a vocal environmental movement has emerged. Some critics, reflecting the traditional anti-imperialist attitude of Indian intellectuals, blame Western corporations for the problem, as in the highly publicized case of leakage from a foreign-owned chemical plant at Bhopal. In reality, much of the problem comes from state-owned factories erected with Soviet aid or—more recently—from the millions of small India-made automobiles that now clog the streets of the major cities around the country. And not all the environmental damage can be ascribed to industrialization. Millions of Indians rely on small charcoal stoves to heat their meals and their homes, spewing toxic gases into the atmosphere. The Ganges River—sacred to Hindus for centuries—is so polluted by human overuse that it is risky for Hindu believers to bathe in it, while air and water pollution is so extensive that it constitutes a severe health problem in urban areas throughout the subcontinent. On some days, New Delhi is the most polluted city on Earth.

Moreover, many Indians have not benefited from the new prosperity. Nearly one-third of the population lives

Two Indias

Q *In what other regions of the world is lack of water a serious problem?*

Earth & Environment **CONTEMPORARY INDIA** is a study in contrasts. In Image 13.3a, middle-class students learn to use a computer, a symbol of their country's recent drive to join the global technological marketplace. Yet India today remains primarily a nation of villages. Image 13.3b shows women in colorful saris filling their pails with water at the village well. As in many developing countries, the scarcity of clean water is one of India's most crucial problems.

IMAGE 13.3a

IMAGE 13.3b

below the national poverty line. Millions continue to live in urban slums, such as the famous "City of Joy" in Kolkata (Calcutta), and most farm families remain desperately poor. In India's countless villages, millions of rural people rely—like the women in Image 13.3b from a village near Aurangabad—on local wells for their access to a clean water supply (see Comparative Illustration, "Two Indias," above). Despite the socialist rhetoric of India's leaders, the inequality of wealth in India is as pronounced as it is in capitalist nations in the West. Indeed, India has been described as two nations: an educated urban India of 100 million people surrounded by more than nine times that many impoverished peasants in the countryside.

Such problems are even more serious in neighboring Pakistan and Bangladesh. As we have seen above, the overwhelming majority of Pakistan's citizens are poor, and at least half are illiterate. Meanwhile, typhoons are frequent in the Bay of Bengal and often cause severe damage and loss of life in low-lying areas of Bangladesh.

Prospects for the future are not bright, for both countries have high birth-rates and lack a modern technological sector to serve as a magnet for the emergence of an educated middle class.

Caste, Class, and Gender The Indian constitution of 1950 guaranteed equal treatment and opportunity for all, regardless of caste, and prohibited discrimination based on untouchability. In recent years, the government has enacted a number of laws guaranteeing access to education and employment to all Indians, regardless of caste affiliation, and a number of individuals of low caste have attained high positions in Indian society. Nevertheless, prejudice is hard to eliminate, and the problem persists, particularly in rural areas, where *dalits* (see "The Post-Nehru Era," p. 324) still perform menial tasks and are often denied fundamental rights by their fellow villagers. Educated Indians often resent the fact that positions in education and the civil service are reserved for low-caste applicants.

Gender equality has also been difficult to establish. After independence, India's leaders also sought to equalize treatment of the sexes. The constitution expressly forbade discrimination based on gender and called for equal pay for equal work. Laws prohibited child marriage, *sati*, and the payment of a dowry by the bride's family. Women were encouraged to attend school and enter the labor market.

Such laws, along with the dynamics of economic and social change, have had a major impact on the lives of many Indian women. Middle-class women in urban areas are much more likely to seek employment outside the home, and some hold managerial and professional positions, although many couples still consult with their parents or an astrologer before deciding whether to go through with a marriage. Like other aspects of life, the role of women has changed much less in rural areas. Female children are still much less likely to receive an education. The overall literacy rate in India today is about 60 percent, but it is less than 50 percent among women. Laws relating to dowry, child marriage, and inheritance are routinely ignored in the countryside. The young bride in the photograph shown here may have played little role in the selection of her future husband (see Image 13.4). There have been a few highly publicized cases of sati, although undoubtedly more women die of mistreatment at the hands of their husband or of other members of his family.

13-1e South Asian Literature Since Independence

Recent decades have witnessed a prodigious outpouring of literature in India. Because of the vast quantity of works published (India is currently the third-largest publisher of English-language books in the world), only a few of the most prominent fiction writers can be mentioned here. Anita Desai (b. 1937) was one of the first prominent female writers to emerge from contemporary India. Her writing focuses on the struggle of Indian women to achieve a degree of independence. In her first novel, *Cry, the Peacock*, the heroine finally seeks liberation by murdering her husband, preferring freedom at any cost to remaining a captive of traditional society (see Historical Voices, "A Marriage of Convenience," p. 332).

The most controversial writer from India today is Salman Rushdie (b. 1947).

In *Midnight's Children* (1980), he linked his protagonist, born on the night of independence, to the history of modern India, its achievements, and its frustrations. Rushdie's later novels have tackled such problems as religious intolerance, political tyranny, social injustice, and greed and corruption. His attack on Islamic fundamentalism in *The Satanic Verses* (1988) won plaudits from literary critics but provoked widespread criticism among Muslims, including a death sentence by Iran's Ayatollah Khomeini.

HISTORIANS DEBATE 13-1f **What Is the Future of India?**

Today, Indian society looks increasingly Western in form, if not in content, and the distinction between traditional and modern, or local and cosmopolitan, sometimes seems to be a simple dichotomy between rural and urban. The major cities appear modern and westernized, while many villages have changed little since precolonial days.

William J. Duiker

IMAGE 13.4 Young Hindu Bride in Gold Bangles. Awaiting the marriage ceremony, a young bride sits with her female relatives at the Meenakshi Hindu temple, one of the largest in southern India. Although child marriage is illegal, Indian girls are still married at a young age. With the marital union arranged by the parents, this young bride may never have met her future husband. Bedecked in gold jewelry and rich silks—part of her dowry—she nervously awaits the priest's blessing before she moves to her husband's home. There she will begin a life of servitude to her in-laws' family.

 How would you compare the position of women in South Asia with what you have encountered in other parts of the world today? What accounts for the differences?

A Marriage of Convenience

 What is the source of Mrs. Rupa Mehra's objection to her daughter's planned marriage? How does her daughter respond?

Art & Ideas **ONE OF INDEPENDENT INDIA'S** foremost challenges has been to realize Mahatma's Gandhi's dream of integrating the country's multiple ethnic and religious groups into a cohesive society. Among the most serious issues is the uneasy relationship between the Muslim community and the Hindu majority. In *A Suitable Boy*, author Vikram Seth (b. 1952) describes the dilemma faced by a Hindu family when a daughter wishes to marry her Muslim boyfriend. Rupa Mehra is the mother of two daughters, Savita and Lata. Savita has married Pran, a fellow Hindu, but Lata has fallen in love with Kabir, a Muslim student at her university.

In the passage presented here, the author portrays the anguish experienced by family members as they seek to resolve the problem. At the end of 1,500 pages, Lata finally agrees to follow family tradition and marry the young Hindu her mother has chosen. Although it will initially be a "marriage of convenience," she hopes that respect for her husband will eventually turn to love, as happened with her sister Savita.

A Suitable Boy

Mrs. Rupa Mehra was not more prejudiced against Muslims than most upper-caste Hindu women of her age and background. As Lata had inopportunely pointed out, she even had friends who were Muslims, though almost all of them were not orthodox at all. The Nawab Sahib was perhaps, quite orthodox, but then he was, for Mrs. Rupa Mehra, more a social acquaintance than a friend.

The more Mrs. Rupa Mehra thought, the more agitated she became. Even marrying a non-kshatriya Hindu was bad enough. But this was unspeakable. It was one thing to mix socially with Muslims, entirely another to dream of polluting one's blood and sacrificing one's daughter.

Whom could she turn to in her hour of darkness? When Pran came home for lunch and heard the story, he suggested mildly that they meet the boy. Mrs. Rupa Mehra threw another fit. It was utterly out of the question. Pran then decided to stay out of things and to let them die down. He had not been hurt when he realized that Savita had kept her sister's confidence from him, and Savita loved him still more for that. She tried to calm her mother down, console Lata, and keep them in separate rooms—at least during the day.

Lata looked around the bedroom and wondered what she was doing in this house with her mother when her heart was entirely elsewhere, anywhere but here—a boat, a cricket field, a concert, a banyan grove, a cottage in the hills, Blandings Castle, anywhere, anywhere, so long as she was with Kabir. No matter what happened, she would meet him as planned, tomorrow. She told herself again and again that the path of true love never did run smooth.

Source: From V. Seth, *A Suitable Boy* (New York: Harper Collins, 1993), pp. 197–198.

Yet traditional practices appear to be more resilient in India than in many other societies, and the result is often a synthesis rather than a clash between conflicting institutions and values. Clothing styles in the streets (where the *sari* and the *dhoti* continue to be popular), religious practices in the temples, and social relationships in the home all testify to the importance of tradition in India.

One disadvantage of the eclectic approach, which seeks to blend the old and the new rather than choosing one over the other, is that sometimes contrasting traditions cannot be reconciled. In his book *India: A Wounded Civilization*, V. S. Naipaul (1932–2108), a well-known Trinidadian author of Indian descent, charged that Mahatma Gandhi's glorification of poverty and the simple Indian village was an obstacle to efforts to overcome the poverty, ignorance, and degradation of India's past and build a prosperous modern society. Gandhi's vision of a spiritual India, Naipaul complained, was a balm for defeatism and an excuse for failure.

Yet the appeal of Gandhi's philosophy remains a major part of the country's heritage. In July 2006, at a time when growing despair at economic conditions in the countryside resulted in a rash of suicides by poor farmers, Prime Minister Manmohan Singh called on the Indian people to reject the America model of "wasteful" consumer spending and return to the frugal teachings and spiritual vision of Mahatma Gandhi, which were, in his words, a "necessity" for a country as poor in material goods as India.[4] Tragically, poverty conditions in the Indian countryside continue to afflict much of the country's rural population today.

Certainly, India faces a cruel dilemma. As historian Martha Nussbaum points out in *The Clash Within: Democracy, Religious Violence, and India's Future*, much of India's rural population continues to hold traditional beliefs, such as the concept of *karma* and inherent caste distinctions, that are incompatible with the capitalist work ethic and the democratic belief in equality before the law. Yet these beliefs provide a measure of identity and solace often lacking in other societies where such traditional spiritual underpinnings have eroded.

India also faces other serious challenges. Gandhi's vision of a diverse society composed of many distinct ethnic and religious communities is increasingly at odds with the virulent spirit of nationalism and religious identity sweeping the region today. It must also cope with severe environmental difficulties, including land erosion, overcrowding, and a scarcity of water and other vital resources, which will place severe limitations on the country's ability to transform itself into an advanced industrial society. As a democratic and pluralistic society, it is unable to launch major programs without popular consent and thus cannot move as quickly or often as effectively as an authoritarian system like China's. On the other hand, India's institutions provide a mechanism to prevent the emergence of a despotic government interested only in its own survival. Rich in tradition and experience, India must seek its own path to the future.

13-2 SOUTHEAST ASIA

 Focus Question: What kinds of problems have the nations of Southeast Asia had to face since 1945, and how did they attempt to solve them?

The Japanese wartime occupation had a great impact on attitudes among the peoples of Southeast Asia. It demonstrated the vulnerability of colonial rule in the region and showed that an Asian power could defeat Europeans. The Allied governments themselves also contributed—sometimes unwittingly—to rising aspirations for independence by promising self-determination for all peoples at the end of the war. Although Winston Churchill later said that the Atlantic Charter did not apply to the colonial peoples, it would be difficult to put the genie back in the bottle again.

13-2a The End of the Colonial Era

Some did not try. In July 1946, the United States granted total independence to the Philippines. The Americans maintained a military presence on the islands, however, and U.S. citizens retained economic and commercial interests in the new country.

The British too, under the Labour Party, were willing to bring an end to a century of imperialism in the region. In 1948, the Union of Burma received its independence. Malaya's turn came in 1957, after a Communist-led guerrilla movement had been suppressed.

The French and the Dutch, however, regarded their colonies in the region as economic necessities as well as symbols of national grandeur and refused to turn them over to nationalist movements at the end of the war. The Dutch attempted to suppress a rebellion in the East Indies led by Sukarno (1901–1970), leader of the Indonesian Nationalist Party. But the United States, which feared a Communist victory there, pressured the Dutch to grant independence to Sukarno and his non-Communist forces, and in 1950, the Dutch finally agreed to recognize the new Republic of Indonesia. As we have seen, the situation was even more complicated in Vietnam, where the French refused to recognize Ho Chi Minh's provisional government in Hanoi in the fall of 1945 and sought to reimpose colonial rule. Only in 1954 would Vietnam, temporarily divided into two zones, receive its independence under the Geneva Accords (see Chapter 7).

13-2b In the Shadow of the Cold War

Unfortunately, the new nations of Southeast Asia faced the initial challenges of independence during an era of intense global turmoil because of the outbreak of the Cold War. Although some anti-colonialist leaders within the region (see Map 13.2) admired Western political institutions and hoped to adapt them to their own countries, others were influenced by the Marxist critique of world capitalism and sought to bring about revolutionary changes on the model of the Soviet Union or Communist China. Within a few years after the end of World War II, the Cold War was raging in Southeast Asia.

The Search for a New Political Culture In the immediate aftermath of independence, most new nations in the region adopted constitutions patterned on Western democratic models, and multiparty political systems quickly sprang into operation. By the 1960s, however, many of these budding experiments in pluralist democracy had

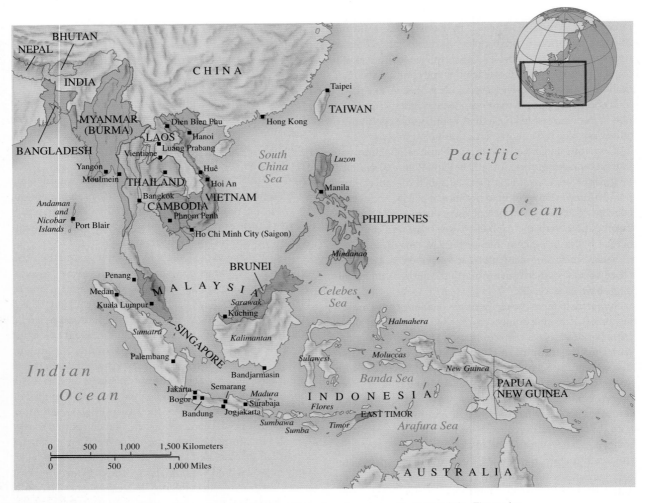

MAP 13.2 Modern Southeast Asia. Shown here are the countries of contemporary Southeast Asia. The major islands that make up the Republic of Indonesia are indicated in yellow.

Q *Which of the countries in Southeast Asia have functioning democratic governments? Which appear to be the most prosperous?*

been abandoned or were under serious threat. Some had been replaced by military or one-party autocratic regimes. In Burma, a moderate government based on the British parliamentary system and dedicated to Buddhism and nonviolent Marxism had given way to a military dictatorship. In Thailand too, the military ruled. In the Philippines, President Ferdinand Marcos (1917–1989) discarded democratic restraints and established his own centralized control. In South Vietnam, under pressure from Communist-led insurgents, Ngo Dinh Diem and his successors paid lip service to the Western democratic model but ruled by authoritarian means.

One key reason why democratic institutions failed to take root in postwar Southeast Asia was that independence had not brought material prosperity in its wake, nor had

it ended economic inequality and the domination of the local economies by foreign interests. Most economies in the region were still characterized by tiny industrial sectors; they lacked technology, educational resources, and capital investment. Disillusionment that the bright promise of independence was not being fulfilled was quick to spread among the general population.

The presence of widespread ethnic, linguistic, religious, and economic differences also made the transition to Western-style democracy difficult. In Malaya, for example, the majority Malays—most of whom were farmers and virtually all of whom were (and still are) Muslims—feared economic and political domination by the local Chinese minority, who were much more experienced in industry and commerce. In 1961, the new Federation of

Malaya, whose ruling party was dominated by Malays, integrated former British possessions on the island of Borneo into the new Union of Malaysia in a move to increase the non-Chinese proportion of the country's population. Yet periodic conflicts persisted as the Malaysian government adopted a program of affirmative action to grant favoritism in the economic sphere to Malays while seeking to guarantee Malay control over politics.

It was unfortunate that the new nations of Southeast Asia were seeking to realize their ambitious objectives in a time of intense Great Power rivalry throughout Asia. While their leaders were under severe pressure to take sides in the Cold War, revolutionary parties—many of them influenced by the Maoist strategy of "people's war"—operated outside the system as they sought to bring about drastic change on the model of the new China. These revolutionary parties drew support not only from China but also from North Vietnam, where Communist leaders openly rejected the Western model and opted for the Leninist pattern of national development based on Communist Party rule. In 1958, North Vietnamese leaders launched a three-year plan to lay the foundations for a fully socialist society. Collective farms were established in rural areas, and all industry and commerce above the family level were nationalized. To worried U.S. officials in Washington, a "red tide" threatened to overrun the entire region of Southeast Asia.

Sukarno and "Guided Democracy" The most prominent example of a failed experiment in democracy was in Indonesia. In 1950, the new Indonesian leaders drew up a constitution creating a parliamentary system under a titular presidency. Sukarno was elected the first president. A spellbinding orator, Sukarno played a major role in creating a sense of national identity among the disparate peoples of the Indonesian archipelago (see Historical Voices, "The Golden Throat of President Sukarno," p. 336).

But Sukarno grew exasperated at the incessant maneuvering among devout Muslims, Communists, and the army, and in the late 1950s, he dissolved the constitution and attempted to rule on his own through what he called **guided democracy**. As he described it, guided democracy was closer to Indonesian traditions and superior to the Western variety. The weakness of the latter, he argued, was that it allowed the majority to dominate the minority, whereas guided democracy would reconcile different opinions and points of view in a government operated by consensus. Highly suspicious of the West, Sukarno nationalized foreign-owned enterprises and sought economic aid from China and the Soviet Union while relying for domestic support on the Indonesian Communist Party.

The army and many devout Muslims resented Sukarno's increasing reliance on the Communists, and devout Muslims were further upset by his refusal to consider a state based on Islamic principles. In 1965, a few leftist military officers launched a coup d'état that provoked a military takeover of the government and a mass popular uprising, which resulted in the slaughter of several hundred thousand suspected Communists, many of whom were overseas Chinese, long distrusted by the Muslim majority (see Movies & History, *The Year of Living Dangerously*, p. 337). After passions had cooled, in 1967, a military government under General Suharto (1921–2008) was installed.

The new government made no pretensions of reverting to democratic rule, but it did restore good relations with the West and sought foreign investment to repair the country's ravaged economy. It also sought to placate demands from some Muslim groups for a state based on strict Islamic principles, a demand that ran counter to one of the core principles of the 1945 constitution—the concept of "Five Principles" (or **Panca Sila**)—that called for a secular state that would reconcile the diverse religious beliefs that characterized the population of the country. In a few areas, notably in western Sumatra, militant Muslims took up arms against the state.

13-2c Southeast Asia in the New Millennium

With the end of the Vietnam War and the gradual rapprochement between China and the United States that began in the late 1970s, the ferment and uncertainty that had marked the first three decades of independence in Southeast Asia gradually gave way to an era of greater political stability and material prosperity. In the Philippines, the dictatorial regime of Ferdinand Marcos was overthrown by a massive public uprising in 1986 and replaced by a democratically elected government under President Corazon Aquino (1933–2009), the widow of a popular politician assassinated a few years earlier. Aquino was unable to resolve many of the country's chronic economic and social difficulties, however, and political stability remained elusive. The current president, Rodrigo Duterte (b. 1945), is an outspoken populist who has sought popularity by vigorously pursuing drug pushers and other criminal elements in the country. A long-running dispute rages on the southern island of Mindanao, where dissident Muslim groups have mounted a terrorist campaign in their effort to obtain autonomy or independence from the central government.

Similar trends are at work elsewhere in the region. Malaysia is a practicing democracy, although the ruling coalition of various ethnic groups has long experienced chronic difficulties in satisfying demands by militant Muslims to create an Islamic state—an eventuality that would arouse deep unease among the country's many

The Golden Throat of President Sukarno

 Does Sukarno's argument that Western-style democracy allows the majority to tyrannize the minority have any merit? If not, why not?

Politics & Government **PRESIDENT SUKARNO OF INDONESIA** was a spellbinding speaker and a charismatic leader of his nation's struggle for independence. These two excerpts are from speeches in which Sukarno promoted two of his favorite projects: Indonesian nationalism and "guided democracy." The force that would guide Indonesia, of course, was to be Sukarno himself. While Sukarno tried to justify his plan to strengthen his own authority by harking back to local village traditions, his real objective was one that is shared by would-be autocrats throughout the world.

Sukarno on Indonesian Greatness

What was Indonesia in 1945? What was our nation then? It was only two things, only two things. A flag and a song. That is all. (Pause, finger held up as afterthought.) But no, I have omitted the main ingredient. I have missed the most important thing of all. I have left out the burning fire of freedom and independence in the breast and heart of every Indonesian. That is the most important thing—this is the vital chord—the spirit of our people, the spirit and determination to be free. This was our nation in 1945—the spirit of our people!

And what are we today? We are a great nation. We are bigger than Poland. We are bigger than Turkey. We have more people than Australia, than Canada, we are bigger in area and have more people than Japan. In population now we are the fifth-largest country in the world. In area, we are even bigger than the United States of America. The American Ambassador, who is here with us, admits this. Of course, he points out that we have a lot of water in between our thousands of islands. But I say to him—America has a lot of mountains and deserts, too!

Sukarno on Guided Democracy

Indonesia's democracy is not liberal democracy. Indonesian democracy is not the democracy of the world of Montaigne or Voltaire. Indonesia's democracy is not à la America, Indonesia's democracy is not the Soviet—NO! Indonesia's democracy is the democracy which is implanted in the breasts of the Indonesian people, and it is that which I have tried to dig up again, and have put forward as an offering to you. . . . If you, especially the undergraduates, are still clinging to and being borne along the democracy made in England, or democracy made in France, or democracy made in America, or democracy made in Russia, you will become a nation of copyists!

Source: From Howard Jones, *Indonesia: The Possible Dream* (New York: Harcourt Brace Jovanovich, Hoover Institute, 1971), pp. 223, 237.

ethnic and religious minorities. Critics argue that the program that assigns employment preferences for indigenous Malays appears above all to benefit the traditional ruling elites. In 2018, for the first time the government was voted out of office on charges of chronic corruption. In neighboring Thailand, fragile democratic forces are observed warily by the military, which recently declared martial law over the country after a series of massive antigovernment protests.

In Burma (renamed Myanmar in 1989), the forces of greater popular participation were long silenced by a repressive military regime known as SLORC. Recently, however, the military junta agreed to a gradual transition to civilian leadership under the National League for Democracy. Led by Aung San Suu Kyi, the admired daughter of a World War II nationalist leader, the new government faces intimidating challenges from anemic economic growth and a bitter conflict between the country's Buddhist majority and a widely distrusted Muslim minority group known as the Rohingya. Government efforts to expel the Rohingya from the country have aroused widespread criticism from civil rights groups abroad.

Indonesia after Suharto For years, a major exception to the trend toward political pluralism in the region was Indonesia, where Suharto ruled virtually without restraints. But in 1997, protests against widespread official corruption (several members of Suharto's family had

MOVIES & HISTORY

The Year of Living Dangerously (1983)

President Sukarno of Indonesia was one of the most prominent figures in Southeast Asia in the first two decades after World War II. A key figure in the nationalist movement while the country was under Dutch colonial rule, he was elected president of the new republic when it was granted formal independence in 1950. The charismatic Sukarno initially won broad popular support for his efforts to end colonial dependency and improve living conditions for the impoverished local population. But the government's economic achievements failed to match his fiery oratory, and when political unrest began to spread through Indonesian society in the early 1960s, Sukarno dismantled the parliamentary system that had been installed at independence and began to crack down on dissidents.

These conditions are the setting for the Australian film *The Year of Living Dangerously*. Based on a novel of the same name by Christian Koch, the movie takes place in the summer of 1965, at a time when popular unrest against the dictatorial government had reached a crescendo and the country appeared about to erupt in civil war. The newly arrived Australian reporter Guy Hamilton (Mel Gibson) is befriended by a diminutive Chinese Indonesian journalist Billy Kwan, effectively played by Linda Hunt, who received an Academy Award for her performance. Kwan, who has become increasingly disenchanted with Sukarno's failure to live up to his promises, introduces Hamilton to the seamy underside of Indonesian society as well as to radical elements connected to the Communist Party who are planning a coup to seize power in Jakarta.

The movie reaches a climax as Hamilton—a quintessentially ambitious reporter out to get a scoop on the big story—inadvertently becomes involved in the Communist plot and arouses the suspicion of government authorities. As Indonesia appears ready to descend into chaos, Hamilton finally recognizes the extent of the danger and manages to board the last plane from Jakarta. Others are

Photographer Billy Kwan (Linda Hunt) and reporter Guy Hamilton (Mel Gibson) film a political protest.

not so fortunate, as Sukarno's security police crack down forcefully on critics of his regime.

The Year of Living Dangerously (the title comes from a remark made by Sukarno during his presidential address in August 1964) is an important if underrated film that dramatically portrays a crucial incident in a volatile region caught in the throes of the global Cold War. The beautiful scenery (the film was shot in the Philippines because the story was banned in Indonesia) and a haunting film score help create a mood of tension spreading through a tropical paradise.

 Do you think this film provides justification for the decision by the Indonesian army to step in and overthrow the Sukarno regime?

reportedly used their positions to amass considerable wealth), coupled with Muslim demands for a larger role for Islam in society, led to violent street riots and calls for Suharto's resignation. Forced to step down in the spring of 1998, Suharto was replaced by his deputy B. J. Habibie (1936–2019), who called for the establishment of a national assembly to select a new government based on popular

aspirations. The new government faced internal challenges from dissident elements seeking autonomy or separation from the republic, as well as from religious forces seeking to transform the country into an Islamic state. Under pressure from the international community, Indonesia finally agreed to grant independence to the onetime Portuguese colony of East Timor, where the majority of the people are Roman Catholics. But violence provoked by pro-Indonesian militia units forced many refugees to flee the island. Religious tensions also erupted between Muslims and Christians elsewhere in the archipelago, and Muslim rebels in western Sumatra continued to agitate for a new state based on strict adherence to fundamentalist Islam. In 2002, a terrorist attack directed at tourists on the island of Bali aroused fears that Indonesia had become a haven for terrorist elements throughout the region.

In direct elections held in 2004, General Susilo Yudhyono (b. 1949) defeated Sukarno's daughter Megawati Sukarnoputri and ascended to the presidency. The new chief executive inaugurated an era of economic reform and political stability, and power was transferred peacefully ten years later to his successor, the mayor of Jakarta, Joko Widodo. Pressure from militant Muslim groups to abandon the country's secular tradition continues, however, and was recently punctuated by bloody terrorist attacks on the islands of Java and Bali. Still, the fact that democratic elections can take place holds promise for the future.

Vietnam and Cambodia: The God that Failed

As always, Vietnam is a special case. After achieving victory over South Vietnam with the fall of Saigon in the spring of 1975 (see Chapter 7), the Communist leaders in Hanoi, heady with success, decided to carry out the rapid reunification of the two zones into a new Socialist Republic of Vietnam (SRV). Simultaneously they also laid plans to begin the process of socialist transformation throughout the country. The result was a disaster, as the economy virtually stalled, creating widespread hunger and provoking the exodus of thousands of refugees to neighboring countries. In 1986, party leaders finally recognized reality and—following the example of Mikhail Gorbachev in Moscow—introduced their own version of *perestroika* in Vietnam (see Chapter 9).

The turn toward moderation succeeded, and the trend in recent years has been toward a mixed capitalist-socialist economy along Chinese lines and a greater, but still limited, popular role in the governing process. Elections for the unicameral parliament are more open than in the past, but the government remains suspicious of Western-style democracy and represses any opposition to the Communist Party's guiding role over the state.

An even greater tragedy took place in neighboring Cambodia, where a brutal revolutionary regime under the leadership of Pol Pot, the dictatorial head of the Khmer Rouge ("red Khmer" in French), took power in the spring of 1975. The new regime, which had established close ideological ties with Mao Zedong during the Cultural Revolution in China, proceeded to carry out the massacre of more than one million Cambodians in pursuit of the perfect communist society (see Image 13.5). Eventually, dissident elements led by the ex-Khmer Rouge cadre Hun Sen revolted against the regime's excesses, and with the aid of a

William J. Duiker

IMAGE 13.5 Holocaust in Cambodia. When the Khmer Rouge seized power in Cambodia in April 1975, they immediately emptied the capital of Phnom Penh and systematically began to eliminate opposition elements throughout the country. Thousands were tortured in the infamous Tuol Sleng prison and then marched out to the countryside, where they were summarily executed. Many of the victims had been arrested simply because they wore eyeglasses or had soft hands, indicating that they were members of the bourgeois class. Their bodies were thrown into massive pits. The remains were disinterred after the fall of the Khmer Rouge regime and are now displayed at an outdoor museum on the site.

Q *How would you compare the extermination of class enemies by the Khmer Rouge in Cambodia with the mass executions that took place in Nazi Germany and in the Soviet Union under Stalin? Were they similar in scope and intent, or were there significant differences?*

IMAGE 13.6 A Forest Fire on the Island of Sumatra. Man-made forest fires are one of the most prevalent forms of environmental pollution in Southeast Asia today, as precious rainforests are clear-cut to make room for valuable export crops such as rubber, coffee, and palm oil. Shown here, a forest fire on the Indonesian island of Sumatra casts a pall of acrid smoke over neighboring communities.

 How do you think the destruction of the rainforest in Southeast Asia compares with the clearing of land for economic use that often takes place in the United States?

William J. Duiker

Vietnamese invading force brought an end to the reign of terror. Almost forty years later, Hun Sen still rules in the capital of Phnom Penh.

Financial Crisis and Recovery The trend toward more representative systems of government in the region has been due in part to increasing prosperity and the growth of an affluent and educated middle class. Although Myanmar, the Philippines, and the three Indochinese states (Cambodia, Laos, and Vietnam) are still struggling, the remaining states in the region have been undergoing relatively rapid economic development.

In the summer of 1997, however, a financial crisis swept throughout the region, triggered by growing budget deficits and irresponsible investment practices by financial institutions. Recovery from the shockwaves was delayed by a massive tsunami that struck the western islands of Indonesia and the Malay Peninsula a few years later, and caused heavy casualties as well as inflicting substantial economic damage.

Eventually, the region managed to weather both crises. Blessed with abundant natural resources, the nations of Southeast Asia today enjoy an annual growth rate greater than most parts of the world. As they reap the benefits of these resources, however, progress in the region is endangered by growing environmental pollution. One key cause for concern is the widespread practice of cutting down rainforests to clear land for the cultivation of profitable tropical products such as rubber, coffee, and palm oil. The disappearance of the forest cover has cut down on the natural absorption of carbon dioxide gases. On some days, a heavy pall of smoke hangs over the entire region (see Image 13.6). Meanwhile, the draining of underground aquifers and the rise in sea levels throughout the region has led to chronic flooding in low-lying major cities such as Bangkok and Jakarta.

13-2d Regional Conflict and Cooperation: The Rise of ASEAN

Southeast Asia has historically been vulnerable to outside interference because of the absence of powerful states within the region. Recent efforts by local governments to protect themselves from hostile foreign influence have often failed because of the political, ethnic, and religious diversity that characterizes the population in the area. Sometimes that diversity has led to the outbreak of serious internal disputes. Some of these disputes have been caused by historical rivalries and territorial disputes that had been submerged during the long era of colonial rule. In the 1960s, Indonesian president Sukarno briefly launched a policy of confrontation with the Federation of Malaya, contending that the Malay peninsula had once been part of long-ago empires based on the Indonesian islands. The claim was dropped after Sukarno's fall from power in 1965. Another chronic border dispute has long existed between Cambodia and two of its neighbors, Thailand and Vietnam, both of which once exercised suzerainty over Cambodian territories. The frontiers established at the moment of Cambodian independence were originally drawn up by French colonial authorities for their own convenience.

After the Communist victories in Vietnam and Cambodia in 1975, the lingering border dispute between the two one-time ideological allies briefly erupted into violence, when the Khmer Rouge dictator Pol Pot claimed that vast territories in the Mekong delta had been seized from Cambodia by the Vietnamese in previous centuries. When the Khmer Rouge launched attacks across the common border, Vietnamese forces invaded Cambodia in December 1978 and installed a pro-Hanoi regime in Phnom Penh. Fearful of Vietnam's increasing power in the region, China launched a brief but bloody attack on Vietnam to demonstrate its displeasure. Although the dispute was quickly resolved, mutual suspicions between the two Communist countries continue to linger.

The outbreak of war among the erstwhile Communist allies aroused serious concern from other countries in the neighborhood. In 1967, several countries in the region had established the Association of Southeast Asian Nations, or **ASEAN**. Composed of Indonesia, Malaysia, Thailand, Singapore, and the Philippines, ASEAN at first concentrated on cooperative social and economic endeavors, but after the end of the Vietnam War, it recognized the need to broaden the scope of its efforts.

The ASEAN alliance has thus grown from a weak collection of diverse states into a stronger organization whose ten members—Vietnam, Laos, Myanmar, Thailand, and Brunei have joined the original five countries—cooperate militarily and politically to provide the nations of Southeast Asia with a more cohesive voice to represent their interests on the world stage. They will need it, for disagreements with Western countries over global economic issues and the rising power of China present major challenges to their well-being. The admission of Vietnam into ASEAN in 1995 was especially important, since it provided both Hanoi and its neighbors with greater leverage in dealing with their powerful neighbor to the north, whose claims of ownership over islands in the South China Sea have aroused widespread concern throughout the region.

13-2e Daily Life: Town and Country in Contemporary Southeast Asia

The urban–rural dichotomy observed in India is also found in Southeast Asia, where the cities resemble those in the West while the countryside often appears little changed from precolonial days. In cities such as Bangkok, Manila, and Jakarta, broad boulevards lined with skyscrapers alternate with muddy lanes passing through neighborhoods packed with wooden shacks topped by thatch or rusty tin roofs. Nevertheless, in recent decades, millions of Southeast Asians have fled to these urban slums. Although most available jobs are menial, the pay is better than in the villages.

Traditional Customs, Modern Values   The urban migrants change not only their physical surroundings but their attitudes and values as well. Sometimes the move leads to a decline in traditional religious faith. Belief in natural and ancestral spirits, for example, has declined among the urban populations of Southeast Asia. In Thailand and Myanmar, Buddhism has come under pressure from the rising influence of materialism, although temple schools still educate thousands of rural youths whose families cannot afford the cost of public education. In Indonesia, reverence for the past is undermined by the fact that ancient Hindu and Buddhist kingdoms on the islands have been replaced by the relatively recent arrival of Islam. On the predominantly Hindu island of Bali, however, traditional values and practices fill the everyday lives of the population (see Image 13.7).

Nevertheless, Buddhist, Muslim, and Confucian beliefs still remain strong, even in cosmopolitan cities such as Bangkok, Jakarta, and Singapore. This preference for the traditional also shows up in lifestyle. Traditional dress—or an eclectic blend of Asian and Western dress—is still common. Asian music, art, theater, and dance remain popular, although Western music has become fashionable among the young, and Indonesian filmmakers complain that Western films are beginning to dominate the local market.

The increasing inroads made by Western culture have caused anxiety in some countries. In Malaysia, for example, fundamentalist Muslims criticize the prevalence of pornography, hedonism, drugs, and alcohol in Western culture and have tried to limit their presence in their own country. The Malaysian government has attempted to limit the number of U.S. entertainment programs shown on local television stations and has replaced them with shows on traditional themes.

Changing Roles for Women   One of the most significant changes that has taken place in Southeast Asia in recent decades is in the role of women in society. In general, women in the region have historically faced fewer restrictions on their activities and enjoyed a higher status than women elsewhere in Asia. Nevertheless, they were not the equal of men in every respect. With independence, Southeast Asian women gained new rights. Virtually all of the constitutions adopted by the newly independent

IMAGE 13.7 Tourism and Tradition in Bali. The influence of modern Western culture has had a corrosive effect on contemporary societies throughout Southeast Asia. Traditional forms of art and architecture, music, and film have been replaced by their modern Western equivalents. The small island of Bali in eastern Indonesia has managed to preserve much of its traditional way of life by presenting it to visitors as a tourist experience. Although the tourist district in the capital of Denpasar is overrun with modern hotels, bars, and tourist shops, residents of the island still seek to preserve elements of their heritage as an outpost of Hindu culture in a country with 90 percent Muslim citizens. This photo shows Balinese actors at a theatrical performance on a familiar theme from the classical Indian repertoire. In an ironic twist, tourism in Bali helps to preserve traditional culture even as it undermines its relevance in the daily lives of the islanders.

 Is it important for societies to maintain their traditional values and customs, even as the world is changing so rapidly under the challenge of globalization?

states granted women full legal and political rights, including the right to work. Today, women have increased opportunities for education and have entered careers previously reserved for men. Women have become more active in politics, and as we have seen, some have served as heads of state.

Yet women are not truly equal to men in any country in Southeast Asia. Sometimes the distinction is simply a matter of custom. In Vietnam, women are legally equal to men, yet until recently no women had served in the Communist Party's ruling Politburo. In Thailand, Malaysia, and Indonesia, women rarely hold senior positions in government service or in the boardrooms of major corporations. Similar restrictions apply in Myanmar, although Aung San Suu Kyi, the daughter of a respected nationalist leader, is currently head of state.

Sometimes, too, women's rights have been undermined by a social or religious backlash. The revival of Islamic

fundamentalism has had an especially strong impact in countries like Indonesia and Malaysia, where women are expected to cover their bodies and wear the traditional Muslim headdress (see Image 13.8). Even in non-Muslim countries, women are expected to behave demurely and exercise discretion in all contacts with the opposite sex.

13-2f Cultural Trends

In most countries in Southeast Asia, writers, artists, and composers are attempting to synthesize international styles and themes with local tradition and experience. The novel has become increasingly popular as writers seek to find the best medium to encapsulate the dramatic changes that have taken place in the region in recent decades.

The best-known writer in postwar Indonesia—at least to readers abroad—was Pramoedya Toer (1925–2006). Born in eastern Java, he joined the Indonesian nationalist

IMAGE 13.8 Behind the Veil. Until fairly recently, women in Muslim-majority countries in Southeast Asia have tended to dress in the manner that had existed in colonial and pre-colonial times. But since the Iranian Revolution of 1979 (see Chapter 15), Muslim women all over Asia have begun to follow stricter dress codes in imitation of practices in the Middle East. While full-body coverings like the burka and the chador are rarely seen in the region, head scarves are commonplace. In the image shown here, a group of young girls from a Muslim school on the Malaysian island of Penang pay a tourist visit to the city of Malacca, once a major entrepot for the spice trade with Europe. The bright colors of their footwear and handbags offer a startling contrast with the jet black of their cloaks.

 Do you believe that a veil or a full body covering is inherently demeaning to a woman, or do you feel that women in any society should be allowed to dress as they please, or in accordance with religious tradition?

movement in his early twenties. Arrested in 1965 on the charge of being a Communist, he spent the next several years in prison. While incarcerated, he began writing his four-volume *Buru Quartet*, which recounts in fictional form the story of the struggle of the Indonesian people for freedom from colonial rule and the autocratic regimes of the independence period.

Among the most talented of contemporary Vietnamese novelists is Duong Thu Huong (b. 1947). A onetime member of the Vietnamese Communist Party who served on the front lines during the Sino-Vietnamese war in 1979, she later became outspoken in her criticism of the party's failure to carry out democratic reforms and was briefly imprisoned in 1991. Undaunted by official pressure, she

has written several novels that express the horrors experienced by guerrilla fighters during the Vietnam War and the cruel injustices perpetrated by the regime in the cause of building socialism. She has recently written a fictional biography of Ho Chi Minh entitled *The Zenith* (2012).

13-2g A Region in Flux

Today, the Western image of a Southeast Asia mired in the Vietnam conflict and the tensions of the Cold War has become a distant memory. In ASEAN, the states in the region have created the framework for a regional organization that can serve their common political, economic, technological, and security interests. A few members of ASEAN are already on the road to advanced development. The remainder are showing some indications of undergoing a similar process within the next generation. Although ethnic and religious tensions continue to exist in most ASEAN states, there are promising signs of increasing political stability and pluralism throughout the region.

To be sure, there are challenges to overcome. The financial crisis that erupted in the fall of 2008 continues to test the resilience of local economies that depend on robust foreign markets for their exports. Myanmar is only beginning to emerge from a long period of isolation and is still mired in a state of chronic underdevelopment. The Indochinese countries remain potentially unstable and have not been fully integrated into the region as a whole. Finally, terrorist activity, especially in Indonesia, has not been brought to an end. Although most Muslims in Southeast Asia have traditionally embraced moderate political, social, and religious views, radical agitators have made inroads through the increasing numbers of Muslim schools, many of them financed by fundamentalist Islamic groups in the Middle East, in the region.

All things considered, however, the situation is more promising today than would have seemed possible half a century ago. For the most part, the nations of Southeast Asia have put aside the bitter legacy of the colonial era and appear capable of coordinating their efforts to erase the internal divisions and conflicts that have brought so much tragedy to the peoples of the region for centuries. Most have abandoned the bitter divisions of the Cold War to embrace the wave of globalization that has been sweeping the world in recent years.

MAKING CONNECTIONS

At the beginning of the twentieth century, virtually all of South and Southeast Asia was under colonial rule. The regional economy was primarily rural and based on the export of natural resources, the local population was mainly poor and illiterate, and power and influence resided in a colonial authority or a discredited ruling elite. The once-vibrant region that had historically served as the fulcrum of the Eurasian supercontinent, uniting great empires from the Mediterranean Sea to the shores of the Pacific in a global network for the exchange of goods, technology, and ideas had declined into a sleepy "periphery," a backdoor to the "center" of global power and influence, then located in Western Europe.

Today, many of the nations in Asia have passed through the stage of industrialization and a few have taken their places in the forefront of the technological age. In parts of the region, a younger generation is proving to be as adept at mastering the challenges of new information technology as their counterparts in the United States and Western Europe. To many observers today, British poet Rudyard Kipling's famous phrase, "East is East and West is West, and ne'er the twain shall meet," seems both racially colorblind and a gross failure to recognize the ability of societies to adapt themselves to changing circumstances.

A closer look at the situation, however, reveals that there remain some significant differences between the independent nations of southern Asia and the advanced societies in the West. Whereas most of Europe and the Western hemisphere is now fully industrialized and well embarked into the next stage of technological revolution, significant segments of the population in southern Asia—and especially in rural areas—are still living in pre-industrial conditions, a reality which will make it much more difficult for governments to carry out measures to eliminate poverty and prepare their society for the transformation into the industrial age. Not every Asian nation can become a Little Tiger.

At the same time, the tenacity of tradition is arguably stronger in many Asian countries than it is in the West. After all, the Industrial Revolution in Europe emerged from within European tradition, rather than being imported from the outside, as was the case in much of Asia. The values and institutions that characterized traditional Asian societies were a product of internal conditions and many of them have survived, even under the impact of globalization. The fact is, culture still matters, and Asians, like Europeans and Americans, will each seek to adopt their own path into an uncertain future.

Still, for the moment the trend lines are clear. Barring unforeseen events, the nations of Asia are currently on a path to evolve in a manner similar to, if not identical with, their counterparts in Europe and the Western Hemisphere. In so doing, Asia is preparing to take its place in the forefront of human achievement, a position the continent had proudly occupied prior to the Industrial Revolution in Europe. The powerful force of globalization, combined with the countervailing efforts on the part of those who are determined to resist it, is now a common phenomenon that unites East and West, for good or for ill.

Whether the current trends will continue to remain in effect, of course, is the key issue here. So far, the Industrial and Technological Revolutions of the past two centuries have driven the trajectory of human civilization in the direction of globalization, but in the process they have given birth to the emergence of powerful countervailing forces throughout the world. We will discuss this issue in more detail in the final chapter of this book.

REFLECTION QUESTIONS

Q How have the nations of South and Southeast Asia dealt with the challenge of integrating their ethnic and religious minorities into their multi-ethnic societies? Have some nations done better than others?

Q How has independence affected the role of women in contemporary South and Southeast Asia? How does their role compare with that in other parts of the world?

Q What kinds of environmental problems do the nations of South and Southeast Asia face today? How have the region's governments sought to deal with such challenges? To what degree have they been successful?

CHAPTER TIMELINE

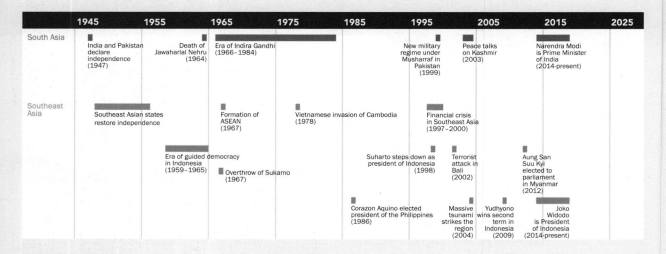

CHAPTER NOTES

1. *New York Times*, May 2, 1996.
2. Quoted in Larry Collins and Dominique Lapierre, *Freedom at Midnight* (New York, 1975), p. 252.
3. Cited in Somini Sengupta, "In World's Largest Democracy, Tolerance Is a Weak Pillar," *New York Times*, October 29, 2008.
4. From Pankaj Mishra, "Impasse in India," New York Review of Books, June 28, 2007, p. 51.

EMERGING AFRICA

Chapter Outline and Focus Questions

14-1 Uhuru: *The Struggle for Independence in Africa*

Q What role did nationalist movements play in the transition to independence in Africa, and how did such movements differ from their counterparts elsewhere?

14-2 *The Era of Independence*

Q In what diverse ways has the emergence of independent states affected the peoples of Africa? What explains the different strategies that various African leaders have adopted in seeking to carry out their nation's destiny?

14-3 *Continuity and Change in Modern African Societies*

Q How would you compare living conditions in Africa with those that you have observed in South and Southeast Asia? What accounts for the differences?

IMAGE 14.1 Morning in Timbuktu

William J. Duiker

Connections to Today

In what ways has the modern history of Africa differed from other parts of the world? How have these differences affected the situation on the continent today?

ON TAKING OVER THE CITY, they began to terrorize the inhabitants—cutting off the hands of suspected thieves, stoning adulterous couples to death, forbidding the playing of any kind of musical instrument, and desecrating the shrines of local Sufi mystics. The invaders were probably fanatical Berber warriors who sought to impose their strict version of Islam on the population throughout the region. The city was Timbuktu, once a fabled caravan stop on a major trade route snaking through the Sahara and more recently a sleepy river port in the central African country of Mali. The time was January 2013.

Timbuktu lies in the **Sahel**, a grassy region just south of the Sahara that stretches from the western tip of the African continent to the Nile River valley in the east. A geographic fault line between the arid desert and the rich tropical forest lands along the Atlantic coast to the south, it has historically marked the division between predominantly Muslim pastoral peoples to the north and farming communities, many of them Christians or followers of indigenous faiths, to the south. When these areas were placed under European rule in the late nineteenth century,

345

colonial authorities ignored these cultural and environmental differences and drew their boundary lines based simply on the extent of their conquests.

In recent times the Sahel has become a political and ideological battleground as well, as Muslim pastoralists compete with Christian and animist farmers for scarce fertile land and access to precious water reserves. The struggle has been going on for centuries, but it has intensified in recent years as a result of the increasing desiccation of the region. As grasslands dry up along the edge of the Sahara, pastoral peoples are forced to move southward in search of adequate pasture lands, where they encounter agriculturalists reluctant to give up their farms. It is one of the political and environmental challenges that many nations in Africa face today.

14-1 *UHURU:* THE STRUGGLE FOR INDEPENDENCE IN AFRICA

 Focus Question: What role did nationalist movements play in the transition to independence in Africa, and how did such movements differ from their counterparts elsewhere?

After World War II, some European governments reluctantly recognized that the end result of colonial rule in Africa would be African self-government, if not full independence. The war had imposed enormous strains on the economies of the colonial countries, and the costs of maintaining their empires had become prohibitive. Accordingly, in their view, colonial rule had to be brought to an end and the African population would have to be trained to handle the responsibilities of representative government. As a result, during the 1950s most British colonies introduced reforms that increased the representation of the local population. Members of legislative and executive councils were increasingly chosen through elections, and Africans came to constitute a majority of these bodies. Elected councils at the local level were introduced in 1950s to reduce the power of the chiefs and clan heads, who had controlled local government under indirect rule. An exception was South Africa, where full European domination continued. In the Union of South Africa, the franchise was restricted to whites except in the former territory of the Cape Colony, where persons of mixed ancestry had enjoyed the right to vote since the mid-nineteenth century. Black Africans did win some limited electoral rights in Northern and Southern Rhodesia (now Zambia and

Zimbabwe, respectively), although whites generally dominated the political scene.

A similar process of political liberalization was taking place in the French colonies. At first, the French tried to integrate the African peoples living under the French flag—or at least their traditional elites—into French culture. By the 1920s, however, racist beliefs in Western cultural superiority and the tenacity of traditional beliefs and practices among Africans had somewhat discredited this ideal (see Chapter 2). The French therefore substituted a more limited program of assigning a limited number of French-educated elites as administrators at the local level as a link to the rest of the population. The remaining European colonial powers, notably Belgium and Portugal, made little effort to prepare their subject peoples in the Congo and southern Africa for independence.

14-1a The Colonial Legacy

As in Asia, colonial rule had a mixed impact on the societies and peoples of Africa. The Western presence brought some short-term and long-term benefits to Africa, such as improved transportation and communication facilities, and in a few areas laid the foundation for a modern industrial and commercial sector. Improved sanitation and medical care increased life expectancy. The introduction of some modern schools and selective elements of Western political systems laid the groundwork for the future creation of democratic societies.

Yet the benefits of westernization were distributed very unequally, and the vast majority of Africans found their lives little improved, if at all (see Chapter 2). Many suffered under harsh European colonial regimes. Only South Africa and French-held Algeria, for example, developed modern industrial sectors, extensive railroad networks, and modern communications systems. In both countries, European settlers were numerous, most investment capital for industrial ventures was European, and whites comprised almost the entire professional and managerial class. Members of the local population were generally restricted to unskilled or semiskilled jobs at wages less than one-fifth of those enjoyed by Europeans.

Many colonies concentrated on export crops—peanuts in Senegal and Gambia, cotton in Egypt and Uganda, coffee in Kenya, palm oil and cocoa products in the Gold Coast. In some cases, the crops were grown on plantations, which were usually owned by Europeans. But plantation agriculture was not always suitable in Africa, and much farming was done by free or tenant farmers. In some areas, where land ownership was traditionally vested in the community, the land was owned and leased by the corporate village. The vast majority of the profits from the exports, however, accrued to Europeans or to merchants from other foreign countries, such as India and the Arab emirates.

While a fortunate few benefited from the increase in exports, the vast majority of Africans continued to be subsistence farmers growing food for their own consumption. The gap was particularly wide in places like Kenya, where the best lands were reserved for European settlers to make the colony self-sufficient. As in other parts of the world, the early stages of the Industrial Revolution were especially painful for the rural population, and ordinary subsistence farmers reaped few benefits from colonial rule. Thousands were pressed into gang labor to work on plantations or infrastructure projects. To make matters worse, in some areas—notably in West Africa—the cultivation of cash crops eroded the fragile soil base and turned farmland into desert.

14-1b The Rise of Nationalism

Political organizations for African rights did not arise until after World War I, and then only in a few areas, such as British-ruled Kenya and the Gold Coast. At first, organizations such as the National Congress of British West Africa (formed in 1919 in the Gold Coast) and Jomo Kenyatta's Kikuyu Central Association focused on improving living conditions in the colonies rather than on national independence. After World War II, however, following the example of independence movements elsewhere, these groups became organized political parties with independence as their objective. In the Gold Coast, Kwame Nkrumah (1909–1972) led the Convention People's Party, the first formal political party in black Africa. In the late 1940s, Jomo Kenyatta (1894–1978) founded the Kenya African National Union (KANU), which focused on economic issues but had an implied political agenda as well.

For the most part, these political activities were nonviolent in their tactics and were led by Western-educated African intellectuals. Their constituents were primarily urban professionals, merchants, and members of labor unions. But the demand for independence was not entirely restricted to the cities. In Kenya, for example, the widely publicized Mau Mau movement among the Kikuyu people used guerrilla tactics as an element of its program to achieve *uhuru* (Swahili for "freedom") from the British. One of the primary reasons for the revolt was to protest against the unlawful seizure of African lands by European plantation owners. In an initial uprising in 1952, the Mau Mau killed about 100 Europeans and an estimated 2,000 Africans. The specter of a nationwide revolt alarmed the European population and led the Kenyan colonial government to declare an official emergency in 1952. In the subsequent fighting, which lasted into 1956, about 600 soldiers and policemen and 2,000 civilians were killed, along with about 10,000 Mau Mau. The emergency ended in 1959, and Kenyan independence came in 1963. Yet the scale of the conflict is only recently becoming publicly known. In 2011, the Kenyan Human Rights Commission alleged that more than 90,000 Kenyans were executed, tortured, or mutilated by security forces during the emergency, and that perhaps 160,000 were detained in poor conditions. The recent discovery of secret British colonial archives from the Kenyan Emergency, revealed during recent court cases brought by Kenyans against the British government, has confirmed some of these allegations.

In South Africa and Algeria, where the political system was also dominated by European settlers, the transition to independence was more complicated. In South Africa, political activity by African peoples began with the formation of the African National Congress (ANC) in 1912. Initially, the **ANC** was dominated by Western-oriented intellectuals and had limited mass support. Its goal was to achieve economic and political reforms, including full equality for educated Africans, within the framework of the existing system. Some of its key leaders had been influenced by Mohandas Gandhi and his program of nonviolence. But the ANC's efforts to protect African land rights and to gain voting rights met with little success, while conservative white parties managed to stiffen the segregation laws and impose a policy of full legal segregation, called **apartheid**, in 1948. In response, the ANC became increasingly radicalized, and by the 1950s, many ANC leaders such as Nelson Mandela had given up on the non-violent approach and decided to adopt the strategy of workers' strikes, demonstrations, and civil disobedience. Nelson Mandela was arrested and sentenced to life in prison.

In Algeria, resistance to French rule by Berbers and Arabs in rural areas had never ceased. After World War II, urban agitation intensified, leading to a widespread rebellion against colonial rule in the mid-1950s. At first, the French government tried to maintain its authority in Algeria, which was considered an integral part of metropolitan France. But when Charles de Gaulle became president of France in 1958, he reversed French policy, and Algeria became an independent republic four years later, with Ahmad Ben Bella (1918–2004) as its president. The armed struggle in Algeria hastened the transition to statehood in its neighbors as well. Tunisia won its independence in 1956 after some urban agitation and rural unrest but retained close ties with Paris. The French attempted

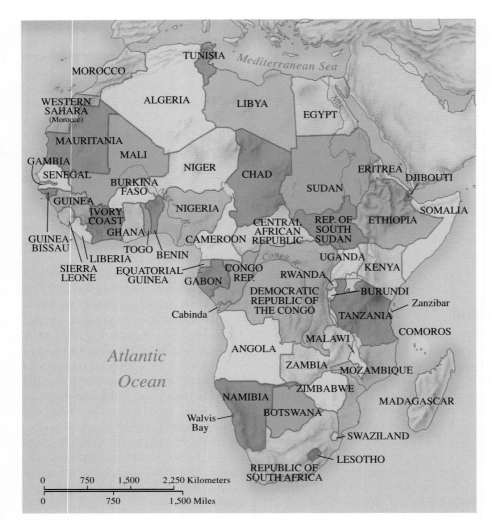

MAP 14.1 Contemporary Africa. This map shows the independent states of Africa today.

 Why was the goal of African unity so difficult to achieve after the rise of independent states?

to suppress the nationalist movement in French Morocco by sending Sultan Muhammad V into exile, but the effort failed, and in 1956, he returned as the ruler of the independent state of Morocco.

Most black African nations achieved their independence in the late 1950s and 1960s, beginning with the Gold Coast, renamed Ghana, in 1957 (see Map 14.1). It was soon followed by Nigeria; the Belgian Congo, renamed Zaire and then the Democratic Republic of the Congo; Kenya; Tanganyika, later joined with Zanzibar and renamed Tanzania; and several other countries. Most of the French colonies agreed to accept independence within the framework of de Gaulle's French Community. By the late 1960s, only parts of southern Africa and the Portuguese possessions of Mozambique and Angola remained under European rule.

Independence thus came later to Africa than to most of Asia. Several factors help explain the delay. For one

thing, colonialism was established in Africa somewhat later than in most areas of Asia, and the inevitable reaction from the local population was consequently later in coming. Furthermore, with the exception of a few areas in West Africa and along the Mediterranean, coherent states with a strong sense of cultural, ethnic, and linguistic unity did not exist in most of Africa during precolonial times. Most traditional states, such as Ashanti in West Africa, Songhai in the southern Sahara, and Kongo in the Congo River basin, were collections of heterogeneous peoples with little sense of national or cultural unity. Even after colonies were established, the European powers often practiced a policy of "divide and rule," and the British encouraged political decentralization by retaining the authority of the traditional local chieftains. It is hardly surprising that when opposition to colonial rule emerged, unity was difficult to achieve.

14-2 THE ERA OF INDEPENDENCE

 Focus Questions: In what diverse ways has the emergence of independent states affected the peoples of Africa? What explains the different strategies that various African leaders have adopted in seeking to carry out their nation's destiny?

The newly independent African states faced intimidating challenges. They had been profoundly affected by colonial rule, but for the most part, the experience had been detrimental to their interests. Although Western political institutions, values, and technology had been introduced, the exposure to European civilization had been superficial at best for most Africans and tragic for many. At the outset of independence, most African societies were still primarily agrarian and traditional, and their modern sectors depended mainly on imports from the West.

HISTORIANS DEBATE 14-2a The Destiny of Africa: Unity or Diversity?

Like their counterparts in South and Southeast Asia, most of Africa's new leaders came from the urban middle class. They had studied in Europe or the United States and spoke and read European languages. Although most were profoundly critical of colonial policies, they had been influenced by Western civilization and appeared for the most part to accept the Western model of governance and Western democratic values.

Their views on economics were somewhat more diverse. Some, like Jomo Kenyatta of Kenya and General Mobutu Sese Seko (1930–1997) of Zaire, were advocates of Western-style capitalism. Others, like Julius Nyerere (1922–1999) of Tanzania, Kwame Nkrumah of Ghana, and Sékou Touré (1922–1984) of Guinea, preferred an "African form of socialism," which bore scant resemblance to the Marxist-Leninist socialism practiced in the Soviet Union. According to its advocates, it was descended from traditional communal practices in precolonial Africa.

At first, most of the new African leaders accepted the national boundaries established during the colonial era. But as we have noted, these boundaries were artificial creations of the colonial powers. Virtually all of the new states included widely diverse ethnic, linguistic, and territorial groups. Zaire, for example, was composed of more than 200 territorial groups speaking seventy-five different languages. For some African observers, the fact that the continent was not historically divided into a number of clearly defined nation-states suggested that a different pattern might be appropriate for African peoples as they entered a new stage of independence. After all, they reasoned, the power of nationalism in Europe had been a double-edged sword—it had united diverse peoples according to their cultural or ethnic identity but then divided them into squabbling contestants for control over territory and resources. The result had been two disastrous world wars.

Pan-Africanism was a theory that originated among a number of African intellectuals during the first half of the twentieth century. A basic component of the idea was the conviction that there was a distinctive "African personality" that owed nothing to Western materialism and provided a common sense of destiny for all black African peoples. According to Aimé Césaire, a West Indian of African descent and a leading ideologist of the movement, while Western civilization prized rational thought and material achievement, African culture emphasized emotional expression and common sense of humanity.

The concept of a unique African destiny—known to its originators by the French term *négritude*, or "blackness" (a concept on which the English-language "Black is Beautiful" movement was based)—was in part a natural defensive response to the social Darwinist concept of Western racial superiority that was popular in Europe and the United States during the early years of the twentieth century. But the pan-African movement was also stimulated by growing self-doubt among many European intellectuals after World War I, who feared that Western civilization was a path of self-destruction. To such critics of Western civilization, the Western drive for economic profit and political hegemony was like a plague that threatened ultimately to destroy all civilization. To like-minded African intellectuals like Aimé Césaire, it was the obligation of Africans to use their own humanistic and spiritual qualities to help save the human race. In his words:

> Those who invented neither gunpowder nor compass
> those who tamed neither steam nor electricity
> those who explored neither sea nor sky
> but those who know the humblest corners of the country suffering
> those whose only journeys were uprooting
> those who went to sleep on their knees
> those who were domesticated and christianized
> those who were inoculated with degeneration.[1]

The idea had more appeal to Africans from French colonies than to those from British possessions. Yet it also found some adherents in the British colonies, as well as in the United States and elsewhere in the Americas. African-American intellectuals such as W.E.B. Dubois and George Padmore and the West Indian politician Marcus Garvey attempted to promote a "black renaissance" by popularizing the idea of a distinct African personality.

Toward African Unity

 What are the key objectives expressed in this charter? To what degree have they been achieved?

Interaction & Exchange **IN MAY 1963,** the leaders of thirty-two African states met in Addis Ababa, the capital of Ethiopia, to discuss the creation of an organization that would represent the interests of all newly independent African countries. The result was the Organization of African Unity. An excerpt from its charter is presented here. Although the organization did not realize all of its founders' aspirations, it provided a useful forum for the discussion and resolution of common problems. In 2001, it was replaced by the African Union, which was designed to bring about increased cooperation among the states on the continent; unlike the OAU, the African Union has recognized the need on occasion to intervene in the internal affairs of member nations.

Charter of the Organization of African Unity

We, the Heads of African States and Governments assembled in the City of Addis Ababa, Ethiopia;

CONVINCED that it is the inalienable right of all people to control their own destiny;

CONSCIOUS of the fact that freedom, equality, justice, and dignity are essential objectives for the achievement of the legitimate aspirations of the African peoples;

CONSCIOUS of our responsibility to harness the natural and human resources of our continent for the total advancement of our peoples in spheres of human endeavor;

INSPIRED by a common determination to promote understanding among our peoples and cooperation among our States in response to the aspirations of our peoples for brotherhood and solidarity, in a larger unity transcending ethnic and national differences;

CONVINCED that, in order to translate this determination into a dynamic force in the cause of human progress, conditions for peace and security must be established and maintained;

DETERMINED to safeguard and consolidate the hard-won independence as well as the sovereignty and territorial integrity of our States, and to fight against neocolonialism in all its forms;

DEDICATED to the general progress of Africa; . . .

DESIROUS that all African States should henceforth unite so that the welfare and well-being of their peoples can be assured;

RESOLVED to reinforce the links between our states by establishing and strengthening common institutions;

HAVE agreed to the present Charter.

Source: J. Woronoff, *Organizing African Unity* (Scarecrow Press, 1980), pp. 642–649.

A number of African political leaders—including Nkrumah of Ghana, Touré of Guinea, and Kenyatta of Kenya—were also enticed by the dream of **Pan-Africanism**, a concept of continental unity that transcended national boundaries and, with their encouragement, was to find its first concrete manifestation in the Organization of African Unity (OAU), which was founded in Addis Ababa, Ethiopia in 1963 (see Historical Voices, "Toward African Unity," above).

14-2b Dream and Reality: Political and Economic Conditions in Independent Africa

The program of the OAU called for an Africa based on freedom, equality, justice, and dignity and on the unity, solidarity, prosperity, and territorial integrity of African states. It did not take long for reality to set in. Vast disparities in education and wealth and the lingering effects of colonial domination made it hard to establish material prosperity in much of Africa. Expectations that independence would lead to stable political structures based on "one person, one vote" were soon disappointed as the initial phase of pluralistic governments gave way to a series of military regimes and one-party states. Between 1957 and 1982, more than seventy leaders of African countries were overthrown by violence, and the pace has not abated in recent years.

The Problem of Neocolonialism Part of the problem could be (and was) ascribed to the residual impact of colonialism. Most new countries in Africa were dependent on the export of a single crop or natural resource. When prices fluctuated or dropped, these countries were at the mercy of international markets. In several cases, the resources were

HISTORICAL VOICES

Stealing the Nation's Riches

 According to Ayi Kwei Armah, who was to blame for conditions in his country?

Art & Ideas   **AFTER 1965, AFRICAN NOVELISTS** transferred their anger from the foreign oppressor to their own national leaders, deploring their greed, corruption, and inhumanity. One of the most pessimistic expressions of this betrayal of newly independent Africa is found in *The Beautiful Ones Are Not Yet Born*, a novel published by the Ghanaian author Ayi Kwei Armah in 1968. The author decried the government of Kwame Nkrumah and was unimpressed with the rumors of a military coup, which, he predicted, would simply replace the regime with a new despot and his entourage of "fat men." Ghana today has made significant progress in reducing the level of corruption.

Ayi Kwei Armah, *The Beautiful Ones Are Not Yet Born*

The net had been made in the special Ghanaian way that allowed the really big corrupt people to pass through it. A net to catch only the small, dispensable fellows, trying in their anguished blindness to leap and to attain the gleam and the comfort the only way these things could be done. And the big ones floated free, like all the slogans. End bribery and corruption. Build Socialism. Equality. Shit. A man would just have to make up his mind that there was never going to be anything but despair, and there would be no way of escaping it. . . .

In the life of the nation itself, maybe nothing really new would happen. New men would take into their hands the power to steal the nation's riches and to use it for their own satisfaction. That, of course, was to be expected. New people would use the country's power to get rid of men and women who talked a language that did not flatter them. There would be nothing different in that. That would only be a continuation of the Ghanaian way of life. But here was the real change. The individual man of power now shivering, his head filled with the fear of the vengeance of those he had wronged. For him everything was going to change. And for those like him who had grown greasy and fat singing the praises of their chief, for those who had been getting themselves ready for the enjoyment of hoped-for favors, there would be long days of pain ahead. The flatterers with their new white Mercedes cars would have to find ways of burying old words. For those who had come directly against the old power, there would be much happiness. But for the nation itself there would only be a change of embezzlers and a change of the hunters and the hunted. A pitiful shrinking of the world from those days Teacher still looked back to, when the single mind was filled with the hopes of a whole people. A pitiful shrinking, to days when all the powerful could think of was to use the power of a whole people to fill their own paunches. Endless days, same days, stretching into the future with no end anywhere in sight.

Source: From *The Beautiful Ones Are Not Yet Born* by Ayi Kwei Armah (Heinemann, 1989).

---

still controlled by foreigners, leading to the charge that colonialism had been succeeded by **neocolonialism**, in which Western domination was maintained primarily by economic rather than political or military means. To make matters worse, most African states had to import technology and manufactured goods from the West, and the prices of those goods rose more rapidly than those of their export products.

In some cases, the new states contributed to their own problems. Scarce national resources were squandered on military equipment or expensive consumer goods rather than used to create the infrastructure needed to support and sustain an industrial economy. Corruption, a painful reality throughout the modern world, became almost a way of life in Africa as bribery became necessary to obtain even the most basic services (see Historical Voices, "Stealing the Nation's Riches," above).

External Interference, Internal Division Many of the problems encountered by the new nations of Africa were also ascribed to the fact that independence did not bring an end to Western interference in Africa's political affairs. During the Cold War, both superpowers routinely interfered in the internal affairs of African states, notably when the United States engineered the overthrow of the leftist leader Patrice Lumumba (1925–1961) in the Congo, and the Soviet Union similarly interfered in Ethiopia and Angola. Most African countries adopted a neutral stance in the Cold War, but competition between Moscow and

Washington throughout the region was fierce, often undermining the efforts of fragile governments to build stable new nations.

To make matters worse, new African nations had difficulty achieving a united position on many issues, and their disagreements left the region vulnerable to external influence and conflict. Border disputes festered in many areas of the continent, and in some cases flared into outright war—as in Morocco (where a rebel movement in the Western Sahara fought against Moroccan control), in the Horn of Africa (where Muslim guerrillas fought against the Christian government in Ethiopia), and between Kenya and Uganda in a dispute over boundaries in the lake district of East Africa.

The concept of nationhood was also undermined by the lingering force of regionalism or ethnic rivalries. Nigeria, with the largest population on the continent, was rent by civil strife during the late 1960s when dissident Ibo groups in the southeast attempted unsuccessfully to form the independent state of Biafra. Another force undermining nationalism in Africa was that of **pan-Islamism**. Its prime exponent in Africa was the Libyan president Muammar Qaddafi (1942–2011), whose ambitions to create a greater Muslim nation in the Sahara under his authority led to conflict with neighboring Chad. Pan-Islamic ideas have also recently surfaced in Nigeria and other nations of West Africa, where divisions between Muslims and Christians have recently erupted into violence (see "Tensions in the Desert," p. 356).

The Population Bomb Finally, rapid population growth has crippled efforts to create modern economies. By the 1980s, annual population growth averaged nearly 3 percent throughout Africa, the highest rate of any continent. Unfortunately, drought conditions and the inexorable spread of the Sahara (usually known as **desertification**), caused partly by overcultivation of the land, led to widespread hunger and starvation, first in West African countries such as Niger and Mali and then in Ethiopia, Somalia, and the Sudan (see Image 14.2).

Predictions are that the population of Africa will increase by at least 200 million over the next ten years, but that estimate does not take into account the prevalence of AIDS, which has reached epidemic proportions in Africa. According to a United Nations study, at least 5 percent of the entire population of sub-Saharan Africa is infected with the virus, including a high percentage of the urban middle class. Some observers estimate that without measures to curtail the effects of the disease, it will have a significant impact on several African countries by reducing population growth.

Although economic growth has quickened in recent years, poverty is still widespread in Africa, particularly

IMAGE 14.2 Manioc, Food for the Millions. Manioc (also called cassava or yuca), a tuber like the potato, was brought to Africa from South America soon after the voyages of Columbus. Although low in nutrient value, it can be cultivated in poor soil with little moisture and is the staple food for nearly one-third of the population of sub-Saharan Africa. Manioc is also widely grown in tropical parts of Asia and South America and is familiar to Westerners as the source of tapioca. In this photograph, village women in Senegal, dressed in the colorful clothing so characteristic throughout the continent, rhythmically pound manioc to remove traces of naturally occurring cyanide that would otherwise poison those who rely on the tuber as a basic commodity. As the threat of chronic drought becomes an ever more common reality in parts of Africa, dry crops like manioc will acquire increasing importance in the diet of the African people.

 What types of staple foods can you think of that are widely cultivated in other parts of the world for the purpose of providing sustenance to the local population?

among the three-quarters of the population still living off the land. Urban areas have grown tremendously, but as in much of Asia, most are surrounded by massive squatter settlements of rural peoples who have fled to the cities in search of a better life. The expansion of the cities has overwhelmed fragile transportation and sanitation systems and led to rising pollution and perpetual traffic jams, while millions are forced to live without running water and electricity. Meanwhile, the fortunate few (all too often government officials on the take) live the high life and emulate the consumerism of the West (in a particularly expressive phrase, the rich in many East African countries are known as *wabenzi*, or "Mercedes-Benz people").

In "Pedestrian, to Passing Benz-Man," the Kenyan poet Albert Ojuka voiced the popular discontent with economic inequality in the 1970s:

You man, lifted gently
out of the poverty and suffering

we so recently shared; I say—
why splash the muddy puddle on to
my bare legs, as if, still unsatisfied
with your seated opulence
you must sully the unwashed
with your diesel-smoke and mud-water
and force him to buy, beyond his means
a bar of soap from your shop?
A few years back we shared a master
today you have none, while I have
exchanged a parasite for something worse.
But maybe a few years is too long a time.[2]

It is a lament still voiced today.

14-2c The Search for Solutions

While the problems of nation building described here have to one degree or another afflicted all of the emerging states of Africa, each has sought to deal with the challenge in its own way, sometimes with strikingly different consequences. Some African countries have made dramatic improvements in the past two decades, but others have encountered increasing difficulties. Despite all its shared problems, Africa today remains one of the most diverse regions of the globe.

Tanzania: An African Route to Socialism   Concern over the dangers of economic inequality inspired a number of African leaders to restrict foreign investment and nationalize the major industries and utilities while promoting democratic ideals and values. Julius Nyerere of Tanzania was the most consistent, promoting the ideals of socialism and self-reliance through his Arusha Declaration of 1967, which set forth the principles for building a socialist society in Africa. Nyerere did not seek to establish a Leninist-style dictatorship of the proletariat in Tanzania, but neither was he a proponent of a multiparty democracy, which in his view would be divisive under the conditions prevailing in Africa:

> Where there is one party—provided it is identified with
> the nation as a whole—the foundations of democracy
> can be firmer, and the people can have more opportunity
> to exercise a real choice, than when you have two or
> more parties.

To import the Western parliamentary system into Africa, he argued, could lead to violence because the opposition parties would be viewed as traitors by the majority of the population.[3]

Taking advantage of his powerful political influence, Nyerere placed limits on income and established village collectives to avoid the corrosive effects of economic inequality and government corruption. Sympathetic foreign countries provided considerable economic aid to assist the experiment, and many observers noted that levels of corruption, political instability, and ethnic strife were lower in Tanzania than in many other African countries. Nyerere's vision was not shared by all of his compatriots, however. Political elements on the island of Zanzibar, citing the stagnation brought by two decades of socialism, agitated for autonomy or even total separation from the mainland. Tanzania also has poor soil, inadequate rainfall, and limited resources, all of which have contributed to its slow growth and continuing rural and urban poverty (see Historical Voices, "Socialism Is Not Racialism," p. 354).

In 1985, Nyerere voluntarily retired from the presidency. In his farewell speech, he confessed that he had failed to achieve many of his ambitious goals to create a socialist society in Africa. In particular, he admitted that his plan to collectivize the traditional private farm (*shamba*) had run into strong resistance from conservative peasants. "You can socialize what is not traditional," he remarked. "The *shamba* can't be socialized." But Nyerere insisted that many of his policies had succeeded in improving social and economic conditions, and he argued that the only real solution was to consolidate the multitude of small countries in the region into a larger East African Federation. Today, a quarter of a century later, Nyerere's party, the Party of the Revolution, continues to rule the country.

Kenya: The Perils of Capitalism   The countries that opted for capitalism faced their own dilemmas. Neighboring Kenya, blessed with better soil in the highlands, a local tradition of aggressive commerce, and a residue of European settlers, welcomed foreign investment and profit incentives. The results have been mixed. Kenya has a strong current of indigenous African capitalism and a substantial middle class, mostly based in the capital, Nairobi. But landlessness, unemployment, and income inequities are high, even by African standards (almost one-fifth of the country's 41 million people are squatters, and unemployment is currently estimated at 40 percent). The rate of population growth—about 2.5 percent annually—is one of the higher rates in the world. Almost 80 percent of the population remains rural, and 50 percent of the people live below the poverty line. The result has been widespread unrest in a country formerly admired for its successful development.

Kenya's problems have been exacerbated by chronic disputes between disparate ethnic groups and simmering tensions between farmers and pastoralists, leading some to question whether the country is capable of achieving political stability. For many years, the country maintained a fragile stability under the dictatorial rule of President Daniel arap Moi (b. 1924), one of the most authoritarian of African leaders.

Socialism Is Not Racialism

 How does African socialism, as described in this excerpt, compare with the version practiced in the Soviet Union and in China today? What are the key differences?

Politics & Government **AT ARUSHA, TANZANIA, IN 1967,** Julius Nyerere, the president of Tanzania, set forth the principles of building a socialist society in Africa. An African style of socialism, he explained, would put the country's wealth in the hands of the people rather than in the hands of foreign capitalists. Under Nyerere and his successors, the country has taken a socialist approach to economic development. The results have been mixed: the country is not wealthy, but there are few extremes of wealth and poverty.

Julius Nyerere, The Arusha Declaration

The Arusha Declaration and the actions relating to public ownership were all concerned with ensuring that we can build socialism in our country. The nationalization and the taking of a controlling interest in many firms were a necessary part of our determination to organize our society in such a way that our efforts benefit all of our people and that there is no exploitation of one many by another.

Yet these actions do not in themselves create socialism . . . The basis of socialism is a belief in the oneness of man and the common historical destiny of mankind. Its basis, in other words, is human equality.

Acceptance of this principle is absolutely fundamental to socialism. The justification of socialism is Man—not the State, not the flag. Socialism is not for the benefit of black men, nor brown men, nor white men, nor yellow men. The purpose of socialism is the service of man, regardless of color, size, shape, skill, ability, or anything else . . .

Socialism has nothing to do with race, nor with country or origin. In fact any intelligent man, whether he is a socialist or not, realizes that there are socialists in capitalist countries—and from capitalist countries. Very often such socialists come to work in newly independent and avowedly socialist countries like Tanzania because they are frustrated in their capitalist homeland . . .

Neither is it sensible for a socialist to talk as if all capitalists are devils. It is one thing to dislike the capitalist system and to try and frustrate people's capitalist desires. But it would as stupid for us to assume that capitalists have horns as it is for people in Western Europe to assume that we in Tanzania have become devils.

In fact the leaders in the capitalist countries have now begun to realize that communists are human beings like themselves—that they are not devils. It would be very absurd if we react to the stupidity they are growing out of and become equally stupid ourselves in the opposite direction! We have to recognize in our words and our actions that capitalists are human beings as much as socialists. They may be wrong; indeed by dedicating ourselves to socialism we are saying that they are. But our task is to make it impossible for capitalism to dominate us.

Source: From Julius Nyerere, "The Arusha Declaration" in *Freedomways* (magazine) (Dar es Salaam: Second Quarter, 1970), pp. 124–127.

Plagued by charges of corruption, Moi finally agreed to retire in 2002, but under his successor, Mwai Kibaki (b. 1931), the twin problems of political instability and widespread poverty continue to afflict the country. When presidential elections held in December 2007 led to a victory for Kibaki's party, opposition elements—angered by the government's perceived favoritism toward Kibaki's Kikuyu constituency—launched numerous protests, and violent riots occurred throughout the country. A fragile truce was eventually put in place, but popular anger at current conditions smolders just beneath the surface. In March 2013, another disputed presidential election

resulted in a victory for Uhuru Kenyatta (b. 1961), the son of the country's popular first president. Although Kenyatta's party has been plagued with charges of corruption, ethnic favoritism, and election irregularities, it comfortably won re-election in 2018.

South Africa: An End to Apartheid Perhaps Africa's greatest success story is in South Africa, where the white government, which long maintained a policy of racial segregation (apartheid) and restricted black sovereignty to a series of small "Bantustans" in relatively infertile areas of the country, finally accepted the inevitability of African involvement in the political process and the national economy. A key factor in the decision was growing international pressure in the form of a campaign to persuade foreign investors to withdraw funds from the country. In 1990, the government of President F. W. (Frederik Willem) de Klerk (b. 1936) released African National Congress leader Nelson Mandela (1918–2013) from prison, where he had been held since 1964. In 1993, the two leaders agreed to hold democratic national elections the following spring. In the meantime, ANC representatives agreed to take part in a transitional coalition government with de Klerk's National Party. Those elections resulted in a substantial majority for the ANC, and Mandela became president (see Image 14.3).

In May 1996, a new constitution was approved, calling for a multiracial state. The National Party immediately went into opposition, claiming that the new charter did not adequately provide for joint decision-making by members of the coalition. But the new ANC-dominated government won broad support from many groups within the country, and in 1999, a major step toward political stability was taken when Nelson Mandela stepped down from the presidency and was replaced by his long-time disciple Thabo Mbeki (b. 1942). The new president faced a number of intimidating problems, including rising unemployment, widespread lawlessness, chronic corruption, and an ominous flight of capital and professional personnel from the country. Mbeki's conservative economic policies earned the support of some white voters and the country's new black elite but were criticized by labor unions, which contended that the benefits of the new black leadership were not seeping down to the poor. The government's promises to carry out an extensive land reform program—aimed at providing farmland to the nation's 40 million black farmers—were not fulfilled, leading some squatters to seize unused private lands near Johannesburg.

In 2008, Mbeki was forced out of office by disgruntled ANC party members. A year later, his one-time vice president and rival Jacob Zuma (b. 1942) was elected president. Zuma won reelection six years later, but high unemployment and charges of government corruption have tarnished the image of the ANC, and Zuma was forced to resign. Still, South Africa remains the wealthiest and most

IMAGE 14.3 An End to Apartheid. In 1994, Nelson Mandela, the long-time head of the African National Congress (ANC), was elected president of the Republic of South Africa and the policy of apartheid officially came to an end. Shown here in an iconic photograph, Mandela stands between his predecessor F. W. de Klerk and his chief lieutenant and eventual successor as chief of state, Thabo Mbeki. The ANC remains in power today, twenty-five years later.

 Why do you think Nelson Mandela, a one-time member of a radical organization, was elected as president of South Africa to widespread acclaim?

industrialized state in Africa and the best hope that a multiracial society can succeed on the continent. The country's black elite now number nearly one-quarter of its wealthiest households, compared with only 9 percent in 1991.

Nigeria: A Nation Divided   If the situation in South Africa provides grounds for modest optimism, the situation in Nigeria provides reason for serious concern. Africa's largest country in terms of population and one of its wealthiest because of substantial oil reserves, Nigeria was for many years in the grip of military strongmen. During his rule, General Sani Abacha (1943–1998) ruthlessly suppressed all opposition and in late 1995 ordered the execution of author Ken Saro-Wiwa (1941–1995) despite widespread protests from human rights groups abroad. Saro-Wiwa had criticized environmental damage caused by foreign oil interests in southern Nigeria, but the regime's major concern was his support for separatist activities in the area that had launched the Biafran insurrection in the late 1960s. When Abacha died in 1998 under mysterious circumstances, national elections led to the creation of a civilian government under Olusegun Obasanjo (b. 1937).

Civilian leadership has not been a panacea for Nigeria's problems, however. Although Obasanjo promised reforms to bring an end to the corruption and favoritism that had long plagued Nigerian politics, the results were disappointing (the state power company—known as NEPA— was so inefficient that Nigerians joked that the initials stood for "never expect power again").

Equally serious has been the challenge of resolving the country's territorial and religious disputes. Unified in 1914 into a single colony by the British for their own convenience, Nigeria has been faced since independence with the uneasy reality of a Muslim north and a predominantly Christian south. In early 2000, religious tensions between Christians and Muslims began to escalate when riots broke out in several northern cities as a result of the decision by some Muslim provincial officials to apply strict Islamic law throughout their jurisdictions. Although the violence abated when local officials managed to craft a compromise that limited the application of some of the harsher aspects of Muslim law, it arose again during the presidency of Goodluck Jonathan (b. 1951), a Christian. Churches and mosques were bombed by extremists in the northern sections of the country and massacres took place on both sides of the religious divide. The unrest has been fueled in part by the terrorist activities of **Boko Haram**, an al-Qaeda affiliate active in the region. But after terrorist cells identified with Boko Haram kidnapped thousands of students and converted them to Islam, efforts by the government to recover the victims have been hindered by reports of widespread brutality committed by Nigerian military units on the civilian population. The replacement of Jonathan by the one-time military strongman Muhammadu Buhari in 2015 aroused hopes that a new administration could calm tensions and restore some semblance of order to the country, but so far passions have not diminished; meanwhile, the nation's economy is slumping because of a drop in oil prices.

Tensions in the Desert The religious tensions that erupted in Nigeria have spilled over into neighboring states on the border of the Sahara. Pressure to apply Shari'a has spread to the neighboring state of Mali, where a radical Islamic group has seized power in the northern part of the country, applying strict punishments on local residents for alleged infractions against Shari'a law and destroying Muslim shrines in the historic city of Timbuktu. Unrest in the area is also fomented by the efforts of ethnic Tuareg peoples (related to the Berbers) to obtain independence from the state of Mali. French military units were dispatched to the region in January 2013 and drove the rebels out of the major population centers, but the threat of Islamic radicalism has not subsided.

A similar rift has been at the root of the lengthy civil war in Sudan. Conflict between Muslim pastoralists— supported by the central government in Khartoum—and predominantly Christian black farmers in the southern part of the country raged for years until the government finally agreed to permit a plebiscite in the south under the sponsorship of the United Nations to determine whether the local population there wished to secede from the country. In elections held in early 2011, voters overwhelmingly supported independence as the new nation of the Republic of South Sudan, but tribal disputes and clashes along the disputed border continue to provoke tensions in the region. In 2019, widespread public protests forced the resignation of the long-time dictator Omar Hassan al-Bashir of the Republic of Sudan, but the future remains uncertain.

The dispute between Muslims and Christians throughout the southern Sahara is a contemporary African variant of the traditional tensions that have existed between farmers and pastoralists throughout recorded history. Muslim cattle herders, migrating southward to escape the increasing desiccation of the grasslands south of the Sahara, compete for precious land with primarily Christian farmers. As a result of the religious revival now under way throughout the continent, the confrontation often leads to outbreaks of violence with strong religious and ethnic overtones.

Central Africa: Cauldron of Conflict   But perhaps the most tragic situation took place in the central African states of Rwanda and Burundi, where a chronic conflict between the minority Tutsis and the Hutu majority has led to a bitter civil war, with thousands of refugees fleeing to neighboring Zaire. The predominantly pastoral Tutsis, supported by the colonial Belgian government, had long dominated the sedentary Hutu population. The Hutus' attempt to bring an end to Tutsi domination initiated the conflict, which was marked by massacres on both sides. The presence of large numbers of foreign troops and refugees intensified centrifugal forces inside Zaire, where General Mobutu Sese Seko had long ruled with an iron hand. In 1997, military forces led by Mobutu's long-time opponent Laurent-Désiré Kabila (1939– 2001) managed to topple the general's corrupt government. Once in power, Kabila renamed the country the Democratic Republic of the Congo and promised a return to democratic practices. But the new government systematically suppressed political dissent, and in January 2001, Kabila was assassinated. He was succeeded by his son Joseph Kabila (b. 1971). Peace talks to end the conflict began that fall, but the fighting has continued, leading to horrific casualties among the civilian population. An election held in 2019 has resulted in a disputed result, and the situation remains uncertain.

14-2d Africa: A Continent in Flux

The brief survey of events in some of the more important African countries provided here illustrates the enormous difficulty that historians of Africa face in drawing any general conclusions about the pace and scope of change that has taken place in the continent in recent decades. Progress in some areas has been countered by growing problems elsewhere, and signs of hope in one region contrast with feelings of despair in another.

The shifting fortunes experienced throughout the continent are most prominently illustrated in the political arena. Over the past two decades, the collapse of one-party regimes has led to the emergence of fragile democracies in several countries. In other instances, however, democratic governments erupted in civil war or were replaced by authoritarian leaders. One prominent example of the latter is the Ivory Coast, long considered one of West Africa's most stable and prosperous countries. After the death of President Félix Houphouet-Boigny in 1993, long-simmering resentment between Christians in the south and newly arrived Muslim immigrants in the north erupted into open conflict. National elections held in 2010 led to sporadic violence and a standoff between opposition forces and the sitting president, who was forced to resign the following year. By contrast, Ghana, once one of the most fragile countries in West Africa, has shown signs of making the transition to a stable democracy. Even in Liberia, a bitter civil war recently gave way to the emergence of a stable democratic government under Ellen Johnson-Sirleaf (b. 1938), the continent's first female president.

In general, then, the political picture in Africa is cloudy. Although many African leaders voice their support for the principles of democracy and human rights, such concepts clearly have not yet struck deep roots in the soil of the continent. Efforts to build a foundation for stable and effective governments are undermined by rampant corruption and widespread popular dissatisfaction with the quality of leadership. An additional obstacle to progress is the fact that the lingering influence of ethnic and tribal differences prevents the emergence of a broader commitment to a sense of shared national identity. In that sense, advocates of pan-Africanism, who argued that the peoples of the continent should avoid the pitfall of nationalism, have gotten their wish.

Similarly, the economic picture in Africa has also been mixed. Until recently, high growth rates in some of the continent's largest economies gave rise to the popular slogan "Africa Rising," but falling commodity prices (by far Africa's greatest export earner) as a result of the recent economic slowdown in China and Europe have tarnished that image and induced a more sober assessment of the situation. Most African states are still poor and their populations often are illiterate. Infrastructure is still primitive in many areas, and agricultural yields are low by global standards. More than half a century since the end of the colonial era, the industrial revolution has not transformed the continental landscape the way it has in many other parts of the world.

Unfortunately, African concerns carry little weight in the international community. A recent agreement by the World Trade Organization (WTO) on the need to reduce agricultural subsidies in the advanced nations has been widely ignored. In 2000, the General Assembly of the United Nations passed the Millennium Declaration, which called for a dramatic reduction in the incidence of poverty, hunger, and illiteracy worldwide by the year 2015, but the appeal for foreign assistance was widely ignored by the world's wealthier nations.

Over the years, some foreign governments have sought to respond to requests for help, but aid from the United States and Europe has been on the decline, as many argue that external assistance cannot succeed unless the nations of Africa adopt measures to bring about good government and sound economic policies. The largest amount of foreign investment today seems to come from China, which has recently signed agreements with several African governments to invest in various infrastructure projects. China's objectives in extending its increasingly powerful reach to Africa are reminiscent of those that inspired the era of Western imperialism: broadening its political influence on the international stage and gaining access to the continent's vast store of natural resources. The scope of Chinese assistance has recently been reduced, however, as a result of the economic slowdown in China combined with growing African concerns about a potential loss of sovereignty. In the meantime, Russia has sought to enter the competition by offering military equipment and advisers to authoritarian governments who view military prowess as the best defense against rivals at home and abroad. The Cold War is back in Africa, but now under a different name.

In sum, the African continent still suffers from a number of chronic political and economic problems, but there are some signs of hope. The overall rate of economic growth for the region as a whole is twice what it was during the 1980s and 1990s and even today remains on a par with the rest of the world. As a result, Africans have been lifted out of poverty by the millions (see Comparative Illustration "New Housing for the Poor," p. 358). Although poverty, AIDS, and a lack of education and infrastructure are still major impediments in much of the region, rising commodity prices—most notably, an increase in oil revenues—could enable many countries to make additional investments and reduce their national debt. One promising sign is that the African people are not about to despair. In a recent survey of public opinion throughout the continent, the majority of respondents were optimistic about the future and confident that they would be economically better off in five years.

The African Union: A Glimmer of Hope   A significant part of the problem is that Africans must find better ways to cooperate with one another and to protect and promote

New Housing for the Poor

Q *Why do you think the segregated housing facilities known as "townships" developed in the first place in South Africa? For whom were they designed?*

Family & Society | **UNDER APARTHEID,** much of the black population in South Africa was confined to so-called townships, squalid slums located along the fringes of the country's major cities. Image 14.4a shows a crowded

IMAGE 14.4b

township on the edge of Cape Town, one of the most modern cities on the continent of Africa. Today, the government is actively building new communities that provide better housing, running water, and electricity for their residents. Image 14.4b shows a new township rising on the outskirts of the city of New London. The township has many modern facilities and even a new shopping mall with consumer goods for local residents.

IMAGE 14.4a

their own interests. A first step in that direction was taken in 1991, when the OAU agreed to establish the African Economic Community (AEC). In 2001, the OAU was replaced by the **African Union**, which is intended to provide greater political and economic integration throughout the continent on the pattern of the European Union (see Chapter 10). The new organization has already sought to mediate several of the conflicts in the region.

As Africa evolves, it is useful to remember that economic and political change is often an agonizingly slow and painful process. Introduced to industrialization and concepts of Western democracy only a century ago, African societies are still groping for ways to graft Western political institutions and economic practices onto a structure still significantly influenced by traditional values and attitudes.

14-3 CONTINUITY AND CHANGE IN MODERN AFRICAN SOCIETIES

Q **Focus Question:** How would you compare living conditions in Africa with those that you have observed in South and Southeast Asia? What accounts for the differences?

In general, the impact of the West has been greater on urban and educated Africans and more limited on their rural and illiterate compatriots. One reason is that the colonial presence was first and most firmly established in the cities. Many cities, including Dakar, Lagos, Johannesburg, Cape Town, Brazzaville, and Nairobi, are direct products of the colonial experience. Most African cities today look like their counterparts elsewhere in the world. They have high-rise buildings, blocks of residential apartments, wide boulevards, neon lights, movie theaters, and traffic jams.

14-3a Education

The educational system has been the primary means of introducing Western values and culture. In the precolonial era, formal schools did not really exist in Africa except for parochial schools in Christian Ethiopia and academies to train young males in Islamic doctrine and law in Muslim societies in North and West Africa. For the average African, education took place at the home or in the village courtyard and stressed socialization and vocational training. Traditional education in Africa was not necessarily inferior to that in Europe. Social values and customs were transmitted to the young by storytellers, often village elders and frequently women, who could gain considerable prestige through their performance.

Europeans introduced modern Western education into Africa in the nineteenth century. At first, the schools concentrated on vocational training, with some instruction in European languages and Western civilization. Eventually, pressure from Africans led to the introduction of professional training, and the first institutes of higher learning were established in the early twentieth century.

With independence, African countries established their own state-run schools. The emphasis was on the primary level, but high schools and universities were established in major cities. The basic objectives have been to introduce vocational training and improve literacy rates. Unfortunately, both funding and trained teachers are scarce in most countries, and few rural areas have schools (see Image 14.5). As a result, illiteracy remains high, estimated at about 40 percent of the population across the continent. There has been a perceptible shift toward education in the vernacular languages. In West Africa, about one in four adults is conversant in a Western language.

14-3b Urban and Rural Life

The cities are where the African elites live and work. Affluent Africans, like their contemporaries in other developing countries, have been strongly attracted to the glittering material aspects of Western culture. They live in

IMAGE 14.5 Learning the ABCs in Niger. Educating the young is one of the most crucial problems for many African societies today. Few governments are able to allocate the funds necessary to meet the challenge, so religious organizations—Muslim or Christian—often take up the slack. In this photo, students at a madrasa—a Muslim school designed to teach the Qur'an—are learning how to read Arabic, the language of Islam's holy scripture. Madrasas are one of the most prominent forms of schooling in Muslim societies in West Africa today.

 Do you feel that African nations are justified in approving the establishment of schools based on religious teachings in the absence of sufficient funds to build a more extensive public school system?

Western-style homes or apartments and eat Western foods stored in Western refrigerators, and those who can afford to drive Western cars. It has been said, not wholly in praise, that there are more Mercedes-Benz automobiles in Nigeria than in Germany, where they are manufactured.

Outside the major cities, where about three-quarters of the continent's inhabitants live, Western influence has had less impact. Millions of people throughout Africa live much as their ancestors did, in thatched huts, such as the one shown being built here by this young man in Kenya (see Image 14.6). Many are without modern plumbing and electricity: they farm or hunt by traditional methods, practice time-honored family rituals, and believe in the traditional deities. Even here, however, change is taking place. Economic need has brought about massive migrations in parts of Africa as some leave their home village to work on plantations, others move to the cities, or flee abroad or to refugee camps to escape hunger or starvation. The drying up of arable lands in the Sahel areas of West Africa has prompted a mass exodus of refugees northward to the Mediterranean coast, where they hope—often in vain—to find overseas transportation to the continent of Europe. Migration itself is a wrenching experience, disrupting familiar family and village ties and enforcing new social relationships.

William J. Duiker

IMAGE 14.6 Building His Dream House. In Africa, the houses of rural people are often constructed with a wood frame, known as wattle, daubed with mud, and then covered with a thatched roof. Such houses are inexpensive to build and remain cool in the hot tropical climate. In this Kenyan village not far from the Indian Ocean, a young man is applying mud to the wall of his future home. Houses are built in a similar fashion throughout the continent, as well as in much of southern Asia.

Nowhere, in fact, is the dichotomy between old and new, local and foreign, rural and urban so clear and painful as in Africa. Urban dwellers regard the village as the repository of all that is backward in the African past, while rural peoples view the growing urban areas as a source of corruption, prostitution, hedonism, and the destruction of communal customs and values. The tension between traditional ways and Western culture is particularly strong among African intellectuals, many of whom are torn between their admiration for things Western and their desire to retain an African identity.

14-3c Religious Belief

Before the arrival of the world religions like Christianity and Islam, most of the 800 different ethnic communities in Africa had their own well-developed religious systems. Like other aspects of life, African religious beliefs varied considerably, but certain characteristics were shared throughout much of the continent. One common feature was pantheism, the belief in a single creator god from whom all things come. This transcendent figure was generally not accessible to communication with individual human beings, except through intermediary deities, who

also served a variety of purposes, some in connection with Nature, while others provided other benefits, such as good health or human fertility.

Belief in an afterlife was closely connected to the importance of ancestors and the **lineage group** or clan. Each lineage could trace itself back to a founding ancestor or group of ancestors. These ancestral souls would not be extinguished as long as the group continued to perform rituals in their name (see Image 14.8). The rituals could also benefit the lineage group on Earth because the ancestral souls, being closer to the gods, had the power to influence the lives of their descendants for good or evil.

Such beliefs have often been challenged but by no means replaced in those parts of the continent that have been affected by the arrival of Christianity and Islam. Although both "Great Tradition" religions reject the idea of spirit worship and the concept of lesser deities, such indigenous traditions have often survived through synthesis with the imported faiths to create a unique brand of Africanized religion.

14-3d African Women

As noted in Chapter 2, one of the consequences of colonialism in Africa was a change in the relationship between men and women. Some of these changes could be described as beneficial, but others were not. Women were often introduced to Western education and given legal rights denied to them in the precolonial era. But they also became a labor source and were sometime recruited or compelled to work on construction projects.

Independence also had a significant impact on gender roles in African society. Almost without exception, the new governments established the principle of sexual equality and permitted women to vote and run for political office. Yet as elsewhere, women continue to operate at a disability in a world dominated by males. In general, politics remains a male preserve, and although a few professions, such as teaching, child care, and clerical work, are dominated by women, most African women are employed in menial positions such as agricultural labor, factory work, and retail trade or as domestics. Education is open to all at the elementary level, but women comprise less than 20 percent of students at the upper levels in most African societies today.

Urban Women Not surprisingly, women have made the greatest strides in the cities. Most urban women, like men, now marry on the basis of personal choice, although a significant minority are still willing to accept their parents' choice. After marriage, African women appear to occupy a more equal position than their counterparts in most Asian countries. Each marriage partner tends to maintain a separate income, and women often have the right to possess property separate from their husbands. Though many wives still defer to their husbands in the traditional manner, others are like the woman in Abioseh Nicol's story "A Truly Married Woman," who, after years of living as a common law wife with her husband, is finally able to provide the price and finalize the marriage. After the wedding, she declares, "For twelve years I have got up every morning at five to make tea for you and breakfast. Now I am a truly married woman, [and] you must treat me with a little more respect. You are now my husband and not a lover. Get up and make yourself a cup of tea."[4]

In the cities, a feminist movement is growing, but it is firmly based on conditions in the local environment. Many African women writers, for example, opt for a brand of African feminism much like that of Ama Ata Aidoo (b. 1942), a Ghanaian novelist, whose ultimate objective is to free African society as a whole, not just its female inhabitants. After receiving her education at a girls' school in the preindependence Gold Coast and attending Stanford University in the United States, she embarked on a writing career. Every African woman and every man, she insists, "should be a feminist, especially if they believe that Africans should take charge of our land, its wealth, our lives, and the burden of our development. Because it is not possible to advocate independence for our continent without also believing that African women must have the best that the environment can offer."[5]

Women in Rural Areas Feminism has had less impact on women in rural areas, where traditional attitudes continue to exert a strong influence. In some societies, female genital mutilation, the traditional rite of passage for a young girl's transit to womanhood, is still widely practiced. Polygamy is also not uncommon, and arranged marriages are still the rule rather than the exception. In some Muslim societies, efforts to apply *Shari'a* law have led to greater restrictions on the freedom of women. As we have seen, in northern Nigeria, Boko Haram terrorists recently kidnapped hundreds of Christian school children and converted them to Islam in preparation for a life of prostitution or marriage to their followers. A Muslim woman was recently sentenced to death for committing adultery. The sentence was later reversed on appeal.

The dichotomy between rural and urban values can lead to acute tensions. Many African villagers regard the cities as the fount of evil, decadence, and corruption. Women in particular have suffered from the tension between the pull of the city and the village. As men are drawn to the cities in search of employment and excitement, their wives and girlfriends are left behind, both literally and figuratively, in the village. In some areas, African women become active in commerce while their husbands labor in the fields. Often, however, women perform heavy work along with the male counterparts. In this photograph of a salt mine in Senegal, men are assigned to unearth salt from the lake bed, while women carry it to the shore (see Image 14.7).

14-3e African Culture

Inevitably, the tension between traditional and modern, local and foreign, and individual and communal that has permeated contemporary African society has spilled over into culture. In general, in the visual arts and music, utility and ritual have sometimes given way to pleasure and decoration. In the process, Africans have been affected to a certain extent by foreign influences but have retained their distinctive characteristics. Wood carving, metalwork,

William J. Duiker

IMAGE 14.7 Salt of the Earth. During the precolonial era, many West African societies were forced to import salt from Mediterranean countries in exchange for tropical products and gold. Today, the people of Senegal satisfy their domestic needs by mining salt deposits contained in lakes like this one in the interior of the country. These lakes are the remnants of vast seas that covered the region of the Sahara in prehistoric times. Note that women are sharing the heavy labor, while men occupy the managerial positions. In mining the salt, men and women have clearly assigned roles, with men dislodging the salt from the lake bed and women carrying it to shore.

Can you think of cases in other countries where women are routinely assigned to carry on heavy labor? Do you feel that the practice in African societies is justified or not?

painting, and sculpture, for example, have preserved their traditional forms but are now increasingly adapted to serve the tourist industry and the export market. One of the most renowned artists in Africa today is the Ghanaian-born El Anatsui (b. 1944), whose monumental draperies made of stapled aluminum bottle caps evoke the tapestry of many traditional African societies. Stunningly majestic, these dramatic panels recall the colorful patterns of traditional African textiles.

Literature   No area of African culture has been so strongly affected by political and social events as literature. Except for Muslim areas in North and East Africa, precolonial Africans did not have a written literature, although their tradition of oral storytelling served as a rich repository of history, custom, and folk culture. The first written literature in the vernacular or in European languages emerged during the nineteenth century in the form of novels, poetry, and drama.

Angry at the negative portrayal of Africa in Western literature (see Opposing Viewpoints, "Africa: Dark Continent or Radiant Land?" p. 363), African authors initially wrote primarily for a European audience as a means of establishing black dignity and purpose. In response to condescending Western attitudes about African history, many glorified the emotional and communal aspects of the traditional African experience. The Nigerian Chinua Achebe (1930–2013) is considered the first major African novelist to write in the English language. In his writings, he attempted to interpret African history from an African perspective and to forge a new sense of African identity. In his trailblazing novel *Things Fall Apart* (1958), he recounted the story of a Nigerian who refused to submit to the new British order and eventually committed suicide. Criticizing his contemporaries who accepted foreign rule, the protagonist lamented that the white man "has put a knife on the things that held us together and we have fallen apart."

In recent decades, the African novel has turned its focus from the brutality of the foreign oppressor to the shortcomings of African leaders. Having gained independence, African politicians are portrayed as mimicking and even outdoing the injustices committed by their colonial predecessors. A prominent example of this genre is the work of the Kenyan Ngugi Wa Thiong'o (b. 1938). His first novel, *A Grain of Wheat*, takes place on the eve of independence. Although Ngugi mocks local British society for its racism, snobbishness, and superficiality, his chief interest lies in the unsentimental and even unflattering portrayal of ordinary Kenyans in their daily struggle for survival.

Like most of his predecessors, Ngugi initially wrote in English, but he eventually decided to write in his native Kikuyu as a means of broadening his readership. For that reason, perhaps, in the late 1970s, he was placed under house arrest for writing subversive literature. There, he secretly wrote *Devil on the Cross*, which urged his compatriots to overthrow the ruling government. Published in 1980, the book sold widely and was eventually read aloud by storytellers throughout Kenyan society. Fearing an attempt on his life, Ngugi has since lived in exile.

Many of Ngugi's contemporaries have followed his lead and focused their frustration on the failure of the continent's new leadership to carry out the goals of independence. One of the most outstanding is the Nigerian Wole Soyinka (b. 1934). His novel *The Interpreters* (1965) lambasted the corruption and hypocrisy of Nigerian politics. Succeeding novels and plays have continued that tradition, resulting in a Nobel Prize in Literature in 1986. In 1994, however, Soyinka barely managed to escape arrest, and he entered a self-imposed exile abroad until the Abacha regime in Nigeria came to an end. In a protest against the brutality of the regime, he published from exile a harsh exposé of the crisis. His book, *The Open Sore of a Continent*, placed the primary responsibility for failure not on Nigeria's long list of dictators but on the very concept of the modern nation-state, which was introduced to Africa arbitrarily by Europeans. A nation, he contends, can only emerge spontaneously from below, as the expression of the moral and political will of the local inhabitants; it cannot be imposed artificially from above.

Recently, novelists in Nigeria have addressed a number of other controversial subjects, like polygamy and violence against women, topics which are politically sensitive because of Muslim taboos. Ayobami Adebayo's *Stay With Me* (2017), for example, portrays the struggle of an infertile wife to prevent her husband from taking a second spouse.

A number of Africa's most prominent writers today are women. Traditionally, African women were valued for their talents as storytellers, but writing was strongly discouraged by both traditional and colonial authorities on the grounds that women should occupy themselves with their domestic obligations. In recent years, however, a number of women have emerged as prominent writers of African fiction. Two examples are Buchi Emecheta (1940–2017) of Nigeria and Ama Ata Aidoo (b. 1942) of Ghana. Beginning with *Second Class Citizen* (1975), which chronicled the breakdown of her own marriage, Emecheta published numerous works exploring the role of women in contemporary African society and decrying the practice of polygamy. Ata Aidoo has focused on the identity of today's African women and the changing relations between men and women in society. In her novel *Changes: A Love Story* (1991), she chronicles the lives of three women, none presented as a victim but all caught up in the struggle for survival and happiness. Of late, two young authors have

Africa: Dark Continent or Radiant Land?

 Compare the depiction of the continent of Africa in these two passages. Is Laye making a response to Conrad? If so, what is it?

Interaction & Exchange **COLONIALISM CAMOUFLAGED ITS ECONOMIC OBJECTIVES** under the cloak of a "civilizing mission," which in Africa was aimed at illuminating the so-called Dark Continent with Europe's brilliant civilization. In 1899, the Polish-born English author Joseph Conrad (1857–1924) fictionalized his harrowing journey up the Congo River in the novella *Heart of Darkness*. Conrad's protagonist, Marlow, travels upriver to locate a Belgian trader who has mysteriously disappeared. The novella describes Marlow's gradual recognition of the egregious excesses of colonial rule, as well as his realization that such evil lurks in everyone's heart. The story concludes with a cry: "The horror! The horror!" Voicing views that expressed his Victorian perspective, Conrad described an Africa that was incomprehensible, sensual, and primitive.

Over the years, Conrad's work has provoked much debate. Author Chinua Achebe, for one, lambasted *Heart of Darkness* as a racial diatribe. Since independence, many African writers have been prompted to counter Conrad's portrayal by reaffirming the dignity and purpose of the African people. One of the first to do so was the Guinean author Camara Laye (1928–1980), who in 1954 composed a brilliant novel, *The Radiance of the King*, which can be viewed as the mirror image of Conrad's *Heart of Darkness*. In Laye's work, Clarence, another European protagonist, undertakes a journey into the impenetrable heart of Africa. This time, however, he is enlightened by the process, obtaining self-knowledge and ultimately salvation.

Joseph Conrad, *Heart of Darkness*

We penetrated deeper and deeper into the heart of darkness. It was very quiet there. At night sometimes the roll of drums behind the curtain of trees would run up the river and remain sustained faintly, as if hovering in the air high over our heads, till the first break of day. Whether it meant war, peace, or prayer we could not tell. . . . But suddenly, as we struggled round a bend, there would be a glimpse of rush walls, of peaked grass-roofs, a burst of yells, a whirl of black limbs, a mass of hands clapping, of feet stamping, of bodies swaying, of eyes rolling, under the droop of heavy and motionless foliage. The steamer toiled along slowly on the edge of a black and incomprehensible frenzy. The prehistoric man was cursing us, praying to us, welcoming us—who could tell? We were cut off from the comprehension of our surroundings; we glided past like phantoms, wondering and secretly appalled, as sane men would be before an enthusiastic outbreak in a madhouse.

Camara Laye, *The Radiance of the King*

At that very moment the king turned his head, turned it imperceptibly, and his glance fell upon Clarence. . . .

"Yes, no one is as base as I, as naked as I," he thought. "And you, lord, you are willing to rest your eyes upon me!" Or was it because of his very nakedness? . . . "Because of your very nakedness!" the look seemed to say. "That terrifying void that is within you and which opens to receive me; your hunger which calls to my hunger; your very baseness which did not exist until I gave it leave; and the great shame you feel. . . ."

When he had come before the king, when he stood in the great radiance of the king, still ravaged by the tongue of fire, but alive still, and living only through the touch of that fire, Clarence fell upon his knees, for it seemed to him that he was finally at the end of his seeking, and at the end of all seekings.

Sources: "Joseph Conrad Selection": From *Heart of Darkness* by Joseph Conrad. Penguin Books, 1991. "Camara Laye Selection": From *The Radiance of the King* by Camara Laye, translated from the French by James Kirkup. New York: Vintage, 1989.

garnered great acclaim for their novels about Nigeria's political and social upheavals—Chimamanda Ngozi Adichie (b. 1977) in *Half a Yellow Sun* (2006) and Sefi Atta (b. 1964) in *Everything Good Will Come* (2005).

Music Contemporary African music also reflects a hybridization or fusion with Western culture. Traditional music in Africa was closely connected with every aspect of daily life. Through music and dance, Africans recalled

William J. Duiker

IMAGE 14.8 African Dance Today. Group dancing has always played an important role in sub-Saharan African society. Traditionally it has served several functions, including religious performance, ceremonies celebrating rites of passage, and the portrayal of local history. As many Africans have moved away from their rural villages into the cities, they have created "dance clubs" in their new environment as a means of maintaining ties with their ancestral village while creating a substitute community in their new environment. Shown here, members of a Zulu village in South Africa perform a warrior dance to recall the glorious history of Zulu warriors defending their homeland against European invaders.

Q *Does music and dance in the United States play a similar role in maintaining tradition and linking performers with their past?*

Even as African societies evolve and absorb multiple forms of influence from abroad, African dance survives today as a means of uniting the peoples of the continent to their cultural traditions of the past. Traditional dance continues to be a key instrument in preserving African traditions and way of life in a world marked by rapid change (see Image 14.8).

Having traveled to the Americas via the slave trade centuries earlier, African drum beats evolved into North American jazz and Latin American dance rhythms, only to return to reenergize African music. In fact, one of the most vibrant aspects of African culture today is its thriving musical scene, as it has become one of the continent's most effective weapons for social and political protest. One can find **Afropop** groups at almost every major music festival these days, and performers like Angelique Kidjo from Benin and Cesaria Evora of Cape Verde are truly global superstars. Recently, the "desert blues" style of the West African nation of Mali has found its way onto the airwaves in the United States and Europe with the songs of the Tuareg

their local history, expressed reverence for their ancestors, marked important social rituals, and maintained contact with the world of the spirits. A wide variety of instruments were used, including woodwinds, strings, "talking drums," and other percussion instruments. A strong rhythmic pattern was an important feature of most African music, although the desired effect was achieved through a wide variety of means, including gourds, pots, bells, sticks beaten together, and hand clapping, as well as the talking drums. Much was produced in the context of social rituals such as weddings and funerals, religious ceremonies, and inaugurations.

Music could also serve an educational purpose by passing on to the young generation information about the history and social traditions of the community. In the absence of written language in sub-Saharan Africa, music and dance served as the primary means of transmitting folk legends and religious traditions from generation to generation.

musical collective Tinariwen, Ali Farka Touré, and the *kora* player Toumani Diabeté, all of whom have won Grammy awards. Many of the lyrics are openly political and serve as a call to action (some of the musicians are actively fighting for the independence of the Tuareg peoples against the government in Mali), while others simply evoke the realities and the challenges of contemporary African life.

Easily accessible to all, African music, whether Afro-beat in Nigeria, rai in Algeria, or reggae in Benin, represents the "weapon of the future," say contemporary musicians; "it helped free Nelson Mandela" and "will put Africa back on the map." Censored by all the African dictatorial regimes, these courageous musicians persist in their struggle against corruption, what one singer calls the second slavery, "the cancer that is eating away at the system." Their voices echo the chorus "Together we can build a nation/Because Africa has brains, youth, knowledge."[6]

MAKING CONNECTIONS

Nowhere in the developing world is the dilemma of continuity and change more agonizing than in Africa. Mesmerized by the spectacle of Western affluence yet repulsed by the bloody trail from slavery to World War II and the atomic bombs over Hiroshima and Nagasaki, African intellectuals have been torn between the dual images of Western materialism and African uniqueness. For the average African, of course, such intellectual dilemmas pale before the daily challenge of survival. But the fundamental gap between traditional and modern is perhaps wider in Africa than anywhere else in the world and may well be harder to bridge.

What is the future of Africa? It seems almost foolhardy to seek an answer to such a question, given the degree of ethnic, linguistic, and cultural diversity that exists throughout the vast continent. Not surprisingly, visions of the future are equally diverse. Some Africans still yearn for the dreams embodied in the program of the OAU in the hope that the continent might avoid the dual pitfalls of virulent nationalism and industrialization. Novelist Ngugi Wa Thiong'o, for one, does not despair, and calls for "an internationalization of all the democratic and social struggles for human equality, justice, peace, and progress."[7] But others have discarded the democratic ideal and turned their attention to autocratic systems as the most effective guiding principle of national development. As both China and Russia intensify their efforts to gain political influence on the continent, the statist model that they project has proven attractive to political forces that seek a shorter and surer route to power than the ballot box. Like all peoples, however, Africans must ultimately find their own solutions within the context of their own traditions, not by seeking to imitate the example of others.

REFLECTION QUESTIONS

Q To what degree have the nations of Africa managed to achieve political stability and economic prosperity since achieving independence after World War II?

Q What are some of the key challenges facing African nations and peoples today? How are they attempting to address them?

Q Why has the idea of the nation-state been so slow to take root in Africa since the end of World War II? Do you think that nations are the most effective way to organize human society or not?

Q How have African writers sought to portray the political and social realities of the continent since the inauguration of the era of independence? Does African literature play a role similar to that of the United States?

CHAPTER TIMELINE

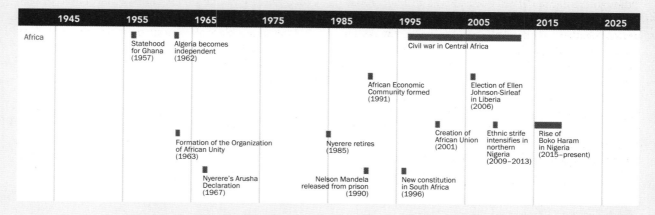

CHAPTER NOTES

1. Aimé Césaire, *Cahier d'un retour du pays natal*, trans. John Berger and Anna Bostock (Harmondsworth, England,1969), p. 10, quoted in Emmanuel N. Obiechina, *Language and Theme: Essays on African Literature* (Washington, D.C. 1990), pp. 78–79.

2. Albert Ojuka, "Pedestrian, to Passing Benz-Man," quoted in A. Roscoe, *Uhuru's Fire: African Literature East to South* (Cambridge, England, 1977), p. 103.

3. Cited in Martin Meredith, *The Fate of Africa* (New York, 2004), p. 168.

4. Abioseh Nicol, *"A Truly Married Woman"* and Other *Stories* (London, 1965), p. 12.

5. Ama Ata Aidoo, *No Sweetness Here* (New York, 1995), p. 136.

6. Gilles Médioni, "Stand Up, Africa!" *World Press Review*, July 2002, p. 34.

7. Ngugi Wa Thiong'o, *Decolonising the Mind: The Politics of Language in African Literature* (Portsmouth, N.H., 1986), p. 103.

Chapter Outline and Focus Questions

15-1 *Crescent of Conflict*

Q Why does the Middle East appear to be one of the most unstable and conflict-ridden regions in the world today? What historical factors might help explain this phenomenon?

15-2 *Society and Culture in the Contemporary Middle East*

Q How have religious issues affected political, economic, and social conditions in the Middle East in recent decades?

IMAGE 15.1 Answering the call of the muezzin

William J. Duiker

"WE MUSLIMS ARE OF ONE FAMILY even though we live under different governments and in various regions."[1] So said Ayatollah Ruholla Khomeini, the Islamic religious figure and leader of the 1979 revolution that overthrew the shah in Iran. The ayatollah's remark was dismissed by some as just a pious wish by a religious mystic. In fact, however, it illustrates a crucial aspect of the political dynamics in the Middle East: if the concept of cultural uniqueness represented a potential alternative to the system of nation-states in Africa, then the desire for Muslim unity has played a similar role for many people in the Middle East. In both regions, a yearning for a sense of community beyond national borders tugs at the emotions and intellect of their inhabitants and counteracts the dynamic pull of nationalism that has provoked political turmoil and conflict in much of the rest of the world.

Connections to Today

What possible strategies might the peoples of the Middle East adopt to assist them in restoring peaceful conditions and stable societies throughout the region today?

367

15-1 CRESCENT OF CONFLICT

 Focus Questions: Why does the Middle East appear to be one of the most unstable and conflict-ridden regions in the world today? What historical factors might help explain this phenomenon?

A dramatic example of the powerful force of pan-Islamic sentiment took place on September 11, 2001, when Muslim terrorists hijacked four U.S. airliners and turned them into missiles aimed at the center of world capitalism. Although the headquarters of the organization that carried out the attack—known as al-Qaeda—was located in Afghanistan, the militants themselves came from several different Muslim states. In the months that followed, popular support for al-Qaeda and its mysterious leader, Osama bin Laden (1957–2011), intensified throughout the Muslim world. To many observers, it appeared that the Islamic peoples were embarking on an era of direct confrontation with the entire Western world.

What were the sources of Muslim anger? In a speech released on videotape shortly after the attack, bin Laden declared that it was a response to the "humiliation and disgrace" that have afflicted the Islamic world for more than eighty years, a period dating back to the end of World War I (see Historical Voices, "I Accuse!", p. 369). Although that was clearly not the only motive, there seems little doubt that the rage that has spread through much of the Islamic world has deep historical roots and will not be easily quenched.

For the Middle East, the period between the two world wars was an era of transition. With the fall of the Ottoman and Persian Empires, new modernizing regimes emerged in Turkey and Iran, and a more traditionalist but fiercely independent government was established in Saudi Arabia. Elsewhere, however, European influence continued to be strong; the French and British had mandates in Syria, Lebanon, Jordan, and Palestine, and British influence persisted in Iraq and southern Arabia and throughout the Nile valley. **Pan-Arabism**—the concept of the unity of all Arab peoples—was on the rise, but it lacked focus and coherence (see Map 15.1).

During World War II, the Middle East became the cockpit of European rivalries, as it had been during World War I. The region was more significant to the

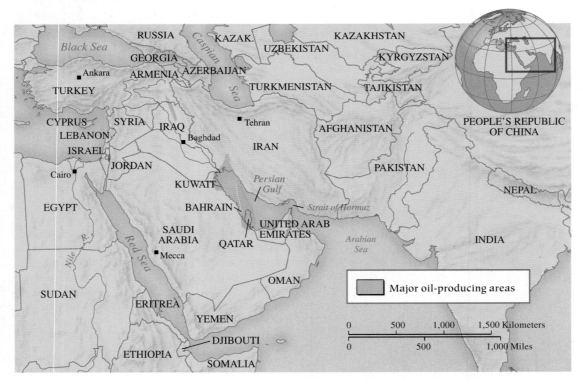

MAP 15.1 The Modern Middle East. Shown here are the boundaries of the independent states in the contemporary Middle East.

 Which are the major oil-producing countries?

I Accuse!

 What reasons did Osama bin Laden present to justify the terrorist attacks carried out by his followers around the world? How would you respond to his charges?

Politics & Government

IN 1998, OSAMA BIN LADEN was virtually unknown outside the Middle East. But this scion of a wealthy industrialist from Saudi Arabia was on a mission—to avenge the hostile acts perpetrated on his fellow Muslims by the United States and its allies. Having taken part in the successful guerrilla war against Soviet occupation troops in Afghanistan during the 1980s, bin Laden now turned his ire on the tyrannical regimes in the Middle East and their great protector, the United States. In the following excerpts from a 1998 interview, he defended the use of terror against those whom he deemed enemies of Islam. Three years later, his followers launched the surprise attacks that led to more than 3,000 deaths on September 11, 2001.

Interview with Osama bin Laden by His Followers (1998)

What is the meaning of your call for Muslims to take up arms against America in particular, and what is the message that you wish to send to the West in general?

The call to wage war against America was made because America has spearheaded the crusade against the Islamic nation, sending tens of thousands of its troops to the land of the two Holy Mosques [Saudi Arabia], over and above its meddling in its affairs and its politics and its support of the oppressive, corrupt, and tyrannical regime that is in control. These are the reasons behind the singling out of America as a target. And not exempt from responsibility are those Western regimes whose presence in the region offers support to the American troops there. We know at least one reason behind the symbolic participation of the Western forces and that is to support the Jewish and Zionist plans for expansion of what is called the Great Israel. Surely, their presence is not out of concern over their interests in the region. . . . Their presence has no meaning save one and that is to offer support to the Jews in Palestine who are in need of their Christian brothers to achieve full control over the Arab Peninsula

which they intend to make an important part of the so called Greater Israel.

Many of the Arabic as well as the Western mass media accuse you of terrorism and of supporting terrorism. What do you have to say to that?

Every state and every civilization and culture has to resort to terrorism under certain circumstances for the purpose of abolishing tyranny and corruption. Every country in the world has its own security system and its own security forces, its own police, and its own army. They are all designed to terrorize whoever even contemplates an attack on that country or its citizens. The terrorism we practice is of the commendable kind for it is directed at the tyrants and the aggressors and the enemies of Allah, the tyrants, the traitors who commit acts of treason against their own countries and their own faith and their own prophet and their own nation. Terrorizing those and punishing them are necessary measures to straighten things and to make them right. Tyrants and oppressors who subject the Arab nation to aggression ought to be punished. . . . America heads the list of aggressors against Muslims. The recurrence of aggression against Muslims everywhere is proof enough. For over half a century, Muslims in Palestine have been slaughtered and assaulted and robbed of their honor and of their property. Their houses have been blasted, their crops destroyed. And the strange thing is that any act by them to avenge themselves or to lift the injustice befalling them causes great agitation in the United Nations, which hastens to call for an emergency meeting only to convict the victim and to censure the wronged and the tyrannized whose children have been killed and whose crops have been destroyed and whose farms have been pulverized. . . .

In today's wars, there are no morals, and it is clear that mankind has descended to the lowest degrees of decadence and oppression. They rip us of our wealth and of our resources and of our oil. Our religion is under attack. They kill and murder our brothers. They compromise our honor and our dignity and if we dare to utter a single word of protest against the injustice, we are called terrorists. This is compounded injustice. And the United Nations insistence to convict the victims and support the aggressors constitutes a serious precedent that shows the extent of injustice that has been allowed to take root in this land.

Source: From Khater, Sources in the History of the Modern Middle East, 2nd Edition. © 2011 Cengage Learning.

warring powers than previously because of the growing importance of oil and the Suez Canal's position as a vital sea route. For a brief period, the Afrika Korps, under the command of the brilliant German general Erwin Rommel, threatened to seize Egypt and the Suez Canal, but British troops defeated the German forces at El Alamein, west of Alexandria in 1942, and gradually drove them westward until their final defeat after the arrival of U.S. troops in Morocco under the field command of General George S. Patton. From that time until the end of the war, the entire region from the Mediterranean Sea eastward was under secure Allied occupation.

15-1a The Question of Palestine

With the end of World War II, a number of independent states emerged in the Middle East: Jordan, Lebanon, and Syria, all European mandates before the war, became independent. Egypt, Iran, and Iraq, though still under a degree of Western influence, became increasingly autonomous. Sympathy for the idea of Arab unity led to the formation of the Arab League in 1945, but different points of view among its members prevented it from achieving anything of substance.

The one issue on which all Muslim states in the area could agree was the question of Palestine. As tensions between Jews and Arabs in that mandate intensified during the 1930s, the British attempted to limit Jewish immigration into the area and firmly rejected proposals for independence, despite the promise made in the 1917 Balfour Declaration that Palestine should become a national home for the Jewish people (see Chapter 5).

After World War II ended, the situation drifted rapidly toward crisis, as thousands of Jewish refugees, many of them from displaced persons camps in Europe, sought to migrate to Palestine despite Palestinian Arab complaints and British efforts to prevent their arrival (see Opposing Viewpoints, "The Arab and the Jewish Case for Palestine," p. 371). As violence between predominantly Muslim Palestinian Arabs and Jews intensified in the fall of 1947, the issue was taken up in the United Nations General Assembly. After an intense debate, the assembly voted to approve the partition of Palestine into two separate states, one for the Jews and one for the Palestinian Arabs. The city of Jerusalem was to be placed under international control. A UN commission was established to iron out the details and determine the future boundaries.

During the next several months, growing hostility between Jewish and Palestinian Arab forces—the latter increasingly supported by neighboring Muslim states—caused the British to announce that they would withdraw their own peacekeeping forces by May 15, 1948.

Shortly after the stroke of midnight, as the British mandate formally came to a close, the **Zionist** leader David Ben-Gurion (1886–1973) announced the independence of the state of Israel and established its temporary capital at Tel Aviv. Later that same day, the new state was formally recognized by the United States, while military forces from several neighboring Muslim states—all of which had vigorously opposed the formation of a Jewish state in the region—entered Israeli territory but were beaten back. Thousands of Arab residents of the new state fled. Internal dissonance among the Arabs, combined with the strength of Jewish resistance groups, contributed to the failure of the invasion, but the bitterness between the two sides did not subside. The Muslim states refused to recognize the new state of Israel, which became a member of the United Nations, legitimizing it in the eyes of the rest of the world. The stage for future conflict was set.

The exodus of thousands of Palestinian refugees into neighboring Muslim states had repercussions that are still felt today. Jordan, which had become an independent kingdom under its Hashemite ruler, was flooded by the arrival of one million urban Palestinians. They overwhelmed the country's half million residents, most of whom were Bedouins. To the north, the state of Lebanon had been created to provide the local Christian community with a country of their own, but the arrival of the Palestinian refugees upset the delicate balance between Christians and Muslims. Moreover, the creation of Lebanon had angered the Syrians, who had lost that land as well as other territories to Turkey as a result of European decisions before and after World War II.

15-1b Nasser and Pan-Arabism

The dispute over Palestine placed Egypt in an uncomfortable position. Technically, Egypt was not an Arab state. King Farouk (1920–1965), who had acceded to power in 1936, had frequently declared support for the Arab cause, but the Egyptian people were not Bedouins and shared little of the culture of the peoples across the Red Sea. Nevertheless, Farouk committed Egyptian armies to the disastrous war against Israel.

In 1952, King Farouk, whose corrupt habits had severely eroded his early popularity, was overthrown by a military coup engineered by young military officers ostensibly under the leadership of Colonel Muhammad Nagib. The real force behind the scenes was Colonel Gamal Abdul Nasser (1918–1970), the son of a minor government functionary who, like many of his fellow officers, had been angered by the army's inadequate preparation for the war against Israel four years earlier. In 1953, the monarchy was replaced by a republic.

The Arab and the Jewish Case for Palestine

 How did the authors of these documents justify their position on the issue of Palestine? What counterarguments could be advanced in each case?

Politics & Government

AFTER THE BRITISH GOVERNMENT issued the Balfour Declaration in 1917 recognizing the right of the Jewish people to a homeland in Palestine, the Zionist organization issued a memorandum making the case for the idea. But as more and more Jews began to immigrate to Palestine after World War II, the Arab Office in Jerusalem issued a statement defending the right of the indigenous inhabitants to preserve its traditional character.

Memorandum to the Peace Conference in Versailles
The Historic Title

The claims of the Jews with regard to Palestine rest upon the following main considerations:

1. The land is the historic home of the Jews; there they achieved their greatest development; from the centre, through their agency, there emanated spiritual and moral influences of supreme value to mankind. By violence they were driven from Palestine, and through the ages they have never ceased to cherish the longing and the hope of a return.

2. In some parts of the world, and particularly in Eastern Europe, the conditions of life of millions of Jews are deplorable. Forming often a congested population, denied the opportunities which would make a healthy development possible, the need of fresh outlets is urgent, both for their own sake and the interests of the population of other races, among whom they dwell. Palestine would offer one such outlet. To the Jewish masses it is the country above all others in which they would most wish to cast their lot. By the methods of economic development to which we shall refer later, Palestine can be made now, as it was in ancient times, the home of a prosperous population many times as numerous as that which now inhabits it.

3. Palestine is not large enough to contain more than a proportion of the Jews of the world. The greater part of the fourteen millions or more scattered throughout all countries must remain in their present localities, and it will doubtless be one of the cares of the Peace Conference to ensnare for them, wherever they have been oppressed, as for all peoples, equal rights and humane conditions. A Jewish National Home in Palestine will, however, be of high value to them also. Its influence will permeate the Jewries of the world, it will inspire these millions, hitherto often despairing, with a new hope; it will hold out before their eyes a higher standard; it will help to make them even more useful citizens in the lands in which they dwell.

4. Such a Palestine would be of value also to the world at large, whose real wealth consists in the healthy diversities of its civilizations.

5. Lastly, the land itself needs redemption. Much of it is left desolate. Its present condition is a standing reproach. Two things are necessary for that redemption—a stable and enlightened Government, and an addition to the present population which shall be energetic, intelligent, devoted to the country, and backed by the large financial resources that are indispensable for development. Such a population the Jews alone can supply.

The Problem of Palestine

1. The whole Arab People is unalterably opposed to the attempt to impose Jewish immigration and settlement upon it, and ultimately to establish a Jewish State in Palestine. Its opposition is based primarily upon right. The Arabs of Palestine are descendants of the indigenous inhabitants of the country, who have been in occupation of it since the beginning of history; they cannot agree that it is right to subject an indigenous population against its will to alien immigrants, whose claim is based upon a historical connection which ceased effectively many centuries ago. Moreover they form the majority of the population; as such they cannot submit to a policy of immigration which if pursued for long will turn them from a majority into a minority in an alien state; and they claim the democratic right of a majority to make its own decisions in matters of urgent national concern. . . .

2. In addition to the question of right, the Arabs oppose the claims of political Zionism because of the effects which Zionist settlement has already had upon their situation and is likely to have to an even greater extent in the future. Negatively, it has diverted

(continued)

the whole course of their national development. Geographically Palestine is part of Syria; its indigenous inhabitants belong to the Syrian branch of the Arab family of nations; all their culture and tradition link them to the other Arab peoples; and until 1917 Palestine formed part of the Ottoman Empire which included also several of the other Arab countries. The presence and claims of the Zionists, and the support given them by certain Western Powers have resulted in Palestine being cut off from the other Arab countries and subjected to a regime, administrative, legal, fiscal, and educational, different from that of the sister-countries. Quite apart from the inconvenience to individuals and the dislocation of trade which this separation has caused, it has prevented Palestine participating fully in the general development of the Arab world.

Sources: From David Hunter Miller, *My Diary at the Conference of Paris* (New York, 1924), V, pp. 15–29, as printed in Akram F. Khater, *Sources in the History of the Modern Middle East*, 2nd ed. (Cengage, 2011), pp. 152–153. From Akram Khater, *Sources in the History of the Modern Middle East*, 2nd ed. (Cengage, 2011), pp. 179–190.

In 1954, Nasser seized power in his own right and immediately instituted a land reform program. He also adopted a policy of neutrality in foreign affairs and expressed sympathy for the Arab cause. The British presence had rankled many Egyptians for years, for even after granting Egypt independence, Britain had retained control over the Suez Canal to protect its route to the Indian Ocean. In 1956, Nasser suddenly nationalized the Suez Canal Company, which had been under British and French administration. Seeing a threat to their route to the Indian Ocean, the British and the French entered into a secret agreement with Israel, inviting Israel to attack Egypt to give Britain and France a pretense for deploying peacekeeping forces to the canal zone, thereby protecting their investment. Exasperated at sporadic Arab commando raids on Israeli territory, Israel agreed to participate. In late 1956, Israel attacked Egypt, and France and Britain seized the canal. But the Eisenhower administration in the United States, concerned that the attack smacked of a revival of colonialism, supported Nasser and brought about the withdrawal of foreign forces from Egypt and of Israeli troops from the Sinai peninsula.

The United Arab Republic   Nasser now turned to pan-Arabism. In 1958, Egypt united with Syria in the United Arab Republic (UAR). The union had been proposed by members of the Ba'ath Party, which advocated the unity of all Arab states in a new socialist society. In 1957, the Ba'ath Party assumed power in Syria and opened talks with Egypt on a union between the two countries, which took place in March 1958 following a plebiscite. Nasser, despite his reported ambivalence about the union, was named president of the new state.

Egypt and Syria hoped that the union would eventually include all Arab states, but other Arab leaders, including young King Hussein of Jordan and the kings of Iraq and Saudi Arabia, were suspicious. The latter two in particular understandably feared pan-Arabism on the assumption that they would be asked to share their vast oil revenues with the poorer states of the Middle East.

Nasser opposed the existing situation, in which much of the wealth of the Middle East flowed into the treasuries of a handful of wealthy feudal states or, even worse, the pockets of foreign oil interests. In his view, through Arab unity, this wealth could be put to better use to improve the standard of living in the area. To achieve a more equitable division of the wealth of the region, natural resources and major industries would be nationalized; central planning would ensure that resources were exploited efficiently, but private enterprise would continue at the local level.

In the end, however, Nasser's determination to extend state control over the economy brought an end to the UAR. When the government announced the nationalization of a large number of industries and utilities in 1961, a military coup overthrew the Ba'ath leaders in Damascus, and the new authorities declared that Syria would end its relationship with Egypt.

The breakup of the UAR did not end Nasser's dream of pan-Arabism. In 1962, Algeria finally received its independence from France and, under its new president, Ahmad Ben Bella (1918–2004), established close relations with Egypt, as did a new republic across the Red Sea in Yemen. During the mid-1960s, Egypt took the lead in promoting Arab unity against Israel. At a meeting of Arab leaders held in Jerusalem in 1964, the Palestine Liberation Organization (PLO) was set up under Egyptian sponsorship to represent the interests of the Palestinians. According to the charter of the PLO, only the Palestinian people (and thus not Jewish immigrants from abroad) had the right to form a state in the old British mandate. A guerrilla movement called al-Fatah, led by the dissident PLO figure Yasir Arafat (1929–2004), began to launch terrorist attacks on Israeli territory, prompting Israel to raid PLO bases in Jordan in 1966.

15-1c The Arab-Israeli Dispute

Growing Arab hostility was a constant threat to the security of Israel. In the years after independence, Israeli leaders dedicated themselves to creating a Jewish homeland. Aided by reparations paid by the postwar German government and private funds provided by Jews living abroad, notably in the United States, the government attempted to build a democratic and modern state that would be a magnet for Jews throughout the world and a symbol of Jewish achievement.

But ensuring the survival of the tiny state surrounded by antagonistic Muslim Arab neighbors was a considerable challenge, made more difficult by divisions within the Israeli population. Immigrants from Europe tended to be secular and even socialist in their views, whereas those from the Middle East were often politically and religiously conservative. The state was also home to Christians as well as many Muslim Palestinians who had not fled to other countries. To balance these diverse interests, Israel established a parliament, called the Knesset, on the European model, with proportional representation based on the number of votes each party received in the general election. The parties were so numerous that none ever received a majority of votes, and all governments had to be formed from a coalition of several parties. As a result, moderate secular leaders such as long-time prime minister David Ben-Gurion had to cater to more marginal parties composed of conservative religious groups.

The Six-Day War During the late 1950s and 1960s, the dispute between Israel and other states in the Middle East escalated in intensity. Essentially alone except for the sympathy of the United States and several Western European countries, Israel adopted a policy of determined resistance and immediate retaliation against PLO and Arab provocations. By the spring of 1967, relations between Israel and its Arab neighbors had deteriorated as Nasser attempted to improve his standing in the Arab world by intensifying military activities and imposing a blockade against Israeli commerce through the Gulf of Aqaba.

Concerned that it might be isolated, and lacking firm support from Western powers (which had originally guaranteed Israel the freedom to use the Gulf of Aqaba),

in June 1967 Israel suddenly launched air strikes against Egypt and several of its Arab neighbors. Israeli armies then broke the blockade at the head of the Gulf of Aqaba and occupied the Sinai peninsula. Other Israeli forces attacked Jordanian territory on the West Bank of the Jordan River (Jordan's King Hussein had recently signed an alliance with Egypt and placed his army under Egyptian command), occupied the whole of Jerusalem, and seized Syrian military positions in the Golan Heights along the Israeli-Syrian border.

Despite limited Soviet support for Egypt and Syria, in a brief six-day war, Israel had mocked Nasser's pretensions of Arab unity and tripled the size of its territory, thus enhancing its precarious security (see Map 15.2). Yet Israel had also aroused more bitter hostility among the Arabs and brought an additional million Palestinians inside its borders, most of them living on the West Bank.

During the next few years, the focus of the Arab-Israeli dispute shifted as Arab states demanded the return of the territories lost during the 1967 war. Meanwhile, many Israelis argued that the new lands improved the security of the beleaguered state and should be retained.

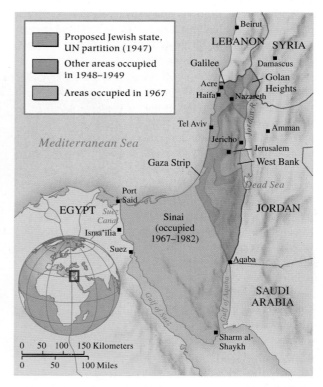

MAP 15.2 Israel and Its Neighbors. This map shows the evolution of the state of Israel since its founding in 1948. Areas occupied by Israel after the Six-Day War in 1967 are indicated in green.

Q *What is the significance of the West Bank?*

Concerned that the dispute might lead to a confrontation between the superpowers, the Nixon administration tried to achieve a peace settlement. The peace effort received a mild stimulus when Nasser died of a heart attack in September 1970 and was succeeded by his vice president, ex-general Anwar al-Sadat (1918–1981). Sadat soon showed himself to be more pragmatic than his predecessor, dropping the now irrelevant name United Arab Republic in favor of the Arab Republic of Egypt and replacing Nasser's socialist policies with a new strategy based on free enterprise and encouragement of Western investment. He also agreed to sign a peace treaty with Israel on the condition that Israel withdraw to its pre-1967 frontiers. Concerned that other Arab countries would refuse to make peace and take advantage of its presumed weakness, Israel refused.

Rebuffed in his offer of peace, smarting from criticism of his moderate stand from other Arab leaders, and increasingly concerned over Israeli plans to build permanent Jewish settlements in the West Bank, Sadat attempted once again to renew Arab unity through a new confrontation with Israel. In 1973, on Yom Kippur (the Jewish Day of Atonement), an Israeli national holiday, Egyptian forces suddenly launched an air and artillery attack on Israeli positions in the Sinai just east of the Suez Canal. Syrian armies attacked Israeli positions in the Golan Heights. After early Arab successes, the Israelis managed to recoup some of their losses on both fronts. As a superpower confrontation between the United States and the Soviet Union loomed, a cease-fire was finally reached. In the next years, a fragile peace was maintained, marked by U.S. "shuttle diplomacy" (carried out by Secretary of State Henry Kissinger) and the rise to power in Israel of the militant Likud Party under Prime Minister Menachem Begin (1913–1992).

The Camp David Agreement After his election as U.S. president in 1976, Jimmy Carter began to press for a compromise peace based on Israel's return of territories occupied during the 1967 war and Arab recognition of the state of Israel. In September 1978, Sadat and Begin met with Carter at Camp David in the United States and agreed on a framework for peace in the region (see Image 15.2). A year later, in the first treaty signed with a Muslim Arab state, Israel agreed to withdraw from the Sinai, but not from other occupied territories unless it was recognized by other Arab countries.

The promise of the Camp David agreement was not fulfilled, however. One reason was the assassination of Sadat by Islamic militants in October 1981. But there were deeper causes, including the continued unwillingness of many Muslim governments to recognize Israel and the Israeli government's encouragement of Jewish settlements in the occupied West Bank.

The PLO and the *Intifada* During the early 1980s, the militancy of the Palestinians increased, leading to rising unrest, popularly labeled the ***intifada*** (uprising), among PLO supporters living inside Israel. To control the situation, a new Israeli government under Prime Minister Itzhak Shamir (1915–2012) invaded southern Lebanon to destroy PLO commando bases near the Israeli border. The invasion aroused controversy abroad and further destabilized the perilous balance between Muslims and Christians in Lebanon. As the 1990s began, Israel and a number of its neighbors engaged in U.S.-sponsored peace talks, but progress was slow. Terrorist attacks by Palestinian militants resulted in heavy casualties and

IMAGE 15.2 The Camp David Accords. Prime Minister Menachim Begin of Israel and President Anwar al-Sadat hold a joint press conference after the signing of the Camp David Accords in September 1978. U.S. President Jimmy Carter is seated between them. Tragically, Sadat (on Carter's right) paid a high price for his courage in signing the agreement, for he was assassinated in Cairo by a Muslim terrorist two years later.

Q *Why do you think the Camp David agreement did not resolve the Palestinian dispute?*

shook the confidence of many Jewish citizens that their security needs could be protected. National elections held in 1996 led to the formation of a new government under Benjamin Netanyahu (b. 1949), which adopted a tougher stance in negotiations with the Palestinian Authority under Yasir Arafat.

In 1999, a new Labour government under Prime Minister Ehud Barak (b. 1942) sought to revitalize the peace process. Negotiations resumed with the PLO and also got under way with Syria over a peace settlement in Lebanon and the possible return of the Golan Heights. But the talks broke down over the future of the city of Jerusalem (see Image 15.3), leading to massive riots by Palestinians and a dramatic increase in bloodshed on both sides. The death of Yasir Arafat in 2004 and his replacement by Palestinian moderate Mahmoud Abbas (b. 1935), as well as the withdrawal of Israeli settlers from Gaza in 2005, raised modest hopes for progress, but the victory of **Hamas**, a radical organization dedicated to the destruction of the state of Israel, in Palestinian elections in 2006 undermined the search for peace.

IMAGE 15.3 **The Temple Mount at Jerusalem.** The Temple Mount is one of the most sacred places in the city of Jerusalem. Originally, it was the site of a temple built during the reign of Solomon, king of the Israelites, about 1000 B.C.E. The Western Wall, built during the reign of King Herod, is shown in the foreground. Beyond the wall is the Dome of the Rock complex, built on the place from which Muslims believe that Muhammad ascended to heaven. Sacred to both religions, the Temple Mount is now a major bone of contention between Muslims and Jews and a prime obstacle to a final settlement of the Arab-Israeli dispute. In 2018, the Trump administration suddenly announced that the U.S. Embassy would be shifted from Tel Aviv to Jerusalem, a clear sign that the United States recognizes Israeli ownership of the entire city of Jerusalem.

 What is the significance of the Temple Mount in the context of the Arab-Israeli dispute?

Also in 2006, radical Muslim forces, known as **Hezbollah** and operating in southern Lebanon, launched massive attacks on Israeli cities. In response, Israeli troops crossed the border in an effort to wipe out the source of the assault. Two years later, Hamas militants in the Gaza Strip launched their own rocket attacks on sites in southern Israel. The latter responded forcefully, thereby raising the specter of a wider conflict. As attitudes hardened, Israeli elections in early 2009 led to the return to office of former prime minister Benjamin Netanyahu and a virtual stalemate in the peace process. Apparently convinced that a peace settlement is increasingly unlikely, the Israeli government has continued to expand the number of Jewish settlements in the occupied West Bank—home to almost five million Muslims—and recently passed legislation declaring that Israel is "the nation-state of the Jewish people." Weary of war but pessimistic about the prospects of finding a solution, Israeli voters in 2019 returned Benjamin Netanyahu to office for another five-year term.

15-1d Revolution in Iran

As it intensified, the Arab-Israeli dispute sent shockwaves throughout the region. In 1960, a number of oil-producing states formed the Organization of Petroleum Exporting Countries (OPEC) to gain control over oil prices, but the organization was not recognized by the foreign oil companies. In the 1970s, a group of Arab oil states established the Organization of Arab Petroleum Exporting Countries (OAPEC) to use as a weapon to force Western governments to abandon pro-Israeli policies. During the 1973 Yom Kippur War, some OPEC nations announced significant increases in the price of oil to foreign countries. The price hikes were accompanied by an apparent oil shortage and created serious economic problems in the United States and Europe, as well as in the Third World.

One of the key oil-exporting countries was Iran (see Map 15.3). Under the leadership of Shah Mohammad Reza Pahlavi (1919–1980), who had taken over from his father in 1941, Iran had become one of the richest countries in the Middle East. Although relations with the West had occasionally been fragile (especially after Prime Minister Mohammad Mosaddeq had briefly attempted to nationalize the oil industry in 1951), during the next twenty years, Iran became a prime ally of the United States in the Middle East. With encouragement from Washington, which hoped that Iran could become a force for stability in the Persian Gulf, the shah attempted to carry through a series of social and economic reforms to transform the country into the most advanced in the region.

On paper, it appeared that his efforts were succeeding. Per capita income increased dramatically, literacy rates improved, a modern communications infrastructure took shape, and an affluent middle class emerged in the capital of Tehran. Under the surface, however, trouble was brewing. Despite an ambitious land reform program, many peasants were still landless, unemployment among intellectuals was dangerously high, and the urban middle class was squeezed by high inflation. Housing costs had skyrocketed, in part because of a massive influx of foreigners attracted by oil money.

Some of the unrest took the form of religious discontent as millions of devout Shi'ite Muslims looked with distaste at what they viewed as a new Iranian civilization based on greed, sexual license, and material accumulation. Conservative *ulama* (Muslim scholars) opposed rampant government corruption, the ostentation of the shah's court, and the extension of voting rights to women. Some opposition elements resorted to terrorism against wealthy Iranians or foreign residents in an attempt to initiate social and political disorder. In response, the shah's U.S.-trained security police, the SAVAK, imprisoned and sometimes tortured thousands of dissidents.

The Fall of the Shah Leading the opposition was Ayatollah Ruholla Khomeini (1900–1989), an austere Shi'ite cleric who had been exiled to Iraq and then to France because of his outspoken opposition to the shah's regime. From Paris, Khomeini continued his attacks in print, on television, and in radio broadcasts. By the late 1970s, large numbers of Iranians began to respond to Khomeini's diatribes against the "satanic regime," and demonstrations by his supporters were repressed with ferocity by the police. But workers' strikes (some of them in the oil fields, which reduced government revenue) grew in intensity. In January 1979, the shah appointed a moderate, Shapur Bakhtiar (1914–1991), as prime minister and then left the country for medical treatment.

MAP 15.3 Iran

Bakhtiar attempted to conciliate the rising opposition and permitted Khomeini to return to Iran, where he demanded the government's resignation. With rising public unrest and incipient revolt within the army, the government collapsed and was replaced by a hastily formed Islamic republic. The new government, which was dominated by Shi'ite *ulama* under the guidance of Ayatollah Khomeini, immediately began to introduce traditional Islamic law (see Movies & History, *Persepolis*, p. 377). A new reign of terror ensued as supporters of the shah were rounded up and executed.

Though much of the outside world focused on the U.S. embassy in Tehran, where militants held a number of foreign hostages, the Iranian Revolution involved much more. In the eyes of the ayatollah and his followers, the United States was "the great Satan," the powerful protector of Israel, and the enemy of Muslim peoples everywhere. Furthermore, it was responsible for the corruption of Iranian society under the shah. Now Khomeini demanded that the shah be returned to Iran for trial and that the United States apologize for its acts against the Iranian people. In response, the Carter administration stopped buying Iranian oil and froze Iranian assets in the United States.

The effects of the disturbances in Iran quickly spread beyond its borders. Sunni militants briefly seized the holy places in Mecca and began to appeal to their brothers to launch similar revolutions in Islamic countries around the world, including far-off Malaysia and Indonesia. At the same time, ethnic unrest emerged among the Kurdish minorities along the border. In July 1980, the shah died of cancer in Cairo. With economic conditions in Iran rapidly deteriorating, the Islamic revolutionary government finally agreed in January 1981 to free the 52 remaining U.S. citizens and diplomats held hostage in the U.S. Embassy in return for the release of Iranian assets in the United States. During the next few years, the intensity of the Iranian Revolution moderated slightly, as the government displayed a modest tolerance for a loosening of clerical control over freedom of expression and social activities. But rising criticism of rampant official corruption and a high rate of inflation sparked a new wave of government repression; newspapers were censored, the universities were purged of disloyal or "un-Islamic" elements, and religious militants raided private homes in search of blasphemous activities.

MOVIES & HISTORY
Persepolis (2007)

The Iranian author Marjane Satrapi (b. 1969) has recre-ated *Persepolis*, her autobiographical graphic novel, as an enthralling animated film of the same name. Using simple black-and-white animation, the movie recounts key stages in the turbulent history of modern Iran as seen through the eyes of a spirited young girl, also named Marjane. The dia-logue is in French with English subtitles (a version dubbed in English is also available), and the voices of the characters are rendered beautifully by Danielle Darrieux, Catherine Deneuve, Chiara Mastroianni, and other European film stars.

In the film, Marjane is the daughter of middle-class left-wing intellectuals who abhor the dictatorship of the shah and actively participate in his overthrow in 1979.

After the revolution, however, the severity of the ayatol-lah's Islamic rule arouses their secularist and democratic impulses. Encouraged by her loving grandmother, who reinforces her modernist and feminist instincts, Marjane resents having to wear a head scarf and the educational restrictions imposed by the puritanical new Islamic regime, but to little avail. Emotionally exhausted and fear-ful of political retribution from the authorities, her family finally sends her to study in Vienna.

Study abroad, however, is not a solution to Marjane's problems. She is distressed by the nihilism and emotional shallowness of her new Austrian school friends, who seem oblivious to the contrast between their privileged lives and her own experience of living under the shadow of a tyrannical regime. Disillusioned by the loneliness of exile and several failed love affairs, she descends into a deep depression and then decides to return to Tehran. When she discovers that her family is still suffering from politi-cal persecution, however, she decides to leave the country permanently and settles in Paris.

Observing the events, first through the eyes of a child and then through the perceptions of an innocent schoolgirl, the viewer of the film is forced to fill in the blanks, as Marjane initially cannot comprehend the meaning of the adult conversations swirling around her. As Marjane passes through adolescence into adulthood, the realization of the folly of human intransigence and superstition becomes painfully clear, both to her and to the audience. Although animated films have long been a staple in the cinema, thanks in part to Walt Disney, both the novel and the film *Persepolis* demonstrate how graphic design can depict a momentous event in history with clarity and compassion. After it began to appear in movie theaters in some cities in the Middle East, protests based on its depiction of Muhammed and the Islamic religion were a factor in inciting the riots that inaugurated the Arab Spring.

 Why might a devout Muslim find some aspects of life in modern Western society morally unacceptable today?

Presidential elections held in 2004 brought a new hard-line leader Mahmoud Ahmadinejad (b. 1956), to power in Tehran. A new wave of official repression soon ensued. The new president immediately inflamed the situation by increasing support for terrorist groups in the region and calling publicly for the destruction of the state of Israel; his government also aroused unease throughout the world by proclaiming its determination to develop a nuclear energy program, ostensibly for peaceful purposes. Blessed with the support of the conservative religious leadership, Ahmadinejad was reelected in 2009, but worsening economic conditions inside Iran—in part the consequence of a trade embargo enforced by the United States and several other major nations—eroded the government's popularity and led to the victory of a moderate candidate, Hassan Rouhani (b. 1948) in presidential elections held in 2013.

With his election came a sliver of hope that the era of confrontation with Western nations might be brought to an end, as much of the younger generation appeared anxious to end the country's isolation from the rest of the world. In 2015, a breakthrough agreement between Iran and a coalition of global nations was signed, bringing an end to the trade embargo in return for a halt in Iran's nuclear program. But the determination of the country's religious leadership to spread Iran's influence throughout the region appeared undiminished. In retaliation, in 2018 the administration of U.S. President Donald Trump reinstated its sanctions against Iran, and the issue was at a stalemate once again. Periodic clashes between naval forces of Iran and Western nations in the Persian Gulf have introduced the specter of military conflict to the dispute.

15-1e Crisis in the Persian Gulf

Although much of the public anger was directed against the United States during the early phases of the Iranian revolution, Iran had equally hated enemies closer to home. To the north, the immense power of the Soviet Union, driven by atheistic communism, was viewed as a modern-day version of the Russian threat of previous centuries. To the west was a militant and hostile Iraq, now under the leadership of the ambitious Saddam Hussein (1937–2006). Problems from both directions appeared shortly after Khomeini's rise to power. Soviet military forces occupied Afghanistan to prop up a weak Marxist regime there. The following year, Iraqi forces suddenly attacked along the Iranian border.

Iraq and Iran had long had an uneasy relationship, fueled by religious differences (Iranian Islam is predominantly Shi'ite, while the ruling class in Iraq was Sunni) and a perennial dispute over borderlands adjacent to the Persian Gulf, the vital waterway for the export of oil from both countries (see Map 15.1). Like several of its neighbors, Iraq had long dreamed of unifying the Arabs but had been hindered by internal factions and suspicion among its neighbors.

During the mid-1970s, Iran gave some support to a Kurdish rebellion in the mountains of Iraq. In 1975, the government of the shah agreed to stop aiding the rebels in return for territorial concessions at the head of the gulf. Five years later, however, the Kurdish revolt had been suppressed, and President Saddam Hussein, who had assumed power in Baghdad in 1979, began to persecute non-Arab elements in Iraq, including Persians, Kurds, and the country's small Christian community. A fervent believer in the Ba'athist vision of a single Arab state in the Middle East, Saddam then turned his sights to the east, accusing Iran of violating the territorial agreement and launching an attack on his neighbor. The war was a bloody one and lasted nearly ten years; poison gas was used against civilians, and children were sent out to clear minefields. Other countries, including the two superpowers, watched nervously in case the conflict spread throughout the region. Finally, with both sides virtually exhausted, a cease-fire was arranged in the fall of 1988.

The Vision of Saddam Hussein   The bitter conflict with Iran had not slaked Saddam Hussein's appetite for territorial expansion in the form of a Ba'athist state that would dominate the Middle East. In early August 1990, Iraqi military forces suddenly moved across the border and occupied the small neighboring country of Kuwait at the head of the gulf. The immediate pretext was the claim that Kuwait was pumping oil from fields inside Iraqi territory. Baghdad was also angry over the Kuwaiti government's demand for repayment of loans it had made to Iraq during the war with Iran. But the underlying reason was Iraq's contention that Kuwait was legally a part of Iraq. Kuwait had been part of the Ottoman Empire until the beginning of the twentieth century, when the local prince had agreed to place his patrimony under British protection. When Iraq became independent in 1932, it claimed the area on the grounds that the state of Kuwait had been created by British imperialism, but opposition from major Western powers and other countries in the region, which feared the consequences of a "greater Iraq," prevented an Iraqi takeover.

The Persian Gulf War   The Iraqi invasion of Kuwait sparked an international outcry, and the United States amassed an international force that liberated the country and destroyed a substantial part of Iraq's armed forces. But the allied forces did not occupy Baghdad at the end of the war because allied leaders feared that doing so would cause a total breakup of the country, an eventuality that would operate to the benefit of Iran. They hoped instead that the Hussein regime would be ousted by an internal revolt. In the meantime, harsh economic sanctions were imposed on the Iraqi government as the condition for peace. The anticipated overthrow of Saddam Hussein did not materialize, however, and his tireless efforts to evade the conditions of the cease-fire continued to bedevil the administrations of Presidents Bill Clinton and George W. Bush.

15-1f Turmoil in the Middle East

The terrorist attacks launched against U.S. cities in September 2001 added a new dimension to the Middle Eastern equation. The operation had been orchestrated by an organization called al-Qaeda that, under the leadership of Osama bin Laden, had begun to recruit followers from all over the Muslim world with the intention of waging terrorist attacks against prominent targets in Europe and the United States. Al-Qaeda's ultimate objective was to destabilize those governments that—in the eyes of bin Laden and his associates—were propping up dictators in the Middle East and weakening the forces of the true faith of Islam (see Historical Voices, "I Accuse!" p. 369).

Conflicts in Afghanistan and Iraq   After the failure of the Soviet Union to quell the rebellion in Afghanistan during the 1980s (see Chapter 7), a fundamentalist Muslim group known as the Taliban, which had been supported covertly by the United States during the revolt, seized power in Kabul and began to rule the country with a fanaticism reminiscent of the Cultural Revolution in China. Backed by conservative religious forces in Pakistan, the Taliban provided a base of operations for Osama bin Laden's al-Qaeda terrorist network. After the attacks of September 11, however, a coalition of forces led by the United States drove the Taliban out of Kabul and attempted to build a new and moderate government in Afghanistan. But the country's history of bitter internecine warfare among tribal groups presented a severe challenge to those efforts, and although al-Qaeda was dealt a major blow in May 2011 when Osama bin Laden was killed by U.S. special operations forces during a raid on his hideout in northern Pakistan,

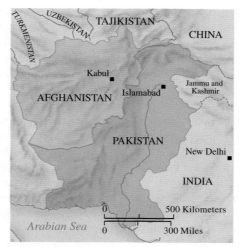

MAP 15.4 Afghanistan

Taliban forces have managed to regroup among tribal communities in Afghanistan and continue to operate in mountainous areas of the country. With the U.S. military presence in the mountainous country now stretching almost two decades, peace talks have been held without success (see Map 15.4).

Emboldened by its initial success in evicting the Taliban from its dominant position in Afghanistan, the administration of George W. Bush broadened its regional objectives. In March 2003, the Bush administration ordered U.S.-led forces to occupy Iraq and topple the Saddam Hussein regime. To justify the action, the White House charged that Iraqi dictator Saddam Hussein had not only provided support to bin Laden's terrorist organization but also stockpiled weapons of mass destruction for use against his enemies. Although the plan was controversial among the American public and was opposed by many U.S. allies, administration strategists hoped that the overthrow of the Iraqi dictator would promote the spread of democracy throughout the region. In the months that followed, U.S. occupation forces sought to restore stability to the country while setting out plans to transform Iraq into a democratic society. But although Saddam Hussein was captured by U.S. troops and later executed, armed resistance by militant Muslim elements continued, while the new Iraqi government soon descended into turmoil as sectarian clashes took place between Sunnis and the majority Shi'ite population.

On assuming office in 2009, President Barack Obama promised to bring about the withdrawal of U.S. combat forces from Iraq, while training an Iraqi military force capable of defeating the remaining insurgents. But as the final U.S. combat forces departed Iraq, the situation inside the country was slow to stabilize as Sunni militants, some of them infiltrated from neighboring Syria, unleashed attacks that threatened to undermine the fragile stability of the Shi'ite-dominated Iraqi regime (see Map 15.5).

Predominantly Sunni areas
Predominantly Shi'ite areas
Predominantly Kurdish areas

MAP 15.5 Iraq

False Dawn: The Arab Spring   As the wave of unrest threatened to engulf the entire region, popular protests against current conditions broke out in several countries in the Middle East. Beginning in Tunisia, the riots spread rapidly to Egypt—where they forced the abrupt resignation of long-time president Hosni Mubarak (b. 1929)—and then to other countries in the region, including Syria, Libya, and Yemen, where political leaders sought to quell the unrest, often by violent means. The uprisings (dubbed by pundits the "Arab Spring") aroused hopes around the world that the seeds of democracy had been planted in a region long dominated by autocratic governments (see Image 15.4).

It soon became clear that such optimism was drastically misplaced, as the unstable conditions led rapidly to the outbreak of civil wars in several countries in the region. In Egypt, a newly elected government under Prime Minister Mohamed Morsi (1951-2019), a member of the one-time radical Muslim Brotherhood, antagonized moderates by seeking to install a strict interpretation of Islamic law, and another round of popular protests led to his overthrow and a return to military rule. A new government under General Abdel Fattah el-Sisi has suppressed protest and restored the autocratic rule practiced by his predecessor Hosni Mubarak.

A bloodier confrontation took place in neighboring Libya, where the long-time dictator Muammar Qaddafi was toppled by a popular revolt with the assistance of NATO air strikes, but a fragile peace has since descended into civil war. In Yemen, a mountainous state along the southern coast of the Arabian peninsula, bitter fighting between the established Sunni-based government and a rebel Shi'a group known as the **Houthi** has resulted in thousands of civilian casualties. The conflict has serious regional implications, with Saudi Arabia backing the Sunni-based government forces, while the Houthis—who currently occupy the capital of Sana'a—have received support from their co-religionists in Iran.

The consequences of spreading violence were most ominous in Syria, where a variety of ethnic groups rose up in opposition to the minority Shi'ite government led by President Bashir al-Assad (b. 1965). Although some resistance forces sought to form a more pluralist society or, like the Kurds, were struggling to realize their dream of creating an independent Kurdistan carved from several neighboring states, other resistance groups allied with militants operating in neighboring Iraq to form a new terrorist organization, popularly called the Islamic State of Iraq and Syria (ISIS). The goal of the ISIS leadership was to create a caliphate that would rule the entire region according to the tenets of fundamentalist Islam. As ISIS began to seek recruits among restive Muslims elsewhere, terrorist attacks carried out by its supporters spread rapidly throughout the world. Meanwhile, casualties resulting from the civil war within Syria numbered in the hundreds of thousands, unleashing a mass migration of frightened refugees into continental Europe (see Image 15.5).

Today, the situation throughout the Middle East remains unstable, with autocratic governments ruling with ruthless determination against restive populations suffering under economic

Claudia Wiens/Alamy Stock Photo

IMAGE 15.4 Tahrir Square: Ground Zero for the Arab Spring. When popular demonstrations broke out against the regime of Egyptian president Hosni Mubarak in early 2011, Tahrir Square, in the heart of the teeming metropolis of Cairo, was at the epicenter of the protests. For weeks, supporters and opponents of the regime clashed periodically in the square, resulting in severe casualties. After the overthrow of Mubarak, the square continued to provide a venue for public protests against the new government of President Mohamed Morsi, leader of the Muslim Brotherhood, and when public protests against the latter escalated, the army stepped in to depose President Morsi.

Why were the demonstrations in Tahrir Square not successful in changing the trajectory of Egyptian politics?

IMAGE 15.5 **The Destruction of Aleppo.** One of the most disastrous consequences of the civil war in Syria has been its effect on the people living in that war-torn country. With casualties numbering in the hundreds of thousands, and countless others fleeing for safety abroad, those remaining in ancient cities like Aleppo are caught in the crossfire of tenacious opposing forces, as this photograph graphically demonstrates.

underdevelopment, high rates of unemployment, and widespread civic unrest. Even countries that have long appeared to be unaffected by the turmoil in the region have now caught the virus. Young people in the fundamentalist Islamic kingdom of Saudi Arabia—where the unemployment rate is alarmingly high, especially among the young—have begun to clamor for greater freedom of thought and action, while in the one-time French possession of Algeria, massive popular demonstrations brought about the resignation of the aging ruler Abdelaziz Bouteflika, who had presided over a repressive military regime since the end of the twentieth century. It is no exaggeration to say that the situation in the Middle East is more dangerous than it has been for decades.

15-2 SOCIETY AND CULTURE IN THE CONTEMPORARY MIDDLE EAST

Q **Focus Question:** How have religious issues affected political, economic, and social conditions in the Middle East in recent decades?

In the Middle East today, all aspects of society and culture—from political and economic issues to literature, art, and the role of the family—are intertwined with questions

of religious faith. Whereas in much of the rest of the world, the center of popular attention is usually focused on political or economic issues as sometimes related but ultimately separate from religious beliefs and practices, in most countries of the Middle East, Islam is at the center of social, political, and economic life.

15-2a Varieties of Government: The Politics of Islam

When U.S. forces invaded Iraq in 2003, Bush administration officials argued that the overthrow of the Saddam Hussein regime would open the door to the spread of democratic values throughout the region. In the eyes of many seasoned observers, however, ambitious schemes drafted by outsiders to remake the Middle East in the Western image are unrealistic, since Western-style democratic values are not deeply rooted in the culture of the region. Although the popular uprisings that have taken place in many countries in recent years are a clear sign that the autocratic ways of the past are no longer as effective as they had been in the past, few countries in the Middle East have managed to make the transition to broad-based pluralistic societies based on the concept of equal rights and a peaceful transfer of power. A few Arab nations, such as Jordan and the Persian Gulf mini-states of Bahrain, Kuwait, and the United Arab Emirates (UAE), have engaged in limited forms of democratic experimentation, but they too continue to repress dissident activities. The Crown Prince of the Kingdom of Saudi Arabia, Muhammad bin Salman, has recently declared his intention to introduce political reforms in his once-closed kingdom, but even here, his autocratic tendencies and brutal suppression of critics raises doubts among many about his ultimate intentions.

Some tolerance for political dissent and religious pluralism appears to prevail in the North African nations of Tunisia and Morocco. In general, however, Muslim leaders like ex-President Hosni Mubarak of Egypt usually insist that only authoritarian rule can prevent the spread of civil disorder and Islamic radicalism throughout the region. To some, the recent rise of ISIS in the aftermath of the U.S. invasion of Iraq has appeared to justify those fears.

But is autocracy the only answer, or is it only a band aid applied to a deep flesh wound? Syria's Bashar al-Assad (b. 1965) once remarked that he would tolerate only "positive criticism" of his policies. "We have to have our own democracy to match our history and culture," he said, "arising from the needs of our people and our reality."[2] Today, Assad's regime is on life support as the result of the series of popular uprisings that have destabilized his country, and the only peace in Syria today is the peace of death.

For many years, the shining exception to the general rule appeared to be Turkey, where—after a long period of military rule—free elections and the sharing of power had recently tended to become more prevalent. For decades, the military had played the dominant role in Turkish politics, enforcing Kamal Ataturk's policy of secularism and ethnic tolerance with a sometimes iron hand, but in 2007 a Muslim-based political party won peaceful elections and took power in the capital of Ankara. The new government, under the direction of Prime Minister Recep Erdogan (b. 1954), earned popular support by combining a moderate stance on religious issues with a number of economic reforms.

As time went on, however, Erdogan's autocratic instincts became more in evidence. Official corruption, a pronounced favoritism to traditional Islam, and the brutal suppression of dissenting voices have severely tested the government's popularity, which is based primarily in religiously conservative rural areas on the Asian peninsula of Anatolia. Erdogan—who has now assumed the presidency to perpetuate his power—appears unfazed by such criticism and openly promotes the past glories of the Ottoman Empire as a potential model for a new Turkey. But Erdogan's tough stance toward his opponents has not always worked to his benefit. Many of Turkey's most enterprising people have left the country, and the economy has been badly damaged by the flight of capital toward more secure locations. With the population of Turkey bitterly divided and a destructive civil war in Syria still being waged at its doorstep, it remains an open question whether Turkey's recent experiment with political pluralism will succeed.

HISTORIANS DEBATE **Islam and Democracy: Are They Compatible?** Is it still possible to turn Muslim countries like Iraq into democratic nations, as President George W. Bush and his advisers believed? Or are critics correct that states in which a majority practice the Islamic faith are not fertile ground for the establishment of democratic institutions? For many years, most Western governments followed the assumption that only a strong paternal government could rule effectively in the Middle East,

provoking some observers to charge that they coddled Middle Eastern dictatorships as a means of preserving access to the vast oil reserves in the region (see Historical Voices, "Islam and Democracy," p. 383). The recent wave of popular unrest initially aroused hopes that a new order awaited in the wings, but as sectarian conflicts have spread rapidly throughout the region, the current signs suggest that this wave of political and social instability is likely to continue for the indefinite future. Effective democracy relies for its survival on a shared sense of national destiny, and any public agreement on such issues is in short supply these days.

Certainly there is nothing inherent in the religion of Islam that is contrary to democratic principle and practice. There are no privileged castes or classes recognized in Muslim society, and all believers are theoretically equal in the eyes of God. Muslim countries in Southeast Asia like Indonesia and Malaysia are obvious testimonials to the fact that free elections can take place in Muslim-majority countries with a minimum of violence and public dispute. On the other hand, the treatment of religious minorities in many states in the Middle East leaves much to be desired, while the position of women remains an obvious affront to the basic democratic principle of sexual equality.

The crux of the problem, then, appears to lie not in the Islamic creed itself but in the inherited crust of tradition that has accompanied its rise to prominence as a world religion. Many Muslim religious figures in the Middle East seem intent on enforcing a rigid interpretation of Islam that is often based not on scripture but on ancient practice. And many politicians in the region appear unwilling to risk antagonizing such voices, out of fear of the political consequences. As Islamic societies are buffeted by the countervailing winds of globalization and traditional resistance, the fate of the region hangs in the balance.

15-2b The Economics of the Middle East: Oil and Sand

Few areas exhibit a greater disparity of individual and national wealth than the Middle East. While millions live in abject poverty, a fortunate few rank among the wealthiest people in the world. The primary reason for this disparity is oil. Unfortunately for most of the peoples of the region, oil reserves are distributed unevenly and all too often are located in areas where the population density is low (see Map 15.1). Egypt and Turkey, with more than 75 million inhabitants apiece, have almost no oil reserves. The combined population of Kuwait, the United Arab Emirates, and Saudi Arabia is about 45 million people. This disparity in wealth inspired Nasser's quest for Arab unity but has also posed a major obstacle to that objective, as oil-rich states proved unwilling to share the largess that lay

Islam and Democracy

 Q *How does the author answer the charge that democracy and Islam are incompatible? To what degree is the West responsible for the problems of the Middle East?*

Religion & Philosophy ONE OF GEORGE W. BUSH'S KEY OBJECTIVES in launching the invasion of Iraq in 2003 was to promote the emergence of democratic states throughout the Middle East. According to U.S. officials, one of the ultimate causes of the formation of terrorist movements in Muslim societies is the prevalence in such countries of dictatorial governments that do not serve the interests of their citizens. According to the author of this editorial, an Indian Muslim, the problem lies as much with the actions of Western countries as it does with political attitudes in the Muslim world.

M. J. Akbar, "Linking Islam to Dictatorship"

Let us examine a central canard, that Islam and democracy are incompatible. This is an absurdity. There is nothing Islamic or un-Islamic about democracy. Democracy is the outcome of a political process, not a religious process.

It is glibly suggested that "every" Muslim country is a dictatorship, but the four largest Muslim populations of the world—in Indonesia, India, Bangladesh, and Turkey—vote to change governments. Pakistan could easily have been on this list.

Voting does not make these Muslims less or more religious. There are dictators among Muslims just as there are dictators among Christians, Buddhists, and Hindus (check out Nepal). . . . Christian Latin America has seen ugly forms of dictatorship, as has Christian Africa.

What is unique to the Muslim world is not the absence of democracy but the fact that in 1918, after the defeat of the Ottoman Empire, every single Muslim in the world lived under foreign subjugation.

Every single one, from Indonesia to Morocco via Turkey. The Turks threw out their invaders within a few years under the great leadership of Kemal Atatürk, but the transition to self-rule in other Muslim countries was

slow, uncertain, and full of traps planted by the world's preeminent powers.

The West, in the shape of Britain, France, or America, was never interested in democracy when a helpful dictator or king would serve. When people got a chance to express their wish, it was only logical that they would ask for popular rule. It was the street that brought Mosaddeq to power in Iran and drove the shah of Iran to tearful exile in Rome. Who brought the shah of Iran and autocracy back to Iran? The CIA.

If Iranian democracy had been permitted a chance in 1953, there would have been no uprising led by Ayatollah Khomeini in 1979. In other countries, where the struggle for independence was long and brutal, as in Algeria and Indonesia, the militias who had fought the war institutionalized army authority. In other instances, civilian heroes confused their own well-being with national health. They became regressive dictators. Once again, there was nothing Islamic about it.

Muslim countries will become democracies, too, because it is the finest form of modern governance. But it will be a process interrupted by bloody experience as the street wrenches power from usurpers.

Democracy has happened in Turkey. It has happened in Bangladesh. It is happening in Indonesia. It almost happened in Pakistan, and the opportunity will return. Democracy takes time in the most encouraging environments.

Democracy has become the latest rationale for the occupation of Iraq. . . . Granted, democracy is always preferable to tyranny no matter how it comes. But Iraqis are not dupes. They will take democracy and place it at the service of nationalism. A decade ago, America was careless about the definition of victory. Today it is careless about the definition of democracy.

There is uncertainty and apprehension across the Muslim nations: uncertainty about where they stand, and apprehension about both American power and the repugnant use of terrorism that in turn invites the exercise of American power. There is also anger that a legitimate cause like that of Palestine can get buried in the debris of confusion. Muslims do not see Palestinians as terrorists.

Source: From M. J. Akbar, "Linking Islam to Dictatorship" in *World Press Review*, May 2004. Reprinted by permission.

From Rags to Riches in the Middle East

 Q *Which are the wealthiest states in the Middle East? Which are the poorest?*

Politics & Government **FEW PARTS OF THE WORLD** exhibit such a glaring contrast between conditions of wealth and poverty as the contemporary Middle East. Although much of the population in the region still lives in

impoverished conditions barely above the means of subsistence, a fortunate few possess among the highest standards of living in the entire world. Image 15.6a shows a shepherd with his donkey and two camels in the Arabian desert scratching out a living near the coast of Yemen. Image 15.6b shows the skyline of the modern city of Abu Dhabi in the United Arab Emirates.

IMAGE 15.6a

IMAGE 15.6b

under their soil (see Comparative Illustration "From Rags to Riches in the Middle East," above).

Economics and Islam The Qur'an provides little guidance to Muslims searching for economic policies appropriate to their faith, although it is clear in its concern for the overall welfare of the community. Thus, it is no surprise that the states of the Middle East have adopted diverse approaches to the challenge of developing strong and stable economies. Some, like Nasser in Egypt and the leaders of the Ba'ath Party in Syria, were attracted to a form of Arab socialism with a high degree of government intervention in the economy to relieve the inequities of the free enterprise system. Others have turned to the capitalist model to maximize growth while using taxes or massive development projects to build a modern infrastructure, redistribute wealth, and maintain political stability and economic opportunity for all.

Regardless of the strategy employed, many Middle Eastern states have been plagued with problems of rapid

population growth, widespread corruption, and a lack of adequate educational and technological skills, all of which have acted as a drag on economic growth (see Image 15.7).

One key problem is rural poverty. Arable land is in short supply throughout the region and is often concentrated in the hands of wealthy absentee landlords. Some countries such as Egypt and Iran have adopted ambitious land reform programs, although with mixed success. In any case, there are many structural obstacles to rural prosperity, including rapid population growth, low agricultural productivity, and a lack of water resources. Much of the Arabian Peninsula is desert, and those who inhabit the area—like the lonely shepherd shown in the comparative illustration above—are barely able to scratch out a livelihood. Agricultural productivity throughout the region has been plagued by a lack of water. With populations growing at more than 2 percent annually on average in the Middle East (more than 3 percent in some countries), several governments have tried

IMAGE 15.7 An Unlimited Resource: School Children in Yemen. One of the chief sources of political unrest in many Middle Eastern countries is the high level of unemployment, especially among the young. Almost one-half of the total population of 30 million people in Yemen today are under the age of 15, and the average Yemeni woman produces almost five children, one of the highest fertility rates in the world. Tragically, the current civil war in the country has led to the death by violence or starvation of thousands of civilians, certainly a brutal way to control population growth.

Q *Are countries faced with high birth rates and stagnant economies justified in adopting population control problems, as has been the case in China?*

to increase the amount of water available for irrigation. Many attempts have been sabotaged by government ineptitude, political disagreements, and territorial conflicts, however. For example, disputes between Israel and its neighbors over water rights and between Iraq and its neighbors over the exploitation of the Tigris and Euphrates Rivers have caused serious tensions in recent years. Today, the dearth of water in the region is reaching crisis proportions.

Emigration to the cities has not been a panacea, as few Middle Eastern leaders have managed to adopt policies calculated to place their country on a path of sustained economic growth. Another way that governments have attempted to deal with rapid population growth is to encourage emigration. Oil-producing states with small populations, such as Saudi Arabia and the United Arab Emirates, have imported labor from other countries in the region, mostly to work in the oil fields. Since the mid-1980s, the majority of the population in those states has been composed of foreign nationals, who often send the bulk of their salaries back to their families in their home countries. When oil revenues declined in the 1980s and 1990s, however, several governments took measures

to reduce their migrant population. Today migrant workers are a volatile force in the politics of the region.

15-2c The Islamic Revival

In recent years, developments in the Middle East have often been described in terms of a resurgence of traditional values and customs in response to Western influence. Indeed, some conservative religious forces in the area have consciously attempted to replace foreign culture and values with allegedly "pure" Islamic forms of belief and behavior. Such views have undoubtedly been a major factor in the recent popularity of terrorist movements such as al-Qaeda and ISIS.

Modernist Islam In the early twentieth century, many Muslim intellectuals responded to Western influence by trying to create a "modernized" set of Islamic beliefs and practices that would not clash with the demands of the twentieth century. This process was particularly espoused in countries with modernizing leaders like Turkey, Egypt, and Iran. Mustafa Kemal Atatürk embraced the strategy when he attempted to secularize the Islamic religion in the new Turkish republic (see Image 15.8). The Turkish model was followed by Shah Reza Khan and his son Mohammad Reza Pahlavi in Iran and then by Nasser in postwar Egypt, all of whom attempted to honor Islamic values while asserting the primacy of other issues such as political and economic development. Religion, in effect, had become the handmaiden of political power, national identity, and economic prosperity.

These secularizing trends were particularly noticeable among the political, intellectual, and economic elites in urban areas. They had less influence in the countryside, among the poor, and among devout elements within the clergy. Many Muslim clerics believed that Western influence in the cities had given birth to political and economic corruption, sexual promiscuity, hedonism, individualism, and the prevalence of alcohol, pornography, and drugs. Although such practices had long existed in the Middle East, they were now far more visible and socially acceptable.

William J. Duiker

IMAGE 15.8 Santa Sophia: Symbol of Religious Tolerance in Turkey. The Church of Holy Wisdom (Hagia Sofia in Greek) was built by the sixth-century Byzantine Emperor Justinian in the center of his capital of Constantinople to proclaim the glories of Christianity throughout the eastern Mediterranean. After the fall of the Byzantine empire in 1453, the Ottomans turned the magnificent church into a mosque, but Kemal Ataturk, modern Turkey's first president, ordered that it be made a museum to symbolize his country's recent embrace of secular governance. Visitors today are awestruck by the magnificent Christian mosaics in the interior, which vie for attention with gigantic discs in gilded Arab script praising the glories of Allah.

Q *Do you believe that a constitutional provision to guarantee the separation of church and state is desirable in all countries that seek to govern by democratic means?*

Return to Tradition Reaction among conservatives against the modernist movement in the Middle East gradually built up after World War II and reached its zenith in the late 1970s with the return of the Ayatollah Khomeini to Iran. It is not surprising that Iran took the lead in light of its long tradition of ideological purity within the Shi'ite sect as well as the uncompromisingly secular character of the shah's reforms in the postwar era. Over forty years later, key elements within the Iranian political and religious leadership continue to enforce traditional Islamic customs and beliefs despite a growing counter-reaction from among the younger generation, many of whom are increasingly drawn to the glittering Western lifestyle they see on social media.

The cultural and social effects of the Iranian Revolution soon began to spread. In Algeria, the political influence of fundamentalist Islamic groups enabled them to win a stunning victory in the national elections in 1992. When the military stepped in to cancel the second round of elections and crack down on the militants, the latter responded with a campaign of terrorism against moderates that claimed thousands of lives. A similar trend emerged in Egypt, where militant groups such as the Muslim Brotherhood engaged in terrorism, including the assassination of President Anwar al-Sadat and attacks on foreign tourists, who are considered carriers of corrupt Western influence. Military rule over both countries has been justified by the fear of a recurrence of the civil unrest.

Even in Turkey, generally considered the most secular of Islamic societies, the victory of the Islamic Justice and Development Party (AKP) in recent elections has led to efforts on their part to guarantee the rights of devout Muslims to display their faith publicly. Such policies have opened a growing divide between secular elements among the middle class and more traditionalist forces in the countryside that represent the base of President Erdogan's political authority.

The shift from secularism to fundamentalist Islam has had a perceptible influence within the region. The Erdogan government has adopted a pro-Arab stance in foreign affairs, while threatening to reduce the country's economic and political ties to Europe and the United States. Worried moderates increasingly voice concern that the secular legacy of Kemal Atatürk was being eroded, but an abortive coup d'etat led to the arrest of many of Erdogan's enemies in government and the professions and an effort to silence critical voices in the media.

15-2d Women in the Middle East

Nowhere have the fault lines between tradition and modernity in the Middle East been so sharp as in the ongoing debate over the role of women in a Muslim society. At the beginning of the twentieth century, women's place in Middle Eastern society had changed little since the death of the prophet Muhammad. Women were secluded in their homes and had few legal, political, or social rights.

During the first decades of the twentieth century, advocates of modernist views began to contend that Islamic doctrine was not inherently opposed to women's rights. To modernists, Islamic traditions such as female seclusion, wearing the veil, and polygamy were actually pre-Islamic folk traditions that had been tolerated in the early Islamic era and continued to be practiced in later centuries. Such views had a considerable impact on a number of Middle Eastern societies, including Turkey and Iran. As we have seen, greater rights for women were a crucial element in the social revolution promoted by Kemal Atatürk in Turkey. In Iran, Shah Reza Khan and his son granted female suffrage and encouraged the education of women. In Egypt, a vocal feminist movement arose in educated women's circles in Cairo as early as the 1920s. With the exception of Orthodox religious communities, women in Israel have achieved substantial equality with men and are active in politics, the professions, and even the armed forces. Golda Meir (1898–1978), prime minister of Israel from 1969 to 1974, became an international symbol of the ability of women to be world leaders.

In recent years, a more traditional view of women's role has tended to prevail in many Middle Eastern countries. Attacks by religious conservatives on the growing role of women contributed to the emotions underlying the Iranian Revolution of 1979. Iranian women were instructed to wear the veil and to dress modestly in public. Films produced in post-revolutionary Iran rarely featured women, and when they did, physical contact between men and women was prohibited. The events in Iran had repercussions in secular Muslim societies such as Egypt, Turkey, and far-off Malaysia, where women began to dress more modestly in public and criticism of open sexuality in the media became increasingly frequent.

Still, women's rights have been extended in a few countries. In 1999, women obtained the right to vote in Kuwait, and they have been granted an equal right with their husbands to seek a divorce in Egypt. In Iran, women have many freedoms that they lacked before the twentieth century; for example, they can receive military training, vote, practice birth control, and publish fiction. Most important, today nearly 60 percent of university entrants in Iran are women.

The most conservative nation with respect to social relations in the Middle East has long been Saudi Arabia where, following Wahhabi tradition, women have not only been segregated and expected to wear the veil in public but also restricted in education and employment and forbidden to drive automobiles (see Historical Voices, "Keeping the Camel Out of the Tent," p. 388). Even there, however, there are tantalizing signs that change is in the air. In recent years, laws restricting women's right to work in commercial establishments have been loosened, and women have been given formal permission to drive vehicles as well

as to attend soccer matches in public in 2017. That dramatic change in policy seems to reflect the determination of the kingdom's new ruler, Crown Prince Mohammed bin Salman (b. 1985) to bring his country into the modern world. Once granted, rights are difficult to suppress, and women in Saudi Arabia today continue their efforts to obtain full civil rights equal to those possessed by their male counterparts.

15-2e Literature and Art

As in other areas of Asia and Africa, the encounter with the West in the nineteenth and twentieth centuries stimulated a cultural renaissance in the Middle East. Muslim authors translated Western works into Arabic and Persian and began to experiment with new literary forms.

National Literatures   Since World War II, Iranian literature has been hampered somewhat by political considerations, since it has been expected to serve first the Pahlavi monarchy and then the Islamic republic. Nevertheless, Iran has produced one of the most prominent national literatures in the contemporary Middle East.

Despite the male-oriented nature of Iranian society, many of the new writers are women. Since the revolution, the veil and the *chador*, an all-enveloping cloak, have become the central metaphor in Iranian women's writing. Advocates praise these garments as the last bastion of defense against Western cultural imperialism and the courageous woman's weapon against Western efforts to dominate the Iranian soul. Behind the veil, the Islamic woman can breathe freely, unpolluted by foreign exploitation and moral corruption. Other Iranian women, however, consider the veil and *chador* a "mobile prison" or an oppressive anachronism from the Dark Ages. A few use the pen as a weapon in a crusade to liberate their sisters and enable them to make their own choices. As one writer, Sousan Azadi, expressed it, "As I pulled the *chador* over me, I felt a heaviness descending over me. I was hidden and in hiding. There was nothing visible left of Sousan Azadi."[3]

Like Iran, Egypt in the twentieth century experienced a flowering of literature accelerated by the establishment of the Egyptian republic in the early 1950s. The most illustrious contemporary Egyptian writer was Naguib Mahfouz (1911–2006), who won the Nobel Prize in Literature in 1988. His *Cairo Trilogy* (1952) chronicles three generations of a merchant family in Cairo during the tumultuous years between the world wars. Mahfouz was particularly adept at blending panoramic historical events with the intimate lives of ordinary human beings. Unlike many other modern writers, his message was essentially optimistic and reflected his hope that religion and science could work

Keeping the Camel Out of the Tent

 According to Geraldine Brooks, do women in Saudi Arabia have an opportunity to receive an education? To what degree do they take advantage of it?

Family & Society **"ALMIGHTY GOD CREATED SEXUAL DESIRE** in ten parts; then he gave nine parts to women and one to men." So pronounced Ali, Muhammad's son-in-law, as he explained why women are held morally responsible as the instigators of sexual intercourse. Consequently, over the centuries, Islamic women have been secluded, veiled, and in many cases genitally mutilated in order to safeguard male virtue. Women are forbidden to look directly at, speak to, or touch a man prior to marriage. Even today, they are often sequestered at home or limited to strictly segregated areas away from all male contact. Women normally pray at home or in an enclosed antechamber of the mosque so that their physical presence will not disturb men's spiritual concentration.

Especially limiting today are the laws governing women's behavior in Saudi Arabia. Schooling for girls has never been compulsory because fathers believe that "educating women is like allowing the nose of the camel into the tent; eventually the beast will edge in and take up all the room inside." The country did not establish its first girls' school until 1956. The following description of Saudi women is from *Nine Parts Desire: The Hidden World of Islamic Women* by the journalist Geraldine Brooks.

Geraldine Brooks, *Nine Parts Desire*

Women were first admitted to university in Saudi Arabia in 1962, and all women's colleges remain strictly segregated. Lecture rooms come equipped with closed-circuit TVs and telephones, so women students can listen to a male professor and question him by phone, without having to contaminate themselves by being seen by him. When the first dozen women graduated from university in 1973, they were devastated to find that their names hadn't been printed on the commencement program. The old tradition, that it dishonors women to mention them, was depriving them of recognition they believed they'd earned. The women and their families protested, so a separate program was printed and a segregated graduation ceremony was held for the students' female relatives. . . .

But while the opening of women's universities widened access to higher learning for women, it also made the educational experience much shallower. Before 1962, many progressive Saudi families had sent their daughters abroad for education. They had returned to the kingdom not only with a degree but with experience of the outside world. . . . Now a whole generation of Saudi women have completed their education entirely within the country. . . .

Lack of opportunity for education abroad means that Saudi women are trapped in the confines of an education system that still lags men's. Subjects such as geology and petroleum engineering—tickets to influential jobs in Saudi Arabia's oil economy—remain closed to women. . . . Few women's colleges have their own libraries, and libraries shared with men's schools are either entirely off limits to women or open to them only one day per week. . . .

But women and men sit for the same degree examinations. Professors quietly acknowledge the women's scores routinely outstrip the men's. "It's no surprise," said one woman professor. "Look at their lives. The boys have their cars, they can spend the evenings cruising the streets with their friends, sitting in cafés, buying black-market alcohol and drinking all night. What do the girls have? Four walls and their books. For them, education is everything."

Source: From *Nine Parts Desire: The Hidden World of Islamic Women*, by Geraldine Brooks (Doubleday, 1996).

together for the overall betterment of humankind. One of the most popular contemporary authors presents a more pessimistic view. In *The Yacoubian Building*, Alaa al-Aswany (b. 1957) deplored the problems of political corruption and religious fundamentalism that plagued Egypt under Mubarak's regime. After the arrest of demonstrators who had taken part in the uprising in Tahrir square, he expressed criticism of restoration of the autocratic, and has been prosecuted for his comments. No woman writer has played a more active role in exposing the physical and psychological grievances of Egyptian women than Nawal el-Saadawi (b. 1931). For decades, she has battled against the injustices of religious fundamentalism and a male-dominated society—even enduring imprisonment for promoting her cause. In 1982 she established the Arab Women's Solidarity Association, which promotes the cause of women in society and politics, and is still in operation today. In *Two Women in One* (1985), el-Saadawi follows the struggle of a young university student as she rebels against the life her father has programmed for her, striking out instead on an unchartered independent destiny.

The emergence of a modern Turkish literature can be traced to the establishment of the republic in 1923. The most popular contemporary writer is Orhan Pamuk (b. 1952), whose novels attempt to capture Turkey's unique blend of cultures. "I am living in a culture," he writes, "where the clash of East and West, or the harmony of East and West, is the lifestyle. That is Turkey."[4] His novel *Snow* (2002) dramatizes the conflict between secularism and radical Islam in contemporary Turkey. Pamuk was awarded the Nobel Prize in Literature in 2006.

The current turmoil in the Middle East has been explored by a number of writers from the region. Mohsin Hamid (b. 1971), a Pakistani author, has explored recent global issues in his two novels *The Reluctant Fundamentalist* (2007) and *Exit West* (2017). In the latter, he encapsulates the forced emigration of millions of refugees forced to flee their homes because of war or environmental degradation. Hamid then describes their brave struggle to adapt to a foreign culture in exile.

Although Israeli literature arises from a totally different tradition from that of its neighbors, it shares with them certain contemporary characteristics and a concern for ordinary human beings. Early writers identified with the aspirations of the new nation, trying to find a sense of order in the new reality, voicing terrors from the past and hopes for the future.

Some contemporary Israeli authors, however, have taken controversial positions on sensitive national issues. Their works address the difficulties of the Israeli situation as well as the bitterness of Palestinians living under Israeli occupation. In his extraordinary novel, *To the End of the Land* (2010), David Grossman (b. 1954) weaves together the daily joys and sorrows of an ordinary Israeli family with the constant undercurrent of conflict and loss. Having lost his own son in battle in 2006, Grossman has been labeled by some the moral conscience of his country. With the Arabs feeling victimized by colonialism and the Jews by Nazi Germany, each side believes that it alone is the rightful proprietor of ancient Palestine.

Music   Popular music in the contemporary Middle East reflects worldwide trends because it blends global and local musical elements. Hip-hop is especially popular because it allows the disadvantaged to express their grievances and yearnings in hypnotic rhymes and rhythms. In Israel, some groups rely on the shock value of their music to pillory the country's political and social shibboleths. Palestinian hip-hop projects the despair and rage of the performers as they portray the misery and futility of their everyday lives. In *"Sham put the soul in the 47,"* the widely popular group Sham has recently lauded the Palestinian resistance fighters who resisted the establishment of the state of Israel in 1948.

As the shockwaves from the Arab Spring spread from Tunisia and Egypt throughout the region, many other performers were inspired to use their music for openly political purposes. One song, entitled "Come on Bashar, Leave," became popular as a rallying cry for dissidents during the civil war in Syria.

MAKING CONNECTIONS

The Middle East is one of the most unstable regions in the world today. This turbulence is due in part to the continued interference of outsiders attracted by the massive oil reserves under the Arabian peninsula and the Persian Gulf. Outside interference has underlined the humiliating weakness of Muslim nations in their relationship with the West, and also identified Western policy toward the Middle East with unpopular dictators in the region.

But internal factors are equally if not more important in provoking the chronic turmoil in the region. One divisive issue is the tug-of-war between the sense of ethnic identity in the form of nationalism and the intense longing to be part of a broader Islamic community, a dream that dates back to the time of the Prophet Muhammad. Although the motives for seeking that Arab unity are sometimes self-serving—two such examples are Nasser and Saddam Hussein—there is no doubt that the sentiment is widespread within the population and has fueled the recent support for ISIS, whose stated objective is to produce a caliphate that will erase national boundaries throughout the region.

Another reason for the current unrest in the Middle East is the intense debate over the role of religion in civil society. Muslims, of course, are not alone in believing that a purer form of religious faith is the best antidote for such social evils as hedonism, sexual license, and political corruption. But it is hard to deny that the issue has been pursued with more anger and passion in the Middle East than in almost any other part of the world. In fact, many Muslim societies in the region have yet to accept the reality of a world characterized by dramatic social and technological change. One of the consequences of such a view is stagnant economies and the emergence of a deep-seated sense of anger and frustration, especially among the young, that is surging through the Islamic world today, a sense of resentment that is directed as much at the region's internal leadership as at allegedly hostile forces in the West. Today, the world is reaping the harvest of that bitterness, and the consequences cannot yet be foreseen.

REFLECTION QUESTIONS

Q Why does the Middle East appear to be one of the most unstable and conflict-ridden regions in the world today? What historical factors might help explain this phenomenon?

Q What are some of the key reasons advanced to explain why democratic institutions have been slow to take root in the Middle East?

Q Why do you think religious and ethnic issues play such a significant role in provoking conflict in the Middle East today? How do such issues contribute to the popularity of radical terrorist organizations in the region?

Q Do you feel that U.S. policies in the Middle East contributed to the rise of al-Qaeda and other terrorist groups in recent years?

CHAPTER TIMELINE

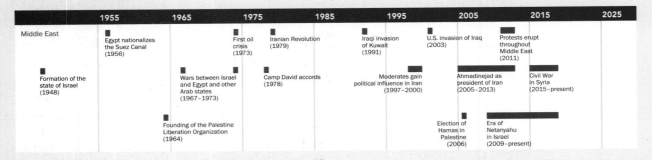

CHAPTER NOTES

1. Quoted in R. R. Andersen, R. F. Seibert, and J. G. Wagner, *Politics and Change in the Middle East: Sources of Conflict and Accommodation*, 4th ed. (Englewood Cliffs, N.J., 1982), p. 51.

2. Susan Sachs, "Assad Looks at Syria's Economy in Inaugural Talks," *New York Times*, July 18, 2000.

3. Sousan Azadi, with Angela Ferrante, *Out of Iran* (London, 1987), p. 223, quoted in *Stories by Iranian Women Since the Revolution*, ed. S. Sullivan (Austin, Tex., 1991), p. 13.

4. Brian Lavery, "In the Thick of Change Where Continents Meet," *New York Times*, August 27, 2003.

PART IV
REFLECTIONS

IN THE ATLANTIC CHARTER, issued after their meeting near the coast of Newfoundland in August 1941, Franklin Roosevelt and Winston Churchill set forth a joint declaration of their peace aims calling for the self-determination of all peoples and self-government and sovereign rights for all nations that had been deprived of them. Although Churchill later disavowed the assumption that he had meant these conditions to apply to colonial areas, Roosevelt on frequent occasions during the war voiced his own intention to bring about the end of colonial domination throughout the world at the close of the conflict. In his mind, Churchill's nostalgia for the past glories of the British Empire could safely be ignored.

It took many years to complete the process, but the promise contained in the Atlantic Charter to bring an end to the colonial era was eventually fulfilled. Although some powers were reluctant to divest themselves of their colonies, World War II had severely undermined the stability of the colonial order, and by the end of the 1940s, most colonies in Asia had received their independence. Africa followed a decade or two later. In a few instances—notably in Algeria, Indonesia, and Vietnam—the transition to independence was a violent one, but for the most part, it was realized by peaceful means.

THREE WISHES What did the leaders of these new nations hope to achieve, now that they had the opportunity? Based on their writings, their speeches, and especially their actions, it seems that they harbored three broad goals at the outset of independence: to throw off the shackles of Western economic domination and ensure material prosperity for all their citizens; to introduce new political institutions that would enhance the right of self-determination of their peoples; and to develop a sense of nationhood and establish secure territorial boundaries. How did they choose to get there? Not surprisingly, given their background and experience, most of them opted to follow a capitalist or moderately socialist path toward economic development. Only in a few cases—North Korea and Vietnam being the most notable examples—did revolutionary leaders decide to pursue the Communist model of development. For them, the example set by the Soviet Union, or by China, would be the path to follow.

It did not take long for reality to set in, as most of the new governments in Asia and Africa quickly fell well short of their ambitious goals. Virtually all remained economically dependent on the advanced industrial nations. Several faced severe problems of urban and rural poverty. Fledgling democratic governments soon proved ineffective and were gradually replaced by military dictatorships or one-party regimes that dismantled representative institutions and oppressed dissident elements and ethnic minorities within their borders. Only in a few cases—notably with Japan and the Little Tigers—were many of the initial aspirations actually fulfilled.

THEORIES OF DEVELOPMENT What had happened to tarnish the bright dreams of the post-colonial leaders for material affluence, national unity, and political self-determination? During the 1950s and 1960s, one school of thought was dominant among scholars and government officials in the United States as they contemplated the challenge of preventing a Communist takeover of the Third World. Advocates of **modernization theory**, as it was known, believed that the political and economic problems faced by the newly independent countries were a consequence of the difficult transition from a traditional agrarian to a modern industrial society. Although they expected most newly independent countries in Asia and Africa to follow a path toward the creation of modern industrial societies on the capitalist model, they would need both time and substantial amounts of economic and technological assistance to complete the journey. It was the duty of the United States and other advanced capitalist nations to provide such assistance while encouraging the leaders of these states to follow the path already adopted by the West. In cases where Communist meddling threatened to derail the process, direct intervention—political and even military—was justified to keep the process of modernization on track.

As it turned out, modernization theory had only limited success in the practical arena (Vietnam was a prime example of its limitations), and it soon came under attack from a younger generation of revisionist scholars, many of whom had reached maturity during the Vietnam War and who argued that the prime responsibility for continued political unrest and economic underdevelopment in the developing world lay not with the new countries themselves but with their continued domination by the former colonial powers. In this view, known as **dependency theory**, the countries of Asia, Africa, and Latin America were the victims of the international marketplace, which charged high prices for the manufactured goods of the West while paying low prices for the raw material exports of preindustrial countries. Efforts by these countries to build up their own industrial sectors and move into the stage of self-sustaining growth were hampered because many of their resources were still controlled by European and American corporations. To end this "neocolonial"

relationship, dependency theory advocates argued, developing societies should reduce their economic ties with the West and adopt a policy of economic self-reliance, thereby taking control of their own destinies.

FROM THEORY TO PRACTICE Either way, it was clear that most newly independent African and Asian countries faced severe challenges in forging political and economic policies responsive to their citizens' needs. And it was also evident that a one-size-fits-all approach was not the answer. A few countries had adapted rapidly to the changing environment and entered a stage of political stability and sustaining economic growth, but many others had not.

In 1991, the Cold War suddenly came to an end. The Soviet Union disintegrated into multiple independent nations, while China abandoned its emphasis on "people's war" and embraced a new strategy based on peaceful economic development. With the decline in ideological tensions and in great power rivalry, the nations of Asia and Africa could shift their attention to more practical concerns about achieving political stability, promoting economic development, and enacting social reforms to improve the lives of their citizens. As we have seen in the chapters above, some states have made substantial progress in what was once described as "modernizing" their societies. Where Japan and the Little Tigers were the first, other nations eventually began to follow, although in many cases the progress was uneven. In much of South and Southeast Asia, a peaceful transition of power is now the general rule for governments, and the standard of living has been improving steadily, although there are still pockets of extreme poverty in some areas. Clashes over ethnic and religious issues still occur with regularity in a number of countries, but territorial conflicts between neighboring nations have declined simultaneously as a sense of nationhood generally prevails.

One of the most dramatic and momentous transformations that has taken place in Asia is in China. Once a predominantly rural country with wide areas of poverty and rural illiteracy, China today is an advanced industrial power and has taken its place at the forefront of the technological revolution now sweeping across the world. With its increasingly affluent middle class and its hard-working and relatively well-educated labor force, it is a vital component driving the globalization process. On the other hand, Beijing's single-minded commitment to achieving national "wealth and power," carried out under the direction of an exclusive ideological elite with seemingly limitless power poses an existential challenge to its competitors in a multipolar world.

OBSTACLES TO CHANGE IN AFRICA AND THE MIDDLE EAST Not all the important regions of the world have shared in the general trend toward political stability and socio-economic progress. In the contemporary Middle East, protracted ethnic and religious unrest has resulted in chronic economic underdevelopment and an almost constant state of civil conflict. In Africa, widespread poverty and a political culture characterized by endemic corruption and mismanagement have undermined the continent's effort to carry out measures to build a modern manufacturing industry and take an active part in the technological revolution.

Why have the nations of Africa and the Middle East experienced greater difficulties in taking an active part in the global transformation that is occurring elsewhere in the world? A couple of salient issues are perhaps worthy of particular attention here. As we have seen above, in the Middle East, religious tradition has been a powerful barrier to political, economic, and social change. Social practices that prevailed in nomadic communities during the pre-Islamic era are still promoted as the only proper standard for contemporary behavior. Even Muslim countries located thousands of miles away from the Middle East have not been immune to such teachings, which are promoted in local madrasas by puritanical Wahhabi instructors imported from Saudi Arabia. Many politicians and government officials are undoubtedly skeptical that such mores have relevance in the modern world but, fearful of provoking a violent public reaction, they are often intimidated against announcing their opposition.

In sub-Saharan Africa, one key factor that may have hindered the capacity of the region to adapt quickly to the rapid pace of global change may have been its ethnic and linguistic diversity, which undoubtedly hindered the ability of the African peoples to effectively counter the Western onslaught and ultimately led to the particularly rapacious character of the colonial enterprise there. Even today, half a century after the end of formal colonial rule, much of the continent of Africa is still locked into an unequal relationship with the former colonial powers, a relationship which has been exacerbated by the rapid pace of technological change that has been taking place elsewhere in recent years.

HALF THE SKY One of the most important signposts that helps us to determine the success of a particular country or a region in coping with the challenges of global change is in how it defines the proper role of the sexes in society. In most traditional societies, the sole responsibility of a woman was to be a proper daughter, wife, and mother. Women's activities were restricted to the home, and outside of educating their children,

they made few contributions to the broader society.

In premodern times, Europe was a patriarchal society, but with the advent of the Industrial Revolution the role of women gradually began to change, and today women in Western countries have reached a point where they can, if they wish, play almost any role in society that is open to a man. While many still experience cultural, religious, or political resistance to their expanding role, women in Western societies today are active, and often prominent, in such important fields as politics, education, business, law, and the arts. And Western society is the better for it.

In many Asian countries, women's role in society has steadily expanded in recent years. Although women still confront persistent obstacles to advancement, their position has improved as these nations enter the ranks of advanced industrial societies. China, the new superpower, was traditionally a highly patriarchal society, and in some respects it still is. But Chinese leaders have come to recognize the importance of women in participating in the process of building a modern nation. Even the Communist leader Mao Zedong, an outright chauvinist in his personal behavior, conceded as much when he quoted a Chinese proverb to the effect that women "make up half the sky." While women continue to suffer from many disadvantages in China, they have begun to play a significant role in the economy, notably as workers in factories, much as female silk workers in Japan helped to fuel the Meiji revolution in the nineteenth century. The much-criticized "one child per family" policy set the stage for the process by enabling Chinese women to leave the home and seek employment in the workplace. China's future success in emerging as one of the world's most advanced nations is largely dependent upon its capacity to recognize the important role that women can play in all aspects of government and society.

In the Middle East and Africa, women are beginning to knock on the door to demand equality, but to a large extent have not yet been admitted. In much of the Middle East, many traditional limitations still apply. Women are not even equal in the mosque, where they are assigned a separate room for prayer so that they will not present a temptation to the male worshipper. Their prospects are measurably better in Africa, since the obstacles there are founded not on religion, but on custom. Even there, women have traditionally been active in commerce, and have been honored as educators and storytellers for generations. Their role in society will undoubtedly expand as the continent seeks to adjust to the rapidly changing conditions that characterize our present age.

GLOBALIZATION AND TRADITION How will the nations of Asia and Africa be affected by the dramatic changes taking place in the world today? Future trends remain difficult to predict, since the impact of globalization simultaneously provokes both rapid change and bitter resistance. Like the advanced industrial regions in Europe and the Western hemisphere, they will need to learn how to maximize the opportunities of global change while minimizing its disruptive effects on society. The wild card in the deck is the potential impact of climate change, which almost inevitably will affect many of the political, economic, and social realities that we take for granted today. Many areas of Asia and Africa have already been seriously affected by climate change, and the consequences have had global repercussions. We will deal with this important issue in the final chapter of the book.

PART V

THE NEW MILLENNIUM

16 The Challenge of a New Millennium

William J. Duiker

The Guggenheim Museum in Bilbao, Spain

CHAPTER 16

THE CHALLENGE OF A NEW MILLENNIUM

Chapter Outline and Focus Questions

AP Images/Carmen Taylor

IMAGE 16.1 Terrorist attack on the World Trade Center in New York City, September 11, 2001

Connections to Today

Do you believe that the system of liberal democracy that exists in the continent of Europe and much of the Western Hemisphere is capable of resolving the problems that are discussed in this chapter? What changes would you suggest to improve the system to make it more effective?

ON SEPTEMBER 11, 2001, two commercial airliners skyjacked by Islamic terrorists slammed into the twin towers of the World Trade Center in New York City (see Image 16.1). Another struck a side wall of the Pentagon outside Washington, D.C. A fourth crashed in a field in central Pennsylvania. These heinous attacks ushered in a new era for the United States—and for the world at large. The Cold War had ended a decade earlier, encouraging prognosticators to predict the advent of a new world order marked by global peace and prosperity. But the fallout from the stunning attacks on the power centers of the United States, along with the unleashing of two new wars in the Middle East and President George W. Bush's declaration of a global "war on terror," aroused new questions and anxieties about the future. Would the new century introduce an era of international peace and relative stability, such as had occurred after the end of the Napoleonic wars in nineteenth-century Europe? Or would the end of the Cold War signal the rise of a new spirit of rivalry and national competitiveness, leading to destructive wars reminiscent of the last century? Would the dramatic expansion of trade among nations lead to global prosperity and material accumulation, or would the Technological Revolution already under way lead to the kinds of political, social, and cultural ferment that had characterized the Industrial Revolution of the nineteenth century?

Certainly, at the turn of the century there were sufficient grounds to adopt any or all of these points of view. As the new millennium dawned, the United States bestrode the world like a colossus, unchallenged in its military and economic might and sufficiently confident in its destiny to play the role of global policeman. Yet there were already disquieting signs—in the form of ethnic and religious clashes in Eastern Europe, the Middle East, and Africa—that the vision of a new era of peace and stability might turn out to be a mirage. By the same token, the expansion of world trade was already beginning to produce victims as well as beneficiaries, and competition among nations over access to crucial resources was beginning to intensify. **Globalization**, like the Industrial Revolution of an earlier age, was not a tide that lifted all boats.

In the meantime, other issues—some of them virtually ignored by world leaders during the era of the Cold War—were increasingly in need of attention. Environmental degradation, rapid population growth, and the projected shortage of many precious natural resources, including liquid energy and fresh water, were now widely viewed as serious threats to the future success of the human experiment. And behind all of these pressing concerns lay a more existential one—how to seek out the underlying purpose and meaning of life in a world increasingly defined by the voracious accumulation of material goods. Was the rise of the consumer society the ultimate objective of all humankind, or could ultimate happiness be achieved only through the emergence of a new spiritual civilization?

Such questions were undoubtedly in the minds of many as they faced the challenges of a new millennium.

Today, more than two decades later, they have taken on even greater relevance as the world faces the future with ever-increasing concern and trepidation.

16-1 AFTER THE COLD WAR: THE REVENGE OF HISTORY

 Focus Question: Why did the end of the Cold War not lead to the "new world order" that many observers at the time anticipated?

With the end of superpower rivalry and the collapse of the Soviet Union in 1991, the attention of the world shifted to the new post-Cold War era. For many observers, the prognosis was excellent. George H. W. Bush, the U.S. president at the time, looked forward to a new era of peace and international cooperation that he labeled the **"new world order,"** while pundits predicted the advent of a new "American century," marked by the victory of liberal democratic values and free enterprise capitalism.

The wave of optimism that accompanied the end of the Cold War was all too brief. After a short period of euphoria, it soon became clear that forces were now being released that had long been held in check by the ideological rigidities of the Cold War. The era of conflict that had characterized much of the twentieth century was not at an end; it was simply taking a different form. In effect, the ideological issues that had defined the Cold War were being replaced by a series of ethnic or national disputes that were reminiscent of those that had taken place during the first half of that turbulent century.

The first major eruption took place in a familiar venue: the Balkans, where the Yugoslavian Federation—long held together by the transcendent personality of Marshal Tito—broke apart in a bitter conflict that has yet to be finally resolved. An even more dangerous arena of discord exhibited familiar signs of turmoil: in the Middle East, where historical ethnic and religious animosities spread rapidly throughout the region and culminated in the outbreak of civil war in a number of countries. Finally, another development revived worries over the possible resumption of the Cold War itself: after a brief flirtation with democracy, Russia turned back to its familiar refuge of autocratic rule under the leadership of the ex-KGB official Vladimir Putin. Putin looked longingly at the past as he hoped to revive the empire that had once flourished under the tsars and the commissars. Even in East Asia, where an atmosphere of peace and cooperation had briefly reigned after the restoration of U.S.–Chinese relations, new territorial disputes between

China and its neighbors over ownership of the South China Sea threatened to embroil the Pacific region in a new round of dangerous conflicts. As the world began to show signs of returning to the threatening image of warring nations that had characterized the first half of the twentieth century, many observers expressed concern that the new world order was beginning to look a lot like the old one.

Are we headed, then, toward the emergence not of a new world order, but of a more familiar one characterized by an uneasy balance between competing power blocs intent on imposing their will on an uncertain world? Or are there significant differences in the contemporary situation that will enable policy makers in world capitals to avoid some of the disastrous mistakes of the past? We will seek answers to these questions, and to their implications, during the remainder of this chapter.

16-2 CONTEMPORARY CAPITALISM AND ITS DISCONTENTS

 Focus Questions: Based on the conditions that exist around the world today, do you believe that capitalism is the best economic system for improving the lives of human populations? Are there ways in which capitalism should be changed to improve its performance?

During the slightly more than half-century that divided the end of World War II from the beginning of the new millennium, capitalism proved itself to be—at least in terms of the rise of global GDP per capita—a highly productive system for promoting economic growth and prosperity in countries where it was practiced. Although the degree to which the goods produced in the factories of capitalist countries were distributed in a reasonably equitable manner is a matter of debate, there is general agreement that the postwar era has seen more progress in bringing about the elimination of world poverty than any other period in recorded history (see "The Elimination of Poverty and Disease," p. 401). An outside observer seeking to single out the primary reason for the victory of the West over the socialist camp—a reversal of the Maoist parlance that the East Wind would triumph over the West Wind—would find it difficult to avoid the conclusion that the material benefits provided by a global capitalist system was one of the key factors for the victory of the West in the Cold War.

By the opening of the new century, however, a generation of rapid growth in the capitalist states in Europe and North America began to give way to a general decline in economic performance. This slowdown gave rise to a number of related problems, several of them containing serious social and political implications. These problems included an increase in the level of unemployment; government belt-tightening policies to reduce social services and welfare and retirement benefits; and in many countries, growing popular resentment against minority groups or recent immigrants, who were blamed by some for their deteriorating economic prospects.

There are several reasons for the declining productivity of most Western economies, including a gradual reduction in consumer demand (caused partly by a period of stagnant wages), increased competition from low-wage countries in Asia, and lower levels of government investment in infrastructure projects. One flagrant symptom of the problem was the widening financial gap between the wealthy minority and the remainder of the population. As consumer demand declined, corporation executives had little incentive to place their savings in capital investment projects, and turned their attention to investment overseas, or wealth accumulation for themselves.

The financial meltdown that struck first in the United States and then spread to the rest of the world in the fall of 2008 added a new sense of urgency to the challenge. Declining revenues resulting from the economic downturn forced business owners to cut back on their payrolls and made it more difficult for governments to meet their own financial responsibilities. At the same time, the globalization of world markets limited the ability of world leaders to insulate their peoples from the vicissitudes of the marketplace at a time of heightened instability. The dream of a crisis-free form of capitalism came to an abrupt end.

16-2a The View from the Top

In the advanced industrial countries around the world today, the primary economic challenge lies not so much in levels of production as in the means of distribution, a striking similarity to the situation in Europe in the middle of the nineteenth century (see Chapter 1). There is an abundance of goods in the economy, certainly more than sufficient to feed, clothe, and house virtually every member of the population. But how can governments ensure that the material benefits of the capitalist system will be divided on a reasonably equitable basis among the entire community? A healthy economy is a prosperous consumer, but with income levels flat, the equation becomes broken. In seeking to rise to the challenge, capitalist nations around the world have adopted a variety of strategies.

Europe: Speed Bumps on the Road to the Welfare State   In Europe, the challenge of harnessing capitalist productivity to the needs of the general population has been shaped by the fact that growth rates in Europe have traditionally been kept artificially low because of the persistent fear of inflation (rampant inflation, it is widely believed, was a major factor in the rise of Hitler in Germany in the 1930s), and also because welfare payments have been more generous than in most other capitalist countries. Ever since the start of the Industrial Revolution two centuries ago, European governments have accepted the necessity of taming the market in order to minimize the risk of social unrest. In seeking to maintain a balance between promoting unbridled growth and protecting the general welfare, European governments have consistently placed a higher emphasis on the latter.

Today, however, with the threat of a demographic crunch on the horizon, European governments have been compelled to face the realization that a cutback in their generous welfare programs will be required to keep their economies on a sound footing. As they grapple with solutions to this dilemma, they have exposed one of the underlying weaknesses of the European Union as it has attempted to integrate the economies of its various members under a single set of principles. While the economies of most northern European states are sufficiently robust to manage the challenge, governments in the southern tier like Greece, Italy, and Spain have been unable to trim social benefits because of stiff public opposition, despite the growing risk of bankruptcy. Even in France, one of the most important economies in the EU, recent cuts to the country's generous welfare programs ignited social unrest with the outbreak of the "yellow vest" protest movement (see Chapter 10).

Compounding the problem is the fact that the European Union, as a multinational organization, lacks a centralized executive body authorized to make difficult decisions in a time of crisis. The nations most affected by the economic downturn have appealed for assistance from their more fortunate counterparts, notably Germany, but the latter have been reluctant to sacrifice their own well-being in an effort to save what they regard as their more profligate neighbors. The expansion of the EU into Eastern Europe, where economies are more vulnerable and capitalist practices are a comparatively recent phenomenon, only adds to the complexity of the issue. Today, in both economic and structural terms, the continent of Europe is facing its most serious internal challenge since the end of World War II.

The United States: Capitalism Ascendant? As we have seen above, the United States fared better than many other capitalist states in the 1990s, since the economic revival at that time—stimulated by technological advances—enabled the Clinton administration to reduce budget deficits without having to engage in substantial tax increases or a massive reduction in welfare spending. During the first decade of the new century, however, the federal deficit

began to rise again, a consequence of growing entitlement costs and the Bush administration policy of reducing taxes while simultaneously trying to wage two wars abroad. Although gross domestic product continued to grow, economic growth did not lead to increased prosperity for all Americans. While the rich were getting richer, the poorest 20 percent of the population saw little benefit.

The financial crisis that struck in the fall of 2008 was the result of several factors, including the collapse of a housing bubble (the result of easier access to money for home mortgages), lax government regulatory procedures on lending, and a steady increase in household debt. Although the Bush administration belatedly announced a major federal bailout to prevent additional losses on Wall Street, the stock market suffered its largest collapse since the Great Depression. After the presidential elections in November, the incoming Obama administration prepared a major stimulus package to jump-start the economy. These measures were successful in reversing the downward trend in the stock market and production began slowly to recover. But because the program had been scaled back from its original planned size and scope in deference to political realities, growth rates were insufficient to reduce the unemployment rate, which was still close to 8 percent at the beginning of President Obama's second term in office. At the root of the problem was the age-old debate between Democrats and Republicans over the proper role of government and the relative importance of entitlement spending and deficit reduction. As the two parties locked horns over the issue in Congress, the danger of political paralysis loomed.

The Trump administration followed party precedent by seeking to stimulate economic growth through a tax cut, combined with a roll back of government regulations that inhibit entrepreneurs from investing in job-creating projects. The administration also followed GOP orthodoxy by issuing periodic threats to cut back on social entitlement programs like Social Security and Medicare. Heartened by continued public resistance to the "individual mandate" requirement in the Affordable Care Act, the administration particularly focused its attention on cutting government health-care spending, and planned deep cuts in other social programs to reduce the federal budget deficit.

But the Trump administration broke with the Republican playbook on trade policy by raising tariffs on goods imported from other countries—some of them key U.S. allies like Canada and the EU. The White House argued that raising tariffs would serve to protect working-class jobs in the United States, while discouraging U.S. corporations from shipping their factories to lower-wage countries abroad. In line with that strategy, the administration announced its decision to abandon the Obama administration's plan to join with other Asian nations in a Trans-Pacific Partnership (TPP), and called for a renegotiation of the NAFTA treaty with U.S. neighbors in the Western Hemisphere. The administration focused particular attention on trade relations with China, contending that the long-standing U.S. trade deficit with that country was too large to sustain. It also charged that the economic relationship between the two countries was not based on a level playing field, since China's state capitalist economy openly manipulates the markets in order to promote Beijing's ambitious political and foreign policy objectives.

Another element in the Trump administration's strategy was to impose severe limits on immigration into the United States from across the border with Mexico. As the volume of unauthorized migrants arriving at the border (some of them traveling in family groups from conflict-prone countries in Central America) has increased, the White House responded by demanding funds from Congress to build a concrete wall along the border to deter future arrivals. Resistance to the plan from Democratic members of Congress—who argue that other means to control the level of immigration are more effective—has been steadfast, and the issue has not yet been resolved.

Although the issue of immigration into the United States has often been framed by many politicians in terms that exploit raw emotion and seek political advantage, it also contains major economic implications. Since most immigrants from Mexico and Central America gravitate to low-paying jobs that are not appealing to most Americans, they have historically been tacitly accepted by the public and the government alike as a necessary reality. But as their numbers have increased, some Americans point to the financial burden that the new arrivals place on the nation's educational and medical systems. In recent years, centrist members of Congress from both parties have attempted to craft a compromise solution which reconciles the political, economic, and moral aspects of the issue, but as the positions on both sides have hardened, a solution today appears as far away as ever.

How successful has the Trump administration been in achieving its economic objectives? At first, in raw statistical terms the results were relatively promising. The stock market rose steadily on positive economic news, as the country enjoyed an annual growth rate of just under three percent, while unemployment figures dipped to a fifty-year low. But the outbreak of the Coronavirus pandemic—also known as Covid-19—in early 2020 (see "The Elimination of Poverty and Disease" below) brought an abrupt halt to the upward trends in the U.S. economy, as official efforts to contain and slow the spread of the deadly new virus brought about a dramatic increase in unemployment, while similar conditions in countries around the globe resulted in an abrupt drop in the level of international trade.

Even before the sudden shock of the pandemic, however, the economic gains in recent years for the average American have been marginal, at best. While the already-rich have gotten even wealthier in recent decades, salaries for the middle class and the poor have been relatively stagnant and often have not matched the steady increase in retirement and health-care costs. Most new job opportunities in the contemporary economy are at salary levels that are barely adequate to meet the needs of the average family, while poverty levels in the U.S., particularly among children and the elderly, are alarmingly high for a nation of our overall wealth and resources.

Future prospects for the U.S. economy are uncertain, and are highly dependent upon political trends. As we have seen earlier (see Chapter 8), economic policy in the United States has always followed a pattern of pendulum swings from a laissez-faire approach to one of active government intervention. So long as the U.S. economy maintains a level of steady growth, most Americans have usually been satisfied with an emphasis placed on the former, but a new economic crisis could signal the onset of a strong public demand for greater government intervention.

Capitalism in Asia: From Low Wage to High End   One area in the capitalist world that has so far been able to avoid the worst consequences of the global economic slowdown is East Asia, where most of the industrializing nations have managed to maintain steady economic growth with a minimum of social unrest and an impressive record of political stability. During the 1990s, pundits opined that the "East Asian miracle" was a product of the amalgamation of capitalist economic techniques and a value system inherited from Confucianism that stressed hard work, frugality, and the subordination of the individual to the community—all reminiscent of the "Puritan work ethic" of the early capitalist era in the West.

An important corollary of the region's achievements has been the capacity of Asian governments to use the advantage of their relatively low-wage working force as a means of gaining entrée into the global marketplace. First it was the Japanese; then South Korea, Taiwan, and Singapore stepped in; finally China, by being accepted into the World Trade Organization in 2000, found the key to escaping its own poverty trap. Today other nations throughout the continent are following a now familiar pattern.

There is an inherent risk in such a strategy, of course. As noted just above, where one treads, others may follow. Then, as wages rise, Asian economies are forced to seek foreign markets for more high-end products—a strategy that puts them in direct competition with their Western counterparts. The riskiest consequence of this export-driven strategy is that it exposes the practitioner to the rapid swings of the international marketplace. To apply a well-worn metaphor,

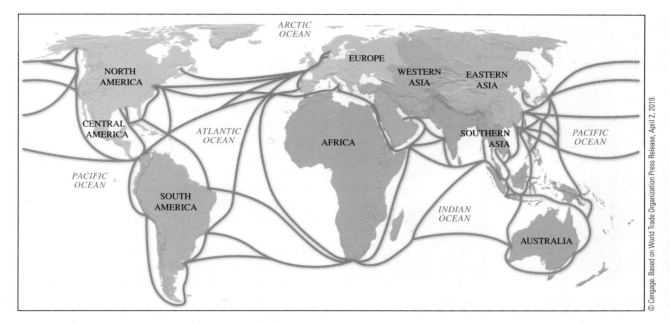

MAP 16.1 Global Patterns of Trade. International trade is the engine that drives the expansion of economic growth all over the world. This map shows major trade routes around the globe. The vast majority of trade consists of liquid energy, mining, goods and services, and agricultural products. In 2018 the total value of merchandise trade was almost $20 trillion dollars, 98% of which took place among members of the World Trade Organization. The major countries involved in world trade are China, the European Union, Japan, and the United States. International trade grew by 4.6% in 2017 but dropped to about 3% growth in 2018 because of slack economies and trade tensions between major partners.

Q *Do you believe that active participation in world trade is beneficial for all nations? If not, why not?*

during a global economic downturn, advanced economies may catch a slight cold; their competitors develop a high fever (see Map 16.1).

The financial crises of 1997 and 2008 (see Chapter 13) demonstrated that the Pacific nations were not immune to the vicissitudes of capitalism, but (with the exception of Japan), they rapidly recovered and have now resumed the steady growth that had characterized their performance during the last quarter of the twentieth century. China in particular has become a major force in the global economy, replacing Japan and Germany as the world's largest exporter of goods and serving as an engine of growth for nations throughout the region (see Image 16.2). Many observers see China, with its growing industrial base and abundant supply of cheap labor, as the most serious threat to the U.S. economic hegemony. But China has a number of its own vulnerabilities (see Chapter 12), and a further slowdown in the global economy could have a chilling effect on its already declining pace of growth.

16-2b Life on the Margins of Capitalism

Capitalism has always had winners and losers. That generalization is true of countries and regions as well as of

individuals. And it is an unfortunate reality that some regions of the world have not experienced the degree of rapid economic growth and political stability that has been experienced in the most highly industrialized parts of the world. For reasons that we have discussed above, the most prominent regions that have not shared in the rise of global prosperity over the past few decades are in Africa and the Middle East. Some countries in Asia and Latin America fall into the same category.

The Elimination of Poverty and Disease One of the greatest challenges facing the global economy today is to reduce the high level of poverty that persists in many parts of the world. In 1990, about 36 percent of the total population of the world lived in conditions of extreme poverty (as defined by the World Bank Group in terms of a daily salary of $1.90). An approximately equal number were illiterate, while hundreds of thousands died annually from malnutrition, hunger, or disease. At a Millennium Summit in 2000, the United Nations adopted a plan calling for advanced nations to double their financial assistance to poorer countries, while taking measures to equalize the playing field in the realm of trade to assist the developing

William J. Duiker

IMAGE 16.2 Silk Workers of the World Unite! In recent years, many critics have charged that Chinese factories are able to market their goods at cheap prices abroad because their employees are paid low wages and often must work in abysmal conditions. The silk industry, which produces one of China's key high-end exports, is a case in point. At this factory in Wuxi, women workers spend ten-hour days with their hands immersed in boiling water as they unwind filaments from cocoons onto a spool of silk yarn. Their blistered red hands testify to the difficulty of their painful task.

Q *Are developing nations like China justified in placing male and female workers in low-wage jobs under challenging conditions in order to improve their competitiveness in world markets?*

countries in working their way out of debt. The declared goal was to reduce the number of those suffering extreme poverty and hunger by half by the year 2015, while reducing infant mortality and ensuring basic education for all the world's children.

It has not been easy. When the UN General Assembly returned to the issue five years later the acrimony of the debate demonstrated how difficult it would be to carry the plan from dream to reality. Disagreements over how to fight terrorism and protect human rights, combined with the reluctance of industrial countries to open their markets to agricultural imports, prevented the delegates from implementing a specific plan.

Still, recent figures show that the incidence of extreme poverty had been reduced in the year 2015 to about ten percent of the total population of the world, or a total of about 735 million people. That figure indicated that the level of global poverty had declined an average of about one percent a year since 1990. During that 25-year period, a total of over one billion people raised themselves from impoverished conditions. One troubling factor, however,

is that today the incidence of poverty is now concentrated in specific regions, with over forty percent of the world's extreme poor living in sub-Saharan Africa. Another 12 percent are located in the countries of South Asia.[1]

Steady progress is being achieved in improving health conditions around the world as well. The threats from dangerous diseases such as pneumonia and HIV are gradually declining, while deaths from that old scourge malaria have dropped by nearly one-half since the beginning of this century, leading to increased life expectancy in almost every country around the world. According to World Health Organization estimates, the number of children who die before the age of five has declined by at least 50 percent in the last three decades. One warning sign, however, is the continuing threat of the pandemic spread of bacterial and viral infections. The recent outbreak of Covid-19, a novel coronavirus that first appeared in central China in late 2019 and has raced with lightning speed around the globe, is a clarion warning that while the rise of globalization offers great benefit for human progress, it also presents huge risks and challenges in the realm of fighting infectious diseases on this planet.

A key reason for the improving quality of global health care is the growing use of vaccinations. With substantial help from international agencies, medicines are more widely available in afflicted areas, leading to a decrease in the number of women dying in childbirth. Yet, as health-care professionals and advocates emphasize, much more needs to be done, including improved medical qualifications for health workers and better diagnoses of illnesses. Some of the potential solutions are difficult to achieve because of the spread of smoking and the popularity of fast-food restaurants in emerging countries. Tobacco companies have reacted to a decline in smoking in the West by actively marketing their goods in Africa and Asia.

There has also been some good news on the literacy front. Rising literacy levels are one of the key signals that a given area is climbing out of poverty. Since the early nineteenth century, the rate of literacy around the globe has risen from only 12 percent in 1820 to about 83 percent today. Since 1960, global literacy has increased by an average of almost one percent per year. Not surprisingly, the regions of the world where literacy rates are low are also those where extreme poverty is common. To reduce one problem is to reduce the other. Efforts are underway to promote more universal education for both boys and girls at the elementary and the secondary level, but when local funding is absent—notably in Africa—progress is slow (see Chapter 14).

One key reason for the continued prevalence of poverty and illiteracy in the developing world is the lack

Women on the Front Lines of Development

 What are some of the various ways that East Asian countries have sought to engage women in the developmental process, according to the authors of this book? Why are women so important in the effort to improve economic conditions around the world today?

Family & Society **IN THEIR HIGHLY PRAISED BOOK** *Half the Sky,* authors Nicholas Kristof and Sheryl WuDunn explore the challenges and opportunities for women in the developing world today. Partly an appeal for global attention to the plight of women in many countries as they struggle against generations of oppression, the book also highlights ways in which women have become a key resource for nations that seek to pass from an agrarian to an advanced industrial economy.

Half the Sky

Women are…a linchpin of [East Asia's] development strategy. Economists who scrutinized East Asia's success noted a common pattern. These countries took young women who previously had contributed negligibly to gross national product (GNP) and injected them into the formal economy, hugely increasing the labor force. The basic formula was to ease repression, educate girls as well as boys, give the girls the freedom to move to the cities and take factory jobs, and then benefit from a demographic dividend as they delayed marriage and reduced childbearing. The women meanwhile financed the education of younger relatives, and saved enough of their pay to boost national savings rates. This pattern has been called "the girl effect…"

Evidence has mounted that helping women can be a successful poverty-fighting strategy anywhere in the world, not just in the booming economies of East Asia. The Self-Employed Women's Association was founded in India in 1972 and ever since has supported the poorest women in starting businesses—raising living standards in ways that have dazzled scholars and foundations. In Bangladesh, Muhammad Yunus developed microfinance at the Grameen Bank and targeted women borrowers…

Eighty percent of the employees on the assembly lines in coastal China are female, and the proportion across the manufacturing belt of East Asia is at least 70 percent. The economic explosion in Asia was, in large part, an outgrowth of the economic empowerments of women…

[T]he case for investing in girls' education is still very, very strong. Anecdotally, we know of many women who, with education, were able to obtain jobs or start businesses and transform their lives and the lives of those around them. More broadly, it's generally accepted that one of the reasons East Asia has prospered in recent decades is that it educates females and incorporates them into the labor force, in a way that has not been true of India or Africa…

The challenges are manifest: Of the 115 million children who have dropped out of elementary school, 57 percent are girls. In South and West Asia, two-thirds of the children who are out of schools are girls…

One of the most cost-effective ways to increase school attendance is to deworm students. Intestinal worms affect children's physical and intellectual growth. Indeed, ordinary worms kill 130,000 people a year, typically through anemia or intestinal obstruction, and the anemia particularly affects menstruating girls…

Another cost-effective way of getting more girls to attend high school may be to help them manage menstruation. African girls typically use (and reuse) old rags during their periods, and they often have only a single torn pair of underwear. For fear of embarrassing leaks and stains, girls sometimes stay home during that time.

Source: Nicholas D. Kristof and Sheryl WuDunn, *Half the Sky: Turning Oppression into Opportunity for Women Worldwide* (New York: Random House, 2010), pp. xix–xx, 170–172.

of educational opportunities for women. In 2006, the United Nations Development Program declared that "women's empowerment helps raise economic productivity and reduce infant mortality. It contributes to improved health and nutrition. It increases the chances for education for the next generation."[2] In their book *Half the Sky: Turning Oppression into Opportunity for Women Worldwide*, Nicholas Kristof and Sheryl WuDunn described the lack of medical facilities and the deplorable health conditions in many rural areas of Africa and Asia (see Historical Voices,

"Women on the Front Lines of Development," above). In many areas, women suffer myriad illnesses as a result of cooking on traditional wood-burning stoves that produce smoke containing carbon monoxide and other pollutants. To alleviate the problem, the Global Alliance for Clean Cookstoves is developing and marketing efficient and low-cost cook-stoves, with the goal of producing 100 million stoves by the year 2020.

The Great Escape: The Migration of Peoples   People have been migrating from place to place, as individuals, as families, or in larger groups, since prehistorical times. They are motivated by a variety of causes—by war, by pestilence, by economic need, or more recently by climate change—and in the process they have profoundly shaped the character of the human experience throughout the world. After a great wave of migration during the Middle Ages—much of it composed of pastoral peoples emanating from Central Asia—the process decelerated during the early modern period. It resumed during the era of war and revolution in the first half of the twentieth century. But during the Cold War, migration almost came to a halt as the two opposing ideological blocs huddled behind their respective boundaries on both sides of the invisible iron curtain.

Since the beginning of the new millennium, people have been on the move once again, migrating in a steady stream from the poorer regions of the world toward the advanced nations of the West. In the past few years, the trickle has turned into a flood. Statistics tell the story: from 2010 to 2013, almost one and one-half million refugees from Africa and the Middle East crossed the borders into the European Union each year. Some of them came from the Middle East via the Anatolian Peninsula and into the Balkans. Others risked their lives by crossing the Mediterranean Sea in flimsy boats, hoping to arrive safely on the beaches of Greece, Italy, and Spain (see Map 16.2).

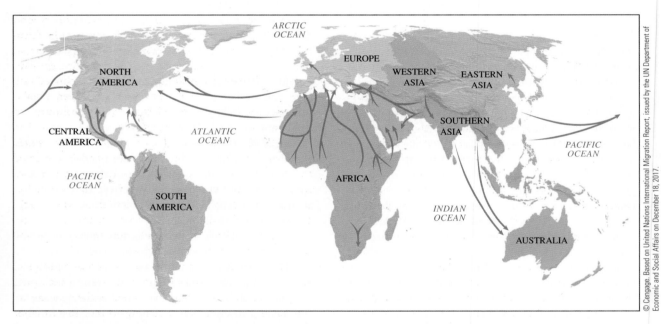

© Cengage. Based on United Nations International Migration Report, issued by the UN Department of Economic and Social Affairs on December 18, 2017.

MAP 16.2 Patterns of International Migration. According to a recent United Nations report, there were over 250 million people living outside their country of birth in 2017, an increase of almost 50% since the year 2000. About 64% of them live in high-income countries and about half live in ten countries, most importantly Saudi Arabia, Germany, Russia, and the United States. In the past few years the pace of migration has quickened, as more and more people flee war, climate change, and terrorism. Almost 50% of all international migrants are women, while 74% of migrants are of working age. Among all international migrants, a total of 26 million are classified as refugees. Although the refugee issue attracts much attention in Europe and the United States, over 80% of refugees worldwide are currently settled in low-income countries.

Q *Where do you think most refugees are coming from these days, and why are they leaving their home countries?*

Why do they come? As in all cases involving mass movement, there are undoubtedly many reasons, but a few key factors stand out. Refugees from the Middle East fled from the civil wars in Syria, Iraq, and Afghanistan, or have sought to escape the activities of Islamic terrorists in the region; those coming from Africa are more likely motivated by economic reasons and climate change. With the increasing desiccation of the Sahara and its environs, individuals and families are fleeing their homes in search of jobs to improve their livelihood, or to escape the growing conflict between farmers and pastoralists in Nigeria and other states in Central Africa (see Historical Voices, "Migration and Climate Change," p. 406).

Migration is taking place in other areas of the globe as well. Substantial numbers of migrants from South Asian countries cross the Indian Ocean to seek asylum in Australia or Southeast Asia; others head west in the hopes of finding temporary employment in the oil-rich states of Saudi Arabia and the Persian Gulf. And there has been a steady movement of peoples from Mexico and Central America northward toward the United States. Some are seeking employment opportunities and plan to return home when conditions at home improve. Others seek permanent residence in the United States. Most recently, thousands of families have left their homes in poor regions of Central America to escape gang warfare and widespread government corruption. South America itself is not immune to the pattern of migration and resettlement, as a flood of refugees have left the conflict-ridden state of Venezuela for neighboring countries in South America.

Large-scale human migration, of course, can be a double-edged sword. On the positive side, for the receiving countries it provides an influx of low-wage workers to help fuel the local economy and support the generous welfare programs that characterize many industrialized societies. But it can have a destabilizing effect as well, since it arouses resentment among local residents in areas where high unemployment is a matter of popular concern. And, as we have seen, it can have a particularly unsettling effect when the new arrivals are ethnically or culturally distinct from the majority population of their host countries. In such cases, migration on a large scale can tend to intensify feelings of uneasiness and popular resentment against the new arrivals (see "16-4 Democracy in Crisis," later in this chapter).

The Danger of Overpopulation It is no accident that some of the poorest countries in the world have the highest rate of population growth. Part of the reason for that reality is the fact that in many poor rural societies large families are required to support the household. One of the consequences of such traditional practices, of course, is that women in such societies are viewed almost exclusively as mothers, and their role in society is restricted to the home and the nurturing of their children.

At some point, poor countries run the risk of allowing the local population to outstrip its capacity to feed itself. Concern over excessive population growth dates back to the early nineteenth century, when the British economist Thomas Malthus worried that the population of the world would increase more rapidly than the food supply. Such fears peaked in the decades immediately following World War II, when a rise in world birthrates and a decline in infant mortality combined to fuel a dramatic increase in population in much of the developing world. The concern was alleviated after the 1970s, when the so-called green revolution improved crop yields, and statistical evidence began to suggest that the rate of population growth was declining in many countries of Asia and Latin America.

Yet some experts question whether increases in food production, through technological innovation in farming practices as well as genetic engineering of crops, can keep up indefinitely with global population growth, which continues today, though at a slightly reduced rate from earlier levels. In recent years, the green revolution has been supplemented by a "blue revolution" to increase food yields from the world's oceans, seas, and rivers. From a total of 2.5 billion people in 1950, world population rose to 7.1 billion in 2013 and is predicted to exceed 9 billion by the middle of this century. Today, many eyes are focused on India, where the population recently surpassed 1.2 billion, and on Africa, where rapid rates of growth are expected to continue for the foreseeable future (see Image 16.4). Both areas are faced with the danger of dramatic climate change.

Many European countries have the opposite problem, as low fertility rates among European-born women raise the prospect of lower population levels in the near future. A decrease in population not only would lead to labor shortages, thereby increasing the need for "guest workers" from Africa and the Middle East, but also would reduce the number of employed workers paying taxes, making it difficult to maintain expensive welfare programs (see Chapter 10). Many Europeans feel, however, that introducing more refugees from strife-torn areas of Africa and the Middle East is not the best answer to the problem. Some European countries like France are now providing financial incentives to encourage young European citizens to have larger families.

Migration and Climate Change

 What parts of the world are currently experiencing dramatic population movements? Do you agree with the solutions offered in this document?

Earth & Environment | **ONE OF THE PRIMARY CAUSES** of the large-scale migration of peoples that is taking place these days can be ascribed to dramatic climate change and its impact in certain parts of the world, notably in North Africa and the Middle East. Drought conditions and shortage of water have become commonplace in these regions, and as conditions continue to deteriorate, the pace of departure to more hospitable parts of the world is likely to rise accordingly. A recent report issued by the UN Migration, Environment and Climate Change Division sought to bring public attention to the problem. The following document contains excerpts from a statement by Dina Ionesco, the chairperson of the division.

IMAGE 16.3 Refugees fleeing flood conditions in eastern India.

Dina Ionesco, Climate Change and Global Migration

...Environmental changes and natural disasters have played a role in how the population is distributed on our planet throughout history.... However, it is highly likely that undesirable environmental changes directly created by, or amplified by, climate change, will extensively change the patterns of human settlement. Future degradation of land used for agriculture and farming, the disruption of fragile ecosystems and the depletion of precious natural resources like fresh water will directly impact people's lives and homes....

There are predictions for the twenty-first century indicating that even more people will have to move as a result of these adverse climate impacts.... The World Bank...has put forward projections for internal climate migration amounting to 143 million people by 2050 in three regions of the world, if no climate action is taken.... However, our level of awareness and understanding of how environmental factors affect migration, and how they also interact with other migration drivers such as demographic, political and economic conditions, has also changed. With enhanced knowledge there is more incentive to act urgently, be prepared, and respond.

...The main priority is to find solutions that allow people to stay in their homes and give them the means to adapt to changing environmental conditions. [This] approach aims to avoid instances of desperate migration and its associated tragedies.... However, where climate change impacts are too intense, another priority...is to enhance availability and flexibility of pathways for regular migration....

A last resort measure is to conduct planned relocations of population—this means organizing the relocation of entire villages and communities away from areas bearing the brunt of climate change impacts....

There is no one single solution to respond to the challenge of environmental migration, but there are many solutions that tackle different aspects of this complex equation. Nothing meaningful can ever be achieved without the strong involvement of civil society actors and the communities themselves who very often know what is best for them and their ways of life....

I also think that we need to stop discourses that focus only on migrants as victims of tragedy. The bigger picture is certainly bleak at times, but we need to remember that migrants demonstrate everyday their resilience and capacity to survive and thrive in difficult situations.

Source: UN News, Migration and the climate crisis: the UN's search for solutions, 31 July 2019. (https://news.un.org/en/story/2019/07/1043551).

William J. Duiker

IMAGE 16.4 India's Hope, India's Sorrow. In India, as in many other societies in South Asia, overpopulation is a serious obstacle to economic development. The problem is particularly serious in large cities where thousands of poor children are forced into begging or prostitution. Shown here are a few of the thousands of street children in the commercial hub of Mumbai. With the Indian economy experiencing rapid growth, the national government is aggressively addressing the issue of poverty.

 Do you believe that countries like India that have a high birth rate are justified in establishing family planning programs to control population growth? Why or why not?

16-3 FROM THE INDUSTRIAL TO THE TECHNOLOGICAL REVOLUTION

Q Focus Questions: In what ways is technology having an effect on economic systems around the world today? On balance, do you believe that new technology should be adopted whenever it can improve productivity in a particular branch of the economy?

Technology has always been the engine that drives the capitalist machine. In its early stages it was the steam engine that dug the coal, and the railroad car that carried it to the factory. It was the incandescent bulb that lit the factory floor, and the truck that delivered the finished product to the consumer. More recent inventions increasingly allow the individual worker to be replaced by the machine, and enable the movement of goods, services, and ideas from one end of the world to another in hours, minutes, or even a split second. But as technology creates, it also destroys. In the name of efficiency and productivity, old ways are abandoned to give way to new methods and new possibilities.

Jobs are lost, and new ones appear. The essence of technology, as of capitalism itself, is creative destruction.

Part of the trouble is, many human beings are—sometimes understandably—resistant to change. When the first automated looms and knitting frames began to appear in British factories in the early nineteenth century, local weavers—who had spent a lifetime perfecting their craft—began to attack the machines and burn down the factories that contained them. Known as Luddites (from a possibly fictitious character Ned Ludd who had allegedly engaged in the protests himself), they attempted to halt the advance of technology in the textile industry in order to protect their livelihood. Not surprisingly, factory owners did not agree, and called out the police to confront the strikers, who died by the hundreds for their pains. In the end, the mechanization of the textile industry led to cheaper and better products, and more employment in the factories.

The adoption of the machine spread inexorably from England across the Atlantic to the United States. In 1900, there were twelve million Americans farmers who (like their counterparts the world over) tilled their fields with horse and plow. But in the first quarter of the twentieth century, tractors and combines from newly established factories began to replace human labor, and today agriculture in the United States employs only about two million people, many of them immigrants from Latin America. But jobs lost were jobs gained, since many of those who left the fields found new employment in the booming factories. And as farm machines led to increased food production, marketed at lower prices, farmers, factory workers, and consumers alike profited, to the ultimate benefit of the U.S. economy as a whole.

As many observers have noted, the world economy today is in the process of transition to what has been called a "postindustrial age," characterized by the emergence of a system that is not only increasingly global in scope but also increasingly technology intensive. This process, which futurologist Alvin Toffler dubbed the Third Wave (see Chapter 1), offers the promise of bringing about increased global economic growth and human prosperity on a massive scale.

For many observers of the process, in most respects the transition from the Industrial to the Technological Revolution will thus be a positive development. Jobs lost are jobs gained, and they are better jobs, with better working conditions and higher salaries. As had occurred in the factories of nineteenth-century England and in the field of American agriculture in the early twentieth century, society as a whole stands to benefit from the entire process.

There is certainly much to be said for the argument that the shift from an industrial to a technological age has been, on balance, of benefit to the vast majority of people in the world. It is certainly responsible for the flood of consumer goods that permeate so much of the world today. In the years following the end of World War II, television offered easy access to the news of the day and provided cheap entertainment to millions. Jet planes enabled the tourist and the business traveler alike to cover thousands of miles around the Earth between breakfast and dinner (or, sometimes, between dinner and breakfast). The invention of the shipping container—and its inevitable spin-off, the container ship (see Image 16.5)—made it possible to transport vast amounts of manufactured products from place to place at an affordable cost, bringing a smile to the face of every defender of the free trade philosophy of the famous Scotsman Adam Smith.

In the past few decades, the pace of technological change has increased exponentially. The invention of the personal computer has provided its user with access to vast stores of useful (and useless) information, all of which can be quickly and easily dispatched immediately to recipients anywhere on the globe. It simplifies the workload in small businesses and large corporations worldwide by providing

IMAGE 16.5 The Container Ship: Delivery Truck of the Seven Seas. The shipping container was invented in the 1950s by Malcom P. McLean, the owner of an American trucking company in North Carolina. It soon revolutionized the shipping industry, enabling U.S. companies to box their products at their factory and then ship the container by truck to what was now a container port, where the box was loaded onto a container ship to be transported to a far-off destination. Although labor unions initially resisted the new invention (it reduced the amount of human labor involved in the process at portside), it dramatically lowered the cost to transport goods long-distance and has become the standard means of shipping bulk goods from one port to another. As such, it ranks as one of the most important inventions of the modern age.

 How do you think labor unions justified their opposition to the invention of the container? Were they justified in their opposition?

an alternative to the now antiquated postal service. It provides jobs and educational opportunities to ambitious young people living in India and the Philippines, who can politely inform a consumer in Europe or the United States with the comforting news that "your package is on its way," often from a Chinese port (see Chapter 13).

Today cell phones, tablets, and other mobile devices are nothing short of "mini-computers in the pocket," putting the world at one's fingertips and enabling communication with friends, family, or business associates at a fraction of the cost of Alexander Graham Bell's now-outmoded land-line telephone. Robots have begun to replace human labor on the factory floor and to speed up the manufacturing process. Drones (officially known as "unmanned aerial vehicles") serve a wide variety of useful purposes: scouring the world above the treetops, they monitor the movements of endangered wildlife species, seek out and destroy nests of dangerous terrorists, assist farmers in trying to anticipate weather and crop conditions, identify egregious polluters, patrol national borders to pinpoint drug dealers, and monitor our air quality and water supply. Drones are also used as carriers—delivering goods to customers in hard-to-reach places, assisting paramedics by providing them with equipment and medications, and engaging in firefighting and rescue operations. They even pollenate our plants when bees are unavailable. In China, they have been especially useful in delivering precious life-saving medicines to outlying areas of the country that are inaccessible to motorized vehicles.

The most recent technological miracle is known as Artificial Intelligence (AI). It offers the promise of boosting labor productivity in the United States by 40 percent and is already being utilized in the fields of education, health, politics, national security, criminal justice, and the military. But, as the name implies, there are dangers inherent in its widespread use, including those of data bias, lack of transparency, and unequal distribution. Ill-informed use can lead to bad judgment. There are also unanswered questions about the social and ethical impact of a system that revolves around human interaction with machine intelligence. The full implications of recent advances in artificial intelligence are yet to be determined, but are enormous in their potential.

16-3a Is Technology a Magic Wand?

Despite the manifold benefits that much new technology brings, some critics take issue with the glib assumption that technology is an unalloyed benefit to the human community. Even in the United States, where Schumpeter's philosophy of "creative destruction" commands general acceptance, some critics complain that the slavish devotion to the gods of technology have imposed serious costs, not only on the U.S. economy but beyond that, on the American way of life (see "16-5c Technology and Society," later in this chapter). The same complaint could be equally applied to many other parts of the world. Although new technology provides high-wage jobs to those with the training to master its often-complex requirements, it drives many other workers who previously occupied well-paying jobs off the factory floor and into low-wage employment in service industries. Similarly, countless numbers of middle-aged office employees have seen the number of available jobs shrink as computers accelerate worker productivity and, lacking retraining for a modern workforce, are forced into retirement or compelled to work as clerks in Walmart, or in competition with teenagers looking for summer jobs in the fast-food industry.

There is no way to halt the process, because in today's competitive marketplace business owners must automate wherever and whenever they can in the search to benefit the bottom line. After all, new technologies and new ways of doing things are the primary mechanism that drives the capitalist machine. But in many advanced countries today, the view is growing that increased automation in the office or the manufacturing process no longer provides clear benefits to the society at large. The reality is that in the contemporary economy, when automation takes place productivity growth is often sluggish. As the economist Lawrence Summers (a former Secretary of the Treasury in the Clinton administration) remarked recently: "Until a few years ago, I didn't think this was a very complicated subject; the Luddites were wrong and the believers in technology and technological progress were right. I'm not so completely certain now."[3]

Societal Consequences The hidden social costs of technology have provoked growing anger throughout the advanced industrialized countries, where access to a job with middle-class wages and benefits is viewed by many as a social right. And it is undoubtedly a major factor in provoking the decline in public confidence toward government and the bureaucratic elites that fuels the populist revolt now taking place in many industrialized countries. The reality is, of course, that it is now increasingly clear that the Technological Revolution, like the Industrial Revolution that preceded it, will entail enormous societal consequences and—unless solutions can be found—may ultimately give birth to a level of social and political instability that has not been seen in the developed world since the Great Depression of the 1930s. The success of the advanced capitalist states in the second half of the twentieth century was built on the foundations of a broad consensus on several propositions: (1) the importance of limiting income inequities to reduce the threat of political instability while maximizing domestic consumer demand; (2) the need for high levels of government investment in infrastructure projects such as education, communications, and transportation as a means of coping with the challenges of continued economic growth and technological innovation; and (3) the desirability of cooperative efforts in the international arena as a means of maintaining open markets for the free exchange of goods. The ultimate purpose of these principles was to create the conditions for the continued spread of the social benefits of the Industrial Revolution while at the same time minimizing the material inequities and disruptive market cycles that are endemic to the capitalist system.

Recent events graphically demonstrate that these principles remain of crucial importance as the world enters the next stage of the Technological Revolution. Yet as the new century gains momentum, all of these assumptions are increasingly coming under attack. Citizens are reacting with growing hostility to the high tax rates needed to maintain the welfare state, refusing to support education and infrastructure development, and opposing the formation of trade alliances to promote the free movement of goods and labor across national borders. Such attitudes are being expressed by individuals and groups on all sides of the political spectrum, making the traditional designations of left-wing and right-wing politics increasingly meaningless. Although most governments and political elites have continued to support most of the programs that underpin the welfare state and the global marketplace, they are increasingly attacked by groups in society that feel they have been victimized by the system. The breakdown of the public consensus that brought modern capitalism to a pinnacle of achievement raises serious questions about the likelihood that society can meet the coming challenge of the Third Wave without increasing political and social tensions in both the domestic and international arenas.

Can anything be done to soften the powerful but disruptive economic effects of the Technological Revolution? Can the global effort to improve conditions for human life on this planet keep pace with the voracious demand for new technology that envelops the global marketplace? It seems obvious that any decision to turn away from the wondrous advances that technology has to offer would be impractical and, regardless, almost certainly impossible. Some level of division in society between high-skilled and lower-skilled jobs is inevitable, and not everyone benefits in an equal manner to changes taking place in the global marketplace. The most sensible and practical solution is to find ways to reward workers in all economic fields with a living wage and a ladder to seek a life of personal satisfaction and material comfort. It also entails the need to provide educational opportunities for workers at all levels of the economic spectrum. As many observers have noted, not every young person needs, or even wants, a college degree. Statistics suggest that the global marketplace—in the advanced industrialized countries as well as in the developing world—requires middle-skilled workers more than it does applicants with graduate degrees. Adequate funding for education to provide technological skills at the secondary or at the community college level and at an affordable cost would go a long way to providing job opportunities for the young, and qualified applicants for employers in the new highly competitive environment.

Over a century ago, prescient governments in Western Europe and the United States successfully prevented the collapse of the capitalist system by adopting measures to improve living conditions and salaries for the working population of those countries. They also opened up the political system to enable working men and women to play an active role in bringing about changes to improve their own betterment. Today, sensible solutions such as those that have been discussed above are badly needed to help preserve the current capitalist system that, with all its faults, has provided so many benefits to the world.

The Technological Revolution is already posing a number of other serious consequences in contemporary society—notably in the realm of politics and social attitudes and behavior. I will discuss some of these implications in a later section of this chapter (see "16-5c Technology and Society," later in this chapter).

16-4 DEMOCRACY IN CRISIS

 Focus Questions: What are some of the reasons for the attacks on liberal democratic systems and values that are taking place around the world today? What do these attacks have in common?

Government is the most important tool available in human societies to establish and guarantee public order, as well as to protect the welfare of their inhabitants. And since the outbreak of the European Enlightenment and the cataclysmic popular revolutions to which it gave birth, most thoughtful observers in Western civilization have concluded that the best system of governance in the modern world, by far, is the system that we know as liberal democracy. As defined by political philosophers, liberal democracy is a form of government based on the will of the people that seeks to provide equal protection for all citizens under the law. It is based on the principle that the separation of powers and the creation of a representative government is the best guarantee that the civil rights and liberties of all will be protected. It operates under the principles of classical liberalism which seek to uphold the sanctity of individual liberty, private property, and the market economy (see Chapter 1).

Based on the historical record over the past two centuries, those countries that have adopted a liberal democratic system of government have tended to be stable, peaceful, and reasonably efficient in creating conditions that promote the betterment of the lives of their citizens. During the twentieth century, the community of liberal democratic nations faced severe threats from proponents of rival political systems, who trumpeted the superiority of fascist, communist, or other autocratic ideologies, but they have emerged victorious on all occasions. It is not surprising that since the end of World War II, many nations and peoples in other parts of the world—headed by the advanced industrialized societies in East Asia—have come to view the liberal democratic system of government with admiration, and have sought to emulate it.

In retrospect, the high point for public confidence in the superiority of liberal democracy probably occurred at the end of the Cold War, when the collapse of the Soviet Union and is satellites confirmed to many observers at the time that no other form of government presented a realistic alternative to the dominance of liberal democracy throughout the world. In 1989, the political philosopher Francis Fukuyama voiced these views in a famous magazine article. He argued that the decline of communism demonstrated conclusively that the advanced capitalist democracies of the West had triumphed in the war of ideas and would now proceed to remake the rest of the world in their own image. Three years later, in a widely discussed book entitled, *The End of History and the Last Man*, Fukuyama contended that capitalism and liberal democracy, while not necessarily ideal mechanisms to satisfy all human aspirations, were more effective than any rival doctrine and deserved consideration as the best available ideology to be applied universally throughout the globe.[4]

Even at the time, not all commentators agreed with Fukuyama's prognosis. Some questioned whether the triumph that he had predicted was as complete as he contended. Autocratic practices still flourished in many other parts of the world, and their incapacity to provide for the needs of the local population had not yet been demonstrated. Others pointed out some of the alleged weaknesses in liberal democracy—its relatively laissez-faire attitude toward systemic problems in human society, or its dismissal of the role of religion and the life of the spirit as a force for stability and change in society. Others pointed out that greater human freedom and increasing material prosperity had not led to a heightened level of human achievement and emotional satisfaction, but rather to increasing alienation and a crass pursuit of hedonistic pleasures. Some concluded that a new and perhaps "postmodernist" paradigm for the human experience must be found.

Still, confidence that liberal democracy was the most appropriate form of government for all peoples and nations remained high among most members of Western society, and the promotion of democratic institutions and values around the world has remained a bedrock principle of the foreign policy of most Western nations ever since. The British politician and statesman Winston Churchill put it succinctly in 1947 when he remarked: "No one pretends that Democracy is perfect or all-wise. Indeed it has been said that Democracy is the worst form of Government except for all those other forms that have been tried from time to time."[5]

But in recent years, for the first time since the perilous era of the 1930s, the assumption that liberal democracy is superior to all of its alternatives is in serious doubt. Political leaders in Moscow and Beijing, in particular, shrug off demands that they adopt democratic institutions and practices and have openly declared their preference for a more autocratic form of government—a system which, they maintain, is more appropriate to their own historical and cultural traditions.

China has been the most open in taking the argument a step further, proposing itself as an alternative to the Western model, and it has not been shy at promoting its case (notably through the establishment of so-called "Confucian Institutes" in willing foreign nations) to the rest of the world. In a visit to the United States in 1997, China's then-president Jiang Zemin declared that human rights were something that should be determined by individual societies on the basis of their own traditions and course of development, rather than being dictated by the powerful nations of the world. China's current leader, Xi Jinping, has sought to refine the issue. To Xi and other Chinese observers, by defining human rights almost exclusively in terms of individual freedom, Western commentators ignore the importance of providing adequate food and shelter for all members of society, an achievement that China has singularly brought about in the course of one generation.

16-4a Europe Today: Nationalism Redux

The contention in Moscow and Beijing that liberal democracy is not the only—or even necessarily the best—way to govern a society has attracted favorable attention elsewhere. Many political leaders in Africa, Asia, and Latin America have openly declared their preference for a more centralized form of government, describing it as a better means of pursuing their multiple objectives in a complex world. This preference has even spread to Europe, where newly established political parties and governments in virtually every country on the continent have openly flouted liberal democratic norms as they seek to promote what they proclaim to be their national destiny. The trend is most pronounced in Eastern Europe, where government leaders in countries like Poland and Hungary imprison or force into exile their opponents, undermine the system of justice, and attack the news media for publishing "fake news." The idea of "the Nation" is sacred, and resistance to the admission of immigrants from non-European countries is running strong among the local populace.

Although democratic institutions are still relatively healthy in Western Europe, restive populations there have begun to complain about foreigners in their midst and to rail against the overreach of EU functionaries in Brussels. One of the most familiar complaints about the European Union from among its citizens is that its bureaucrats try to micromanage behavior and attitudes in total disregard of local customs and patterns of behavior. Recently established political parties today openly resort to nationalist appeals to earn popular support, and in Italy influential political figures have reminisced about the fascist era and the strong leadership qualities of Benito Mussolini (see Chapter 6). Even in Great Britain, perhaps the birthplace of modern pluralistic democracy, one of the most powerful messages expressed by those who favor a British exit from the EU has been the desire to cut off the flow of migrants from the European continent into the British Isles.

16-4b The Making of Two Americas

Populism, which is generally defined as a political approach directed at ordinary people who feel that their concerns are ignored by establishment elites, has been a familiar historical factor in U.S. politics, but for the most part its influence has been limited. Fear of mob rule was one of the concerns that inspired the Founding Fathers to draft a constitution containing the sovereign principle of separation of powers, as well as instituting a representative government which was designed to enable debate on crucial issues to take place, removed from the passions of the crowd.

On the whole, most Americans have accepted these principles embodied in the U.S. Constitution and have resisted the appeal of a strong chief executive who might manipulate the popular passions of the moment to take actions beyond established law. They have also accepted the bedrock principle inherent in liberal democracy that while the voice of the majority must be heard, the rights of the minority must also be respected. In a nation composed of immigrants, and blessed with a plethora of wide-open spaces, most Americans have accepted the view that there is plenty of room for everybody.

In difficult times, however, the American people have not been immune to the siren lure of a powerful chief executive who will cut through the bureaucratic red tape and follow "the will of the people." During the late nineteenth century, harsh economic conditions stemming from the transition to an industrial society gave rise to populist movements that demanded drastic change and a return to economic fairness. Often the anger was directed at foreigners (favorite targets were Irish immigrants in eastern cities or Asian workers on the west coast). Only after the passage of reformist legislation during the early twentieth century were conditions alleviated, allowing the movements to subside.

Populist unrest revived again during the Great Depression of the 1930s, when strident voices from both the right and the left began to lose faith in the American system of government (much of the anger at the time was focused directly on capitalist moguls or on the then-current occupant of the White House—Franklin D. Roosevelt) claiming that only drastic change could bring about the creation of a government that would look out for the interests of the American people. That radical frenzy began to fade when economic conditions slowly improved and, perhaps more importantly, when the country was suddenly faced with a serious threat from abroad. Many who were alive during those years are convinced that at no time in U.S. history were the American people as united in purpose as they were during World War II.

In recent years, there have been multiple warning signs that a populist fervor is once again on the rise in the land. The creation of the Tea Party was an early sign, since it attained wide popularity after the 2008 election by focusing public anger on an allegedly oppressive federal government that routinely interfered in the private lives of U.S. citizens. In the minds of many supporters of the movement was the contention that the country was dominated by liberal elites who favored the interests of minorities over the needs of ordinary people in the American heartland. Although there was a whiff of racism in the movement, the concerns expressed by supporters more often focused on economic concerns or on the tendency of the government to interfere in the personal lives of individual citizens.

Trumpism: Symptom or Cause?   As a presidential candidate in 2016, Donald J. Trump played effectively on the populist emotions that were rapidly being injected into the bloodstream of the country. Running as an outsider, he criticized "the Establishment," composed of the bureaucracy and the politicians in Washington, which included not only his Democratic opponent but also prominent members (and previous presidents) of his own Republican Party. In Trump's view and that of many of his supporters, the bureaucrats in Washington D.C. were determined to defend their privileges, and routinely ignored the wishes and the interests of average Americans. The Washington bureaucracy, he warned his followers—quoting the phrase of Steve Bannon, one of his key supporters and advisors—was a "deep state," which would use every technique at its disposal to resist all efforts by his administration to serve the will of the people.

On entering the White House, Trump followed through on the populist aspect of his campaign, testing many of the key norms of the country's liberal democratic system of government. He attacked judges whose legal decisions were at variance with his wishes, and when his own Attorney General appointed a special counsel, ex-FBI director Robert Mueller, to investigate charges that his presidential campaign had colluded with Russian sources to obtain derogatory information on his Democratic opponent, he openly sought to sabotage the investigation. He adopted a classical populist tactic by focusing public anger on alleged "outsiders"—Muslim terrorists from the Middle East, or gang members and drug pushers who entered the country illegally from Mexico. At a time when job security had been a matter of widespread public concern for many years, such inflammatory messages found a willing audience in the broader population.

The tendency of the new administration to overthrow established norms spilled over into foreign policy. President Trump broke postwar precedent by downplaying the importance of relations with leaders of key Western allies like Chancellor Angela Merkel of Germany and Theresa May of Great Britain, and publicly suggested that the NATO alliance no longer deserved U.S. support, since most of the organization's European members have lagged in providing financial support for the common defense. In an additional slap at the U.S. foreign policy establishment, he behaved as if his closest ally and confidante on the world stage was Russia's president Vladimir Putin, a man whose autocratic proclivities openly run counter to the Western political principle of the separation of powers, and whose recent actions threatened to undermine the alliance of democratic nations established at the end of World War II.

As opposition to its actions mounted, the Trump administration persistently attacked the mainstream media, among whose ranks were some of its severest critics. The press, the White House declared, was the purveyor of "fake news" designed to undermine and distort the president's achievements, and his supporters were encouraged to obtain their information on national issues from sources that had openly supported him from the start of his campaign.

Under the circumstances, it was probably inevitable that the president's critics, whether within the political establishment or in the press, relentlessly attacked virtually all of the administration's initiatives, an understandable reaction but one that left little room for those Americans who were hoping for a sober evaluation of the facts. The attacks from the media also convinced Trump's supporters that his opposition was out to destroy him, regardless of the cost to the country. In consequence, the level of partisanship in Washington politics, already at a high pitch since the 1990s, has reached the point where compromise on almost any issue became virtually impossible in Washington, D.C.

Some of President Trump's most fervent critics concluded that the political crisis in the United States was a consequence of the unique character of the president himself, a man who cannily manipulated the emotions and fears of the American people to satisfy his own narcissistic and autocratic impulses. They dismissed his followers as racists and Bible-toting rednecks who have been left behind in the historic struggle to build a better and more efficient society. As we have seen above, however, the rise of populism today is a phenomenon common to almost all liberal democratic countries, which suggests that Donald Trump is more a symptom of weaknesses in the system than a cause. I shall return to this issue briefly in the concluding section of this book.

16-5 A TRANSVALUATION OF VALUES: SOCIAL CHANGE IN THE TECHNOLOGICAL ERA

 Focus Question: How have social institutions and values been affected by the dramatic changes taking place in the world today?

As should be clear from the chapters above, not all the problems and concerns facing human societies today can be ascribed directly to economic factors. It is one of the paradoxes of the modern world that at a time of almost unsurpassed political stability and relative economic prosperity for the majority of the population in most Western countries, public cynicism about the system is increasingly widespread. Many people appear to tune out the litany of political and social commentary and focus exclusively on their own personal concerns. Although the levels of alienation and cynicism might seem to run higher in Western societies, the problem has begun to appear in relatively prosperous Asian countries as well. It almost seems to be the price human beings pay for affluence.

16-5a Family and Society

The reasons that have been advanced to explain this paradox vary widely. Some observers place the responsibility for many contemporary social problems in Western societies on the decline of the traditional family system. With the family now increasingly deprived of its historic role of providing a moral grounding to its younger members, they argue, children grow up without moorings in a soulless and impersonal world. The statistical evidence is clear. There has indeed been a steady rise in the percentage of out-of-wedlock births and single-parent families in countries throughout the Western world. In the United States, 40 percent of all births were out of wedlock in 2014, compared with about 7 percent in 1960. The percentage is even higher in Europe. Between 1980 and 2005, the proportion of single-parent households doubled in the Western world. Approximately half of all marriages in the United States end in divorce, although the rate has declined somewhat in recent years. Even in two-parent families, both parents often work full time, thus leaving their children with too much unsupervised time and limited opportunity to benefit from parental guidance at a critical time in their young lives.

On the other hand, there is scant evidence that long-term partnerships are less effective in raising healthy and well-adjusted children than are their traditional counterparts. Same-sex parents often work out as well or even better than is the case with conventional relationships. What is important, many feel, is the quality of the parental experience and the nature of the guidance that is provided rather than the formal character of the parental relationship itself.

The decline in the traditional family is not so prevalent in many other parts of the world. In much of Africa and Asia, the nuclear family still functions as an important building block of contemporary society. In China, India, and Africa, for example, only about one percent of children are born out of wedlock. By the same token, divorce rates in most Asian and African countries are much lower than in the Western world. Only about four percent of marriages in China end in divorce. Curiously, while in the United States divorce is more common among relatively uneducated families, in China it is almost exclusively an urban phenomenon (a common joke in Beijing ends with "have you had your divorce today?"). Still, given the large numbers of people in China, those small percentages translate to nearly four million couples applying for divorce each year.

Why are divorce and out-of-wedlock births relatively uncommon in most Asian and African societies? Undoubtedly part of the reason is the residual force of tradition, since divorce in such areas can bring shame on both parties, and especially on the woman. Economic necessity is also an important factor, since the wife is often economically dependent upon her husband and would struggle to secure a livelihood as a single woman. Strong family ties, it should be kept in mind, are often achieved at the expense of the degradation of women, and are not necessarily an indication of a healthy society.

It should also be noted that although the traditional family system is more resilient in Africa and Asia than it is in the West, there are perceptible signs of change. Divorce is on the rise in some major East Asian countries and, despite the Confucian tradition of filial piety, more and more elderly parents have begun to complain that they are being ignored by their children, many of whom have abandoned their rural birthplace to seek employment in the cities (see Chapters 12 and 13). Not surprisingly, older citizens frequently react by complaining that Asian youth of today are too materialistic, faddish, and steeped in the individualistic values of the West. It is a concern that would probably be shared in many other parts of the world, including the Middle East, Africa, and Latin America. The trend away from the traditional family is a world-wide phenomenon, but at varying rates of change and with varying consequences.

Observers point to several factors as an explanation for these conditions: the increasing mobility of the world's population, as increasing numbers of people move from the countryside to the cities; the growing emphasis (especially in advanced capitalist states around the world) on an individualistic lifestyle devoted to instant gratification, a phenomenon promoted vigorously in the West by the advertising media, and in places like China by the state; the rise of feminist advocacy for shared responsibilities between male and female parents, which is sometimes mischaracterized as an effort to remove women from responsibility for the care and nurturing of the next generation altogether; and the increasing mobility of contemporary life, which disrupts traditional family ties and creates a sense of rootlessness and impersonality in the individual's relationship to the surrounding environment.

16-5b Religion: A Matter of Faith

While some analysts cite the reduced role of the traditional family as a major factor in the widespread sense of malaise in the contemporary world, others point to the decline in religious faith and the increasing secularization of world society. It seems indisputable that one of the causes of the widespread feeling of alienation in many societies is the absence of any sense of underlying meaning and purpose in life, a quality which religion often provides. Religious faith not only offers belief in a universal moral order, it also creates a sense of belonging among a community of believers. The members of a church, a temple, or a mosque provide the faithful with a built-in support group that can serve as a surrogate family in times of need. A community of faith also imparts a set of values that give every young member a roadmap for proper behavior in the process of entering adulthood.

Historical experience suggests, however, that there can be a price to pay for an enhanced sense of community, since it can result in the heightened intolerance of "outsiders" or unbelievers. History is replete with examples of religious differences that escalate into bloody conflict. The religious wars in Europe during the Medieval and early modern eras, the ongoing clash of faiths in the Middle East, and the religious divide that still plagues the subcontinent of South Asia are only some of the most flagrant examples. Many of these historical confrontations have not yet been resolved, and continue to poison the politics of many regions in the world today. In virtually every continent on this Earth, religious differences still present a flashpoint for conflict within otherwise peaceful communities.

The issue of religion and its implications for social policy are thus quite complicated. Although the percentage of people attending church on a regular basis or professing firm religious convictions has been dropping steadily in most Western countries, the intensity of religious belief appears to be growing in many individual communities. In the United States, the evangelical movement has become a significant force in politics and an influential factor in defining many social issues. In Europe, Christian groups have begun to organize in opposition to the immigration of migrants of other faiths. In Latin America, a decline in membership in the Roman Catholic Church in some countries has been offset by significant increases in the popularity of evangelical Protestant sects. In predominantly Muslim countries like Egypt and Turkey, a growing intensity of religious belief in some communities has led to stricter behavioral codes and growing suspicion of fellow citizens of other faiths.

In parts of Africa and Asia as well, there are clear signs that organized religion is expanding in scope and influence. Both Christianity and Islam are gaining adherents in Africa, and the intense competition between the two faiths is one reason for the increased violence along the southern rim of the Sahara. Throughout the Muslim world, conflict between Sunnis and Shi'ites, and between traditionalists and modernists, has reached crisis proportions in many countries. In India, Hindu revivalist groups seek to change the secular character of the Indian republic, while sporadic outbreaks of violence among Hindus, Muslims, Christians, and Sikhs are increasingly common in various parts of the country.

IMAGE 16.6 A Prayer to the Buddha. Religion continues to play a major role in the lives of many peoples throughout the world today, and is even reviving in countries living under Communist rule, such as contemporary China and Vietnam. Although the practice of religion has long been officially discouraged in both countries, the government has relaxed its restrictions in recent years, and attendance at religious functions is increasing steadily. Some observers speculate that religious faith provides a sense of purpose and the meaning of life in societies where the dialectical materialism of Karl Marx has long been official doctrine. Shown here, two Vietnamese are praying at a brightly decorated Buddhist temple in the commercial center of Ho Chi Minh City—the one-time Saigon.

 Which are the major Buddhist societies in the world today?

Even in China, where the Communist government long imposed strict limitations on the practice of any organized religion, attendance at Buddhist temples and Christian churches has been steadily increasing in recent years, especially among members of the growing and highly influential middle class, who often view their faith as a stepping-stone to higher status and achievement in Chinese society (see Image 16.6). In the meantime, dissident nationalities like the Tibetans and the Muslim minorities in Xinjiang province turn to traditional religion as a symbol for their demand for greater autonomy or independence from the People's Republic of China. Throughout the world, religion, politics, and national identity are increasingly intertwined.

Not long ago, there was a common assumption in secular circles that religious faith was in decline around the world. As attendance at church in Western countries dropped and peoples living in countries ruled by communist parties were presumably convinced to adopt the Marxist theory of historical materialism, many observers believed that in a modern world governed by scientific achievement and the theory of evolution, religion would become a relic of the past. Even in Muslim countries, the rise of Modernist Islam was cited as tacit evidence that fervent belief was headed toward the dust heap of history.

That assumption is no longer tenable. As we have noted above, religious belief is alive and well in many regions of the world, even in secular societies where attendance at religious ceremonies has declined and more people adopt a secular lifestyle. Vast numbers of people once living behind the Iron Curtain have been attracted to religion as an alternative to the Marxist-Leninist shibboleths of the past. Even in Russia, Christianity has become an important attribute of Vladimir Putin's strategy to rebuild the once-powerful Russian empire, and it is flourishing in Moscow's one-time satellites in Eastern Europe. For many peoples on Earth today, religion provides a vital sense of community and defines their own place in the world.

The truth is that the divide between the secular and the religious in many countries is one aspect of the larger divide that is taking place as a consequence of the technological revolution. In urban areas and within educated communities, religious belief often no longer occupies an important position, although in parts of Asia, organized religions like Christianity and Buddhism are sometimes viewed as a ticket to the good life. In rural areas and in smaller communities where respect for tradition continues to hold sway, religion plays a central role in the community. To ride on the wave of change that is sweeping across the modern world is to adopt a secular world view that is characterized by a belief in science and confidence in the power of technology to improve the human condition. Whether that is a reasonable assumption is one of the central questions facing us today. Billions of people in all regions of the world are convinced that religious faith is what provides meaning in their lives.

16-5c Technology and Society

It goes without saying that new scientific and technological discoveries will exert a continuing impact on our changing world. We have already discussed some of the economic repercussions in an earlier section (see "16-3a Is Technology a Magic Wand?" earlier in this chapter). But the political and social reverberations are equally significant. Advances in human communication like the Internet have provided people living even in isolated areas with easy access to information and communication (see Image 16.7). On the other hand, the social media have sometimes inflamed historic antagonisms and enabled terrorist groups to spread their message throughout the world. Dictatorial regimes have with varying degrees of success sought to screen out critical opinions on local websites and freely use the new technology to spread their own propaganda among their citizens. For the purveyors of "fake news" worldwide, the social media are an ideal platform to broadcast their alternative views.

Social media also can have an influential effect on human behavior. The Internet provides users with the opportunity to seek out others with common interests, but often to the exclusion of hearing and considering differing viewpoints. It can also discourage face-to-face communication by encouraging individuals to bury their heads in their electronic devices. Who isn't familiar with the cartoon that shows a family of four spending their vacation at a beautiful beach, yet all of whom have hardly looked up from their cell phones? Millions of parents around the world are faced with the need to insist that their children put aside their electronic devices and take part in a family discussion.

IMAGE 16.7a

IMAGE 16.7b

IMAGE 16.7 Hello, World. In the twenty-first century, the entire world is becoming wired, as peoples in the developing nations realize that economic success depends increasingly on information technology. Few countries have embraced the Internet as enthusiastically as China. Millions of Chinese citizens—sometimes to the discomfort of their government—now turn to the electronic media for their chief source of information about the wider world. In Image 16.7a, an Apple store on a major shopping street in Shanghai displays the new iPhone (a device itself manufactured in Chinese factories) to potential buyers. The response to the new technology has been enthusiastic all over the world. Image 16.7b shows young Buddhist monks in Bagu, a city in south Myanmar, communicating with their friends on their ubiquitous cellphones.

Ⓠ *Do you think that Apple is justified in permitting its products to be manufactured in China? What are the benefits and disadvantages in doing so?*

Governments and the major social media platforms are well aware of the promise and the risk of the new communications technology, and government hearings have been held in many countries to seek out solutions. But technology is notoriously difficult to control, and common sense suggests that no simple nostrum will be found. Like so many other scientific advances that have marked the human quest for knowledge, the benefits and the costs of communications technology cannot be easily measured, and easy solutions for the latter are most often elusive.

As we have discussed, these questions have inspired some people to express serious doubts about the role of science and technology and its impact on the contemporary world. Nuclear power has been targeted by environmental groups for decades. Many people express distrust of all genetically modified food products. Voices across the political and social spectrum have begun to complain that technological advances are at least partly responsible for the psychological malaise now so prevalent in much of the contemporary world. The criticism dates back at least to the advent of television. Television, in the eyes of its critics, has contributed to a decline in human communication and turned viewers from active participants in the experience of life into passive observers. With the advent of the computer and products like the smart phone, the process has accelerated as recent generations of young people raised on video games and surfing the Web find less and less time for personal relationships or creative activities away from their computers. Many older observers find the current popular use of "selfies" as the height of self-absorption.

But nowhere is the suspicion of modern science more pronounced than it is in devout communities where it contradicts deeply held convictions based on an interpretation of holy writ. In Christian evangelical communities, many devout believers take issue with one of the most fundamental assumptions of modern science: the concept of the evolution of species. Evangelical Christian groups have opposed the teaching of evolutionary theory in the classroom, or have demanded that public schools also present the biblical interpretation of the creation of the Earth, and qualify evolution as only one theory. In adopting such attitudes, conservative Christians share their convictions with devout believers in other faiths such as Islam and Judaism. The sense of mutual distrust and discomfort between the world of science and the world of faith is not a new phenomenon, of course (dating back at least to the early years of Christianity), but it seems to have become increasingly prevalent in recent years.

16-6 ONE WORLD, ONE ENVIRONMENT

 Focus Question: How persuasive to you is the warning by many climate scientists that human action is at least partly responsible for global warming?

In the opinion of many climatologists, no single factor is more likely to affect future events on this Earth than significant changes taking place in the global environment. If the scientific community is correct in asserting that global warming is currently underway and will probably intensify in the coming decades, it will inevitably have dramatic and possibly catastrophic effects on all living things on this Earth. Climate change will impact societies on every continent, albeit in different ways in different areas. While a warmer Earth may provide benefits to some peoples and some countries, others may suffer from highly negative effects, with serious consequences on their political and social stability. In that event, the political ramifications could be significant: collapsed economies, widespread political conflict and social unrest, intensified competition for dwindling natural resources, and massive migration of peoples out of adversely affected countries seeking a safe haven. The first signs of such a movement are now clearly visible in parts of Africa, the Middle East, and southern Asia (see "The Great Escape: The Migration of Peoples," p. 404). If global warming is as likely and widespread as some scientists warn, it could eventually transform the human experience in multiple and unforeseen ways and bring an end to the world as we now know it (see Map 16.3).

Climate change, of course, has been taking place since the original creation of the Earth. It has continued to occur on a regular basis in historical times, bringing about the rise and fall of civilizations, the migration of peoples, and the opening of new historical eras. It can be beneficial or harmful in its impact. Widespread drought in the Middle East may have precipitated the movement of the first farmers into the European continent several thousand years ago. Dramatic climatic changes triggered by El Nino events probably led to the collapse of advanced civilizations along the Pacific coast of South America. A period of cold weather called the Little Ice Age led to crop failures and unsettled conditions in Europe during the Middle Ages, followed by a warming trend that played a significant role in giving birth to the modern world.

Historians have discovered that human beings have often inadvertently played a role in bringing about climate

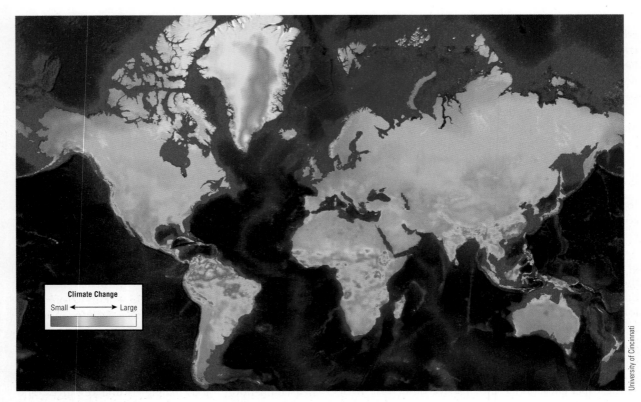

MAP 16.3 Global Climate Change. Climate change is projected to have a major impact all over the world, but some areas will be more adversely affected than others. Using the year 2000 as a baseline, this map shows a projection of the relative degree of change that is currently expected to take place over the first 70 years of the twenty-first century. The areas most affected—many of them in the tropics and the arctic regions—are shown in brown and white. This map image was generated by the Climate Explorer interactive web application developed by Professor Tomasz Stepinski at the University of Cincinnati.

change, and sometimes human action has caused significant damage to the natural surroundings. It may first have occurred when Neolithic peoples began to practice slash-and-burn agriculture or when excessive hunting depleted the herds of bison and caribou in the Western Hemisphere. Silting up of the irrigation systems almost certainly played a major role in the decline of the ancient civilizations in the Persian Gulf region, and soil erosion and other consequences of human action may have contributed to the fall of the Roman Empire. Overplanting and excessive population growth probably caused the erosion of cornfields and the ultimate collapse of Mayan civilization in Central America. Never before, however, has the danger of significant ecological damage been as serious as it has during the past century.

The underlying culprit, without a doubt, is the Industrial Revolution. The effects of chemicals introduced into the atmosphere or into rivers, lakes, and oceans have increasingly threatened the health and well-being of all living species. For many years, the main focus of environmental concern was in the developed countries of the West, where industrial effluents, automobile exhausts, and

the use of artificial fertilizers and insecticides led to urban smog, extensive damage to crops and wildlife, poisoned rivers and streams, and a major reduction of the ozone layer in the upper atmosphere. In recent decades, however, as the Industrial Revolution has spread to other areas of the world, the problem has become global in scope and has finally led to demands for vigorous action to counter the danger to peoples and societies around the world.

Awareness of the increasing damage to the environment first came to public attention in the 1950s, when Rachel Carson pointed to the dangers that the widespread use of some pesticides posed for animal and human life (see Chapter 8). Then, the opening of Eastern Europe after the revolutions of 1989 brought to the world's attention the incredible environmental destruction in that region caused by unfettered industrial pollution. Communist governments had obviously operated under the assumption that production quotas were much more important than environmental protection. The nuclear power disaster at Chernobyl in Ukraine in 1986 made Europeans acutely aware of potential environmental hazards, and 1987 was touted as the "year of the environment." In response, many European states, following the lead of the United States, implemented new regulations to protect the environment and established government ministries to oversee environmental issues. Green movements and political parties played an important role in bringing the issue to public attention.

16-6a A Nightmare Scenario

In recent years, recognition of the problem has spread to all parts of the world. China's headlong rush to industrialization has resulted in major ecological damage in that country. Industrial smog, caused by the widespread use of coal as a source of energy, has created almost unlivable conditions in many cities, and hillsides denuded of their forest cover have experienced severe erosion that has led to the destruction of thousands of acres of farmland. Although the Chinese government has invested heavily in tree planting and "clean coal" technology, levels of pollution in China are already higher than in the fully developed industrial societies of the West (see Chapter 11 and Image 16.8a).

Destruction of the world's forest cover is a problem of equal importance in many parts of the world, notably in the Amazon rainforest of Brazil and on the islands of the Indonesian archipelago. With the rapid decline in the forest cover throughout the Earth, there is less plant life to perform the crucial process of reducing carbon dioxide levels in the atmosphere. In 1997, forest fires on the Indonesian islands of Sumatra and Borneo created a blanket of smoke over the entire region, forcing schools and offices to close and causing respiratory ailments in thousands of people. Some of the damage could be attributed to the traditional slash-and-burn techniques used by subsistence farmers to clear forest cover for their farmlands, but the primary cause was the clearing of forests to create or expand palm oil plantations, one of the region's major sources of export revenue (see Image 16.8b).

Most of the attention concerning threats to the climate in recent years has been focused on the threat of global warming. Global temperatures caused by the emission of greenhouse gases have been rising steadily (climatologists routinely announce that the most recent five years are among the hottest on record), resulting in warmer ocean temperatures, a melting ice pack in the polar regions, and a steady rise in the sea level. Consequences could include the periodic inundation of densely populated coastal areas around the world, flooding in river basins, and the very disappearance of low-lying islands in the seas and oceans. A significant rise in sea level could force the evacuation and relocation of peoples living in coastal areas along the eastern and gulf states of the United States and along the perimeter of Asia.

16-6b Facing the Prospect of Climate Change

Governments and peoples around the world have been slow to recognize the threat posed by changes in the environment. Because catastrophic events such as hurricanes, floods, and droughts occur frequently in nature, it is tempting to view these kinds of discrete weather

IMAGE 16.8a

IMAGE 16.8b

IMAGE 16.8 **The Face of Climate Change.** The impact of climate change on the global environment takes various forms and imposes different costs on society as a whole. Image 16.8a shows the skies over the city of Shanghai covered with its familiar blanket of smog. High levels of greenhouse gases are commonplace in many Asian cities today, and no more so than in China, where carbon effluents from factories, power plants, and automobile exhausts combine to make Chinese cities among the most unhealthy environments in the world today. Image 16.8b shows a wildfire in the nation of Chile. Trees are an important mechanism for absorbing harmful greenhouse gases, and their destruction caused by acts of nature or by deliberate human activity removes an important natural tool in the struggle to limit the effects of global warming in the years to come.

Q *Do you believe that it is possible to counter the trend toward global warming? If so, how?*

events as either evidence for or against a major change in the overall climate. Climate change, however, actually refers to trends that are measured over decades. One cold winter in parts of the United States is not an indication that global warming is a hoax. Warming and cooling patterns have taken place before and throughout all of our recorded weather history, and unusual weather changes can easily be passed off as a statistical anomaly. Scientists who voice concern over global climate trends are sometimes dismissed by critics as alarmists. Examples of scientific exaggeration that never came to pass remain in the public memory, notably when some researchers predicted the return of a new Ice Age in the latter half of the twentieth century. However, overall advances in our understanding of climate dynamics in recent years make it far less likely that scientists are misinterpreting the signs of climate change today.

Still, as scientific evidence and understanding about the growing risk of environmental catastrophe has continued to accumulate, political leaders in many countries have begun to pay more attention to the problem. After several efforts to bring the environmental issue to the conference table were aborted, an international conference on the subject was finally convened in Kyoto, Japan, in 1997.

It is one thing to recognize a problem, however, and quite another to resolve it. The Kyoto conference was marked by bitter disagreement among delegates over the degree to which developing countries should share the burden of cleaning up the environment. Nations such as China and India expressed the view of many smaller countries in the developing world when they objected to being held to the same standards as their more industrialized counterparts. The latter, they argued, bore primary responsibility for starting the Industrial Revolution in the first place. As a result, few nations expressed a willingness to take unilateral action that might pose an obstacle to their economic development plans or could lead to a rise in unemployment. Measures to reduce the release of harmful gases into the atmosphere are costly and can have significant negative effects on economic growth. Thus, politicians who embraced such measures risked political suicide, despite the evident severity of the problem.

What was most needed was to reach a level of international cooperation that would bring about major efforts to reduce pollution levels throughout the world. After several further international conferences yielded only limited agreements to preserve tropical forests and develop clean energy, years of talks finally managed to forge wide agreement on a number of key issues, and in December 2015 a conference was convened in the city of Paris where it brought about an agreement to adopt major steps to address the problem.

The **Paris Climate Agreement** committed 175 signatory countries, including the Earth's two major polluters, China and the United States, to set specific goals to bring about reductions in the emissions of harmful gases. While the goals established at the conference were voluntary in nature, signatory countries were committed to providing targets for further action every five years. The overall objective at the conference was to limit global warming to a level below two degrees centigrade, cutting greenhouse gas emissions to reach a net-zero emissions target by the last half of this century.

16-6c The Debate over Global Warming

Problems were not long in coming. In 2017, the Trump administration announced that the United States intended to withdraw from the Paris Climate Agreement. The decision was not a complete surprise since, as a candidate, Donald Trump had openly expressed his doubts on the topic of global warming during the presidential campaign. In explaining the decision to abandon the treaty, he declared that he did not necessarily dispute the fact that the Earth's temperature was rising, but he dismissed the evidence that it was being caused by human action. In any case, he added, the climate may turn colder again, as it has periodically throughout history.

The decision by the Trump administration to withdraw from the climate agreement was a severe blow to its prospects of success, and highlighted one of the key challenges for those who hope to engage the nations of the world in a concerted effort to address the problem. Although a substantial majority of Americans consistently agree with the proposition that global warming is currently taking place, there is less agreement about the role of human action in bringing it about. Since many of the skeptics support the President's party, the issue has been firmly imbedded in the partisan deadlock that has poisoned the political scene in Washington since the beginning of the new century.

The issue of climate change has not always been subject to partisan disagreement in American politics. In the past, leaders of both major parties have supported legislation to clean up the environment and address the climate issue. But the increasing influence of evangelicals within the Republican Party—many of whom are already suspicious of science because of its rejection of biblical explanations for the creation of the Earth—has led the party leadership to adopt a position skeptical of climate science, thus rendering a bipartisan solution more difficult to achieve. In their resistance to the adoption of measures to control climate change, climate-deniers are joined by powerful forces within the business community, who are concerned at the costs that decisive action would entail, and at the prospective impact that it would impose on their own economic interests.

One of the issues that originally drove the movement to bring an end to the planet's reliance on sources of liquid energy was the fear that such sources around the world were drying up. As supplies of oil and natural gas dwindled, the cost of fuel periodically increased, thus threatening the ability of governments and consumers alike to manage their expenses. But the invention of horizontal drilling and **fracking**—a process involving the use of a pressurized liquid to fracture rock formations containing shale oil deposits—has opened up new sources of natural gas and petroleum and led to a steady reduction in the cost of these products to the consumer. Critics have pointed out that the environmental risks posed by the use of such a process are substantial, in the form of oil spills, air and water pollution, and the increased potential for triggering earthquakes under the Earth's crust, but the political and economic advantages posed by fracking are so self-evident that the process is now widespread. Science can give, and science can take away.

As world leaders flounder over how to address the climate crisis, some optimists have expressed the hope that new technology will eventually step in to resolve the debate. After all, the introduction of safer pesticides in the 1960s and 1970s brought an end to the widespread use of DDT, thus reducing the threat of polluted waters and skies. Stricter gasoline requirements in the United States lowered the presence of carbon dioxide in automobile exhausts, thus clearing the atmosphere over cities like Los Angeles (car companies have successfully reduced the level of carbon dioxide emanating from their vehicles by over 90% in the past fifty years). The skies over the city of Pittsburgh, once heavily laden with coal dust particles emanating from the steel mills nearby, have also improved in recent years, reducing the threat of respiratory ailments to people living in the area.

Optimists also point to the fact that with the help of government subsidies that were negotiated under previous administrations, alternative energy sources like wind and solar power are becoming cheaper to produce, and some analysts predict that they will overtake and eventually bring to an end the world-wide reliance on traditional energy sources like coal, oil, and natural gas. Even today, in the United States there are more job opportunities in the field of wind and solar power than there are in the oil and gas industry. Electric cars, once a dream sitting on a drawing board, are now a realistic alternative to the internal combustion engine. Even the giant oil companies have begun to recognize the fact that change is on the way, and have begun to invest in alternative sources of energy themselves. As a result of such factors, some climate scientists are hopeful that economic realities—always a driving force for change in capitalist societies—will eventually resolve the debate in a favorable manner.

Many environmentalists warn, however, that the world is in a race against time in the fight against climate change, and is currently losing the competition. Bill McKibben, one of the most outspoken writers on the environmental front, argues that at the current pace of change, the world will not be able to prevent major and perhaps catastrophic damage from environmental pollution before the benefits of new discoveries take hold. He warns that scientists, far from exaggerating the dangers, have "routinely underestimated the pace of planetary disruption," which is currently taking place at a faster rate than even many alarmists in previous years had predicted. And because the fossil fuel industry is reluctant to change (more financial profit comes from the continuing exploitation of an oil field than from the one-time installation of a wind or solar farm), firm and rapid government intervention is still needed to push the widespread transition to renewable energy along at a faster pace.[6]

In May 2019, a United Nations report on the current state and future prospects of the Earth's climate presented a stark warning that the decline of animal species around the world has reached dangerous proportions, and that "transformative changes" in global policy with regard to global warming were needed to restore and protect nature from potentially catastrophic consequences. (see Historical Voices, "The UN Raises the Alarm," p. 422).

16-6d Population Growth and the Environment

One aspect of the debate on the environment that has sometimes been underestimated is the role which population growth plays in the process of climate change. As the world population continues to rise, the demand for food increases steadily. Today, the replacement of forest land for agriculture and pastureland is estimated to account for up to 25% of the greenhouse gases released on Earth each year. Half a century ago, predictions that population growth would outstrip the capacity of the Earth to feed its inhabitants raised expressions of alarm in some quarters. Fortunately, those warnings were somewhat overdrawn, as new genetically engineered crops led to an increase in food production, while family planning programs and the shift of millions of people from farming to other occupations led to a decline in the rate of population growth (see "The Danger of Overpopulation," p. 405). Still, the Earth's population continues to rise, particularly in regions where local peoples are vulnerable to the risk of starvation.

Adding to the serious implications of the problem is the fact that as the standard of living in many parts of the

The UN Raises the Alarm

> **Q** *What does this report indicate are the primary threats to the global environment in the present day? How, according to the author of this report, is global warming likely to harm the world's economy?*

 Earth & Environment **IN THE SPRING OF 2019,** a United Nations committee on the environment issued a report on the current state of biodiversity on this planet. The report warned that the damage now being inflicted on nature was unprecedented in its severity, and that current efforts to control it were insufficient. It concluded that "transformative changes" were needed to restore nature to a point where it could meet human requirements.

A Report on Biodiversity and Ecosystem Services

…The assessment's authors have ranked, for the first time at this scale and based on a thorough analysis of the available evidence, the five direct drivers of change in nature with the largest relative global impacts so far. These culprits are, in descending order: (1) changes in land and sea use; (2) direct exploitation of organisms; (3) climate change; (4) pollution and (5) invasive alien species.

The Report notes that, since 1980, greenhouse gas emissions have doubled, raising average global temperatures by at least 0.7 degrees Celsius—with climate change already impacting nature from the level of ecosystems to that of genetics—impacts expected to increase over the coming decades, in some cases surpassing the impact of land and sea change and other drivers.

Despite progress to conserve nature and implement policies, the Report also finds that global goals for conserving and sustainably using nature and achieving sustainability cannot be met by current trajectories, and goals for 2030 and beyond may only be achieved through transformative changes across economic, social, political and technological factors…it is likely that most will be missed by the 2020 deadline. Current negative trends in biodiversity and ecosystems will undermine progress towards 80% of the assessed targets of the Sustainable Development Goals, related to poverty, hunger, health, water, cities, climate, oceans and land. Loss of biodiversity is therefore shown to be not only an environmental issue, but also a developmental, economic, security, social and moral issue as well.

Three-quarters of the land-based environment and about 66% of the marine environment have been significantly altered by human actions. On average these trends have been less severe or avoided in areas held or managed by Indigenous Peoples and Local Communities…

Land degradation has reduced the productivity of 23% of the global land surface, up to US$577 billion in annual global crops are at risk from pollinator loss and 100–300 million people are at increased risk of floods and hurricanes because of loss of coastal habitats and protection.

In 2015, 33% of marine fish stocks were being harvested at unsustainable levels; 60% were maximally sustainably fished, with just 7% harvested at levels lower than what can be sustainably fished.

Urban areas have more than doubled since 1992.

Plastic pollution has increased tenfold since 1980, 300–400 million tons of heavy metals, solvents, toxic sludge and other wastes from industrial facilities are dumped annually into the world's water, and fertilizers entering coastal ecosystems have produced more than 400 ocean 'dead zones', totally more than 245,000 square kilometers—a combined area greater than that of the United Kingdom.

Negative trends in nature will continue to 2050 and beyond in all of the policy scenarios explored in the Report, except those that include transformative change—due to the projected impacts of increasing land-use change, exploitation of organisms and climate change, although with significant differences between regions.

Source: Media Release by the Intergovernmental Science-Policy Platform on Biodiversity and Ecosystem services, Food and Agriculture Organization of the United Nations, pp. 1–3.

world continues to rise, more and more consumers turn to meat products, thus putting farmers under pressure to turn their lands into pasture for livestock, which is statistically the most wasteful use of land in terms of the amount of protein produced per acre. The problem is particularly serious in developing countries like China, where millions of people turn away from staple products like wheat and rice in favor of meat products like beef, chicken, and pork.

Today the debate over the environment is growing in intensity, and if the vast majority of climate scientists are correct in their predictions, it may eventually dwarf in importance many of the other issues facing the world today. It is an unfortunate characteristic of human nature to avoid facing an uncomfortable reality until a moment of crisis has arrived. It may be that the peoples of the Earth still have time to take action to avoid the worst of the calamity that threatens their future livelihood. The next few years are likely to provide us with a greater awareness of the scope of the problem and, depending on our ability to act, the range of possible outcomes.

16-7 THE ARTS: MIRROR OF THE AGE

 Focus Question: How do the current trends in the art world reflect the age that we live in today?

If, as has been observed, the arts are the signature of their age, what has been happening in literature, art, music, and architecture in recent decades is a reflection of the evolving global response to the rapid changes taking place in human society today. This reaction has sometimes been described as Postmodernism, although today's developments are much too diverse to be placed under a single label. Some of the arts are still experimenting with the Modernist quest for the new and the radical. Others have begun to return to more traditional styles as a reaction against globalization and a response to the search for national and cultural identity in a bewildering world.

The most appropriate label for the contemporary cultural scene, in fact, is probably pluralism. The arts today are an eclectic hybrid, combining different movements, genres, and media, as well as incorporating different ethnic or national characteristics. There is no doubt that Western culture has strongly influenced the development of the arts throughout the world in recent decades. In fact, the process has gone in both directions as art forms from Africa and Asia have profoundly enriched the cultural scene in the West. One ironic illustration is that some of the best literature in the English and French languages today is being written in the nations that were once under British or French colonial rule. Today, global interchange in the arts is playing the same creative role that the exchange of technology between different

regions played in stimulating the Industrial Revolution. As one Japanese composer declared not long ago, "I would like to develop in two directions at once: as a Japanese with respect to tradition, and as a Westerner with respect to innovation. . . . In that way I can avoid isolation from the tradition and yet also push toward the future in each new work."[7]

Such a globalization of culture, however, has its price. Because of the popularity of Western culture throughout the developing world, especially among young people, local cultural forms are being eroded and destroyed as a result of contamination by Western music, mass television, and commercial hype. Although what has been called the "McWorld culture" of cola drinks, denim jeans, and rock music is considered merely cosmetic by some, others see it as cultural neo-imperialism and a real cause for alarm (see Image 16.9). How does a society preserve its traditional culture when the young prefer to spend their evenings at a rock concert rather than attend a traditional folk opera or *wayang* puppet theater? Although there is sometimes local resistance to outside cultural influence, especially in the Middle East where religious traditionalists see the hand of Satan in all forms of Western culture, it is an uphill battle—as we saw in Chapter 15, young Palestinians are using hip-hop to convey their anti-Israeli message.

William J. Duiker

IMAGE 16.9 Ronald McDonald in Indonesia. The giant statue shown in this photograph welcomes patrons to a McDonald's restaurant in Jakarta, the capital city of Indonesia. Fast-food restaurants like McDonald's and Kentucky Fried Chicken have served as beacons for those who not only appreciate the taste, but also wish to be seen as members of a new generation of citizens of the world. As they symbolize the globalization of today's world civilization, these restaurants also inspire resentment on the part of those who lament the decline of traditional culture and the delights of experiencing a local cuisine.

 Do you see the proliferation of fast-food restaurants around the world as a positive development, or as a sign of the emergence of a world devoid of cultural uniqueness?

World conferences have been convened to safeguard traditional cultures from extinction, but is there sufficient time, money, or inclination to turn back the tide?

What do contemporary trends in the art world have to say about the changes that have occurred since the beginning of the twentieth century? One reply is that the euphoric optimism of artists during the age of Picasso and Stravinsky has been seriously tempered more than a century later. Naiveté has been replaced by cynicism or irony as protection against the underlying pessimism of the current age. Conceptual art has become dominant, setting ideas above aesthetic pursuits. Installation art and videos best express these artists' desire to confront the social, economic, and political injustices of the era. Some critics on the Left even declare that the exclusive purpose of art is to serve the cause of political reforms. Until the Beijing regime began to crack down on its critics, Chinese writers and artists followed a similar path, mocking the excesses of state capitalism and the corrupt practices of many of the country's communist leaders, while African artists echo some of the same themes, blending traditional African motifs with multimedia compositions that confront the social and political issues that characterize contemporary life on the continent.

By the 1990s, some critics began to call the contemporary art scene "the art of distemper," focused exclusively on expressing the anxiety and disaffection of our age, no longer morally uplifting but devoid of a pleasure principle or any aesthetic value. Whereas a few painters such as the British artist David Hockney (b. 1937) still create works of stunning beauty, many others offer a tired repetition of the shrill and angry diatribe against the multiple ills afflicting today's world. In fact, anger may be the signature of Western art today, perhaps best reflected in the breathless paintings created by the American artist Jean-Michel Basquiat (1960–1988), which recalls the famous painting of 1893 entitled *"The Scream"* by the Norwegian painter Edvard Munch. It is almost a relief to experience the humorous solid gold, fully operational toilet by the Italian artist, Maurizio Cattelan (b. 1960) at the Guggenheim Museum in New York City. Almost a century later, Duchamp's plain porcelain urinal created in 1917 had been transformed into an ostentatious symbol of the excesses of unbridled capitalism.

What, then, are the prospects for the coming years? One critic has complained that Postmodernism, "with its sad air of the parades gone by,"[8] is spent and exhausted. Others suggest that there is nothing left to say that has not been expressed previously and more effectively. The public itself appears satiated and desensitized after a century of "shocking" art and, as in the case of world events, almost incapable of being shocked any further. Human sensibilities have been irrevocably altered by the media, by technology, and especially by the cataclysmic events that have taken place in our times. Perhaps the twentieth century was the age of revolt, representing "freedom from," while the next hundred years will be an era seeking "freedom for."

What is comforting is that no matter how pessimistic and disillusioned people claim to be, hope springs eternal as young writers, artists, and composers continue to grapple with their craft, searching for new ways to express the human condition. Of all the contemporary arts, architects around the world are producing imaginative and original works that can still inspire wonder and admiration. How can one not be astonished by architect Frank Gehry's Guggenheim Museum in Bilbao, Spain (see the Part V opening photo on p. 395), with its thrusting turrets and billowing sails of titanium? Such exuberance can only testify to humanity's indomitable spirit and ceaseless imagination— characteristics that are badly needed in the world today.

MAKING CONNECTIONS

In the opening chapter of this book, I referred to the paradox of the Industrial Revolution. On the one hand, the creation of advanced industrialized societies that began to emerge in the Western world during the nineteenth century led to an era of unprecedented economic growth and human achievement in those countries affected by the phenomenon. On the other hand, it resulted in abysmal living and working conditions for a substantial proportion of the population in the industrializing countries, as well as in the colonialized territories under their rule. Ultimately the competition for markets and resources among the imperialist nations culminated in two fratricidal wars of unprecedented ferocity. The Industrial Revolution was not only an outstanding achievement, but an appalling tragedy.

As the current wave of globalization and technological change has steadily worked its way through recent history, the world is now at a similar juncture, as the advent of the age of globalization and of its twin, the Technological Revolution, are having a transformative impact of their own, simultaneously creative and destructive, affecting rich and poor nations alike. At the same time, changes in the global environment are a wild card that may ultimately trump all other problems afflicting the world today. The twenty-first century is currently characterized by simultaneous trends toward globalization and fragmentation, as the inexorable thrust of technology transforms societies and individuals seeking to preserve their own identity and a sense of meaning and purpose in a confusing world.

It is a cruel irony that this titanic process is taking place at a time when the liberal democratic nations of the West—the nations that have, for good or ill, provided the primary impetus for global change over the past 200 years—find themselves today afflicted by their own doubts and disagreements, not only over their own internal challenges, but over their proper role and responsibility in the world beyond. If the United States and other advanced liberal democratic nations hope to play an active and influential role in shaping a world marked by rapid globalization and technological change, they must come to terms with the current limitations in their own performance and devise new solutions to their problems. Otherwise, their ability to shape the future will be severely undermined, to the detriment of the world and its peoples.

Coping with the Strains of Globalization

What are some of the chief sources of the malaise that is currently afflicting so many liberal democratic societies around the world today? Certainly one of the key symptoms of their current status is the growing alienation of many individuals and groups from the central government and from the political system that it represents. As we have seen above, countless peoples have become convinced that their voices are not being heard in the cacophony of noise that proliferates in the political arena, and resigned to the fact that their votes do not count in a system where wealth buys enormous influence. As a result, they tune out, rather than paying attention to public affairs, or they listen to angry voices on the left or the right who argue that the only solution is to overthrow the current system and start over.

Although much of the public discontent that has driven the rise of populism is caused by economic insecurity, the reaction often takes on cultural overtones, as people begin to view the "other"—the foreigners in their midst—as the source of the problem. Such is certainly the case in Eastern Europe and in the Mediterranean, where the rapid influx of refugees from Africa and the Middle East has inspired calls to shut the border and send the new arrivals back to their home country. In towns and villages across Europe, long-time residents witness the shuttering of local shops and businesses, and assign blame for the change on the foreign-looking people congregating in the town square, that once-vibrant center of local culture that now too often seems like a forlorn relic of the past. But the primary factor that led to the hollowing-out of the town

center was not the foreigner lingering in the square. It was the big-box shopping center sitting on the outskirts of town, a consequence of globalization that appeals to the local shopper because of its cheap prices and its wide selection of consumer goods. The immigrant is not the source of the problem, but merely a symbol of the globalization process itself.

People living in the larger cities in liberal democratic countries—and especially those residing in affluent communities—are generally less prone to such feelings of cultural malaise. They are normally accustomed to living in a culturally diverse environment, and in many cases they have benefitted from globalization and view the future with a measure of optimism. Where rapid change is a way of life and not a force to be feared, tradition can seem like a force holding back progress and therefore something to be opposed. But for those individuals who reside in ethnically distinct communities and feel exposed to the vicissitudes of the market, the fear is real, and the threat of change has an ominous ring to it. They thereby become vulnerable to the appeals of demagogues, who thrive on public dissent and seek to use it to achieve power and influence.

Most liberal democratic societies have faced such challenges in the past, and have ultimately devised strategies to surmount the problem. As economic conditions gradually improve, the populist wave subsides, and the fear of outsiders declines along with it. The most effective answer to feelings of cultural insecurity is an improvement in the general welfare, wherein most people accept the truism that "a rising tide lifts all boats."

The key to defusing much of the public anger that permeates the political culture today, then, is to find effective ways to protect the economic interests and the needs of the more vulnerable members of society. Sometimes that means heightened attention to depressed minority communities in the larger cities; in others it requires measures to provide economic opportunities in rural areas and small towns that have been adversely affected by the steady thrust of globalization. To achieve maximum effect, it may require putting less emphasis on enhancing the productive capacity of the marketplace than on seeking to manage the destabilizing effects of rapid change on vulnerable groups within the system. Rampant capitalism that ignores its social consequences is not only morally objectionable, it is also counterproductive, for recent history provides ample evidence that, in the long run, capitalism has been at its most effective when the divide between great wealth and poverty has been kept to a moderate level.

The Search for Consensus   The formula used successfully by most liberal democratic societies over the years to resolve such challenges has been by government action. The passage of legislation to eliminate gross economic inequities and the adoption of measures to encourage a broader proportion of the populace encourages people to feel that they have a stake in the system. Unfortunately, one of the most serious weaknesses in many liberal democratic societies today is their blatant failure to meet their most basic responsibilities. The political gridlock in the United States and the United Kingdom, a bleak performance matched in many other European countries as well, leaves many to conclude that a liberal democratic system falls far short of attending to their needs. No wonder political leaders in Moscow and Beijing are encouraged to offer their own systems as an alternative.

The spirit of compromise, of course, is in short supply almost everywhere these days, but nowhere more so than in the Western democracies, where the very search for a middle ground seems to be one of the casualties, as much of the energy in politics gravitates to the extremes. One important reason for the abandonment of the center is the information revolution which is extending its reach around the world. With the rising popularity of social media, more and more people receive their news via their computer or their cell phone, where many sites are blatantly partisan and make no pretense of reporting a balanced presentation of the news. Still, it is important to remember that compromise is the oil that lubricates politics in a liberal democracy, and that without it, the system ultimately cannot survive. Peoples and societies can function effectively for lengthy periods even in the face of unresolved differences within their midst, but without eventual recourse, the system ultimately breaks down. The challenge for political leaders is to find ways to defuse the anger and the mutual distrust, lest demagogic forces find a foothold from which to work their mischief.

How can a consensus on key issues be reached at a time when charges of "fake news" and "alternative facts" are an abrupt impediment to what should be a shared discourse to discover truth? One of the presumed truths of political science theory is that an informed voter is the best defense of a healthy democracy. The most important means of providing accurate information in any society are a free press and an effective educational system. Although both education and the press are under attack today from outside forces, one has to hope that through these mechanisms, most voters will eventually be enabled to make their own individual choices based on an ability to separate truthful evidence from falsehoods, and from innuendos designed to inflame the public debate.

HISTORIANS DEBATE
Can Liberal Democracy be Exported?

As Western nations have sought to project their power and influence abroad since the end of World War II, they have naturally promoted the fundamental principles of liberal democracy as a universal litmus test for achieving political stability and economic prosperity in all countries. Democracy has been seen by most Western thinkers and political leaders as the best means to bring about the creation of a peaceful, stable, and prosperous world. As we have seen in earlier chapters, until recently the strategy has appeared to be fairly successful. The one-time Soviet satellites in Eastern Europe, for the most part, have adopted the model of their Western counterparts. Some of the more advanced industrialized societies in East Asia have introduced their own pluralistic political systems, many of which are currently functioning as well or even more effectively than are their counterparts in the West. India has been a practicing democracy for over seventy years. Democratic forms of government have been successfully installed in Latin America and Africa, although their roots are fragile and could be seriously undermined in the event of a national crisis.

But in light of the recent problems encountered by many liberal democratic societies, some have asked whether the Western model can still serve as a beacon for nations outside the tradition of Western civilization. After all, it runs counter to the historical experience of many regions elsewhere in the world, where until fairly recently the individual has historically been firmly subordinated to the larger community or the state. Many scholars and political pundits have argued that democracy is the best answer for all social ills. But in recent years, a number of knowledgeable observers have pointed out that the installation of Western-style democratic systems continue to face a number of historical and cultural headwinds in other parts of the world. As the TV political commentator Fareed Zakaria has recently pointed out, a benevolent form of autocracy may sometimes by temporarily preferable to an unstable and conflict-ridden democracy. Such views were tacitly held by many senior Middle Eastern specialists in the U.S. foreign policy establishment during and after the Cold War, and some have concluded today that their bleak assessments were justified by the results of the Arab Spring in Egypt. Examples abound of traditional societies that have passed through a stage of autocratic rule en route to the creation of a government characterized by democratic principles and institutions. The challenge, of course, is how to differentiate a soft form of autocratic rule that is open to evolution from its more malignant variant.

As some critics have pointed out, the tendency of many observers in Europe and the United States to promote the Western democratic model to the rest of the world emits a discernible whiff of the same cultural arrogance that characterized the doctrine of social Darwinism at the end of the nineteenth century. Both views take as their starting point the assumption that the Western conceptualization of the human experience is universal in scope and will ultimately, inexorably spread to the rest of the world. Neither gives much credence to the view that other civilizations might have seized on a corner of the truth and thus have something to offer.

Promoters of the liberal democratic model take heart from the fact that the only realistic alternative is a form of autocracy, which by nature has its own limits. Although dictatorships, whether defined by ideology, by faith, or simply by the theory of "might makes right" often possess a short-term advantage by dint of their ability to act quickly and decisively to attack a problem, they tend to be more brittle by nature, since they are not selected through the ballot box, but at the point of a gun. More tolerant of diversity and more open to the dictates of the popular will, liberal democracies are much better prepared to find ways to balance competing forces among the populace, and to craft solutions that can reconcile divergent views with a minimum of political conflict. By contrast, autocracies are more prone to dismiss such concerns as illegitimate efforts to divide the nation and to resort to force to curb any potential form of unrest. There is probably no better example of that tactic today than in the Chinese province of Xinjiang, where the central government's response to the ethnic and religious unrest has been to herd up to one million Muslim Uighurs into re-education camps to enforce their loyalty to the state. When, for whatever reason, discontent rises to the surface—a constant nightmare of the current leaders in Moscow and Beijing—autocrats are directly exposed to the anger of the populace.

The fact remains that although the liberal democratic model appears to be a resilient system of government suited to handle the stresses of globalization and the technological revolution, its current performance has not always been sufficiently effective in mastering the challenge. To put it in the starkest terms: in the eyes of many observers today China currently appears to present a better model for economic development and political stability than do the Western democracies. The latter obviously must improve their performance before one can effectively predict the outcome of the contest.

A Final Word

It will not be easy to manage the stresses and strains that globalization will impose on world societies as it transforms the political, the economic, the social, and the cultural institutions and values that have been crafted and practiced over the centuries. Further advances in technology will complicate the process, simultaneously promoting and inhibiting solutions. Global warming will undoubtedly add significantly to the stresses involved, and may eventually have a game-changing impact on the process. Our generation thus bears an enormous responsibility in seeking the means to navigate our current difficulties and find calm waters on the other side.

A historian seeking to learn from a comparable period in the recent past can do worse than to look back to the era of the Industrial Revolution, itself a global event that over the course of more than a century dramatically changed the human as well as the natural environment in myriad ways. As it worked its way through the historical landscape, industrialization gave rise to a horrific era of total war and violent revolution, but then followed up with a half-century of technological change, growing material prosperity, and the broadening of human freedoms. And nowhere during that process were human beings more often able to rise to the occasion than during those times when the challenge was the greatest, such as during the era of World War II, when countless individuals—political leaders and their constituents alike—were able to rise above their petty disputes and to cooperate in a common effort against the twin evils of racial genocide and fascism. There is reason, then, to hope for the best. Human beings have the capacity to find ways to cooperate on surmounting their differences before the advent of a new world crisis. Perhaps we will not learn how to control the forces of change until they begin to compel us to do so. In the meantime, I recall the words that the talented American actress Bette Davis addressed to her houseguests as she faced the unenviable prospect of aging in the blockbuster film *All About Eve*: "Fasten your seat belts, it's going to be a bumpy night."

REFLECTION QUESTIONS

Q Do you believe that the capitalist system is the best available to human beings as they seek to achieve their ultimate destiny? What are its advantages and its defects?

Q What, in your view, are some of the benefits and risks as the world enters the Technological Revolution? What, if anything, can be done to minimize the risks?

Q How serious is the threat of global warming, and what actions, if any, should the governments of the world adopt to address the challenge?

CHAPTER TIMELINE

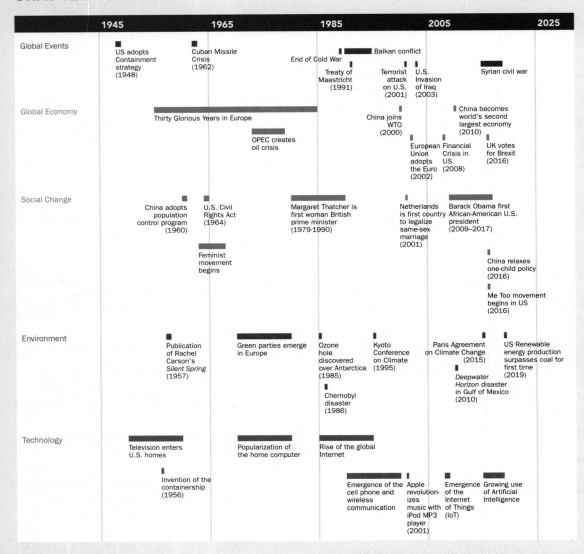

	1945	1965	1985	2005	2025

Global Events

US adopts Containment strategy (1948)

Cuban Missile Crisis (1962)

End of Cold War

Balkan conflict

Treaty of Maastricht (1991)

Terrorist attack on U.S. (2001)

U.S. Invasion of Iraq (2003)

Syrian civil war

Global Economy

Thirty Glorious Years in Europe

OPEC creates oil crisis

China joins WTO (2000)

China becomes world's second largest economy (2010)

European Union adopts the Euro (2002)

Financial Crisis in US (2008)

UK votes for Brexit (2016)

Social Change

China adopts population control program (1960)

U.S. Civil Rights Act (1964)

Margaret Thatcher is first woman British prime minister (1979-1990)

Netherlands is first country to legalize same-sex marriage (2001)

Barack Obama first African-American U.S. president (2009–2017)

Feminist movement begins

China relaxes one-child policy (2016)

Me Too movement begins in US (2016)

Environment

Publication of Rachel Carson's *Silent Spring* (1957)

Green parties emerge in Europe

Ozone hole discovered over Antarctica (1985)

Kyoto Conference on Climate (1995)

Paris Agreement on Climate Change (2015)

US Renewable energy production surpasses coal for first time (2019)

Deepwater Horizon disaster in Gulf of Mexico (2010)

Chernobyl disaster (1986)

Technology

Television enters U.S. homes

Popularization of the home computer

Rise of the global Internet

Invention of the containership (1956)

Emergence of the cell phone and wireless communication

Apple revolutionizes music with iPod MP3 player (2001)

Emergence of the Internet of Things (IoT)

Growing use of Artificial Intelligence

CHAPTER NOTES

1. The World Bank, Press release, dated September 19, 2018. A preliminary estimate suggests that extreme poverty has declined to about 8.6 percent in 2018. The current goal is to reduce it to under 3 percent by 2030.
2. Nicholas D. Kristof and Sheryl WuDunn, *Half the Sky: Turning Oppression into Opportunity for Women Worldwide* (New York, 2009), p. xx.
3. Eduardo Porter "Tech Splits Workers: High Pay for a Few, Low Pay for the Rest," in *The New York Times*, February 5, 2019.
4. In retrospect, Fukuyama now concedes that he might have been overly optimistic in his original analysis. The world today, he admits, has reverted to "a political spectrum organized increasingly around identity issues, many of which are defined more by culture than by economics." Cited in David Frum, "The Case for Liberal Republicanism," in *The Atlantic* (November 2018), p. 15.
5. Richard Langworth (ed.), *Churchill by Himself* (New York: Public Affairs, 2008), p. 574.
6. Bill McKibben, "A Future Without Fossil Fuels?" in *The New York Review of Books*, April 4, 2019.
7. The composer was Toru Takemitsu. See Robert P. Morgan, *Twentieth-Century Music* (New York, 1991), p. 422.
8. Herbert Muschamp, "The Miracle in Bilbao," *New York Times Magazine*, September 7, 1997, p. 72.

A

Abstract Expressionism   a post–World War II artistic movement that broke with all conventions of form and structure in favor of total abstraction.

Abstract painting   an artistic movement that developed early in the twentieth century in which artists focused on color to avoid any references to visual reality.

African National Congress   *see* ANC.

African Union   the organization that replaced the Organization of African Unity in 2001; designed to bring about increased political and economic integration of African states.

Afropop   a general term for contemporary African popular music. Many current stars use their music as a medium for social and political protest.

Ainu   an ethnic minority group in Japan. Descendants of the islands' original settlers, they now live mainly on the island of Hokkaido.

anarchists   people who hold that all government and existing social institutions are unnecessary and advocate a society based on voluntary cooperation.

ANC   the African National Congress. Founded in 1912, it was the beginning of political activity by South African blacks. Banned by the politically dominant whites in 1960, it was not officially "unbanned" until 1990. It is now the majority party in South Africa.

anti-Semitism   hostility toward or discrimination against Jews.

apartheid   the system of racial segregation practiced in the Republic of South Africa until the 1990s; involved political, legal, and economic discrimination against nonwhites.

apparatchik   a government functionary or member of the Communist Party apparatus in the Soviet Union.

appeasement   the policy, followed by the European nations in the 1930s, of accepting Hitler's annexation of Austria and Czechoslovakia in the belief that meeting his demands would ensure peace and stability.

ASEAN   the Association for the Southeast Asian Nations, formed in 1967 to promote the prosperity and political stability of its member nations. Currently, Brunei, Cambodia, Indonesia, Laos, Malaysia, Myanmar, the Philippines, Singapore, Thailand, and Vietnam are members. Other countries in the region participate as "observer" members.

assimilation   the concept, originating in France, that the colonial peoples should be assimilated into the parent French culture.

association   the concept, developed by the French colonial officials, that the colonial peoples should be permitted to retain their precolonial cultural traditions.

Atlantic Charter   a policy statement, drafted by Great Britain and the United States in 1941, that set out the Allies' goals for the post–World War II world, including the self-determination of all peoples.

B

blitzkrieg   "lightning war." A war conducted with great speed and force, as in Germany's advance at the beginning of World War II.

Boko Haram   terrorist group affiliate of al-Qaeda, active in Nigeria and neighboring countries.

Bolsheviks   a small faction of the Russian Social Democratic Party that was led by Lenin and dedicated to violent revolution. The Bolsheviks seized power in Russia in 1917 and were subsequently renamed the Communists.

Brezhnev Doctrine   the doctrine, enunciated by Leonid Brezhnev, that the Soviet Union had a right to intervene if socialism was threatened in another socialist state; used to justify the use of Soviet troops in Czechoslovakia in 1968.

Burakumin   a Japanese minority similar to *dalits* (untouchables) in Indian culture. Past and current discrimination has resulted in lower educational attainment and socioeconomic status for members of this group. Movements with objectives ranging from "liberation" to integration have tried over the years to change this situation.

C

cartel   a combination of independent commercial enterprises that work together to control prices and limit competition.

caste system   a system of rigid social hierarchy in which all members of that society are assigned by birth to specific "ranks" and inherit specific roles and privileges.

chaebol   a South Korean business conglomerate similar to the Japanese *keiretsu*.

civil disobedience   the tactic of using illegal but nonviolent means of protest; designed by the Indian nationalist leader Mohandas Gandhi to resist British colonial rule. The tactic was later adopted by nationalist and liberation forces in many other countries.

civil rights   the basic rights of citizens, including equality before the law, freedom of speech and press, and freedom from arbitrary arrest.

civil service examination   an elaborate Chinese system of selecting bureaucrats on merit, first introduced in 165 C.E., developed by the Tang dynasty in the seventh century C.E., and refined under the Song dynasty. It contributed to efficient government, upward mobility, and cultural uniformity.

Cold War   the ideological conflict between the Soviet Union and the United States between the end of World War II and the early 1990s.

collective farms   large farms created by combining many small holdings into large farms worked by the peasants under government supervision; created in the Soviet Union by Stalin and in China by Mao Zedong.

communalism   in South Asia, the tendency of people to band together in mutually antagonistic social subgroups; elsewhere used to describe unifying trends in the larger community.

Communist International (Comintern)   a worldwide organization of Communist Parties, founded by Lenin in 1919 and dedicated to the advancement of world revolution; also known as the Third International.

conceptual art   an artistic movement beginning in the 1970s in which the emphasis is on conveying a concept and on the means used to create the art rather than on the object that is created.

Confucianism a system of thought based on the teachings of Confucius (551–479 B.C.E.) that developed into the ruling ideology of the Chinese state.

conquistadors "conquerors." Leaders in the Spanish conquests in the Americas, especially Mexico and Peru, in the sixteenth century.

consumer society a term applied to Western society after World War II as the working classes adopted the consumption patterns of the middle class and installment plans, credit cards, and easy credit made consumer goods such as appliances and automobiles widely available.

containment a policy adopted by the United States during the Cold War. It called for the use of any means, short of all-out war, to limit Soviet expansion.

Contras in Nicaragua in the 1980s, an anti-Sandinista guerrilla movement supported by the U.S. Reagan administration.

D

Dadaism an artistic movement in the 1920s and 1930s by artists who were revolted by the senseless slaughter of World War I and used their "anti-art" to express contempt for the Western tradition.

daimyo prominent Japanese landowning families who provided allegiance to the local shogun in exchange for protection; similar to feudal vassals in Europe.

dalits the lowest level of Indian society, technically outside the caste system and considered less than human. Commonly referred to as untouchables, they were renamed *harijans* ("children of God") by Gandhi. They remain the object of discrimination despite affirmative action programs.

deconstruction (poststructuralism) a theory formulated by Jacques Derrida in the 1960s, holding that there is no fixed, universal truth because culture is created and can therefore be analyzed in various ways.

deficit spending the concept, developed by John Maynard Keynes in the 1930s, that in times of economic depression, governments should stimulate demand by hiring people to do public works, such as building highways, even if this increases the public debt.

denazification after World War II, the Allied policy of rooting out all traces of Nazism in German society by bringing prominent Nazis to trial for war crimes and purging any known Nazis from political office.

dependency theory the theory, emerging in the 1960s, that the economic underdevelopment of the developing nations of Asia, Africa, and Latin America is caused by their continued economic domination by the former colonial powers.

descamisados the "shirtless ones." The working-class supporters of Juan Perón during his rise to power in Argentina.

desertification the process of becoming desert, often as a result of mismanagement of the land or climate change; especially, the expansion of the Sahara.

de-Stalinization the policy of denouncing and undoing the most repressive aspects of Stalin's regime; begun by Nikita Khrushchev in 1956.

détente the relaxation of tension between the Soviet Union and the United States that occurred in the 1970s.

direct rule a concept devised by European colonial governments to rule their colonial subjects without the participation of local authorities. It was most often applied in colonial societies in Africa.

E

Einsatzgruppen in Nazi Germany, special strike forces in the SS that played an important role in rounding up and killing Jews.

Elam Tigers a militant separatist organization based in northern Sri Lanka that sought to obtain a separate state for the Tamil people, an ethnic group whose members live in India and Malaysia as well as Sri Lanka; also known as the Tamil Tigers (the formal name is Liberation Tigers of Tamil Eelam).

eta in feudal Japan, a class of hereditary slaves who were responsible for what were considered degrading occupations, such as curing leather and burying the dead; known today as the *Burakumin*.

ethnic cleansing the policy of killing or forcibly removing people of another ethnic group; used by the Serbs against Bosnian Muslims in the 1990s.

existentialism a philosophical movement that arose after World War II and emphasized the meaninglessness of life, born of the desperation caused by two world wars.

F

fascism an ideology that exalts the nation above the individual and calls for a centralized government with a dictatorial leader, economic and social regimentation, and forcible suppression of opposition; in particular, the ideology of Mussolini's Fascist regime in Italy.

favelas slums and shantytowns in and around urban areas in Brazil.

feminism the belief in the social, political, and economic equality of the sexes; also, organized activity to advance women's rights.

Final Solution the Nazis' name for their attempted physical extermination of the Jewish people during World War II.

Five Pillars of Islam the core requirements of the Muslim faith: belief in Allah and his prophet, Muhammad; prescribed prayers; observation of Ramadan; pilgrimage to Mecca; and giving alms to the poor.

five relationships in traditional China, the hierarchical interpersonal associations considered crucial to the social order; consisted of the subordination of son to father, wife to husband, younger brother to older brother, and subject to ruler, and the proper relationship of friend to friend.

Four Modernizations the radical reforms of Chinese industry, agriculture, technology, and national defense instituted by Deng Xiaoping after his accession to power in the late 1970s.

fracking a process involving the use of a pressurized liquid to fracture rock formations containing shale oil and gas deposits.

G

genro the ruling clique of aristocrats in Meiji Japan.

glasnost "openness." Mikhail Gorbachev's policy of encouraging Soviet citizens to openly discuss the strengths and weaknesses of the Soviet Union.

globalization a term referring to the trend by which peoples and nations have become more interdependent; often used to refer to the development of a global economy and culture.

global warming the gradual increase in the overall temperature of the earth's atmosphere, attributed to the greenhouse effect caused by increased levels of carbon dioxide and other pollutants.

Good Neighbor policy a policy adopted by the administration of President Franklin D. Roosevelt to practice restraint in U.S. relations with Latin American nations.

Gosplan in the Soviet Union, the "state plan" for the economy drawn up by the central planning commission.

Great Leap Forward a short-lived radical experiment in China, started in 1958, that created vast rural communes in an attempt to replace the family as the fundamental social unit.

Great Proletarian Cultural Revolution an attempt to destroy all vestiges of tradition in China in order to create a totally egalitarian society. Launched by Mao Zedong in 1966, it devolved into virtual anarchy and lasted only until Mao's death in 1976.

green revolution the introduction of technological agriculture, especially in India in the late 1960s; increased food production substantially but also exacerbated rural inequality because only the wealthier farmers could afford fertilizer.

guided democracy the name given by President Sukarno of Indonesia in the late 1950s to his style of government, which theoretically operated by consensus.

H

Hamas a militant Islamic group, whose goal is to liberate the Palestinian territories from Israel. Hamas has controlled the Gaza Strip since winning elections in 2006.

harijans "children of god." A name used by Mohandas Gandhi to refer to the *dalits* (untouchables) in India.

Hezbollah a radical Islamist political party and militant group based in Lebanon.

high culture the literary and artistic culture of the educated and wealthy ruling classes.

hijab a traditional head, face, or body covering worn in public by some Muslim women.

Hinduism the main religion in India. It emphasizes reincarnation, based on the results of the previous life, and the desirability of escaping this cycle. Its various forms feature both asceticism and the pleasures of ordinary life and encompass a multitude of gods as different manifestations of one ultimate reality.

Holocaust the mass slaughter of European Jews by the Nazis during World War II.

Holodomor the man-made famine imposed by Stalin's regime on Soviet Ukraine in 1932–1933, during which millions of Ukrainians died.

Houthi rebel militant Shi'a group that emerged in Yemen in the 1990s, in opposition to the established Sunni-based government.

I

imperialism the policy of extending one nation's power either by conquest or by establishing direct or indirect economic or cultural authority over another. Generally driven by economic selfinterest, it can also be motivated by a sincere (if often misguided) sense of moral obligation.

indirect rule a colonial policy of foreign rule in cooperation with local political elites. Though implemented in much of India and Malaya and in parts of Africa, it was not feasible where resistance was greater.

informal empire the growing presence of Europeans in Africa during the first decades of the nineteenth century. During this period, most African states were nonetheless still able to maintain their independence.

intifada the "uprising" of Palestinians living under Israeli control, especially in the 1980s and 1990s.

Islam the religion derived from the revelations of Muhammad, the Prophet of Allah; literally, "submission" (to the will of Allah); also, the culture and civilization based on the faith.

K

keiretsu a type of powerful industrial or financial conglomerate that emerged in post–World War II Japan following the abolition of the *zaibatsu*.

kokutai in Meiji Japan, the core ideology of the state, embodying the notion of the supreme authority of the emperor.

kowtow the ritual of prostration and touching the forehead to the ground, demanded of all foreign ambassadors to the Chinese court as a symbol of submission.

kulaks prosperous Russian and Ukrainian peasant farmer class who rose from Tsar Alexander II's emancipation of the serfs in the late nineteenth century. By the 1930s, many resisted Stalin's efforts at farm collectivization, and were targeted for punishment by the Soviet regime.

L

laissez-faire French for "leave it alone." An economic doctrine that holds that an economy is best served when the government does not interfere but allows the economy to self-regulate according to the forces of supply and demand.

Lebensraum "living space." A doctrine, adopted by Hitler, that holds that a nation's power depends on the amount of land it occupies. Thus, a nation must expand to be strong.

liberalism an ideology based on the belief that people should be as free from restraint as possible. Economic liberalism is the idea that the government should not interfere in the workings of the economy. Political liberalism is the idea that there should be restraints on the exercise of power so that people can enjoy basic civil rights in a constitutional state with a representative assembly.

liberation theology an activist movement, especially among Roman Catholic clergy in Latin America, that combines Marxist ideas with a call to liberate the oppressed from injustice.

lineage group segment of an African clan. Lineages are traced through a single parent, either father or mother, and trace back many generations to a common ancestor. Lineage remains an important aspect of African social identity.

M

maharaja originally, a king in the Aryan society of early India (a great raja); later used more generally to denote an important ruler.

Marshall Plan the European Recovery Program, under which the United States provided financial aid to European countries to help them rebuild after World War II.

Marxism the political, economic, and social theories of Karl Marx, which included the idea that history is the story of class struggle and that ultimately the proletariat will overthrow the bourgeoisie and establish a dictatorship en route to a classless society.

mass leisure forms of leisure that appeal to large numbers of people in a society, including the working classes; emerged at the end of the nineteenth century to provide workers with amusements after work and on weekends; used during the twentieth century by totalitarian states to control their populations.

mass society a society in which the concerns of the majority—the lower classes—play a prominent role; characterized by extension of voting rights, an improved standard of living for the lower classes, and mass education.

matrilinear passing through the female line—for example, from a father to his sister's son rather than to his own—as practiced in some African societies; not necessarily or even usually combined with matriarchy, in which women rule.

Meiji Restoration the period during the late nineteenth and early twentieth centuries when fundamental economic and cultural changes occurred in Japan, transforming it from a feudal and agrarian society to an industial and technological one.

Mensheviks the faction of the Russian Social Democratic Labor Party that called for the gradual achievement of socialism by democratic means and opposed Lenin's emphasis on violent revolution.

Me Too movement social movement arising in the 2010s to support and give voice to victims of sexual harassment and sexual violence.

minimalism a style of music originating in the 1960s that is characterized by subtle and gradual transformations of musical phrases or rhythmic patterns that are continuously repeated.

ministerial responsibility a tenet of nineteenth-century liberalism that held that ministers of the monarch should be responsible to the legislative assembly rather than to the monarch.

mir a traditional peasant village commune in Russia.

MITI the Ministry of International Trade and Industry in Japan; responsible for formulating and directing much of Japanese industrial policy after World War II.

Modernism the artistic and literary styles that emerged in the decades before 1914 as artists rebelled against traditional efforts to portray reality as accurately as possible and writers explored new forms.

modernization theory the theory, prevalent in the 1950s and 1960s, that the world's newly independent countries would ultimately follow the Western model and create modern industrial societies and that their current economic problems were a consequence of the difficult transition from a traditional agrarian to a modern industrial economy.

Monroe Doctrine for Asia Japan's plan to end Western influence in East Asia while guiding the nations of the region to modernization and prosperity on the Japanese model.

N

Narodnaya Volya the "People's Will." A left-wing Russian terrorist organization that assassinated Tsar Alexander II in 1881.

nationalism a sense of national consciousness based on awareness of being part of a commmunity—a "nation"—that has common institutions, traditions, language, and customs and that becomes the focus of the individual's primary political loyalty.

nationalization the process of converting a busines or industry from private ownership to government control and ownership.

NATO the North Atlantic Treaty Organization, a military alliance formed in 1949 in which the signatories (Belgium, Canada, Denmark, France, Great Britain, Iceland, Italy, Luxembourg, the Netherlands, Norway, Portugal, and the United States) agreed to provide mutual assistance if any one of them was attacked; later expanded to include other nations, including former members of the Warsaw Pact.

natural selection Darwin's idea that organisms that are most adaptable to their environment survive and pass on the variations that enabled them to survive while less adaptable organisms become extinct; known by the shorthand expression "survival of the fittest."

Nazi New Order the Nazis' plan for their conquered territories; included the extermination of Jews and others considered inferior, ruthless exploitation of resources, German colonization in the east, and the use of Poles, Russians, and Ukrainians as slave labor.

neocolonialism the use of economic rather than political or military means to maintain Western domination of developing nations.

new course a short-lived liberalizing change in Soviet policy toward Eastern European allies instituted after Stalin's death in 1953.

New Culture Movement a protest launched by students at Beijing University after the failure of the 1911 revolution; aimed at abolishing the remnants of the old system and introducing Western values and institutions into China.

New Deal the reform program implemented by President Franklin D. Roosevelt in the 1930s; included large public works programs and the introduction of Social Security.

New Democracy the initial program of the Chinese Communist government, from 1949 to 1955; focused on honest government, land reform, social justice, and peace rather than the goal of a classless society.

New Economic Policy a modified version of the old capitalist system introduced in the Soviet Union by Lenin in 1921 to revive the economy after the ravages of the civil war and war communism.

New Order in East Asia Japan's plan in the 1930s to create a Japanese-dominated sphere of influence comprising Japan, Manchuria, and China.

new world order a term used by President George H. W. Bush to refer to the new era of peace and international cooperation that he envisioned would result after the collapse of the Soviet Union.

Nonaligned Movement an organization of neutralist nations established in the 1950s to provide a third alternative to the socialist bloc, headed by the Soviet Union, and the capitalist nations led by the United States. Jawaharlal Nehru of India, Gamal Abdul Nasser of Egypt, and Sukarno of Indonesia were the movement's chief sponsors.

O

Open Door Notes a series of letters sent in 1899 by U.S. Secretary of State John Hay to Great Britain, France, Germany, Italy, Japan, and Russia, calling for equal economic access to the Chinese market for all states and for the maintenance of the territorial and administrative integrity of the Chinese Empire.

organic evolution Darwin's principle that all plants and animals have evolved over a long period of time from earlier and simpler forms of life.

P

pan-Africanism the concept of African continental unity and solidarity in which the common interests of African countries transcend regional boundaries.

pan-Arabism a movement promoted by Egyptian president Gamal Abdul Nasser and other Middle Eastern leaders to unify all Arab peoples in a single supra-national organization. After Nasser's death in 1971, the movement languished.

Panca Sila   the "Five Principles" of Indonesia's state philosophy, formulated by nationalist leader Sukarno.

pan-Islamism   a movement aimed at unifying all Muslim peoples throughout Africa; promoted first by Gamal Abdul Nasser of Egypt and later by Muammar Qaddafi of Libya.

Paris Climate Agreement   international accord signed in 2016 that seeks to mitigate global warming through long-term active measures by 195 signatory countries to reduce greenhouse gas emissions. The United States signed onto the agreement during the Obama administration, but the Trump administration has since taken steps to withdraw the U.S. from the agreement. In the face of the federal government's reversal, many state and local governments and businesses in the U.S. have nonetheless expressed their intent to work toward the Paris agreement goals.

peaceful coexistence   the policy adopted by the Soviet Union under Nikita Khrushchev in 1955 and continued by his successors that called for economic and ideological rivalry with the West rather than nuclear war.

perestroika   "restructuring." The term applied to Mikhail Gorbachev's economic, political, and social reform in the Soviet Union.

polygny   the practice of having more than one wife at a time.

Pop Art   an artistic movement of the 1950s and 1960s in which artists took images of popular culture and transformed them into works of fine art; for example, Andy Warhol's paintings of Campbell's soup cans.

popular culture   as opposed to high culture, the unofficial written and unwritten culture of the masses, much of which was passed down orally and was centered on public and group activities such as festivals; in the twentieth century, the entertainment, recreation, and pleasures that people purchase as part of mass consumer society.

Popular Fronts   governments to be formed by coalitions of leftist parties including Communists in the 1930s as part of Stalin's strategy to form a united front with the capitalist nations against Nazism. Although the strategy did not succeed in most countries, a Popular Front government was formed in France in 1936 and survived until 1938.

Postmodernism   a term used to cover a variety of artistic and intellectual styles and ways of thinking prominent since the 1970s.

poststructuralism   *see* deconstruction.

priyayi   the local landed aristocracy in the Dutch East Indies; used as local administrators by the Dutch East India Company.

proletariat   the industrial working class; in Marxism, the class that will ultimately overthrow the bourgeoisie.

purdah   the Indian term for the practice among Muslims and some Hindus of isolating women and preventing them from associating with men outside the home.

R

raja   originally, a chieftain in the Aryan society of early India, a representative of the gods; later used more generally to denote a ruler.

reparations   payments made by a defeated nation after a war to compensate another nation for damage sustained as a result of the war; required from Germany after World War I.

rural responsibility system   post-Maoist land reform in China, under which collectives leased land to peasant families, who could consume or sell their surplus production and keep the profits.

S

Sahel   the grassy semidesert region extending across Africa south of the Sahara.

samizdat   the clandestine publication and sharing of government-suppressed literature in Eastern Bloc countries.

samurai   "retainers." Japanese warriors who usually served a particular shogun and lived by a strict code of ethics and duty; similar to European knights.

sati   the Hindu ritual requiring a wife to throw herself on her deceased husband's funeral pyre.

satyagraha   "hold fast to the truth." The Hindu term for the practice of nonviolent resistance advocated by Mohandas Gandhi.

self-strengthening   a late-nineteenth-century Chinese policy under which Western technology would be adopted while Confucian principles and institutions were maintained intact.

sepoys   local troops who formed the basis of the British Indian Army; hired by the East India Company to protect British interests in South Asia.

Shari'a   a law code, originally drawn up by Muslim scholars shortly after the death of Muhammad, that provides believers with a set of prescriptions to regulate their daily lives.

Shi'ite   the second largest tradition of Islam, which split from the majority Sunni soon after the death of Muhammad in a disagreement over the succession; especially significant in Iran and Iraq.

Shinto   a kind of state religion in Japan, derived from beliefs in nature spirits and until recently linked with belief in the divinity of the emperor and the sacredness of the Japanese nation.

shogun   a powerful Japanese leader, originally military, who ruled under the titular authority of the emperor.

shogunate system   the system of government in Japan in which the emperor exercised only titular authority while the shoguns (regional military dictators) exercised actual political power.

Sikhism   a religion, founded in the early sixteenth century in the Punjab, that began as an attempt to reconcile the Hindu and Muslim traditions and developed into a significant alternative to both.

social Darwinism   the application of Darwin's principle of organic evolution to the social order; led to the belief that progress comes from the struggle for survival as the fittest advance and the weak decline.

socialism   an ideology that calls for collective or government ownership of the means of production and the distribution of goods.

socialized medicine   health services for all citizens provided by government assistance.

soviets   councils of workers' and solders' deputies formed throughout Russia in 1917; played an important role in the Bolshevik Revolution.

sphere of influence   a territory or region over which an outside nation exercises political or economic influence.

Star Wars   nickname for the Strategic Defense Initiative, proposed by President Ronald Reagan, which was intended to provide a shield that would destroy any incoming missiles; named after a popular science fiction movie series.

sultan   "holder of power." A title commonly used by Muslim rulers in the Ottoman Empire, Egypt, and elsewhere; still in use in parts of Asia, sometimes for regional authorities.

Sunni   the largest tradition of Islam, from which the Shi'ites split soon after the death of Muhammad in a disagreement over the succession.

Surrealism   an artistic movement that arose between World War I and World War II. Surrealists portrayed recognizable objects in unrecognizable relationships in order to reveal the world of the unconscious.

Swahili   a mixed African-Arab culture that developed by the twelfth century along the east coast of Africa; also, the national language of Kenya and Tanzania.

T

Taisho Democracy   following the Meiji period, time from 1912 to 1926 that saw the rise of democratic institutions and political liberalism in Japan, during the reign of Taisho emperor Yoshihito.

tariffs   duties (taxes) imposed on imported goods; usually imposed both to raise revenue and to discourage imports and protect domestic industries.

Tea Party   faction of the Republican Party arising during the Obama administration as a grassroots conservative populist movement.

three obediences   the traditional duties of Japanese women, in permanent subservience: child to father, wife to husband, and widow to son.

Three People's Principles   the three principles on which the program of Sun Yat-sen's Revolutionary Alliance (Tongmenghui) was based: nationalism (meaning primarily the elimination of Manchu rule over China), democracy, and people's livelihood.

totalitarian state   a state characterized by government control over all aspects of economic, social, political, cultural, and intellectual life; subordination of the individual to the state; and insistence that the masses be actively involved in the regime's goals.

trade union   an association of workers in the same trade, formed to help members secure better wages, benefits, and working conditions.

trench warfare   warfare in which the opposing forces attack and counterattack from a relatively permanent system of trenches protected by barbed wire; characteristic of World War I.

Truman Doctrine   the doctrine, enunciated by President Harry Truman in 1947, that the United States would provide economic aid to countries that were threatened by Communist expansion.

U

uhuru   "freedom" in Swahili. A key slogan in African independence movements, especially in Kenya.

ulama   a convocation of leading Muslim scholars. The earliest, which took place shortly after the death of Muhammad, drew up the *Shari'a*, a law code based largely on the Qur'an and the sayings of Muhammad, to provide believers with a set of prescriptions to regulate their daily lives.

unconditional surrender   complete, unqualified surrender of a nation; required of Germany and Japan by the Allies in World War II.

uninterrupted revolution   the goal of the Great Proletarian Cultural Revolution launched by Mao Zedong in 1966.

V

varna   Indian classes or castes. *See also* caste system.

Viet Cong   the forces of the National Liberation Front of South Vietnam (NLF) during the Vietnam War. The term is short for "Vietnamese Communists."

Vietminh Front   the multiparty national alliance led by Ho Chi Minh that took control of northern and central Vietnam after World War II and waged a "people's war" of national liberation against the French.

Vietnam syndrome   the presumption, from the 1970s on, that the U.S. public would object to a protracted military entanglement abroad, such as another Vietnam-type conflict.

W

war communism   Lenin's policy of nationalizing industrial and other facilities and requisitioning the peasants' produce during the civil war in Russia.

war guilt clause   the clause in the Treaty of Versailles that declared Germany (and Austria) responsible for starting World War I and ordered Germany to pay reparations for the damage the Allies had suffered as a result of the war.

Warsaw Pact   a military alliance, formed in 1955, in which Albania, Bulgaria, Czechoslovakia, East Germany, Hungary, Poland, Romania, and the Soviet Union agreed to provide mutual assistance. After it was dissolved in 1991, most former members eventually joined NATO.

welfare state   a social and political system in which the government assumes primary responsibility for the social welfare of its citizens by providing such things as social security, unemployment benefits, and health care.

women's liberation movement   the struggle for equal rights for women, which has deep roots in history but achieved new prominence under this name in the 1960s, building on the work of, among others, Simone de Beauvoir and Betty Friedan.

Y

Young Turks   a successful Turkish reformist group in the late nineteenth and early twentieth centuries.

Z

zaibatsu   powerful business cartels formed in Japan during the Meiji era and outlawed following World War II.

zamindars   Indian tax collectors who were assigned land from which they kept part of the revenue. The British revived the system in a misguided attempt to create a landed gentry.

Zionism   an international movement that called for the establishment of a Jewish state or a refuge for Jews in Palestine.

Architecture: Bauhaus School, 102; the Chicago school, 26; functionalism, 26; in Japan, 71; modernism in, 26, 102; post-World War I, 102; Soviet era, 232
Ardennes forest, 146
Arendt, Hannah, 134
Argentina: autocratic rule in, 127; cattle ranchers, 19; Falkland Islands and, 213; military and, 213; oil industry in, 127; population, 19; trade, 127; urbanization in, 19
Arguedas, José Maria, 217
Aristocracy, in Europe, 7. *See also* Elite class
Armah, Ayi Kwei, 351
Armenia, 112, 238, 261
Arms race, 171, 186–187
Arranged marriages, 69, 123, 124, 313, 361
Art(s): Abstract Expressionists, 207; Abstract paintings, 101; African, 361–362, 424; in China, 123, 316–317; conceptual, 207; contemporary, 422–423; Dadaism, 101; in Japan, 71, 72; late nineteenth century, 24–26, *25*; Mexican, 130; in the 1920s, 101; Pop Art, 207; postwar Europe, 271; post-World War II American, 207; Soviet era, 232; in Soviet Union under Gorbachev, 235–236; Surrealism, 101
Artificial Intelligence (AI), 409
Art-manga, 288
Arusha Declaration of 1967, 353, 354
ASEAN (Association of Southeast Asian Nations), 339, 342–343
Ashanti, 43, 49, 348
Asia: capitalism in, 400–401; Cold War in, 171–176; colonization in, 31; divorce in, 414; events leading to World War II in, 142–144; Lenin and, 116–117; nationalist movements in, 106; religion in, 415; Shidehara diplomacy and, 126; trade with, 3; women and economic development in, 403; women in, 393; World War II in, 149–151, *150. See also* Southeast Asia; specific locations
Al-Assad, Bashir, 380, 382
Assimilation, colonialism and, 32
Association, colonialism and, 32
Association of Southeast Asian Nations (ASEAN), 339, 342–343
Al-Aswany, Alaa, 388
Atatürk. *See* Kemal Atatürk, Mustafa
Atlantic Charter, 152, 333, 391
Atlee, Clement, 154, 254, 322
Atomic bomb: bombing of Japan, 156–157; Hiroshima and Nagasaki, 156; Potsdam Conference and, 154–155
Atta, Sefi, 363
Attenborough, Richard, 109
Aung San Suu Kyi (Burma), 336, 341
Aurora (battleship), 91
Auschwitz-Birkenau death camp, 148
Australia: postwar, 296; women's right to vote in, 10; World War I and, 83; World War II and, 150
Austria: annexation of, 140; events leading to World War I and, 79–80; parliamentary system in, 137; Treaty of Versailles and, 89, 90, 94; uprisings in 1848 and, 13

Austria-Hungary, 14, *15*; in 1871, *15*; collapse of, 63; Industrial Revolution and, 75; Treaty of Versailles and, 89–90; in Triple Alliance, 79; World War I and, 79–80, 81
Authoritarian regimes. *See* Dictatorial regimes
Autocracy, 381–382
Automobile(s): in China, 311; in Cuba, 216; internal combustion engine and, 6; Middle Eastern women driving, 387; new technology in, 206; For plants, 96; in postwar Europe, 264, 266
Automobile industry, 6
Ayodhya, India, 327
Azadi, Sousan, 387
Azerbaijan, 166, 261
Azuelo, Mariano, 130

B

B-29 bombers, 156
Ba'ath Party, 372, 384
Ba'ath vision of Hussein, 378
Babur, 34
Baby boomers, 197
Bacon, Francis, 271
Baghdad, 114, 378
Bahrain, 381
Ba Jin, 124
Bakhtiar, Shapur, 376
Bakunin, Mikhail, 20
Baldwin, James, 208
Balfour Declaration, 115, *116*, 370
Balfour, Lord Arthur, 115
Bali, 338, *341*
Balkans, the: nationalism in, 15–16; Soviet occupation of, 165; territorial changes after World War I, 90; Treaty of Versailles and, 90; World War I and, 79–80, *80*; World War II and, 146. *See also* individual country names
Ballet Russe, 26
Baltic region, 148, 153
Baluchis, the (Pakistan), 325
Al-Bana, Hasan, 115
"Banana Chinese," 121
"Banana republics," 127
Bandung Conference (1955), 324
Bangalore, India, 329
Bangladesh, 324, 330, 403
Banknotes, *95*
Bank of England, 254
Banks and banking: Great Depression and, 97; Latin America borrowing money from foreign, 210
Bannon, Steve, 412
Bantu-speaking peoples, 45
Barak, Ehud, 375
Barth, John, 207
Al-Bashir, Omar Hassan, 356
Basketball, 208
Basquiat, Jean-Michel, 425
Basutoland (Lesotho), 46
Bataan peninsula, 149
Batavia (Jakarta), Java, 40
Bathing Women (Cézanne), *25*
Batista, Fulgenico, 127, 215
Battle at Normandy, 153
Battle of Britain, 146
Battle of Dien Bien Phu, 176

Battle of Kursk, 153
Battle of Masurian Lakes, 81
Battle of Stalingrad, 152
Battle of Tannenburg, 81
Battle of the Bulge, 153
Battle of the Coral Sea, 150
Battle of Waterloo, 12
Bauhaus School, 102
Bay of Bengal, 330
Bay of Pigs (1961), 180–181, 216
The Beautiful Ones Are Not Yet Born (Armah), 351
Beauvoir, Simone de, 268, 269
Bechuanaland (Botswana), 46
Beckett, Samuel, 270–271
Beer Hall Putsch, 135
Begin, Menachem, 374, *374*
Beijing, China, 57, 60
Beijing University, 118–119
Belarus, 240, 261
Belgian Congo, 33, 44, 45, 47, 348, 351
Belgium: colonization in Africa, 44, *44*, 45; in the Common Market, 249; NATO and, 168; steel and, 5; uprising in 1848, 13
Bell, Alexander Graham, 6, 408
Belloc, Hilaire, 49
Bellow, Saul, 208
Ben Bella, Ahmad, 347, 372
Bengali, 326
Ben-Gurion, David, 370, 373
Berbers, 347
Beria, Lavrenti, 221
Berlin Airlift, 168
Berlin Blockade, 168
Berlin Conference (1884), 45
Berlin Crisis (1957), 179
Berlin, Germany, 229; division of, 168, *168*, *169*; at end of World War II, 246
Berlin Wall, 229; fall of, 236–238, *238*
Bernstein, Leonard, 179
Bertolucci, Bernardo, 301
Bey (Turkey), 112
Bharatiya Janata Party (BJP), 325
Bhopal, 329
Bhutto, Benazir, 326
Bhutto, Zulfikar Ali, 326
Biafra, 352, 355
Biao, Lin, speech (1966), 178–179
Bicycle program, Paris, 268
Big Four, 88
Big Three, 88, 153
Binding feet (China), 64, *64*, 65, 123
Bin Laden, Osama, 197, 368, 369, 379
Bin Salman, Muhammad, 381, 387
Biological weapons, 151
Birmingham, England, coal pollution in, 7
Birth rates, 264, *265*
Bismarck, Otto von, 13, 79
Black Africans, voting rights for, 346
Black Lines No. 189 (Kandinsky), *102*
The Black Man's Burden (Morel), *33*
Black Muslims, 193
Blair, Tony, 257
Blitzkrieg, 145, 146
Boers, the, 45, *45*, 47, 49
Boer War, 46
Bohemia, 141
Boko Haram, 356, 361

women in postwar, 267–268, 269; World War II and, 139–142, 146–149, *147*. *See also* Eastern Europe; individual country names; specific locations

European Atomic Energy Community (EURATOM), 261

European Coal and Steel Community (ECSC), 260–261

European Community (EC), 261. *See also* European Union (EU)

European Economic Community (EEC), 261

European Recover Program (Marshall Plan), 167–168

European Union (EU), 249; Brexit and, 257; complaints about, 411–412; creation of, 249; economic downturn and, 399; euro and, 261; expansion of, 261–263; membership (2013), *259*

Euro, the, 261

Evangelical Christians, 417, 420

Evangelical movement, 414–415

Everything Good Will Come (Atta), 363

Evolutionary theory, 417

Evolution, theory of (Darwin), 23, 24

Evora, Cesaria, 364

Executions: Bolshevik Revolution and, 94; in China, 59, 65; under Stalin, 100

Existentialism, 269–270

Exit West (Hamid), 389

Expressionism, 25

F

Factories: child labor in, 8; munition, during World War I, 87; post-World War II Soviet Union, 221; silk industry in China, *402*; Soviet Union, 226–227; textile, 8, 9; women in textile, 8; World War I, 86

"Fake news," 411, 413

Falkland Islands, 213, 256

Family: in China, 312, 313; Confucianism and, 123, 312; decline in size of, in India, 327, 329; decline in traditional, 413–414; in Fascist Italy, 135; Japanese culture and, 282; postwar society and, 276; single-parent, 413; in South Korea, 292, *292*

Family (Ba Jin), 124

Family planning program, in China, 310

Fang Lizhi, 304

Far Eastern Commission, 279

Farming and farmers: in Africa under colonialism, 346–347; in China, 63, 122–123; collective, 100, 299–300, 312, 335; discontent by Chinese, 311; in India, 329; Industrial Revolution in the United States and, 4; in Japan, 126; selling produce on open market, 234, 235; in Southeast Asia, 335

Farouk, King, 370

Fascio di Combattimento (League of Combat), 134

Fascism, 134–135. *See also* Dictatorial regimes; Hitler, Adolf; Mussolini, Benito; Nazi Germany

Fashoda, Sudan, 45

Fast food, in India, 328–329

Fattah el-Sisi, Abdel, 380

Favelas, 214

The Feast of the Goat (Llosa), 217

Federal Republic of Germany (FRG). *See* West Germany

Federal Reserve System, 17

Federation of Malaya, 334–335, 339–340

Female genital mutilation, 361

The Feminine Mystique (Friedan), 202

Feminism, 202; African, 361; in Europe, 9, 268; in the United States, 9–10. *See also* Women's rights movements

Ferdinand, Archduke Francis, 80

Ferdinand, Sophia, 80

Ferguson, Niall, 76

Ferry, Jules, 30

Feudal system, 65–66

Fez, 112

Filial piety, 123

Fillmore, Millard, 66

Final Solution, 148

Financial crisis: in 2008, 247, 275, 398; postwar, in Europe, 265; stock market crash of 1929, 97. *See also* Great Depression, the

Finland, Treaty of Versailles and, 90

First Battle of the Marne, 81

First National, the, 20

First World War. *See* World War I

Five Pillars of Islam, 115

Five relationships, in China, 313

Five-year plan (Soviet Union), 221

Flying shuttle, 3–4

Food riots, 126

Food supply, population and, 405

Football, 208

Foot binding (China), 64, *64*, 65, 123

Forbidden City, 53, 54

Ford, Gerald R.: economy under, 196; Vietnam War and, 185

Ford, Henry, 6, 96, 99

Foreign concession areas, in China, 56–57, 63, 65

Forster, E.M., 36

Fourastié, Jean, 264

"Four Freedoms" speech (Roosevelt), 145

Four Modernizations (China), 303–304

4'33" (Cage), 207

Fourth Republic (France), 249

Fox, Vicente, 215

Fracking, 421

France: Africa and, 43, 44, *44*, 45, 347–348; Algeria and, 43, 249, 347; automobile industry in, 6; bicycle program in Paris, 268, 270; casualties in World War I, 88; colonialism in Southeast Asia, 37, 38–39, 333; colonization by, 31; in the Common Market, 249; conflict in Indochina, 176; declaring war on Germany, 142, 145; demilitarized Rhineland and, 139; direct rule in Africa, 46–47; economy, 250; Eiffel Tower, *6*; French Revolution, 12; government, 13, 16; Great Depression and, 97; immigrants in postwar, 250; imperialism and, 30; League of Nations and, 88; Munich Conference and, 140, 141; Muslims in, *266*; NATO and, 168; Nile valley and, 43; in North Africa, 110; occupation of the Ruhr valley, 95; Paris Peace Conference and, 88; political

reform, 16; Popular Front government in, 140; post-World War I, 96; slave trade and, 42; social benefits, 399; steel and, 5; Suez Canal and, 372; Syria and, 111–112; theory of colonialism, 32; Treaty of Locarno, 95; Treaty of Versailles and, 94–95; in Triple Entente, 79; Tunisian independence and, 347–348; uprisings in 1848 and, 13; U.S. defensive alliance with, 94; Vietnam and, 37, 176; welfare state in, 249–251; women's suffrage in, 268; World War I and, 78, 81, 86; World War II and, 146, 153

Franco, Francisco, 138, 139

Frankfurt, Germany, 13

Free Democratic Party (Germany), 252, 253

"Free French," 249

Free French movement, 153

Free market economy, 258, 294. *See also* Capitalism

French Canadians, 17

French Communist Party, 176

French Community, 348

French Indochina, World War I and, 83. *See also* Cambodia; Indochina; Laos; Vietnam

French Popular Movement, 249

French Revolution, 12, 13

French Socialist Party (FSP), 105, 118

Freud, Sigmund, 23

Friedan, Betty, 202, 269

Fuentes, Carlos, 217

Fukuyama, Francis, 411

Functionalism, 26

Fundamentalist Islam: in Algeria, 386; ISIS and, 380; Middle East politics and, 381–382; Muslim guerilla groups, 186; *The Satanic Verses* (Rushdie) and, 331; Sumatra and, 338; Taliban, 379

G

Galapogas Islands, 23

Gallegos, Rómulo, 130

Gallipoli, 83

Gambia, 346

Gandhi, Indira, 324, 327, 328

Gandhi, Maneka, 328

Gandhi, Mohandas (Mahatma), 108–110, *111*, 322, 323, 332, 347

Gandhi, Rahul, 325

Gandhi, Rajiv, 324–325, 327, 328, 329

Gandhi, Sonia, 328

Ganges River, 329

Gang of Four (China), 303

Gardens, Japanese, 72

The Garlic Ballads (Mo Yan), 317

Garvey, Marcus, 349

Gates, Bill, 206

Gatling gun, 49

GATT (General Agreement on Tariffs and Trade), 191

Gaucho (cowboy), 130

Gay, Peter, 8

Gaza Strip, 375

Geertz, Clifford, 51

Gehry, Frank, 424

General Agreement on Tariffs and Trade (GATT), 191

Serbian Communist Party, 258
Serfs/serfdom, 14, 20
Serialism, 271
Seth, Vikram, 332
Sèvres, Treaty of, 112
Sexual equality, 201–203
Shah Mohammad Reza Pahlavi, 375, 385
Shah Reza Khan, 114, 385, 387
Shaka (Zulu), 45
Sham (music group), 389
Shamba, 353
Shamir, Itzhak, 374
Shandong peninsula, 59
Shandong Province, China, 119, 126
Shanghai, China, 119, 120
Shanghai massacre (1927), 119, 120
Shari'a (Islamic law), 41, 112, 116, 356, 376
Shidehara diplomacy, 126, 138
Shi'ite Muslims, 114, 376, 378, 379, 386, 415
Shimonoseki, Treaty of, 70
Shin, Kyung-Sook, 292
Shinto, 287
Shipping container, 408, *408*
Shipwreck, at Caffard Cove, 42
Shogunate system, 65
Shostakovich, Dmitri, 232
Siberian concentration camps, 221, 222, 226
Sideline industries, 235, 310
Sierra Leone, 43
Sikhs, *35*, 49, *324*, 327
Silent Spring (Carson), 204, 205
Silk industry, 65, 68, *402*
Singapore, 292–293, *293*; in ASEAN, 340; as
    British colony, 37; "Little Tigers" and,
    279; politics and government, 293;
    postwar, 292–293; towers/trees in, 293,
    294; World War II and, 149
Singh, Manmohan, 327, 333
Single-parent households, 413
Six-Day War, 373–374
Sjahrir, Sutan, 108
Skyscrapers, 5, 26, 232
Slash-and-burn agriculture, 418, 419
Slaves and slavery: British settlements for
    freed, 43; European colonialism in
    Africa and, 47; in Latin America, 18;
    textile work by, 8
Slave trade, 41, 42
Slavophiles, 14
SLORC, 336
Slovakia, 258, 261
Slovenia, 258, 261
Smith, Adam, 408
Snow (Pamuk), 389
Social Darwinism, 29, 31, 32, 135
Social Democrats (Germany), 252
Socialism, 22; in Africa, 349, 353, 354; China's
    transition to, 299–300; in India, 327;
    New Economic Policy (NEP) and,
    99; rise of, 19–20; Stalin's policies on
    transition to, 100; in Tanzania, 353
Socialist Party (French), 118
Socialist realism, 232
Socialist Republic of Vietnam (SRV), 338
Socialists (Japan), 281
Socialized medicine, 254
Social media, *416*, 416–417, 426
Social Revolutionaries (Russia), 90, 92

Social Revolutionary Party (Russia), 93, 94
Social Security, 197–198
Social Security Act (1935), 98
Social structures, mass society and, 7–8
Society for Foreign Missions, 36
Sofala, Africa, 41
Soil erosion, 311
Soka Gakkai, 298
Solar power, 421
Solidarity (labor union), 236
Soloman Islands, 150
Solzhenitsyn, Alexander, 225, 226, 233
Somalia, 186
Some Prefer Nettles (Tanizaki), 125
Songhai, 348
Son of the Revolution (Liang Heng), 301–302
Sorokin, Vladimir, 243
Sot-Weed Factor (Barth), 207
South Africa: apartheid and, 347, 354–355;
    British colonization, 46; colonization
    of, 45; European colonialism in, 45, *45*,
    346; Gandhi and, 108, 109; housing, 358;
    transition to independence, 347
South African Republic (Transvaal), 45, 46
South America: immigration from, 405; map,
    210; racial diversity in, 17–18. *See also*
    Latin America
South Asia, 322–333; cotton fibers imported
    from, 4; map of modern, *324*;
    partitioning of, 322. *See also* India;
    Pakistan
Southeast Asia, 333–343; agriculture, 40;
    ASEAN alliance and, 339–340; border
    disputes, 339–340; China and, 56; Cold
    War and, 181–185; colonization in, 31,
    36, *37*, 38–40; cultural trends, 341–342;
    democracy in postwar, 333–335;
    economic development in, 39–40;
    future of, 342–343; Islam in, 36; Japan's
    conquest of, 149, 151; Japan's "southern
    strategy" and, 143–144, 333; in the new
    millennium, 335–339; political culture,
    333–334; rainforests in, *339*; trade, 36;
    urban-rural dichotomy in, 340; women
    in, 340–341
Southern Christian Leadership Conference
    (SCLC), 192
Southern Rhodesia, 46
South Korea, 175, 291; economic growth in,
    291; family in, 292, *292*; "Little Tigers"
    and, 279; North Korea and, 291–292;
    politics and government, 291
South Ossetia, 241
South Vietnam, 176, 182, 183, 185, 334, 338
South Yemen, 186
Soviet Red Army, invasion of Czechoslovakia,
    229
Soviets of Agricultural Laborer's Deputies, 92
Soviets of Deputies of Poor Peasants, 92
Soviets of Workers' Deputies, 92
Soviet Union: Afghanistan and, 186, 379;
    agriculture in, 223, 224, 225, 227;
    Armenia and, 112; arms race and,
    186–187; Berlin Blockade and, 168;
    Berlin Crisis and, 179; Brezhnev and,
    185, 223–227; China and, 171, 173, 180,
    181; Chinese civil war and, 173; Cold
    War and, 169–170, 187; collapse of,

275; collective farms in, 100; creation
of, 98–99; Cuba and, 215–216; Cuban
Missile Crisis and, 180–181; cultural
exchange with U.S., 179; cultural
expression in, 232–233; de-Stalinization,
223; dictatorial regime in, 134;
disintegration of, 234–236; economy,
99, 187, 220–221, 225–227; Ethiopia,
351; expansion into Third World, 186;
Helsinki Accords and, 186, 225; invasion
of Czechoslovakia, 229, 230; Japan and,
143, 280; Khrushchev and, 177–179, 222–
223; Korean War and, 175; Malenkov
and, 222; Marshall Plan and, 168; media,
225, 235; Nazi-Soviet Nonaggression
Pact, 142; New Economic Policy (NEP),
99, 100; nonaggression pact with
Germany, 143; *perestroika*, 187; Poland
and, 145, 165; post-World War II, 221,
222; Potsdam Conference and, 154–155;
SALT I and, 185–186; SALT I and SALT
II, 186; seeking united fronts with
capitalist countries, 140; space program,
181, 206; Stalin and, 221; Stalin's
strategy to build socialism in, 100; threat
of expansion by, 166–167; Vietnam and,
176; Vietnam War and, 182; Warsaw
Pact, 169; women in, 234; World War
II and, 146–148, 152, 153, 221; Yalta
Agreement and, 154. *See also* Cold War;
Lenin, Vladimir; Stalin, Joseph and
Stalinism
Soyinka, Wole, 362
Space program, 181
Space race, 206
Spain: authoritarian government in, 138;
    colonization in Africa, *44*; in the
    European Community (EC), 261; Latin
    America and, 17; social benefits, 399
Spanish-American War, 37–38
Spheres of influence, 59
Spice Islands, 36
Spielberg, Steven, 180
Spinning jenny, 3–4
Spinning wheel, Gandhi's message and, 109
Sports, 208, 233
Spratly Islands, 307
Sputnik I, 206
Sri Lanka, 324–325
Srivijaya, 36
SS (*Schutzstaffel*), 136–137
Stagflation, 196
Stalingrad, Battle of, 152
Stalin, Joseph and Stalinism, 99, 134; death of,
    177, 222; economic recovery program,
    221; on the Great Depression, 139–140;
    Greece and, 167; Khrushchev on, 223,
    224, 225; Korean War and, 175; legacy
    of, 100–101; on Mao Zedong, 171;
    Mao Zedong and, 174; at Potsdam
    Conference, 155; reputation of, under
    Brezhnev, 225; responsibility for the
    Cold War and, 169, 171; seeking united
    fronts, 140; Soviet-U.S. tensions and,
    165; suspicions by, 221–222; on United
    Nations, 154; Yalta Conference and, 164,
    165; Yugoslavia and, 165–166
Standard Oil, 115

Stanton, Elizabeth Cady, 10, 11
Starry Night (van Gogh), 25
Starvation, 100, 300, 352
Star Wars (Strategic Defense Initiative), 187
Stasi, the (East Germany), 230, 253
Steamboat, 4
Steam engine, 4
Steamships, *57*
Steel: Industrial Revolution and, 4–5; in Latin
        America, 127; produced in Russia,
        14; Soviet production of, 100; U.S.
        production of, 17
Sterilization, compulsory (India), 324, 327
Stevens, Hiram, 49
Stilwell, Joseph, 149–150
Stimson, Henry L., 142
Stockhausen, Karlheinz, 271
Stock market: Great Depression and, 97
Strait of Malacca, 37
Straits Times, 293
The Stranger (Camus), 270
Strategic Defense Initiative (SDI), 187
Stravinsky, Igor, 26
Streetcars, 6
Stresemann, Gustav, 95, 96
Sturmabteilung (SS Troops), 135
Submarine warfare, 85
Sub-Saharan Africa, 117, 352
Subways, 6
Sudan, 356
Sudetenland, 140
Suez Canal, 31, 43, *43*, 115, 372, 374
Suez Canal Company, 372
Suffragette (film), 12
Suffrage, women's, 10, 11, 12, 96, 112, 268, 387
Sugar plantations, 42
Suharto, General, 335, 336–337
Suicide: in Japan, 284
A Suitable Boy (Seth), 332
Sukarno (Indonesia), 333, 335, 336, 339–340
Sukarnoputri, Megawati, 338
Sullivan, Louis H., 26
Sumatra, 36, 39, 40, 338, *339*, 419
Sunni Muslims, 114, 379, 415
The Sun Shines over the Sangan River, 316
Sun Yat-Sen, 61, 117, 119; Chiang Kai-shek
        and, *111*; Three People's Principles, 120
Surrealism, 71, 101
"Survival of the fittest," 31
Swahili, 41
Swaziland, 46
Symbolism, 71
Syria, 111–112; Arab-Israeli conflict and,
        374; Arab Spring and, 380; Assad
        regime, 382; civil war within, 380,
        381; independence of, 370; refugees in
        Germany, 254; Six-Day War and, 373;
        United Arab Republic (UAR) and, 372

T

Tabriz, Iran, 114
Tahir Square demonstrations, *380*
Taiping Rebellion, 56–57, 65
Taisho democracy, 125, 126–127
Taiwan, 70, 172, 173; agriculture, 288–289;
        China and, 181, 307, 308; Cold War
        and, 174; Khrushchev and, 181; "Little
        Tigers" and, 279; map of modern,

288; Nationalist Party rule in, 288–290;
        postwar, 288–290; U.S.-China relations
        and, 176, 184, 185, 307; U.S. fears about
        Chinese invasion of, 175
Taliban, 379
Tamil Tigers, 324–325
Tanganyika, 348
Tanizaki, Junichiro, 125
Tannenberg, Battle of, 81
Tanzania, 348, 353
Taoism. *See* Daoism (Taoism)
Tariffs, 97, 399
Taxes/taxation: agricultural, in India, 34;
        agricultural, in Japan, 68; carbon, 204;
        salt, in India, 110
"Tea hair," 284, 315
Tea industry, 56, 68
Tea Party, 198, 412
Teakwood, 39–40
Tea plantations, 40
Technological Revolution, 3, 206, 397
Technology and technological change(s):
        capitalism and, 407; China's use of
        western, 58; in China under Deng
        Xiaoping, 303; criticisms of, 409;
        economy and, 407–408; electronic, in
        China, 416; examples of recent, 408–409;
        impact on, 75; in India, 329; in the past
        few decades, 408–409; in post-World
        War II U.S., 206; religion and, 415–416;
        social and political influences, 416–417;
        societal consequences of, 409–410; in
        Soviet Union, 227
Tehran, Iran, 114, 154
Telephone, invention of, 6
Television, 208, 233, 311, 408, 417
Television shows, 201
Tennyson, Alfred Lord, 8
"Ten thousand-dollar" households
        (China), 310
Terrorism: by al-Qaeda, 379; bin Laden's
        justification for, 369; Boko Haram, 356;
        in France, 251; in Indonesia, 338; by
        Irish Republican Army (IRA), 256; in
        Mumbai, India, 325; Muslim population
        in Europe and, 266; in Nigeria, 356; by
        Palestinian militants, 374–375; PLO
        attacks on Israel, 373; Russian radicals,
        14; September 11th attacks, 188, 197,
        368, 396–397
Tet Offensive, 182
Textile industry: in China, 123; in India, 35;
        inventions leading to, 3–4; in Japan, 69;
        technology in, 407; women working
        in, 8, 86
Thailand, 334; ASEAN and, 340; border
        dispute with Cambodia, 339–340;
        colonialism and, 31, 37
Thakin, Burma, 107
Thatcher, Denis, 256
Thatcher, Margaret, *250*, 256, 257
The Thaw (Ehrenburg), 232
"Theater of the absurd," 270
Theory of evolution, 23, 24
Theory of relativity, 22–23
Theosophy, 101
The Rite of Spring (Stravinsky), 26
Things Fall Apart (Achebe), 362

Third International (Comintern), 117, 118
Third Republic (France), 16
Third Wave, the, 75, 408
Third World: Cold War and, 180; Soviet
        expansion into, 186. *See also* individual
        country names
Three obediences (Japan), 69
Three People's Principles, 61, 120
Thuggee, 34
Tiananmen Square demonstrations (1989),
        304, 305
Tianjin, Treaty of, 57
Tibet, 59, 174, 308, *308*
Tilak, Balwantrao, 108
Timbuktu, 41, 345, *345*
Timor, 36
Tinariwen, 364
The Tin Drum (Grass), 271
Tito (Josip Broz), 165, 167, 258
Toer, Pramoedya, 341–342
Toffler, Alvin, 75, 408
Tokugawa system (Japan), 65, 67
Tokyo, 67, 71, *71*, 156
Tokyo Bay, 66, *66*
Tokyo National University of Fine Arts and
        Music, 72
Tokyo School of Fine Arts, 72
Tools, manufacturing, 7
Totalitarian state, 134
To the End of the Land (Grossman), 389
Touré, Ali Farka, 364
Touré, Sékou, 349
Tourism, 233, 264, 310
Toynbee, Arnold, 79
Trade: in Africa, 41; in Argentina, 127; in
        China, 55, 56, 311; Chinese, 122;
        colonial policy on, 39–40; cotton, 4;
        global patterns of, *401*; industrialization
        and, 6; Japanese, 138–139; Latin
        America, 18, 127; linking Europe with
        other nations, 29–30; opium, 56; in Qing
        China, 55; Qing Dynasty, 53–54, 56–57;
        Southeast Asia, 36, 37; of Southeast
        Asia, 36; spice, 36; in U.S. under Trump,
        399–400
Trade embargo, 378
Trade unions: British, 16
Traditional customs: in Bali, *341*; in India,
        331–332, 333; in Southeast Asia, 340
Trans-Jordan, 115
Trans-Pacific Partnership (TPP), 399–400
Transportation, 4, 6
Trans-Siberian Railway, 70
Transvaal (South African Republic), 45, 46
Treaty of Addis Ababa, 49
Treaty of Kanagawa, 67
Treaty of Lacarno, 95
Treaty of Lausanne, 112
Treaty of Maastricht, 261, 262, 265
Treaty of Nanjing, 56
Treaty of Sèvres, 112
Treaty of Shimonoseki, 70
Treaty of Tianjin, 57
Treaty of Versailles, 89–90
Trench warfare, 82
Trifonov, Yury, 233
Triple Alliance, *15*, 79, *80*
Triple Entente, *15*, 79, *80*